HAMLET'S MOMENT

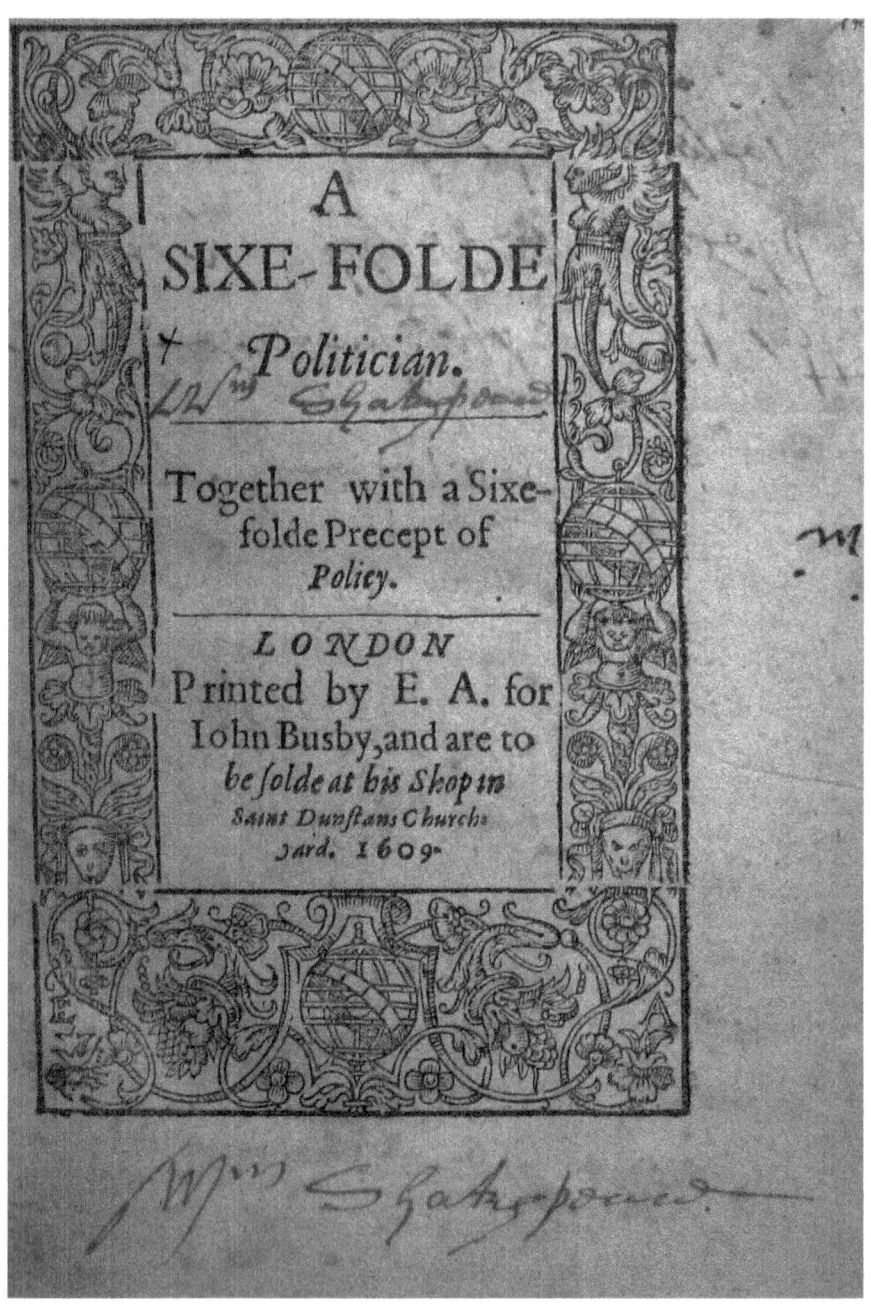

Frontispiece. Shakespeare's signature on the title page of John Melton: *A Sixe-folde Politician: Together with a Sixe-folde Precept of Policy* (London: E.A. for Iohn Busby, 1609), a forgery by William Henry Ireland. Folger STC 17805 copy 1.

Photograph by András Kiséry, from the collection of the Folger Shakespeare Library.

Hamlet's Moment

Drama and Political Knowledge in Early Modern England

ANDRÁS KISÉRY

OXFORD
UNIVERSITY PRESS

Great Clarendon Street, Oxford, OX2 6DP,
United Kingdom

Oxford University Press is a department of the University of Oxford.
It furthers the University's objective of excellence in research, scholarship,
and education by publishing worldwide. Oxford is a registered trade mark of
Oxford University Press in the UK and in certain other countries

© András Kiséry 2016

The moral rights of the author have been asserted

First Edition published in 2016

Impression: 1

All rights reserved. No part of this publication may be reproduced, stored in
a retrieval system, or transmitted, in any form or by any means, without the
prior permission in writing of Oxford University Press, or as expressly permitted
by law, by licence or under terms agreed with the appropriate reprographics
rights organization. Enquiries concerning reproduction outside the scope of the
above should be sent to the Rights Department, Oxford University Press, at the
address above

You must not circulate this work in any other form
and you must impose this same condition on any acquirer

Published in the United States of America by Oxford University Press
198 Madison Avenue, New York, NY 10016, United States of America

British Library Cataloguing in Publication Data

Data available

Library of Congress Control Number: 2015949826

ISBN 978–0–19–874620–1

Printed in Great Britain by
Clays Ltd, St Ives plc

Links to third party websites are provided by Oxford in good faith and
for information only. Oxford disclaims any responsibility for the materials
contained in any third party website referenced in this work.

Acknowledgements

Most of this book was written in 2011–14, but the debts I incurred in the process extend much further back in time. Jean Howard, David Kastan, and Alan Stewart supervised a dissertation which contained early versions of some of the materials here. The three of them remain formative influences. Jean has been a model of commitment, control, and cheer—she taught me to attend to form and argument, both literary and scholarly, but also to attend plays. David's thinking seemed to resonate with my vague ideas about books and writing with surprising and enabling force, but he would also send me out on a limb and then wait for me to realize why it was worth it. If Jean and David were doctoral parents of a whole generation at Columbia, Alan was like an older brother who makes all he is doing seem easy and cool: his attention and generosity opened up a realm of intellectual possibility, making me look for the people who did the reading and writing.

Hamlet's Moment was shaped by other teachers as well. Conal Condren encouraged at important moments, and demanded a conceptual clarity I wish I could muster. Péter Dávidházi's essay about Polonius first alerted me to the play of power in *Hamlet*, but his advice has never been Polonius-like. Heather James listened and helped since a rainy afternoon in D.C., and unlike this book, our friendship will continue. Peter Lake made me understand what I was writing about, and taught me most of what I know about early modern politics and its historians. Many of my ideas came from the work of Fritz Levy, who later also encouraged the formulation of others. Ivan Lupić commented carefully and selectively, and drove me around recklessly, and I expect him to keep doing both. I need to talk to Noah Millstone more often. There is much in this book I wish I had been able to show Dénes Némedi. Joanna Picciotto appeared to believe in the project very early, but her gift helped especially in its final stages: she gave me and my book the most exacting yet most generous reading. Julianne Werlin pointed out what was missing and made me try to fix it. George Donaldson, István Géher, Géza Kállay, Scott Long, John Lyon, Ádám Nádasdy, Bruce Robbins, Kálmán Ruttkay, and Ferenc Takács were my teachers long before this book would have begun, but they are there in how I write and think.

Fellow students Avishek Ganguly, Dehn Gilmore, Rishi Goyal, Musa Gurnis, Matt Sandler, Alex Smith, Eugene Vydrin, and Lauren Walsh deserve equal thanks. With Tiffany Werth, my mediatrix, we share more than our birthday. Allison Deutermann and I have lived parallel lives for well over a decade now. With Matt Zarnowiecki we also shared the experience of southern exposure. The two of them, along with Andrea Walkden, Gavin Hollis, and Vim Pasupathi, read versions of some of the chapters that follow and discussed them over what wines we could afford in Long Island City.

Julie Crawford, Adam Hooks, Lorna Hutson, Jim Shapiro, and Peter Stallybrass read, helped, and supported in ways that were truly crucial. Alan Bryson, Jeff Doty,

Matt Hunter, David Gehring, Penny Geng, Jason Powell, Aaron Pratt, Angus Vine, Lizzy Williamson, and Adam Zucker have been wonderful interlocutors—as were Alan Farmer and Zachary Lesser, whose SAA seminar allowed me to try out a part of what became the first chapter of this book. Tiffany Stern disagreed—this book is a recognition of how right she was. Gabe Cervantes, Jon Farina, Dahlia Porter, Allison Schachter, Sandy Solomon, and Ben Tran helped me refocus, but also made 2008–9 one of the best years I have had.

Personal and intellectual lives are inseparable, and my friends' interest in some part, or none, of what follows, was always a source of pleasure. Zsófi Bán, Ferenc Csirkés, Mikhal Dekel, Rishi Goyal, Zsolt Komáromy, Zoltán Márkus, Kati Orbán, Szilárd Papp, Laurent Stern, and Paul Stewart listened to ideas early and late. For her care and companionship, brilliance and inspiration over twenty years, I will never be able to properly thank Ágnes Berecz.

At City College, Fred Reynolds supported my research and offered shrewd advice, and Eric Weitz helped and pushed me to finish. Renata Miller and Paul Oppenheimer offered useful guidance as my department chairs, and with Emily Greble, Dan Gustafson, Mark Mirsky, and Hap Veeser, were also among the colleagues on whom I was especially dependent as I was writing this book. Liz Mazzola read more, and more quickly, than almost anyone, and has been a model of productivity and determination.

For opportunities to try out parts of this material and for helpful comments, I am grateful to Thomas Fulton and Henry Turner at Rutgers, Peggy Knapp at Carnegie Mellon, the Columbia University Seminar on Shakespeare, the late Gábor Vermes and the Columbia University Seminar on Law and Politics, and the organizers of the Yale Early Modern Colloquium. Shelly Eversley and the members of a CUNY FFPP seminar in spring 2013 helped me recognize what I owed my audience. I am grateful for the opportunity to rework here Chapter 3, published in an earlier form in *English Literary History*, 81 (2014), 29–60. Jacqueline Baker encouraged me to finish, and the two anonymous reviewers for Oxford University Press helped me recast the manuscript into a more coherent final shape. I am truly grateful for their careful and perceptive reading.

Over the years, I enjoyed short-term Folger and Huntington fellowships, and for several years, I depended on the Wertheim Reading Room at NYPL, then managed by Jay Barksdale. The staff of the Cohen Library of CCNY were endlessly patient with interlibrary loan requests. Support for my research was provided by several PSC-CUNY Awards, jointly funded by The Professional Staff Congress and The City University of New York. Hansun Hsiung, Ben Robinson, and Aaron Pratt also helped with images.

DSK has been there since the very beginning of this—in fact, earlier. Without his attention and help at some decisive moments, I would not be writing these acknowledgements. To him, and now also Jane, I cannot offer thanks enough.

Contents

List of Figures — ix
List of Abbreviations — xi
Note on Texts — xiii

Introduction: Hamlet's Moment — 1
Politics on the Stage — 2
Political Competence and Dreams of Mobility — 9
The Moment — 20
This Book — 29

I. *HAMLET* AND THE PROFESSION OF POLITICS

1. **'The Wiser Sort': The Distinction of Politics and Gabriel Harvey's Machiavellian *Hamlet*** — 37
   Harvey's Note — 42
   Political Expertise and the Learning of Mere Scholars — 47
   Politic Learning and Machiavelli — 52
   The Wiser Sort — 58
   A Choice of Tragic Sentences: Political Reading as the Work of Distinction — 61
   Lucrece's Rape and the Trial of Politic Distinction — 72
   Ophelia's Chastity and the Reason of State — 77
   Sorts of Characters — 82

2. **Some Travellers Return: Diplomatic Writing, Political Careers, and the World of *Hamlet*** — 89
   Hamlet in Denmark — 89
   An English Ambassador Explores Denmark — 96
   English Ambassadors and Venetian Relations — 106
   Diplomacy and the Profession of Politics — 112
   Travels, Hopes, and Relations — 117
   Shakespeare's Elsinore: The Rights of Return — 124

3. **'I Lack Advancement': Political Agents and Political Servants in Hamlet's Moment** — 134
   Political Hamlet, 1561 — 134
   Political Hamlet, 1609 — 136
   Polemical Hamlet: Belleforest — 140
   Hamlet's Speeches and Horatio's Silences — 147
   Independence and Dependence: The Fall of the Polonius Clan — 157
   Horatio's Moment — 161

II. POLITICAL KNOWLEDGE AND THE PUBLIC STAGE IN HAMLET'S MOMENT

4. 'Vile and Vulgar Admirations': Chapman and the Public of Political News — 169
   - News — 169
   - On Stages and Bookstalls — 174
   - A Public of Politics and a Scene of Exchange — 179
   - Betrayals — 184
   - Scandalous Relations — 191
   - Denial, Self-Knowledge, and Curiosity — 199

5. 'The Most Matter with Best Conceyt': The Publics of Tacitean Observation and the Margins of Politics in Jonson's *Sejanus* — 206
   - Politic Notes, Politic Readers — 211
   - The Politic Tragedy of *Seianvs His Fall* — 215
   - To Tell the Truth — 224
   - The Knowledge of Power — 227
   - The Distinction of Tragical Satire — 231
   - Popular Dissemination — 237

6. 'For Discourse's Sake Merely': Political Conversation on the Stage and Off — 243
   - Insider Talk and the Interests of Conversation: *The Malcontent* — 248
   - Tobacco and Foreign Affairs: *Monsieur d'Olive* — 256
   - *Volpone* and the Fool's Profession — 261
   - Reading Plays for Discourse's Sake — 266

Bibliography — 281
Index — 319

List of Figures

Frontispiece. Shakespeare's signature on the title page of John Melton: *A Sixe-folde Politician: Together with a Sixe-folde Precept of Policy* (London: E.A. for Iohn Busby, 1609), a forgery by William Henry Ireland. Folger STC 17805 copy 1. ii

1.1. Gabriel Harvey's note including his reference to *Hamlet* in his copy of *The Workes of our Antient and Lerned English Poet, Geffrey Chaucer, Newly Printed*. (Londini: [printed by Adam Islip] impensis Geor. Bishop, anno. 1598) BL Add MS 42518, fol. 394v (sig. 3Z6v). 39

1.2. Gabriel Harvey's notes on sentences and note-taking in *Hecvba, & Iphigenia in Aulide Euripidis Tragoediae in Latinum Tralatae Erasmo Roterodamo Interprete* (Venetiis: Aldvs, 1507), Houghton Library, Harvard University, shelfmark *EC H2623 Zz507e, Folger Shakespeare Library STC 22345 copy 2, sigs. I8v–A1r. 66

1.3. Gnomic pointing in Shakespeare's *Lucrece* (London: Printed by Richard Field, for Iohn Harrison, and are to be sold at the signe of the white Greyhound in Paules Churh-yard [*sic*], 1594), sigs. E1v–E2r. 75

1.4. The sentences of Corambis as marked in the First Quarto of *The Tragicall Historie of Hamlet Prince of Denmarke by William Shake-speare. As It Hath Beene Diuerse Times Acted by His Highnesse Seruants in the Cittie of London: As also in the Two Vniuersities of Cambridge and Oxford, and else-where* (London: Printed for N.L. and Iohn Trundell, 1603), BL C.34.k.1, sig. C2r. 86

2.1. Daniel Rogers's list of Danish notables in *A Discourse Touching the Present Estate and Gouuernement of the Kingdomes of Denmarke… * The Huntington Library, San Marino, California, MS EL 1608, f. 9r. 104

4.1. Intaglio broadsheet about the arrest and execution of the Duke of Biron. Franz Hogenberg: *Spectatori: Carl de Gontaut Her von Biron…*, 1602. Universitäts- und Landesbibliothek Düsseldorf, urn:nbn:de:hbz:061:1-92649. 187

5.1. William Drake's notes from Ben Jonson's *Sejanus*, with the original passages as printed in 1605. William Drake's notebook, Folger Shakespeare Library MS V.a. 263, f. 16v, and *Seianus his fall. VVritten by Ben: Ionson* (London: printed by G. Elld, for Thomas Thorpe, 1605) sigs. D3r, D3v, E1r, E2v. 209

5.2. The title page of the 1604–5 third edition of Henry Savile's *The end of Nero and beginning of Galba. Fovre bookes of the Histories of Cornelius Tacitus…* The Third Edition. Published with: *The Annales of Cornelivs Tacitvs. The Description of Germanie* (London: Printed by Arnold Hatfield for Iohn Norton, 1604–5), Columbia University Rare Book and Manuscript Library, LODGE 1604 T118. 222

5.3. The title page of the 1605 quarto of *Seianus his fall. VVritten by Ben: Ionson* (At London: printed by G. Elld, for Thomas Thorpe, 1605) Beinecke Rare Book and Manuscript Library, Ih J738 605s. 223

List of Abbreviations

CP The Cecil Papers at Hatfield House, accessed through *The Cecil Papers*, http://cecilpapers.chadwyck.com
ODNB *The Oxford Dictionary of National Biography*, http://www.oxforddnb.com
TNA SP The National Archives, State Papers collection, also accessed through *The State Papers Online, The Government of Britain, 1509–1714*, http://gale.cengage.co.uk/state-papers-online-15091714.aspx

Note on Texts

I quote the modernized text of *Hamlet* from Harold Jenkins (ed.), *Hamlet* (The Arden Shakespeare; London: Methuen, 1982); and the writings of Ben Jonson from David M. Bevington, Martin Butler, and Ian Donaldson (eds.), *The Cambridge Edition of the Works of Ben Jonson*. 7 vols. (Cambridge and New York: Cambridge University Press, 2012).

Introduction
Hamlet's Moment

This is a book about early modern plays and political knowledge. It suggests that around 1600, drama as a form of popular entertainment and as the most influential secular public medium was instrumental in familiarizing its audience with *politics as a profession*: with political institutions and offices, with the protocols of political negotiation, and with the kinds of knowledge that were necessary for survival and advancement in political careers. In talking about political knowledge, my aim is not to attribute a political theory or a political position to the theatre in general or to some plays in particular, nor do I seek to discover representations of such positions or theories within plays. And although I think these plays think about politics, I don't want to claim that Shakespeare and his colleagues were original political thinkers, or political philosophers of sorts, either. In this I veer from the approaches that have dominated our thinking about the politics of early modern drama.

Clarifying my own starting point might be easiest through a contemporary analogy. Popular genres familiarize us with areas of society from which we are excluded not by physical distance, cultural difference, or social privilege in general terms, but by the very systems and structures of expert knowledge that constitute them. Detective fiction like Georges Simenon's Maigret stories, Jean-Claude Izzo's Montale trilogy, or Henning Mankell's Wallander novels, and TV series like *Law and Order* and *CSI* have imagined for us the work of police inspectors and professional investigators. Our sense of the practice of the law and of the process of the jury trial has been similarly shaped by movies like *Witness for the Prosecution* and *Twelve Angry Men* and by courtroom drama on television. Such fiction doesn't simply build on what the audience already knows. The opposite is implied by the fact that as a result of the worldwide distribution of American TV shows, people in many civil law countries are now more familiar with the American jury trial than with the protocols of their own legal system.[1] Hospital drama like *ER* has made wide audiences eager to discuss medical procedures they have never undergone, much less studied or performed.[2] Closer to the concerns of this book, our

---

[1] Carol J. Clover, 'Law and the Order of Popular Culture', in Austin Sarat and Thomas R. Kearns (eds.), *Law in the Domains of Culture* (Ann Arbor: The University of Michigan Press, 2000), 97–119 at 97–8; Barbara Villez, *Séries Télé, Visions de la Justice* (Paris: Presses Universitaires de France, 2005).

[2] Pam Belluck, 'A Made-Up Hospital That Offered Real Medicine', *The New York Times*, 4 April 2009, http://www.nytimes.com/2009/04/05/weekinreview/05belluck.html, accessed 15 May 2015; Catherine Belling, 'Reading *The Operation*: Television, Realism, and the Possession of Medical

understanding of intelligence operations is defined by John Le Carré's *oeuvre*, and our sense of the corridors of power is based on television programmes like *The West Wing* and *House of Cards*. Fictions make the professions familiar, invest them with cultural prestige, incite us to talk about them, and invite fantasies of professional careers as exciting paths of social mobility. Few of us would make the mistake of confusing such fiction-based competence with professional expertise, and yet we rely on it in our conversations about Westminster and Washington politics, about open heart surgery, or about the criminal justice system, and ultimately, we depend on it in how we make sense of our world—and none of this would happen if their creators (writers or expert consultants) did not invest substantial professional knowledge in these fictions.

Early modern drama played a role similar to these modern fictional forms, as a channel for the dissemination of knowledge about professional work, and about the business of politics in particular, to a broad and socially inclusive public.[3] The central claim of my book is that this engagement with professional political knowledge informed and shaped the theatrical production of the early years of the seventeenth century, defining some of the greatest plays written in English. In this book, I explore the connections between political knowledge and dramatic form, tracing how plays engaged with (and also contributed to) the professionalization, popular dissemination, and aestheticization of politics. I here begin with an initial look at the role of drama in the dissemination of political knowledge in early modern England, and at the nature and use of political knowledge in circulation outside the realm of politics.

POLITICS ON THE STAGE

We have long taken for granted that the complex political plays that proliferated on the English stage around the turn of the seventeenth century—the works of Christopher Marlowe, William Shakespeare, Ben Jonson, George Chapman,

---

Knowledge', *Literature and Medicine*, 17 (1998), 1–23; Solange Davin, 'Healthy Viewing: The Reception of Medical Narratives', *Sociology of Health & Illness*, 25 (2003), 662–79.

[3] For studies of the intersections of drama with various kinds of expert and professional knowledge, see e.g. Nina Taunton, *1590s Drama and Militarism: Portrayals of War in Marlowe, Chapman and Shakespeare's Henry V* (Aldershot: Ashgate, 2001); Patricia A. Cahill, *Unto the Breach: Martial Formations, Historical Trauma, and the Early Modern Stage* (Oxford: Oxford University Press, 2008); William Kerwin, *Beyond the Body: The Boundaries of Medicine and English Renaissance Drama* (Amherst: University of Massachusetts Press, 2005); Henry S. Turner, *The English Renaissance Stage: Geometry, Poetics, and the Practical Spatial Arts 1580–1630* (Oxford: Oxford University Press, 2006); Edward Gieskes, *Representing the Professions: Administration, Law, and Theater in Early Modern England* (Newark: University of Delaware Press, 2006). The connections between drama and legal culture have received most attention in recent years, including Subha Mukherji, *Law and Representation in Early Modern Drama* (Cambridge: Cambridge University Press, 2006); Bradin Cormack, *A Power to Do Justice: Jurisdiction, English Literature, and the Rise of Common Law, 1509–1625* (Chicago: University of Chicago Press, 2007). Lorna Hutson, *The Invention of Suspicion: Law and Mimesis in Shakespeare and Renaissance Drama* (Oxford: Oxford University Press, 2008) is an exemplary exploration of links between professional knowledge, its familiarity among laypeople, and the impact of such knowledge on literary form.

John Marston, Thomas Middleton, and their contemporaries—were crucial to the political culture and the political imagination of their time, but we rarely consider one of their most basic political functions, namely, that they helped large audiences to understand *what politics was*. Plays about the realm of politics represented intricate political situations, the complications resulting from the delegation of power, negotiations and back-channelling, intelligence gathering, and the interception of communication. In doing so, they allowed paying audiences a glimpse behind the public façades of power, into the world of diplomats and secretaries, of court factions and loyalties, and also provided them with a vocabulary necessary to talk about this world. These plays gave virtual access to statecraft, to the knowledge that defined a trade of high cultural prestige: the profession of politics.

The perceived effect of these sophisticated depictions of the political elite's activities are encapsulated in Henry Wotton's exasperated remarks about a performance of *All Is True*, a play 'representing some principal pieces of the reign of Henry VIII'. Wotton noted the sumptuous theatrical imitation of the 'extraordinary circumstances of pomp and majesty, even to the matting of the stage; the Knights of the Order with their Georges and garters, the Guards with their embroidered coats, and the like; sufficient in truth within a while to make greatness very familiar, if not ridiculous.'[4] The best historicist scholarship of the 1980s focused on the ideological effects of such performances, debating whether they devalued sovereign majesty by demystifying it or confirmed power through making the audience complicit in its production.[5] Whether they made their audiences accept or challenge that power, it is clear that the price of a theatre ticket promised a familiarity with greatness which went well beyond the embroidered coats of guards and the matting of palace floors, and which was until then not offered by any medium to such a wide audience. The *arcana imperii* discussed (or as it often happened, flaunted and withheld) by plays could certainly be seen as secular equivalents of sacred, pontifical mysteries, as

---

[4] Logan Pearsall Smith, *The Life and Letters of Sir Henry Wotton*, 2 vols. (Oxford: Clarendon Press, 1907) 2:32. The formulation used by Wotton about the dangers of people's familiarity with secrets of state continued to be used to argue for controlling the circulation of political information well into the seventeenth century. In 1663, the first issue of *The Intelligencer; published for the Satisfaction and Information of the People* carried an introduction which uses a remarkably similar formulation, and which, coming from the editor of a newspaper, may sound somewhat surprising. In it, Sir Roger L'Estrange writes that a political newspaper 'makes the *Multitude* too *Familiar* with the *Actions*, and *Counsels* of their *Superiours*; too *Pragmaticall* and *Censorious*, and gives them, not only an *Itch*, but a kind of *Colourable Right*, and *Licence*, to be Meddling with the *Government*' (*The Intelligencer*, Monday 31 August 1663, p. 2). L'Estrange explains that this argument would only be relevant if we could suppose 'the *Press* in *Order*; the *People* in their right *Wits*, and Newes, or *No Newes*, to be the *Question*'—which, as he explains, is precisely not the case, and the purpose of the newspaper is to inform the people and set them straight, as it were. When in 1660, *The Parliamentary Intelligencer* was renamed *The Kingdomes Intelligencer*, its purpose stated on the title page similarly switched from 'For Information of the People' into 'To prevent false news.'

[5] Stephen Orgel, 'Making Greatness Familiar', *Genre*, 15 (1982), 41–8; David Scott Kastan, 'Proud Majesty Made a Subject: Shakespeare and the Spectacle of Rule', *Shakespeare Quarterly*, 37 (1986), 459–75; Stephen Greenblatt, *Shakespearean Negotiations: The Circulation of Social Energy in Renaissance England* (Berkeley: University of California Press, 1988) 21–65. Oliver Arnold, in *The Third Citizen: Shakespeare's Theater and the Early Modern House of Commons* (Baltimore: Johns Hopkins University Press, 2007) extends this analysis to the theatre's (and Shakespeare's) representation of Parliament and to its critique of political representation.

King James explicitly and repeatedly insisted they should be, deeming their demystification, their *Entzauberung*, an act of sacrilege—but also (and even some of James's own references to 'mysteries of state' point in this direction) as the trade secrets of the craft or profession of politics, and their revelation as an act not only of symbolic and political, but also of practical and social consequence.[6]

Already in the 1590s, chronicle plays and tragedies of state, from Shakespeare's *Richard III* to *Henry V*, and from Marlowe's *Edward II* to the anonymous *Woodstock*, were paying close attention to the political mechanisms and institutions of the English monarchy: to the responsibility of the Lord Protector during the sovereign's minority, to the council's deliberative and advising powers, to the negotiation of competing claims of succession, but also to the intrigue, coercion, and underhanded dealings used in discharging political office. Around the turn of the century, the theatre came to focus on statecraft and its court settings even more intently. It is not news that Shakespeare's most successful and most influential play is a political tragedy, but it is worth noticing how different its vision of the realm of politics is from earlier drama. Plays like *Hamlet*, Jonson's *Sejanus*, Marston's *The Malcontent*, and Chapman's French tragedies offer richly detailed visions of political activity, putting on display the techniques of gathering and transmitting intelligence, the analysis of political agents' motives and concerns, the shrewd deployment of information, and scenes of instruction in prudent political analysis and conduct. While these early seventeenth-century plays are looking at the court more closely than earlier political drama was, they are also less directly interested in forms of constitution, in questions of sovereignty, in the legitimacy or the personal burden of rule, than were the plays of the 1590s. They attend to the pressures on the servants of the state and on the clients of powerful statesmen, to the activities of secretaries and envoys, and to the instruments with which power is acquired

---

[6] The twofold meaning of the term is recognized by Ernst H. Kantorowicz, 'Mysteries of State: An Absolutist Concept and Its Late Mediaeval Origins', *The Harvard Theological Review*, 48 (1955), 65–91 at 67–8. For the mystery of state as sacred, pontifical *arcanum*, see especially the 'Proclamation touching D. Cowels booke called the Interpreter' (25 March 1610), complaining about the age which 'hath bred such an unsatiable curiosity in many mens spirits, and such an itching in the tongues and pennes of most men, as nothing is left unsearched to the bottome, both in talking and writing. For from the very highest mysteries in the Godhead, and the most inscrutable Councels in the Trinitie, to the very lowest pit of Hell, and the confused actions of the divels there, there is nothing now unsearched into by the curiositie of mens braines ... And therefore it is no wonder, that men in these our dayes doe not spare to wade in all the deepest mysteries that belong to the persons or State of Kings or Princes, that are gods upon Earth: since we see, (as we have already said) that they spare not God himselfe.' James Francis Larkin and Paul L. Hughes (eds.), *Royal Proclamations of King James I, 1603–1625* (Stuart Royal Proclamations, Oxford: Clarendon Press, 1973) 243. But mystery is a term commonly used in the sense of craft—as in other royal proclamations, for example, addressing concerns about 'Trades, Mysteries, or Manufactures of spinning, or making of Gold and Silver Threed, Purles, Plates, Oes, Spangles, or Foliat' (579), and King James himself also talks about the mystery of state in the sense of 'the handicraft or trade of kings' (Kantorowicz 68n10). In his speech in Star Chamber, 1616, he calls the common law 'a mystery and skill best knowen vnto' his audience, just before he would expostulate about his own 'Prerogative or mystery of state': King James VI and I, *Political Writings*, ed. Johann P. Sommerville (Cambridge: Cambridge University Press, 1994) 212. For the traditions connecting divine mysteries and craft secrets as versions of esoteric knowledge, see Pamela O. Long, *Openness, Secrecy, Authorship: Technical Arts and the Culture of Knowledge from Antiquity to the Renaissance* (Baltimore: Johns Hopkins University Press, 2001).

and maintained. They familiarize their audiences with the business of politics, with the practical, moral, and existential quandaries of political service. If Shakespeare's two tetralogies sought to understand what it meant to be king, and what it took to be king, these plays thought about what it meant to be employed, and what it took to be employed. This perspective defines some of the greatest English plays, the tragedies of the early years of the seventeenth century.

Early seventeenth-century plays representing the workings of the realm of politics are part of a larger trend, of a flourishing of genres about affairs of state. Some of the most radically polemical texts of the late sixteenth century were presented as overviews of constitutional issues, and could serve as introductions to theories of government. The last decade of the reign of Elizabeth also saw the emergence of a market in vernacular translations of classical and continental political literature. The publication of English translations of Aristotle's *Politics*, as well as of Tacitus, Livy, and Plutarch, is only the most obvious indicator of the sudden expansion of the accessibility of materials previously restricted to a rather limited academic readership. Translations of Bodin, Lipsius, and Guicciardini, the manuscript circulation of English translations of Machiavelli's *Prince*, as well as the London publication of his major works (albeit in Italian and under false imprints), and the appearance of English works of 'politic history' that were offering lessons from the past for the understanding of contemporary politics, were part of this surge in the circulation of materials that promised instruction in the affairs of state to a broader audience, including people with no hope for putting their knowledge to use in action.

The circulation of the textual instruments and products of political service were another important facet of this widening of access to affairs of state. Political news from abroad was becoming more available in both manuscript and print. Diplomatic surveys of foreign polities (*relazioni*, as we could call them after their Venetian models), the staple products of early modern intelligence gathering and processing, began to enter public circulation. Letters of advice and treatises on politics, on political careers and on the business of government, often in the form of aphorisms, were produced near the centres of political activity, in government circles and at the secretariats of powerful political players, most notably of the Earl of Essex, but they were also copied and soon thereafter also printed. Francis Bacon's *Essays*, in its first edition a series of thematically organized aphorisms, originates in this culture of political instruction, and constitutes a fascinating case of the self-promotion of an expert political advisor through publicity. Manuals specifically written for print circulation, like Lipsius's *Six Bookes of Politics*, Barnabe Barnes's *Foure Bookes of Offices: Enabling Privat Persons for the Speciall Seruice of all Good Princes and Policies*, or John Melton's *The Sixe-fold Politician*, indicate that 'politics' was emerging as a field of specialized knowledge, an area of expertise that required more than good morals and a well-rounded education.[7] Frowned upon by

---

[7] On politic education in the early seventeenth century see Noah Millstone, 'Seeing Like a Statesman in Early Stuart England', *Past & Present*, 223 (2014), 77–127 at 100–12. I am grateful to Noah Millstone for long conversations about our, at points, remarkably convergent projects.

many (as the uses of the word 'policy,' 'politic', and 'politician' indicate, its shades of meaning ranging from 'prudent' to 'diabolic'), politics was nevertheless increasingly recognizable as a profession.[8] Works written in these political genres served as credentials of their authors' quasi-professional expertise, and the knowledge they articulated promised to be helpful in gaining employment in the system of political patronage. To produce them was to engage in what Lisa Jardine and William Sherman term 'knowledge transactions', an outlay of intellectual labour as part of, or in the hope of, employment.[9] When they entered wider circulation, however, such texts were also reaching readers unlikely to enter into such transactions, either as authors or as patrons. In print, such works may have advertised their authors' expertise, but they primarily catered to an audience of readers who did not turn to them for advice on how to act (because they were not in the position to act), but for explanations of what was happening, driven by the desire for the pleasure as well as for the prestige they might derive from discussing political events with their peers. The effect of such publicity was not only the dissemination of knowledge about the art whose rules were thus circulated, however, but also an increase in the public prestige of the profession whose members were obviously in the possession of more than just this (now exoteric) information.[10]

---

[8] For the uses of the word and its associations, see Napoleone Orsini, ' "Policy": Or the Language of Elizabethan Machiavellism', *Journal of the Warburg and Courtauld Institutes*, 9 (1946), 122–34. On the long-term evolution of politics as a profession, see the schematic overview in the early part of 'Politics as a profession': Max Weber, *The Vocation Lectures*, ed. David S. Owen and Tracy B. Strong, trans. Rodney Livingstone (Indianapolis: Hackett, 2004) 38–43. As Weber's lecture indicates, the professionalization of political work is inseparable but distinct from the birth of modern bureaucracy, of civil service; on the British case, A. G. Aylmer's studies are foundational; see especially *The King's Servants: The Civil Service of Charles I, 1625–1642* (New York: Columbia University Press, 1961) and for a useful overview of the transformation from the sixteenth century to the nineteenth century, 'From Office-Holding to Civil Service: The Genesis of Modern Bureaucracy: The Prothero Lecture', *Transactions of the Royal Historical Society*, 5th ser., 30 (1980), 91–108. In the sixteenth century, the ambassador emerged as an exemplary figure of high-prestige professional political expertise; see especially Douglas Biow, *Doctors, Ambassadors, Secretaries: Humanism and Professions in Renaissance Italy* (Chicago: University of Chicago Press, 2002); Timothy Hampton, *Fictions of Embassy: Literature and Diplomacy in Early Modern Europe* (Ithaca: Cornell University Press, 2009); Douglas Biow, *On the Importance of Being an Individual in Renaissance Italy: Men, Their Professions, and Their Beards* (Philadelphia: University of Pennsylvania Press, 2015) 21–114. The extent to which the term 'profession' as used in modern, post-industrial contexts might apply to this setting is discussed in Chapter 2.

[9] Lisa Jardine and William Sherman, 'Pragmatic Readers: Knowledge Transactions and Scholarly Services in Late Elizabethan England', in Anthony Fletcher and Peter Roberts (eds.), *Religion, Culture, and Society in Early Modern Britain: Essays in Honour of Patrick Collinson* (Cambridge: Cambridge University Press, 1994), 102–24; William H. Sherman, 'The Place of Reading in the English Renaissance: John Dee Revisited', in James Raven, Helen Small, and Naomi Tadmor (eds.), *The Practice and Representation of Reading in England* (Cambridge: Cambridge University Press, 1996), 62–76; cp. also Mario Biagioli, *Galileo, Courtier: The Practice of Science in the Culture of Absolutism* (Chicago: University of Chicago Press, 1993).

[10] Millstone, 'Seeing Like a Statesman'; Eric H. Ash, *Power, Knowledge, and Expertise in Elizabethan England* (Baltimore: Johns Hopkins University Press, 2004); and cp. Biow, *On the Importance of Being an Individual in Renaissance Italy* 35–57 on the rhetoric and functions of disclosing knowledge of a craft or art. On the public dissemination of political documents and political knowledge in early modern Europe, see Jacob Soll, *Publishing the Prince: History, Reading, & the Birth of Political Criticism* (Ann Arbor: University of Michigan Press, 2005); Filippo de Vivo, *Information and Communication in Venice: Rethinking Early Modern Politics* (Oxford and New York: Oxford University Press, 2007).

Chapters of this book show how theatrical representations of the realm of politics (whether fictionalizing recent or historical events or embellishing invented scenarios with factual and verisimilar details) drew on the textual tools and products of the profession of politics, putting on display the knowledge embodied in political news, maxims of state, ambassadorial *relazioni*, politic histories—and dramatized the activities they facilitated in the original, courtly context of their production. On-stage political advice is offered in Machiavellian aphorisms, political positions are argued in the terminology of pamphlets about the rights and obligations of the subject and the monarch, while representations of foreign states rely on intelligence reports and newsletters. Commercial drama did not, of course, compete with expert instruction. Rather, the broad, conversation-provoking publicity of performance supplemented and radically expanded the limited manuscript and broader print circulation of expert political knowledge. Plays offered such knowledge for consumption to a paying, non-professional audience. In doing so, they repurposed them from professional tools into the matter of political conversation among those excluded from political activity.

The first scene of *Alphonsus, the Emperor of Germany*, a late sixteenth-century play that combines a revenge plot with a quasi-historical drama of lurid political machinations, is a particularly crude example of the display of political knowledge on the stage, and therefore illuminates very clearly the promises held by such display.[11] The play begins with Alphonsus, whose imperial crown is in danger, asking the secretary Lorenzo for help. Lorenzo, happy to oblige, tells his emperor to

> take paper, pen, and ink,
> Write first this maxim, it shall do you good:
> 1. A prince must be of the nature of the lion and the fox, but not the one without the other. (1.1.99–101)

Alphonsus writes and comments, explaining to himself the point of the instruction; then Lorenzo moves on to the next maxim: '2. A prince above all things must seem devout; but there is nothing so dangerous to his state, as to regard his promise or his oath'—and so on, until he reaches '6. Be always jealous of him that knows your secret.' This is a maxim which Alphonsus quickly puts into practice, poisoning his instructor, committing the set of notes to memory, and—'lest the world should find this little Schedule'—destroying it (1.1.109–11, 173, 197). The rest of the play shows how he uses this secret recipe book for the ruthless and duplicitous

---

[11] *The Tragedy of Alphonsus, Emperour of Germany as it hath been very often Acted (with great applause) at the Privat house in Black-Friers by His Maiesties Servants*. By George Chapman Gent. (London: for Humphrey Moseley, 1654). I am citing the text by act, scene, and line number from the modern edition in Thomas Marc Parrott (ed.), *The Plays and Poems of George Chapman: The Tragedies* (London: George Routledge & Sons, 1910). Parrott rejects the attribution to Chapman (683–92), as does Fredson Bowers in 'The Date and Composition of *Alphonsus, Emperor of Germany*', *Harvard Studies and Notes in Philology and Literature*, 15 (1933), 165–89, who argues—based on internal, mostly stylistic evidence—that the play was written in the late 1590s. Bowers was the last critic to discuss the question of the play's date. It was dated 1594 in Alfred Harbage and Samuel Schoenbaum, *Annals of English Drama, 975–1700* (Rev. edn.; London: Methuen, 1964) and it is not assigned a date in the relevant volumes of Martin Wiggins, *British Drama, 1533–1642: A Catalogue* (Oxford: Oxford University Press, 2012–), that have appeared so far.

pursuit of political success, in his efforts to hold on to his power. These maxims are words with power not unlike the spell Faustus uses for summoning demons—words whose power is inseparable from their status as articulations of forbidden knowledge. If magic was the paradigm of such knowledge, by casting Machiavellian advice as secret, diabolic spells, *Alphonsus* stages the analogy between the promise and the perils of having access to *arcana naturae* (or *arcana Dei*?) and *arcana imperii*.[12]

But the analogy only extends so far. Unlike the words of the secret conjuration in a performance of Marlowe's play, the words of the Italian secretary's advice to the emperor in *Alphonsus* are genuine: they are recognizably derived from another Florentine secretary's work, i.e. from Machiavelli's advice to the prince, as mediated by Innocent Gentillet's *Antimachiavel*.[13] And they are real in a more important sense as well: as words of advice rather than magic spells, they serve as an interpretive tool for the play's audience, who can use them to discuss the deeds of Alphonsus from a privileged perspective. The demonization of secret political knowledge as a source of illicit and underhanded empowerment in *Alphonsus* serves to identify the morsels of knowledge put on theatrical display as craft secrets. It advertises their instrumental efficacy, and proclaims a maxim-based *ars politica* to be a form of expert knowledge whose pronouncements can not only advise princely action but also explain it to those observing it, whether in the form of stage fictions or as real events encountered in the form of news. Rather than following Fredson Bowers, who once argued that certain similarities between *Alphonsus* and *Hamlet* indicate the influence of the *Ur-Hamlet* on the anonymous play,[14] in this book I claim that Shakespeare's play, as we know it, is not only a product of this politically oriented public environment, but also the richest and most complex reflection on the uses of political knowledge that comes down to us from its moment.

By disseminating information about foreign states and constitutions, or ostentatiously rehearsing politic maxims, the stage was helping to create a new public for a professional style of political discussion, a public reading and excitedly discussing materials and judging issues it could not realistically expect to have any direct use for or influence on. And yet the stage appears to be doing more than merely providing its audience with *Ersatz* versions of courtly cultural goods—after all, people hearing or reading the play are offered the very words in which such knowledge was also offered to early modern statesmen and rulers.[15] Political insights copied in

---

[12] On the analogy, see Carlo Ginzburg, 'High and Low: The Theme of Forbidden Knowledge in the Sixteenth and Seventeenth Centuries', *Past & Present*, 73 (1976), 28–41 at 35–8. On magic, secrets, and power, see William Eamon, *Science and the Secrets of Nature* (Princeton: Princeton University Press, 1994) 38–90. Eamon's book explores the early modern idea of secret as a technique or recipe, the notion that underlies my point here.

[13] Several of these widely known Machiavellian aphorisms also appear, for example, in the *Observations* compiled by a certain T.B. and dedicated to the Privy Councillor Lord North. On the MSS of this text see Sydney Anglo, *Machiavelli: The First Century: Studies in Enthusiasm, Hostility, and Irrelevance* (Oxford: Oxford University Press, 2005) 667–9.

[14] Fredson Bowers, '*Alphonsus, Emperor of Germany*, and the *Ur-Hamlet*', *Modern Language Notes*, 48 (1933), 101–8.

[15] Paul Yachnin has compellingly argued that theatre was a purveyor of 'populuxe' cultural goods; cp. Anthony B. Dawson and Paul Edward Yachnin, *The Culture of Playgoing in Shakespeare's England:*

contemporary commonplace books put together by provincial gentlemen with no ties to power indicate that among the members of this wider public, the expertise that was useful in political employment was transformed into a type of cultural capital that I term here 'political competence', by which I mean a familiarity with—and a facility in discussing—the business of politics that is put on display in sociable exchange as a marker of distinction. Once in circulation, words and pieces of information don't reveal their origins: it makes little difference to your ability to use the word 'caviar' whether you know it from a play, from someone who has actually tried it, or from regularly having it yourself. On first hearing about the lion and the fox, or about a castle in a place called Elsinore, you may look puzzled—but once your friend standing next to you in the playhouse has enlightened you, saying something to the effect that this is Machiavel's advice, and that is the royal castle of Denmark, you might start referring to them yourself, and explaining them with a knowing smile to those not in the know. This is a crucial part of the cultural promise and cultural work of the theatre: it incites to inquiry and conversation, and in doing so, both invites and enables the performance of competence.

POLITICAL COMPETENCE AND DREAMS OF MOBILITY

On 2 February 1602, John Manningham, a law student at the Middle Temple, saw Shakespeare's *Twelfth Night* performed, and took note of

> A good practise in it to make the steward beleeve his Lady widdowe was in Love with him, by counterfayting a letter, as from his Lady, in generall termes, telling him what shee liked best in him, and prescribing his gesture in smiling, his apparraile, &c.[16]

The letter asks Malvolio to signal his acceptance of the love thrust upon him by indulging in his secret social aspirations and becoming a caricature of the obnoxiously self-promoting courtier—which this hapless victim of the practical joke will perform to the point, baffling Lady Olivia but pleasing audiences for over four centuries with his smiles and yellow stockings, cross-gartered. One curious element in the script for Malvolio's performance of greatness tends to go unnoticed and unremarked on, partly because the play itself doesn't dwell on it, and partly no

---

A Collaborative Debate (Cambridge: Cambridge University Press, 2001) 38–65; Paul Yachnin, '"The Perfection of Ten": Populuxe Art and Artisanal Value in *Troilus and Cressida*', *Shakespeare Quarterly*, 56 (2005), 306–27. While my sense of the cultural function of the public theatre is close to Yachnin's, I think that around 1600, the theatre's commercial nature has not yet been producing the effects it would a century later: while 'populuxe' is a compelling model, and arguably an *emergent* mode of how the theatre engaged with some aspects of elite culture, in Hamlet's moment, and in the field of politics in particular, it was offering more than mere knock-offs of elite cultural goods. The threat many perceived was precisely that the linguistic and intellectual models offered by the theatre were not cheap replicas that would have been recognizable as such on closer inspection.

[16] Robert Parker Sorlien (ed.), *The Diary of John Manningham of the Middle Temple, 1602–1603: Newly Edited in Complete and Unexpurgated Form from the Original Manuscript in the British Museum* (Hanover, NH: Published for the University of Rhode Island by the University Press of New England, 1976) 48.

doubt because it has lost its perspicacity. He is instructed to 'let thy tongue tang arguments of state', that is, to talk politics. There seems to be little use for political discussion in Olivia's household, or indeed anywhere in the play's Illyria, making the request seem like a strange intruder among the rest of the letter's suggestions. But Malvolio's habit of talking politics is high on the list of social transgressions Maria rehearses as she discusses her plan for the forged letter: she thinks he is 'an affectioned ass, that cons state without book and utters it by great swaths' (2.3.121–2). Malvolio's own lack of surprise confirms the accusation. Having finished reading the letter, he begins to rattle off the ingredients of his metamorphosis, declaring 'I will be proud, I will read politic authors', before he contemplates donning the more spectacular accessories. That we don't get to see Malvolio immersed in his politic authors and quoting from them in 'arguments of state' only goes to indicate that talking politics is the unremarkable, default way of marking status. Like behaviour, dress, comportment, or choices in consumption, political competence appears as an essential part of a complex performative repertoire used to claim high standing in society, and here, a signal that Malvolio's bewildering performance is nothing but a delirious act of social ambition.

John Manningham's interest in the humiliation of Malvolio, the man whom Sir Toby Belch calls a 'mere steward', suggests something about the preoccupations of this son of a yeoman farmer, one of the few low-born young men enrolled in an institution which prepared its mostly gentlemen students for the practice of the common law as well as for membership in a national elite, and which also helped him to rise, by 1619, to the status of armigerous gentleman.[17] In his journal, Manningham collected wise sayings, anecdotes from the country, the theatre, and the court, many of them stories of social mobility through marriage, patronage, and professional success. Carefully noting who shared with him what joke or what piece of gossip, his diary is a register of the daily conversations of the wits of the Inns of Court. Manningham recorded political news and trivia as well as exemplary 'meanes to preferment' (223) that he heard about, showing that the fantasy of advancement through the fortuitous engagement in the exchange of information, the fantasy of entering a political career by engaging in versions of the knowledge transactions that constituted the apprenticeship of professional politicians, was informed by the anecdotes about political careers that were circulating in this environment. Manningham records that Thomas Bodley, 'at first but the sonne of a merchant', was lucky enough to be able to give 'some intelligence of moment to the Counsell, whereupon he was thought worthie employment, whereby he rose'.[18] The importance of knowledge, experience, and information in advancement is emphasized by Bodley's autobiography, an account of one of the more successful cases of social mobility through a career in politics. Bodley

---

[17] Sorlien (ed.), *The Diary of John Manningham* 251–76; Bruce R. Smith (ed.), *Twelfth Night, or, What You Will: Texts and Contexts* (The Bedford Shakespeare, Boston: Bedford/St. Martin's, 2001) 1–25.

[18] Sorlien (ed.), *The Diary of John Manningham* 101. (Parenthetical references to Manningham's diary in this and the next paragraph are by page number to this edition.) Cp. Andrew Mousley, 'Self, State, and Seventeenth-Century News', *Seventeenth Century*, 6 (1991), 149–69 at 150.

abandoned his position as University Orator at Oxford for travelling 'beyond the Seas, for attaining to the knowledge of some speciall moderne tongues, and for the encrease of my experience in managing of affaires, being wholly then addicted to employ my selfe...in the publique service of the State'.[19] With his now 'increased experience' he found employment through Leicester and Walsingham, and in the 1580s, he was sent abroad on a variety of diplomatic missions. The turning point in the narrative of his slowly rising career arrives when he returns home 'to deliver unto [the Queen] some secret overtures'. At that time, 'her Highnesse embracing the fruit of my discoveries', he was sent back to the Hague 'to pursue those affaires to performance, which I had secretly proposed; and according to the project which I had conceived...all things were concluded and brought to that issue that was instantly desired, whereupon I procured my instant revocation'—taking the next step up the ladder of political office.[20]

From time to time, Manningham also took notes from 'politic authors': he read the Instructions of Charles V to Philip II (78–81), John Hayward's answer to Parsons' *Conference about the Succession* (236–44), as well as Thomas Stapleton's oration 'Contra Politicos' (125–30). It would be hard to discern a political agenda or ideology behind these politic notes: in the context of his diary, teeming with the voices of his companions, their purpose seems to be to serve him in later conversations, letting his 'tongue tang with arguments of state'. In Malvolio's Illyria as in Manningham's London, politic authors are not used to advise on actions in government, diplomacy, or to assume a partisan position in a field of political debate. Nor is Manningham so delusional as to undertake such readings with the immediate aim of entering political service—not even Malvolio would be thinking of that. Stories like Bodley's only serve to bestow authority and prestige upon arguments of state, confirming their status as an important element in the performative repertory of a gentleman, manifestations of a competence that entitles one to membership in a select company. The ability to talk politics is a form of cultural capital and a mark of distinction.

The social implications of talking politics can also be gleaned from such exasperated comments as the following passage appearing in another play written around 1601, John Marston's *Jack Drum's Entertainment*. Early in the play Sir Edward Fortune responds to the usurer Mamon's question, 'what news at court?', by erupting in an angry tirade about presumptuous and indiscriminate talk about affairs of state:

> What news at court? ha, ha, now Jesu God,
> Fetch me some Bordeaux wine—what news at court?
> Reprobate fashion, when each ragged clout,
> Each cobbler's spawn and yeasty boozing bench
> Reeks in the face of sacred majesty
> His stinking breath of censure—Out upon't!   *He drinks*

---

[19] *The Life of Sr Thomas Bodley, the Honourable Founder of the Publique Library in the Vniversity of Oxford. VVritten by Himselfe* (Oxford: Henry Hall, 1647) sig. B2v.
[20] *The Life of Sr Thomas Bodley*, sig. B4v.

> Why, by this Bordeaux juice, 'tis now become
> The shoeing-horn of bezzlers' discourse,
> The common food of prate: what news at court?
> But in these stiff-necked times, when every jade
> Huffs his upreared crest, the zealous bent
> Of Counsellors' solid cares is trampled on
> By every hackney's heels: Oh I could burst
> At the conjectures, fears, preventions
> And restless tumbling of our tossed brains:
> Ye shall have me an empty cask that's fur'd
> With naught but barmy froth, that ne'er travelled
> Beyond the confines of his Mistress's lips,
> Discourse as confident of peace with Spain,
> As if the Genius of quick Machiavel
> Ushered his speech.[21]

Political news is the shoehorn which eases one into the sociability of an inn or an alehouse, where the beer on tap will quickly turn everyone into an expert in secret diplomacy, its mere froth making even an empty wooden mug (or someone as empty-headed as one) talk like Machiavelli, identified here neither as a demonic figure nor a revolutionary analyst of statecraft, but as the patron saint of fast-talking politicos.

The existence of such public conversation is implied by the Queen's famous complaint, in 1585, that 'she heard how parliament matters was the common table-talk at ordinaries'.[22] The sociability and newsmongering Sir Fortune and his contemporaries were remarking on might remind the modern reader of the coffee-house culture that arose several decades later, and thus of the frequently made point that the history of the modern public sphere reaches further back in time than Jürgen Habermas thought half a century ago. Coffee-house conversations, in the familiar account, disregarded status as sources of discursive authority, creating a new space in which ideas could be exchanged, debated, and judged critically.[23] Sir Fortune's commentary on alehouse politicos is precisely directed against, and

---

[21] *Iacke Drums Entertainment: or The Comedie of Pasquill and Katherine* (London: Richard Oliue, 1601) sigs. A3r–v, modernized. Note that 'barmy froth' is among the words and phrases of which Marston/Crispinus is purged in *Poetaster*; see Chapter 6.

[22] Cp. also Robert Cecil's later remark, namely, that 'whatsoever is subject to public expression cannot be good. Why! Parliament matters are ordinarily talked of in the streets', quoted in J. E. Neale, *The Elizabethan House of Commons* (Rev. edn.; Harmondsworth: Penguin Books, 1963) 401–2, where Neale also quotes the 1589 claim that parliamentary proceedings are 'made or used as table-talk'. See also Chapters 4 and 6 of this book.

[23] Jürgen Habermas, *The Structural Transformation of the Public Sphere: An Inquiry into a Category of Bourgeois Society* (Cambridge, MA: MIT Press, 1989) 30–43; Richard Sennett, *The Fall of Public Man* (Cambridge: Cambridge University Press, 1977) 80–2; Steve Pincus, '"Coffee Politicians Does Create": Coffeehouses and Restoration Political Culture', *The Journal of Modern History*, 67 (1995), 807–34. Sennett relies on Aytoun Ellis, *The Penny Universities: A History of the Coffee-Houses* (London: Secker & Warburg, 1956), while Habermas's dependence on the nostalgic nineteenth-century revaluation of the coffee house is highlighted by Markman Ellis, 'Coffee-Women, *The Spectator*, and the Public Sphere in the Early Eighteenth Century', in Elizabeth Eger et al. (eds.), *Women, Writing and the Public Sphere, 1700–1830* (2001), 27–52 at 44–5.

thus clearly registering, the kind of social levelling that we have learnt to associate with the public sphere as materialized in the coffee house—and it does so in terms rather similar to the contemporary satirical accounts of the emblematic scene of the Restoration public sphere as the chaotic setting for unruly interaction across status boundaries.[24]

To alarmed contemporary commentators, the most objectionable indicator of there being 'no respect of persons' or 'no distinction of persons' at the coffee house was the unbridled curiosity for political information this encouraged.[25] A 1673 tract suggests that in the coffee house,

> all the Rooms rung with nothing but a continued Noise of Arcana Imperii, and Ragioni di stato (in these places some think, most of our late Forms of Government were model'd, and there are, that say, Machiavel the Florentine was born in a Coffee-house).[26]

There is a remarkable continuity between the scandalous political curiosity embodied by early seventeenth-century alehouse Machiavels and by late seventeenth-century coffee-house politicos, and also between the vibrant scenes of political discussions and public exchanges in which they thrived. The late seventeenth-century perception of the deep involvement of the coffee house in the culture of news, as a setting for an often raucous and scandalous discussion of the secrets of politics, of the reason of state, may thus appear to be an extension and expansion of earlier views of earlier settings. My argument is not, however, that we ought therefore read the 1601 settings through the cultural–historical topos of the coffee house, and through the model of the public sphere that topos has helped to formulate. The culture of the coffee house was defined by newsprint and by the partisanship characteristic of representative politics, an environment rather different from the pre-newspaper

---

[24] Lawrence E. Klein, 'Coffeehouse Civility, 1660–1714: An Aspect of Post-Courtly Culture in England', *Huntington Library Quarterly*, 59 (1996), 31–51 at 32–43. It is in a truly vitriolic pamphlet, for example, that we find a reference to the 'great privilege of equality' as something 'only peculiar to the Golden Age, and to a coffee house', see M.P., *A Character of Coffee and Coffee-Houses* (London, 1661) sig. A4v.

[25] M.P., *A Character of Coffee and Coffee-Houses*, sig. A4r, and Samuel Butler, *Characters*, ed. Charles W. Dawes (Cleveland: Press of Case Western Reserve University, 1970) 256–7, cited by Pincus, ' "Coffee Politicians Does Create" ', 815. Pincus's quotations de-emphasize just how scathing some of the contemporary satirical accounts are. So when in one often-quoted passage, the commentator declares 'there's no needing / Of complements or gentile breeding, / For you may seat you any where, / There's no respect of persons there'; what is perhaps not always recognized is how threatening this description really finds the scene. The reference to 'gentile breeding' of course invokes the fuller context of the formulation 'there is no respect of persons with God', Paul's assertion of the absence of any distinction between Jew and Gentile—a distinction which only disappears, however, before God (Romans 2:1–16). The Biblical resonance of 'no respect of persons' in this description of the coffee-house setting does not therefore so much signal a suspension of status difference as a religious confusion triggered by the Turkish brew, whereas the absence of 'complements' is, again, a signal of the suspension not of status difference but of the rules of civility. On coffee houses and newsmongering, cp. Brian Cowan, 'Mr. Spectator and the Coffeehouse Public Sphere', *Eighteenth-Century Studies*, 37 (2004), 345–66 at 349–57; Joanna Picciotto, *Labors of Innocence in Early Modern England* (Cambridge, MA: Harvard University Press, 2010) 301–3.

[26] *The Transposer Rehears'd: or the Fifth Act of Mr. Bayes's Play* (Oxford: 1673) 36, quoted by Michael McKeon, *The Secret History of Domesticity: Public, Private, and the Division of Knowledge* (Baltimore: Johns Hopkins University Press, 2005) 76.

world of political conversation whose logic I am tracing in this book.[27] The lessons of 1601 can be used to revisit the (often normatively oriented) account of the early modern public sphere that is based on the Restoration and post-Restoration situation. Changing our perspective from social effects to the forces underlying them, they encourage us to examine the participants' motives in joining the conversation, to identify the interests and social ambitions driving the engagement in public discussion—all forcibly obscured by such accounts of the public sphere as are focused on its function as constitutive of modern representative democracy.

Before the first coffee houses opened, taverns (places licensed to serve wine) and alehouses served as scenes of conviviality and discussion—and recent scholarship has emphasized the extent to which these scenes of sociability were producing, and were understood to be producing, social distinction. The tavern scene was associated with the deployment of wit, the faculty of distinction and discrimination, which in turn served to distinguish the community of tavern wits from the disorderly, often riotous, unsophisticated, and decidedly plebeian communality of the alehouses, these 'headquarters of popular political opposition and discontent', and also from the nostalgic, patriarchal fantasies of inclusive, ale-drinking rural conviviality—neither of which were imaginable as settings for legitimate political discussion and critical debate.[28] But the intellectually and politically charged culture of conversation of the tavern was defined not by some form of civic rationality, much less by political partisanship, but by a satiric and ludic performance aimed at social and cultural distinction and aesthetic discrimination.[29] An attention to the logic of such discrimination may supplement and correct a more general understanding of early modern critical conversation and satiric performance as responses to social and political phenomena driven by a civic animus, by a concern about injustice or corruption.[30] It may, of course, be all that—but it is also a social game whose motives are not all civic and public-minded. In early seventeenth-century taverns, wine and wit, markers of an emerging form of public sociability, served to distinguish participants from other social groups as well as from each other. Conversations about politics had an obvious place in these convivial environments, but they did not necessarily, or even primarily, take the form of what we would now call political discussion. That is to say, their function was not necessarily or typically to find

---

[27] For a compelling account of print, partisanship, and adversarial public discussion in the late seventeenth century, see Mark Knights, *Representation and Misrepresentation in Later Stuart Britain: Partisanship and Political Culture* (Oxford: Oxford University Press, 2005) 220–71.

[28] Peter Clark, *The English Alehouse: A Social History, 1200–1830* (London and New York: Longman, 1983) 123–94, the quote at 158; Judith Hunter, 'English Inns, Taverns, Alehouses and Brandy Shops: The Legislative Framework 1495–1797', in Beat Kümin and B. Ann Tlusty (eds.), *The World of the Tavern: Public Houses in Early Modern Europe* (Aldershot: Ashgate, 2002), 65–82; Cedric C. Brown, 'Sons of Beer and Sons of Ben: Drink as a Social Marker in Seventeenth-Century England', in Adam Smyth (ed.), *A Pleasing Sinne: Drink and Conviviality in Seventeenth-Century England* (Cambridge: D. S. Brewer, 2004), 3–20.

[29] Michelle O'Callaghan, *The English Wits: Literature and Sociability in Early Modern England* (Cambridge: Cambridge University Press, 2007) 2–8; Adam Zucker, *The Places of Wit in Early Modern English Comedy* (Cambridge: Cambridge University Press, 2011), and recent work by Ian Munro.

[30] For such an earnest understanding of political satire, see e.g. Andrew McRae, *Literature, Satire, and the Early Stuart State* (Cambridge: Cambridge University Press, 2004).

solutions to problems of common concern, they were not opportunities for judging, articulating, and creating possibilities of change: rather, they were understood as discussions about politics as an art, science, or profession. They were conversations about a field of knowledge in which competence could be demonstrated and performed.[31]

Early seventeenth-century observers understood the conceptual and social potential of the philosophical, literary, and political discussion that took place in the tavern and the alehouse in terms markedly different from the late seventeenth- and eighteenth-century intellectual tradition influentially outlined by Habermas. They saw its significance not in its promise of a status-blind discursive equality, not as a political and intellectual opportunity (or fantasy: fantasies have their own discursive and regulative reality) for the formation of a public abstracted from social distinction and difference.[32] Rather, they understood them as spaces in which inherited social and cultural distinction and authority were challenged in order to then be produced and reproduced discursively, to the advantage of those most adept at such discursive production and reproduction.

Such distinction and authority is clearly on Sir Fortune's mind. Beer froth is the emblem of vacuous talk: for Sir Fortune, however, booze does more than lubricate or generate the conversation. Like one's profession or ancestry, one's drink of choice also classifies—not for nothing does he call emphatically for a Bordeaux to fortify him in holding forth against the presumption of common beer-guzzling prattlers.[33] The complaint about the public disregard for the painstaking work of legitimate politicians combines with an assertion of class- (or rather, status-) based discernment, of a judgement of competence and incompetence. Sir Fortune identifies the beer-fuelled talk about politics as a breach of social decorum, a challenge to the system used to demarcate status difference, and thus to the kind of traditional authority held by Sir Fortune as the cheerfully hospitable and generous lord of an ancient household.

In *Jack Drum's Entertainment* as in *Twelfth Night*, political statements are understood not as political but as social acts: neither of these plays view political discussion as something aimed at intervention in a conflict, they don't consider political comment as public action intended to achieve change in matters of common concern, but rather as a personal claim upon a place in society, upon some sort of prestige, authority, or quality, upon something we could describe as class status. This understanding of political discussion inverts the relationship between

---

[31] For a *Begriffsgeschichte* of the three concepts of politics, as discipline, field, and activity, see Kari Palonen, *The Struggle with Time: A Conceptual History of 'Politics' as an Activity* (Hamburg: Lit, 2006) 33–72.

[32] This rational public space or sphere would be analogous with Hannah Arendt's truly political 'arena in which at least few or the best can interact with one another as equals among equals', an equality that has 'of course, nothing to do with justice'. Hannah Arendt, *The Promise of Politics*, ed. Jerome Kohn (New York: Schocken Books, 2005) 118.

[33] Keith Wrightson, *Earthly Necessities: Economic Lives in Early Modern Britain* (The New Economic History of Britain; New Haven: Yale University Press, 2000) 298–300; Adam Fox, 'Food, Drink and Social Distinction in Early Modern England', in Steve Hindle, Alexandra Shepard, and John Walter (eds.), *Remaking English Society: Social Relations and Social Change in Early Modern England* (Cambridge: Boydell & Brewer, 2013), 165–87.

social status and politics that is habitually assumed, where political talk appears as a (however distorted or ideologically displaced) function of one's class position or identity.[34] Instead of being an expression of where one stands, or believes to stand, in society, in these plays, talking politics is an activity through which people actually attempt to claim a social position independent of, and even above, their means and inherited status. The significance of the prattlers' comments on the impending peace with Spain is not the specific view they take on the issue, but the fact that they even presume to have a view. Sir Fortune's diatribe seeks to discredit what he sees as a newly popular habit by describing it as newfangled and evoking a classification system presumed to be beyond dispute—but even in his claims, the winning argument in the debate between the natural authority of hereditary status and the understanding of class as a culturally produced form of social identity appears to be the latter, not the former. When Sir Fortune dismisses alehouse prattlers as inexperienced and empty-headed, he implicitly acknowledges competence rather than entitlement as the criterion for distinction and exclusion. If the difference between careful counsellors and hackneys is one of knowledge and experience, then we are witnessing the emergence of a new regime of authority and legitimacy: a system in which domination is predicated on the claims of competence, on the implicit and treacherous premise of inherent merit, and on the no less treacherous promise of mobility through acquiring it.

Such a system is described in *Distinction: a Social Critique of the Judgment of Taste*, Pierre Bourdieu's most influential book, a study of French culture in the third quarter of the twentieth century. Bourdieu's study explores how choices made in the consumption of cultural goods (understood as the culture of the consumption of goods of any kind, including abstract art, movies, clothing, and services) define one's position in the class system of a modern capitalist society, and how culture as a system of preferences and judgements produces and legitimates social difference and ultimately, social domination. For Bourdieu, just as there is no disinterested judgement of taste, there is also no disinterested political opinion: just as there is no autonomous sphere of the aesthetic, there is also no autonomous sphere of the political. He shows that one's ability to make political arguments, to judge and comment on political questions, is another competence like one's taste in music, food, or shoes, in that it classifies us through the quality and nature of our opinions and choices. By being able to make the appropriate political distinctions, we achieve social distinction.

Starting from the analysis of who responds 'I don't know' to questions in opinion polls, Bourdieu reflects on how claims of competence and incompetence serve as mechanisms to exclude, and make people exclude themselves, from political discussion. In a society where domination takes the form of cultural classification, class intervenes in the formation of political opinion at the level of the ascription of competence in forming such an opinion. The ability to speak politically, to feel capable of forming an opinion on issues identified as political on the one hand,

---

[34] The classic instance of such a political sociology can be found in Marx's *Eighteenth Brumaire*.

and the entitlement to use that knowledge on the other, are mutually reinforcing, and participate in regulating society through the ascription of status.[35]

Hamlet's Moment is not a work of Bourdieusian cultural sociology, but a literary–historical project which traces how plays drew on and broadcast political knowledge, and how this engagement shaped both the plays of the golden age of English drama and the nature of public political discussion. The book does nonetheless take up Bourdieu's suggestion that we think not only about the social roots but also about the social uses of political talk. It assumes that we better understand the politics performed on the stage if we recognize that off-stage political comment is not merely expressive of, or motivated by social status, but also performative of, and even establishing or producing, such status. *Twelfth Night* and *Jack Drum's Entertainment* are not, of course, produced in the kind of self-regulating environment of classifying competences that Bourdieu saw in operation in twentieth-century France: rather, they witness the *emergence* of a system of such competences. Along with other satires of would-be politicians and newsmongering busybodies, these plays register the beginning of the wide dissemination of political knowledge, the emerging sense of the utility of political competence as a marker of distinction, and the attempts to acquire and display political competence beyond the circles of those traditionally entitled to wield it.

Shakespeare's *Hamlet* and other political tragedies of the early seventeenth century were releasing political knowledge into the social interactions captured by these comedies. In this pivotal moment, the stage helped to make politics into an appealing subject, a topic of conversation, transforming knowledge about statecraft from a quasi-professional, instrumental expertise into a form of cultural capital useful in making one's mark in everyday sociable interaction. While such an assessment obviously swerves from an understanding of the public sphere as a critical setting oriented towards an ideal of rationality and universality, aiming to negotiate and adjudicate between a plurality of interests, and to thus articulate the public interest, this shift in the emphasis is not meant to imply that the socially motivated interest in political knowledge had no public, political consequences. Looking ahead to the upheavals of the seventeenth century, we recognize that the dissemination of political vocabularies and political information could lead to political debates and rebellions: as seventeenth-century commentators from Boccalini to Hobbes realized, in early modern states such knowledge was a necessary precondition of challenges to monarchical rule.

The emergence of the English public sphere cannot, of course, be simply understood as the politicization of the sociable discussion of 1601, and an exclusive historiographical focus on political discussion, on the secrets of state, cannot explain

---

[35] Pierre Bourdieu, *Distinction: A Social Critique of the Judgement of Taste*, trans. Richard Nice (London: Routledge and Kegan Paul, 1984) 397–465. Where Bourdieu's work on distinction is providing a conceptual grounding for cultural criticism, Paul Fussell, *Class: A Guide through the American Status System* (New York: Summit Books, 1983) and Michael Thompson, *Rubbish Theory: The Creation and Destruction of Value* (Oxford: Oxford University Press, 1979) would often serve the purpose equally well. The choice of the French over the home-grown is itself illustrative of how such decisions classify.

the emergence of the rational and emancipatory ideals which, as Habermas and others have argued, were structuring bourgeois society in spite of the fact that its own logic obviously compromised and contradicted them.[36] Developments in distinct spheres of intellectual inquiry and knowledge-production were fertilising each other, although our own disciplinary rigour often makes us blind to these effects. The Machiavellian analysis of state secrets performed by those entitled to do so by their office served as a methodological model for the Baconian project of experimental science as formulated in *The Advancement of Learning* in 1605.[37] Over the course of the century that followed, the public—in the Habermasian sense of 'inofficial'—performance of such political analysis and discussion was redeemed from its abjection as idle, transgressive chatter, frivolous and disruptive political curiosity, partly by its assimilation to scientific curiosity as another version of the excavation of truth.[38] Once the inquiry into the secrets of nature was redeemed by Baconian science as the labour of innocent curiosity, and transformed into a model for civil, polite, and policed public interaction, then the excited public discussion of politics could be reimagined as a homologous activity, as the rational inquiry into public interest, as an interminable search for a shared truth that is to emerge from the negotiation and evaluation of competing individual claims and interests. The liberal ideals intended to govern the public use of reason, the normative bracketing of status and of individual interest are therefore best understood as attempts at the domestication of political talk by the emerging protocols of the public sphere of natural science: in other words, the transgressive political curiosity of the busybodies of Hamlet's moment was redeemed by its conceptual assimilation to the culture of scientific curiosity. What distinguishes the coffee house of 1661 from the tavern and the alehouse of 1601, then, is not the content, the critical implications, or even the style of political discussion there, but the ideals legitimating it: the modern, liberal vision of political engagement which an association between coffee-house culture and scientific inquiry, between coffee-house public and the public of Gresham College and the Royal Society helped into being.[39]

---

[36] I am paraphrasing Michael Warner, *Publics and Counterpublics* (New York: Zone Books, 2002) 46.

[37] Cp. Bacon's recurrent insistence on the usefulness of Machiavelli as a model; e.g. 'Is not the ground which Machiavill wisely and largely discourseth concerning Gouernments, That the way to establish and preserve them, is to reduce them ad Principia: a rule in Religion and Nature, as well as in Ciuill administration?' *Two Bookes of Francis Bacon of the Proficience and Aduancement of Learning, Diuine and Humane* (London: 1605) sig. 2F1v. I am quoting the text as presented in Michael Kiernan (ed.), *The Advancement of Learning* (The Oxford Francis Bacon, Oxford: Oxford University Press, 2000). Bacon's conception of the inquiry into natural law is based on the analogy with human law, a notion which 'confines the idea within the horizon of the political thought of the time'—Hans Blumenberg, *The Legitimacy of the Modern Age*, trans. Robert M. Wallace (Cambridge, MA: MIT Press, 1983) 387. John Michael Archer's important *Sovereignty and Intelligence: Spying and Court Culture in the English Renaissance* (Stanford: Stanford University Press, 1993), which covers some of the same ground as the present book from a different, but closely related perspective, locates the rise of modern rationality and political intelligence in the sixteenth century, and the origins of modern scientific observation in the methodologies of surveillance and political knowledge-production by and for the state.

[38] See Knights, *Representation and Misrepresentation in Later Stuart Britain* 335–60 on the process of the idealization and polite moderation of political discussion.

[39] This passage summarizes one of the implications of the chapter on 'The Culture of Curiosity' in Picciotto, *Labors of Innocence* 255–319, and to some extent McKeon, *The Secret History of*

Introduction 19

But the new normative ideals did not transform or erase the interests that animated the continuing discussion of affairs of state—that is simply not what ideals do.[40] It is precisely for a clearer sense of the transformation and radicalization of public political discussion in the seventeenth century, and for an understanding of the emergence of the mode of discussion about the public interest, that we also need to attend to the non-political, self-interested motives that drove early modern publics to desire and acquire an understanding of the realm of politics—attend to interests which the setting of 1601, the setting before the emergence of those powerful alternative descriptions about public discussion, makes so clearly visible.

And we might go further. The competitive sociability as the setting for the circulation of political knowledge around the turn of the century may in fact serve as a starting point for the revision of several narratives about the culture of early modernity. The discernment on display in the acuity of political judgement, in the detached, cynical, 'politic' commentary which proceeded by the ostentatious piercing of illusions and the revelation of secret motives, was loosely analogous to the indifference or objectivity cultivated by seventeenth-century virtuosi, but in a more emphatically, even flamboyantly aesthetic register. The politic comment authorized itself as a form of technical analysis, but it was recognizable as a style of discourse and of argument. Its claim to realism, to an insight into the true nature or 'inside' of things, became inseparable from its distinctive formal quality, Machiavellian analysis from the maxim, turning the search for truth into a search for formal accomplishment. The politic mode therefore deserves our attention as part of a genealogy of the rational, critical public sphere.

This account also impinges on narratives about the changing functions of literariness. The stylization of political argument was only made possible by the political–analytic work of the pointed politic style, its ability to trouble or unpick established, familiar judgements and categories by means of its characteristic working through distinctions and divisions. It is therefore not a resistance to specialized, technocratic, utilitarian knowledge production that creates a need for the unsettling work of form, its restless questioning and productivity, and thus for the quality most readily identified with the literary

---

Domesticity 347–57, on disinterestedness in science and politics. Both of them are, of course, circumspect enough not to make a claim as crude as my formulation here. They are both also anticipated by remarks in David Zaret, 'Religion, Science and Printing in the Public Spheres in Seventeenth-Century England', in Craig Calhoun (ed.), *Habermas and the Public Sphere* (Cambridge, MA: MIT Press, 1992), 212–35. In his later book, Zaret chose to focus on the civil war years and the impact of print, although in his conclusion he offers a further abbreviated version of his argument about the role of science: *Origins of Democratic Culture: Printing, Petitions, and the Public Sphere in Early-Modern England* (Princeton: Princeton University Press, 2000) 272–3. The connection with scientific inquiry might also explain the emergence of the ideal type of the bourgeois public sphere in England rather than elsewhere. Of course I am not making a case for a mono-causal explanation here; for a socio-economical explanation, see Steve Pincus, 'The State and Civil Society in Early Modern England: Capitalism, Causation and Habermas's Bourgeois Public Sphere', in Peter Lake and Steve Pincus (eds.), *The Politics of the Public Sphere in Early Modern England* (Manchester: Manchester University Press, 2007), 213–31.

[40] On efforts at, and failures of, civilizing public political talk, cp. Klein, 'Coffeehouse Civility, 1660–1714'; John Barrell, 'Coffee-House Politicians', *Journal of British Studies*, 43 (2004), 206–32; Cowan, 'Mr. Spectator and the Coffeehouse Public Sphere'.

as the operation of peculiarization and defamiliarization, but professional analysis. Qualities of drama we associate with literary or philosophical tendencies are thus revealed to be active in the work of political analysis and social self-promotion. This is not, of course, to question the histories of the rise of the literary in modernity, only to point to the sometimes surprising plurality of its genealogies.

In such reconstruction of the dissemination of political knowledge and the creation of a politic style, formal literary analysis aligns with Bourdieusian analysis, and together they can find their place in a Habermasian account much as the plurality of individual interests behind aesthetic competition can be joined in the regulating ideal of the public good. The comedy of *Twelfth Night* and the satire of *Jack Drum's Entertainment* allow us to recognize the motives of conversations about politics that were social and sociable but not public-oriented or political at all—motives and conversations which nonetheless made possible, in the long run, well beyond the chronological limits of this book, the eruption of public-minded popular political discussion.

THE MOMENT

The dissemination and re-functioning of political knowledge I have been describing is a long-term process—whereas the plays involved in it are the products of a brief period. The years at the turn of the seventeenth century when Shakespeare's *Hamlet* was written, first performed, and published in two different editions, are at the conjuncture of independently occurring transformations in public political discussion and in theatrical culture. This conjuncture is Hamlet's moment.

In its approach to this moment, this book is contextualist. It seeks to make audible again some of what Lionel Trilling called 'the voice of multifarious intention and activity...all the buzz of implication...coming to us from what never gets fully stated', the distracting noise that informed, and was implied in, everything that got written in the past, a noise that has long stopped, leaving us 'only with what has been fully phrased and precisely stated'—the literary text itself.[41] It has an unapologetically historicist bias in that it seeks to listen to the plays against— and also for—the noise of the moment of their initial production and reception, even though that noise itself often includes the reception, the reading and rewriting, the anachronic reverberations, of much earlier texts, an irony that might immediately put the logical priority (and indeed the very identity) of the primary context into question. But *Hamlet's Moment* is also keen to avoid the suggestion that this context would exhaust or explain the difference *Hamlet* and other plays made to their cultural and political moment, not to mention literary history. What justifies our close attention to the plays is precisely that

> innovation is a kind of secular miracle: secular, because it happens amid the humdrum machinery of life getting along, and virtually everything about it is comprehensible without

---

[41] 'Manners, morals and the novel', in Lionel Trilling, *The Liberal Imagination: Essays on Literature and Society* (New York: New York Review Books, 2008), 206.

recourse to any notion of supernatural mystery or fated destiny; miraculous, not only because it can change things dramatically, but because none of that machinery suffices to explain why it had to happen this way.[42]

The book's narrowly contextualist historicism is motivated by a different mode of historical thought, and by what I perceive as the shortcomings of its current manifestations. Like so many, I also understand the years I call Hamlet's moment as pivotal, as a turning point: if it is not exactly the moment of the birth of modernity (the nature of modernity is that it is constantly being born), it is at least a moment in time in which some of the aspects of that birth can be grasped—in which some moments of this complex notion, now using the non-temporal sense of the word 'moment', become visible. The two, closely related moments of the birth of modernity whose interrelatedness *Hamlet's Moment* explores are the birth of modern politics and the birth of the modern public sphere.

Some of the most important recent literary scholarship on the origins of political modernity has been informed by (or is squarely in the field of) intellectual history. The focus of this research is on political theology, centrally concerned with the links between sovereignty and religion, between the secular and the sacred, and between the pre-modern and the modern—via the explorations of Weimar-era German critics of the liberal tradition.[43] Not least because Carl Schmitt devoted a lecture to *Hamlet*, the play and its moment have been particularly important to this new body of work.[44] Studies of early modern English literature in this intellectual–historical mode have mostly turned away from versions of historicism which sought to understand political actions as well as cultural representations with the help of anthropology, sociology, and social and economic history, and which relied on the concepts of ideology and of culture as mediations between representations and practices.[45] Historicist scholarship has on occasion been criticized for reducing representations to practices, texts to their contexts: reading the new, at times starkly anti-historicist, and decidedly non-contextualist intellectual history, one now occasionally gets the impression that contrary to

---

[42] Kirk Varnedoe, *A Fine Disregard: What Makes Modern Art Modern* (New York: Abrams, 1990), 10–11.

[43] For a representative collection, see Graham L. Hammill and Julia Reinhard Lupton (eds.), *Political Theology and Early Modernity* (Chicago: University of Chicago Press, 2012), and for a helpful survey of the field, Jennifer Rust, 'Political Theology and Shakespeare Studies', *Literature Compass*, 6/1 (2009), 175–90. The early modern engagements of the scholars whose intellectual origins, if not their entire, or even most important, output, can be traced to the Weimar years, i.e. of Carl Schmitt, Ernst Kantorowicz, and Walter Benjamin, as well as of Hannah Arendt and Leo Strauss, and, perhaps surprisingly, of Freud, are discussed in Victoria Kahn, *The Future of Illusion: Political Theology and Early Modern Texts* (Chicago: University of Chicago Press, 2014). Julia Lupton has sought to recuperate and reorient this intellectual tradition for writing the early modern genealogy of liberalism, especially in her *Thinking with Shakespeare: Essays on Politics and Life* (Chicago: University of Chicago Press, 2011).

[44] Carl Schmitt, *Hamlet oder Hekuba: Der Einbruch der Zeit in das Spiel* (Düsseldorf–Köln: Eugen Diederichs Verlag, 1956); now available as *Hamlet or Hecuba: The Intrusion of the Time into the Play*, trans. David Pan and Jennifer R. Rust (New York: Telos Press, 2009).

[45] It is important to note that in the 1920s and 1930s, Schmitt repeatedly described his enterprise as sociological.

what the Marx of the Feuerbach-theses thought, early modern philosophers, jurists, and poets were not only interpreting the world, but changing it already.[46]

Because it is less interested in, for example, early modern theories of sovereignty, and more in how such theories would have socially benefited those familiar with them, this book only overhears this current conversation, without hoping to be able to participate in it. But it might be worth pointing out that the current separation of the study of political theology, and of the history of political thought and political philosophy in this reinvigorated tradition of intellectual history, from the ongoing research into social and political practices in general, and into the problem of the nature, history, and function of the public sphere in particular[47] is far from inevitable. These areas of research are linked through their histories, and the intellectual genealogies can be the ground for a *rapprochement*. In terms of its intellectual lineage, after all, Habermas's early work now seems indebted not only to the first generation of the Frankfurt School, but also to Carl Schmitt and especially to the thought of Hannah Arendt, whose work helped him turn away from a Marxist *Ideologiekritik*. More importantly, a mode of literary scholarship that still seeks to discern the links between the history of society and the histories of languages, concepts, and ideas—between practices and representations[48]—will still find the history of communication, of the institutions, techniques, and protocols of reading and writing and conversation and performance a powerful way to do so. Such research promises to return the ideas to their historical contexts without necessarily reducing them to those contexts, as crude uses of the notion of ideology arguably did. And this is where Habermas might serve as one source of inspiration, if not a model. His ambition to link the history of capitalism, the history of communication, and the history of political ideas and of philosophy as mutually informing, points to an ideal against which to measure the historicist enterprise. The ambition of this book is, of course, much more modest, but it attempts to link social, intellectual, and literary history by examining the circulation of knowledge in print and

---

[46] The one major critic of early modern English writing that I am aware of who has engaged with this intellectual history while paying a continued attention to economic and social processes, to the processes of work and of communication, and putting conceptual transformations in relation to those processes, is Richard Halpern, whose work on early modernity over the past quarter of a century shows a remarkable continuity—see especially *The Poetics of Primitive Accumulation: English Renaissance Culture and the Genealogy of Capital* (Ithaca: Cornell University Press, 1991); 'Marlowe's Theater of Night: *Doctor Faustus* and Capital', *English Literary History*, 71 (2004), 455–95; 'Eclipse of Action: *Hamlet* and the Political Economy of Playing', *Shakespeare Quarterly*, 59 (2008), 450–82; 'The King's Two Buckets: Kantorowicz, *Richard II*, and Fiscal *Trauerspiel*', *Representations*, 106 (2009), 67–76.

[47] In addition to titles cited elsewhere in this introduction, see also Joad Raymond, *News, Newspapers, and Society in Early Modern Britain* (London and Portland: Frank Cass, 1999); Bronwen Wilson and Paul Edward Yachnin, *Making Publics in Early Modern Europe: People, Things, Forms of Knowledge* (New York: Routledge, 2010); Massimo Rospocher, *Beyond the Public Sphere: Opinions, Publics, Spaces in Early Modern Europe* (Annali dell'Istituto Storico Italo-Germanico in Trento; Bologna and Berlin: Il Mulino and Duncker & Humblot, 2012); Christian Emden and David R. Midgley (eds.), *Beyond Habermas: Democracy, Knowledge, and the Public Sphere* (New York: Berghahn Books, 2013).

[48] Samuel Moyn, 'Imaginary Intellectual History', in Darrin M. McMahon and Samuel Moyn (eds.), *Rethinking Modern European Intellectual History* (Oxford: Oxford University Press, 2014), 113–30.

manuscript, in professional and fictional forms, and by attending to the interest in, and utility of, this circulation in a particular historical moment.[49]

It is perhaps time to locate Hamlet's moment in history. English politics of the last decades of the sixteenth century was defined by the problem of the succession of the childless Queen. The issue was debated in government circles, and the arguments were also made public by the monarch's counsellors, thus calling into being a public whose opinion could exert pressure in factional conflicts. Since public political debate was incited and managed by elements within the regime, its ebb and flow was largely the function of the changing positions of those capable of controlling the discussion by releasing information and arguments into public circulation, and of the fractures and tensions within this elite. The last years of Elizabeth's reign were defined by the competition between Robert Cecil and the Earl of Essex: a competition for the Queen's favour, for control over the court and over English foreign relations, and also for the attention of James. Cecil's and Essex's assertions of loyalty to the King of Scotland always implied a threat to his claims to the throne from other claimants supported by other members of the English elite, so factional conflict also helped to keep alive the anxieties over the succession, and with it, theories of resistance, of election, as well as a strategically invoked civic rhetoric for the description of the government of England. In 1601, the fall of Essex thus put an end to years of debate and anxiety: now that his competitor was gone, Robert Cecil could engineer the smooth and uncontested accession of James Stuart, obviating public arguments about how the person of the next monarch should be determined. The lively and decidedly risky debate about theories of sovereignty and the subjects' right to participate, fraught with implications of confessional difference, appeared to be coming to an end.[50]

---

[49] In a series of programmatic articles, Warren Boutcher has argued for such an approach to historical interpretation; see especially 'Humanism and Literature in Late Tudor England: Translation, the Continental Book and the Case of Montaigne's *Essais*', in Jonathan Woolfson (ed.), *Reassessing Tudor Humanism* (Basingstoke: Macmillan, 2002), 243–68; 'Literature', in Jonathan Woolfson (ed.), *Palgrave Advances in Renaissance Historiography* (Basingstoke: Palgrave, 2005), 210–40; 'Unoriginal Authors: How to Do Things with Texts in the Renaissance', in Annabel S. Brett, James Tully, and Holly Hamilton-Bleakley (eds.), *Rethinking the Foundations of Modern Political Thought* (Cambridge: Cambridge University Press, 2006), 73–92.

[50] Patrick Collinson, 'The Monarchical Republic of Queen Elizabeth I', *Bulletin of the John Rylands Memorial Library*, 69 (1986–7), 394–424; Patrick Collinson, *De Republica Anglorum or, History with the Politics Put Back* (Cambridge: Cambridge University Press, 1990); Patrick Collinson, 'The Elizabethan Exclusion Crisis and the Elizabethan Polity', *Proceedings of the British Academy*, 84 (1994), 51–92; John Guy (ed.), *The Reign of Elizabeth I: Court and Culture in the Last Decade* (Cambridge: Cambridge University Press, 1995); Jean-Christophe Mayer (ed.), *Breaking the Silence on the Succession: A Sourcebook of Manuscripts and Rare Elizabethan Texts (c.1587–1603)* (Montpellier: Université Paul-Valéry Montpellier 3, 2003); Jean-Christophe Mayer (ed.), *The Struggle for the Succession in Late Elizabethan England: Politics, Polemics and Cultural Representations* (Montpellier: Université Paul-Valéry Montpellier 3, 2004); Peter Lake, 'The King (the Queen) and the Jesuit: James Stuart's *True Law of Free Monarchies* in Context/s', *Transactions of the Royal Historical Society*, 14 (2004), 243–60; Peter Lake, 'The Politics of "Popularity" and the Public Sphere: The "Monarchical Republic" of Elizabeth I Defends Itself', in Peter Lake and Steve Pincus (eds.), *The Politics of the Public Sphere in Early Modern England* (Manchester: Manchester University Press, 2007), 59–94; John F. McDiarmid, *The Monarchical Republic of Early Modern England: Essays in Response to Patrick Collinson* (Aldershot: Ashgate, 2007); Jeffrey S. Doty, *Shakespeare, Popularity, and the Public Sphere* (Cambridge: Cambridge University Press, forthcoming).

England's engagement with the continent also entered a new phase at the turn of the century. Open war among Spain, France, the Netherlands, and England was drawing to a close. 1598–9 ended the French civil wars and brought the peace of Vervins between Spain and France, England's most important wartime ally, as well as the first overtures for negotiation from Archduke Albert in the Low Countries. England began to withdraw active military support from France and the States General, and by the time of James's accession, the pacification of Ireland and the negotiation of the peace treaty with Spain were well under way.

Accounts of the dramatic and literary landscape of early modern England often use the onset of hostilities to explain intellectual changes and shifts of mentality. The success of the heroic drama of the early 1590s, and the often jingoistic nationalism of the English history play has been convincingly traced to the political climate of the period following 1588 and the militarization of the late Elizabethan state.[51] But if the repeated Armada threats, the military engagements in France and in the Netherlands, and the naval expeditions against Spain all had an unmistakable impact on life, writing, and performance in England, so did their passing.[52]

The importance of James's posturing as *rex pacificus* has of course been commented upon, and the Jacobean peace (however uncertain and transient) shaped early seventeenth-century political culture in other ways as well. Although the pressures of ongoing warfare were keenly felt by the English until the turn of the century, with a significant number of men drafted for military service through the late nineties, the peak of the Irish wars,[53] the same period also saw a dramatic expansion of diplomatic activity, providing an expanding circle of more privileged men with avenues of advancement. While Essex's failure in Ireland clearly helped to divest militaristic attitudes of their lustre and public appeal, the diplomatic service he operated (and attempted to use in his efforts to establish himself as Burghley's potential successor as the Queen's most influential counsellor) attracted an important group of young men looking to launch themselves on political careers.

The competing secretariats and intelligence networks of Essex and the Cecils were the most visible opportunities for political employment in the last decade of Elizabeth's reign. The fall of Essex reshuffled these patronage networks, subordinating them to a single centre, but the reorientation of English foreign policy under Robert Cecil promised more opportunities for political service. With permanent embassies and missions established in Venice, Madrid, and elsewhere, the diplomatic corps underwent a sudden large-scale expansion, opening up possibilities for

---

[51] John S. Nolan, 'The Militarization of the Elizabethan State', *Journal of Military History*, 58 (1994), 391–420; David M. Bevington, *Tudor Drama and Politics: A Critical Approach to Topical Meaning* (Cambridge, MA: Harvard University Press, 1968) 301; James Shapiro, 'Revisiting *Tamburlaine*: *Henry V* as Shakespeare's Belated Armada Play', *Criticism*, 31 (1989), 351–66.

[52] Paul A. Jorgensen, *Shakespeare's Military World* (Berkeley: University of California Press, 1956) 118.

[53] Mark Charles Fissel, *English Warfare, 1511–1642* (Warfare and History; London and New York: Routledge, 2001) 96–105. About pressing men into service in the 1590s and the anxieties surrounding the practice, see also James Shapiro, *1599: A Year in the Life of William Shakespeare* (London: Faber, 2005) 71–8.

entry into the patronage system surrounding court and diplomatic offices.[54] The demilitarization of English politics and the heightened visibility of diplomatic careers resulted in a shift of the dominant cultural model for social advancement from the soldier–courtier to the diplomat–politician.

The shift I am talking about is therefore perceptible in the short-term history, the *histoire événementielle*, of cultural representation—but it is embedded in long-term processes. What Keith Thomas terms 'the waning of the military ideal', for example, is a transformation on a much longer scale, taking place over many decades, even centuries.[55] Importantly for my purposes, Thomas links this transformation to the professionalization of the military, to its change from a generally defining activity into a separate trade. This book is about a related, although not entirely analogous, development: the professionalization of politics and the democratization of political commentary. But my focus on Hamlet's moment is prompted by the recognition of the extent to which these long-term processes were impelled and articulated by local, momentary exigencies.

Just as agitated debate about the succession was terminated and jingoistic militarism was sidelined by new realities around the turn of the century, these same new realities were drawing attention to the business of politics, to the successful navigation of political careers, especially to the competences and knowledge associated with employment in diplomacy, the political activity most clearly associated with expertise. The tide would of course soon turn again: after the turn-of-the-century shift I have been describing, public controversy would pick up again in the 1610s and 1620s, when reactions to dynastic marriages, domestic religious tensions, the rule of royal favourites, the re-confessionalization of international politics, and the onset of the Thirty Years War galvanized the English public sphere. Court and parliamentary scandal and the rapid expansion of the marketplace of news mark the eruption of public political debate ahead of its revolutionary transformation in the 1640s.[56]

---

[54] Garrett Mattingly, *Renaissance Diplomacy* (London: Jonathan Cape, 1955) 195–7; Wallace T. MacCaffrey, *Elizabeth I: War and Politics, 1588–1603* (Princeton: Princeton University Press, 1992) 196–245, 515–20; Paul E. J. Hammer, *Elizabeth's Wars: War, Government and Society in Tudor England, 1544–1604* (Basingstoke: Palgrave Macmillan, 2003) 204–6, 215–16, 221, 229–35; Shapiro, *1599: A Year in the Life of William Shakespeare* 50–4; Paul E. J. Hammer, 'The Crucible of War: English Foreign Policy, 1589–1603', in Susan Doran and Glenn Richardson (eds.), *Tudor England and Its Neighbours* (Basingstoke: Palgrave, 2005), 235–66; Pauline Croft, 'Rex Pacificus, Robert Cecil, and the 1604 Peace with Spain', in Glenn Burgess, Rowland Wymer, and Jason Lawrence (eds.), *The Accession of James I: Historical and Cultural Consequences* (Basingstoke: Palgrave Macmillan, 2006), 140–54.

[55] Keith Thomas, *The Ends of Life: Roads to Fulfilment in Early Modern England* (Oxford: Oxford University Press, 2009) 62–76. This is a change closely linked to the memorable account of the transformation of the nobility by Norbert Elias.

[56] David Norbrook, *Poetry and Politics in the English Renaissance* (Rev. edn.; Oxford: Oxford University Press, 2002) 179–98; Hans Werner, 'The Hector of Germanie, or the Palsgrave, Prime Elector and Anglo–German Relations of Early Stuart England', in R. Malcolm Smuts (ed.), *The Stuart Court and Europe: Essays in Politics and Culture* (Cambridge: Cambridge University Press, 1996). Richard Cust and Ann Hughes (eds.), *Conflict in Early Stuart England: Studies in Religion and Politics, 1603–1642* (London and New York: Longman, 1989); Thomas Cogswell, *The Blessed Revolution: English Politics and the Coming of War, 1621–1624* (Cambridge: Cambridge University Press, 1989); Kevin Sharpe, *The Personal Rule of Charles I* (New Haven: Yale University Press, 1992) 1–63; Ethan

The transformative effect of print—and particularly of printed news, of printed pamphlets and petitions, and of the periodical press—on the public sphere of politics is now a commonplace. This book looks at a moment when print is still only one among several, equally important public media, when the political imaginary is as preoccupied with the restricted circulation of manuscripts as it is with the publicity of print, and when drama, a genre existing both in the theatre and in print, is a defining constituent of the political mediascape, and recognized as a powerful medium of political publicity.[57] Late sixteenth- and early seventeenth-century theatre and conversation often anticipate or at least precede print, this inky owl of Minerva, who won't catch up with other media through the diurnal (or at least periodical) production of information until the mid-century. In this same period, the theatre was also a more up-to-date school of discourse than any conversation manual could hope to be—well into the seventeenth century, as we shall see, conversation manuals in fact imitated, and borrowed from, the fashionable language of the stage. Conversation was modelled on stage discourse, and it is the contention of this book that political conversation, with its complicated, often apolitical motives, was as well. Noah Millstone's research has unearthed a whole discursive universe of politic analysis practised not only by diplomats, courtiers, and worldly sophisticates, but also by students and provincial gentlemen. The evidence for this thriving, indeed popular, form of discussion comes mostly from the 1620s and 1630s.[58] What is important to recognize here is that the stage is not lagging behind but seems to be driving the trend, with the most astutely politic plays pre-dating the bulk of the surviving manuscript material: the separates, newsletters, and news diaries that register the widespread popularity of this mode.

It is a significant fact that the commercial theatre created some of its most compelling representations of the realm of politics, and enlisted characters like Hamlet and Sejanus, Bussy d'Ambois and the Duke of Byron, Malevole and Bosola, Macbeth and Coriolanus, in a moment of calm between two periods of agitated political discussion, between the passing of heated controversy at the turn of the century and the re-animation of the public sphere from the second decade of the seventeenth century on.[59] That the political drama of Hamlet's moment is the

---

H. Shagan, 'Introduction: English Catholic History in Context', in Ethan H. Shagan (ed.), *Catholics and the 'Protestant Nation'* (Manchester and New York: Manchester University Press, 2005), 1–21 at 9; Chris R. Kyle, *Theater of State: Parliament and Political Culture in Early Stuart England* (Stanford: Stanford University Press, 2012); Jason Peacey, *Print and Public Politics in the English Revolution* (Cambridge: Cambridge University Press, 2013).

[57] See especially F. J. Levy, 'How Information Spread among the Gentry, 1550–1640', *Journal of British Studies*, 21 (1982), 11–34; Fritz Levy, 'The Decorum of News', in Joad Raymond (ed.), *News, Newspapers, and Society in Early Modern Britain* (London and Portland, OR: Frank Cass, 1999), 12–38; Fritz Levy, 'Staging the News', in Arthur Marotti and Michael Bristol (eds.), *Print, Manuscript and Performance* (2000); Douglas Bruster, 'The Structural Transformation of Print in Late Elizabethan England', in *Shakespeare and the Question of Culture: Early Modern Literature and the Cultural Turn* (Basingstoke: Palgrave Macmillan, 2003), 65–93; Doty, *Shakespeare, Popularity, and the Public Sphere*.

[58] Noah Millstone, *Manuscript Circulation and the Invention of Politics in Early Stuart England* (Cambridge: Cambridge University Press, 2015).

[59] Peter Lake and Steve Pincus, 'Rethinking the Public Sphere in Early Modern England', *Journal of British Studies*, 45 (2006), 270–92 at 279.

political drama of an apparent lull in public controversy frustrates our desire to see plays about politics as interventions in a field of debate, with ideological positions and stakes. The plays of the 1590s have long been seen as energized by public political polemics,[60] and the political drama of the 1610s and 1620s has also been discussed in the context of the emerging public sphere,[61] but the political plays written during the first decade of the seventeenth century appear to resist being situated in public discussion.[62]

That resistance is overcome if we realize that many of the conversations these plays were tapping into—and more importantly feeding into and also generating—were of a different nature: they were conversations about the means, not necessarily about the ends of political action. They were not the heated polemics, the partisan position-takings of those periods of high-pitched debate, but sociable yet self-interested exchanges about politics as field of opportunities for advancement, and about politics as a field to be observed, judged, and commented upon in efforts to cultivate and display discernment. Such conversations are themselves displays of cultural capital, of a familiarity with the business of politics, of an access to inside information: of political competence that draws on professional forms of political knowledge. The theatres of the turn of the century were located at the intersection between the court and a wider commercial public, and were thus particularly well placed to disseminate such knowledge. Their engagement with the political culture of urban and court elites consisted partly in reflecting the discourses and practices of the professionalizing political class back at this defining segment of their constituency—but in holding a mirror up to this insider group, they were also refracting those discourses and practices outward, to an audience recruited from outside those circles, who thus became spectators and judges of a world represented to them. In the audience, courtiers, would-be courtiers, and sceptical spectators stood shoulder to shoulder, competing in their judgement of

---

[60] Bevington, *Tudor Drama and Politics*; Marie Axton, *The Queen's Two Bodies: Drama and the Elizabethan Succession* (London: Royal Historical Society, 1977); Mayer (ed.), *The Struggle for the Succession in Late Elizabethan England* 299–432; Chris Fitter, 'Emergent Shakespeare and the Politics of Protest: *2 Henry VI* in Historical Contexts', *English Literary History*, 72 (2005), 129–58; Jeffrey S. Doty, 'Shakespeare's *Richard II*, "Popularity," and the Early Modern Public Sphere', *Shakespeare Quarterly*, 61 (2010), 183–205.

[61] Jerzy Limon, *Dangerous Matter: English Drama and Politics in 1623/24* (Cambridge: Cambridge University Press, 1986); Ian Munro, 'Making Publics: Secrecy and Publication in *A Game at Chess*', *Medieval & Renaissance Drama in England*, 14 (2001), 207–26; Alastair Bellany, *The Politics of Court Scandal in Early Modern England: News Culture and the Overbury Affair, 1603–1660* (Cambridge: Cambridge University Press, 2002) 1–3; Thomas Cogswell and Peter Lake, 'Buckingham Does the Globe: Henry VIII and the Politics of Popularity in the 1620s', *Shakespeare Quarterly*, 60 (2009), 253–78.

[62] Topical readings of plays, efforts to read them as coded commentary on contemporary events, seem to be the significant exception to this. Characteristically, however, the most important systematic treatment of topical political meaning in early modern plays stops short of the turn of the century; see Bevington, *Tudor Drama and Politics*. The difficulty is best explained by Swinburne (and Bevington's book starts with quoting him): he suggested (tongue in cheek, of course) that Romeo is clearly an image of Burghley, precisely because there appears to be no resemblance whatsoever. In the absence of evidence of public discussion whose terms could be on display in the drama, topical meaning cannot be anchored in contemporary reality. For a recent, rich and compelling yet problematic effort at reading *Volpone* as topical satire, see Richard Dutton, *Ben Jonson, Volpone and the Gunpowder Plot* (Cambridge: Cambridge University Press, 2008).

the competences performed on stage, and in doing so, acquiring the very competences they were judging.

This theatre of political judgement, an incarnation of the most powerful metaphor for the public world in the early modern period, was helped into being by a specifically aesthetic, theatrical event involved in the conjuncture of Hamlet's moment. In the theatres, the turn of the century saw an intense rivalry among repertories, among acting and writing styles. The revival of the boys' companies around 1599–1600 created a highly competitive theatre scene in London, a competitiveness that was manifested in the 'war of theatres', a series of plays clearly responding to and making sometimes quite scathing fun of each other.[63] The on-stage caricatures of dramatists as well as of writing and performance styles that served as the artillery in this 'war' helped to create a highly self-reflective and sharply critical culture of playmaking and playgoing, a theatrical culture driven by the desire to explore, formulate, and judge strategies and competences necessary for achieving distinction in dramatic, literary, cultural, and social terms. When Rosencrantz explains that the boys' companies 'so berattle the common stages...that many wearing rapiers are afraid of goose-quills and scarce come thither,' (2.2.340–2) he is describing a scene where the cultural habits of gentry audiences are pinpointed and indeed skewered in the name of decorum.

The theatres' participation in the production of social distinction is signalled by a passage at the end of *Jack Drum's Entertainment*—where the difference between habits of consumption that Sir Edward Fortune used to distinguish between legitimate and illegitimate political commentary is invoked again, this time to distinguish between gentle and unsophisticated performances, companies and audiences.

> SIR ED.... I saw the Children of Paul's last night,
> And troth they pleased me pretty, pretty well,
> The Apes in time will do it handsomely.
> PLA. I'faith I like the audience that frequenteth there
> With much applause: A man shall not be choked
> With the stench of garlic, nor be pasted
> To the barmy jacket of a beer-brewer.
> BRA. JU. Tis a good gentle audience, and I hope the Boys
> Will come one day into the Court of requests.

Judgement and discernment in this play do of course serve to achieve and signal distinction—

> BRA. SIG. I and they had good plays, but they produce
> Such musty fopperies of antiquity,
> And do not suit the humorous age's backs
> With clothes in fashion.
> PLA. Well Brabant well, you will be censuring still,
> There lies a jest in steep will whip you for't.[64]

---

[63] Matthew Steggle, *Wars of the Theatres: The Poetics of Personation in the Age of Jonson* (Victoria, BC: University of Victoria, 1998); James P. Bednarz, *Shakespeare & the Poets' War* (New York: Columbia University Press, 2001).

[64] Marston, *Iacke Drums Entertainment*, sigs. A3r–v.

So ill-advised censure will not only distinguish but will itself also draw censure: in the logic of the war of the theatres, the whip of satire will lash at the critic. Such exchanges, however, also serve to further clarify the distinctions and articulate the differences.

If, as recent criticism has pointed out, the comedies of this moment helped to formulate the standards and uses of social competencies, created communities through judgements of wit, and guarded discernment with the help of satire,[65] the authors of *Hamlet*, *Sejanus*, *The Malcontent*, and *Bussy d'Ambois* were applying the same theatrical lens to the affairs of state, to the practices of sharing and withholding knowledge in politics, and the successes and failures of its self-interested uses. In a remarkable series of tragedies and tragicomedies about court politics, Shakespeare, Ben Jonson, John Marston, and George Chapman foregrounded the knowledge and competences necessary for success and survival in political employment, and subjected them to an analysis in the terms of discernment and distinction developed by the theatres.

THIS BOOK

Hamlet's Moment reads drama in its engagement with professional political knowledge, revealing how plays written in the first decade of the seventeenth century were shaped by the forms of this knowledge and by the social promises such knowledge held. This argument presupposes that there was such a thing as a political profession, however loosely understood: that there was a career path associated with political employment that was assumed to be a path to social advancement, and that there was a recognizable body of knowledge and mode of thinking defining it. To show this, the first half of the book focuses on *Hamlet* and its reflection on the conditions of political employment, on the characteristics of thinking in a politic manner, and on the education and intellectual work required for advancement in political careers. In the second half of the book I turn to plays that follow in the wake of Shakespeare's path-breaking tragedy, and engage with the kinds of knowledge associated with political education and political careers. Like *Hamlet*, these plays rely on political modes of reading and writing and display the textual products of the profession of politics, but they also reflect on the circulation of such texts and knowledge outside their limited, professional sphere, whether they are imagining it, paradoxically, as a political threat, or more realistically, as conversational ammunition. Read in their intellectual and communicative contexts, these plays afford us a view of the place of drama in the public dissemination and uses of political knowledge, and of the nature of political discussion in Hamlet's moment.

[65] Leo Salingar, 'Jacobean Playwrights and "Judicious" Spectators', *Renaissance Drama*, 22 (1991), 209–34; Mary Bly, *Queer Virgins and Virgin Queans on the Early Modern Stage* (Oxford: Oxford University Press, 2000); Lucy Munro, *Children of the Queen's Revels: A Jacobean Theatre Repertory* (Cambridge: Cambridge University Press, 2005) 55–95; Zucker, *The Places of Wit* 54–101; Allison K. Deutermann, *Audiences to This Act: Listening for Form in Early Modern Theater* (Edinburgh: Edinburgh University Press, forthcoming).

In the first chapter, I examine the question of the education of those aspiring to succeed in political service, and the emerging understanding of politics as a distinct mode of thinking and area of expertise. My starting point is the first and most-quoted early comment on Shakespeare's *Hamlet*, a note by Gabriel Harvey, who praised it as a work that can 'please the wiser sort'. A humanist famously eager for a political career, Harvey left copious marginalia in his books, which are often seen as exemplary of late sixteenth-century practices of reading in the contexts of political patronage. These notes help me insert *Hamlet* in the contexts of late sixteenth-century political education, of the emerging discussion about the reason of state, and of the culture of extracting *sententiae* from literary texts. Sententious statements and arguments provide a formal link between tragic drama and the focus on aphoristic formulations in Machiavelli's sixteenth-century reception. To read tragic drama like Harvey meant developing a textual hermeneutics whose purpose was political education and whose main task was making a distinction between moral or philosophical considerations on the one hand and the principles of political action on the other—all this in an effort to make up for the failure of humanist schooling to provide pragmatic, material guidance, and to serve as a method for the training of a political elite. Harvey's note implies a similarity between the utility of Shakespeare's *Lucrece* and *Hamlet*. But when we read them in the context of the discussion about the reason of state, it turns out that the public, polemical modality of *Lucrece* flatly refuses to distinguish between moral and political obligations, whereas *Hamlet* reveals itself as a text structured precisely by the tensions between religious–ethical and political norms and arguments, and by the conflicting claims they make on dramatic characters and on play readers.

While in my first chapter I seek to discern politics in abstract terms, as a form of judgement and kind of expertise, in the second chapter, I turn to diplomacy, the field in which people entering political careers were trained and tested. Diplomacy in general, and the ways in which foreign intelligence is gathered, transmitted, and used at home, is a major preoccupation of Shakespeare's *Hamlet*. Using documents related to Daniel Rogers's 1588 embassy to Denmark, I establish the play's indebtedness for foreign intelligence to the textual products of diplomatic service: to the genre of ambassadorial *relazioni*, descriptions of foreign states written by diplomats as well as would-be diplomats on their return from foreign states. *Hamlet* thus both represents the secretive world of diplomacy for the play's public, and joins other publications in divulging information derived from the textual products of this world.

Since diplomatic service was the main training field of people entering political careers, the production and circulation of such documents was a crucial way of claiming the political expertise necessary for gaining advancement or employment. The hopes of advancement are central to the play's own engagement with diplomacy and travel: in the world of *Hamlet*, characters' social advancement and political empowerment is enabled by their return from abroad. This avenue of empowerment defines the spatial logic of the play, its rarely if ever noted unity of place: set in and around Elsinore castle throughout, the play treats foreign locations only as they affect Denmark. Although everything in Denmark depends on it, the foreign world remains unseen—it remains that 'which passeth show', and, like the characters' often-discussed inwardness, only makes a mediated appearance, a mediation that is the crux of both political action and social advancement in the play.

The focus of the third chapter is the transformation of the understanding of the political agent in public discussion and in stage representation. The chapter explores how Shakespeare's *Hamlet* departs both from earlier English dramatic representations of the world of politics, and from previous treatments of the story of the Prince of Denmark. These departures describe Hamlet's moment as a turn away from public-minded polemic, and towards the pressures on the self-interested subject. In earlier plays, as in Marlowe's *Edward II*, in the anonymous *Thomas of Woodstock*, or in Shakespeare's *2 Henry VI*, the structures of the monarchical republic, the forms of legitimate public control over the monarch featured centrally, providing the institutional basis for the public contestation of power. The narrative source of *Hamlet* participates in a similar polemical context: the *histoire tragique* of Amleth by François de Belleforest directly links the play's plot to the intense international polemics about hereditary monarchy and about the subjects' right to resist and depose the monarch that was prompted by the problems of the Scottish and the English succession and of the French wars of religion. By the turn of the century, the changing international situation and the impending Stuart succession extinguished the open debate, and Shakespeare's play adjusts the dramatic templates for the representation of politics to this new situation by deflecting the polemical intervention made by its source about the English succession, and even distancing itself from the very idea of public political controversy.

The play's inward turn is a function of a change in the dominant understanding of the political realm. *Hamlet* understands politics as a career, as an opportunity for individual success or failure, rather than the field of public action performed in the name or interest of the community. Following *Hamlet*, playwrights' attention turned from the contestation of legitimacy and sovereignty to the tensions and dilemmas of living a political life under the status quo, focusing on the competences and forms of expertise associated with the profession of politics and the networks of patronage defining it. In the figure of Horatio, Shakespeare's *Hamlet* even creates a character who advances himself to a key position by his competent service and his ability to keep quiet about controversial issues.

The second part of the book revisits the forms of knowledge explored in the example of *Hamlet*, and considers their transformations in public circulation, tracing the emergence of a politic style of conversation. In Chapter 4, I examine the consequences of the escape or 'betrayal' of foreign intelligence to a public beyond court circles, and to the problems and anxieties attendant upon such wide, commercial, anonymous circulation—problems and anxieties that register the inception of the early modern public sphere. In Hamlet's moment, the stage was one of the most important public media for the dissemination of political news from abroad. The five tragedies written by George Chapman during the first decade of the reign of James Stuart constitute the largest surviving corpus of early modern English plays that engage with French court politics. A reconstruction of Chapman's connections to a group of booksellers reveals how accounts of French politics were transferred from diplomatic correspondence and ambassadorial reports to the public stage via the marketplace of news and of books centred around St Paul's Cathedral, creating diplomatic scandals through the representation of disreputable events of the recent past. The plays' predicament as a commercial medium for the dissemination of political intelligence is reflected by the fraught involvement of Chapman's tragic heroes in the knowledge economy of their own courtly environment. The plays about Bussy d'Ambois and the Duke of Biron tap into a thriving marketplace of news: and they do not only stage recent events, but also examine the circulation of foreign intelligence, its escape from government circles and entry into public circulation—that is, the plays' own condition of existence.

Although they were considered as the secrets of princes, sententious political observations, 'maxims of state' were produced and collected by secretaries and scholars like Harvey and enjoyed wide circulation across all social and cultural registers, gracing courtly political discussion as well as the talk of fashionable gallants and—as satirists were eager to point out—also the gossip of barbers, porters, and cobblers. In the early years of the seventeenth century, many English playbooks were also studded with such aphoristic materials, offering typographically highlighted political maxims to be copied into the notebooks of their readers, and thus disseminating a mode of thinking about the motives and actions of political agents. In Chapter 5, I look at Ben Jonson's 1603–5 *Sejanus*, the play that is most insistent on displaying these markers, and engages most closely with the problem of the public access to the *arcana principii* it formulates. *Sejanus* presents itself as a piece of authoritative Tacitean historiography, and its maxims part of the play's effort to align itself with the 'politic' historiography of Tacitus, Commynes, or Guicciardini—historians valued for the aphoristic materials that could be extracted from their texts. In spite of its ostentatious display of sententious commentary of unflinching realism, however, Jonson's tragedy suggests that such unmasking of power is practically inconsequential. In *Sejanus*, the fearless analysis of the political world is the ineffectual activity of powerless outsiders, a source of intellectual and aesthetic pleasure, not of political change—so in a sense, Jonson's tragedy found its ideal reader in Sir William Drake, who read and re-read *Sejanus* alongside other politic authors without any thought of putting the copious political notes he took from his readings to use in political action.

In spite of what Harvey's early praise implied, in spite of how much political information the stage divulged, and in spite of how closely drama modelled the prudential use of political knowledge, then, plays did not emerge as a medium for serious political education, they did not become the texts to which political agents turned for instruction. This does not, however, mean that they had no impact on the political culture of the time. In the final chapter of the book I look at what little evidence we have from traces of playreading and from the plays themselves about the effects of the circulation of political knowledge by the stage and by printed drama on the conversations among its audience. Like Shakespeare's *Hamlet*, John Marston's *The Malcontent* and Chapman's *Monsieur d'Olive* also participate in the war of the theatres, this short period of intensely and competitively self-reflective playmaking that transformed the stage into a medium of cultural and social criticism, and plays into models for social and conversational competence. In my final chapter, I show how these plays link the forms of political knowledge explored in this book—diplomacy and Machiavellian prudence—to agonistic and self-interested models of conviviality and conversation, and how they police the porous boundary between professional knowledge and conversational competence, a boundary so blatantly ignored by the secret hero of this book, Sir Politic Would-be, who at last makes his appearance here.

In this early-seventeenth century moment, the stage transforms politic wit into a conversational asset, into the currency of social self-advancement. So much so that some playreaders scouring plays for conversational ammunition, for apt turns of phrase and sharp repartee, were extending the same reading techniques to politic authors, copying novel expressions and witty formulations from their English editions of Machiavelli and Tacitus, aiming to cultivate a style of conversation modelled on them. My account of the early seventeenth-century popularity of Machiavellian maxims in this final chapter thus encapsulates the argument of the book as a whole: the widespread success of this quintessentially political genre depends on its social and conversational utility.

PART I

HAMLET AND THE PROFESSION OF POLITICS

1

'The Wiser Sort'
The Distinction of Politics and Gabriel Harvey's Machiavellian *Hamlet*

The most frequently quoted English literary marginalium is marginal only in a generic sense: it covers more than half of a folio page at the end of a copy of the 1598 edition of the *Workes* of Chaucer. It is in the middle of this long impromptu survey of contemporary English authors, probably dating from the early years of the seventeenth century, that Gabriel Harvey makes a distinction between two types of Shakespearean writing pleasing two different types of readers, namely, *Venus and Adonis* the 'younger sort' and *Lucrece* and *Hamlet* the 'wiser'.[1]

Harvey was a voracious reader and obsessive note-taker, marking up his books using a set of shorthand symbols, making brief comments on people and events

---

[1] Harvey's copy of *The Workes of Our Antient and Learned English Poet, Geffrey Chaucer, Newly Printed* (London, 1598) is now BL Add. MS 42518. The note is on sig. 3z6v, transcriptions are published in G. C. Moore Smith, *Gabriel Harvey's Marginalia* (Stratford-upon-Avon: Shakespeare Head Press, 1913) 232–3; Harold Jenkins (ed.), *Hamlet* (Arden Shakespeare, London: Methuen, 1982) 573–4. The reference has been central to the debates around the date of *Hamlet*, although the recent consensus is that Harvey's note 'is really of little use in trying to date *Hamlet*'. Philip Edwards (ed.), *Hamlet* (Cambridge: Cambridge University Press, 1985) 5. The same point was made by Leo Kirschbaum, 'The Date of Shakespeare's Hamlet', *Studies in Philology*, 34 (1937), 168–75. Cp. also E.A.J. Honigmann, 'The Date of *Hamlet*', *Shakespeare Survey*, 9 (1956), 24–34; Jenkins (ed.), *Hamlet* 3–6; Thomas Fulton, 'Speculative Shakespeares: The Trials of Biographical Historicism', *Modern Philology*, 103 (2006), 385–408 at 395–8. Michael J. Hirrel, 'When Did Gabriel Harvey Write His Famous Note?' *Huntington Library Quarterly*, 75 (2012), 291–9, is an effort to date specific segments of the note, and reconstruct a staggered composition where new material was added every few years, but this is hampered by the absence of supporting evidence beyond the fact that difference in the darkness of the ink implies pauses between segments (without any hint whether pauses of minutes or of decades), and quite possibly also by Harvey's habit (discussed by Kirschbaum 172–4, and debated but not, *pace* Jenkins, refuted by Honigmann 25–6) of using present tense to talk about dead people. This is particularly important because Harvey seems to be referring to the Earl of Essex in the present tense—a fact often used to argue that Essex was still alive when Harvey mentioned the play as Shakespeare's.

A point that often seems to escape attention is that there is no example from the period of anyone referring to a play by the name of the play's author unless they are referring to the (published) text. Plays seen at the theatre but not read were simply not talked about as plays written by someone. In conversation among the audience, they seem to have been referred to by title, or what is practically the same: subject, by playing company, and were on occasion even associated with the lead actor—but not with the author. The important exception is, of course, when legal action was taken against offending plays—and even then, it was the offending playbook, a text and material object, that was subject to censure, not someone authoring a performance. But the juridical discourse has not, at this point, begun to transform public conversation and popular notions of authorship. Which means that rather than using Harvey's note to date the manuscript of Shakespeare's *Hamlet*, we probably ought to use what we know about the publication of Shakespeare's *Hamlet* to date Harvey's note.

described in the text, adding topic headings in the margins, and also recording his reflections in carefully phrased sentences in the blank spaces above, below, between, before and after the printed text. These marginalia are probably Harvey's most fascinating writings and have by now become also his most widely read.[2] In both their general obsessiveness and particular obsessions, they add up to an obviously troubled and occasionally troubling textual performance. But Harvey's idiosyncrasies are in fact elaborations of vocabularies and patterns of thought that were widely shared in their period, and—as Lisa Jardine and Anthony Grafton have shown in an essay that has come to define how we study the practices of reading—with their help we can reconstruct a world of reading as a world of social and political relationships.[3]

Gabriel Harvey's marginalia are intense efforts at inhabiting and organizing an intellectual universe. In the note reproduced here in Figure 1.1, an English commercial play—that is, a kind of text often said to be habitually disparaged by contemporaries for its lack of literary merit—is mentioned alongside major works of poetry, thus appearing to receive early recognition for its seriousness and intellectual value. Harvey cites *Venus and Adonis*, *Lucrece*, and *Hamlet* at the end of a distinct part of the note, a survey of contemporary poetry in print, where he enumerates

> owre best Inglish, aunciont & moderne. Amongst which, the Countesse of Pembrokes Arcadia, & the Faerie Queene ar now freshest in request: & Astrophil, & Amyntas ar none of the idlest pastimes of sum fine humanists. The Earle of Essex much commendes Albions England: and not vnworthily, for diuerse notable pageants, before, & in the Chronicle. Sum Inglish, & other Histories nowhere more sensibly described, or more inwardly discouered. The Lord Mountioy makes the like account of Daniels peece of the Chronicle, touching the Vsurpation of Henrie of Bullingbrooke. Which in deede is a fine, sententious, & politique peece of poetrie: as proffitable, as pleasurable. The younger sort takes much delight in Shakespeares Venus, & Adonis: but his Lucrece, & his tragedie of Hamlet, Prince of Denmarke, haue it in them, to please the wiser sort. Or such poets: or better: or none.[4]

Shakespeare has a unique place in Harvey's note—not only is he featured with multiple works, he is also the one poet who is seen as addressing distinct segments of the reading public, 'the younger' and 'the wiser'. The binary of Shakespeare's two narrative poems, *Venus and Adonis* and *Lucrece* (and incidentally, his earliest publications, which also remained his most successful in his lifetime) as lusty and chaste,

---

[2] For a reading of Harvey's marginalia that makes this argument, see H. R. Woudhuysen, 'Gabriel Harvey', in Andrew Hadfield (ed.), *The Oxford Handbook of English Prose 1500–1640* (Oxford: Oxford University Press, 2013), 611–30. In 'Bibliographical musings', Adorno writes about Marx that his 'texts read as though they had been written hastily on the margins of the texts he was studying, and in his theories of surplus value this becomes almost a literary form'. Theodor W. Adorno, *Notes to Literature*, ed. Rolf Tiedemann, trans. Shierry Weber Nicholsen, 2 vols. (New York: Columbia University Press, 1991) 2:25. Harvey's most important work remains, physically, in the margins of the texts he was studying, not written hastily at all, and never transferred into texts of 'his own'.

[3] Lisa Jardine and Anthony Grafton, '"Studied for Action": How Gabriel Harvey Read His Livy', *Past & Present*, 129 (1990), 30–78.

[4] BL Add. MS 42518, sig. 3z6v.

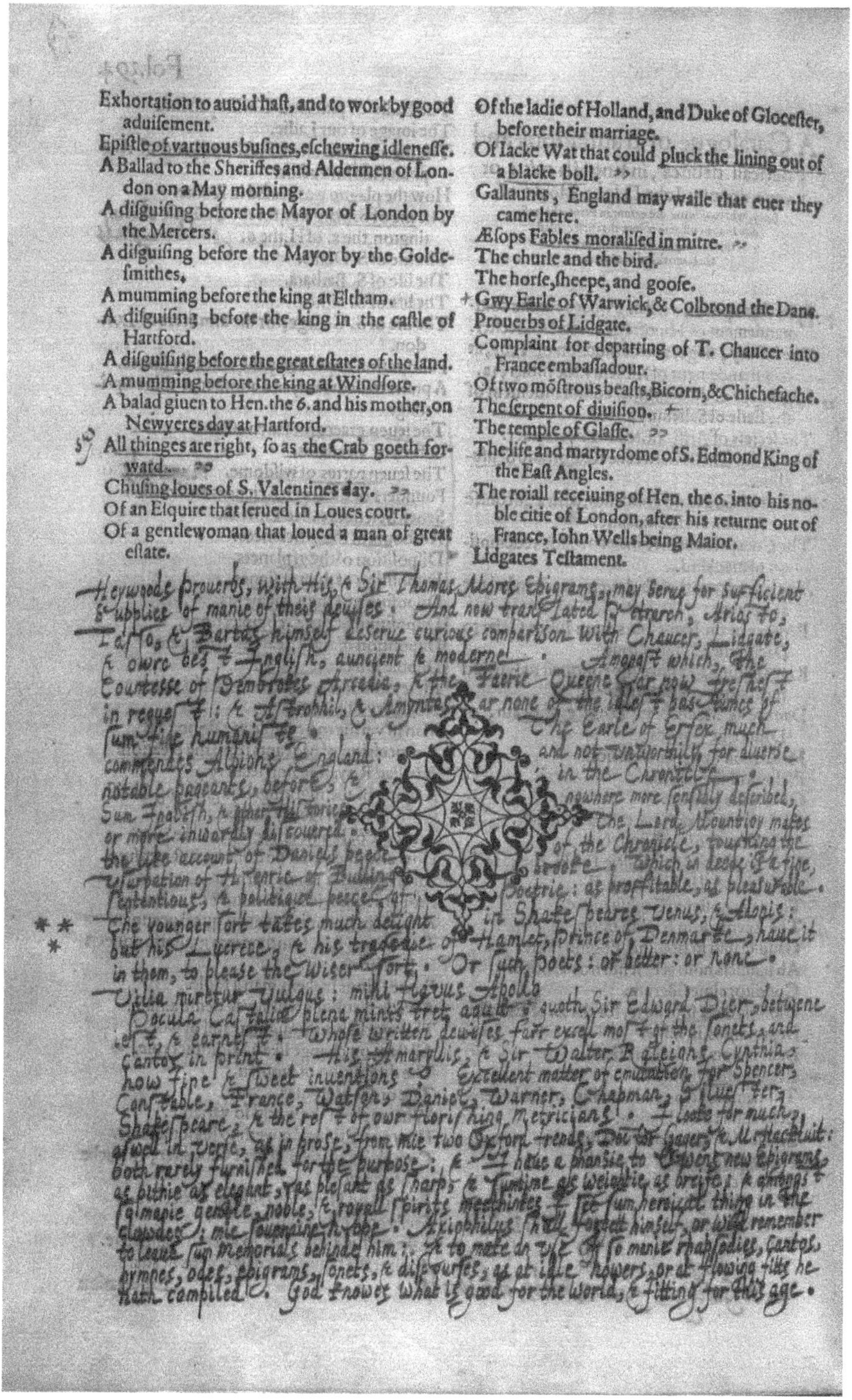

Exhortation to auoid haſt, and to work by good aduiſement.
Epiſtle of vartuous buſines, eſchewing idleneſſe.
A Ballad to the Sheriffes and Aldermen of London on a May morning.
A diſguiſing before the Mayor of London by the Mercers.
A diſguiſing before the Mayor by the Goldeſmithes.
A mumming before the king at Eltham.
A diſguiſing before the king in the caſtle of Hartford.
A diſguiſing before the great eſtates of the land.
A mumming before the king at Windſore.
A balad giuen to Hen. the 6. and his mother, on Newyeres day at Hartford.
All thinges are right, ſo as the Crab goeth forwatd.
Chiuſing loues of S. Valentines day.
Of an Eſquire that ſerued in Loues court.
Of a gentlewoman that loued a man of great eſtate.

Of the ladie of Holland, and Duke of Gloceſter, before their marriage.
Of Iacke Wat that could pluck the lining out of a blacke boll.
Gallaunts, England may waile that euer they came here.
Æſops Fables moraliſed in mitre.
The churle and the bird.
The horſe, ſheepe, and gooſe.
Gwy Earle of Warwick, & Colbrond the Dane.
Prouerbs of Lidgate.
Complaint for departing of T. Chaucer into France embaſſadour.
Of two môſtrous beaſts, Bicorn, & Chichefache.
The ſerpent of diuiſion.
The temple of Glaſſe.
The life and martyrdome of S. Edmond King of the Eaſt Angles.
The roiall receiuing of Hen. the 6. into his noble citie of London, after his returne out of France, Iohn Wells being Maior.
Lidgates Teſtament.

Fig. 1.1. Gabriel Harvey's note including his reference to *Hamlet* in his copy of *The Workes of our Antient and Lerned English Poet, Geffrey Chaucer, Newly Printed*. (Londini: [printed by Adam Islip] impensis Geor. Bishop, anno. 1598) BL Add MS 42518, fol. 394v (sig. 3Z6v).
© The British Library Board.

bawdy and morally serious, was a familiar one, clearly formulated for example in Thomas Freeman's epigram 'To Shakespeare':

> Who loves chaste life, there's Lucrece for a Teacher:
> Who list read lust there's Venus and Adonis,
> True model of a most lascivious leatcher.[5]

The contrast between these two texts was also emphasized by Shakespeare himself: dedicating *Venus and Adonis* to Southampton, he announced a forthcoming 'graver labour'. When it was published the following year, the tragic gravity of *Lucrece* was actually highlighted through its typography: double inverted commas printed in the margin of twenty-five of its lines marked them as weighty, sententious matter.[6] This typographic feature allows us to integrate *Hamlet* into Harvey's equation, since fourteen lines of sententious wisdom are highlighted in the first quarto of *Hamlet*, and seven lines in the second quarto, and *Lucrece* and *Hamlet* are the only two works by Shakespeare that had been printed with gnomic pointing at the time Gabriel Harvey was writing his note.[7] (See Figures 1.2 and 1.3.) By mentioning them together Harvey was registering something *Hamlet* and *Lucrece* had in common—a particular gravity these texts' printers or publishers were also aware of.

The story of the rise of English commercial drama to 'literary' status has been told frequently and compellingly, and the careful documentation of the efforts made by authors and publishers to achieve this transformation has been one of the central contributions of book history to the history of early modern English literature. Harvey's note has often been used to emphasize the poetical and philosophical value of *Hamlet*, and the early recognition of Shakespeare's plays, or of plays in general, for their literary qualities.[8] Using the link between the typography of

---

[5] Thomas Freeman: *Rubbe, and a Great Cast* (London: [Nicholas Okes], to be sold [by L. Lisle], 1614) sigs. K2v–K3r. On the early seventeenth c. perceptions and uses of the two poems, see Sasha Roberts, *Reading Shakespeare's Poems in Early Modern England* (New York: Palgrave Macmillan, 2003) 20–142.

[6] On the marking of sententiae, see G. K. Hunter, 'The Marking of Sententiae in Elizabethan Printed Plays, Poems, and Romances', *The Library 5th ser.*, 6 (1951), 171–88. The changing uses of this marker—the *diple*—in typography, and some alternative ways of marking sententiae, are discussed in M. B. Parkes, *Pause and Effect: An Introduction to the History of Punctuation in the West* (Berkeley: University of California Press, 1993) 57–61.

[7] The coincidence has also been noted by Zachary Lesser and Peter Stallybrass, 'The First Literary *Hamlet* and the Commonplacing of Professional Plays', *Shakespeare Quarterly*, 59 (2008), 371–420 at 394. The only other Shakespeare playbook with gnomic pointing before the 1623 Folio is the 1609 *Troilus*, and Harvey's note seems to be registering the literary world of several years earlier—most scholars agree on 1604 as *ante quem*.

[8] Most recently by Lukas Erne, *Shakespeare and the Book Trade* (Cambridge: Cambridge University Press, 2013) 18. Erne's reference to Harvey is a symptom of a continuing tension in the field of Shakespeare studies. David Scott Kastan formulated the now standard narrative of the rise of drama from subliterary to canonical, see especially 'Shakespeare in Print', in his *Shakespeare after Theory* (London: Routledge, 1999), 71–92, and cp. Zachary Lesser, 'Playbooks', in Joad Raymond (ed.), *The Oxford History of Popular Print Culture, Vol 1: Britain and Ireland to 1660* (Oxford: Oxford University Press, 2011), as well as the recent debates about this narrative: David Scott Kastan, *Shakespeare and the Book* (Cambridge: Cambridge University Press, 2001); Lukas Erne, *Shakespeare as Literary Dramatist* (Cambridge: Cambridge University Press, 2003); David Scott Kastan, 'Humphrey Moseley and the Invention of English Literature', in Sabrina Alcorn Baron, Eric N. Lindquist, and Eleanor F. Shevlin (eds.), *Agent of Change: Print Culture Studies after Elizabeth L. Eisenstein* (Amherst & Boston:

The Distinction of Politics and Gabriel Harvey's Machiavellian Hamlet 41

late sixteenth-century playtexts and contemporary reading practices, Zachary Lesser and Peter Stallybrass have sharpened this reading of Harvey's note as a symptom of the elevation of drama to literary status by arguing that the marked sententiousness of playbooks like the first quarto of *Hamlet* should itself be seen as a mark of distinction, the sign of the effort of early modern publishers to heighten the (presumably low) cultural prestige of these texts by associating them with scholarly reading—and Harvey's note as a possible recognition of their success.[9]

While my argument builds on theirs, it seeks to discern not the distinction of learning, but the distinctions within the field of learning, and show how *Hamlet* produces them. I argue that the gravity of *Lucrece* and *Hamlet* for Harvey, and for readers like Harvey, is the distinction of the political—it is what distinguishes politics from other spheres and modalities of thought, 'from the pastimes of sum fine humanists', and also, what distinguishes those engaged in political discussion from other sorts of people. In its concerns, although not in its specifics, my argument is therefore parallel with John Guillory's major essay on the play which also takes its cue from Harvey's note, linking the play's preoccupations to the political setting of the moment, and to the intellectual world of the same courtly elite I am also linking it to. Guillory's emphasis is on dissident politics and the unspeakable truths that cannot be uttered or resolved through rebellion, a situation in which philosophy becomes the alternative to action.[10] Rather than seeking to explore the dialectic of violence and philosophy, my effort is to establish a closer, more practical and pragmatic link between text and context, trying to understand texts as they are implicated in human agency by attending to the emergent formation of disciplinarity and the material and intellectual practices of reading.[11] I identify the wisdom of the play as political, as distinct from philosophical or literary in some general sense—ultimately, as the wisdom that can inform political activity (which may not be independent political *action* in the strong sense) and can entitle one to

---

University of Massachusetts Press, 2007), 105–24. An exchange between Kastan and Erne captures the reaction to the wide acceptance of the story about the originally low cultural prestige and subsequent rise of Shakespearean drama, and the reassertion of the old—new orthodoxy of Shakespeare's dramatic output as self-consciously authorial, and therefore, presumably, literary enterprise: see Erne, 'Reconsidering Shakespearean Authorship', *Shakespeare Studies*, 36 (2008), 26–36, and Kastan, ' "To Think These Trifles Some-Thing": Shakespearean Playbooks and the Claims of Authorship', *Shakespeare Studies*, 36 (2008), 37–48. Closely relevant is the account of print and stage as rival disseminative markets in Joseph Loewenstein, *Ben Jonson and Possessive Authorship* (Cambridge: Cambridge University Press, 2002). Adam Hooks's forthcoming *Vendible Shakespeare* argues that instead of the rise of drama to literary status, the narrative ought to be about the consolidation of drama, of plays, as a distinct field of writing. Like Hooks, I find that the term 'literary' is often elastic and imprecise in these debates, and that disagreement is sometimes the product of a lack of conceptual clarity.

[9] Lesser and Stallybrass, 'The First Literary *Hamlet*', 394.

[10] See John Guillory, ' "To Please the Wiser Sort": Violence and Philosophy in *Hamlet*', in Carla Mazzio and Douglas Trevor (eds.), *Historicism, Psychoanalysis, and Early Modern Culture* (New York: Routledge, 2000), 82–109. Guillory's is the most elegant and most powerful formulation of the cold-war-style interpretation of *Hamlet*.

[11] In recent essays informed by the work of Alfred Gell, Warren Boutcher makes a case for an interpretation of material texts as agentive and networked objects; see Boutcher, 'L'Objet Livre à l'Aube de l'Époque Moderne', *Terrain*, 59 (2012), 88–103; 'Literary Art and Agency? Gell and the Magic of the Early Modern Book', in Liana Chua and Mark Elliott (eds.), *Distributed Objects: Meaning and Mattering after Alfred Gell* (New York and Oxford: Berghahn Books, 2013), 155–75.

such activity: to service, advising, analysis. The distinction of *Hamlet* and *Lucrece* depends not on their literariness as such, but on the pragmatic, political utility of specific formal qualities we identify as literary. They are texts distinguished by qualities which are used by characters in the works—and which can also be used by such readers of those works as Gabriel Harvey—in making political distinctions, in articulating politic judgement, and ultimately, in articulating the distinction of the political.

HARVEY'S NOTE

Harvey's note, part of a meandering meditation on his own poetic output (or rather, on the lack thereof) and on the works of contemporary English poets, is a roll-call of golden age talents. This list of names belongs to a characteristic genre of the 1590s: the catalogues that both reflected on and shaped the contemporary scene of writing, lists produced by such writers as Thomas Nashe, Edmund Spenser, Thomas Edwards, Richard Carew, or Francis Meres.[12] In a list predictably headed by Sidney and Spenser, the seemingly prescient, indeed modern-looking inclusion of *Hamlet* reassuringly accords with our expectation of the rise of English poetry as a national enterprise, and Shakespeare's role in it. But the context of this note indicates that we ought to look more closely at Harvey's understanding of the matter and uses of literature, and at the importance and specific value he might be attributing here to *Hamlet*. His comments are, after all, inscribed in the blank spaces between sections of the antiquarian apparatus of the 1598 Chaucer, between catalogues and lists of works of learning produced in medieval England.[13] This is a volume in which Harvey found a prose tract on astronomy, *The Treatise on the Astrolabe*, the single most interesting text, and marked it attentively and heavily, while leaving long stretches of the narrative poetry untouched, maybe even unread.[14]

---

[12] See Nashe's 1589 preface to Greene's *Menaphon*, Thomas Edwards's 'L'envoy' to his 1593 *Narcissus*, Spenser's 1595 *Colin Clouts Come Home Againe*, Richard Carew's 1596 'Epistle on the excellency of the English tongue', as well as Meres's *Palladis Tamia*. Carew's epistle was first published in the second edition of William Camden's *Remaines, concerning Britaine but especially England, and the inhabitants thereof* (London: John Leggatt for Simon Waterson, 1614) sigs. F2v–G2v; on its date, see Richard Foster Jones, *The Triumph of the English Language: A Survey of Opinions Concerning the Vernacular from the Introduction of Printing to the Restoration* (Stanford: Stanford University Press, 1953) 244.

[13] Expanding the single-author *oeuvre* into an archive of medieval English writing, Speght includes Lydgate's *Fall of Thebes* (369r–393v), followed by a catalogue of Lydgate's writings (394r–v). Harvey sets to work in the blank area of 393v, facing the printed catalogue, and when he runs out of space, continues in the blank space at the end of the catalogue on 394v, his own catalogue framing the printed list.

[14] But cp. Megan Cook, 'How Francis Thynne Read His Chaucer', *Journal of the Early Book Society for the Study of Manuscripts and Printing History* (2012), 215–43 especially at 221–4. In Cook's careful study, a comparison between Thynne's and Harvey's annotations identifies a contrast 'between a materialist-antiquarian and a philosophic-humanistic reading paradigm' (222). The traces of reading in books are manifold—while the marginal notes certainly indicate Harvey's attention to issues other than the pragmatic, the sheer amount of ink spilled on the pages of the *Treatise of the Astrolabe* in the form of underlining indicates a concentration unmatched by his attention to the rest of *Works*, and as Cook also notes, Harvey frequently refers to the *Treatise* in his marginalia in other books as well. And

Harvey's reading of poetry is informed by his attention to specific areas of competence: in his copy of *The Surueye of the World* (1572), he praises Chaucer's 'Astronomical descriptions' and his 'conclusions of the Astrolabie' and explains that unlike those who commend poets 'for their witt, pleasant veine, varietie of poetical discourse, & all humanitie: I specially note their Astronomie, philosophie, & other parts of profound or cunning art', adding that 'it is not sufficient for poets, to be superficial humanists'. He accordingly proceeds to make a catalogue of poems valuable for astronomical learning—he calls them 'excellent Cantiques for a mathematicall witt'—based on the recommendations of his learned friends: thus he mentions that the mathematician Thomas Digges 'hath the whole Aquarius of Palingenius bie hart: & takes mutch delight to repeate it often', explaining on the verso of the same page that Digges 'esteemes [Palingenius] abooue all moderne poets, for a pregnant introduction into Astronomie, & both philosophies'.[15] In poetical form, knowledge becomes a source of delight any good reader will recognize, but it is the endorsement of expert practitioners in a particular field that establishes the utility of the matter articulated through the 'witt, pleasant veine, varietie of poetical discourse'. For Harvey, poetry is valuable as the formulation of its matter—not as the passive container but as the productively pleasing thought of specialized expert knowledge.

Rather than imagining literary writing as freely and almost endlessly adaptable to the needs of each member of their stratified audience—that is, seeing it, in classic humanist fashion, as a collection of flowers from which bees can gather their honey even as spiders will suck their poison, and as one that has value for any reader or writer—Harvey envisions a textual universe divided into distinct fields, where any writing is appropriate for certain specific uses and perhaps even resistant to others, according to the matter it is concerned with. The assumptions underlying his reading practice challenge any understanding of literature, of philosophy, of the liberal arts, of the humanities as intellectual forces contravening such specialization.[16] His thought is marked by an incipient but already keen disciplinary desire, by a perceived necessity of the division of intellectual labour as a precondition of its efficacy.

---

as I am trying to argue here, even his literary–historical notes are underwritten by an attention to pragmatic, professional interests. The contrast, in other words, while undeniable, might be less stark than Cook's excellent essay implies.

[15] Smith, *Gabriel Harvey's Marginalia* 160–1. On Harvey's engagement with Chaucer's *Treatise*, see Jessica Wolfe, *Humanism, Machinery, and Renaissance Literature* (Cambridge: Cambridge University Press, 2004) 151–60.

[16] We could add to this list humanism (*Humanismus*, in the post-renaissance sense of the word forged in 1808 by Friedrich Immanuel Niethammer). As Horkheimer and Adorno put it, 'philosophy refers, among other things, to thinking which refuses to capitulate to the prevailing division of labour and does not accept prescribed tasks. The existing order coerces people not merely by physical force and material interests but by overwhelming suggestion. Philosophy is not a synthesis, a basic science, or an overarching science but an effort to resist suggestion, a determination to protect intellectual and actual freedom.' Max Horkheimer and Theodor W. Adorno, *Dialectic of Enlightenment: Philosophical Fragments*, ed. Gunzelin Schmid Noerr, trans. Edmund Jephcott (Stanford: Stanford University Press, 2002) 202.

As a closer look at its context in the long note in his Chaucer reveals, Harvey's mention of Shakespeare is also implicated in his efforts at textual discipline by division. He finds *Hamlet* and *Lucrece* notable because of their potential for political instruction and political advice. The specific nature of their appeal to the wise is indicated by his organization of the catalogue of poets and titles into two large categories. After mentioning the *Faerie Queene* and *Arcadia*, the two big, encyclopaedic fictions of the period, Harvey proceeds to love poems, the 'pastimes of sum fine humanists', and contrasts these to some examples of political–historical poetry recommended by members of the political elite not only for the pleasures, but also, and it seems primarily, for the profits they have to offer as sources of historical descriptions and of political prudence.[17] The ensuing comment on Shakespeare is structured by this opposition between frivolous love poetry and the texts commended by Essex and Mountjoy: those who enjoy *Amyntas* will presumably also like *Venus and Adonis*, and avid readers of Samuel Daniel's 'fine, sententious, and politique' *Civil Wars* and of *Albion's England*—whose author, William Warner, was called by Francis Meres in 1598 'the most sententious' among the English poets[18]—will find similar pleasures and uses in *Lucrece* and *Hamlet*, as texts offering political insight, opportunities, and sententious tools for the analysis of matters of state.

The list in his 1598 Chaucer is typical of Harvey's obsessive tendency to use the margins and other blank spaces of his books for lists of authors on particular topics, lists of indispensable books and of the best authorities. Whether they rework or expand catalogues in the texts in whose margins they appear (as the list in his Chaucer clearly does), or simply serve as reminders of books related to the one in which they are inscribed, these lists establish both the canon of a field of knowledge and Harvey's expertise in that field—rehearsing a list of authorities is Harvey's own claim upon authority.[19] But whereas the various branches of rhetoric are literally mastered by Harvey, who derives their canons either from common humanistic knowledge or from the classics themselves, in the case of extracurricular topics or fields of knowledge in which expertise is based on personal experience rather than on book learning, his catalogues tend to be sourced to the recommendations of specific people knowledgeable in the subject.[20]

Harvey's lists of authors who provide guidance in matters of state are anchored in the recommendations of diplomats and statesmen, rather than in the judgement of people who are merely 'fine humanists' without the practical experience to supplement their learning. For example, in the survey of ancient and modern historiography he inscribes in his Livy, he specifically derives the authority of Sir Thomas Smith's suggestions from his political experience, not from his considerable and

---

[17] William Scott also selects these two works by Daniel and Warner as the examples of poetry that are 'more Historicall and lesse Fiction (like Lucan)': BL Add. MS 81083, now published as William Scott, *The Model of Poesy*, ed. Gavin Alexander (Cambridge: Cambridge University Press, 2013), f. 10v.
[18] *Palladis Tamia* (London: P. Short, for Cuthbert Burbie, 1598) sig. 2O1v.
[19] Nicholas Popper, 'The English Polydaedali: How Gabriel Harvey Read Late Tudor London', *Journal of the History of Ideas*, 66 (2005), 351–81.
[20] See e.g. his list of the makers of instruments: Smith, *Gabriel Harvey's Marginalia* 211–12.

The Distinction of Politics and Gabriel Harvey's Machiavellian Hamlet   45

well-known erudition, scholarship, and theoretical insight. Although Smith is an admired scholar, it is practice that orients learning here, not the other way round:

> Sir Thomas Smyth, the Queenes principal secretarie; … especially in his ambassages in Scotland, Fraunce, and Netherlande; found no sutch use of anie autours, as I heard himself say, as of Liuie, Plutarch, and Justinian. He mutch commended Sallust, Suetonius, Tacitus, and sum other of the best: but his classical and statarie historians were Liuie, Plutarch, Halicarnasseus; and verie fewe other. Of the new, Cominaeus, Guicciardine, Jouius, Paulus Aemilius, Egnatius, and but fewe other.[21]

History is, of course (as any reader or writer of the turn of the century, anyone reading and writing in what I am calling 'Hamlet's moment' would suppose) 'the imitator of time, the storehouse of actions, and the witness of the past'.[22] According to Harvey, however, the value of these histories consists not simply in the past experience they contain and preserve, but in a very particular way in which they are *magistra vitae*, that is, in their tested practical, pragmatic utility: in the guidance successful political agents claim these authors can provide, and have provided, for doing political business.[23]

The selection of 'sententious, politic' English writers 'much commended' by Essex and Mountjoy that he entered in his copy of Chaucer is closely analogous to the list of Thomas Smith's recommendations: the reference to *Hamlet* and *Lucrece* appears in the formal context of the suggestions of people whose own actions and position bestow upon them an unquestionable authority in matters military and political. Of the two leaders he mentions there, Charles Blount, the eighth baron Mountjoy, was not only the dedicatee of Daniel's truly 'sententious, and politique' *Civil Wars* (a poem whose sentiousness was signalled, from the 1605 edition onwards, by gnomic pointing): beyond his military valour and political leadership, the baron was also famous for his habit of politically oriented reading, prompting Daniel in his funeral poem on Blount to recall the 'many volumes whereto thou / Hast set thy notes vnder thy learned hand' as further evidence of his nobility.[24] The centrality of Essex to late Elizabethan political culture, and more specifically, to a whole circle of politic readers, is well known. Crucially, he was (to an extent of

---

[21] Harvey's copy of *T. Liuii Patauini Romanae Historiae Principis Decades Tres* (Basileae: Per Ioannes Heruagios, 1555): Princeton University Library Rare Books (Ex) Oversize PA 6452.A2 1555q, sig. 3A1r, quoted also in Jardine and Grafton, '"Studied for Action": How Gabriel Harvey Read His Livy', 54.

[22] Miguel de Cervantes Saavedra, *The Ingenious Hidalgo Don Quixote de La Mancha*, trans. Roberto González Echevarría (New York: Penguin Books, 2001) 76. This passage from Part I Chapter IX is quoted and discussed in 'Pierre Menard, author of the *Quixote*': Jorge Luis Borges, *Collected Fictions*, trans. Andrew Hurley (New York: Penguin Books, 1998) 94.

[23] On the fate of the *magistra vitae* topos, see Reinhart Koselleck, *Vergangene Zukunft: Zur Semantik geschichtlicher Zeiten* (Frankfurt am Main: Suhrkamp, 1979) 38–66. On versions of the understanding of the pragmatic uses of history in the century around 1600, Anthony Grafton, *What Was History? The Art of History in Early Modern Europe* (Cambridge: Cambridge University Press, 2007). On the lasting relevance of classical political history, see also Iggy Pop, 'Caesar Lives', *Classics Ireland*, 2 (1995), 94–6.

[24] Samuel Daniel, *A Funerall Poem Vppon the Death of the Late Noble Earle of Deuonshyre* (London: 1606), sig. A3r; Boutcher, 'Humanism and Literature in Late Tudor England', 261; Fred Schurink, '"Like a Hand in the Margine of a Booke": William Blount's Marginalia and the Politics of Sidney's *Arcadia*', *Review of English Studies*, 59/238 (2008), 1–24.

course vicariously, through the agency of his amanuenses, secretaries, advisors, and friends, most importantly Francis Bacon) the author of several letters of advice to young noblemen, instructing them on their studies—on what to read and how in order to become able and well-regarded members of the political class.[25] The genre of such instructions on studies includes Philip Sidney's letters to Edward Denny and to Robert Sidney, and its best examples might be the letters produced at Essex's secretariat and addressed to Fulke Greville and to the young Roger Manners, Earl of Rutland—pragmatically oriented private syllabi stressing the importance of modern languages, military theory, and most importantly and centrally, political history and theory.[26] As a record of his betters' recommendations, Harvey's list of politic, sententious poems, a list that includes *Hamlet* as well as *Lucrece*, aligns itself with such reading lists as a vernacular programme of reading coming from great political leaders and appropriate for the 'institution' of statesmen and military commanders.

That Harvey singles out *Hamlet* and *Lucrece* for their field-specific, political utility, affords us a glimpse at the engagement of drama and fictional writing with this cordoning off of the matters and problems of government as a distinct field of knowledge, and with an emerging system of education, canon of texts and, most importantly, ways of reading contributing to this work of distinction, predicated upon the field's exceptional status as well as upon its analogy with other areas of expert knowledge. This also means that Harvey, and the moment he is a part of, understands politics not as public agency, but as a specialized field of knowledge, distinct from other types of knowledge and competence. In what follows, I will establish the place of political knowledge in the field of learning, show how Harvey's note is informed by his engagement with Machiavelli's importance to political education, and in the second half of the chapter, reveal how *Lucrece* and *Hamlet* exemplify the capacity of literature, and *Hamlet* the particular capacity of drama, to exercise the faculty of political judgement, of distinction and decision as identified by Harvey.

Policy or statecraft, the mode of thinking that Harvey is seeking to articulate through his politically oriented reading practice, is defined through its distinction from the study of the humanities and of philosophy, and through its efforts at marking that distinction. In Harvey's reading of *Hamlet*, 'policy' is the figure as well as the agent of distinction between fields of competence. And he considers

---

[25] Paul E. J. Hammer, 'The Use of Scholarship: The Secretariat of Robert Devereux, Second Earl of Essex, c. 1585–1601', *The English Historical Review*, 109 (1994), 26–51; Paul E. J. Hammer, 'The Earl of Essex, Fulke Greville, and the Employment of Scholars', *Studies in Philology*, 91 (1994), 167–80; Alexandra Gajda, *The Earl of Essex and Late Elizabethan Political Culture* (Oxford: Oxford University Press, 2012). Such mediated and collaborative authorship has been explored and conceptualized by Alan Stewart, 'The Making of Writing in Renaissance England: Re-Thinking Authorship through Collaboration', in Margaret Healy and Thomas Healy (eds.), *Renaissance Transformations: The Making of English Writing (1500–1650)* (Edinburgh: Edinburgh University Press, 2009), 81–96, and they were the subject of Ann Blair's 2014 Rosenbach Lectures, 'Hidden Hands: Amanuenses and Authorship in Early Modern Europe' at the Kislak Center of the University of Pennsylvania Libraries (17–20 March).

[26] R. J. P. Kuin (ed.), *The Correspondence of Sir Philip Sidney*, 2 vols. (Oxford: Oxford University Press, 2012) 980–5, 1005–10.

these competences as marks of distinction which sort people into categories; divide them into 'sorts' in the emerging early modern terminology of 'radical differentiation' and dissociation.[27] The distinction among fields of reading and writing, between fields of knowledge thus informs a new system of social distinction.

POLITICAL EXPERTISE AND THE LEARNING OF MERE SCHOLARS

The need to produce extracurricular reading lists like Harvey's at a moment when the profession of humanistic education was flourishing seems to call for some comment. We think of the late sixteenth century as the period when a system of grammar schools and universities was solidly established, defining the textual and intellectual culture of England, inculcating habits of thought, ways of reading and writing, but also shaping sexual identities, and creating and marking social distinction. Humanist education served as a rite of passage that marked cultural superiority, and while it helped to reaffirm pre-existing status differences, it also promised meritocratic mobility. The linguistic and rhetorical skills imparted by this system of education were supposed by the ideology of the system itself to prepare pupils morally and intellectually for an active civic existence, for entry into a political life and professional training. But in the lasting and familiar paradox of education in the humanities and the liberal arts, the training provided by the grammar schools and universities did not directly fulfil any of these promises. The glut of jobless graduates indicated that education did not automatically lead to social mobility or active life in some form of employment.[28] The primarily literary (that is, grammatical, rhetorical, and poetical) skills could be valuable only if applied well in the right context, but the schools did not prepare students for such application. When thinking about Jonson's or Shakespeare's grammar school experience it is easy to forget about their classmates: for many (or perhaps most) grammar school students, these future merchants and craftsmen, the literary skills themselves were spectacularly useless to begin with. Double translation from and then back into Latin, preferably in distichs, was not something they were ever likely to attempt again. Humanist education created expectations the institutions of education failed to fulfil: their version of humanist training was thoroughly impractical and could be a deeply unsatisfactory avenue for those who aspired to rise with its help.[29] Writing in 1611, Bacon argued that 'the great number of schools' causes a want of employable 'servants for husbandry and apprentices for trade' while

---

[27] On the early modern language of 'sorts' as a language of differentiation, capturing changing early modern social identities, creating groupings across the boundaries of estates and degrees, and as a terminology 'pregnant with actual or potential conflict' see Keith Wrightson, '"Sorts" of People in Tudor and Stuart England', in Jonathan Barry and Christopher Brooks (eds.), *The Middling Sort of People* (New York: St. Martin's Press, 1994), 28–51, at 38.

[28] Mark H. Curtis, 'The Alienated Intellectuals of Early Stuart England', *Past & Present*, 23 (1962), 25–43.

[29] On humanism as a marker of status, bestowing identity of rank and worth, promising general education to anyone suitable yet guarding the threshold of suitability closely, and on the limitations of

there being more scholars red than the state can prefer and employ, and the active part of that life not bearing a proportion to the preparative, it must needs fall out that man persons will be bred unfit for other vocations, and unprofitable for that in which they are brought up; which fills the realm full of indigent, idle, and wanton people, which are but *materia rerum novarum*.[30]

Because of the shape of grammar school and university curricula in late sixteenth- and early seventeenth-century England, experience-based expertise and formal education came to be seen as quite a bit at odds. The title page of the 1640 edition of Bacon's *Advancement of Learning*, a reworking of the more familiar earlier image, encapsulates this clearly. In this version, the pillars of Hercules, beyond which the ship of discovery is seen sailing happily, are inscribed Oxford and Cambridge.[31] Bacon himself opens the 1597 first edition of his *Essays* with 'Of studies', and that piece by making a distinction between study and expertise. He suggests that 'expert men can execute, but learned men are fittest to judge or censure', and then goes on to warn that 'To spend too much time in [studies] is sloth; to use them too much for ornament is affectation; to make judgment wholly by their rules is the humour of a scholar.'[32] In his copy of John Blagrave's *Mathematicall Iewel*, Harvey recorded his admiration for the author's achievement, noting that he was 'An youth: & no Vniuersity-man. the more shame for sum Doctors of Vniuersities, that may learn of him.' And after the brief list of Blagrave's books, 'His sole, or principal Autors', Harvey points out: 'Schollars haue the bookes: & practitioners the Learning.'[33]

---

the programme itself, see Anthony Grafton and Lisa Jardine, *From Humanism to the Humanities: Education and the Liberal Arts in Fifteenth- and Sixteenth-Century Europe* (London: Duckworth, 1986) 29–57; Halpern, *The Poetics of Primitive Accumulation* 21–45; Colin Burrow, 'Shakespeare and Humanistic Culture', in Charles Martindale and A. B. Taylor (eds.), *Shakespeare and the Classics* (Cambridge: Cambridge University Press, 2004) at 17. On the political and psychic dimensions of grammar school education as a rite of passage see Walter J. Ong, 'Latin Language Study as a Renaissance Puberty Rite', *Rhetoric, Romance, and Technology: Studies in the Interaction of Expression and Culture* (Ithaca: Cornell University Press, 1971), 113–41; Alan Stewart, *Close Readers: Humanism and Sodomy in Early Modern England* (Princeton: Princeton University Press, 1997) 88–104; Lynn Enterline, *Shakespeare's Schoolroom: Rhetoric, Discipline, Emotion* (Philadelphia: University of Pennsylvania Press, 2012).

[30] 'Advice to the King, touching Sutton's estate' in James Spedding (ed.), *The Letters and the Life of Francis Bacon Including All His Occasional Works* (London: Longmans, Green, Reader, and Dyer, 1868) 4:249–55, at 252–3. On the unemployment of grammar school- and university-educated intellectuals, see L. C. Knights, *Drama and Society in the Age of Jonson* (London: Chatto & Windus, 1937) 324–6; Curtis, 'The Alienated Intellectuals of Early Stuart England'.

[31] Francis Bacon, *Of the Advancement and Proficience of Learning* (Oxford: Leon: Lichfield, for Rob: Young & Ed: Forrest., 1640). This is the first English translation of the longer, later version called *De Augmentis*. Obviously, the title page of the Latin original, intended as much for a European as for an English audience, could not have made this gesture at the two Universities.

[32] Brian Vickers (ed.), *Francis Bacon: The Major Works*, ed. Brian Vickers (2nd, Rev. edn.; Oxford: Oxford University Press, 2002) 81.

[33] Smith, *Gabriel Harvey's Marginalia* 212. Gresham College, the institution which is often seen as a precursor to the Royal Society, opened in 1597, and it has often been understood as offering a practical, experiential curriculum, as an institution that linked school learning to mathematical practice, and thus became the starting point of the intellectual but also educational transformation that came to be termed the scientific revolution. A ballad from the 1660s celebrated 'Gresham, for thy Colledge / From whence must issue soe much Knowledg', and which must be seen as the modern alternative to the Universities: 'Thy Colledg, Gresham, shall hereafter / Be the whole world's Universitie, / Oxford

In the late sixteenth century, the (whether justified or unfounded) sense of a growing gap between the pedantry of school education and pragmatic knowledge was not unique to the practitioners of natural philosophy and the mathematical arts: it was also very much present in the courtly, political environment. Essex's recently discovered second letter of advice to Rutland (presumably drafted by Bacon) makes this particularly clear. There, Essex proposes a personalized course of study that the young earl should follow with the help of a reader, and repeatedly advises him against studying with a 'meer scholler', arguing that '*sonitus* or *fluens verborum* is noe parte of true knowledge. But he is the true oratour whoe seekes to be rich in matters and not in wordes.'[34] The commonplace opposition between matter and words, used to formulate differences between styles of training and expertise, and even to draw lines between fields of study and writing, is in Essex's letter used to comment on the results of the grammar school curriculum, and specifically, of the effort to prioritize the use of language over the manipulation of ideas. The competitive emulation of stylistic models and especially the emphasis on linguistic *copia*, on the analysis of texts into fragments to be organized under subdivisions, juxtaposed and compared with analogous formulations, and redeployed in the amplification of written composition, necessarily dissolved the matter of writing in an intertextual web of signifiers cut free from their referents.[35] This is the condition Gabriel Harvey reflected on in his inaugural oration of the Easter term, 1576, at the end of his professorship of rhetoric at Cambridge, when he described humanist study as a time when he valued 'words more than matter, language more than thought, the one art of speaking more than the thousand subjects of knowledge'.[36]

---

and Cambridge are our laughter; / Their learning is but Pedantry.' See Dorothy Stimson, *Scientists and Amateurs: A History of the Royal Society* (New York: H. Schuman, 1948) 56–63. The assumption that around 1600, the curriculum of Gresham College was closely linked to the activities of London mathematical practitioners, was called into question by Mordechai Feingold, *The Mathematicians' Apprenticeship: Science, Universities and Society in England, 1560–1640* (Cambridge: Cambridge University Press, 1984) 166–89. On scientific education inside and outside the universities, see also Deborah E. Harkness, *The Jewel House: Elizabethan London and the Scientific Revolution* (New Haven: Yale University Press, 2007) 97–141, and on the mid-seventeenth-century intellectual setting in which the late sixteenth-century efforts at educational reform really began to flourish, Picciotto, *Labors of Innocence* 147–78.

[34] 'resounding or fluent with words'—Stewart conjectures 'fluens' where the MS has 'fuens': Alan Stewart (ed.), *The Oxford Francis Bacon I: Early Writings, 1584–1596* (Oxford: Clarendon Press, 2012) 970. For an ambitious intellectual history of the rise of modernity as a shift of emphasis from trivial to quadrivial arts, from verbal to mathematical learning within humanism, see Timothy J. Reiss, *Knowledge, Discovery, and Imagination in Early Modern Europe: The Rise of Aesthetic Rationalism* (Cambridge: Cambridge University Press, 1997).

[35] Nor was this 'destruction of content' an unintended side effect only: rhetorical analysis into topics and commonplaces was expressly proposed as a way to divert attention from the troubling matter found in classical texts, thus sanitizing them for classroom use. Such literary gymnastics were intended as a training in textual skills and good morals, not as a form of material instruction. I am indebted for this argument to Halpern, *The Poetics of Primitive Accumulation* 45–60; cp. also Ann Moss, *Printed Commonplace-Books and the Structuring of Renaissance Thought* (Oxford: Clarendon Press, 1996) 105–6.

[36] 'Pluris verba, quam res; linguam, quam mentem; vnam dicendi artem, quam mille intelligendi doctrinas faciebam', Harold S. Wilson (ed.), *Gabriel Harvey's Ciceronianus*, trans. Clarence A. Forbes (University of Nebraska Studies, Studies in the Humanities, Lincoln: The University of Nebraska,

For Essex, a 'meer scholler' is someone who has no experience or substantial knowledge to complement his linguistic and rhetorical training, and who can therefore offer little in terms of advice or instruction to a nobleman seeking to enter an active life in politics. Although he was concerned not with the training of an elite, but with maintaining the boundaries of what was admissible in public discussion, King James used the same argument. In his 1610 proclamation 'touching D. Cowels booke called the Interpreter' he complains that 'there is nothing now unsearched into by the curiositie of mens braines... men in these our dayes doe not spare to wade in all the deepest mysteries that belong to the persons or State of Kings or Princes, that are gods upon Earth.' In practical terms, James's objection to curiosity—a term he still associates with opprobrium[37]—hinges on the question of expertise, and on the distinction between school learning and political knowledge:

> this licence that every talker or writer now assumeth to himselfe, is come to this abuse, that many Phormio's will give councell to Hanibal, and many men that never went out of the compasse of Cloisters or Colledges, will freely wade by their writings in the deepest mysteries of Monarchie and politique government: Whereupon it cannot otherwise fall out, but that when men goe out of their element, and meddle with things above their capacitie; themselves shall not onely goe astray, and stumble in darknesse, but will mislead also divers others with themselves into many mistakings and errours.[38]

The mysteries of state are above and beyond the capacity of those whom Essex had called 'mere scholars'. Scholarly pretensions to political insight are transgressions driven by curiosity, and the depth of ignorance they reflect is indicated, first and foremost, by the failure to recognize the distinction between the two spheres or elements. People who live in 'cloisters and colledges' lack the competence to discuss the business of government and affairs of state.[39]

1945) 69. Both the Latin and English text are from this edition, although I have slightly modified the translation.

[37] On the history of the concept of curiosity and its seventeenth-century re-valorization or indeed redemption, a change that was central to the scientific revolution and to the rise of the modern public sphere, see Blumenberg, *The Legitimacy of the Modern Age* 229–401; Picciotto, *Labors of Innocence* 3–4, 193–8, 255ff, and cp. also Barbara M. Benedict, *Curiosity: A Cultural History of Early Modern Inquiry* (Chicago: University of Chicago Press, 2001) 1–70.

[38] Larkin and Hughes (eds.), *Royal Proclamations of King James I, 1603–1625* 243.

[39] In discussions of the concept of curiosity, the emphasis on the discovery of the secrets of nature often obscures the fact that in late sixteenth-century contexts, as a negative term, curiosity had a primarily social and political valence, and was referring to a social, rather than theological transgression, as prying into the business and lives of others. The Augustinian association of curiosity with temptation and the fall is here combined by James with the Greek concept of *polypragmosyne*, a concept whose historical trajectory reaches from eager political engagement to meddling in politics, and later, of being a busybody or gossip. The source of this latter notion is found in Plutarch's essay appearing as 'Of Curiosity' in *The Philosophie, Commonlie Called, the Morals Written by the Learned Philosopher Plutarch of Chaeronea. Translated ... by Philemon Holland* (London: Arnold Hatfield, 1603) 133–44, and now translated as 'On being a busybody' in Plutarch, *Moralia*, trans. W. C. Helmbold (Loeb Classical Library 337, VI; Cambridge, MA: Harvard University Press, 1939) 469–517. See Victor Ehrenberg, 'Polypragmosyne: A Study in Greek Politics', *The Journal of Hellenic Studies*, 67 (1947), 46–67; Blumenberg, *The Legitimacy of the Modern Age* 298; Neil Kenny, *Curiosity in Early Modern*

Earlier in the sixteenth century, English humanists advertised themselves as educators of the perfect governor, and promoted their brand of education in virtue through classical erudition as the ideal training for that purpose. People like Roger Ascham were arguing for the humanistic education of the nobility by pointing out that low-born men were supplanting the aristocracy in high office by means of their learning.[40] But if formal education was conceived and advertised as a status marker and a tool for cultural assimilation to the elite, in our late sixteenth-century moment, it also becomes a mark of vulnerability, at least in the absence of other qualifications. As L. C. Knights noted long ago, 'apart from the army and the learned professions an administrative career was the only one open to men of education and social standing, and there was far greater number of aspirants than there were places for them to fill.'[41] Under such circumstances, school learning is, at best, a necessary but insufficient first step that promises the linguistic and moral fashioning of gentlemen before they acquire more substantial knowledge, and, at worst, a synonym for futility, a pastime without purpose or instrumental justification, learning without useful content. Schooling claims to be a mark of social distinction, but being a 'meere scholler' means being stuck on the wrong side of yet another line of social distinction.[42]

Alternative educational models were striving to address the fundamental shortcoming of the emphasis on the *trivium* and of school education being cut off from practical application. Curricula aiming to provide a pragmatic education were first drawn up as part of the intense discussion that took place in the second half of the sixteenth century, both in England and on the Continent, about the form and substance of the training of the political elite at special academies. In the early 1570s, Humphrey Gilbert proposed the establishment of such an institution, intended for the education of royal wards. He suggested that 'whereas in the vniversities men studie onely schole lerninges, in this Achademy they shall study matters of accion meet for present practize, both of peace and warre.' As he explained, the emphasis would be on foreign languages, law, mathematics (i.e. the mechanic arts) and the martial arts. Logic and rhetoric were to be taught in English,

Europe: Word Histories (Wolfenbütteler Forschungen; Wiesbaden: Harrassowitz, 1998) 35. While it may also imply the ambitious and foolhardy violation of boundaries, the Greek term was redeemed by Gabriel Harvey, who calls Cromwell *polypragmaticus* in true admiration; see Smith, *Gabriel Harvey's Marginalia* 149; Wolfe, *Humanism, Machinery, and Renaissance Literature* 140.

[40] Ruth Kelso, *The Doctrine of the English Gentleman in the Sixteenth Century: With a Bibliographical List of Treatises on the Gentleman and Related Subjects Published in Europe to 1625* (Urbana: University of Illinois Press, 1929) 113–14; Stewart, *Close Readers* xxxiv–xxxix.

[41] Knights, *Drama and Society in the Age of Jonson* 327.

[42] Elizabeth Hanson looks at the universities in the shifting system of social distinction in the early modern period in 'Fellow Students: Hamlet, Horatio, and the Early Modern University', *Shakespeare Quarterly*, 62 (2011), 205–29. As growing numbers of noblemen were entering colleges, she argues, sons of the nobility could no longer be readily contrasted to the figure of the poor scholar, the cleric of lowly origin, and their relationship can be described in terms of a hierarchical supplementarity rather than a distinction. As her focus is on the experience of the coexistence of young noblemen and poor students within the universities, and on the implications of this experience for our understanding of the relationships among the play's current students (Hamlet, Horatio, Rosencrantz, and Guildenstern), the significance of her argument will be of particular importance to mine when it comes to the figure of Horatio in Chapter 3.

and philosophy to focus on the 'politique parte of' moral philosophy, divided into 'two sortes—The one concerning Ciuill pollicie, The other concerning Martiall pollicy'.[43] In France, the demand for such finishing schools for the nobility led to the establishment and flourishing of academies throughout the country.[44] In England, similar institutions were not set up until the 1630s, and then with more emphasis on civility and graceful deportment than on 'matters of action',[45] but the plans for such alternatives or at least complements to 'schole learninges,' i.e. to grammar school and university education, registered a growing demand for a pragmatically oriented training. The public appeal of proposals for the formalization and institutionalization of the training of gentlemen resided in the notion that they were building on the experience of the private education of the aristocracy, and were therefore making available the private curriculum of those destined for political office by birth.[46] In the late sixteenth and especially in the early seventeenth century, advice on the education of gentlemen started to enjoy wide circulation in print, providing models for self-fashioning, and shaping the reading and self-education of a wider audience of socially aspiring readers.[47] It is largely as part of this movement that political knowledge comes to be recognized as a field of extramural study.

POLITIC LEARNING AND MACHIAVELLI

In a marginal note, Harvey brings to this widespread perception of the uselessness of school learning the clarity of those who are at the receiving end of it:

> Common Lerning, & ye name of A good schollar, was neuer so much contemn'd, & abiectid of princes, Pragmaticals, & common Gallants, as nowadayes; jnsomuch that it necessarily concernith, & importith ye lernid ether praesently to hate yr books; or

---

[43] 'The erection of an Achademy in London, for educacion of her Maiesties Wardes, and others the youth of nobility and gentlemen,' drafted by Humphrey Gilbert. BL MS Lansdowne 98, ff. 2–7, published in *Queene Elizabethes Achademy (by Sir Humphrey Gilbert) & c*, ed. F J Furnivall (London: for the Early English Text Society by Kegan Paul, Trench, Trübner & Co., 1869) 1–12, the quoted passages at 10 and 3, respectively. Gilbert's proposal was probably building on Sir Nicholas Bacon's earlier draft, now BL Add. 32379, ff. 29–33: 'Articles devised for the bringinge vp in vertue and lerninge of the Queenes Majestys wardes beinge heires males.' Mark H. Curtis, *Oxford and Cambridge in Transition, 1558–1642: An Essay on the Changing Relations between the English Universities and English Society* (Oxford: Clarendon Press, 1959) 63–8. On the importance of the mechanical arts for the 'new humanism' of the late sixteenth c., see Wolfe, *Humanism, Machinery, and Renaissance Literature* 17–28, 88–124.

[44] Mark Edward Motley, *Becoming a French Aristocrat: The Education of the Court Nobility, 1580–1715* (Princeton: Princeton University Press, 1990).

[45] Jean E. Howard, *Theater of a City: The Places of London Comedy, 1598–1642* (Philadelphia: University of Pennsylvania Press, 2007) 162–208.

[46] Curtis, *Oxford and Cambridge in Transition, 1558–1642* 126–48; Patricia-Ann Lee, 'Some English Academies: An Experiment in the Education of Renaissance Gentlemen', *History of Education Quarterly*, 10 (1970), 273–86.

[47] Kelso, *The Doctrine of the English Gentleman in the Sixteenth Century*; Frank Whigham, *Ambition and Privilege: The Social Tropes of Elizabethan Courtesy Theory* (Berkeley: University of California Press, 1984) 1–31; Boutcher, 'Humanism and Literature in Late Tudor England'.

actually to insinuate, & enforce themselues, by uery special, & singular propertyes of emploiable &, necessary vse, in all affaires, as well priuate, as publique, amounting to any commodity, ether oeconomical, or politique.[48]

Many of the traces of Harvey's reading can be understood as signs of his effort to 'enforce' himself by 'very special, and singular properties of employable and necessary use', turning from a traditional notion of erudition to a more pragmatic one—and here we should remember that Harvey's 'pragmaticals' are advisors and aides, people performing expert (political, legal) work in the service of others.[49] Reflecting on the careers of those he considered the greatest statesmen, the 'right politiques'[50] of Tudor England (not incidentally all low-born, upwardly mobile figures), Harvey insisted that they rose by pragmatic, politic skill rather than by learning. As he says, Thomas Cromwell by 'the only promptnes of his wit, facility of speach, & a pragmatical dexterity to all purposes, ouershadowed & obscured, euen our greatist clarkes', and for the sake of making the same point, he downplays the actual education of William Cecil, Lord Burghley, claiming that he achieved the same 'by semblable meanes, with sum lytle more lerning, & lyke politique Method'.[51]

Harvey himself spent his life between the world of scholarship and that of 'princes, Pragmaticals, & common Gallants'. In 1580, he briefly served Robert Dudley, Earl of Leicester as his secretary, and he was also expecting to be sent abroad with a diplomatic mission—the kind of employment that, as I will show in the second chapter of this book, often served as the first step towards a career in government employment.[52] It wasn't his decision not to follow through with these career plans: in a marginal note that seems to date from the early seventeenth century, he still asserts that 'I don't much care to become the king's professor [Regius Professor], I would much rather be the King's procurator.'[53] If Harvey lived at the cusp of this divide, some of his colleagues succeeded in crossing it, although such success did not always lead to long-term felicity. Henry Cuffe, the Regius Professor of Greek at Oxford, became one of Essex's secretaries and close political advisors. Among other services, he was sent by Essex to Paris to read Louis Le Roy's 'expositions of Aristotle' with Henry Wriothesley, the Earl of Southampton, and he was also the scholar—clearly not considered by Essex as a 'mere scholler'—assigned to read with Rutland, and thus presumably charged with putting into effect Essex's instructions. And although in the Essex trial Cuffe defended himself by effectively claiming to be a 'mere scholler', arguing that on the day of the rebellion he was

---

[48] In Ramus's *Oeconomia*, bound with Harvey's copy of Foorth, currently at the Saffron Walden museum. I thank Adam Hooks for information about these volumes. Smith, *Gabriel Harvey's Marginalia* 151. On Harvey's praise of experience over bookishness, see Wolfe, *Humanism, Machinery, and Renaissance Literature* 136–41.
[49] Jardine and Sherman, 'Pragmatic Readers', 114–15, esp. n141.
[50] Smith, *Gabriel Harvey's Marginalia* 192.
[51] Commonplace book, BL MS Add 32494 f. 16v, Smith, *Gabriel Harvey's Marginalia* 91.
[52] Virginia F. Stern, *Gabriel Harvey, His Life, Marginalia and Library* (Oxford: Clarendon Press, 1979) 39, 46, 68.
[53] 'non curo esse regius professor / malo esse regius procurator', Folger MS H.a. 2, f. 118r. Regius professor indicates the professorship sponsored by the monarch. 'Procurator' here might stand either for attorney general, or, perhaps, simply for counsellor.

'locked up in my chamber amongst my books', the prosecution saw his participation in political consultation with the rebel lords reason enough to convict him and sentence him to death. They clearly saw him 'rich in matters and not [just] in wordes', a scholar who was made influential and dangerous by his political expertise.[54]

Anxious over the apparent failure of humanist training in rhetoric to propel him into the political employment this ideology promised, and disillusioned with literary art as a master discipline, Harvey was eager to try and achieve 'pragmatical dexterity' and learn 'politique method', the competence he saw as key to advancement in a political career. Political training was only one of his many interests: his notes and books are a paradoxical testimony to his efforts at experiential, material self-education in a variety of fields. The reading lists found among his marginalia and the catalogue of his surviving books outline a course of study that his contemporaries would have recognized as appropriate to the multifaceted pragmatic education of noblemen.[55] While the titles that can be ascertained to have belonged to him include a small set of books on rhetoric, the books directly relevant to his scholarly education are complemented by a solid list of titles on military issues, horsemanship, history and political topics, mathematical arts and sciences, and civil conversation, reflecting his strong interest in extramural subjects—these are the books that promised to fill his eloquence with matter.

But this is also to say that in his effort to move away from book learning, Harvey still found himself reading and compiling reading lists. Reading is the only action he could expertly perform, and to modern scholars he is best known for a pragmatic humanism that aimed to establish reading as the experiential, action-oriented exercise of military and political prudence. After his time teaching at Cambridge, when he was employed in Leicester's household, he was called upon for his services as a scholar–reader who studied with young noblemen in preparation for their political and military careers as well as for specific impending missions. As Lisa Jardine and Anthony Grafton have shown in their seminal article, he was reading Livy with Philip Sidney and with Thomas Smith Jr, using Machiavelli's *Discourses* as a commentary—and in preparing his aristocratic students for a life in politics, he was also training himself for such a career.[56] For Harvey, 'pragmatical dexterity' and 'politique method' were interpretive skills, inseparable from the practice of reading: in fact, they *were* a practice of reading, although one markedly different from what was undertaken in university classrooms.

---

[54] The information derives from Thomas Arundell's note to Robert Cecil, 18 February 1600/01, Bodleian MS Ashmole 1729, f. 190r, quoted in Jardine and Grafton, ' "Studied for Action": How Gabriel Harvey Read His Livy', 33; Alan Stewart, 'Instigating Treason: The Life and Death of Henry Cuffe, Secretary', in Lorna Hutson and Erica Sheen (eds.), *Literature, Politics and Law in Renaissance England* (Basingstoke: Palgrave, 2005), 50–70 at 54.

[55] See the list of Harvey's books in Stern, *Gabriel Harvey, His Life, Marginalia and Library* 198–241. Harvey's marginalia attest to his interest in, and awareness of, contemporary European academies as institutions of vernacular education. At the bottom of the last page of his Quintilian (now BL shelfmark C 60 l 11) he notes (referring to Thomas's description of Italy): 'The Academy in Florence, A braue Theater of domestical eloquence. Will. Thomas.'

[56] Jardine and Grafton, ' "Studied for Action": How Gabriel Harvey Read His Livy'. See also Lisa Jardine, 'Gabriel Harvey: Exemplary Ramist and Pragmatic Humanist', *Revue des Sciences Philosophiques et Théologiques*, 70 (1986), 36–48; Jardine and Sherman, 'Pragmatic Readers'.

The Distinction of Politics and Gabriel Harvey's Machiavellian Hamlet   55

Harvey captures that difference by outlining an emerging canon of texts that exemplify pragmatic reading and interpretation. In a draft letter, talking about the state of scholarship, he notes the tendency of 'scholars in ower age' to be 'rather active then contemplaitve philosophers: coveting above all things under heaven to appear somwhat more than scholars if themselves wiste how.' The debate about the active and contemplative lives does not merely crop up in the world of contemplation, in the groves of academe, but disrupts its routines. Harvey also describes the shift in the attention of the learned: a situation where the old staples of school learning (holdovers from a pre-humanist curriculum) are supplanted by political literature as

> Aristotles Organon is nighhand as little redd as Dunses Quodlibet. His oeconomicks and politiques every on hath by rote. You can not stepp into a schollars studye but (ten to on) you shall likely finde open ether Bodin de Republica or Le Royes Exposition vppon Aristotles Politiques or sum other like Frenche or Italian Politique discourses.[57]

Harvey identifies the central text of this emerging alternative curriculum with circumspect disingenuousness. As he says, 'sum good fellowes amongst us begin nowe to be pretty well acquayntid with a certayne parlous booke callid, as I remember me, Il Principe di Niccolo Macchiavelli.'[58] Contrary to what his hesitation signals, Harvey was of course closely familiar not only with the *Discorsi* and the *Art of War* but also with *The Prince*, and by the 1580s, Machiavelli emerges as the most frequently referenced authors in his marginalia.[59] The appeal of Machiavelli's writing to people aiming to 'appear somwhat more than scholars' or 'fine humanists' is explained by Machiavelli himself, who asserts in his dedication to Lorenzo de'Medici that 'I have not embellished this work by filling it with rounded periods, with high-sounding words or fine phrases, or with any of the other beguiling artifices of apparent beauty which most writers employ to describe and embellish their subject; for my wish is that, if it is to be honoured at all, only the variety of its matter

---

[57] Edward John Long Scott (ed.), *Letter-Book of Gabriel Harvey, A.D. 1573–1580* (Camden N.S. 33, London: Camden Society, 1884) 78–9. For a similar account of the shift from the ancients to the moderns, but without the political specificity, the letter to Spenser in Alexander B. Grosart (ed.), *The Works of Gabriel Harvey, D.C.L.*, 3 vols. (London and Aylesbury: Printed for private circulation only, 1884) 1:68–9.

[58] Scott (ed.), *Letter-Book of Gabriel Harvey* 78–9.

[59] *The Prince* was a book that Harvey, like many others, demonized in publication but perused eagerly in private, as is evidenced in the draft letter from 1573, in which he is begging Master Remington to lend him his copy of Machiavelli, explaining that 'I purpose to peruse him only, not to misuse him; and superficially to surveie his forrests of pollicie, not guilefully to conveie awaie his interest in them', that is, that his aim is only to know the much-talked about dangerous material, the supposed manual of Catholic conspirators and enemies of the state: Scott (ed.), *Letter-Book of Gabriel Harvey* 174. His account of the habits of university scholars, quoted above, is presumably from a few years later. In 1578, he addresses a long satire to Leicester and prints it the same year in *Gratulationes Valdenses*. This poem, partly written in Machiavelli's person, testifies to his close familiarity with the anti-machiavellian view of the Florentine secretary's work and puts it to political use in arguing against the French match; see *Gabrielis Harueij Gratulationum Valdinensium libri quatuor* (London: Henry Binneman, 1578), sigs. E4r–F2v, and T. H. Jameson, 'The "Machiavellianism" of Gabriel Harvey', *PMLA*, 56 (1941), 645–56. By the late 1580s, Machiavelli is among the most frequently mentioned authors in Harvey's marginalia, cited as the best and greatest authority on policy.

and the gravity of the subject should make it acceptable.'[60] Machiavelli advertises his work as a text that Essex would have commended as 'rich in matters and not in wordes', as a text offering what the Queen, despairing over Polonius's elaborately drawn out praise of brevity as the 'soul of wit', calls 'more matter with less art' (2.2.95). And indeed, the text of *The Prince* is sharply distinguished from ornately erudite humanist prose by the vernacular simplicity of its vocabulary, metaphors, and syntax.[61]

Harvey stages his account of the recent intellectual fad, the obsession with political literature, as a revelation of the behind-the-scenes life of scholars, disclosing a scene of learning taking place in private rooms, an immersion in pragmatic study as a secret alternative to the curriculum delivered in the lecture halls. His mention of Machiavelli as a text 'sum good fellowes amongst us begin nowe to be pretty well acquayntid with' is a performative gesture that asserts the programme's esoteric nature. Harvey's predilection for third-person references to himself has been remarked upon by both his earliest and his twenty-first-century critics, and the 'schollars studye' described here might just be a case in point: it seems to serve both as a convenient buffer of deniability, but also as a gesture that establishes the status of Machiavelli's book as the central—and hence most arcane—text of the arcane field of political knowledge. It is a book that promises entry to this exclusive world, and at the same time marks the boundary between those in the know (and entitled to be in the know), and the daylight innocence of academic existence. The distinction between these two worlds, between an everyday public world and a world of political discussion, is also one that Machiavelli himself articulates in his most famous letter to his friend Francesco Vettori, where he describes how in the evening, returning home after a day defined by work, social encounters, and reading, he removes his everyday clothes and puts on clothes fit for a royal court—and in his solitude, enters 'the ancient courts of men of old' and engages them in conversation, asking them 'why they acted as they did'. As he explains, *The Prince* is the record of 'what has been valuable in their conversations', that is, of what he learnt from his inquiries into the motives and reasons of the political agents of the past.[62] In Harvey as in Machiavelli's letter—which Harvey could not have known—the interpretation of political activities is imagined as a world apart, a realm that has its own protocols, dress codes, norms, and rituals.

How Harvey understood the realm of politics is signalled by the centrality of Machiavelli's work to how he describes the readings of those scholars who aspire to become more than scholars: 'active philosophers'. The purpose of the study of political authors, of Bodin and of Le Roy's commentary on Aristotle, was not to

---

[60] Niccolò Machiavelli, *The Prince*, ed. Quentin Skinner, trans. Russell Price (Cambridge: Cambridge University Press, 1988) 3, translation modified.
[61] August Buck, *Machiavelli* (Darmstadt: Wissenschaftliche Buchgesellschaft, 1985) 163–4, citing Fredi Chiappelli, *Studi sul Linguaggio del Machiavelli* (Firenze, 1952) and Chiappelli, *Nuovi Studi sul Linguaggio del Machiavelli* (Firenze: Felice Le Monnier, 1969) 24ff.
[62] 10 December 1513; quoted from Machiavelli, *The Prince* 93.

acquire theoretical knowledge either of the diversity of constitutions or of good government (neither of which concern Machiavelli in *The Prince*), but to become successful in political conduct, or at least in advising on it. Harvey's notes in John Foord's *Synopsis Politica*, a brief Aristotelian compendium of political institutions and offices notable for its broadly republican perspective that even includes the description of kingship as elective, are evidence of this focus and show the intellectual consequences of the pragmatic orientation of political study.[63] As he points out, Aristotle only knows about forms of government, not about stratagems,[64] and most of Harvey's own marginal notes seem to be trying to make up for this imbalance. Harvey doesn't reflect on constitutional ideas, and of the virtues, he focuses not on the ones that prop up the commonwealth, but on those facilitating personal advancement, using the margins of Foord's discussion of republican offices and of the classification of Roman citizens to think about upward mobility, about the way to rise to nobility through office, culminating in this blunt 'Regula regularum: To seeke & enforce all possible aduantage.'[65]

At the end of his copy Harvey notes that he finished reading the *Synopsis* and 'mastered' its subject in three hours in August 1582. He clearly spent more time than that inscribing the margins of the book, perhaps even years after that first read-through. His reflections repeatedly turn to the examples of Thomas Cromwell and Burghley. As Harvey would have realized, Lord Treasurer Burghley was well versed in the civic–humanist rhetoric that underpins Foord's book.[66] Indeed, Foord's idea of an 'interrex' remarkably anticipates the monarchical republicanism of the emergency scenario that Burghley proposed for the case of an interregnum in the Bond of Association a couple of years later—the scenario that serves as the evidentiary cornerstone of Patrick Collinson's reconstruction of the conception of England as a 'monarchical republic'.[67] But Harvey's comments on Burghley in the margins of Foord's text are admiring for a reason other than this aspect of his political vocabulary. His interest is in politics that is understood not as public, participatory action but as prudent, self-interested activity in government employment. A mere dozen or so pages after Foord's disquisitions on the intellectual and moral virtues that are to govern civic life, in the margin of the chapter on church government, we find Harvey reminding himself not only of the necessity to refrain from having too much food or sleep or alcohol or any sex whatsoever if one is to succeed

---

[63] On Foord's *Synopsis*, see Markku Peltonen, *Classical Humanism and Republicanism in English Political Thought, 1570–1640* (Cambridge: Cambridge University Press, 1995) 20, 25–6, 45, 47, 49. Harvey's copy, bound with Ramus's *Oikonomia*, is preserved at the Saffron Walden Museum; the marginalia are transcribed in Smith, *Gabriel Harvey's Marginalia* 189–203.

[64] Smith, *Gabriel Harvey's Marginalia* 191.

[65] Smith, *Gabriel Harvey's Marginalia* 191, 196, 200.

[66] Stephen Alford, *The Early Elizabethan Polity: William Cecil and the British Succession Crisis, 1558–1569* (New York: Cambridge University Press, 1998); Stephen Alford, 'The Political Creed of William Cecil', in John F. McDiarmid (ed.), *The Monarchical Republic of Early Modern England: Essays in Response to Patrick Collinson* (Aldershot: Ashgate, 2007), 75–90.

[67] I discuss what ramifications the monarchical republican scenario outlined in that document had for the stage in Chapter 3.

in a career, but also of 'my Lord Treasurers compendious method', namely, 'the use of virtues and vices as the occasion demands'.[68]

For late sixteenth-century readers like Harvey, Machiavelli's radical (exhilarating or demonic) innovation was what they perceived as an unapologetic bracketing of the considerations of ordinary morality in his advice on 'the art of the state', that is, on how a prince ought to act in order to acquire or retain power.[69] The novelty of Machiavelli's writing for the late sixteenth century was its suggestion that successful political activity follows its own, distinct logic. It is the pragmatic art of the prudent handling of contingent situations, and it is controlled by a single-minded dedication to success, not by higher principle. The diabolic image of Machiavelli as 'Machiavel' or 'Old Nick' shows how prone such a position is to moralistic objection and critique.[70]

THE WISER SORT

Although the divide between moral instruction on the one hand and political advice on the other, as posited by sixteenth-century readers of Machiavelli, was logically compatible with the tenets of pragmatic political education as they emerged in the late sixteenth century, the discursive innovation of this Machiavellism, also exemplified by Harvey's notes, was still massively controversial. It is the reaction to Machiavelli in a highly successful proposal on the military and political education of the nobility that will help us clarify the significance of Harvey's distinction between the younger and the wiser sort of Shakespeare's readers.

---

[68] Smith, *Gabriel Harvey's Marginalia* 202. The 'method' he attributes to Burghley combines the suggestion Machiavelli makes at the end of Chapter 15 of *The Prince*, where he points out that 'doing some things that seem virtuous may result in one's ruin, whereas doing other things that seem vicious may strengthen one's position and cause one to flourish', and the famous argument of Chapter 25 about the necessity of adjusting one's nature to the circumstances; see Machiavelli, *The Prince* 55, 85–6.

[69] Conal Condren, *Argument and Authority in Early Modern England: The Presupposition of Oaths and Offices* (Cambridge: Cambridge University Press, 2006) 219–27. In his letter to Vettori of 10 December 1513, Machiavelli calls the subject of his studies 'l'arte dello stato'.

[70] Some of the most important works in the vast literature on the subject include Edward Stockton Meyer, *Machiavelli and the Elizabethan Drama* (Weimar: E. Felber, 1897); John Wesley Horrocks, 'Machiavelli in Tudor Political Opinion and Discussion' (University of London, 1908); Nadja Kempner, *Raleghs Staatstheoretische Schriften: Die Einführung des Machiavellismus in England* (Beiträge zur Englischen Philologie; Leipzig: B. Tauchnitz, 1928); Orsini, '"Policy": Or the Language of Elizabethan Machiavellism'; Mario Praz, 'The Politic Brain: Machiavelli and the Elizabethans', in *The Flaming Heart* (New York: Doubleday, 1958), 90–145; Felix Raab, *The English Face of Machiavelli: A Changing Interpretation, 1500–1700* (London: Routledge and Kegan Paul, 1964); N. W. Bawcutt, 'Machiavelli and Marlowe's *The Jew of Malta*', *Renaissance Drama*, n.s. 3 (1970), 3–49; Christopher Morris, 'Machiavelli's Reputation in Tudor England', *Machiavellismo e Antimachiavellismo nel Cinquecento* (Firenze: Olschki, 1970), 87–105; Emile Gasquet, *Le Courant Machiavelien dans la Pensée et la Littérature Anglaises du XVIe Siècle* (Études Anglaises 51; Paris, Montréal, Bruxelles: Didier, 1974); Victoria Kahn, *Machiavellian Rhetoric: From the Counter-Reformation to Milton* (Princeton: Princeton University Press, 1994); N. W. Bawcutt, 'The "Myth of Gentillet" Reconsidered: An Aspect of Elizabethan Machiavellism', *The Modern Language Review*, 99 (2004), 863–74; Anglo, *Machiavelli: The First Century*.

Written by François de La Noue, a Huguenot soldier–statesman of legendary valour and considerable learning, the *Discours Politiques et Militaires*, published in 1587 and translated into English in the same year, is a plan for the restoration of France, and of its nobility in particular, to its past 'justice and valiance', partly through a pragmatically oriented vernacular programme of instruction for the political elite to replace the current fashion of simply sending young men on their travels hoping this will somehow educate them.[71] The academies La Noue proposes would offer a well-rounded pragmatic curriculum, including martial arts as well as,

> in our own language, lectures out of the auncient writers that intreat of moral vertues, policy, & war. They might also be instructed in ye Mathematiks, Geography, fortification, & some most vsual languages. And this is profitable for a gentleman, I meane to know so much as he can make vse of (sig. G2r).

La Noue's sixth discourse addresses the question of what readings might be profitable for a gentleman, but its beginning is couched in starkly moral terms. Promising a discussion of what is not profitable at all, the title suggests: 'That the reading of the bookes of Amadis de Gaule, & such like is no lesse hurtful to youth, than the works of Machiauel to age.' La Noue admits that both kinds of writing are in genuine demand: young people crave romantic fiction and end up reading Iberian romances. More importantly, he admits that himself 'delighted in reading' Machiavelli, who 'intreateth of high & goodly politicke & martial affaires, which many Gentlemen are desirous to learne, as matters meete for their professions'. As he says, only with riper judgement—which was confirmed by the admonitions of Innocent Gentillet's *Antimachiavel*, one of the most influential responses to the success and novelty of Machiavelli's work—did he realize the perniciousness of *The Prince* and *The Discourses* (sig. G4r). Machiavelli is associated with ripeness—his work is dangerous for the mature interest in the responsible conduct of one's affairs, and this danger can only be averted by the application of the same mature judgement. Machiavellian thought is an autoimmune disease of the characteristic concerns of age, understood as the source of the practical wisdom that depends on experience. Old age around 1600 did not mean retirement age: it meant having reached maturity, having mastered one's trade or profession.[72]

La Noue's claim about *Amadis* being 'no less hurtful to youth' than 'Machiavel to age' soon became a genuine commonplace of cultural commentary. In 1598, it is quoted by Francis Meres in *Palladis Tamia*,[73] and around the same time also in William Scott's 'Modell of Poesye'.[74] The observation of the French advocate of a vernacular education can thus be found cropping up in the writings of the authors who were engaged in harnessing English vernacular writing, including commercial

---

[71] *The Politicke and Militarie Discourses of the Lord de La Nouue*. ... All faithfully translated out of the French by E. A. (London: for T[homas]. C[adman] and E[dward]. A[ggas] by Thomas Orwin, 1587) sig. F4r.
[72] Gilbert Creighton, 'When Did a Man in the Renaissance Grow Old?', *Studies in the Renaissance*, 14 (1967), 7–32; Keith Thomas, *Age and Authority in Early Modern England* (Proceedings of the British Academy: The Raleigh Lecture on History; London: Oxford University Press, 1976).
[73] *Palladis Tamia* sigs. 2M4r–v.   [74] Scott, *The Model of Poesy* f. 41r.

drama, for similar purposes. But the utility and value of drama remains a divisive issue, and La Noue—who does not consider the theatre—is quoted by writers on both sides of that debate. In 1603, the sentence is appropriated by Henry Crosse, the puritan author whose 1603 *Vertues Common-wealth* is usually remembered for its attack on the stage. But Crosse's book does not spare the products of the printing press, either: he comments scathingly on 'those vaine, idle, wanton Pamphlets and lasciuious loue-bookes, which as fire-brands, inflame the concupiscence of youth', books that are 'as hurtful to youth, as *Machauile* to age',[75] a passage then borrowed by James Cleland in the 1607 *Hero-paideia, or The Institution of a Young Noble Man*.[76] What might be ruinous for younger readers remains an unstable category in this tradition, but more mature readers are persistently imagined as threatened by the 'politic' writing emblematized by Machiavelli.

Harvey was an admirer not only of Machiavelli but also of 'the braue Monsieur de la Nöe',[77] and the long note inscribed on the last pages of his Chaucer witnesses how he seeks to negotiate the conflicting demands of the two authorities. Writing about Shakespeare's best-known works, Harvey reworks La Noue's now commonplace observation about the dangerous appeal of particular types of books for particular audiences. In the contrast between younger readers eager for erotic poetry and the 'wiser sort' mining their books for sententious politic insights, he retains La Noue's assumption about books projecting a particular use and readership for themselves, but removes the moral taint by turning the warning about the threatening harms of two types of texts into the promise of the specific kinds of pleasure they hold.[78] Crucially, in Harvey's version of La Noue's template, the 'parlous booke' of Machiavelli is replaced by Shakespeare's *Lucrece* and *Hamlet*: the central text about the secret arts of power by the works of a commercial poet and playwright, a man of no political experience, who until very recently was not even an armigerous gentleman.

By reading Harvey's reference to *Hamlet* as part of a political reading list, and as a revised reference to La Noue, we are locating the play right at the heart of the discussion about the 'institution' of a national elite, whether understood as a programme of education for the children of the aristocracy, or as an avenue of advancement for people aspiring to court employment, or indeed as a continuing personal effort to perfect one's prudence and civility. Harvey's substitution of Shakespeare for Machiavelli implies that the wisdom-pleasing aspect of *Hamlet* and *Lucrece* is

---

[75] Henry Crosse, *Vertues Common-vvealth: or The High-way to Honour* (London: Printed [by Thomas Creede] for Iohn Newbery, 1603) sig. N4r.

[76] James Cleland, *Hero-paideia, or The Institution of a Young Noble Man* (Oxford: Ioseph Barnes, 1607) sig. V1v. Crosse's sentence goes; 'for in my opinion nothing doth more corrupt and wither greene and tender wits, then such vnsauoury and vituperable bookes, as hurtful to youth, as *Machauile* to age, a plaugh dangerous, and as common as dangerous' (N4r). Cleland, who borrows freely from Montaigne as well as others, also includes La Noue (T4v) in his reading list of vernacular authors one 'should read privately by yourselfe' (T1v), although he considers him 'somewhat difficil for some men' (T4v).

[77] Barnaby Barnes's epistle to Harvey, in Harvey, *Pierces Supererogation or A New Prayse of the Old Asse* (London: Iohn VVolfe, 1593) sig. ***2v.

[78] Although he does so in a piece of private writing that was only circulated, if at all, among his friends: on the last page of the book we find 'gabrielis harueij, et amicorum. 1598.'

not their literary or philosophical quality, but the pragmatic, prudential instruction in the profession of politics they might offer.

Literariness is central to all this nonetheless: the political distinction in Harvey's note is a distinction made on a body of poetic texts, and specifically, within a list of poems. Since the political instruction of these fictions cannot be a function of Shakespeare's own experience, and since, therefore, the value of his poem and his play cannot possibly consist in the authoritativeness of their content, their political matter, it must be a function of the specific use of language, the particular shapes of the claims and situations, and the practice of the kind of reading these words and claims and situations require. In other words, in Harvey's thought, the political matter of writing, the reason why and how art matters politically, turns out to be a function of its artifice: the political value of literature must therefore ultimately consist in what we understand as these texts' formal, rhetorical, literary qualities. Not qualities that are decorative or external to the content, not even features expressive of it, but the qualities of discourse that enable and produce its distinctive matter.[79] It is to these qualities—the qualities that constitute what we may call a politic style—that I will now turn.

A CHOICE OF TRAGIC SENTENCES: POLITICAL READING AS THE WORK OF DISTINCTION

Harvey's notion that a tragedy like *Hamlet* may cater to a desire for political materials and serve as a stand-in for Machiavelli, as the English equivalent of the Florentine secretary's works, follows from the logic of the contemporary understanding of the forms and genres in question, and of their uses. Both Machiavelli's *Prince* and tragic drama were considered storehouses of sententious observations, of aphoristic formulations, of maxims or 'politic sentences'. The prudential instruction offered by Shakespeare's writing for the wiser sort can thus be expected to appear in such maxims, while Harvey's remarks about reading sententious utterances in dramatic texts will also turn out to be concerned with the political insight they contain.

Prudential, action-oriented political writing was closely associated in the period with a particular mode of sententiousness: the 'Machiavellian maxim' was the emblematic form of critical and cynical analysis of politics that focused on the agents' interests and motives, and the object of an entire culture of circulation and collection. The maxim as a form was appropriate to the fundamentally unsystematic nature of such political thought: maxim-based prudential arguments were mobile, flexible, and portable, not only in terms of the situations to which they

---

[79] The notion of literariness invoked here is a broadly formalist or structuralist one: it is the peculiarity of the utterance, the quality that diverges from the norm, the aspect that solicits interpretation. There is no hint, of course, of this being an inherent feature of the text—rather, it emerges at the intersection of the text and its uses. How such a notion might have been conceivable by Harvey and his contemporaries is implied by Derek Attridge, *Peculiar Language: Literature as Difference from the Renaissance to James Joyce* (London: Methuen, 1988) 17–45.

applied, but also in their transferability to new fields of activity. Nonetheless, Machiavellian maxims were also contrasted to moral sentences and wise sayings, and a notion appropriate to one setting may very well have turned out to be scandalous when invoked in another. As Harvey's own sententious formulations of politic insight show, the implicit generic promise of the *sententia*—viz. that it was a form for advice of general validity, regardless of context—was made conspicuously untenable by the separation of the art of the state from the field of general discourse. Propositions that were intended to offer guidance in politics—like Burghley's 'compendious method' or Harvey's *regula regularum*—were not transferable to other areas of human experience without being marked by the opprobrium that attaches to crude immorality.

Perhaps no text helped to codify more forcefully the association between Machiavelli and the kind of sententiously mobile and morally unorthodox maxims that Harvey inscribed in the margins of his copy of *Synopsis Politica* than Innocent Gentillet's 1576 *Discours sur les Moyens de Bien Gouverner et Maintenir en Bonne Paix un Royaume*, published in an English translation in 1602, just a year before Shakespeare's *Hamlet* was first printed—and no book has done more to associate political maxims with the separation of political thought from the consideration of ordinary morality. Gentillet's book is best known as *Antimachiavel* and as this abbreviated version of its subtitle implies, it was conceived as a refutation of the Florentine thinker, whose writings Gentillet considers as 'beastlie vanitie and madnesse, yea, full of extreame wickednesse', a condition made more disturbing by their enormous popularity. He suggests that Machiavelli's 'bookes rightly may be called, The French Courtiers *Alcoran*, they have them in so great estimation; imitating and observing his principles and Maximes, no more no lesse than the Turkes doe the *Alcoran* of their great Prophet *Mahomet*.'[80] To counter the popular discourse which uses Machiavelli's principles and maxims as its diabolic scripture, Gentillet chooses to take on the challenge posed by the courtiers' Alcoran in its own terms. He claims first to 'have extracted and gathered, that which is properly [Machiavelli's] owne, and have reduced and brought it to certaine Maximes' (sig. A3r), in order to then subject them to a critique from the perspective of Christian morality, ignoring—it sometimes seems wilfully—the fact that Machiavelli's suggestions are uniquely tailored to the special situation and needs of rulers, without even a hint at their transferability to everyday human interactions. It is through denying the claims of the casuistry of office, of there being distinct conditions under which actions in conflict with ordinary morality might be considered as prudent and advisable, that Gentillet's reading of Machiavelli produces the sinister figure of the Machiavel as a promoter of immoral self-interest.

Nevertheless, by reducing Machiavelli to maxims, Gentillet actually provided his readers with easy access to the discourse he so forcefully and influentially

---

[80] Innocent Gentillet: *A Discourse vpon the Meanes of VVel Governing and Maintaining in Good Peace, a Kingdome, or Other Principalitie ... Against Nicholas Machiavell the Florentine. Translated into English by Simon Patericke* (London: Adam Islip, 1602) sig. A2v. For accounts of Gentillet's book and its English readers, see Gasquet, *Le Courant Machiavelien* 169–83; Anglo, *Machiavelli: The First Century* 271–324; Bawcutt, 'The "Myth of Gentillet" Reconsidered'.

critiqued, in precisely the form in which it was sought—as a series of decontextualized, quotable maxims.[81] The rhetoric of the printed page of Gentillet, both in the 1576 French and the 1602 English editions, further emphasizes the paradoxical utility of the book: each chapter begins with a maxim taken from or based on Machiavelli, printed in a large italic font and serving as a title and the text to be discussed; this is followed first by Gentillet's summary of Machiavelli's reasons and examples supporting the maxim in a smaller roman font, and then, finally, by Gentillet's refutation in a much smaller typeface. The book is completed by a table of the maxims, rehearsing, once again, the ostensible targets of criticism, but this time even without the small print that would qualify them—a telegraphic manual of political prudence.

As a parallel to the aphoristic quality of Machiavellian writing, the sententiousness of tragic drama is also something of a commonplace in the period, and over the course of the seventeenth century, this parallelism actually becomes a convergence.[82] In the vast manual of *Poetices Libri Septem*, Julius Caesar Scaliger claims that *sententiae* are the pillars, the columns that prop up the fabric of a tragedy,[83] and for contemporary readers, these 'stately speeches and well-sounding phrases' were among the main sources of the 'notable morality'[84] tragedy was supposed to communicate: 'fulness and frequency of sentence' (as Jonson puts it) is one of the chief 'offices of the tragic writer'—signs of the genre's seriousness and the vehicles of the wisdom it was meant to impart.[85]

Although it has been described as a sign that served to assimilate commercial drama to other forms of erudite production, the gnomic pointing of printed play texts is actually dramatic, indeed tragic in its origin.[86] The two earliest

---

[81] Edmond M. Beame, 'The Use and Abuse of Machiavelli: The Sixteenth-Century French Adaptation', *Journal of the History of Ideas*, 43 (1982), 33–54; Victoria Kahn, 'Reading Machiavelli: Innocent Gentillet's Discourse on Method', *Political Theory*, 22 (1994), 539–60.

[82] The seventeenth-century German *Trauerspiel*, with its focus on 'Staats- und Hauptaktionen', is the genre where this convergence concludes. The genre and its investment in the representation of political action through its focus on the tyrant and the intriguer is still usefully described in the first part of the section on 'Trauerspiel und Tragödie' in Walter Benjamin, *The Origin of German Tragic Drama* (London: NLB, 1977) esp. 62–8, 95–8. But Benjamin's theorization of sententiousness depends on his notion of the allegory, not on Machiavellian political knowledge. The centrality of *Hamlet* to Benjamin's book, as both an exemplary *Trauerspiel* and a tragedy contrasted to *Trauerspiele*, cannot be overemphasized.

[83] Lib. III. cap. 97, page 145 col. 1 D. For useful overviews of Scaliger's book, see August Buck's introduction to Julius Caesar Scaliger, *Poetices Libri Septem, Faksimile-Neudruck der Ausgabe von Lyon 1561* (Stuttgart-Bad Cannstatt: Friedrich Frommann, 1964), v–xx, and Marijke Spies, 'Between epic and lyric: the genres in J.C. Scaliger's Poetices Libri Septem', in *Rhetoric, Rhetoricians and Poets: Studies in Renaissance Poetry and Poetics* (Amsterdam: Amsterdam University Press, 1999), 21–8. On the *gravitas* and instruction provided by tragic *sententiae*, see also J. W. Binns, 'Seneca and Neo-Latin Tragedy in England', in C. D. N. Costa (ed.), *Seneca* (London and Boston: Routledge and Kegan Paul, 1974), 205–34.

[84] Philip Sidney, *An Apology for Poetry, or, the Defence of Poesy*, eds Geoffrey Shepherd and R. W. Maslen (3rd edn.; Manchester: Manchester University Press, 2002) 110.

[85] *Sejanus*, 'To the Readers' ll. 13–15.

[86] The argument about the association between gnomic pointing and literariness, by which they mean academic learning, was made powerfully in Lesser and Stallybrass, 'The First Literary *Hamlet*'. In spite of our disagreement about the significance of the typographic device, the account of Lesser and Stallybrass on the early seventeenth-century phenomenon remains authoritative. The classic

texts ever printed with such markers seem to have been two Aldines: the 1502 edition of *Dicta et Facta Memorabilia*, a popular collection of anecdotes and apothegms by Valerius Maximus (where they mark, among others, an observation attributed to Euripides), and the 1503 *editio princeps* of Euripides.[87] Ever since the 1503 Euripides, classical drama, and especially tragedy, continued to be printed with such markers.[88] Over the course of the sixteenth century, the practice was transferred to vernacular drama, whose forms, both literary and typographical, obviously bear the imprint of the tradition of the publication of the classics. So when the first commercial play equipped with gnomic pointing, Jonson's *Every Man Out*, appeared in 1600, its publisher was inserting it in a recognizable tradition, not of a generalized category of 'literary' texts, but of printed drama, the genre that of all types of texts was most consistently equipped with such pointers—a tradition that produced, during the first decade and a half of the seventeenth century, dozens of playbooks so marked, many of them in several editions.

It seems appropriate, then, that Gabriel Harvey, who followed Erasmus's instructions in using a variety of signs to highlight various types of materials throughout his books,[89] chose the opening page of a tragedy, and of none other than Erasmus's translation of the *Hecuba* of Euripides, a 1507 Aldine and among the earliest books printed with gnomic pointing, to remind himself of the significance of such markers:

> Eccè Gnomæ Selectæ, hac notulæ insignitæ, ,, ,,

—that is,

> see the sententiae singled out, marked with this sign, ,, ,,

On the facing page of the same text, he inserts a note in which he formulates a hermeneutics of tragic drama as a form of political analysis that is focused specifically on the dramatic *sententiae*, and on the distinction to be made between points

---

article about English drama and gnomic pointing is Hunter, 'The Marking of Sententiae in Elizabethan Printed Plays, Poems, and Romances'.

[87] In Valerius Maximus, a set of two apothegms titled 'De Euripide philosopho' begins with how the people demanded that Euripides delete a particular *sententia* from a tragedy, whereupon Euripides came on stage and said that he was writing plays to teach them not to learn from them. The section concludes with the story of Alcestis bragging about writing a hundred lines in the three days that it took Euripides to write three, to which Euripides responds, 'your lines will only last three days, mine forever'. The passage closes with the statement that his 'work lucubrated with hesitant pen shall be wafted with sails full of glory through the ages'—a sententious piece of lucubration Aldus marks with double inverted commas in the left margin. *Valerii Maximi Dictorum et Factorum Memorabilium Libri Novem* (Venetiis, 1502) sig. H6r, translation from the Loeb edition.

[88] Moss, *Printed Commonplace-Books* 211n228 mentions a 1506 Seneca published by Giunti as the earliest known such text. On the origins of the practice, see Arrigo Castellani, *Nuovi Saggi Di Linguistica E Filologia Italiana E Romanza (1976–2004)*, eds Valeria Della Valle et al., 2 vols. (Roma: Salerno Editrice, 2009) 1:71–85. I thank Ivan Lupić for calling my attention to this article and for his counsel on topics ranging from *sententiae* to the complications of friendship.

[89] Moss, *Printed Commonplace-Books* 102; Harold S. Wilson, 'Gabriel Harvey's Method of Annotating His Books', *Harvard Library Bulletin*, 2/3 (1948), 344–61.

The Distinction of Politics and Gabriel Harvey's Machiavellian Hamlet 65

of philosophical wisdom and pragmatic political insight (see Figure 1.2). In this carefully wrought passage he states that

> it is useless to read tragedies for someone who cannot distinguish philosophical from tyrannical sentences. One thing is the doctrine of scholars, another the teaching of kings. It calls for politic judgment to distinguish the most prudent sentences from the rest. A tyrant is not always an uneducated brute, nor is the poet or the philosopher always wise, and it will show a sharp judgment if we attend not to who speaks, but rather to what they say, selecting always what is best.[90]

For early modern readers, 'tyrannical sentences' were likely to imply either Machiavellian maxims or sententious material out of Seneca, both of which contexts allowed for generous as well as starkly critical interpretations of the term. Machiavelli's sentences were tyrannical in a very direct sense: Louis Le Roy, in his vast and learned commentary on his 1568 translation of Aristotle's *Politics*—the book Harvey saw open in the rooms of so many scholars, and which Cuffe read with Southampton in 1598—introduced the widespread notion that Machiavelli drew 'most part of his precepts' from Aristotle's discussion of how tyrants preserve their power.[91] Gentillet claimed that *The Prince* 'for the most part containeth nothing but tyrannicall precepts' and in the wake of the *Anti-Machiavel*, a reference to 'maximes tyranniques' became a common way of gesturing at the evils of Machiavellian writing.[92] But classical drama had its share of similar materials. Seneca, whose plays served as a model for the sententiousness of vernacular drama, was also read as a source of exemplary political counsel. The ambiguity of the political purpose of his plays is reflected in the modern critical literature, with scholars debating whether Seneca's aim in writing these tragedies was to advise Nero on the dangers of the abuse of power, or to mobilize the opposition to the emperor, and the scholarship on the reading of Seneca in sixteenth-century England is divided along similar lines.[93] In their sententious scenes of counsel, Seneca's tragedies stage debates about the nature and limits of rule and about the question of what liberties

---

[90] 'Inutiliter tragoedias legit, qui nescit philosophicas sententias a tyrannicis distinguere. Alia scholarum doctrina: alia regnorum disciplina. Politico opus est judicio, ad distinguendum prudentissimas sententias a reliquis. Nec semper tyrannus barbarus: nec semper poeta, aut philosophus sapiens: solertis judicii fuerit, non quis dicat, sed quid dicatur, respicere, et undique optima seligere. Euripidis Jocasta apud Gascognem summa fere tragoediarum omnium' ('Politico opus est iudicio…' might also be construed as 'The politician needs judgment…'). *Hecvba & Iphigenia in Aulide Euripidis Tragoediae in Latinum Tralatae Erasmo Roterodamo Interprete* ([Venetiis]: Aldvs, 1507) Harvard University, Houghton Library, *EC H2623 Zz507e, f. 8v. I thank Adam Hooks for calling my attention to the note about the markers at the bottom of f. 9r, directly facing this passage.

[91] *Aristotles Politiques, or Discourses of Gouernment. Translated out of Greeke into French,… By Loys Le Roy, called Regius. Translated out of French into English. I. D.* (London: Adam Islip, 1598) sig. 2H1r, in the margin of the chapter in question (Book 5, chapter 11). Gentillet suggested that he plagiarized it from the *De Tyrannia* of Bartolus, itself dependent on Aristotle; see Anglo, *Machiavelli: The First Century* 312–14.

[92] Gentillet, *A Discourse vpon the Meanes of VVel Governing* sig. A2v; Anglo, *Machiavelli: The First Century* 340–52.

[93] Jessica Winston, 'Seneca in Early Elizabethan England', *Renaissance Quarterly*, 59 (2006), 29–58; Linda Woodbridge, 'Resistance Theory Meets Drama: Tudor Seneca', *Renaissance Drama*, 38 (2010), 115–40.

66 Hamlet *and the Profession of Politics*

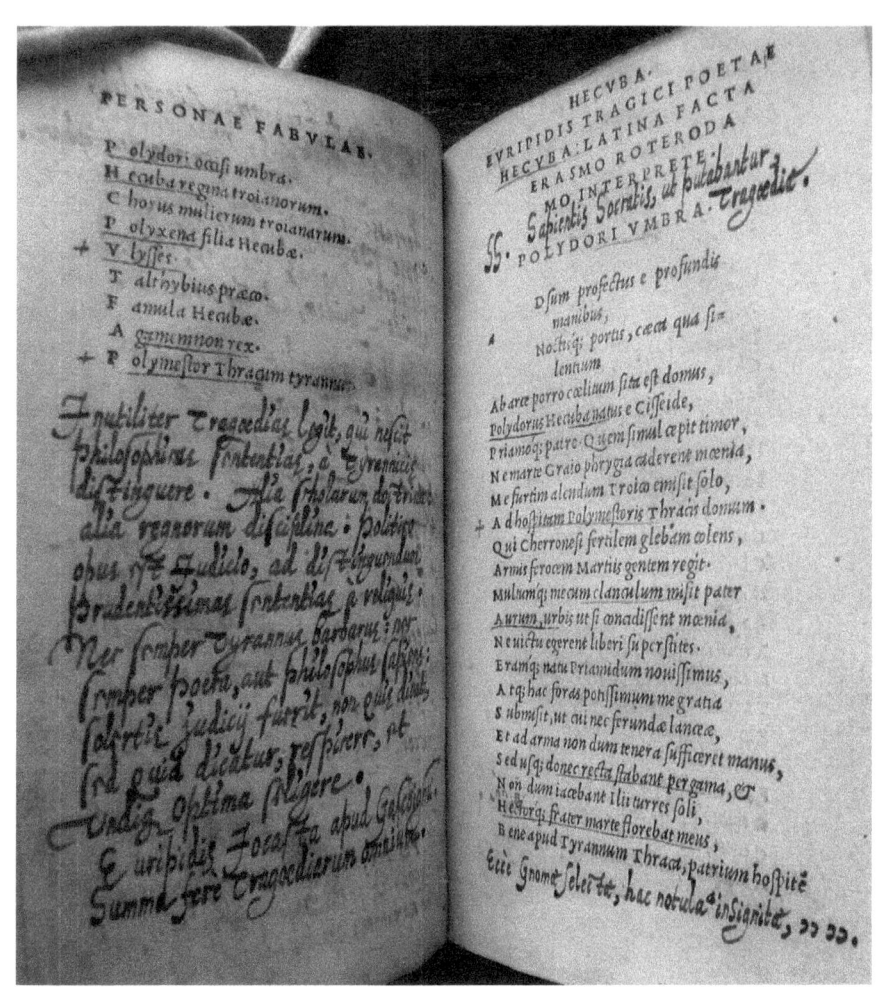

Fig. 1.2. Gabriel Harvey's notes on sentences and note-taking in *Hecvba, & Iphigenia in Aulide Euripidis Tragoediae in Latinum Tralatae Erasmo Roterodamo Interprete* (Venetiis: Aldvs, 1507), Houghton Library, Harvard University, shelfmark *EC H2623 Zz507e, sigs. I8v–A1r.

and obligations are entailed in the king's office, pitting the tyrant's blatant maxims against his counsellor's moral claims.[94]

Harvey's reference to tyrannical maxims invokes both of these traditions and seems to do so without obloquy.[95] That his decisive distinction is between philosopher

---

[94] It is in these scenes that Aristotle's suggestion in the *Rhetoric*, namely, that *sententiae* (*gnomai*) are a device that make an argument compelling through forcefully declaring the speaker's moral preferences, is best illustrated: *Rhetoric* 2.21.15–16 (1395b).

[95] Harvey may be making use of the historical ambiguity of the word—in classical Greek, *tyrannos* was often used as a neutral term for a ruler. As the parallelism between the 'philosophical/tyrannical'

and king, not between tyrant and king, is a clear articulation of the tacit Machiavellian rejection of the distinction made in classical philosophy between tyrants and kings—the rejection which motivates Gentillet's critique and which is even identified by Leo Strauss as the origin of modern political science.[96] The political choice has literary consequences as well: by equating tyrannical maxims with the teaching of kings, Harvey distances himself both from the moralistic tradition in which tragedy 'maketh kings feare to be tyrants, and tyrants manifest their tyranny' and also from the Platonic argument which rejected tyranny and tragic drama as analogous evils.[97] Recognizing the importance of the traditional associations linking tragedies and tyrants, Harvey reverses their implication, turning them into an argument for the utility of tragic drama. Tragedies are not evil, but they are not necessarily mechanisms for moral instruction, either. Instead, Harvey suggests, through their sentences, tragedies can provide guidance in statecraft, which he considers—*pace* Plato—a separate field of useful knowledge following its own principles: the discipline of kings rather than the doctrine of scholars.

In the logic of this note, whether a specific maxim belongs to the field of political expertise or to scholarly learning is not something given a priori: rather, it is established through the judgement of the politician (Harvey's *politicus*, and Hamlet's 'statist', 5.2.33), through his application of his wisdom or prudence.[98] In other words, the politician's prudence is charged with deciding what comes under its own purview and competence, selecting the maxims that are to be followed by a monarch, and separating them from the philosophical rules whose wisdom, although of unquestionable value to private citizens, might be counterproductive in maintaining the power of a ruler.

In Harvey's argument, this work of selection and distinction, this alert application of discrimination and distinction, might in fact be the politician's most important

---

and the 'doctrine of scholars/discipline of kings' binaries indicates, Harvey's knowledge of Greek, and perhaps of Greek tragedy, may have inspired him to use *tyrannus* as an unqualified synonym for *rex*, not an accusatory term.

[96] Strauss claims this *tacit* rejection is central to *The Prince*: Leo Strauss, *On Tyranny: Including the Strauss-Kojève Correspondence*, eds Victor Gourevitch and Michael S. Roth (Rev. and expanded edn.; Chicago: University of Chicago Press, 2000) 23–4. On the problem of tyranny in Machiavelli see Mikael Hörnqvist, *Machiavelli and Empire* (Cambridge: Cambridge University Press, 2004) 194–227. About the assumption shared among a wide range of Machiavelli's critics that *The Prince* is a purely instrumental, cynical handbook of the technology of power, the work of a sinister 'Machiavel', and dependent—in Strauss's terms—on a fateful and immoral separation of facts and values, see Isaiah Berlin, 'The Originality of Machiavelli', *Against the Current: Essays in the History of Ideas* (New York: Viking Press, 1980), 25–79 at 35–6, 40–1; Kahn, *The Future of Illusion* 83–113, and the argument on the conflicting traditions of reading Machiavelli as either classical republican or Machiavel, not as a choice between a correct and a mistaken reading, but as equally produced by Machiavellian rhetoric in Kahn, *Machiavellian Rhetoric* 6–9.

[97] Sidney, *An Apology for Poetry, or, the Defence of Poesy* 98. For an overview of the classical sources of early modern thought about tyranny and its links to the theatre, see Rebecca W. Bushnell, *Tragedies of Tyrants: Political Thought and Theater in the English Renaissance* (Ithaca: Cornell University Press, 1990) 1–36.

[98] Prudence, as Jonson explains, is the true attribute of the prince, 'his chief art and safety', and a quality distinct from being either good or learned—see *Discoveries* ll. 719ff and marginal note (Jonson 2012 7:534), which seems to contradict the body text, although maintains the distinction between prudence and goodness, and calls for both.

and certainly most fundamental intellectual task. The notion of politics being charged with setting the limits for itself, with determining where it applies, without input from philosophers, scholars, or citizens, coincides with a particular understanding of politics: with politics as 'policy' or statecraft, and not with the civic, republican, indeed philosophical idea of politics as the art of good government, as the preservation of the commonwealth of citizens living together in justice, as the actions of public-minded citizens as they negotiate their disagreements in governing their commonwealth.[99] In fact, as an autonomous field setting its own limits, 'policy' or statecraft depends for its success on clearly distinguishing itself from an understanding of politics as an instrument whose use is to be determined by the common good or some other principle external to it.[100]

Harvey's formalization of politic analysis into a maxim, his articulation of the idea of politic analysis or political thinking as the work of distinction, is itself an instance of, and likely shaped by, the style of argument that is so characteristic of the central authority in such analysis, viz. Machiavelli's *Prince*. It has been argued that most, if not all the particular ideas and insights reduced here by Machiavelli 'into a small volume' (as he puts it in the dedication to Lorenzo de'Medici) can be traced to earlier authors—not only to Aristotle, as Louis Le Roy suggested, but also to Cicero, Polybius, Livy, or the sophists.[101] Machiavelli's originality is therefore best located not in the propositional content of his advice, but in the style or form of his thinking. Because my interest is in the smallest, most portable units of Machiavelli's thought, I want to highlight here the most basic aspect of Machiavellian rhetoric—namely, his striking habit of proceeding through the construction of clear, pointed binaries. In Machiavelli's 'dilemmatic technique' or 'dichotomizing mode of argument', issues are reduced to sharp alternatives, antithetical options are highlighted at the expense of compromises.[102] There is no *aurea mediocritas* or ideal middle option as in Aristotle. States are either principalities or republics, either hereditary or new, private citizens become rulers due to their *virtù* or to their *fortuna*, people fail to commit to the new prince either because of pusillanimity and lack of natural spirit or because they are calculating and ambitious, princes have a choice to make

---

[99] For an account which narrativizes this distinction into a transformation of the concept of politics from the latter to the former, see Maurizio Viroli, 'The Revolution in the Concept of Politics', *Political Theory*, 20 (1992), 473–95.

[100] In this respect, Harvey's logic comes very close to Carl Schmitt's suggestion that 'any decision about whether something is *unpolitical* is always a *political* decision'. Carl Schmitt, *Political Theology: Four Chapters on the Concept of Sovereignty*, trans. George Schwab (Chicago: University of Chicago Press, 2005) 2, emphasis in the original. This connection should be unsurprising given Schmitt's well-known effort to define the political by identifying its proper, central principle, which he finds in the distinction between friend and enemy—cp. Carl Schmitt, *The Concept of the Political*, trans. Tracy B. Strong (Chicago: University of Chicago Press, 1996).

[101] Henning Ottmann, 'Was ist neu im Denken Machiavellis?', in Herfried Münkler, Rüdiger Voigt, and Ralf Walkenhaus (eds.), *Demaskierung der Macht: Niccolò Machiavellis Staats- und Politikverständnis* (Baden-Baden: Nomos, 2004), 145–56; and Millstone, 'Seeing Like a Statesman', 86ff.

[102] Federico Chabod, 'Machiavelli's Method and Style', *Machiavelli and the Renaissance* (London: Bowes & Bowes, 1958), 126–48 at 127–8; Buck, *Machiavelli* 46–7, 62–3; Kahn, *Machiavellian Rhetoric* 126.

between individual virtues and their opposites, they may either use law or force, etc.[103]

The dichotomizing style pervades the response to Machiavelli even at the most general level. One way to describe his contribution to Western thought is to see him as shifting the discussion from the distinction between good and evil, from knowing good from evil, to the distinction between what men do and what they ought to do—and attending to the former rather than the latter. As one reader of a translation of *The Prince* that was prepared around 1600 noted, 'Here is shewed that we should not with a rude heate or naturall instinct or by other example but artificially as it were only for a further end follow ether vertue or vice, making noe difference but by the profit we may receiue when we haue occasion to vse them. the Author teacheth what men doe and not what they ought to doe.'[104] When in the margin of Foord's book, Harvey notes that he lives not in Thomas More's Utopia but in Thomas Smith's Commonwealth, he does not merely show he is aware that his is not a country run by philosopher-kings, but a monarchy that is also an aristocratic republic:[105] he is also recalling the moment in Chapter 15 of *The Prince* where Machiavelli insists that it is 'better to concentrate on what really happens rather than on theories or speculations. For many have imagined republics and principalities that have never been seen or known to exist. However, how men live is different from how they should live.'[106]

The characteristic style of *The Prince* registers in many other readers' accounts, although they are rarely capable of sustaining Machiavelli's suspension of moral judgement, his refusal to valorize the branches of his distinctions as good and bad. John Wolfe, the publisher who brought out surreptitious editions of the major political works of Machiavelli,[107] and who was the publisher as well as the employer of Gabriel Harvey (who seems to have lived at his shop in the 1590s), learned from the Florentine 'exactly what difference there was between a just prince and a tyrant, between government by many good men and government by a few bad ones, and between a well-regulated commonwealth and a confused and licentious multitude'.[108] Edward Dacres, the translator of the first printed English version of *The Prince*, insisted that distinctions needed to be made between medicinal and poisonous readings—and what amounted to the same: medicinal and poisonous

---

[103] Machiavelli, *The Prince* 5, 19, 35–6, 55, 61.
[104] Folger MS Y.d.623, folder 16 (photographs of Jules Furthman's copy of a translation based on the Latin version by Sylvester Telius), f. 50v.
[105] Smith, *Gabriel Harvey's Marginalia* 197. Whether this note is meant as a sarcastic comment on Foord's idealistic view of the commonwealth, or a suggestion that it is rather close to what Thomas Smith described, is hard to tell.
[106] Machiavelli, *The Prince* 54.
[107] Denis B. Woodfield, *Surreptitious Printing in England 1550–1640* (New York: Bibliographical Society of America, 1973) 5–18.
[108] 'Lo stampatore al benigno lettore', in *I Discorsi di Nicolo Machiavelli* (Palermo: Heredi d'Antoniello degli Antonielli [in fact, London: John Wolfe], 1584) often bound with Wolfe's edition of *The Prince* of the same year, sig. *2v, as translated by Peter S. Donaldson, *Machiavelli and Mystery of State* (New York: Cambridge University Press, 1988) 93.

uses—of the text.[109] Dacres' comment both registers and anticipates the continuing plurality of the interpretations of *The Prince*—baffling for what appears to be a work of remarkable simplicity and clarity, but ultimately a testimony to the anti-systematic nature of Machiavelli's dilemmatic technique. The one point on which probably all readers agree is just how shocking this little book is.[110] Whether they claim that Machiavelli discovered politics as a sphere separate from ethics, that he distinguished between two different worlds of (say, Christian and pagan–republican) ethics, or that he destroyed the philosophical view of humanity by reducing humans to beings driven by passion and interest, and not by rational, theoretical considerations, interpretations of Machiavelli's significance have been interpretations of the nature of the divide (and contrast, indeed clash) between the actions he recommends and the precepts of common morality. Machiavelli does not seem to spell out a theory of this divide: instead, in the history of his work's reception, he himself has become a figure of division, separation, distinction.[111]

The clearly and pointedly posed alternatives demand decisions. The structure of Machiavelli's argument is directly linked to practice, and is anti-systematic and in this sense also anti-theoretical in nature. Sydney Anglo has pointed out the origins of this disjunctive style in Machiavelli's diplomatic reports and in his other practical political works, in his analysis of the situation of other states, of the conduct of negotiations and of the motives of other agents.[112] The agile, aphoristic grasp of the world of human activity in terms of clearly isolated choices thus finds its origins in political practice: and this might also be the reason why it resists systematization. According to Victoria Kahn, in Machiavelli's arguments, the distinctions themselves cannot ultimately hold and need to be redefined as the opposites turn out to be contained in each other or hidden behind the appearances of each other.[113] Such volatility is a function of the poignant disjunctive style, a thinking that finally refuses to crystallize the dichotomies into trees of hierarchies, and continues its work of assertion and distinction without being able to come to rest. We habitually associate such anti-doctrinal, paradoxical textuality with literariness—but in Machiavellian, 'politic' discourse, the heuristic power of its uncontrollable work is harnessed by prudent, action-oriented deliberation and judgement, where it is uncontainable only up to the moment when it is at last overtaken and extinguished by action.

---

[109] *Nicholas Machiavel's Prince. Translated out of Italian into English; by E.D. With Some Animadversions Noting and Taxing His Errours* (London: R. Bishop, for Wil: Hils, sold by Daniel Pakeman, 1640) sigs. A2r–A3r.

[110] I am taking my cue here from Isaiah Berlin's classic essay, where he sets out to 'account both for the continuing horror and for the differences among the commentators': Berlin, 'The Originality of Machiavelli', 27.

[111] Modern interpretations of this conceptual divide, not incidentally, also tend to be interpretations of the historical divide between, usually, modernity and what went before.

[112] Sydney Anglo, *Machiavelli: A Dissection* (London: Victor Gollancz, 1969) 244–5. Anglo considers this style a weakness, the basis of 'merely assertive, not logically structured, arguments' (244).

[113] Kahn, *Machiavellian Rhetoric* 25–33. Kahn's work is an obviously broader and more ambitious interpretation of the subject, with which I have much (and rather obvious) sympathy, not least for its attention to how this rhetoric was read and reworked over time.

The judgement of the politician is based on experience and analysis, and the political use of tragedies consists precisely in the opportunity that literary representation of action and argument provides for the exercise of political prudence, a critical practice of discrimination and selection that applies to situations and actions as well as to texts, the art of choosing from the available options what is appropriate to our purposes.[114] To read tragedies right is to read them politically, and reading *Hamlet*, and especially reading the *sententiae* in *Hamlet*, is a work of political interpretation in the sense of reading for and in politic terms, and also in the sense of sorting out the political from the rest, of deciding on the distinction between the political and the philosophical—and Harvey's note implies that reading *Lucrece* ought to be no different.[115]

As I have suggested, the form of the Machiavellian maxim, the pointed, aphoristic style, is deeply implicated in the work of division and distinction: it is a form intended to facilitate such work. To call for more matter with less art is, in a sense, to call for the impossible: the sparseness of ornament and the direct approach to the issue of decision in Machiavelli's writing is the artifice that enables the sharp operation of divisions and distinctions. The question is: what kind of art, what kind of artifice can deliver the matter that is called for? What genre of writing is most conducive to the exercise of maxim-based analysis? While Harvey mentions *Lucrece* and *Hamlet* in the same breath, we have seen how closely he follows the logic of generic convention in associating tragic drama with the pleasures of the Machiavellian mode. As he seems to recognize, drama is the form to which Machiavellian reading is native.

To conclude this chapter, I will turn to *Lucrece* and then to *Hamlet* to see how some of their most sententious segments might read if we keep Harvey's distinction between 'the doctrine of scholars' and 'the teaching of kings' in mind. Whether they fall under the jurisdiction of general, philosophical, or of political judgement is a question that troubles a surprising range of situations and scenes in these texts—one that is thus shown central to them and to the moment they inhabit. And the variety of answers they yield, while clearly overdetermined, points to the difference between the capacity of drama and narrative poetry for a productive engagement with the politic style, for a maxim-based analysis in the Machiavellian, politic mode.

---

[114] This is how both Machiavelli and Lipsius explain the term; Machiavelli in *The Prince* defines prudence as 'knowing how to assess the dangers, and to choose the least bad [*il manco tristo*] course of action as being the right one to follow'. Machiavelli, *The Prince* 79. Lipsius defines prudence as 'and understanding & discretion of those things which we ought either to desire or refuse, in publick & in privat. ... with a sound judgment it maketh choise and severeth honest things, from unworthie and dishonest, things profitable, from those that are hurtfull'. Justus Lipsius, *Six Bookes of Politickes or Ciuil Doctrine* (London: Richard Field for William Ponsonby, 1594), 1:7, sigs. C2r–v.

[115] Harvey would have been reflecting on *Hamlet* as text, not as performance, not least because by the time he purchased his Chaucer, he had already moved from London to Saffron Walden. Not much of a playgoer anyway, he remained interested in printed drama throughout his life—in another, later marginal note, he reminds himself of a recent play by Middleton as 'Its a madd world mie masters. The title of a new booke' (Folger MS H.a. 2, f. 48r).

LUCRECE'S RAPE AND THE TRIAL OF POLITIC DISTINCTION

The importance of *Lucrece* for England's 'republican moment' has now become part of the scholarly consensus.[116] The interpretive challenge posed by the poem seems to be how to negotiate between the Ovidian focus on sexual trauma and the Livian emphasis on the political crisis, that is, how *not* to extricate the personal from the political or vice versa.[117] The poem is bookended by the prefatory 'Argument', which sets the narrative firmly in the context of its constitutional consequences, and the concluding scene of Brutus advancing to political leadership, proposing the oath to revenge Tarquin's deed, and leading the citizens to 'show her bleeding body through Rome', using it 'to publish Tarquin's foul offence'. What takes place in between is set in a domestic space, but the poem's insistence on the image of a city under siege as a powerful metaphor for violation, culminating in Lucrece's self-identification with the besieged and invaded city of Troy (464–74, 481–2, 719–28, 1366–561),[118] guarantees that her pain is never fully withdrawn into the domestic realm, and that her own self-understanding is continuous with the language used by the narrative voice that is 'publishing' her shame.[119]

To claim that the politicization of Lucrece's rape is others' doing would also be to ignore the central, dramatic scene of the poem, where Lucrece, at once terrified and bashful, stumblingly begins to address Tarquin—'twice she doth begin ere once she speaks'—but rises to sententious heights in pleading with him. The scene is a scene of tragic counsel, not unlike such scenes in Senecan tragedy as Act 2 of *Thyestes* where the counselling servant's arguments about virtuous government are rebuffed by Atreus's crudely cynical points. Although the narrative poem can't accommodate stichomythic exchanges, in this scene of *Lucrece* the disputing parties are nonetheless allowed the pointed formulations readers so eagerly marked in and copied from Seneca.[120] The debate between Lucrece and Tarquin concludes in what is its logical vanishing point: the tyrant, having run out of arguments, stops

---

[116] Annabel M. Patterson, *Reading between the Lines* (Madison: University of Wisconsin Press, 1993) 297–312; Martin Dzelzainis, 'Shakespeare and Political Thought', in David Scott Kastan (ed.), *A Companion to Shakespeare* (Oxford: Blackwell, 1999), 100–16 at 106–14; Andrew Hadfield, *Shakespeare and Republicanism* (Cambridge: Cambridge University Press, 2008) 130–53.

[117] For the range of responses to this problem, see Ian Donaldson, *The Rapes of Lucretia: A Myth and Its Transformations* (Oxford: Clarendon Press, 1982); Stephanie H. Jed, *Chaste Thinking: The Rape of Lucretia and the Birth of Humanism* (Bloomington: Indiana University Press, 1989); Coppélia Kahn, *Roman Shakespeare: Warriors, Wounds, and Women* (New York: Routledge, 1997) 27–45; Lynn Enterline, *The Rhetoric of the Body from Ovid to Shakespeare* (Cambridge: Cambridge University Press, 2000) 152–97.

[118] I cite *Lucrece* by line number from Colin Burrow (ed.), *The Complete Sonnets and Poems* (The Oxford Shakespeare, Oxford: Oxford University Press, 2002).

[119] For the significance of the poem's language of 'publication' see Patrick Cheney, *Shakespeare, National Poet-Playwright* (Cambridge: Cambridge University Press, 2004) 108–42. Oliver Arnold's reading of *Lucrece* (against *Titus Andronicus*) is closely and pessimistically attuned to the politics of representation and publication in the poem; see *The Third Citizen* 118–28.

[120] In sixteenth- to seventeenth-century copies of Seneca, Act 2 of *Thyestes* is the most often and most intensely marked, underlined, etc.

the mouth of his good counsellor and rapes her, making the rape, the subject of the debate, also its violent extinction.

The words of a desperate counsellor to a lord unable to govern his own passions, the advice Lucrece delivers here is, in Colin Burrow's words, 'a textbook example of political oratory in this period'[121]—and its failure a sure sign of Tarquin's tyrannical bent. In a series of well-turned *sententiae*, Lucrece argues that Tarquin owes it to his 'princely name' to restrain himself, and discusses the consequences of his transgression: the contemplated 'outrage' foreshadows even worse deeds he will commit when he becomes king, and since 'kings' misdeeds cannot be hid in clay', (609) his subjects will be encouraged to commit like transgressions by his example: 'For princes are the glass, the school, the book, / Where subjects' eyes do learn, do read, do look' (615–16). Tarquin's deeds will therefore have consequences that point well beyond his or Lucrece's personal fate: he will become 'the school where lust shall learn', the 'glass wherein it shall discern / Authority for sin' (619–20). Lucrece's account of the consequences is relentless: 'Thy princely office how canst thou fulfil, / When patterned by thy fault foul sin may say / He learned to sin, and thou didst teach the way?' (628–30). By creating an example that will destroy the moral fabric of the realm, Tarquin proves himself incapable of governing: by raping Lucrece, he actively refuses to fulfil, and thus effectively relinquishes, his office. But Lucrece's own assumed persona, her office as a counsellor, does not allow her to raise the possibility of the banishment of the (future) king—the moment she would do so, she would be out of office, and therefore without authority to speak. Lucrece cannot be a republican, certainly not in the sense of advancing anti-monarchical arguments.[122] Instead, this virtuous *matrona* belongs to the great line of stalwart female supports of crumbling conciliar monarchy (a line whose best-known representative in the Shakespearean corpus might be the Paulina of *The Winter's Tale*), begging Tarquin to restore himself to the office (and which amounts to the same, to his better self) he seems to be casting off: 'I sue for exiled majesty's repeal: / Let him return, and flatt'ring thoughts retire' (640–1). Andrew Hadfield identifies the troubling linkage between the rape of Lucrece and the foundation of the republic by calling the new constitutional form 'the child of a rape'—we should add that, uniquely in the long tradition of the story of Lucrece, in Shakespeare's poem, the violent politicization of Lucrece's body is accompanied and preceded by her active political mind's pained acquiescence to regicide as a last resort, with her suicide as a sign of the tragic nature of this change of political conscience.[123]

Lucrece's grave and sententious political oration is based on the idea that the prince is the mirror of the commonwealth, the model after whom his subjects fashion themselves: successful government is guaranteed by princely virtue. For the

---

[121] 'Introduction' in Burrow (ed.), *The Complete Sonnets and Poems* 52.
[122] For an important reminder of the distinct meanings of the term 'republican' see David Wootton's review of *Republicanism: A Shared European Heritage*, edited by Martin Van Gelderen and Quentin Skinner, *The English Historical Review*, 120/485 (2005), 135–9. What Lucrece's position as a counsellor allows her is what Collinson termed a monarchical–republican understanding of the polity.
[123] Hadfield, *Shakespeare and Republicanism* 147; cp. Jed, *Chaste Thinking*.

prince to lead by personal example, his deeds must be judged by the same standards as those of his subjects: he must be following the same moral code as his subjects, except more so. Such mimetic leadership depends on the prince's behaviour being open for all to see—hence Lucrece's reliance on the mirror imagery and her insistence that misdeeds will out. In this view, tyranny disrupts the conditions of good government through opacity. To rape Lucrece, Tarquin puts out the light, and darkness becomes emblematic of the breakdown of the conciliar vision, 'For light and lust are deadly enemies. / Shame folded up in blind concealing night, / When most unseen, then most does tyrannize' (675–6). The second half of *The Rape of Lucrece* is the drama of bringing truth to light: as Lucrece is forced to recognize, keeping her shame secret would mean siding with the rapist.

Lucrece's argument about the connection between transparency and virtuous behaviour responds to Tarquin's attempt to blackmail her into submission with the suggestion that they would be both off the hook if they could just keep quiet about what is about to happen:

> But if thou yield, I rest thy secret friend:
> The fault unknown is as a thought unacted.
> 'A little harm done to a great good end,
> For lawful policy remains enacted.
> 'The pois'nous simple sometime is compacted
> In a pure compound; being so applied
> His venom in effect is purified. (527–9)

As Martin Dzelzainis has noted in his essay on Shakespeare and Lipsius, Tarquin's politic argument—which, as Figure 1.3 shows, is marked by gnomic points in the 1594 text—draws directly on Justus Lipsius's influential collection of political maxims woven together into a political manual, *The Six Books of Politics*, and specifically, on Lipsius's famous chapter on the notion of mixed prudence, on the question whether, having offered 'the best and purest wine' drawn from the spring of prudence, 'May it be lawfull for me to mingle lightly, and ioyne with it some dregs of deceipt?' After considering the issue by dialectically moving through the alternation of sententious points representing opposing sides of the case (in the course of which movement he also invokes Machiavelli's famous point about how the prince needs to have the nature of the lion as well as of the fox), Lipsius concludes: 'Wine, although it be somewhat tempered with water, continueth to be wine: so doth prudence not change her name, albeit a few drops of deceipt bee mingled therewith: For I always meane but a small deale, and to a good end.' In the next chapter, where Lipsius discusses the categories and acceptable limits of deceit, he turns to a characteristically Machiavellian metaphor also used by Tarquin in Shakespeare's poem, i.e. the metaphor of using poison to wholesome effect: 'as in the application of medicines, they do with approbation mingle venomous drugs for the good of the patient, so these things do seeme profitable as it were a medicine.'[124]

---

[124] Lipsius, *Sixe Bookes of Politickes* 4:13, sigs. P4v–Q1v, Q4r; cp. Dzelzainis, 'Shakespeare and Political Thought', 111–13.

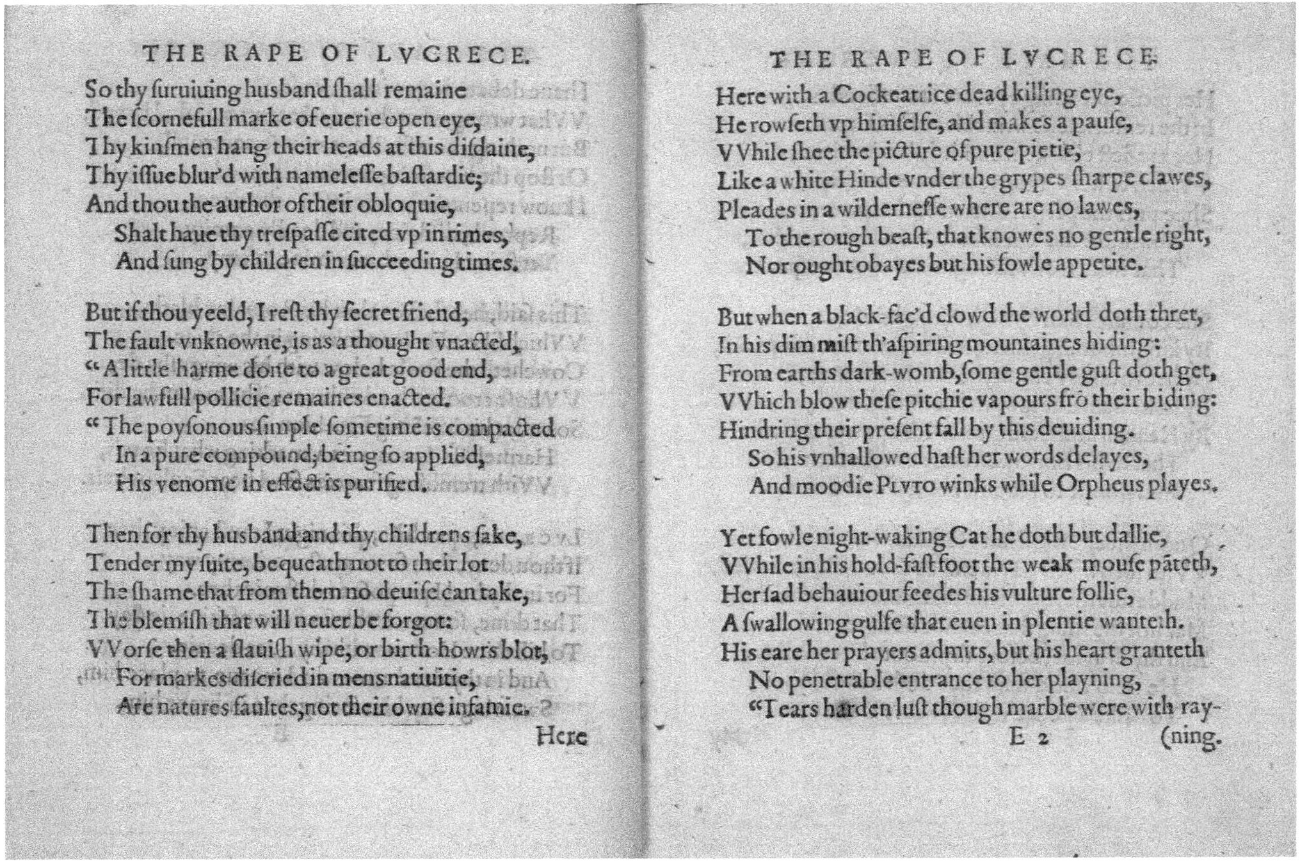

THE RAPE OF LVCRECE.

So thy suruiuing husband shall remaine
The scornefull marke of euerie open eye,
Thy kinsmen hang their heads at this disdaine,
Thy issue blur'd with namelesse bastardie:
And thou the author of their obloquie,
 Shalt haue thy trespasse cited vp in rimes,
 And sung by children in succeeding times.

But if thou yeeld, I rest thy secret friend,
The fault vnknowne, is as a thought vnacted,
"A little harme don'te to a great good end,
For lawfull pollicie remaines enacted.
"The poysonous simple sometime is compacted
 In a pure compound; being so applied,
 His venome in effect is purified.

Then for thy husband and thy childrens sake,
Tender my suite, bequeath not to their lot
The shame that from them no deuise can take,
The blemish that will neuer be forgot:
VVorse then a slauish wipe, or birth-howrs blot,
 For markes discried in mens natiuitie,
 Are natures faultes, not their owne infamie.

Here

THE RAPE OF LVCRECE.

Here with a Cockeatrice dead killing eye,
He rowseth vp himselfe, and makes a pause,
VVhile shee the picture of pure pietie,
Like a white Hinde vnder the grypes sharpe clawes,
Pleades in a wildernesse where are no lawes,
 To the rough beast, that knowes no gentle right,
 Nor ought obayes but his fowle appetite.

But when a black-fac'd clowd the world doth thret,
In his dim mist th'aspiring mountaines hiding:
From earths dark-womb, some gentle gust doth get,
VVhich blow these pitchie vapours fro their biding:
Hindring their present fall by this deuiding.
 So his vnhallowed hast her words delayes,
 And moodie Pluto winks while Orpheus playes.

Yet fowle night-waking Cat he doth but dallie,
VVhile in his hold-fast foot the weak mouse paiteth,
Her sad behauiour feedes his vulture follie,
A swallowing gulfe that euen in plentie wanteth.
His eare her prayers admits, but his heart graunteth
 No penetrable entrance to her playning.
"Teares harden lust though marble were with ray-
 (ning.

E 2

Fig. 1.3. Gnomic pointing in Shakespeare's *Lucrece* (London: Printed by Richard Field, for Iohn Harrison, and are to be sold at the signe of the white Greyhound in Paules Churh-yard [*sic*], 1594), sigs. E1v–E2r.
By permission of the Folger Shakespeare Library.

Lipsius makes it clear throughout that the use of mixed prudence, the overriding of conventional morality for a political purpose, is only acceptable as means to a necessary and legitimate end, which can only be the preservation of the state.[125] His work is one of the most important examples of the late sixteenth-century rationalization and moralization of Machiavelli, of the effort to explicitly articulate the conditions, clearly implied but not explained and certainly not theorized by Machiavelli, under which the bracketing of ordinary morality can be allowed, and allowed even in moral terms. In other words, Lipsius's *Politica* can be described as one of the key texts about the reason of state. Counter-reformation theorists of the reason of state produced a religious casuistry, legitimating Machiavelli's suggestions by putting them in the service of a Christian agenda. Lipsius developed a secular version of the same idea, an explicit version of the casuistry of political office, where political necessity, the interests and security of the state, make deceit not only politically but also morally acceptable.[126] This is how John Donne, in his learned polemical tract *Pseudo-Martyr* of 1610, understood the 'rules...vulgarly called *Ragion di stato*', which 'seeme to be within the compasse of deceite and falshood, yet the end, which is maintenance of lawfull Authoritie, for the publike good, justifies them so well, that the Lawyers...define *Ragion di stato* to be, *Cum aliud agitur, aliud simulatur, bono publico*',[127]

Although his argument is clearly indebted to Lipsius, in Shakespeare's *Lucrece*, Tarquin's sententious reasoning produces no legitimating end that would justify the expediency of the secretive operation of policy: 'the great good end' he invokes as the necessary peg on which to hang his argument can only be understood as adultery. It is pleasure, and not pleasure for the wiser sort. As a 'great good end', it is exclusively private, it is self-interest at odds with the interests of others. But there is something perversely self-fulfilling about this invocation of the 'great good end' here. Tarquin's lines contain the implicit suggestion that by consenting to his desire, Lucrece could turn the transgression into a shared and consensual end, and

---

[125] Richard Tuck, *Philosophy and Government, 1572–1651* (Cambridge: Cambridge University Press, 1993) 57–8.

[126] For a brief overview of the terminology, see Peter Burke, 'Tacitism, Scepticism, and Reason of State', in J. H. Burns and Mark Goldie (eds.), *The Cambridge History of Political Thought, 1450–1700* (Cambridge: Cambridge University Press, 1991), 479–98. The classic study is Friedrich Meinecke, *Machiavellism: The Doctrine of Raison d'État and Its Place in Modern History*, trans. Douglas Scott (New Haven: Yale University Press, 1957). For a survey of responses to this curious history of an idea that is 'beyond the reach of historical change' (16) see Michael Stolleis, *Staat und Staatsräson in der Frühen Neuzeit: Studien zur Geschichte des Öffentlichen Rechts* (Frankfurt am Main: Suhrkamp, 1990) 135–65, and for a more recent corrective, also Maurizio Viroli, 'The Revolution in the Concept of Politics' and *From Politics to Reason of State: The Acquisition and Transformation of the Language of Politics, 1250–1600* (Cambridge: Cambridge University Press, 1992). On the reason of state, Donaldson, *Machiavelli and Mystery of State* 111–40; Tuck, *Philosophy and Government* 31–119; Yves Charles Zarka (ed.), *Raison et Déraison d'État: Théoriciens et Théories de la Raison d'État aux XVIe et XVIIe Siècles* (Paris: Presses Universitaires de France, 1994); Kahn, *Machiavellian Rhetoric* 60–84; H. M. Höpfl, 'Orthodoxy and Reason of State', *History of Political Thought*, 23 (2002), 211–37; Conal Condren, 'Reason of State and Sovereignty in Early Modern England: A Question of Ideology?', *Parergon*, 28/2 (2011), 5–27.

[127] i.e. 'when, for the common good, one thing is done, and another pretended': John Donne, *Pseudo-Martyr*, ed. Anthony Raspa (Montreal and Buffalo: McGill-Queen's University Press, 1993) 56–7.

thus create a community that would legitimate the adultery. From the perspective of the poem, however, Lucrece's hypothetical consent—her genuine, honest, happy consent—would only make the situation worse, turning Tarquin's tyrannical act into conspiracy against the household of Collatine, the upright Roman citizen. From such a political perspective, the non-consensual nature of Tarquin's act is not the biggest problem with it—the real issue is that as a fundamental breach of trust between Tarquin and Collatine, a fundamental breach of unquestioned social norms, it is by necessity an act that needs to remain secret. This is why in her effort to repel Tarquin, Lucrece must propose a principled rejection of the basic premise of Tarquin's argument, viz. the very principle of mixed prudence as proposed by Tarquin, and not merely debate its application to the particular case.

In *Lucrece*, then, the politic mode of argumentation, the suggestion that under certain conditions one might legitimately override the demands of conventional morality, is discredited as perverse, tyrannical sophistry by the very circumstances under which it is uttered. In *The Rape of Lucrece*, 'policy', the discourse of political prudence associated with Machiavelli, is the circular, self-confirming ideology of the rapist, and Lucrece's suicide the force that condemns and ultimately dispels it. Under its pressure, even the morally irreprehensible Brutus's pretended folly, 'wherein deep policy did him disguise' (1815) must give way to the regime of transparent virtue. Arguably, this is what makes the poem compatible with a republican outlook, in spite of its complicated, perhaps evasive take on the change in the constitutional form of government. Through its insistence on truthfulness being the cardinal political virtue and the only antidote to tyranny, *The Rape of Lucrece* is clear about the continuity between personal and political responsibilities and obligations, allowing no exception, no distinction to be made under any circumstances.[128] Policy, as a separate and exceptional mode of action and thought, is by this poem banished from society.

We must also notice that in *Lucrece*, Harvey's political distinctions are produced by, called for, or hinge on, an effectively dramatic argument taking place between two major characters, a scene that would take little to be rendered as a scene of counsel in a Senecan tragedy. A full-fledged tragic conflict offers more opportunity for the unfolding of conflicting, perspectivally defined arguments, and it is perhaps as a result of this, that dramatic writing is more open to the claims of the political. In spite of their superficial similarities, in political terms, Shakespeare's *Hamlet* is of a different nature than *Lucrece*: it is a play whose central problems revolve precisely around the political distinction.

OPHELIA'S CHASTITY AND THE REASON OF STATE

A prince, heir to the crown, is burning with desire for a chaste woman. His violence and her unspeakable loss force her to commit suicide. This is a reign under

---

[128] On the problem of truthfulness and politics, see Bernard Williams, *Truth and Truthfulness: An Essay in Genealogy* (Princeton: Princeton University Press, 2002) 206–32.

which people have found it necessary to hide their intentions behind a pretended madness: her family's righteous anger now helps to bring the smouldering political crisis to a head and put an end to tyranny.

With its conservative evasiveness about the rape, this synopsis of *Lucrece* might be seen as a fitting summary of *Hamlet* as well, although perhaps not from Hamlet's perspective. For him, the sexual transgression that corrupts the state of Denmark is the transgression of the King and the Queen. But to Laertes and his followers, unconcerned with the incestuous nature of the King's marriage, but painfully aware of Ophelia's anguish, it would likely appear accurate. When we first hear about Laertes's rebellion, it is not understood as motivated by Ophelia's distress, nor does Laertes mention her when he bursts on the stage, but as soon as she enters, she becomes an emblem of the injustice Laertes seeks to redress: 'Hadst thou thy wits and didst persuade revenge, / It could not move thus' (4.5.167–8).

Ophelia is on the verge of following Lucrece and the Lavinia of *Titus Andronicus* as the female figurehead of the play's abortive 'republican moment', a woman whose grief—unspeakable, inscrutable, yet vividly present in her song—is promptly appropriated by the political movement which claims to be discharging the magistrates' office by revenging injustice:

> Her speech is nothing,
> Yet the unshaped use of it doth move
> The hearers to collection. They yawn at it,
> And botch the words up to fit their own thoughts,
> which, as her winks and nods and gestures yield them,
> Indeed would make one think there might be thought,
> though nothing sure, yet much unhappily. (4.5.7–13)

So pervasive is the perception of Ophelia's song-speech as a 'nothing' redolent with provocative meaning that Laertes, who wasn't present to hear this account of the public perception of Ophelia, nonetheless echoes it when he reasserts that he hears in her sibylline lines a call for justice: 'This nothing's more than matter' (4.5.173). Her nothing: this performance of words not hers, this early modern mixtape of popular ballads[129] becomes for Laertes what the king of nothing, the ghostly matter is for Hamlet: a prompt to inquire into Claudius's conduct as well as a call for action, a prompt of which of course nothing comes.

As with Lucrece and Lavinia, the public display of Ophelia's sexualized body, a body spoken for by the male agents of political change, seems essential to her role in the formulation of a political position. In her madness, Ophelia's song-speech is dense with sexualized allusion—and yet the violation that would transform her into the emblem of tyrannical rule remains strategically unspoken. In a play that is replete with movements and gestures arrested mid-air, Ophelia's song about the maid at the window asking to be a man's Valentine, who 'Let in the maid that out a maid / Never departed more' (4.5.54–5) remains a hint at the loss of her

---

[129] Scott A. Trudell, 'The Mediation of Poesie: Ophelia's Orphic Song', *Shakespeare Quarterly*, 63 (2012), 46–76.

virginity. Whether this is an image of frustrated desire, of consensual fulfilment, or of rape, is a question that characteristically divides modern interpreters of the text, although from an early modern perspective, the difference between the latter two options may not have been decisive: her chastity would have been lost either way. Her acute description of Hamlet's visit to her closet—'No hat upon his head, his stockings foul'd…and with a look so piteous in purport / As if he had been loosed out of hell / To speak of horrors', staring at length at Ophelia's face (2.1.75–100)— is a strong suggestion of their history of unsupervised, intimate interactions, but the play also refrains from making more of this. Her presumed suicide: her 'doubtful' death (5.1.220) is a similarly evasive gesture that allusively aligns her with Lucrece without quite claiming to be the conscious, and definitely not the political act that would clinch that analogy.

As a revision of the Lucrece narrative, Ophelia's fate is emblematic of the inward-turning political perspective of Shakespeare's *Hamlet* that will be a recurrent theme of the following chapters. It is a perspective characterized by a withdrawal from public political action. Her suffering and death seem to be gesturing at a partisan agenda but end up strongly refusing to align with it. *Hamlet* is a play that is clearly cognizant of England's late sixteenth-century republican moment, but rather than participating in that vision, it enacts a turning away from it. This does not mean, however, that Ophelia's entanglement in the political world of the play, in the intense discussion of political issues with which Elsinore reverberates, and in the implications of a potential analogy with Tarquin's rape of Lucrece, would be a matter of retrospective appropriation only. In their engagements with Ophelia, both Laertes and Polonius consider her sexuality in sharply political terms from the very beginning—although each of them do so differently.

Hamlet's dangerous desire is discussed closely in the Polonius family's scene of instruction in 1.3, a scene where we witness the imparting of much wisdom, with brother and sister warning each other against imprudent sexual engagements before receiving their share of paternal advice. This is the scene that is marked as sententious both in Q1 and in Q2; but whereas Q1 marks Polonius's famously sententious advice about prudent conduct to Laertes, in Q2, it is Laertes's words to Ophelia that are distinguished by a handful of gnomic points, as if the two versions of the text were offering two distinct readings of the scene, Q1 a paternal, Q2 a fraternal one.

In their instructions, Laertes and Polonius both advise Ophelia against yielding to Hamlet too soon or indeed at all, but they do so pursuing two distinct lines of argument, and the apparent reduplication of their advice actually serves to distinguish their concerns.[130] Polonius worries that Ophelia does not 'understand yourself so clearly / As it behooves my daughter and my honour' (1.3.96–7) and orders her to 'Tender yourself more dearly or…you'll tender me a fool' (1.3.107–9). He doesn't exactly seem particularly anxious 'to remove her from the world', as

---

[130] For an illuminating reading of the fate of Ophelia, her distributing flowers as the decomposition of the *florilegium* of 'prescripts' she has received, see Margreta de Grazia, Hamlet *without Hamlet* (Cambridge: Cambridge University Press, 2007) 108–18.

Margreta de Grazia suggested about his efforts[131]—instead, he seeks to maintain the value of her currency by controlling her rate of exchange. Thinking about ill-advised circulation, he claims to know (perhaps remember?) 'When the blood burns, how prodigal the soul / Lends the tongue vows'—his point being that Hamlet is a young man Ophelia ought to beware of—because he is a young man.

The pecuniary banality of Polonius's argument is especially striking as it comes at the end of the scene that begins with his son's incisive comments on the same relationship. Laertes's worry that Ophelia might 'with too credent ear…list [Hamlet's] songs' (1.3.30) not only shows actual care for the future of Ophelia, it results in an exemplary moment of political analysis. In thoroughly realistic terms, Laertes warns Ophelia of Prince Hamlet's limited ability to keep his promises to marry her in the future. Before yielding to Hamlet, he suggests, she ought to remember that he is the heir to the throne, which paradoxically means that 'His greatness weigh'd, his will is not his own.' As Laertes explains, Hamlet is constrained by the fact that

> …on his choice depends
> The safety and health of this whole state;
> And therefore must his choice be circumscrib'd
> Unto the voice and yielding of that body
> Whereof he is the head, (1.3.20–4)

—and not, shall we add, unto the voice and yielding of his own body, 'For he is himself subject to his birth' (1.3.18), his hereditary status and office as prince constraining his decisions as a private person.[132] In his series of remarks about Hamlet, each of which could readily be extracted as a generalized point about the predicament of the monarch of a realm, Laertes rehearses the argument that the obligations of one's office, and the obligations of the office of the prince in particular, may justify—and demand—a conduct otherwise considered immoral, and that the obligation of a Prince to keep his word might always be trumped by the interest and the will of the state. Unlike Polonius, whose prudence does not extend to making the distinction between the mode of operation of a private individual and a prince, Laertes clearly recognizes that even Hamlet's most private acts are thoroughly political, inflected as they are by the reason of state.

Machiavelli was widely understood to be the founding father and greatest master of the reason of state, and his suggestions about the prince's obligation to keep his word often taken to be emblematic of the entire discourse. In the eighteenth chapter of *The Prince*, Machiavelli argues that people in general are treacherous and therefore the prince ought not feel bound to keep his promises to them either. In the *Anti-Machiavel* Gentillet quotes Machiavelli's maxim as 'A wise prince ought

---

[131] de Grazia, Hamlet *without Hamlet* 111.
[132] The reader of the Meisei copy of F1 notes at the top of 2N6v, 'The kingdome hes Interest in the choice of kings wife' but does not follow Laertes to the more provocative conclusion from this; see Akihiro Yamada, *The First Folio of Shakespeare: A Transcript of Contemporary Marginalia in a Copy of the Kodama Memorial Library of Meisei University* (Tokyo: Yushodo Press, 1998) 235.

not to keepe his Faith, when the observation therof is hurtful unto him.'[133] But contrary to Gentillet's ensuing accusation, in recommending the prince this prudent course of action Machiavelli does not condone immoral behaviour as such: as we have seen, *The Prince* is not a work of moral philosophy or even a theory of politics, but a book about statecraft—although it is couched in a rhetoric that prompts theorization and systematization without at the same time quite allowing for its completion.[134] Limiting himself to the actions of princes, and more specifically, to the actions of the new prince, whose situation is predicated upon the interruption of established social norms and customs, Machiavelli considers how the prince may maintain control over a principality and secure the continuing existence of that principality under his control. In other words, Machiavelli's arguments are about the preferable course of action in a situation which is delegitimized to begin with—hence the literally paradoxical nature of his recommendations, i.e. their divergence from received wisdom.[135]

Giovanni Botero, the best-known late sixteenth-century theoretician of the reason of state, opened the series of 'Prudential maxims' in his *Della Ragion di Stato* with the following formulation of Machiavelli's suggestion: 'in the decisions made by princes, interest will always override every other argument; and therefore he who treats with princes should put no trust in friendship, kinship, treaty nor any other tie which has no basis in interest.'[136] Here, a course of action recommended by Machiavelli *to the new prince* as particularly effective is presented as standard procedure, a distinctive characteristic of how rulers (as opposed to private individuals) operate. In *Della Ragion di Stato*, Botero suggested that all that is done for the preservation and extension of a state 'is said to be done for Reasons of State, yet this is said rather of such actions as cannot be considered in the light of ordinary reason'.[137] As he later explained, looking at events in the light of the reason of state is the interpretation of political action based on interest[138]—which makes this opening maxim a cornerstone of the reason of state understood as a specialized hermeneutics of the field of political action. The discovery of 'the autonomy of politics', what some interpreters saw as Machiavelli's signal achievement, is in this sense the product of this late sixteenth-century moment.

Laertes's lines reflect a further inflection of this turn in late sixteenth-century thought. When he introduces politic considerations into the discussion of his sister's sex life, he does so in marked contradistinction to Tarquin's cynically self-interested argument. Rather than simply assuming that Hamlet might break his word because he can do so, he proceeds in a casuistic manner, separating the

---

[133] Gentillet, *A Discourse vpon the Meanes of vvel Governing*, sig. 2K3r.
[134] Viroli, *From Politics to Reason of State* 126–77.
[135] J. G. A. Pocock, *The Machiavellian Moment: Florentine Political Thought and the Atlantic Republican Tradition* (2nd (1st 1975) edn.; Princeton: Princeton University Press, 2003) 156–82.
[136] Giovanni Botero, *The Reason of State*, trans. P. J. Waley and D. P. Waley (New Haven: Yale University Press, 1956) 41.
[137] Botero, *The Reason of State* 3.
[138] In his *Aggiunte ... alla sua Ragion di Stato* (1598), quoted by Noel Malcolm, *Reason of State, Propaganda, and the Thirty Years' War: An Unknown Translation by Thomas Hobbes* (Oxford: Clarendon Press, 2007) 94.

Prince's person from his office, and thus allowing an ultimately ethical explanation to what Gentillet presents as a transparent case of immorality, and what Botero recognizes as a case of two fields following two different types of logic. Laertes's concern is not that Hamlet is dishonest, but that it does not matter whether he is or not, because it is not up to him to keep his word: as future king, he might owe it to Denmark to break it. Unlike Tarquin, Lucrece, or Polonius, Laertes is in direct agreement with Lipsius and other theorists of the reason of state here, who codified and moralized Machiavellian prudence into the protocol of a particular kind of obligation the political leader owes not to himself but to his state and to the common good.[139] Advising his sister on her private life, Laertes uses an exemplary form of the political distinction Harvey is calling for, a mode of argument to which the conflicts and dilemmas of the play respond strikingly well.

SORTS OF CHARACTERS

The political action of the play can readily be parsed in terms of the distinction between ordinary morality and the reason of state as an exceptional mode of operation, and some of the characters' choices between them can be linked to how they are defined by their education and their office. Unlike Hamlet, who attended, and desires to return to, a Protestant university in Germany, Laertes comes from and returns to France, the country known for its academies—indeed, the praise of Laertes's talent with the rapier by the ominously named Lamord, himself famous for his horsemanship, associates Laertes with the kind of elite education offered by the French academies in the period. Although the fencing lessons leave him unprepared for the incident of the exchanged rapiers, his competent evocation of the reason of state, his understanding of the constraints this imposes on the Prince's ability to follow his personal interest, will, desire, or the normal requirements of honesty, provides a powerful analytic perspective on the entire sequence of scenes in Act 1 of Shakespeare's *Hamlet*.

Claudius gestures at the constraints of state interest on his choice in his announcement of his marriage with Gertrude in Act 1 scene 2, the announcement made with 'an auspicious and a dropping eye' of a marriage ratified by the 'better wisdoms' of his counsellors. Whereas Claudius asserts the selflessness of his marriage with the help of the notion of the necessary subordination of the private interest of the Prince to the interest of the state, his brother's ghost attempts to sweep aside the same: his deeply personal indignation and exclusive focus on the adulterous passion of Claudius and his wife makes him completely indifferent to

---

[139] Just how bold Laertes's argument is, is indicated by the editorial tradition which habitually emends Q2's 'safty' to 'sanity' in 'The safety and health of this whole state', blunting the clearly political edge of the line by removing an expression both meaningful and consistent with what late sixteenth- and early seventeenth-century readers would have understood as a characteristically politic perspective. I am reverting to the Q2 reading here, as does the Q2-based Arden 3; influential editions like Jenkins's Arden 2 as well as Wells-Taylor Oxford and thus Norton 1–2 follow Hanmer's and Theobald's authority, domesticating the scene of instruction.

his country's fate, which Horatio in 1.1 assumed he might be trying to help avert. But as he enjoins Hamlet to revenge his death, the Ghost shows no concern for what effect the regicide might have on the future of Denmark or on the lands he acquired from Norway, nor does he invoke Hamlet's claim to the throne as a factor (as does Amleth in Belleforest's narrative). This purgatorial spirit is oblivious not only of Christian ethics and the proscription of blood vengeance, but also of the argument from state interest that would make the bracketing of such injunctions possible.[140] If we are inclined to think about *Hamlet* as a tragedy about Hamlet's obligation to revenge and his unwillingness to do it, Laertes's argument about the Prince's will not being his own makes for incisive commentary here. Granted that Hamlet gave his word to the Ghost, from the perspective of the reason of state introduced by Laertes in the scene preceding the Ghost's encounter with Hamlet, we must ask whether keeping faith and following the commandment is really in the interest of Denmark and of its future king. Would pursuing revenge or rather abstaining from it prove him, in the words of Fortinbras, 'most royal'? Would the revenge be in the political interest of the state and of his own royal status? Wouldn't breaking his oath benefit the state of Denmark and therefore be the way for Hamlet to proceed? But does the school philosopher in Hamlet allow him to argue his way out of his predicament?

Claudius is the character in the play most exercised by the public perception of political acts and political figures, and throughout Acts 4–5, we see him expertly managing the turning tide of public opinion, the aftermath of Polonius's murder. Although he immediately realizes that he was the real target of Hamlet's attack, his direct concern is: 'how shall this bloody deed be answer'd? / It will be laid to us, whose providence / Should have kept short, restrain'd, and out of haunt / This mad young man' (4.1.16–19). Sending Hamlet to England becomes part of his effort to protect his own reputation, both within the court and in wider circles. In language that resonates with Machiavelli's point about success being a result of suiting one's deeds to the time and circumstances, he decides to 'call up our wisest friends, / And let them know both what we mean to do / And what's untimely done' (4.1.38–40). In his meeting with his Lords, he explains his sending Hamlet away as a publicity stunt, a 'desperate appliance' used to control a man who cannot be punished for his deed because he is 'lov'd of the distracted multitude' (4.3.1–11). One of the important repercussions of Polonius's murder is that it transforms Claudius from a torn conscience into a politic prince, constantly adjusting his course to the changing situation. It has often been observed that Claudius is the most 'Machiavellian' of the play's characters, and the language in which he describes the nature of the plan of using an unbated and poisoned blade in the duel is particularly resonant with a situation *cum aliud agitur, aliud simulatur*, 'when one thing is done, and another pretended':

> Let's further think of this,
> Weigh what convenience both of time and means

---

[140] See the discussion in Chapter 3 of this book.

> May fit us to our shape. If this should fail,
> And that our drift look through our bad performance,
> 'Twere better not essay'd. (4.7.147–51)

That Laertes turns out to be so receptive to Claudius's explanations and stratagems might now be understood as a function of his willingness to distinguish between ordinary reason and the reason of state, and to endorse deeds that seem immoral in the light of ordinary reason, making an exception when they are done by the monarch. His willingness to conspire with Claudius is of a piece with his astute analysis of Hamlet's promises.

In conversation with Laertes, Claudius shows himself as the earliest and sharpest critic of the kind of delay of which Hamlet has long been the proverbial example:

> That we would do,
> We should do when we would: for this 'would' changes
> And hath abatements and delays as many
> As there are tongues, are hands, are accidents,
> And then this 'should' is like a spendthrift sigh
> That hurts by easing. (4.7.117–22)

This activist political maxim is in striking agreement with Machiavelli's recommendation, viz. that instead of postponing action, successful agents ought to rely 'on their own strength [*virtù*] and prudence; because time brings all things with it, and can produce benefits as well as evils, evils as well as benefits.'[141] When juxtaposed with Hamlet's self-accusations for his supposed inaction, this argument suggests a vivid contrast between the tyrannical King and the philosopher Prince who intends to go 'back to school in Wittenberg' (1.2.113): a contrast between politic action and scholarly reflection. This distinction is important to keep in mind, even though in the play, their outcome will be the same.[142]

Not that Prince Hamlet is unaware of the problems that beset the world of political action, and the note-taking habits presumably inculcated at Wittenberg reveal him an eager analyst. Such note-taking is central to the scenes of paternal instruction in *Hamlet*. The typographic emphasis on useful *sententiae* demands the attention of note-taking readers, and the advisees in the play are also demanded to take note of them. Polonius enjoins Laertes 'these few precepts in thy memory / Look thou character' (1.3.58–9). His precepts are carefully marked as notable in Q1 (in that version, he is called Corambis—see Figure 1.4) and a little later he even refers to his moral instructions to Ophelia as his 'prescripts' (2.2.142). The play's other important scene of paternal instruction also prompts frenzied note-taking, albeit with some interesting complications. When he orders Hamlet to revenge his murder, the Ghost orders him to ignore the practices of the court and the requirements of office. To follow the Ghost's command, Hamlet would need to forget his notes of politic prudence, his awareness of the

---

[141] Machiavelli, *The Prince* 11.
[142] We should here recall Machiavelli's admiration for Cesare Borgia in spite of his downfall—although political action is success-oriented, failure does not disprove political greatness.

The Distinction of Politics and Gabriel Harvey's Machiavellian Hamlet   85

special obligations of rule, and also to disregard the basic tenets of Christian morality. Hamlet first eagerly promises 'from the table of my memory' to erase 'all saws of books, all forms, all pressures past / That youth and observation copied there', so that his father's 'commandment all alone shall live / Within the book and volume of my brain' (1.5.98–103). The single-mindedness of this rash promise of making *tabula rasa* doesn't last, however: a few lines later Hamlet starts literally taking notes, reaching for 'My tables—meet it is I set down / That one may smile, and smile, and be a villain', and only then proceeding to jotting down the paternal commandment: 'Now to my word. It is "Adieu, adieu, remember me." / I have sworn't' (1.5.107–12). Rather than making it his singular motto, Hamlet here complements his father's command to take direct action with a note about dissimulation. Hamlet does not, after all, wipe everything away, and continues to build his personal manual of prudent notes which reflects an understanding of life at court that is only matched by Claudius's.[143] Hamlet's deliberate unwillingness to stop the sententious reflections on the events he has been told to revenge rather than analyse, however, is curiously devoid of 'politic' overtones. In the politic mode, dissimulation—as suggested by the sentence usually attributed to Louis XI and copied and re-copied so often that it appears to be the period's most widely circulated piece of sententious politic wisdom—is understood to be the very essence of rule: *qui nescit dissimulare, nescit regnare*.[144] But Hamlet's note about dissembling is a general moral observation, not a maxim of reason of state. Throughout the play, the *sententiae* that are marked as notable, either by the dramatic dialogue or by the marginal commas, are pieces of prudent advice that make no distinction between political and ordinary action, whereas the thoroughly politic suggestions, including the observations discussed above, are not imagined as being inscribed at all.

An important sense in which *Hamlet* is a political play, then, is that it understands the possibility of politics as a world apart, or more modestly, as a distinct field, considers this possibility as a critical problem, and explores its consequences through opening up simulation and dissimulation to commentary from the points of view both of ordinary reason or morality and the reason of state. Gabriel Harvey no doubt appreciated this, along with the play's demand that the reader distinguish between politic and philosophical sentences, but such a reading would have revealed to him the world of *Hamlet* as a world curiously topsy-turvy in generational terms. Having interrogated Ophelia about her encounter with a seemingly disturbed Hamlet, Polonius pronounces:

---

[143] My argument here is almost the opposite of Aysha Pollnitz's, who suggests that Hamlet is here discarding what he learnt at university to make room for his father's command, turning 'from philosophy to the practices of the court', and identifies this turn with a loss of self-control; see Aysha Pollnitz, 'Educating Hamlet and Prince Hal', in David Armitage, Conal Condren, and Andrew Fitzmaurice (eds.), *Shakespeare and Early Modern Political Thought* (Cambridge: Cambridge University Press, 2009), 119–38 at 134–5.

[144] On the origin of the sentence, which is also quoted by Puttenham as exemplary of princely wisdom, see the long note in Frank Whigham and Wayne A. Rebhorn (eds.), *The Art of English Poesy by George Puttenham: A Critical Edition* (Ithaca: Cornell University Press, 2007) 408–9.

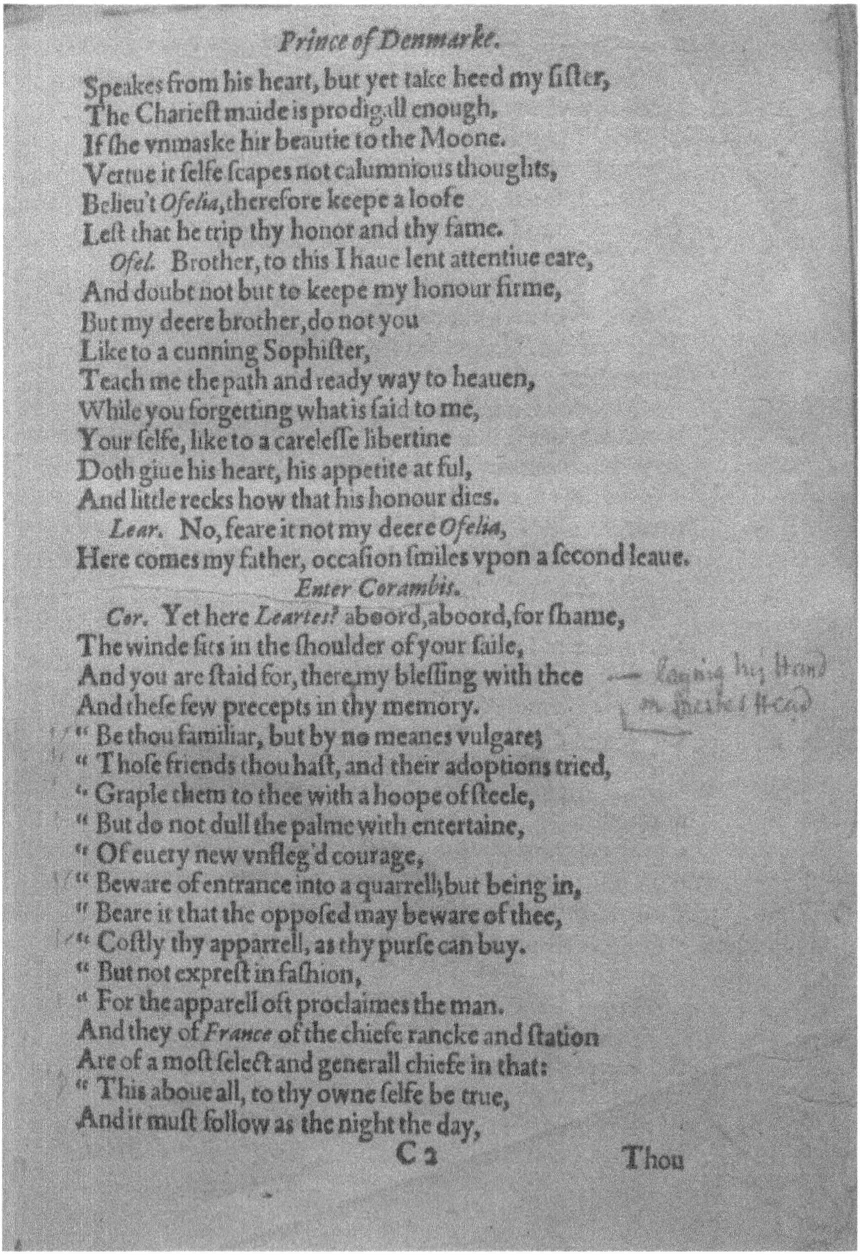

Prince of Denmarke.

Speakes from his heart, but yet take heed my sister,
The Chariest maide is prodigall enough,
If she vnmaske hir beautie to the Moone.
Vertue it selfe scapes not calumnious thoughts,
Belieu't *Ofelia*, therefore keepe a loofe
Lest that he trip thy honor and thy fame.

 Ofel. Brother, to this I haue lent attentiue eare,
And doubt not but to keepe my honour firme,
But my deere brother, do not you
Like to a cunning Sophister,
Teach me the path and ready way to heauen,
While you forgetting what is said to me,
Your selfe, like to a carelesse libertine
Doth giue his heart, his appetite at ful,
And little recks how that his honour dies.

 Lear. No, feare it not my deere *Ofelia*,
Here comes my father, occasion smiles vpon a second leaue.

   Enter Corambis.

 Cor. Yet here *Leartes?* aboord, aboord, for shame,
The winde sits in the shoulder of your saile,
And you are staid for, there my blessing with thee
And these few precepts in thy memory.
" Be thou familiar, but by no meanes vulgare;
" Those friends thou hast, and their adoptions tried,
" Graple them to thee with a hoope of steele,
" But do not dull the palme with entertaine,
" Of euery new vnfleg'd courage,
" Beware of entrance into a quarrell, but being in,
" Beare it that the opposed may beware of thee,
" Costly thy apparrell, as thy purse can buy,
" But not exprest in fashion,
" For the apparell oft proclaimes the man.
And they of *France* of the chiefe rancke and station
Are of a most select and generall chiefe in that:
" This aboue all, to thy owne selfe be true,
And it must follow as the night the day,

    C 2   Thou

Fig. 1.4. The sentences of Corambis as marked in the First Quarto of *The Tragicall Historie of Hamlet Prince of Denmarke by William Shake-speare. As It Hath Beene Diuerse Times Acted by His Highnesse Seruants in the Cittie of London: As also in the Two Vniuersities of Cambridge and Oxford, and else-where* (London: Printed for N.L. and Iohn Trundell, 1603) sig. C2r.
© The British Library Board.

> ...it is as proper to our age
> To cast beyond ourselves in our opinions
> As it is common for the younger sort
> To lack discretion. (2.1.114–16)

This is of course closely similar to the distinction Harvey makes between the wiser and the younger sort. But Shakespeare's *Hamlet* flips Polonius's and Harvey's terms: in the play, the older and supposedly 'wiser' sort, the generation of fathers, Polonius and Old Hamlet, distinguish themselves through their conspicuous lack of discretion, whereas Laertes and Hamlet obviously cast beyond themselves in their opinions. If generational difference is inscribed in Shakespeare's *Hamlet* as the difference between sons' and fathers' habits of thought, then it is between, on one hand, Laertes's and Hamlet's efforts to discern the relative scope of applicability of ordinary reason and the reason of state, their attempts to determine the possibility of distinguishing between matters of state and matters of moral concern, and on the other, their fathers' tendency to category confusion which makes them incapable of the same. (Claudius is in this, as in everything else, a generational interloper.) That Polonius sends a spy after his son and delivers an elaborate lecture on the wisdom of statesmen to Reynaldo, the character about to do the job of a private eye and check on Laertes's sexual and moral transgressions, is a striking example of the misapplication of indubitable political experience, but nowhere is the confusion clearer than when he declares that he is prepared to use Ophelia as a ploy, or as he puts it, to 'loose my daughter' (2.2.162) to Hamlet in order to figure out his secret, and bets that 'If he love her not, / And be not from his reason fall'n thereon, / Let me be no assistant for a state, / But keep a farm and carters' (2.2.164–7). It is for the reader to try and collect on the bet Polonius proposes here: his confusion and mistaken perception explicitly classifies the old counsellor not as a politician, not even as a scholar, but as someone appropriately belonging to what Shakespeare's contemporaries called 'the meaner sort'. In such moments, the comically obvious category confusion alerts us to the clarity with which the play distinguishes between two modes of thinking: on one hand, the politic understanding of people as instruments, and the concomitant bracketing of their dignity, and on the other, a fuller view of human motives and reasoning, something that may appear to modern readers as the philosophical recognition of people not as means but as ends, a recognition which forbids such bracketing.

Polonius's category confusion in this scene ultimately also returns us to Harvey's note and the distinction he is making there between the two kinds of Shakespearean writing. Polonius's 'I will be brief' (2.2.92) echoes the Ghost's 'Brief let me be' (1.5.59)—these are the unheld promises of two garrulous old men, who both lose control of their tongue when they start thinking about the love life of royalty—the Ghost's lengthy speech is a discussion of Gertrude's secret adultery, whereas Polonius is obsessing over Hamlet and Ophelia's love affair. As we have seen, the Queen's request for 'more matter with less art' is a reminder of the counsellor's office to dispense useful advice in the very terms Essex was using. But the reason Polonius fails to discharge his duty adequately is also explicable in those same terms. He gets caught up in an exercise of stylistic analysis—'*To the celestial and my soul's idol, the most beautified Ophelia*—that's an ill phrase, a vile phrase, "beautified" is a vile phrase, but you shall hear—' (2.2.109–11). Attention to the verbal surface diverts attention from the political problem of the troubled mind of the heir apparent—and that verbal surface is the language of love poetry, Hamlet's only literary product, the poem

> *Doubt thou the stars are fire,*
> *Doubt that the sun doth move,*
> *Doubt truth to be a liar,*
> *But never doubt I love.*

—about which Hamlet in his letter immediately admits that he is 'ill at these numbers' (2.2.115–19, italics in the original). Harvey's distinction between the politic mode of *Lucrece* and *Hamlet* and of *Venus and Adonis*, an erotic epyllion, a love poem, turns out to be a polar opposition, two modes that threaten and even extinguish one another. Polonius's failure is his neglect of the matter of policy for what Harvey called the 'pastimes of sum fine humanists'. While his son is able to think about love in terms of policy, the elder statesman proves himself not to be of the wiser sort.

So having begun by thinking about how Gabriel Harvey may have read his *Hamlet*, and having recognized the passages marked by gnomic points as a possible key to his admiration, are we now to conclude that he missed the point of the play itself, viz. that it is the younger sort who are characterized by an ability to perform the kind of politic reading that is a sign of wisdom, and the older by a curious blindness to the distinctions involved? Before we would do so, we should recall that Harvey did not think that sententious insights should be judged according to the person uttering them: he suggested precisely that 'it will show a sharp judgment if we attend not to who says something, but rather to what they say, selecting always what is best.' In other words, Harvey would not have read the play as I have here, reading tragic sentences as symptomatic of characters' ways of thinking, but rather, through decontextualizing them, recognizing that some lines might please the wiser sort even if they are spoken in the play by the younger. In this sense, Harvey would have read tragedy as if it were not drama at all, but source material for the 'Courtiers' *Alcoran*'.[145]

---

[145] As I will show in Chapter 5, he wasn't the only one to do so.

2

Some Travellers Return
Diplomatic Writing, Political Careers, and the World of *Hamlet*

HAMLET IN DENMARK

'Who's there?'—these first words of Shakespeare's *Hamlet* are emblematic not only of 'the interrogative mood' in which the play is supposedly written, but also of its critical interrogation in the nineteenth and twentieth centuries. The question has even served as the opening of a metacritical parable about the dialogic nature of reading, a dialogue between the interpreter and the book, a dialogue in which the book itself takes up the challenge and throws the question back at the interpreter: 'Nay, answer me. Stand and unfold yourself.'[1] The interpretive unfolding of the secrets of the play is usually understood as the unfolding of the self, as asking, in various ways, who might be there, and asking further what such a question might mean. One could, however, also begin by asking back and inquiring (perhaps somewhat tangentially and definitely less momentously): why *there*? *Hamlet* is a play heavily invested in questions of location, displacement, travel: students leave and return, ambassadors come and go, players arrive, an army passes through, and people one after another are dispatched to the undiscovered country. Granted that 'Hamlet's world is pre-eminently in the interrogative mood'—why is it in Elsinore of all places? What does it mean for the play to go to Elsinore? And what does it mean for its characters to be returning to Elsinore, one after the other, in what seems to be a compulsive pattern?

While politically oriented criticism has explored how the Denmark of Shakespeare's *Hamlet* reflects early modern England, Scotland, or indeed post-republican Rome, little has been made of the often-remarked fact that the Denmark of the play most obviously resembles early modern Denmark.[2] Not only are

---

[1] Maynard Mack, 'The World of *Hamlet*', *The Yale Review*, 41 (1952), 502–23 at 504; Harry Levin, *The Question of Hamlet* (New York: Oxford University Press, 1959) 20–1; Geoffrey H. Hartman, *The Fate of Reading and Other Essays* (Chicago: University of Chicago Press, 1975) 3–19; James L. Calderwood, *To Be and Not to Be: Negation and Metadrama in Hamlet* (New York: Columbia University Press, 1983) 114–16; Annabel Patterson, *Shakespeare and the Popular Voice* (Oxford: Basil Blackwell, 1989) 30, 98.

[2] The literature on the British analogies is vast, with discussions of topical allusions to and resonances with Essex, Burghley, Mary Queen of Scots, and King James VI and I, through the drowning of Katherine Hamlett and the death of Hamnet Shakespeare to the play's references to the boy companies and to the 'war of the poets', etc. Honigmann long ago insisted that we take the Danish

Denmark and Elsinore words in everyone's mouth,[3] Shakespeare's *Hamlet* also seems to make a real effort to use these words as signifiers of a specifically recognizable place. The play updates the legendary ancient Nordic setting of its sources to an early modern one that is firmly anchored in geography.[4] In the literary history of Hamlet, Shakespeare's play is the first to move the scene to Elsinore from Jütland, where it is set both in the thirteenth-century chronicle of Denmark by Saxo Grammaticus and in the sixteenth-century *histoire tragique* by François de Belleforest. It is the English play that elaborates the geopolitical setting by including references not only to Norway and England, but also to Poland, and to Wittenberg, the university in Saxony founded in 1502, where much of the Danish Lutheran elite was educated. It is the English play that puts flesh on the bare bones of topography by adding further details—like the pirates, the source of constant diplomatic conflict between England and Denmark in the sixteenth century, or the gestures at the elective monarchy, of which Denmark was a textbook example. And let's not forget the names: not only such first names thought to be common in Denmark as Cornelius and Voltemand, Reynaldo, Johan (the Yaughan to whom the first gravedigger sends his associate for 'a stoup of liquor') or perhaps even Yorick (if it is indeed a rendering of Jörg),[5] but also the family names of Rosencrantz and Guildenstern, names of people who were on the royal council of Denmark, names that are—unlike the name Claudius, to which occasionally a lot of significance is attributed, but which is not a word ever actually uttered in *Hamlet*[6]—put on ostentatious and perhaps comic display the moment they first enter:

> KING: Welcome, dear Rosencrantz and Guildenstern!
> ...
> KING: Thanks, Rosencrantz and gentle Guildenstern.

constitution of the play seriously, but John Dover Wilson's claim, that 'Hamlet is an English prince, the court of Elsinore is modelled upon the English court, and the Danish constitution that of England under the Virgin Queen' still articulates the tacit assumption of much historicist criticism of the play, and so the Danish material John Dover Wilson himself was compelled to recognize as unusually rich is relegated to the status of local colour. See E.A.J. Honigmann, 'The Politics of *Hamlet* and "the World of the Play"', *Stratford-upon-Avon Studies*, 5 (1963), 129–47 at 147; John Dover Wilson, *What Happens in Hamlet?* (Cambridge: Cambridge University Press, 1935) 28; John Dover Wilson (ed.), *Hamlet* (The Works of Shakespeare, Cambridge: Cambridge University Press, 1934) lvn.1. On Roman connections see most recently Andrew Fitzmaurice, 'The Corruption of *Hamlet*', in David Armitage, Conal Condren, and Andrew Fitzmaurice (eds.), *Shakespeare and Early Modern Political Thought* (Cambridge: Cambridge University Press, 2009), 139–56 at 142; Drew Daniel, '"I Am More an Antique Roman Than a Dane": Suicide, Masculinity and National Identity in Hamlet', in Maria Del Sapio Garbero (ed.), *Identity, Otherness and Empire in Shakespeare's Rome* (Farnham: Ashgate, 2009), 75–87.

[3] 'Denmark' is spoken twenty-three times, 'Dane' or 'Danes' ten times, 'Elsinore' four times.
[4] For overviews of the Danish references, see Gunnar Sjögren, 'The Danish Background in *Hamlet*', *Shakespeare Studies*, 4 (1968), 221–30; Cay Dollerup, *Denmark, Hamlet, and Shakespeare: A Study of Englishmen's Knowledge of Denmark Towards the End of the Sixteenth Century with Special Reference to Hamlet*, 2 vols. (Salzburg: Universität Salzburg, 1975).
[5] Dollerup, *Denmark, Hamlet, and Shakespeare* 188–91.
[6] On the other hand, 'Claudio' is: it is the name of a character who gave Hamlet's letter to the messenger who delivers it to Horatio. This Claudio is only mentioned by the messenger (4.7.39) and never does appear on stage. Is he Hamlet?

QUEEN: Thanks, Guildenstern and gentle Rosencrantz:
And I beseech you instantly to visit
My too much changed son. (2.2.1, 35–8)

These names are part of the play's effort at achieving local specificity. They are Danish, foreign matter. Foreign names, like the objects in a cabinet of curiosities, create the effect of the reality of faraway places.

Beyond using names, locations, and other information to suggest a contemporary Denmark, the play modernizes the story of Hamlet in several other ways. Whereas the epistolary exertions of Belleforest's and Saxo's Danes involve ancient Nordic runes engraved in pieces of wood, Shakespeare's play is famously engaged with modern textual culture. Hamlet jots down his father's commandment in his table-books, and the next time we see him on stage his mother points him out saying 'look where sadly the poor wretch comes reading'. On this cue, 'Enter Hamlet reading on a Booke', only to declare that what he finds in it are 'words, words, words' (2.2.168, 192). Signalling a world where private reading is a common pastime or form of devotion, Ophelia is instructed by Polonius to 'read on this book, / That show of such an exercise may colour / Your loneliness' (3.1.44–5).[7] Books however are not the only, and not even the most important texts staged by Shakespeare's play. As Alan Stewart has shown in admirable detail, *Hamlet* puts a noticeable emphasis on the contemporary technologies of writing—on writing and signing and folding and sealing letters and documents.[8]

The careful attention to a specific foreign location and to the materiality of writing point to the third novel feature of *Hamlet* that I want to bring into play here, namely, its interest in the modern business of diplomacy, and in how foreign intelligence is gathered and transmitted. Ambassadors and envoys are of course coming and going in many other plays, but their role is often limited to the introduction of new information: the diplomatic dispatches are not thematized, the focus is on the message they deliver, not on the channel of delivery.[9] *Hamlet*, by contrast, clearly foregrounds the formalities, protocols, rituals, and scripts of diplomatic missions. When in 1.2, Claudius sends an embassy to defuse the Norwegian threat, Cornelius and Voltemand receive both a letter addressed to Norway (1.2.27: 'we have here writ to Norway') and the 'dilated articles' of their instructions (1.2.38). On their successful return, they are formally debriefed: Voltemand's report on what they have achieved and his delivery of the King of Norway's written 'entreaty' for the peaceful passage of Fortinbras, his nephew, through Denmark to Poland, signal the efficiency of Claudius's government and the initial success of his handling of the exterior threat to his reign (2.2.58–85). Claudius intends to 'read, answer, and think upon' Norway's letter (2.2.82), only to be distracted by yet another letter, that of Hamlet to Ophelia, being gloatingly read out by Polonius as evidence of the Prince's love melancholy—as if to call

---

[7] P. K. Ayers, 'Reading, Writing, and *Hamlet*', *Shakespeare Quarterly*, 44 (1993), 423–39.
[8] Alan Stewart, *Shakespeare's Letters* (Oxford: Oxford University Press, 2008) 231–94.
[9] Hampton, *Fictions of Embassy: Literature and Diplomacy in Early Modern Europe* 146.

attention to the pieces of paper in which the royal court transacts both political and sexual business.

The written text is crucial to the operation of diplomacy in *Hamlet*—in the play, diplomacy is so thoroughly mediated that in spite of all the frenzied diplomatic activity we never actually see ambassadors in the course of their negotiations. As if in anticipation of the eighteenth-century formation of the word 'diplomacy' which etymologically implies a business that has to do with written documents or charters, Shakespeare's *Hamlet* represents the conduct of foreign affairs as paperwork, as the production, reproduction, and transmission of documents, observing in careful detail the material processes involved and their effects on the characters' lives.

This is most obvious in the case of Rosencrantz and Guildenstern, on whom the play's interest in diplomatic writing is most directly focused. In Belleforest's narrative, Amleth's companions on his journey to England carry a secret letter from Fengon that instructs the English king to murder Amleth, but the overt purpose of the trip is not mentioned. In Shakespeare's *Hamlet*, in keeping with the play's meticulous attention to the business of politics, it is clearly conceived as a formal embassy sent 'for the demand of our neglected tribute' (3.1.171), which is why Hamlet is mentioned later as 'the ambassador that was bound for England' (4.6.10). Rosencrantz and Guildenstern carry the King's 'commission' (3.3.3), in the form of 'letters seal'd' (3.4.204), a 'sovereign process' or mandate, which 'imports at full, / By letters congruing to that effect, the present death of Hamlet' (4.3.66–8). Their repeated mention turn these letters into a kind of Chekhov's gun. After his return, Hamlet explains to Horatio how he averted and redirected the danger enclosed in them: having unsealed the 'grand commission' they were carrying and realized its import, he substituted an expertly produced new letter for Claudius's original, inserting the names of Rosencrantz and Guildenstern instead of his own in this 'earnest conjuration from the king' (5.2.38), sending off his two friends to be executed.

Hamlet's revision of the King's commission amounts to the rewriting of the events that are to take place on their arrival in England, and thus to a radical revision of the plot Claudius so carefully scripted against him. In conclusion of his careful reading of the episode, Alan Stewart suggests that through his treatment of the scene of writing here, changing the medium from letters engraved in wood that can be erased and re-inscribed to ink and paper that require rewriting, Shakespeare is reflecting on the problem of erasure and revision.[10] Stewart links the rewriting of the sealed commission to the erasable tables of Hamlet's memory, but the metaphor Hamlet uses to describe the moment of his revision

---

[10] Stewart, *Shakespeare's Letters* 279. On the materiality of writing and erasure in Saxo, Belleforest, and Shakespeare, see also Joanna Craigwood, 'Shakespeare's Kingmaking Ambassadors', in Jason Powell and William T. Rossiter (eds.), *Authority and Diplomacy from Dante to Shakespeare* (Farnham: Ashgate, 2013), 199–217. As we both rely on Hampton and Stewart in linking Hamlet's revisions to diplomatic writing, the argument of Jo Craigwood's essay and the present chapter mirror each other remarkably.

of the commission he finds on Rosencrantz and Guildenstern alerts us to another analogy:

> Being thus benetted round with villainies—
> Ere I could make a prologue to my brains,
> They had begun the play—I sat me down,
> Devis'd a new commission (5.2.29–32)

By explaining Hamlet's situation in theatrical terms, and his devising a new letter as the revision of a performance he is perforce part of and whose course he needs to alter by rescripting it, the parenthetical clause links this moment of textual intrigue to the other crucial moment of revision in the play: namely, Hamlet's addition of 'some dozen or sixteen lines' (2.2.535) to the play called *The Murder of Gonzago*, to be performed by the travelling players at Elsinore. Although there is no indication in Shakespeare's play as to what Hamlet may have inserted in the script, the dramatic point of his request is clear: it signals that *The Mousetrap* is a revised version of *The Murder of Gonzago*, that it is Hamlet who transforms a tragedy in the travelling players' repertory into the play wherein to 'catch the conscience of the king' (2.2.601).

The revision of a play and of a letter: these are Hamlet's two major interventions in the course of events that are premeditated.[11] It is the dexterity he shows in altering scripts first written by others that most clearly distinguishes him from Claudius, in spite of the obvious parallelism of their plots against each other. Theatre and diplomacy, Hamlet's and Claudius's respective areas of expertise, emerge in the first half of the play as the major, and finally problematic, alternatives to open violence. As Timothy Hampton observes, the two are in fact analogous since both can be understood as fields of scripted performance, where success depends on the control and manipulation of the script. Claudius's instructions to Cornelius and Voltemand are paralleled by Hamlet's instruction to the players: both King and Prince emphatically warn their actors not to deviate from what is set down for them. Claudius gives his ambassadors 'no further personal power / To business with the King, more than the scope / Of these dilated articles allow' (1.2.36–8) whereas Hamlet asks the players to 'let those that play your clowns speak no more than is set down for them' (3.2.31–2).[12] This balance between Hamlet and Claudius is overthrown when Hamlet draws the obvious conclusion from the analogy and wrests control of diplomacy from Claudius by doing to the embassy what he has done successfully to the play—that is, by revising its script. That this moment occurs during Hamlet's trip to England, and that it thus coincides with what has often been seen as the turning point in the play

---

[11] Halpern, in 'Eclipse of Action' at 479–82 also links these acts of rewriting, identifying them as instances of the play's suggestion that all writing is rewriting, and more generally, that all decomposition is recomposition and all making remaking. According to Halpern's important essay, in these moments, the workmanlike bureaucratic activity, the business of paperwork is transfigured into action: as he says, phrasing it in the Arendtian terminology in which his argument is couched, here 'writing is no longer making but doing—an act' (481). These moments of action are political acts in the strong sense: they are, as Jo Craigwood puts it, moments when diplomats 'author their Kings'. Craigwood, 'Shakespeare's Kingmaking Ambassadors', 217.

[12] Hampton, *Fictions of Embassy* 149, 155–6.

in terms of both structure and Hamlet's character, further emphasizes the importance of this revisionary moment to Shakespeare's *Hamlet*.[13]

Critics have argued that the complications of Shakespeare's play and especially our perception of Hamlet's complexity of character are a result of Shakespeare's revisionary imposition of new motives and concerns upon the 'intractable' materials of an earlier play—in other words, that *Hamlet* is best understood as a play obviously marked, even marred, by the traces of the underlying old play, or what amounts to the same thing: by Shakespeare's revision.[14] There is a rich and closely related tradition of reading the play's theatrical self-reflexivity in the terms of Shakespeare's and Hamlet's revision of older dramatic models, genres, and styles of performance.[15] But whereas such readings usually discuss Hamlet's revisionary efforts either as part of the larger issue of mourning and memory, or as a matter of his performative engagement with the old role of the revenger he feels obliged to play, these two textual interventions show Hamlet as a reviser in a different, more directly practical, textual, and material sense. When he asks the players to 'study a speech of some dozen or sixteen lines, which I would set down and insert in't' (2.2.535–6), he describes himself as a reviser working not through subtle modifications or wholesale rewriting, not by the thorough reshaping of his materials, but by the deft insertion of a detail that completely changes the import of the otherwise unaltered whole. And although he takes great pleasure in rehearsing to Horatio how he 'devis'd a new commission, wrote it fair...folded the writ up in the form of th'other, subscrib'd it, gave't th'impression' (5.2.32–52), the point is precisely that the actual content of the revised commission is the same as that of the original, with the exception, of course, of the names of the people it concerns.

Shakespeare's own tactics and strategies of revision are of course nothing like Hamlet's efficiently local interventions. But, since the names of Rosencrantz and Guildenstern were first introduced in the Hamlet story by the English play to make the world of the story geo-politically verisimilar, these names are sites where the revisions of the dramatist and his character coincide.[16] If Hamlet's and Shakespeare's work overlap here, showing the names of Rosencrantz and Guildenstern as emblematic of the revisions of *Hamlet*, they also force us to think

---

[13] On the sea voyage as turning point in the play, see e.g. Mack, 'The World of *Hamlet*', 520–3; Calderwood, *To Be and Not to Be* 34–47.

[14] Emma Smith, 'Ghost Writing: *Hamlet* and the *Ur-Hamlet*', in Andrew Murphy (ed.), *The Renaissance Text: Theory, Editing, Textuality* (Manchester: Manchester University Press, 2000), 177–90 at 179–82. Zachary Lesser, *Hamlet after Q1: An Uncanny History of the Shakespearean Text* (Philadelphia: University of Pennsylvania Press, 2015) provides an excellent account of the disintegrationist position at 172–9.

[15] A chronological list of the major interpretations based on the notion of revision shows a shift, over time, from seeing it as the source of the play's failure to seeing it as the source of its brilliance: T. S. Eliot, 'Hamlet', *Selected Essays* (London: Faber and Faber, 1951), 141–6; William Empson, '*Hamlet* When New', *Sewanee Review*, 61 (1953), 15–42, 185–205; Mark Rose, '*Hamlet* and the Shape of Revenge', *English Literary Renaissance*, 1 (1971), 132–43; Howard Felperin, 'O'erdoing Termagant: An Approach to Shakespearean Mimesis', *The Yale Review*, 63 (1974), 372–91; David Scott Kastan, '"His Semblable in His Mirror": *Hamlet* and the Imitation of Revenge', *Shakespeare Studies*, 19 (1987), 111–24.

[16] As Empson puts it: here, 'the character does what the author is doing: altering an old play to fit an immediate political purpose.' Empson, '*Hamlet* When New', 18.

more closely about Shakespeare's motive for this revision—or, more modestly perhaps, about the possible early modern response to Shakespeare's introduction of these new elements.

Shakespeare's name here is admittedly just a convenient shorthand for the potentially plural and definitely unknown agency behind the revision. The play we believe that Shakespeare revised, the *Ur-Hamlet*, is lost. Scholars tend to assume that the *Hamlet* seemingly referred to by Nashe in 1589, recorded by Henslowe as performed at Newington Butts in 1594, and memorably alluded to by Thomas Lodge, who mentions a ghost 'which cried so miserably at the Theatre, like an oysterwife, *Hamlet, revenge*' in 1596, must be an earlier, different play. Scholars also tend to assume that this earlier play was written by someone other than Shakespeare. While on stylistic grounds I think it is reasonable to assume that the 1589 play was different from the Q2 text, we have no idea who its author may have been—we don't even have a reason to exclude Shakespeare from the list of candidates.[17] We also don't know whether the 1589 play included the names Rosencrantz and Guildenstern. What we do know is that they are not in Belleforest, and that they are in the 1603 and 1604 quartos. Although I am talking about the revision as Shakespeare's, the agency behind the various aspects and phases of that revision, that transformation from the prose narrative to stage play, remains impossible to pin down. Rosencrantz and Guildenstern, along with the entire set of Danish references, may very well have entered the play as early as 1589: they could have been put there by Shakespeare or by someone else at any time between 1588 and 1603. But my argument does not depend on a specific agent or a specific date. Muriel Bradbrook suggested that '*Hamlet* is not so much a play as a geological deposit of accumulated dramatic experience', and I would argue that it is also a geological deposit of accumulated political experience.[18] What matters here is that this accumulated experience would have made the play particularly appealing to audiences of the turn of the century, Hamlet's moment.

To trace how these names ended up in the play, and to understand why it would have mattered for an early modern play to feature them, means to explore how the play is implicated in the practices, cultures, and social significance of the production and circulation of knowledge about foreign states in late sixteenth-century England, and to consider the power such knowledge may have held for its bearer—that is, to read *Hamlet* as a play about the returns that could be expected around 1600 on the return from abroad. As I have suggested, the presence of the matter of

---

[17] The widely accepted argument about Thomas Kyd's authorship is based on a tenuous reading of Nashe's preface to Greene's *Menaphon* now ossified to literary–historical verity; see the summary (and full references to the evidence) in Jenkins (ed.), *Hamlet* 82–5. As Andrew Hadfield points out, 'Nashe's comments have an energy and purpose that make sense in terms other than a subtle and clever means of naming the author of a bad play': Andrew Hadfield, 'The *Ur-Hamlet* and the Fable of the Kid', *Notes & Queries*, 53 (2006), 46–7 at 47. I can only echo and simplify here the brilliant critique of the entire literary–historical shadow-play of the *Ur-Hamlet* put forward in James J. Marino, *Owning William Shakespeare: The King's Men and Their Intellectual Property* (Philadelphia: University of Pennsylvania Press, 2011) 75–9.

[18] Muriel C. Bradbrook, *Shakespeare the Craftsman* (London: Chatto & Windus, 1969) 122. I want to thank Goran Stanivuković for calling my attention to Bradbrook's formulation.

Denmark, and of the names Rosencrantz and Guildenstern in Shakespeare's *Hamlet*, are closely linked to the play's interest in embassies and diplomacy, to the work of actual English diplomats, and to the textualized culture of early modern political work. In what follows I turn to the examples of English ambassadors and travellers to explore how knowledge gained through travel and presented in the form of well-researched reports could empower its bearers and help them advance in political careers. As the last part of this chapter shows, the play's thematic interest in, and indebtedness to, the products and effects of foreign travel is inextricable not only from the play's concern with preferment and the sources of power, but from its interrogation of selfhood as the unfolding of a hidden interiority as well.[19] In this reading, 'Who's there?' and 'Why there?' yield similar answers, or rather answers whose shape, if questionable, is nonetheless the same.

AN ENGLISH AMBASSADOR EXPLORES DENMARK

When *The Tragedie of Hamlet Prince of Denmark* was first published in 1603, and then in a longer version in 1604/5, the only other publications about Danish matters were two other stories of princes of Denmark, *The Historie of the Tvvo Valiant Knights, Syr Clyomon Knight of the Golden Sheeld, Sonne to the King of Denmarke: and Clamydes the White Knight, Sto the King of Suauia*, an old play of chivalric romance published in 1599, set in a world where Macedonia seems to border on Denmark, and the 1605 *History of the Famous Euordanus Prince of Denmark With the Strange Aduentures of Iago Prince of Saxonie*, a prose romance with giants and knights errant. On the stage, Henry Chettle's *The Tragedy of Hoffman or a Reuenge for a Father*, not published until 1631, seems to have competed with *Hamlet* not only in its focus on revenging a murdered father, but also in its rehearsal of a couple of Danish place names. Usually thought to be the 'Danyshe tragedy' for which Henslowe paid Henry Chettle £1 on 7 July 1602,[20] Chettle's work can hardly be blamed for making an undue effort to imagine a Denmark in any historical or political detail.[21] Denmark was of course an important transit point of the Baltic trade, and English readers could learn about the country not only from sailors returning from the east via the Sound, but also from printed publications, from navigational treatises like the English translation of Cornelis Antoniszoon's *The Safegard of Sailers*. Such works, however, focused on the country from the perspective

---

[19] Instead of considering such empowerment through return as a transhistorical phenomenon, a function of the cosmology of traditional societies where knowledge of geographically distant things enforces and legitimates political power, I am interested in the *moyenne durée* and even the short-term changes in culture, the phenomena that might explain the short-term fluctuations of literary tastes, fashions, topics, and concerns. For a compelling anthropological treatment of these connections, see Mary W. Helms, *Ulysses' Sail: An Ethnographic Odyssey of Power, Knowledge, and Geographical Distance* (Princeton: Princeton University Press, 1988).

[20] E. K. Chambers, *The Elizabethan Stage* (Oxford: Clarendon Press, 1945) 3:264. Delius considered it as the Admiral's Men's production to rival the Chamberlain's Men's *Hamlet* in their repertory: *Shakespeare Jahrbuch*, 9 (1874) 166ff.

[21] Dollerup, *Denmark, Hamlet, and Shakespeare* 50–2.

of trade and navigation—Denmark itself, its contemporary political world remained an undiscovered country to people trying to educate themselves from publicly available materials until the seventeenth century, making *Hamlet* an exceptional play in the attention it pays to it.

The Danish materials in *Hamlet* appear to be largely unmotivated by the plot: with the exception of the references to the election, they are like the 'useless details' in Roland Barthes's famous notion of the 'reality effect'. Barthes argued that details like the presence of barometers and hats and peeling wallpaper that make no apparent difference to the shape of the plot are gestures at a stubborn material world unaffected by the fictional creation, and that through the artifice of invoking such unmotivated detail, the text creates the illusion of an extratextual presence— what Barthes calls a 'referential illusion'. The illusory referent of the Danish matter in *Hamlet* is, of course, not 'the real' as such (as in Barthes's account of realist prose fiction), but a recognizable historical world—what we are dealing with here is not so much an *effet de réel*, but an *effet d'un Danemark réel*, as it were.[22] And whereas Barthes's 'useless details' are references to a material world immediately and commonly shared by novels' readers, the useless details of a foreign historical world are emphatically intertextual. They refer to people and places and customs and political institutions that are only known—if indeed they are known—through texts, and evoking them evokes the whole network of their transmission: the kinds of sources from which you would, could, or should know about 'these things of Denmark'.[23] How, then, could people know about these things in England? What textual networks, and through those, what personal connections did this kind of knowledge evoke? To establish this, I will trace a possible route in which the Danish materials, the names, and other, country-specific political references, might have reached Shakespeare's play.

Daniel Rogers was one of the period's most learned English diplomats, an expert on relationships with the Holy Roman Empire, and in the late 1580s he also became a specialist in Danish matters. He was born in Wittenberg as the son of the Flemish Adrienne van Werden and of Melanchthon's English disciple, John Rogers, in 1538. John Rogers left the university where Hamlet and Horatio, as well as many actual Englishmen and even more Danes, including people called Guildenstern and Rosencrantz, also studied,[24] to serve as a minister at the parish of Meldorf. Meldorf is a village in Dithmarsch, a territory annexed to Denmark in 1559, and having spent much of his childhood there, Daniel Rogers would have been in a familiar land during his embassies to the region in the 1580s. But the Rogers were not people destined for a settled life. John Rogers was among the Protestant

---

[22] Roland Barthes, 'The Reality Effect', in *The Rustle of Language* (Oxford: Blackwell, 1986), 141–8.

[23] 'thes things of France' is what Cotton calls a collection of MSS about contemporary France: BL MS Cotton Vespasian F v, prelim., and see Chapter 4 of this book.

[24] F. A. Leo, 'Rosenkrantz und Guldenstern', *Jahrbuch der deutschen Shakespeare-Gesellschaft*, 25 (1890), 281–6; F. A. Leo, 'Rosenkrantz und Gyldenstern', *Jahrbuch der deutschen Shakespeare-Gesellschaft*, 26 (1891), 325–36; Johann Huizinga, 'Rosenkranz und Güldenstern', *Jahrbuch der deutschen Shakespeare-Gesellschaft*, 46 (1910), 60–8; Preserved Smith, 'Rosencrantz and Guildenstern', *Modern Language Notes*, 36 (1921), 374.

intellectuals Cranmer invited, or invited back, to England under the reign of Edward VI: he returned to London in 1548. His preaching and his defence of the Edwardian church settlement after the succession of Mary led to his imprisonment, and in 1555, he became the first martyr of the Marian persecutions. On 4 February 1555, his seventeen-year-old son Daniel watched him burn at the stake in Smithfield.

Daniel Rogers spent his youth studying and travelling on the Continent, a poor scholar making his name as a modern polyglot and erudite antiquarian. He emerged as a well-regarded member of an international network of radical Protestant intellectuals that also included Languet and Sidney, whom he also accompanied on his continental travels in the early 1570s. Over the years, Rogers's private service to various English diplomats—whether he was carrying their messages, conducting negotiations in their name, providing them with valuable intelligence, or advising them on various issues in the Low Countries, where he was extremely well-connected through colleagues, friends, and family—earned him the admiration of his employers and confirmed him as an authority on Dutch, German, and later also Danish affairs, but still no formal accreditation and no government pay. It was only after being held in prison as an English spy in Germany for four years, precisely for carrying the Queen's letters without official accreditation, that he was rewarded by grants of land and finally, in 1587, by appointment to the clerkship of the Privy Council.[25] By then, he had established himself as England's greatest expert—perhaps next to Robert Beale—on German diplomacy, and this expertise was invaluable in the negotiations with Denmark, the most powerful Lutheran state in Europe, a monarchy deeply entangled in the politics of the northern states of the Empire. In the last two decades of the century, Denmark became more than a problem for English trade: it emerged as an important focus of Anglo-German diplomatic efforts.

Rogers first travelled to Denmark in an official capacity in 1587.[26] In the summer of 1588, the King of Denmark died, and Elizabeth dispatched Rogers once again, 'to declare our sorrowe for the death of our most loving brother King Frederic as also to require some remedie for diuerse griefes of our Merchauntes'.

---

[25] J. A. van Dorsten, *Poets, Patrons, and Professors: Sir Philip Sidney, Daniel Rogers, and the Leiden Humanists* (Leiden: Published for the Sir Thomas Browne Institute at the University Press, 1962) 9–75; F. J. Levy, 'Daniel Rogers as Antiquary', *Bibliothèque d'Humanisme et Renaissance*, 27 (1965), 444–62; Gary McClellan Bell, 'The Men and Their Rewards in Elizabethan Diplomatic Service, 1558–1585', PhD thesis (UCLA, 1974) 378–86; David Scott Gehring, *Anglo-German Relations and the Protestant Cause: Elizabethan Foreign Policy and Pan-Protestantism* (London: Pickering & Chatto, 2013) 61–76.

[26] His account of that embassy, 'A report of his negociations in Denmark', dated from Stade, Jan. 5, 1587/8, is BL MS Cotton Nero B III, ff. 246–9]. On the embassy, see Gehring, *Anglo-German Relations and the Protestant Cause* 120–1. Gehring's book is invaluable here, as it discusses the Danish affairs in the German context. Peregrine Bertie, Lord Willoughby, had been Elizabeth's ambassador to Denmark on multiple occasions earlier in the 1580s and even installed King Frederick II into the Order of the Garter. Daniel's brother, Dr John Rogers, was also employed on more than one occasion. Daniel Rogers rose to become the primary expert partly because of Willoughby's unavailability, and partly because his knowledge of German politics was invaluable in navigating the Danish environment.

The instructions he received for his 1588 embassy provided Rogers with clear guidelines for his address to the Danes at the public audience in Elsinore. Drafted by Burghley, they stipulate that he should start by offering his condolences to the young King, then 'addresse yoursellfe to the Queene his Mother, Widow of the late King, whom you may let understand, that...we have expressely forbidden you to use anie large Speech in opening our said Greef, least it should revive in hir the Wound which we wish thoroughly cured', and 'the best Remedye we can thinke of for the Cure of the said Greef...is to looke not upon our Losse, but his Gayne, and the Hapyenes he [that is, the late King] is no doubt entered into', having 'in his End receaved the Fruit and Comfort of a most honorable and Christian Lyfe'. After making this point about looking on losses and gains with what Shakespeare calls 'an auspicious and a dropping eye' (1.2.11), and about the good fortune of the late king not having been, as was Hamlet Sr, 'cut off even in the blossoms of [his] sin' (1.5.76), the ambassador Rogers was to consult with the four elected Governors of the realm who ruled Denmark during the King's minority, express to them the English grief over the loss of an old ally, and to explain that the English were willing to 'yield satisfaction' or 'convenient Redresse of such as have been don, or may hereafter happen to be don by some disordered Persons'—namely, by English pirates committing 'some Outrages uppon divers Subjects of the Danish Crown', and last but not least to discuss the situation of English merchants getting themselves into trouble by evading the toll due at Elsinore.[27]

Unlike Cornelius and Voltemand, Rogers wasn't particularly rigid in how he followed his instructions—in fact, he felt himself obliged to go off his script right at the very beginning: 'I addressed myselfe, first to the Queene, perceauing that the cheifest honnor was giuen to her, althoughe mine instruccions did prescribe, that I should first address myselfe vnto the kinge.'[28] More significantly, in the course of his negotiations with the four Governors Rogers also 'touched divers thinges whereof I had no charge, and yet could not but move them, having regarde unto the circumstances of this present time'.[29] But while he may have acted without formal, written authorization, he seems to have been following both the drift of his 1587 negotiations with Frederick II and Queen Elizabeth's private oral instructions when he sought once again, unsuccessfully, to revive the old idea of a Protestant alliance in meetings with members of the Danish nobility and, using his invaluable old contacts, with some of the princes and ambassadors from the Protestant states of the Empire who were in Denmark condoling with the royal family.[30]

---

[27] Cecil Papers 16/100. A transcript of the instructions was printed in *A Collection of State Papers Relating to the Reign of Queen Elizabeth, from the Year 1571 to 1596. Transcribed from Original Papers and other Authentic Memorials*, ed. by William Murdin (London, 1759), 627–9. Another copy of the instructions is in a collection of documents related to Denmark, BL MS Cotton Nero B III, f. 258.

[28] Rogers to Walsingham, 24 July 1588, TNA SP 75/1 f. 259v.

[29] Rogers to Burghley, 10 August 1588, BL MS Lansdowne 57/30 (f. 79r).

[30] Arthur J. Slavin, 'Daniel Rogers in Copenhagen, 1588: Mission and Memory', in Malcolm R. Thorp and Arthur J. Slavin (eds.), *Politics, Religion and Diplomacy in Early Modern Europe: Essays in Honor of De Lamar Jensen* (Sixteenth Century Essays and Studies; Kirksville, MO, 1994), 247–66, suggests that Rogers acted without authorization, see 260–4. But as David Gehring has pointed out, Rogers repeatedly insisted that he was acting 'as partelie mine instructions

Rogers needed less justification for exceeding his instructions in another matter. While Denmark was mourning, Europe was preparing for war. By the time Rogers left England for Elsinore, the Armada had already left Lisbon, and England was desperately preparing for the threatening invasion. According to his reports, when he learnt that 'certaine which had receaved Commissions from the Kinge of Spaine to serve him with certaine shippes, mariners, and souldiors uppon the seas, which being invited with great stipends, thought they might so doe', Rogers insisted to the Danish government that such recruitment should be stopped, and at the end of July he reported home that the Governors issued an order forbidding Danish subjects to serve against England.[31] His efforts here anticipated the moves of the English government: on 11 August (OS), two weeks after the English gunfire battered the Armada at Gravelines, and three days after Elizabeth's speech to the anti-invasion forces gathered at Tilbury, Thomas Bodley was dispatched to the north to learn as much as possible about the course the Spanish fleet may have taken after being chased north by the English navy, and persuade the city of Hamburg 'not victuall or any waie to relieve the Spanyard the Common enemie of the Christian Religion'. And in case he found out that the Spanish fleet appeared to be seeking succour further east, he was to continue to Denmark and help Rogers 'sollicite the said King and Gouvernors to forbeare to yeald reliefe to the Spaniards'.[32] That is to say, Bodley was to aid Rogers in what he in fact was already doing, but what quickly lost its vital importance when it turned out that instead of looking for relief in Danish or Hanse ports, the Spanish navy decided to sail home around Scotland. So in spite of going significantly beyond the scope of his instructions, beyond achieving its nominal purpose of offering the condolences of the Queen and preventing Danes from entering Spanish service, Rogers achieved very little of substance he could report on his arrival home: by the time he got home, the anxieties about Denmark's involvement in the war with Spain were a moot point. As the contemporary record states, 'he returned a Kinde answer from the Gouernors concerning our sorrowfullness of the death of the late Kinge, but to the griefe of the merchauntes he returned nothing that imported.'[33] There was also no

---

did prescribe, and her Maiestie priuatelie had commaunded me', Rogers to Walsingham, 24 July 1588, TNA SP 75/1 f. 261v. See Gehring, *Anglo-German Relations and the Protestant Cause* 203n239. For earlier attempts, see James M. Osborn, *Young Philip Sidney: 1572–1577* (New Haven: Yale University Press, 1972) 492–5; Bodley to Walsingham, 25 June 1585, reporting on his embassy to Denmark, TNA SP 75/1/55 ff. 127r–130v, at 128v. Gehring's book now provides a detailed account of these efforts; on the 1587 negotiations, see 120–1. Rogers's service as one of Elizabeth's envoys to the Protestant princes of Germany provided the background for his later missions there—his 1580 mission and his capture, as well as his 1587 and 1588 missions followed from this earlier engagement.

[31] Rogers to Walsingham, 24 July 1588, TNA SP 75/1, f. 262r, and Rogers to Burghley, 10 August 1588, BL MS Lansdowne 57/30, f. 79r.

[32] Instructions to Thomas Bodley going to Denmark, 11 August 1588, BL MS Harley 36, ff. 273–4. By the time Bodley was to leave for Denmark, however, Rogers was already on his way home, and as the Armada was soon known to be sailing north and then west instead of east, it is not even clear that Bodley ever even left—the only surviving evidence of his mission are the instructions. I would like to thank David Gehring for this point and for his thorough reading of this chapter.

[33] BL Add 48094 f. 61r, but cp. Gehring, *Anglo-German Relations and the Protestant Cause* 124.

new treaty with Denmark, and no new Protestant alliance, either. But the embassy allowed him to learn about the country and the regime, and he made good use of this opportunity.

Although he was largely unsuccessful, or perhaps because of that, Rogers generated a substantial paper trail of his embassy. Jean Hotman, in his 1603 treatise *The Ambassador*, points out that 'most commonly it is not knowne what an ambassador doeth in his charge, but by that which himselfe writeth'. Using the example of an Ambassador who was once sent to Denmark and then was almost forgotten because he never wrote home, Hotman further insists that

> in so farre a Countrie, and where the affaires were not very great, an Ambassador hath seldome sufficient occasion to make his vertue knowne, and for that things are worth no more then the value that is made of them, he shall doe well to make himselfe known by his aduises which are looked on and considered by the Secretaries of Estate....[34]

And so Daniel Rogers did. While he was waiting for a formal answer from the Governors of Denmark, he sent home several reports of his reception and his negotiations. Sending these letters meant making specific arrangements, and *Hamlet* is once again accurate when it implies that the trip from Denmark to England was not deemed particularly safe. On 24 July, Rogers concludes his letter to Walsingham explaining that he can only hope the bearer of his letter

> may haue salfe [*sic*] passage: for I vnderstand the seas are verie full of pyrattes, and very few or none dare from hence aduenture by the longe seas towards England, because of newes from all places, that innumerable companies of pyrattes are presentelie at the seas.[35]

After sealing this letter, Rogers takes a new sheet of paper, and starts writing again. He is clearly anxious 'to make his vertue knowne' (as Hotman would require) but has little to show in terms of accomplishment. So, in what is a decided change of tack, in his second letter he starts reporting what he has more of: information. He announces that whereas

---

[34] (London: V[alentine] S[immes] for Iames Shawe, 1603), sig. G6r. Jean Hotman, the son of the great French legal scholar and 'monarchomach' François Hotman, was Leicester's foreign secretary in the 1580s. Although he left England after the death of Leicester, the fact that this treatise was first published, in 1603, in English, and only a year later in French, is suggestive both of Hotman's English connections, and more generally also of the manuscript circulation of such material. The preface of *The Ambassador* explains that the author, 'accounting it a subiect fitte onely for the view of high spirites, and such as already were, or in time might be called to the great affaires of the common wealth: suffered no other copies to be extant then those which he dispersed to his priuate friends...A Gentleman hauing recouered one of them, did at the request of some particular friends, turne it into English, supposing that the scribled copie...might satisfie his iudicious & learned friends' (sig. A4r)—it is this text that is then printed, possibly preceding the first French edition, published in the same year.
[35] TNA SP 75/1 f. 261v.

inn my former letter dated thys day, I haue wrytten at large touchyng the charge committed vnto me, as farre as hetherto I haue been able to negotiate. Now I thinke it my parte to advertise your honour somewhat concerning the state of these kingdoms.[36]

This second letter of 24 July includes information that would qualify as news—there is an outbreak of the plague in Sweden, and Gert Ranzow, the son of the mighty Heinrich Rantzau, 'offreth his service unto her Maiestie, promising to bring unto her Highnes, when she shall require it, 3000 footemen and 1000 horsemen'—but it is intended as much more than a newsletter with the familiar collection of brief notices of whatever came to the writer's attention. It is framed as a brief survey of the government of the country and the political situation there, a synoptic overview that interprets recent developments in the region and is complicated by Rogers's own diplomatic agenda. The two letters are now among the State Papers—suggesting that Rogers's messenger managed to avoid the pirates and, like Rosencrantz and Guildenstern, 'hold [his] course for England' (4.6.25). Enclosed with the second letter, Rogers also sends a list of the notabilities of the Danish court. It is in this list that the names Rosencrantz and Guildenstern—of 'Petrus Guldenstern de Tym, Regni Marescallus', of 'Georgius Rosenkrantz de Rosenholme, Magister Palatii', as well as of 'Axel Guldenstern de Lyngbui, Vicarius regni Norwegiani'—first seem to have made the crossing to England.[37]

Two weeks later, with still nothing new to report, he sends home a copy of the same general description of the country, prefaced by a summary of his negotiations, and once again enclosing the list of *Senatores et Consiliarii Regnorum Daniae Norwegiae etc.*, this time addressing the packet to Burghley.[38] On returning home, and having delivered the politely inconsequential reply from the Danes to his Queen, Rogers sets to work again, and expands the materials included in his reports to Walsingham and Burghley into a systematic account of his view of the state of Denmark in a document dated September 1588, and titled 'A discourse touchinge ye present estate and gouernment of the Kingdomes of Denmarke and Norwegen, with a description of the said realmes and dominions appertayninge unto them.'[39] Rogers states the purpose and scope of his *Discourse* at the beginning:

Hauing been now twise sente from her Maiestie into Denmarke I thinke it good to wryte some discourse touching theise northerne kingdomes and the presente gouuernment of the same... for that there is lyttle wrytten trulie of theise kingdomes

---

[36] TNA SP 75/1 ff.263–6.
[37] Copies of the same list can also be found in BL MS Cotton Nero B III f. 343 [266]. Cp. also BL MS Lansdowne 112, 'Consiliarii et senatores Regnorum Daniae Noruagiae', f. 107. Geoffrey Bullough noted the potential importance of Rogers's letters among the State Papers for the play, and reprinted some excerpts from the *CSP*: Geoffrey Bullough (ed.), *Narrative and Dramatic Sources of Shakespeare* (London: Routledge and Kegan Paul, 1978) 7:184.
[38] Rogers to Burghley, 10 August 1588, BL MS Lansdowne 57/30.
[39] 'A discourse touchinge ye present estate and gouernment of the Kingdomes of Denmarke and Norwegen, with a description of the said realmes and dominions appertayninge unto them written in September Anno 1588', Huntington MS EL 1608. The autograph *Discourse*, a manuscript of twelve folio leaves, was preserved among the Egerton papers at the Huntington; it was presumably written for the use of the Queen's secretaries.

besides that false bruites are spread of them euen by such as persuade they know somewhat.[40]

The recent history of Anglo-Danish negotiations showed that the lack of substantial knowledge of the state made it hard for English envoys to navigate the Danish court and to secure the support of friendly individuals and factions. Rogers's *Discourse* sets out to fill this gap through combining a generalized description with notes about personal experience into a well-organized survey of the country. He uses his long experience in the region, and the information he gathered during his recent embassy from scholars, members of the local political elite, as well as from the foreign ambassadors present, to discuss Denmark's geopolitical situation, its government, its religious and legal institutions, its political and dynastic history (complete with a genealogical table), its engagements with other European nations and recent diplomatic contacts with England, as well as its political elite and the factions within the political class.

In the *Discourse*, Rogers once again incorporates the list of the Danish nobility included with his earlier reports (see Figure 2.1).[41] The presence of the names of Rosencrantz and Guildenstern in Shakespeare's play has been explained by their appearance on the title page of the 1602 edition of Tycho Brahe's 1598 book on astronomical instruments, as well as with reference to the (if the hypothesis is true, astonishingly accurate) memory of travelling players who visited Denmark in the 1580s.[42] But the one channel through which we can actually be sure that their names did enter written circulation in England (however restricted that circulation may have been) early enough to be of use in writing the play was in the missives of Daniel Rogers. The two names which Hamlet inserts in a piece of diplomatic correspondence on board a ship bound for England from Denmark may very well have been inserted in the script by the dramatist from a piece of diplomatic correspondence that arrived from Denmark in 1588, the names having sailed the route the characters are sailing in *Hamlet*. As I have pointed out above, there are some known unknowns at play here, although the five surviving copies of Rogers's list, implying relatively wide dissemination at least within political circles, make it a possible route in which these names entered the English stage. (In Chapter 4, we will see examples of similar materials circulating outside their intended sphere.) My point is not about sources, however, but about the textual universe these names, as touches of authenticity, would have been evoking, about the contexts in which knowledge of such foreign names would have mattered.[43] Whether Rogers's

---

[40] 'A discourse' f. 1.   [41] The list appears on f. 9r.
[42] Possible routes for the transmission of the names have been discussed in Huizinga, 'Rosenkranz und Güldenstern'; Smith, 'Rosencrantz and Guildenstern'; Gunnar Sjögren, '*Hamlet* and the Coronation of Christian IV', *Shakespeare Quarterly*, 16 (1965), 155–60; Dollerup, *Denmark, Hamlet, and Shakespeare* 173–85, 210–12; Jenkins (ed.), *Hamlet* 422–3. The usual assumption of the travelling players bringing the information is no less possible than the scenario I am suggesting here: but the focus on (and transcription of) the names of notables in a foreign environment simply makes better sense in the setting of diplomatic writing.
[43] Anne Barton, *Ben Jonson, Dramatist* (Cambridge: Cambridge University Press, 1984) 170–4; Nicholas Popper, *Walter Ralegh's History of the World and the Historical Culture of the Late Renaissance* (Chicago: University of Chicago Press, 2012) 124–8.

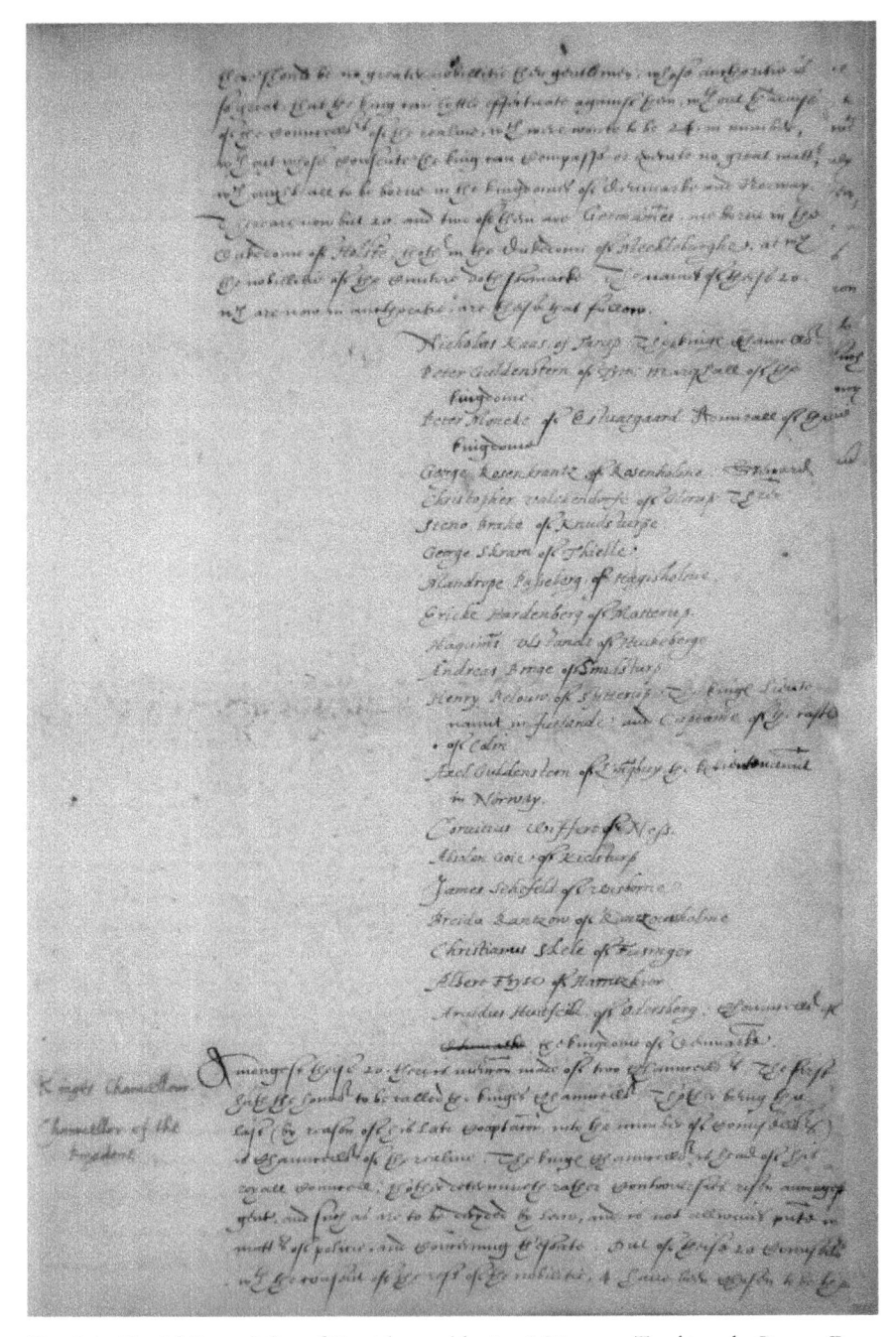

Fig. 2.1. Daniel Rogers's list of Danish notables in *A Discourse Touching the Present Estate and Gouuernement of the Kingdomes of Denmarke*... The Huntington Library, San Marino, California, MS EL 1608, f. 9r.

list is in fact a source or not, it shows the close association of foreign names with the genres and uses of diplomatic writing and diplomatic correspondence.

The 1589 *Certaine Briefe, and Speciall Instructions for Gentlemen, Merchants, Students, Soldiers, Marriners, & c. Employed in Seruices Abrode*, a translation of *Methodus Describendi Regiones* written by a certain Albrecht Meyer under the patronage of Heinrich Rantzau, the puissant Danish statesman, in 1587, is a little pamphlet that consists of a list of things to be observed and taken note of during one's travels, organized into categories that range from the country's topography to its institutions for learning. Here, under the heading for 'The political state', the traveller is among other things also instructed to take note of the 'Proper names of men and women, differing from those that are common in other places'.[44] Meyer's list of topics does not ask the traveller to compile a list of the King's councillors or indeed of specific political notables. But such information was particularly valuable, and was the most obvious reason for the interest in names in political contexts. In 1598, Robert Beale, Clerk of the Privy Council and one of the most experienced politicians of the time, wrote a private memorandum for the inexperienced Lord Zouche who was to travel to Denmark as an ambassador.[45] The memorandum is clearly distinct from the ambassador's official instructions—here, Beale gives Zouche basic practical advice on his assignment: how to prepare, what to pay attention to, what topics to avoid, what positions to take on various political subjects that may come up, how to keep his records, and how to control leaks of sensitive information. The first piece of advice is that Zouche is to learn the titles of the Danish King and how to address him, and 'who are of his Counsell or highe offices in that realme. Learne their titles and addicions.'[46] The names of important people, and names in general, were of special significance in transacting diplomatic business: while the larger political structures may be relatively permanent, who exactly held what office at the given moment could be a decisive question—and could also change very rapidly, which is why Rogers thought it important to enclose his list of names and titles with his missives to each of his contacts at home, why Stephen Lesieur also brought back a list of the councillors of the King of Denmark from his 1599 mission,[47] why someone like Paul Hentzner, an early German traveller to England, concluded his account of the country with a list of English notabilities,[48] and why such lists of names proliferate among early state papers.

If lists of notabilities and their offices were used to keep secretaries of state up to date on their negotiating partners, documents like Daniel Rogers's *Discourse*, aiming to convey an account of the entire Danish polity, helped them situate such information. Rogers incorporates in *Discourse* the list of major officeholders he circulated earlier, and contextualizes names of the Danish political class through his account of the state of Denmark, its political institutions, complete with the loyalties, alliances, grudges, and aspirations of major political players, as well as the

[44] (London: Iohn Woolfe, 1589), C3v–C4r.
[45] Beale took over the responsibility of the northern states after Rogers died in 1591.
[46] BL MS Add 48152 f. 6.   [47] BL MS Add 48152 f. 116v.
[48] *Itinerarium Germaniae; Galliae; Angliae; Italiae; Scriptum Paulo Hentznero* (Nürnberg: Abraham Wagenmann, 1612), 157–8.

country's diplomatic relations with other states. Such a description differs from the descriptions of states offered by the geographies and cosmographies of the period precisely in its attention not only to the more permanent and formal structures, but to the specific political constellation as well: the current balance of powers within the state, the problems, vulnerabilities, and conjunctures, and against this background, the 'very names of the persons'. Ultimately, these mutable specifics distinguished state secrets from public knowledge, the esoteric political information incorporated in a report like Rogers's discourse, from exoteric information about foreign countries. Names like Johan and Jörg (Youghan and Yorick) provided *couleur locale* in a broad sense, and they were names, as their phonetic English spelling suggests, that could be picked up in the harbour—but 'Rosencrantz' and 'Guildenstern' signal state secrets, the kind of valuable intelligence one brought back from abroad on paper. Putting such names on conspicuous display was to bestow upon the play the effect of a real Denmark, to assert the authenticity of the play's Danish materials, to emphasize its insider perspective on international politics, and to assert its indebtedness to diplomatic writing, to the enabling textual products of political careers.

ENGLISH AMBASSADORS AND VENETIAN RELATIONS

Far from being a unique document, Daniel Rogers's tract belongs to a recognizable genre, the pragmatically oriented account of a foreign state. By far the largest known corpus of texts in this genre consists of the *relazioni* that Venetian ambassadors presented to the Council about the countries they were returning from,[49] although similar documents were produced in other countries as well. *Relazioni* described the geography, economy, and demography, the social, religious, political, and military structures of the country visited, and offered an analysis of the nature of the regime, its domestic and especially foreign political ambitions and alliances. Although produced for government use, and supposedly containing the *arcana* of states and princes, the *relazioni* were entering a new life in widely circulating manuscript copies and increasingly also in print, catering to a rapidly growing public demand for political knowledge. They were eagerly bought, copied, and collected in manuscript form throughout Europe, so much so that by the late seventeenth century, demand for them was occasionally satisfied by forgeries.[50]

---

[49] Filippo de Vivo, 'How to Read Venetian *Relazioni*', *Renaissance and Reformation*, 34 (2011), 25–59; Donald E. Queller, 'The Development of Ambassadorial Relazioni', in John Rigby Hale (ed.), *Renaissance Venice* (London: Faber and Faber, 1973), 174–96; Ignazio Toscani, 'Etatistisches Denken und erkenntnistheoretische Überlegungen in den venezianischen Relazionen', in Mohammed Rassem and Justin Stagl (eds.), *Statistik und Staatsbeschreibung in der Neuzeit* (Paderborn: Schöningh, 1980), 111–29.

[50] Queller, 'The Development of Ambassadorial Relazioni', 176–7 and n121; de Vivo, *Information and Communication in Venice* 61. For a still useful anecdotal survey of the circulation, see Armand Baschet, *La Diplomatie Vénitienne: les Princes de l'Europe au XVIe Siècle: François Ier, Philippe II, Catherine de Médicis, les Papes, les Sultans, etc. etc. d'après les Rapports des Ambassadeurs Vénitiens* (Paris: Henri Plon, 1862) 39–53.

Large numbers of sixteenth-, seventeenth- or eighteenth-century scribal copies of *relazioni* can be found in most major collections of early modern manuscripts. Most of these reports have since been published in nineteenth- and twentieth-century scholarly editions, which are themselves less frequently consulted than they would have been a hundred years ago: so the manuscript volumes—their pristine condition and their often sumptuous bindings a testimony to their importance as status objects in eighteenth-century aristocratic libraries—now just sit on the shelves, undisturbed.[51] In the early modern period, however, they were seen as a defining genre of political knowledge production, a genre that was instrumental in the training of the Venetian political class and of European diplomats in general. As late as in 1749, Lord Chesterfield advised his son on his travels in Europe 'to frequent... the Venetian Ministers; who are always better informed of the Courts they reside at, than any other Minister: the strict and regular accounts, which they are obliged to give to their government, making them very diligent and inquisitive.'[52] *Relazioni* transmitted knowledge, but the task of writing them was also seen as a form of training and a routine that kept even the most accomplished diplomats on their toes, a routine that was not only a testimony to the expertise of the producers of these documents, but a key to it.

As Venetian diplomacy became in many ways the model for European practice in general, the Venetian reports served as models as well as sources for political descriptions of foreign states produced in other countries. The 1609 'Account of the state of France' is explicitly advertised by its author, George Carew, as a report after the Venetian model written on his return from his embassy to France. As Carew explains in his dedication to the king, his *Relation* is a compilation based on his 'readings, meditations' and on 'conferences with men of that nation, and of strangers, who in my time followed that court'. He then notes that 'This course of making relations the Venetian Ambassadors always use at their return from their several services, both in a settled and continual speech before the Privy Council of the State, and likewise by reducing it into writing afterwards'—and adds that he hopes 'your Majesty will allow the example, whereby others of better judgment, which serve You in the like places, may be incited to do it better'.[53]

---

[51] See the account of the production and circulation of *relazioni* and their importance as historical documents by the historian who relied on them in his effort to transform early modern political history: Leopold Ranke, *The Ottoman and the Spanish Empires in the Sixteenth and Seventeenth Centuries*, trans. Walter K. Kelly (London: Whittaker and Co., 1853) 1–4; Willy Andreas, *Staatskunst und Diplomatie der Venezianer im Spiegel Ihrer Gesandtenberichte* (Leipzig: Koehler & Amelang, 1943) 73–82; Ugo Tucci, 'Ranke and the Venetian Document Market', in Georg G. Iggers and James M. Powell (eds.), *Leopold von Ranke and the Shaping of the Historical Discipline* (Syracuse: Syracuse University Press, 1990), 99–107.

[52] *Letters Written by the Late Right Honourable Philip Dormer Stanhope, Earl of Chesterfield, to his Son, Philip Stanhope, Esq.*, 2 vols. (4th edn.; London: Printed for J. Dodsley, 1774) 1:399 (Letter 245, 28 February 1749).

[53] Quoted from Thomas Birch, *An Historical View of the Negotiations between the Courts of England, France, and Brussels, from the Year 1592 to 1617* (London: A. Millar, 1749) 415–16. For MS copies of Carew's *Relation* see Beinecke MS Osborn fb20 (which also includes the dedication—I thank Noah Millstone for calling my attention to this copy), BL MSS Add 48062 ff. 60–133b, Add 4466, ff. 22–51v, Add 35846, Add 72390, Egerton 921 ff. 102–27, and Huntington MS HM 41951.

While Carew's *Relation* shows him clearly up to date both on Venetian forms and on French matters, he may appear to be less so on English archival and diplomatic practice. Although his insistence on the exemplarity (and the implied uniqueness) of his report in an English context has often been taken at face value,[54] Carew could so self-consciously seek to excel in the genre precisely because it was already a familiar one in England, its structure and function understood from foreign example and domestic practice. As he returned from France, another resident ambassador, Sir Charles Cornwallis, had just brought home a similar relation from his embassy to Madrid in 1608.[55] A copy of Cornwallis's *Discourse* among the papers of Sir Walter Aston, resident ambassador in Spain in the 1620s, shows that these English *relazioni* served not only as reference works helping the government to conduct business with specific foreign powers, but also as introductory textbooks for newly accredited men to their posts, or indeed as manuals helping them navigate the foreign court.[56] Other examples of the genre also testify to the active use and production of the genre by English diplomats in the late sixteenth century, so Carew's presentation of his account of the state of France as a model for work to be done by his successors turns out to be a promotional tactic rather than a genuine gesture, exemplary as his text was in terms of its sheer length and the quality of research that went into it.

But the output of English diplomats was limited, so English state intelligence relied on other resources, first of all, on copies of *relazioni* acquired in the emerging European marketplace of intelligence, whose most important centre in the period was Venice.[57] Robert Beale's 1592 'Treatise of the office of a Councellor and Principall Secretarie to her Matie' explains that in preparing ambassadors for their missions, 'perhapss your Italian *Relationi* may stande you in some steede for the knowledge of forraine Estates'[58]—implying an archive of copies of Italian (mostly, presumably, Venetian) *relazioni* as a crucial resource at the Secretary's disposal. Italian *relazioni* were present not only among the papers of political figures, but even in academic collections, implying their availability to a broader audience of aspiring young gentlemen: in 1616, Giovanni Battista Lionello, Venetian ambassador

---

[54] See e.g. J. E. Neale, *Essays in Elizabethan History* (London: Jonathan Cape, 1958) 136–42; Queller, 'The Development of Ambassadorial Relazioni', 175.

[55] Charles Cornwallis: *Discourse of the State of Spayne, Written by My Lord aboute the Beginning of this Yeare 1607*, BL MS Cotton Vespasian C x, ff. 1–35. Other copies include BL MSS Add 4149 ff. 132–52, Add 36444 ff. 14–61, Add 39853 ff. 150–62, Add 48062 ff. 326–67, and Bodleian MS Rawlinson C 929. There is a partial reprint in Somers Tracts, 4th collection, vol. ii (1751) 438–52, and vol. iii (1810) 304–15, and a complete Spanish translation based on BL MS Add 39853 ff. 150–62 in I. A. A. Thompson, 'Sir Charles Cornwallis y su "Discurso Sobre el Estado de España" (1608)', in Porfirio Sanz Camañes (ed.), *La Monarquía Hispánica en Tiempos del Quijote* (Madrid: Universidad de Castilla-la Mancha: Sílex, 2005), 65–101 at 77–101.

[56] BL MS Add 36444 ff. 14–61.

[57] Peter Burke, 'Early Modern Venice as a Center of Information and Communication', in John Jeffries Martin and Dennis Romano (eds.), *Venice Reconsidered: The History and Civilization of an Italian State, 1297–1797* (Baltimore: Johns Hopkins University Press, 2000), 389–409; de Vivo, *Information and Communication in Venice*.

[58] BL MS Add 48149, ff. 3v–9v, reprinted in Conyers Read, *Mr. Secretary Walsingham and the Policy of Queen Elizabeth*, 3 vols. (Cambridge, MA: Harvard University Press, 1925) 1:423–43, the quoted passage at 435.

to England, was dismayed enough to discover the presence of a collection of Venetian *relazioni* in the library of the University of Oxford to report its contents to the Venetian Inquisitors of State.[59]

These *relazioni* provided the English with essential political information, and as they did so, they also familiarized them with the characteristics of the genre. There was one important geographical area where English diplomatic efforts were not served well by Italian materials, simply because there were hardly any available. While some papal *nuntii* and German ambassadors visited northern Europe and their reports occasionally entered international circulation, Venetian diplomats rarely visited Denmark, Sweden, Poland, or Russia, and their brief embassies did not allow them to produce the kind of detailed descriptions they put together about the states and the courts of southern and central Europe.[60] English diplomacy, on the other hand, was rather active in northern Europe in the late sixteenth century, allowing English envoys sent there to make a virtue of necessity and produce new reports based on their experiences. It is about this northern area, unexplored by the Italians, that the earliest surviving English *relazioni* were written, pre-dating Carew's work by over two decades. Some earlier examples may have been lost, but the 1588 *Description of Denmark* by Rogers appears to be not only among the earliest surviving English *relazioni*—only Roger Ascham's incomplete 1553 *Report and Discourse... of the Affaires and State of Germany* and Robert Beale's 1569 *The State of Germany* pre-date it[61]—and the earliest *relazione* written by a returning English ambassador, but also the only extant pre-1600 *relazione* about Denmark produced anywhere in Europe.[62] Giles Fletcher's description of Russia, originally presented as an ambassadorial report and soon printed in a revised and somewhat tamed version, while not unique, is also clearly the best and most detailed from the period in any language,[63] and about one third of all the extant

---

[59] *CSP Venice* 14 (1615–17), 285–6, 26 Aug. 1616. The *CSP* entry identifies the MS as Bodleian 911.

[60] A survey of the Venetian *relazioni* that had been made available in print by 1939 shows the difference the Venetian interests made to the coverage: for the sixteenth century, it lists thirty-seven relations about Constantinople, twenty-nine about Rome, twenty-nine about the Empire, twenty-four about France, twenty about Spain, twelve about Savoy, nine about Firenze, nine about England, seven about Syria, six about Hungary (all six of them pre-1523), and only four about Poland, none about Russia, Denmark, or Sweden; see Francesca Antonibon, *Le Relazioni a Stampa di Ambasciatori Veneti* (Istituto Veneto di Scienze Lettere e Arti. Opera della Bibliografia Veneziana. Collana di Bibliografie Minori, 1: Tipografia del Seminario di Padova, 1939).

[61] *A Report and Discourse Written by Roger Ascham, of the Affaires and State of Germany and the Emperour Charles his Court, Duryng Certaine Yeares While the Sayd Roger was There* (London: Iohn Daye, n.d. [1570?]) Beale's report is published in David Scott Gehring (ed.), *Diplomatic Intelligence on the Holy Roman Empire and Denmark During the Reigns of Elizabeth I and James VI: Three Treatises* (Camden Series, Cambridge: Cambridge University Press, forthcoming).

[62] The next diplomatic account of Denmark I am aware of is that of the papal nuntio Bentivoglio, dated 1613 and first published in Bentivoglio's *Relazioni* in 1629, emphatically called 'Breve relazione' and lacking the rich detail Rogers provides.

[63] Giles Fletcher, *Of the Russe Common Wealth. Or, Maner of Gouernement of the Russe Emperour, (Commonly Called the Emperour of Moskouia) with the Manners, and Fashions of the People of that Countrey* (London: Printed by T[homas] D[awson] for Thomas Charde, 1591). There are three earlier versions in manuscript: Queen's College Cambridge MS 25, University College Oxford MS 144, University of Minnesota TC Wilson Library Bell MS 1589 Fl, as well as several modern editions.

accounts of Russia were produced by Englishmen.[64] Finally, Carew's own account of Poland, produced after his 1598 embassy, is the period's most comprehensive political description of that country.[65]

The erudition of these late sixteenth-century English *relazioni* reflects their authors' background. The antiquarian research of Carew, Fletcher, and Rogers—members of the network of scholars whose most prominent member in England was William Camden—both enabled and complemented their more practical work in government employment, even as an alternative route to advancement and patronage.[66] Several other English career politicians had serious scholarly credentials: the diplomat and later founder of the Oxford library that bears his name, Thomas Bodley was a known Hebraist, whereas the historical manuscript collection of Robert Beale was inseparable from the archive of treaties and other state papers he built as a diplomat and formidable Clerk of the Privy Council. Antiquarian research and diplomatic writing were both empirically oriented intellectual practices in which the school learning whose perceived inutility (as we saw in Chapter 1) brought Gabriel Harvey close to despair was applied in uncovering, processing, and organizing new matter that promised to be of pragmatic, profitable use. That Beale's collection of Spanish histories and the French Huguenot diplomat Jacques Bongars's collection of Hungarian histories both came out from the protestant humanist publishing house of André Wechel and his heirs is emblematic not only of how common this link was between diplomatic work and antiquarian historical research, but also of the networked nature of these activities.[67] As nationally oriented antiquarian enterprises were embedded in an international scholarly exchange, antiquarian projects and diplomatic engagements complemented and also supported each other in these people's careers. Participation in scholarly networks of international correspondence, in the international republic of letters, was a crucial vehicle of information exchange, and historical erudition was a form of expertise that was crucial in interpreting and negotiating treaties. And because in

---

[64] Karl Heinz Ruffmann, *Das Russlandbild im England Shakespeares* (Göttingen: Musterschmidt Wissenschaftlicher Verlag, 1952) 48.

[65] George Carew, *Relation of the State of Polonia and the United Provinces of that Crown Anno 1598*, BL MS Royal 18 B. I, printed in *Res Polonicae ex Archivo Musei Britannici I Pars*, ed. Dr Carolus Talbot (Elementa ad Fontium Editiones vol. XIII, Romae, 1965).

[66] Carew edited William Lambarde's influential *Reports: or Causes in Chancery*, and corresponded with Camden and de Thou about contemporary history. Fletcher followed Thomas Norton as Remembrancer of the City of London, he made plans to write an archivally-based history of the reign of Queen Elizabeth in Latin. BL MS Lansdowne 65/59, reprinted in Lloyd E. Berry (ed.), *The English Works of Giles Fletcher, the Elder* (Madison: University of Wisconsin Press, 1964) 383–8. Rogers was encouraged by his cousin Ortelius to write a history of Roman Britain, for which he compiled a considerable amount of material; cp. F. J. Levy, 'The Making of Camden's *Britannia*', *Bibliothèque d'Humanisme et Renaissance*, 26 (1964), 70–97, at 86–8; Levy, 'Daniel Rogers as Antiquary'; Tine Luk Meganck, 'Erudite Eyes: Artists and Antiquarians in the Circle of Abraham Ortelius (1527–1598)', PhD thesis (Princeton University, 2003) 66–74. Rogers's manuscript compilation with some notes by Camden is BL MS Cotton Titus F x.

[67] David J. B. Trim, 'Sir Thomas Bodley and the International Protestant Cause', *Bodleian Library Record*, 16 (1998), 314–40; Cecil Roth, 'Sir Thomas Bodley—Hebraist', *Bodleian Library Record*, 7 (1966), 242–51; Mark Taviner, 'Robert Beale and the Elizabethan Polity', PhD thesis (University of St Andrews, 2000); Ruth Kohlndorfer-Fries, *Diplomatie und Gelehrtenrepublik: Die Kontakte des Französischen Gesandten Jacques Bongars (1554–1612)* (Tübingen: Niemeyer, 2009).

northern Europe, diplomatic transactions were conducted in Latin, the humanist training and connections of these scholar–diplomats was especially vital to successful service in the region.[68]

The sixteenth-century *relazioni* of Rogers, Fletcher, and Carew complemented the available Italian materials, relying on the strengths of English connections in the north and on their authors' scholarship in making up for the limitations of the supply from the Venetian market of documents. Their production also complemented their authors' political employment. They grew out of missions that were at least partial failures: Rogers did not manage to resolve all the issues he was instructed to raise with the Danes;[69] although he tried to present his mission as a success, Fletcher actually failed to deliver on several of his most important charges that concerned the privileges of the Muscovy Company;[70] and during his embassy to Sigismund Vasa, King of Poland and Sweden, Carew not only made the mistake of talking to both sides in the evolving Swedish civil war, but aggravated the mistake by entering into a debate over Elizabeth's titles which angered Sigismund enough to order him to go home.[71] Of course each of the three ambassadors sent home detailed accounts of their negotiations as well as intelligence reports about the countries they visited.[72] But after returning to England, each of them decided to rework these into more systematic and more substantial relations, expanding their earlier reports to put their historical and diplomatic expertise on display, to show themselves as loyal advisors with an encyclopaedic knowledge of the country and capable of shrewd insight into the historical background, the motives and significance of political events there—and offering this work to their superiors, as if to make up for the failure of their negotiations.[73]

---

[68] On the connections between diplomacy and the republic of letters in Europe, see also Natalie Mears, *Queenship and Political Discourse in the Elizabethan Realms* (Cambridge: Cambridge University Press, 2005) 65. On the political uses of historical research, see e.g. Kevin Sharpe, *Sir Robert Cotton 1586–1631: History and Politics in Early Modern England* (Oxford: Oxford University Press, 1979) 27–30; Wyman H. Herendeen, *William Camden: A Life in Context* (Woodbridge: Boydell Press, 2007) 304–33; Grafton, *What Was History?*; Popper, *Walter Ralegh's History of the World*.

[69] William Camden, *The History of the Most Renowned and Victorious Princess Elizabeth, Late Queen of England: Selected Chapters*, ed. Wallace T. MacCaffrey (Chicago and London: University of Chicago Press, 1970) 332–3.

[70] Samuel H. Baron, 'Fletcher's Mission to Moscow and the Anthony Marsh Affair', *Forschungen zur osteuropäischen Geschichte*, 46 (1991), 107–30.

[71] J. K. Fedorowicz, *England's Baltic Trade in the Early Seventeenth Century: A Study in Anglo-Polish Commercial Diplomacy* (Cambridge: Cambridge University Press, 1980) 43–4.

[72] Fletcher's brief of his negotiation in Moscovia: Fletcher to Burghley, 21 September 1589, BL MS Lansdowne 60, no. 59. Fletcher's policy recommendations based on his experience ('Means of decay of the Russe trade' and 'remedies'): Fletcher to the Queen, BL MS Lansdowne 52, no. 37. Both are printed in Berry (ed.), *The English Works of Giles Fletcher, the Elder* 367–81. These notes have been used in English policy making, as indicated by the next ambassador's instructions: see Thomas Stuart Willan, *The Early History of the Russia Company, 1553–1603* (Manchester: Manchester University Press, 1956) 218–19. Carew's reports are TNA SP 88/2 ff. 82–3, endorsed as 'Mr Carewes relacion', and ff. 84–8, 20 January 1598/9, 'De variis rebus a se gestis in Polonia', reprinted in Talbot (ed.), *Res Polonicae Elisabetha I Angliae Regnante Conscriptae ex Archivis Publicis Londoniarum* (Elementa ad Fontium Editiones IV, Romae 1961), 236–8 and 238–51, respectively.

[73] Rogers's manuscript appears to be addressed to his employers. A presentation copy of Fletcher's work addressed to the Queen survives as Queen's College Cambridge MS 25. The only copy of Carew's *Relation of the State of Polonia* is an imperfect, yet sumptuous presentation copy produced by

Following the Venetian example, Carew would have liked the writing of *relazioni* to be a routine part of resident ambassadors' duties, a summation of their work as intelligence-gatherers. In the late sixteenth century, English diplomats only seem to have produced such documents when either the scarcity of information available in England about the country in question or the failure of their own mission (or indeed a combination of the two) made such extra efforts necessary. And it was precisely because in England they were not part of the diplomatic routine (as they were in Venice), and because English diplomacy was not a civic duty (as it was at least nominally in Venice), that the production of *relazioni* in England came to be so closely associated with the demonstration of political competence and diplomatic expertise. It emerged as a tool of self-defence or self-promotion, as a form of self-authentication of politically ambitious English travellers, whether official or private, and thus a genre of political writing redolent with sociocultural significance. In the English context, the function of this quintessential Venetian genre changed: what had been a medium for symbolically discharging an office was repurposed as an occasion to voice one's ambition for preferment, its production a textual emblem of hope for advancement on one's return.[74] Not a ceremonial conclusion, but an effort to prove oneself.

DIPLOMACY AND THE PROFESSION OF POLITICS

In 1585, Alberico Gentili, professor of civil law at Oxford, published *De legationibus*, a foundational work of international law that became one of the period's key authorities on the legal, political and ethical ramifications of diplomacy. In the chapter about the prudence of ambassadors, Gentili invokes Ulysses, whom Homer identified as the most prudent of men by calling him familiar with the mores and cities of many peoples. Travel of course is not only an experience that makes men prudent in general, but also, more specifically, a necessary preparation for diplomatic missions. Gentili asks:

> Why should we send to foreigners one without experience in foreign affairs? By one who has travelled, however, we mean one who gives such indications of his travels as show him to be a man experienced in foreign affairs [*rerum peregrinarum*]. For merely to have been abroad, without having made any effort to acquire knowledge [*scientia*] along this line, is of no significance.[75]

Gentili is here articulating the problem from the perspective of his own patrons, the Earl of Leicester and Sir Francis Walsingham, attending to the needs and

---

a professional with black and gold initials but lacking the dedication and the *explicit*, and containing occasional unfilled blank spaces (11r, 20r etc.) for words the scribe could not make out.

[74] In England, writing *relazioni* is therefore an exemplary instance of the 'knowledge transactions' and the 'textual mode of counsel' described, respectively, by Jardine and Sherman, 'Pragmatic Readers'; Popper, *Walter Ralegh's History of the World* 19–23.

[75] *Alberici Gentilis de Legationibus, Libri Tres* (Londini: Excudebat Thomas Vautrollerius, 1585), sig. Q1v, quoted from Alberico Gentili, *De Legationibus Libri Tres*, trans. Gordon J. Laing, 2 vols. (New York: Oxford University Press, 1924) 2:170, translation slightly modified.

interests of Her Majesty's government, but these interests translate readily to the self-interest of those travelling abroad—if they are to present themselves as employable, they need to produce evidence of their *scientia* of *rerum peregrinarum*.

A survey of the careers of Elizabethan diplomats suggests that Gentili's arguments here do not merely reflect the trajectory of the admired dedicatee of his book, Sir Philip Sidney, but also spell out the rationale of the English government behind selecting and training people for diplomatic missions. That the government paid close attention to the ability and competence of those sent abroad is indicated by the lists kept by Burghley of 'men who are fit to serve' and of 'those that have served' on overseas missions, thus identifying a group of experienced courtier-servants, effectively a *cadre* of diplomats.[76] The 1579 list of those who have served included, among eight noblemen and twenty-four gentlemen, Daniel Rogers, William Davison, Robert Beale as well as Philip Sidney; interestingly, the parallel list of eight noblemen and nineteen gentlemen 'that have not served but are fitt to serve' includes only names of people who would never be employed as ambassadors, thus indicating the importance of foreign experience as preparation for such employment.[77] Nor were people considered fit to serve directly on the basis of their education or other credentials from outside the field. A humanistic education was certainly a valuable foundation for becoming a diplomat (almost all Elizabethan ambassadors coming from the gentry had a university degree), but serving the government abroad still required a specialized form of experience. Previous foreign travel and a documented familiarity with the political conditions of a state or region could lead to employment in the service of accredited ambassadors, and that service was in turn a form of apprenticeship leading to independent appointment. The careers of late sixteenth-century diplomats thus seem to follow a loose template, something like a *cursus honorum*, leading from the subordinate personnel and secretaries accompanying accredited ambassadors on their missions or serving them during their residencies, to special or resident ambassadors.[78] Each step held the promise of the next, but did of course not guarantee it: the outcome depended on performance and on the demonstration of competence, which at the higher stages of the trajectory was to amount to a specialized expertise in the affairs of a specific region.[79]

---

[76] F. Jeffrey Platt, 'The Elizabethan Diplomatic Service', *Journal of the Rocky Mountain Medieval and Renaissance Association*, 9 (1988), 93–116 at 95; Gary M. Bell, 'Elizabethan Diplomacy: A Subtle Revolution', in Malcolm R. Thorp and Arthur J. Slavin (eds.), *Politics, Religion and Diplomacy in Early Modern Europe* (Sixteenth Century Essays and Studies; Kirksville, MO: Sixteenth Century Journal Publishers, 1994), 267–88 at 270.

[77] Bell, 'Elizabethan Diplomacy', 285n282.

[78] Bell, 'Elizabethan Diplomacy', 271–3; Platt, 'The Elizabethan Diplomatic Service', 99–100. For the shape of diplomatic careers under James, see John Stoye, *English Travellers Abroad, 1604–1667: Their Influence in English Society and Politics* (Rev. edn.; New Haven: Yale University Press, 1989) 108–16.

[79] Gary M. Bell, *A Handlist of British Diplomatic Representatives, 1509–1688* (London: Royal Historical Society, 1990); Bell, 'Elizabethan Diplomacy'; Elizabeth Rachel Williamson, 'Before "Diplomacy": Travel, Embassy and the Production of Political Information in the Later Sixteenth Century', PhD thesis (Queen Mary, University of London, 2012) 71–81. I would like to thank Lizzy Williamson for sharing her work with me.

In the terms of the period, we might be tempted to say that it was a craft to be learnt through a prolonged period of apprenticeship, and mastery of the profession was achieved after spending years as a 'journeyman'.[80] But this terminology would evoke the model of medieval and early modern guilds, thus misleadingly implying a trajectory that leads to formal admission to a self-governing body of the members of an occupation, a model that certainly does not apply to people employed in service abroad. Professionalization is another term that has been proposed for the phenomenon, but it needs to be applied here with caution for the same reason.

Even if we recognize a continuity of the professions extending back into the middle ages, and the usefulness of the term for the analysis of pre- and early modern societies, late sixteenth-century diplomacy can only be described as a profession with some rather important qualifications.[81] The lists of criteria by which twentieth-century sociologists sought to define the professions don't apply here easily: people like Rogers are recognized for their expert knowledge and practical competence, but unlike lawyers, doctors, or clerics, early modern English diplomats don't seem to be characterized by an *esprit de corps*, have no jurisdiction over their field of activity, no communal, self-authenticating discourse that would distinguish them from people aspiring to their status—in fact, they do not even have a distinct field of activity or a term for their area of competence: while much is written about the office of the ambassador in the period, 'diplomacy' is a word which only enters circulation in the eighteenth century.[82] Last but not least, recruitment into diplomatic service happened through personal ties, patronage connections: in spite of the powerful and popular aspirational rhetoric, being given a chance to prove yourself was a result of connectedness and privilege.[83] Such discrepancies between modern criteria and early modern occupations have prompted historians of the professions to warn us that unless we want to back-project notions originating in the twentieth-century golden age of the proliferation of the professions, we will need to include in the category 'besides the traditional trinity of church, law, and medicine, all non-mercantile occupations followed by persons

---

[80] Although etymologically, journeyman means 'day-labourer', i.e. someone who is paid by the day, by the *journée*, the German term, 'Wandergeselle', and the word 'Wanderjahre' for the journeyman years, may serve as reminders of the tradition of mastering a trade by going on travels after completing the apprentice years.

[81] The view that professionalization is simply a hallmark of modernity, and professions as social formations only emerged in the eighteenth and especially in the nineteenth century, has frequently been challenged, and the legal, medical, military, and clerical professions have been pointed to as evidence of a much longer history. Cp. Wilfrid R. Prest (ed.), *The Professions in Early Modern England* (London: Croom Helm, 1987); Biow, *Doctors, Ambassadors, Secretaries*; Gieskes, *Representing the Professions*.

[82] On this last point, see Daniela Frigo, 'Prudence and Experience: Ambassadors and Political Culture in Early Modern Italy', *Journal of Medieval and Early Modern Studies*, 38 (2008), 15–34 at 15–16. Eliot Freidson, seeking to discern the ideal type of professionalism, distinguished among three models of controlling labour: in the market model, consumers control work; in bureaucracy, the managers; and in the professionalist model, the members of the occupation. Eliot Freidson, *Professionalism: The Third Logic* (Chicago: University of Chicago Press, 2001) 12. In these terms, early modern diplomacy is simply a bureaucratic occupation—diplomats are civil servants.

[83] I thank Tracey Sowerby for cautioning me on this point.

claiming gentility'.[84] The heavy emphasis on training and Burghley's careful attention to the list of people whose services he could count on, along with the number of people whose lives were spent as civil servants, often in diplomatic service, indicates that the English diplomatic service of the last decades of the sixteenth century nonetheless shows some signs of professionalization. Among long-serving diplomats of the period, there are occasional glimpses of a sense of a shared education and occupation, as when in 1610, Edward Wotton greeted Thomas Edmondes as a diplomat 'bred as it were in the same school with me under Sir Fra. Walsingham'.[85]

But the fact of the matter is that being a diplomat does not seem to have been 'an occupation' and diplomats did not constitute a distinct social group at all. A career that began with performing some basic service abroad could lead in a number of directions other than ambassadorship, and it was not necessarily understood as preparation for a career in foreign service. Because training in diplomacy meant a training in affairs of state in general: not only in the protocols and competences of delegation and representation, but also in politic analysis and prudent negotiation (that is, in the skills supported by the politic wisdom articulated and exercised in the form of Machiavellian maxims)[86] the preparation to serve abroad was preparation for entry not just to the diplomatic corps but to government service and political administration at large. It was the shared background of a large group of people who attempted to rise by making political employment their occupation: the group of 'politicians', a loosely conceived group that included 'men of business', secretaries, and agents, and whose margins were occupied by the facilitators and eager scholars trying to rise by obliging their betters through 'knowledge transactions'.[87] In contemporary literature, these people were understood as counsellors or magistrates, and the criteria for their employment, the specific competences and virtues expected of them, were codified in mirrors of princes and in works specifically describing politicians or counsellors. Lipsius's argument about mixed prudence was most alive as the question of the pressures and definitions of

---

[84] Prest (ed.), *The Professions in Early Modern England* 24. Cp. this rehearsal of the criteria derived from twentieth-century sociology, mollified by a distinction between core definition and the additions that measure the success of the professionalization of a field: 'the professions may be taken as all tertiary-sector occupations that are organised around a formal corpus of specialist knowledge with both a theoretical and a practical bearing ... In addition, there is often a distinctive ethos that focuses upon "service" (rather than production or distribution), indicating not that professionals are individually more altruistic or sweet-natured than others but simply that their occupations are centred upon the provision of expertise. Other correlates include: a high social prestige; a formalised process of training and qualification; and some degree of regulation or control of entry into the business—at its greatest extent leading to outright monopoly. The more successful any given profession, the more likely it was and is to enjoy those last attributes.' Penelope J. Corfield, *Power and the Professions in Britain, 1700–1850* (London: Routledge, 1995) 25–6.

[85] BL MS Stowe 171, f. 316, quoted in Maurice Lee, 'The Jacobean Diplomatic Service', *American Historical Review*, 72 (1967), 1264–82 at 1264.

[86] Cp. Millstone, 'Seeing Like a Statesman in Early Stuart England', 94–100, on politic analysis as practised by seventeenth-century English diplomats.

[87] Patrick Collinson, 'Puritans, Men of Business and Elizabethan Parliaments', *Parliamentary History*, 7 (1988), 187–211; M. A. R. Graves, 'The Management of the Elizabethan House of Commons: The Council's "Men-of-Business"', *Parliamentary History*, 2 (1983), 11–38; M. A. R. Graves, 'The Common Lawyers and the Privy Council's Parliamentary Men-of-Business, 1584–1601', *Parliamentary History*, 8 (1989), 189–215; Jardine and Sherman, 'Pragmatic Readers'.

virtuous action not by monarchs but by the servants of state. The scandal of Henry Wotton's famous quip, viz. that 'an ambassador is an honest man sent to lie abroad for the state' captured the ethical issues at stake, but contemporary and later manuals also explored the knowledge base required for successful service. The analogies with the learned professions were particularly suggestive: when at the beginning of the *Discorsi*, Machiavelli measured the state of political activity and its lack of a proper grounding in classical example to the medical profession as a normative example, he introduced a powerful way of talking about the art of the state. Doctors of the state were charged with keeping their patient healthy, but the metaphor also provided a basis for conceiving of them as a professional group.[88]

These political 'professionals' were not only in and out of service throughout their careers, rising, if they did, from one job to another: their employment abroad also alternated with assignments at home, and these different tasks were clearly understood as part of a single continuum of political service. Once someone had demonstrated his ability to serve in a certain field, the government counted on him, asking for his counsel or service when necessary (and when the factional dynamics allowed): Rogers, Carew, and Fletcher were all repeatedly called upon, sent on missions, or commissioned, either by the government or by one of the trading companies, to negotiate with foreign embassies arriving in England—even as they held various civic and crown offices at home. As the careers of as diverse figures as Stephen Powle, William Davison, Robert Beale, and Henry Wotton show, diplomatic service, whether as the Crown's agent or as resident ambassador, was ultimately expected to be a stepping stone to office or title at home, even though such expectations were often frustrated.[89] A career started in foreign missions could lead all the way up to the position of the secretary of state—a position which in the Elizabethan period was mostly filled by people with extensive diplomatic experience—and other domestic positions also seem to have required such background.[90] So much so, that most major political figures of late Elizabethan and early Stuart England who were not elder sons of aristocratic families began their careers in foreign service, as special envoys, secretaries to ambassadors, or even as secretaries to ambassadors' first secretaries, and even aristocrats used foreign travel as a preparation for a life in politics.[91] And while gentility whether by birth

---

[88] Hans Hattenhauer, *Geschichte des Beamtentums* (Handbuch des öffentlichen Dienstes; Köln, Berlin, Bonn, München: Carl Heymanns Verlag, 1980) 80–9, and the more detailed survey on the (primarily continental) literature, 'Grundzüge der Beamtenethik (1550–1650)', in Stolleis, *Staat und Staatsräson in der Frühen Neuzeit* 197–231.

[89] On their careers, see Virginia F. Stern, *Sir Stephen Powle of Court and Country: Memorabilia of a Government Agent for Queen Elizabeth I, Chancery Official, and English Country Gentleman* (Selinsgrove, PA: Susquehanna University Press, 1992); Nicholas Harris Nicolas, *Life of William Davison, Secretary of State and Privy Counsellor to Queen Elizabeth* (London: J. Nichols & son, 1823); Taviner, 'Robert Beale and the Elizabethan Polity'; Smith, *The Life and Letters of Sir Henry Wotton* 1:8–226.

[90] Most Elizabethan clerks of the Privy Council had substantial foreign experience: Jacqueline D. Vaughan, 'Secretaries, Statesmen and Spies: The Clerks of the Tudor Privy Council, c. 1540–c. 1603', PhD thesis (University of St Andrews, 2006) 46–7, 74–7.

[91] Stoye, *English Travellers Abroad, 1604–1667*; Bell, *A Handlist of British Diplomatic Representatives, 1509–1688*. Examples of foreign travel as initiation of young aristocrats to a political career include, most famously, Philip Sidney, but also people like the third Earl of Rutland, whose later offices did not

or at least by education was clearly a requirement for selection, nobility was not: under Elizabeth's reign, no nobleman was appointed resident ambassador.

In early modern England, then, diplomacy (broadly conceived) became an area where people aspiring to enter a political career could prove themselves, acquire a track record, demonstrate their competence and their willingness to serve. This emphasis on competence and experience as the requirements for political careers had important social consequences: crucially, it contributed to the transformation of the social base of the political class. In contradistinction to many other countries, English foreign service was neither the civic duty of the patriciate, nor the charge of the aristocracy, but mostly the occupation of the gentry, who could hope to convert their years of service to lucrative office and rise to knighthood or even nobility, as did for example Thomas Bodley, John Digby, and Dudley Carleton.[92] And while actual patterns of social mobility through political service may show such expectations to be largely illusory, the promise of social advancement associated with diplomacy nevertheless bestowed considerable social prestige upon the field and upon the competences that could help people enter or advance in foreign service. It is in this context that we ought to consider the circulation, production, and reproduction of diplomatic materials as practices that showed one knowledgeable about foreign affairs and to thus claim eligibility for employment.

TRAVELS, HOPES, AND RELATIONS

Relazioni in England were written as credentials for crown employment, submitted not only, or even primarily, by ambassadors but by other agents and private travellers, as 'masterpieces' produced during their time abroad. The accounts of Italy sent to Burghley by Stephen Powle clearly served such a purpose.[93] In his *Discourse Touching the Office of Principal Secretary of Estate*, Walsingham's secretary Nicholas Faunt surveys the documents to be collected and kept by the First Secretary. At the

---

require an expertise in foreign affairs per se. In the case of Sidney, the discrepancy between the aristocratic family background and the lack of a title which Sidney was trying to make up for with his learning and his display of competence and expertise lead to some famously unpleasant moments; see Jason Powell, 'Astrophil the Orator: Diplomacy and Diplomats in Sidney's *Astrophil and Stella*', in Jason Powell and William T. Rossiter (eds.), *Authority and Diplomacy from Dante to Shakespeare* (Farnham: Ashgate, 2013), 171–84 at 173–7; Mears, *Queenship and Political Discourse in the Elizabethan Realms* 116.

[92] Charles H. Carter, 'The Ambassadors of Early Modern Europe: Patterns of Diplomatic Representation in the Early Seventeenth Century', in Charles H. Carter (ed.), *From the Renaissance to the Counter-Reformation* (New York: Random House, 1965), 269–95 at 283–5.

[93] I thank Lizzy Williamson for calling my attention to these reports. See Stern, *Sir Stephen Powle of Court and Country* 66. A relation of 1583 is Bodleian MS Tanner 309 ff. 97r–115v, another one from 1587 is praised by Burghley in a letter reprinted in Stern, *Sir Stephen Powle of Court and Country* 214. The first of these was written before Powle's visit to Italy, indicating both the extent to which these reports were drawing on research in general and on earlier such relations in particular, and also showing how closely diplomacy and scholarship, reading, and experience were intertwined, and indeed how the work of writing could both prepare for travel and make up for the lack of it.

end of the list, he mentions texts that are both very important and in no short supply, either. As he says, it is important to have

> discripcions most exactly taken of other Countries as well by mappes and Cardes as by discoueringe the present state of their gouerment their alliances dependancs etc. with many other discourses...etc. all which sometimes may serue to verie good purpose, and which wilbee dayly deliuered to the Secr: especially if hee bee knowne to make accompt of vertuous imployment and of men that are liberally brought up,...seeinge there willbee nothinge offered to a personage of his place, that in their Specie may not some way bee proffitable beeinge effected in the ripenes of their witts, and with their greatest industrie and trauell both which...they will as freely bestowe upon him, as hee shalbee willinge to accepte the same at their hands and imploy it to the benefitt and seruice of their Soueraigne and Countrey.[94]

In his memorandum, Faunt singles out the *relazione* as his example of the kind of valuable document that will be 'daily delivered' to the Secretary, provided that he is known to reward such exertions. Established as the most familiar form of political knowledge transactions, it also played a role in patronage-seeking beyond the offices of the state secretariats—reminding us once again that the distinction is not necessarily clear in these cases. As part of his effort to assert himself as a dominant figure in English government, in the 1590s the Earl of Essex was building a new diplomatic and intelligence service, partly complementing, partly in direct competition with the networks run by Burghley.[95] In his efforts to prepare young men for political careers he was relying on the models established by the Queen's secretaries, as well as on the continental experience of such political professionals in his employment as Antonio Perez and Anthony Bacon. The instructions for foreign travel that were written by the earl or his secretaries, and their correspondence with the agents in the field, show that intelligence-gathering was understood both as a form of service and a preparatory exercise for later assignments, and that the *relazione* was the crucial genre in which knowledge was produced in the hope of favour or employment. The examples of *relazioni* produced by English travellers confirm Lizzy Williamson's insight about how little the difference could be between the motives, aims, and even the identities of aristocratic 'educational travellers' and crown servants, between tourists, agents, diplomats, and intelligencers, and also, between the kind of information collected by people on public and on private missions.[96] They also show young aristocrats and aspiring gentleman travellers emulating ambassadors in their textual work. The parallel and interrelated cases of Henry Hawkyns, Essex's agent in Venice, and Francis Davison, a gentleman using his travels to secure the continuing patronage of the earl, illustrate this point well.

---

[94] Bodleian MS Tanner 80, ff. 91–4, published in Charles Hughes, 'Nicholas Faunt's Discourse Touching the Office of Principal Secretary of Estate, &c. 1592', *The English Historical Review*, 20 (1905), 499–508 at 507–8.
[95] Gustav Ungerer, *A Spaniard in Elizabethan England*, 2 vols. (London: Tamesis, 1974, 1976); Paul E. J. Hammer, *The Polarisation of Elizabethan Politics: The Political Career of Robert Devereux, 2nd Earl of Essex, 1585–1597* (Cambridge: Cambridge University Press, 1999) 152–98; Gajda, *The Earl of Essex and Late Elizabethan Political Culture* 66–107.
[96] Williamson, 'Before "Diplomacy": Travel, Embassy and the Production of Political Information in the Later Sixteenth Century'.

In 1595, Essex sent Dr Henry Hawkyns (1553–1630) to work as his agent in Venice. Although Hawkyns was an accomplished and widely travelled civil lawyer, Essex's purpose of employing him in Venice, a 'state with which wee have lytle to doe' was 'rather your inablyinge hereafter then your present service'—that is, to prime him for further, more momentous tasks. The assignment that was to enable Hawkyns for future service included both the gathering of current intelligence (that is, of political news of consequence), and the compiling of a *relazione* of each Italian state 'for your [i.e. Hawkyns's] good and my instruction'. As the earl explained, Hawkyns was to

> gather unto yow suche particuler knowledge of every state in Italy as yow sett me downe the terretorye of every one, the quantitye and greatnes of it, the revenewe and how it is made, the stronge places, and with what garrison they are furnished, the knowne nombers of men of warre that maye be broughte of any sodayne to defende the state or invade any other, and by whome they are commaunded, the portes and havens of every one, and neere what greate towne they are scituated, the comodities that are vented, and whether they be caried, the supplye that it hath from abroade, and whence it commeth, by what lawe or customes every suche estate ys governed and by what ministers the prynce or state is most served.[97]

That he was to write such a report on *each* Italian state clearly implies writing reports based on secondary research—and for such work, Hawkyns was ideally placed. A model state bureaucracy situated at the crossroads of Europe, halfway between London and Istanbul, between Denmark and Sicily, between the Pyrenees and the Carpathians, Venice was home to a bustling informal and technically illegal market of political information, an international clearing house of political intelligence where foreign representatives, Venetian patricians and plebeians, intelligencers and professional scribes circulated and exchanged copies of various documents leaked from government circles—most importantly, ambassadorial *relazioni*.[98] What Hawkyns had to do was compile information from Venetian *relazioni* available at the civic and patrician archives and libraries of the city, or from intelligence professionals and scriveners some of whom 'made a profession of *relazioni*'[99]—but he does not seem to have been particularly successful at hooking up with the right people. Although he claimed to be spending 'almost every daye an houre or 2 in the Venetian libraries', he proceeded very slowly, and was also rebuked by the earl for the little discernment he was showing in gathering news to send home.[100] He dispatched home his first *relazione*, a description of Ferrara, in November 1596.[101]

---

[97] University of London, Senate House Library, MS 187, ff. 9v–11r, published in Paul E. J. Hammer, 'Essex and Europe: Evidence from Confidential Instructions by the Earl of Essex, 1595–6', *The English Historical Review*, 111 (1996), 357–81 at 374–7.

[98] de Vivo, *Information and Communication in Venice*.

[99] Fernand Braudel, *Structures of Everyday Life: The Limits of the Possible*, trans. Siân Reynolds (Civilization and Capitalism, 15th–18th Century; New York: Harper and Row, 1982) 575n104, 576 n127, 584n200, and 585n240.

[100] Ungerer, *A Spaniard in Elizabethan England* 2:171–3; Hammer, 'Essex and Europe: Evidence from Confidential Instructions by the Earl of Essex, 1595–6', 363.

[101] Lambeth Palace Library MS 660 ff. 240–8. See Thomas Birch, *Memoirs of the Reign of Elizabeth, from the Year 1581 Till Her Death*, 2 vols. (London: A. Millar, 1754), 2:204, 255, for Hawkyns's letter

At the same time as Hawkyns, a younger gentleman was also travelling on the Continent, striving to 'show himself to be a man experienced in foreign ways' (as Gentili instructed) and secure the recognition and support of Essex, volunteering the kind of work Hawkyns was employed to do. After passing through Germany, Francis Davison (1575–1613?) and his tutor Edward Smyth arrived in Venice in winter 1595–6, spent about a year there and in Tuscany, and continued to France in 1597.[102]

Davison was linked to the circle of Essex's clients through his membership at Gray's Inn, where along with Francis Bacon he was an important contributor to the revels of 1594–5 recorded in the *Gesta Grayorum*, but the Earl's attention to Francis was primarily due to his father, William Davison. Secretary Davison fell from the Queen's grace for signing the death warrant of Mary Queen of Scots in 1587. In the 1590s, Essex was aggressively campaigning to fill court positions with his own candidates. He advocated William Davison's readmission to court and reappointment as secretary of state, confirming the Davisons as loyal members of his faction.

If William Davison hoped for Essex's help in regaining royal favour, his son clearly perceived Essex's patronage as his chance to rise in politics; he was using his travels to prove himself deserving of the Earl's continuing support by sending home political intelligence. In these efforts, Francis was encouraged by his father, who also helped him with advice on intelligence-gathering. Like Daniel Rogers and others, William Davison started his career in the service of Walsingham in the 1570s, served on various missions to Scotland and the Netherlands from 1574, and finally became a Secretary of State and member of the Privy Council. When he drew up his systematic instructions about travel for his son, detailing in the form of a Ramist bracketed diagram of headings and subheadings what matters should be observed in foreign states, he was relying both on his habit of developing such systematizations of political and other topics and also on decades of diplomatic experience.[103]

Other non-official English travellers to the continent received similar instructions. Methods for travel often reflected a general humanist ideology of civic and moral education,[104] but there is a significant set of letters of advice that aim to

---

dated 29 November 1596, N.S. in which it was enclosed and Anthony Bacon's acknowledgement of its receipt, dated 9 January 1596/7.

[102] The original licence is BL MS Harley 38, f. 188. The best account of Davison's career is Richard McCoy, 'Lord of Liberty: Francis Davison and the Cult of Elizabeth', in John Guy (ed.), *The Reign of Elizabeth I* (Cambridge: Cambridge University Press, 1995), 212–28. The information from Anthony Bacon's papers at Lambeth Palace Library is summarized in Hammer, 'Essex and Europe: Evidence from Confidential Instructions by the Earl of Essex, 1595–6', 364n363.

[103] His advice survives in BL MS Harley 252 f. 123; Harley 290 f. 272 (in the hand of the addressee, Francis); Harley 6893 ff. 169–72; it was published in *Profitable Instructions Describing What Speciall Obseruations Are to be Taken by Trauellers in All Nations, States and Countries; Pleasant and Profitable. By the Three much Admired, Robert, late Earle of Essex. Sir Philip Sidney. And, Secretary Davison* (London: for Beniamin Fisher, 1633), sigs. B1r–C4v. There are several further such Ramist diagrams among the miscellaneous papers of the Davisons, see e.g. BL MS Harley 588 ff. 2–3, and especially f. 4, which is a diagram of the branches and divisions of politics.

[104] On the *ars apodemica*, see Justin Stagl, *A History of Curiosity: The Theory of Travel 1550–1800* (Chur, Switzerland: Harwood Academic Publisher, 1995).

initiate the recipient to the concerns and topics of political information-gathering in a more practical vein: the instructions by William Davison, as well as those by Burghley,[105] Walsingham,[106] Sidney,[107] Essex, or Francis Bacon[108] are examples of such documents, several of which circulated widely in manuscript before they would have reached print several decades or centuries later, if indeed ever. The advice they offer is more concise than the guidelines laid down in some academic books on travel, and often also more pragmatic than methodical. In a letter that enjoyed wide manuscript circulation in the period, with at least a dozen copies surviving, Fulke Greville advised his young cousin Greville Varney then preparing to go to the Continent on how to make himself 'more profitable to his country' by gathering political information abroad. Greville suggests that 'your end must not be, like an Intelligencer, to spend all your time in fishing after the present news, humours, graces, or disgraces of the Court, which happily may change before you come home: but your Lordship's better and more constant ground will be to know the consanguinities, alliances, and estates of their princes, the proportion betwixt the nobility and the magistracy,' and so on[109]—in other words, precisely the kind of information *relazioni* provide instead of what Rogers calls 'false bruites', baseless rumours that have a shorter shelf life than the time it takes to deliver them. Greville's suggestions as to what kind of information would work in the traveller's favour at home are concluded by a note that actually renounces the attempt to be formally organized: 'To be short, because my purpose is not to bring all your observations to heads, but only these few to let you know what manner of return your friends will expect from you.' But even when they insist on the casual nature of the advice, such lists do in fact closely resemble such systematic *aides-mémoire* as the note headed 'Queste cose si ricercano per fare una Relazione', a list of topics drawn up to help the writing of an ambassadorial relation, Venetian style.[110]

---

[105] 'A memoryall for y Earle of Rutland, 20 Januar 1570: thynges to be considered in your travayles'. TNA SP 12/77 no. 6, ff. 10–11.

[106] The letter, now lost, is printed in Read, *Mr. Secretary Walsingham and the Policy of Queen Elizabeth* 18–20.

[107] Letter to Robert Sidney, c.1581, Kuin (ed.), *The Correspondence of Sir Philip Sidney* 878–82, and also printed in *Profitable instructions* (1633).

[108] Essex's instructions were published by Hammer, 'Essex and Europe: Evidence from Confidential Instructions by the Earl of Essex, 1595–6'. Bacon or Essex are the authors of a course of study addressed in three consecutive letters to the Earl of Rutland, moving from general principles through recommendations for reading to observations to be made in travel in the third letter, see Stewart (ed.), *The Oxford Francis Bacon I: Early Writings, 1584–1596* 607–74.

[109] This letter was attributed to Bacon by Spedding, and reprinted until 2012 as the second of the three letters of advice to Rutland; for an edition, see Vickers (ed.), *Francis Bacon: The Major Works* 76–8. In 2009 I stumbled upon the only surviving copy of a letter in Huntington MS EL 2805, ff. 30r–v, which Alan Stewart has since established to be Bacon's hitherto missing second letter to Rutland. See the textual introductions to his edition for the authoritative account of the authorship and transmission of the three letters to Rutland and of the Greville letter in Stewart (ed.), *The Oxford Francis Bacon I: Early Writings, 1584–1596* 651–6, 1006–13. I would like to thank Alan Stewart for sharing with me his work in advance of publication.

[110] Donald E. Queller, 'How to Succeed as an Ambassador: A Sixteenth Century Venetian Document', in Joseph R. Strayer and Donald E. Queller (eds.), *Post Scripta: Essays on Medieval Law and the Emergence of the European State in Honor of Gaines Post* (Studia Gratiana; Roma: Libreria Ateneo Salesiano, 1972), 653–71 at 670–1. The first part of the document transcribed by Queller,

In drafting his first report, the relation of Saxony he sent home to Essex in 1596, Francis Davison was probably organizing his notes with the help of his father's diagram of divisions and subdivisions, and he seems to have done so quite successfully. Anthony Bacon, Essex's secretary certainly praised this *relazione*, 'the first fruites' of Davison's travels, as a piece 'wherein you show no less diligence in observing and collecting, than judgment in orderly disposing the same', advising him 'to proceed and continue'.[111] Davison thanked Bacon for his kind words and 'friendly counsel, of continuing that kind of observation, and making use of my travel' and promised to 'labour to yield... my honourable friends some satisfaction answerable to the expectation you have so unworthily conceived of me'.[112] Eager to please but slow to produce, Davison a couple of months later wrote to Bacon that 'I am ashamed of myself that I have no new relation or discourse ready of some of those parts of Italy, wherby I might both have testified my duty to his lordship, and made some amends for the errors and oversights of the last.'[113]

Throughout his journey, Francis was relying on the support of the Earl of Essex, both financially and also in the form of letters of introduction,[114] and while in his letters he regularly included news, the intellectual products he was offering to deserve the Earl's patronage were clearly meant to be his *relazioni*. His letters to Anthony Bacon and his father mix requests for money with worries about the reception of the first *relazione* he sent and what that meant for his work. As he explained in a letter written to William Davison from Lucca: 'Touching whether I have made the same use of our travel in Italy that it pleased you to think I did in Germany, I have gathered and observed divers particulars, both of Tuscany and some other places, which I forbear to reduce into an absolute discourse before I hear how my Lord accepted of my other.'[115] Beyond the personal gratification and further instructions, a letter from the earl was desirable for two reasons: first, Davison probably realized that his projected Italian *relazioni* were in direct competition with the assignment Essex gave to Dr Hawkyns. As his despairing tutor reported to William Davison from Venice, Francis was already in a scandalous personal quarrel with Hawkyns, so the earl's explicit approval was becoming desperately necessary. The second reason was even more practical: Francis Davison's credit was bad; as his father failed to pay their bills of exchange at home, creditors in Italy were less and less willing to oblige them. A piece of paper indicative of Essex's favour would not only have reignited his hopes for advancement at home

---

'Ricordi per Ambasciatori con un epilogo breve die quelle cose che si ricercan per fare una relazione' also survives in an early modern English translation, 'Remembraunces for dispatche of businesses and suites in Courtes', BL MS Sloane 1710, ff. 37r–v. The English manuscript does not, however, include the 'breve epilogo'.

[111] Anthony Bacon to Francis Davison in Florence, 7 August 1596, excerpted in Birch, *Memoirs*, 2:91. The letter also appears in Francis Davison, *The Poetical Rhapsody: To Which Are Added Several Other Pieces*, ed. Nicholas Harris Nicolas, 2 vols. (London: William Pickering, 1826) xiii.

[112] Francis Davison to Anthony Bacon from Florence, 21 September 1596; Davison, *The Poetical Rhapsody* xvii.

[113] 16 October 1596; Birch, *Memoirs*, 2:178 and Davison, *The Poetical Rhapsody* xix–xx.

[114] Hammer, 'Essex and Europe: Evidence from Confidential Instructions by the Earl of Essex, 1595–6', 364.

[115] 20 November 1596; Davison, *The Poetical Rhapsody* xxxii.

but at the same time also have helped to fix the more immediate problem. As he reminded his father: 'you know the old rule, *haud facile emergunt, quorum virtutibus obstat res angusta domi*[116]—and not only in money but in credit, hope, reputation, and assurance of some kind of recompense of all their pains. A letter from his Lordship would be exceeding welcome, and might work extraordinary effects...'[117]

Essex's reply was delayed because of the Cadiz expedition and its aftermath, but Bacon did not forget Davison's request. In a note of 22 December, he reminded the earl: 'That his lordship would vouchsafe 2 or 3 lines to young Mr. Davison, with some token, as he said he would, for his encouragement.' Essex replied in the margin: 'If I may know by whom Mr. Bacon would make over my bill I would give Sir Gelly Merick order for 200 crowns,'[118] and on 8 January 1596–7 he at last wrote to Davison, thanking him for 'your kindness to myself', and asserting that 'My love to your worthy father, my expectations that you will truly inherit his virtues, and the proof I have seen of your well spending abroad, are the three strong bands to tie my affections unto you.' But the earl would have been hard pressed to reflect in any specificity on the proof of Francis 'well spending abroad', i.e. on the *relazione* of Saxony, because whatever the 'oversights' may have been in the piece, by the time Essex would have looked at it, someone had considered it valuable enough to steal it from his chamber. Writing the next day to Henry Hawkyns, Anthony Bacon explained that in order to prevent similar losses, he had decided to give Hawkyns's relation about Ferrara to the earl only after having made a copy of it.[119]

During their time abroad, Davison and Hawkyns were producing knowledge that was meant to advance them in further employment. Although Davison was on a study trip with his tutor, whereas Hawkyns went to Venice in Essex's employ, they were both sending home materials which were intended to show political expertise and prove them to be more than mere intelligencers. Writing in the genre of the *relazione*, they were effectively inhabiting the role of the professional politician, and it wasn't entirely their fault that the aspirations they inscribed in the form of their reports were crushed soon after their return home in 1598. Francis Davison's situation was made difficult by his own quarrelsome nature and such animosities as he had with the son of a certain Mr Thornelle, which started back in Italy and ended in a fatal duel in England in the summer of 1598, leaving Davison seriously wounded and young Thornelle dead.[120] The decline of his patron's influence at the end of the decade and his fall in 1601 obviously affected his prospects, and although in 1602, Davison's name was briefly floated as a possible member of Sir Thomas Parry's Paris embassy, he was almost immediately dropped from those considered for a job and gave up on his political career, so that on 8 June 1602 John Chamberlain wrote to Dudley Carleton (who was very eager for news about

---

[116] 'Not easily do they rise whose virtues are hindered by the small means of the home' (Juvenal)—or, as Burton translates it in *The Anatomy of Melancholy*: ''tis hard for a poor man to rise'.
[117] 20 November 1596, Davison, *The Poetical Rhapsody* xxxii.
[118] CP 47, no. 45.   [119] Birch, *Memoirs*, 2: 255.
[120] Thomas Ferrers to Humphrey Ferrers, 19 July 1598, BL MS Stowe 150/44, f. 114.

the preparations of the embassy, and was to become Parry's secretary) that 'yt seemes younge Davison meanes to take another course and turne Poet, for he hath lately set out certain sonnets and epigrams'.[121] Dr Henry Hawkyns, whose Italian *relazioni* held the explicit promise of later, more momentous employment, fared even worse. In 1601, he was arrested for his participation in the Essex rebellion, and, with the execution of the earl and the death of Anthony Bacon, he, like Davison, also lost the patrons on whom his political future depended. The knowledge they produced abroad and brought home thus never afforded them the benefits they were hoping for—but even in their failure, their efforts and aspirations exemplify the expectation of domestic empowerment by return from overseas.

SHAKESPEARE'S ELSINORE: THE RIGHTS OF RETURN

Rosencrantz and Guildenstern, the two characters whom I would like to imagine as arriving in the play in a *relazione* written by an aging diplomat to secure the acknowledgement of his service abroad, are also emblematic of the play's attention to the impact of foreign travel and foreign intelligence not only on the state of Denmark but also on those personally involved in them: that is to say, to the rewards and benefits of travel. Reynaldo is the play's intelligencer, whom we only see as he receives his instructions and the promise implicit in Polonius's suggestion that by spying on Laertes, he is becoming like those people 'of wisdom and of reach' who can 'by indirections find directions out' (2.1.64–8). The play's ambassadors, Cornelius and Voltemand, are thanked 'for your well-took labour' and are promised that they will 'feast together' with the king. For their 'visitation' at Elsinore, Rosencrantz and Guildenstern are also promised to 'receive such thanks / As fits a king's remembrance' (2.2.25–6). Eager to serve, they accompany Hamlet on his embassy to England, an 'employment' Hamlet thinks they 'made love to'— but in a frightful departure from the pattern established by Cornelius and Voltemand, the wages of this employment are death. Their embassy becomes an image of unreliable recompense, and thus, of the petty and tragic ways in which our outcomes forever remain beyond our control.

Hamlet's recollection of how he changed the deadly letter carried by Rosencrantz and Guildenstern into their death sentence begins with his recollection of his sleepless night on board the ship, and of his rash indiscretion which made him search his companions and read their grand commission:

> Rashly—
> And prais'd be rashness for it: let us know
> Our indiscretion sometime serves us well
> When our deep plots do pall; and that should learn us
> There's a divinity that shapes our ends,
> Rough-hew them how we will—

---

[121] Norman Egbert McClure (ed.), *The Letters of John Chamberlain*, 2 vols. (Philadelphia: American Philosophical Society, 1939) 1:142, 149, 156.

> HOR. That is most certain.
> HAM. Up from my cabin,
> My sea-gown scarf'd about me, in the dark
> Grop'd I to find out them... (5.2.6–11)

We may have our doubts whether Rosencrantz and Guildenstern agreed with Hamlet on the exact nature and identity of the higher power that shaped their ends, but it is clear that as far as the unpredictable link between expectations and results, between deeds and recompense is concerned, their experience on board that ship mirrors Hamlet's—or rather, their misfortune is the mirror image of Hamlet's luck that night. If anyone, they could complain about 'the spurns / That patient merit of the unworthy takes' (3.1.73–4). They remain so closely associated with frustrated expectations that even bringing news of their death must remain unrewarded. Arriving at the end of the play, and realizing that 'the ears are senseless that should give us hearing / to tell him his commandment is fulfill'd, / That Rosencrantz and Guildenstern are dead', the English Ambassador worries 'Where should we have our thanks?' (5.2.374–7).

The expectation of reward on return structures ambassadors' experience, and it becomes the trope that articulates other types of foreign travel and return from abroad throughout the play. Such coming and going is a particularly striking feature of *Hamlet*, although it is often overlooked as we attend to the claustrophobia of the Danish prison-state and to the tortured interiority of Hamlet and Claudius. Official business in 1.2 involves the sending of ambassadors to Norway, the permission granted to Laertes to go to France, as well as the King denying Hamlet his wish to go to Wittenberg. As soon as the court leaves, we learn that Horatio has just arrived from there. Then Laertes takes off for France, with Reynaldo being sent after him. Having been sent for, Rosencrantz and Guildenstern arrive, presumably also from Wittenberg, followed by the ambassadors returning from Norway. In a theatrically self-conscious gesture, the travelling players talk about the success of the boys' companies of London, as if they were arriving directly from there. When Hamlet is heading down to the harbour to set sail for England, he encounters the army of Fortinbras passing through the country on its way from Norway to Poland. The play concludes with a series of characters returning from abroad. Laertes is back from France, leading a rebellion. Hamlet follows, having dispatched Ros and Guil. Finally, Fortinbras shows up, following hot on the heels of the puzzled English ambassadors. These departures and arrivals are not always rewarded as expected, but each of them links spatial mobility to social mobility or political empowerment, and attending to them closely affords a perspective on the play that expands rather than supersedes the analytic focus on interiority, on 'that within which passes show'.

'So Rosencrantz and Guildenstern go to't' (5.2.56)—Horatio's laconic response to the light-hearted providentialism Hamlet uses to justify the 'defeat' (5.2.58) of Rosencrantz and Guildenstern reflects his situation as another 'fellow student' trying to make himself useful at the Danish court. Although rarely considered in this light, Horatio is a striking example of the uses and rewards of foreign experience in Denmark. Entreated to join Marcellus in his watch on the platform of the castle and confirm whether the apparition they had already seen twice on previous nights is indeed a ghost or only their 'fantasy', Horatio, the scholar, seems well versed in ghost-lore, able to enumerate quickly the various possible reasons for the Ghost's appearance, and to recognize how 'of the truth' of common assumptions about ghosts 'this present object made probation'. Which is not to say that his scholarship is actually able to divine the Ghost's significance. Fortunately, he isn't only, or even primarily, an expert on spirits that walk the night. Unable to decide 'in what particular thought to work', he opines that the apparition 'bodes some strange eruption to our state' (1.1.70–2). And about the matters of state, he is clearly and emphatically knowledgeable. His interlocutors are puzzled by the desperate military effort that 'nightly toils the subject of the land': there is a night watch, cannons are being cast, ammunition being imported, and the shipyards are working 24/7. It is clear that Denmark is anticipating a major invasion from overseas, but the specifics of the threat await the explanation of 'he that knows'. To Marcellus's 'Who is't that can inform me?' Horatio replies with a smug show of modesty: 'That can I—at least the whisper goes so'. and launches on an extended account of Dano-Norwegian relations in bewildering technical detail, reminding his audience not only of the familiar story of the single combat between Hamlet Sr and Fortinbras Sr but also of the 'sealed compact, Well ratified by law and heraldry', which determined the fate of some territories once held by Norway. His familiarity with the dynastic conflict and its background in diplomatic treaties helps him explain the most recent developments: Fortinbras Jr's recruitment of an expeditionary force and his plans to reclaim lands his father lost to Denmark. As readers of Daniel Rogers's *Discourse*, we may note here the play's parallel with the 1588 account. Writing about the 'foure Bishoprickes' of Norway, Rogers notes that they are

> now reduced to the Crowne of Denmarke; for the kingdome of Norway by diuers transactions, hath been made subiecte vnto the realme of Denmarke, by hard Condytions.[122]

In *Hamlet*, Norway only loses territory, but remains a sovereign entity: nonetheless, Rogers's reference to the Kalmar Union of the Scandinavian kingdoms, which serves as an explanation of the present conditions of the region, strongly resonates with Shakespeare's text. Once again: my aim is not necessarily to establish Rogers's *relazione* as a 'source' of the play, but rather, to show that the English scholar–diplomat's display of expertise, a combination of deep historical learning with an awareness of the most current developments, situates Horatio's performance, and so illuminates it.

When early in the next scene, before moving on to his plan for the peaceful resolution of the conflict, the King rehearses a narrative of the events that led to it, his lines verify the accuracy of Horatio's detailed account, showing Horatio a supremely competent analyst, closely acquainted with the esoteric business of regional diplomacy, although obviously not with the King's most recent plans. On his first appearance, then, Horatio is established as 'he that knows', as the character

---

[122] Huntington MS EL 1608, 4v.

who knows what the King knows, as someone familiar with the *arcana imperii*, the motives and intentions of rulers, with the business of politics that is normally hidden from public view. His knowledge puts him on a par with the King and his closest advisors—but his status shows him a marginal entity, moving among people watching on the ramparts while the rest of the court celebrates. He is a recent arrival from Wittenberg, a man whose national identity is unclear, and whose ability to advise and serve, to discuss international affairs, is of a piece with his lack of familiarity with Danish custom, both being a function of his having only recently arrived.

Lest we dismiss his assertion that he is 'more an antic roman than a Dane' as purely figurative, we ought to note that in response to Francisco's 'who's there', he says 'Friends to this ground', leaving 'and liegemen to the Dane' to his friend Marcellus. More strikingly still, he is clearly baffled by the local custom of health drinking accompanied by kettle-drums, trumpets, and a salvo from guns, prompting Hamlet, who is 'native here', to offer the extended self-ethnography of the Danish proclivity to drunkenness. This is the only moment when this play otherwise uninterested in issues of national character makes such an ethnographic gesture, a gesture that is made as if to drive home the point that Horatio is an international student of international relations.[123] He calls the Ghost's voice from the cellarage 'wondrous strange', and Hamlet promptly admonishes him that therefore he should 'as a stranger bid it welcome' (1.5.165), a construction in which 'as a stranger' might be modifying either the subject or the object, and Hamlet seems to actually mean it both ways: you should welcome this strange thing as you would welcome a stranger, and you should welcome this strange thing, being a stranger yourself.

His situation makes Horatio particularly dependent on his learning in establishing social connections: while there may be more things in this heaven and earth than are dreamt of in his philosophy (1.5.166–7), it is this philosophy, and particularly its insight into apparitions, that makes Marcellus ask for Horatio's advice on the Ghost, and it is Horatio's expert knowledge and his dexterity with intelligence that will allow him to move up at the Elsinore court. As an outsider in Denmark, he must rely on his somewhat abstract, deracinated learning to make up for what he is lacking in more practical knowledge to advance himself. Although he had known Hamlet from Wittenberg, that familiarity on its own has not been sufficient for him to reintroduce himself to the Prince, even though he appears to have been in Denmark for a while by the time the play starts. When Marcellus calls upon him for help with foreign states and undiscovered countries, the two being inextricably intertwined in the Denmark whose ghostly king 'was and is the question of these

---

[123] Artillery accompaniment was part of being dined and wined by royalty, and in Denmark there was a heavy emphasis on the wine—King Frederick entertained Thomas Bodley with 'hearty quaffs' and '33 shottes of great artillerie' but the former not the latter was the reason why Bodley then for a day 'was fitte to doe nothinge'; 'drink and gunshot' also rounded off the London visit of Christian IV in 1606. See Gehring, *Anglo-German Relations and the Protestant Cause* 100; Maurice Lee (ed.), *Dudley Carleton to John Chamberlain, 1603–1624: Jacobean Letters* (New Brunswick: Rutgers University Press, 1972) 87, respectively. Even Hamlet's ethnography had serious diplomatic relevance.

wars' (1.1.111), Horatio sees his chance. As the Ghost refuses to yield to his command, he suggests to Marcellus and Bernardo to 'impart what we have seen tonight / Unto young Hamlet' (1.1.169–70), and at the end of the next scene, he volunteers to 'deliver / Upon the witness of these gentlemen / This marvel to' the prince (1.2.193–5). The witnesses, Bernardo and Marcellus, the sentinels to whom the Ghost first appeared, fade out at the end of Act 1, never to re-enter. Horatio, on the other hand, emerges from the ghostly encounter as Hamlet's almost inseparable friend. His curious knowledge transaction with the guards that we witnessed in 1.1 has paid off: through his performance of expertise in political matters, this wandering scholar has been able to emerge as the spokesman of the guards approaching the Prince, and thus launch his career at the court of Elsinore.[124]

Although spatial mobility does not always result in social mobility or in political empowerment in the play, making Horatio's case the exception rather than the rule, Shakespeare's *Hamlet* is nevertheless consistent in associating travel, arrival, and return with a promise of advancement and of attaining political power. As Horatio, Barnardo, and Marcellus puzzle over the Ghost and the predicament of Denmark in the first scene, they link the Ghost to Fortinbras's approach. By invoking the apparitions that portended the fall of Caesar (1.1.116ff), Horatio also indicates that more might be at stake here than some lands lost by old Fortinbras to old Hamlet. His interpretation is quickly marginalized by Hamlet's *tête-à-tête* with the Ghost, which turns Hamlet's attention (and with it, the attention of the interpretive tradition) from the play's present toward the past, from foreign to familiar matters.

But we ought to realize just how prescient Horatio's reading is, with its use of the figure of the Ghost to formulate a link between the fate of the crown and Fortinbras's approach, and recognize the broader purchase of such a link, namely, that throughout the play challenges to Claudius's reign are voiced by characters returning from foreign locations. The analogy between Fortinbras, Hamlet, and Laertes as their fathers' revengers is often remarked upon: but we should also note that each of them voices a claim upon the throne of Denmark as well, and they each do so as they return to Elsinore from abroad. 'Laertes shall be king!' is what his supporters shout when he returns from France in Act 4. Hamlet first talks about his own frustrated ambition for the crown, about Claudius having 'popp'd in between th'election and my hopes' (5.2.65) on arrival from his abortive embassy, and answers Horatio's concern that 'It must be shortly known to him from England / What the issue of the business there,' by asserting that 'It will be short. The interim is mine' (5.2.71–3)—which can only mean that he is now ready to take action, action that will inevitably lead to his challenge of the sovereign.

Of the three sons, it is Fortinbras who makes good on the promise of return, and his success is articulated by his structural association with the Ghost. These two characters frame the play as sudden and threatening appearances, men returning from countries that remain undiscovered in the play, characters whose arrival is linked through staging as well as through the deeds they are known for. As the

---

[124] I will consider his trajectory in the final section of Chapter 3.

Diplomatic Writing, Political Careers, and the World of Hamlet   129

bewildered witnesses put it, the Ghost usurps 'this time of night, / Together with that fair and warlike form / In which the majesty of buried Denmark / Did sometimes march' (1.1.46–9) and they note that the apparition frowns exactly the way Hamlet did 'when in an angry parle / He smote the sledded Polacks on the ice' (1.1.65–6). In the last scene, young Fortinbras is returning from his campaign 'against the Polack' (2.2.63, 75)—their military intervention in the same country, is a source of their charismatic authority, marking them as the two true soldiers of the play.[125] They also look their part: the Ghost's armour is like 'the very armour he had on / When he th'ambitious Norway combated' (1.1.60–1)—that Norway being of course Fortinbras senior. When Fortinbras appears at the end of the play, he will be distinguished from the Danish courtiers by an armour similar to (or perhaps, due to the exigencies of the company wardrobe, the very same as) the Ghost's own. Reverberations of the din of war reinforce the parallel: the brazen cannons that were being daily cast at the beginning of the play and were first fired just before the Ghost enters in 1.4, are part of 'the soldier's music and the rite of war' by the time Fortinbras closes the play by sending someone 'go bid the soldiers shoot'.[126]

Fortinbras's first appearance on stage, in Act 4, follows closely upon the Ghost's fade-out, his disappearance from the play at the end of Act 3. This sequencing opens up the intriguing possibility of the same actor playing the two characters. Less speculatively and more importantly, it invites a reading in which the Ghost is displaced not (or not only) by a Hamlet turned ghostly by his encounter with it,[127] nor perhaps by a Hamlet writing himself into kingship and into his father's role with the help of his father's signet,[128] not even by the skull of the jester,[129] but by the warrior–prince Fortinbras, who (like the Ghost he uncannily and unwittingly doubles, and of whom he is not an heir but rather an equal) unexpectedly returns from beyond the boundaries of the world of this play.[130] Arguably, the closest we get in the play to the fulfilment of the constant movement towards remembrance,

---

[125] Hampton, *Fictions of Embassy* 145–6.
[126] Marcellus inquires about the war preparations at 1.1.70–9, and Horatio explains that they are a response to the threat of Fortinbras's 'list of landless resolutes' (1.1.98). In 1.4 the stage direction says that 'a flourish of trumpets and two pieces goes off' (1.4.6 SD), which gives an opportunity for Hamlet to hold forth about Danish custom, mostly cut in F, and cut off by the Ghost's entrance. Although the SD at 1.4.6 is Q2 only, Horatio's question ('what does this meane my Lord?') and Hamlet's reply ('The King doth wake tonight...') clearly call for some noise. Similarly, the last stage direction of the play, 'Exeunt Marching, after which, a Peale of Ordenance are shot off' is F1 only, but Fortinbras's last line explicitly calls for it.
[127] Barbara Everett, '*Hamlet*: A Time to Die', *Shakespeare Survey*, 30 (1977), 117–23; Marjorie Garber, *Shakespeare's Ghost Writers: Literature as Uncanny Causality* (London: Methuen, 1987) 162.
[128] Garber, *Shakespeare's Ghost Writers* 19; Hampton, *Fictions of Embassy* 158–60.
[129] Peter Stallybrass, '"Well Grubbed, Old Mole": Marx, *Hamlet*, and the (Un)Fixing of Representation', in Jean E. Howard and Scott Cutler Shershow (eds.), *Marxist Shakespeares* (London: Routledge, 2001), 16–30 at 27.
[130] On how closely the two figures are connected to each other, not only via the genealogy of the conflict between Norway and Denmark, i.e. in terms of the plot, but also dramaturgically, see Anselm Haverkamp, 'The Ghost of History: Hamlet and the Politics of Paternity', *Law and Literature*, 18 (2006), 171–98 at 179–82. Haverkamp notes how 'the Ghost accompanies the danger embodied by [Fortinbras]'—I argue that even more is at stake here: they are each other's doubles or ghosts, one fading out (3.4.136) shortly before the other finally enters the stage in person (4.4.1–7).

repetition, recurrence, to an extinction of the past in the fullness of its reoccurrence (of which fullness the political form is succession, *le roi est mort, vive le roi*) is not in Hamlet's work of mourning (which, as David Kastan has recently reminded us, is precisely the work of breaking the cycle of repetition by learning to forget[131]), but rather in the victorious re-entry of Fortinbras. It is Fortinbras, not Hamlet, who, in the last moment of the play, in an outcome discussed and dreaded in Act 1 by everyone except the Ghost and Hamlet, returns to claim his 'rights of memory' (5.2.394), effectively becoming Denmark, the Dane. At the beginning of the play, we see an empty stage, and a figure in armour entering to Horatio and a couple of others. At the end, we see a stage littered with corpses, and a figure in armour entering to Horatio and a couple of others. And if the armour worn by the only father calling for revenge, and the armour worn by the only son the play allows a satisfying revenge[132] might in fact be the same, whoever plays the Ghost may easily play Fortinbras as well. Fortinbras might just be the most uncanny character in this play, no mere double of Hamlet, but a spectral and theatrical iteration (a theatrical rather than dramatic double) of none other than the Ghost.

The play's concern with *repetition* has prompted an entire interpretive tradition, not least through readings of Freud and Marx.[133] Instead of further exploring this concern, I am here interested in a complementary obsession the play has with the figure of *return*, understood not as the temporal recurrence or reoccurrence of an event, but as the spatial reappearance of a person from somewhere else. (The Ghost is the figure that mediates between these two notions—as soon as he speaks, he casts himself not as a repetition of a previous apparition or of a departed person, but as that person returning from beyond the grave, as it were: while his first appearances might imply that it is time that is out of joint, once he starts speaking about Purgatory, it is clear that it is himself who has been dislocated, confined somewhere he is now visiting from.) The trope of political culture that equates return with the promise of advancement controls not only the fortunes and misfortunes of the denizens and strangers at the court of Elsinore, but the fate of the crown of Denmark as well: in Shakespeare's *Hamlet*, return from abroad amounts to a bid for power. Bids for sovereign power, open challenges to the crown, only seem to emerge from outside the world of the play.

The play's insistence on the topology of the hope for empowerment, imagined as a function of one's arrival from abroad, is inscribed in the play's larger mimetic structures, namely, in its rarely noted or discussed persistence in observing the unity of location.[134] Elsinore castle and its surroundings, where characters depart

---

[131] David Scott Kastan, *A Will to Believe: Shakespeare and Religion* (Oxford: Oxford University Press, 2014) 141.

[132] Along with many others that I have happily inhabited and fully assimilated so I no longer even know they were his, this point I also owe to David Kastan: *A Will to Believe* 143.

[133] See e.g. Garber, *Shakespeare's Ghost Writers: Literature as Uncanny Causality* 163–72; Stallybrass, '"Well Grubbed, Old Mole": Marx, *Hamlet*, and the (Un)Fixing of Representation', 23–4.

[134] It was pointed out by Foakes, who interprets it in the framework of claustrophobia and Denmark being a prison: R. A. Foakes, '*Hamlet* and the Court of Elsinore', *Shakespeare Survey*, 9 (1956), 35–43 at 38; cp. also Keith Brown, 'Hamlet's Place on the Map', *Shakespeare Studies*, 4 (1968), 160–82 at 169–72.

Diplomatic Writing, Political Careers, and the World of Hamlet   131

from and return to, are the play's only setting.[135] The fictional topography of the play limits Denmark to Elsinore, where everything that happens further away from the castle than the nearby graveyard or the port which the castle directly overlooks[136] is immediately abroad—and everything that takes place abroad is only related in narrative. The locations that are accessed via the graveyard or the port: the undiscovered countries of Purgatory, of England, Poland, Norway, France, of the London theatre world or of the international waters beset with pirates all remain undiscovered on the stage, their presence in the play being mediated by textual or verbal accounts.[137] After the geographical adventurousness of the history plays, and especially the audacious use of the Chorus in *Henry V* to help 'digest / The abuse of distance' and convey the spectators from London to Southampton to France, in *Hamlet* Shakespeare might seem to have decided to heed Jonson's commentary in the Induction to *Every Man Out of His Humour*, where Mitis and Cordatus, Jonson's commentator–friends discuss the curious fact that in 'some one play we see so many seas, countries, and kingdoms passed over with such admirable dexterity', concluding sarcastically that this 'but shows how well the Authors can travail in their vocation, and outrun the apprehension of their auditory'.[138] In *Hamlet*, no 'Chorus wafts you o'er the seas', as Jonson put it in the 'Prologue' added to *Every Man In His Humour* in the 1616 Folio publication:[139] here, the unity of place is carefully observed, and setting sail means leaving the world of the play.

In other words, the play's topology of power is reflected in the topology of the mode of representation, in a split between *mimesis* and *diegesis*. Whether the classical unity imposed on the play is indeed part of Shakespeare's engagement with the intensely critical and self-reflexive theatrical context often referred to as the 'war of the theatres' (a context that makes an appearance in the play in the Q1/F reference to the boys' companies), *Hamlet* puts this apparent constraint to intense and self-conscious dramatic purpose, using it to motivate the coming and going of emissaries and making it necessary to relate what lies beyond the pale of Elsinore in letters and narratives.[140] In *Hamlet*, dramatic *mimesis* is therefore proper to

---

[135] The castle at Helsingør is called Kronborg, but the play never uses that name.

[136] The presence of all members of the court in the graveyard, and the fact that Yorick is buried there, too, implies that it is in Elsinore. That Fortinbras would have been understood to be landing in Elsinore, and for a clarification of where Shakespeare's contemporaries would have understood his army to pass through, see Gunnar Sjögren, 'The Geography of *Hamlet*', in Gunnar Sorelius (ed.), *Shakespeare and Scandinavia: A Collection of Nordic Studies* (Newark: University of Delaware Press, 2002), 64–71 at 67–70.

[137] Ophelia's drowning is an exception which seems to confirm the rule here.

[138] Jonson (2012) 1:273 (Induction l. 262–5). Later in the play, Jonson also prepares the audience for a change of scene by advising them to 'let your imagination be swifter than a pair of oars, and by this, suppose *Puntarvolo, Brisk, Fungoso*, and the Dog, arrived at the court gate and going up to the great chamber. *Macilente* and *Sogliardo*, we'll leave them on the water till possibility and natural means may land 'em' (4.5.141–5), and cp. Bednarz, *Shakespeare & the Poets' War* 24–6, 72–5.

[139] Jonson (2012) 4:632, l. 15.

[140] This is not to say that *diegesis* is limited to foreign affairs. On the significance of the action we don't get to see, and on its relative prominence in reading, see Stephen Ratcliffe, *Reading the Unseen: (Offstage) Hamlet* (Denver: Counterpath Press, 2010). For a philosophically informed analysis of the play's 'narrative infrastructure' with larger consequences for our understanding of the interdependence

domestic affairs, to the world of Elsinore, and foreign locations are only present in the narratives of stage characters, as stories and events that have some bearing on life at home. In a play so intensely preoccupied with travel, foreign matter matters enormously, but—very emphatically—only as it informs the domestic.

It seems, then, that diplomacy, embassies, travel, and letters, far from being incidental features, trivial touches that help establish an atmosphere, are in fact crucial, structurally determined aspects of the play, although they have been relegated to the margins of our attention by the play's interpretive history. An important strand of this history has concentrated on 'that within which passes show' and how this relates to 'actions that a man might play'—preparing us to reading it as a play about the tortured, inscrutable yet insistently scrutinized psyche, conscience, and intentions of Hamlet and of Claudius, about the secret of old Hamlet's murder, about a world of spying and hiding behind the arras—about the consequences of things that are out of sight, about the threats they pose and how they might come to light.[141] Such readings attend to some hidden interiority, a privileged space that is posited by the play's characters, and understand it as the ultimate object of the anxieties, interrogations, and negotiations that take place in Elsinore, making access to and control over this interior space—and indeed, the very question of its existence—the play's central concern and its master trope. But as I have been arguing here, in *Hamlet*, foreign politics, diplomacy, correspondence, and travel all attempt to control, represent, and negotiate that *without* which passes show, another privileged space which threatens to define or dramatically alter the situation that is in plain view. The interest in the invisible within and in the invisible without are versions of the obsession with verbally or textually mediated spaces and events, with spaces and events that remain out of sight, and with the moments when they might erupt into the world, unto the stage of Elsinore. In this reading, the characters' inwardness and foreign states become analogous spaces, mediated presences of often tragic consequence—they are the spaces of potentiality where life's future course is determined and prepared.

Rather than using a focus on foreign affairs to supplant the familiar concern with the play's interiority, then, I suggest that these two aspects of the play are

---

of narrative and action, see Raphael Falco, '*Hamlet*'s Narrative Infrastructure', *The Shakespearean International Yearbook*, 7 (2007), 123–39. As far as the other plays are concerned: *Titus* leaves Rome and invites us to join Lucius and the Goths, *Othello* shifts from Venice to Cyprus, *Lear* forces us to criss-cross Britain much like the histories do, *Macbeth* moves us around in Scotland, even taking us to England and back, *Coriolanus* shifts back and forth between Rome and the cities of the Volsces, not to mention how *Antony and Cleopatra* crosses the Mediterranean. Even *Romeo and Juliet* manage to leave Verona and take us with them. As spectators of *Hamlet*, we stay put in Elsinore as much as we stay put on Prospero's island in *The Tempest*, or in the Vienna of *Measure for Measure*. Analogies for such unity of place come from Shakespeare's comedies, not from his tragic or historical drama.

[141] Discussions of the problem include e.g. Katharine Eisaman Maus, *Inwardness and Theater in the English Renaissance* (Chicago: University of Chicago Press, 1995); John Lee, *Shakespeare's Hamlet and the Controversies of the Self* (Oxford: Clarendon Press, 2000); de Grazia, *Hamlet without Hamlet*; David Hillman, *Shakespeare's Entrails: Belief, Scepticism and the Interior of the Body* (Basingstoke: Palgrave Macmillan, 2007); Graham Holderness, '"The Single and Peculiar Life": Hamlet's Heart and the Early Modern Subject', *Shakespeare Survey*, 63 (2011), 296–307; Drew Daniel, *The Melancholy Assemblage: Affect and Epistemology in the English Renaissance* (New York: Fordham University Press, 2013) 120–54.

constitutive of each other. The trajectory of Rosencrantz and Guildenstern is emblematic of their connection: they are invited to Elsinore by a king worried about what he calls 'Hamlet's transformation', since 'nor th'exterior nor the inward man / Resembles that it was', and asks them to 'glean / Whether aught to us unknown afflicts him thus, / That opened lies within our remedy' (2.2.5–18). Later in the play, the hapless agents of this exploration become the diplomats who, in the grand commission they carry, provide Hamlet with the hard evidence of the king's guilt, the evidence Hamlet needs to swing into action against him. The threat against the king that he has projected into Hamlet's interiority finally takes shape during the foreign mission, and arrives in Denmark when Hamlet returns from the English embassy. In this reading, the play's intense focus on diplomacy, its obsession with diplomatic writing and with arrivals and departures, rather than remaining peripheral business bedecking the play with the accessories of contemporary court culture, becomes formally integral to Hamlet's mystery. Shakespeare's *Hamlet* aligns the psychological with the diplomatic as the opaque locations that give rise to states of political emergency, to challenges to constitutional order and royal sovereignty, and to life itself.

'And Rosencrantz and Guildenstern go to it.'

3

'I Lack Advancement'
Political Agents and Political Servants in Hamlet's Moment

I gestured at some of the transformations of the Hamlet-story in the previous two chapters—from the chronicle of Saxo Grammaticus and the *histoire tragique* of François de Belleforest through the lost and the extant versions of the English tragedy. What follows is a reading of how the rise of professional politicians to public view is implicated in those transformations. To show the pivotal importance of Shakespeare's *Hamlet* to this narrative, I start with a look at a pair of texts, before-and-after snapshots that highlight the significance of its moment to political culture.

POLITICAL HAMLET, 1561

A collection of political orations published in Venice in 1561, the *Orationi in Materia Civile, e Criminale*, edited and translated by Remigio Nannini, consists of speeches extracted from various classical and modern historians, ranging from Livy's history of Rome to Niccolò Machiavelli's history of Florence, relevant to 'the governments of states and republics, to the accusing and defending of criminals, and to many other things' that can be, as the title page promises, 'useful to anyone who expects to lead a civil life'.[1]

Although he draws most of his materials either from classics or from humanists, Nannini also includes two extracts from the Danish histories of Saxo Grammaticus. Saxo, whose chronicle was written in the thirteenth century and first printed in Paris in 1514, may seem an unlikely choice for an exemplary orator, but he was in some ways as good a modern match for Cassius Dio, Livy, Sallust, or Tacitus, as one could get. Erasmus in his *Ciceronianus* singled him out for his Latin eloquence, for his sententiousness and *copia*, and praised his achievement as especially admirable given the time and place of its writing. Erasmus's endorsement of Saxo's style

---

[1] *Orationi in Materia Civile, e Criminale, Tratte da gli Historici Greci, e Latini, Antichi, e Moderni, Raccolte, e Tradotte per M. Remigio Fiorentino…Nelle Quali, oltre alla Cognitione dell'Historie, S'Ha Notitia di Gouerni di Stati, e di Republiche, d'Accusare, e Difender Rei, e di Molte altre Cose Utili a Ciasuno, ch'Attende alla Vita Ciuile* (Vinegia: Gabriel Giolito de'Ferrari, 1561). The borrowings from Saxo were first noted by Theresa Suriano Ormsby-Lennon, 'Piccolo, Ma Con Gran Vaghezza: A New Source for *Hamlet*?', *The Library Chronicle*, 41/2 (1977), 119–48.

was used as a blurb on the title page of the 1534 Basel edition as well as in the 1576 Frankfurt edition of his *Gesta Danorum*.[2]

Both speeches that Nannini translates are attributed to Amleto (Saxo's Amlethus). In the first (which may be seen to parallel the closet scene in William Shakespeare's *Hamlet*) he berates his mother for her lax morality and explains the rationale of his pretended madness as a ruse that should help him take revenge on Fengon (the prototype of Claudius). In the second, he addresses the assembly of the Danish people after he has killed his usurping uncle. The latter fits especially well in a collection that contains not only Tiberius's speech over the dead Augustus, but also Brutus's oration to the people of Rome after the death of Lucrece, Marc Antony's oration over the dead Julius Caesar, and Cicero's speech to the senate and people of Rome after Caesar's death. Amlethus's speech is a powerful piece of political rhetoric that aims to publicly legitimate his *coup d'état* by casting it as an act of justice, a retribution for the crime of fratricide. Amlethus presents himself to the people not only as the legitimate heir to the throne, but also as the agent who liberated Denmark from the yoke of tyranny. This public scene and Amlethus's public argument are just as important to this story about usurpation and tyrannicide as is the emphatically private (indeed, secret) reasoning about the uses of *simulatio*, about watching one's chances and awaiting the right moment for revenge, that we find in the former selection.

The two speeches, identified in the margin of the early editions of Saxo as 'Amlethi ad matrem verba' and 'Amlethi oratio', also appear in the French rendering of Hamlet's history in the fifth volume of François de Belleforest's *Histoires tragiques*, where they are set off by their separate section titles.[3] The prominence of Hamlet's rhetorical performance in these versions of the narrative and the inclusion of the speeches in Nannini's compilation indicate that late sixteenth-century readers would have considered the history of Hamlet as exemplary not only of the problems that contested sovereignty and succession create for the political agent, but also of the public legitimation of that agent's intervention.[4] In fact, Belleforest's and Nannini's particular interest in this thirteenth-century history of Amlethus

---

[2] Saxo Grammaticus, *Danorum Regum Heroumque Historiae* (Paris: Jodocus Badius, 1514); Saxo Grammaticus, *Danorum Historiæ Libri xvi* (Basel: Johannes Bebel, 1534); Saxo Grammaticus, *Danica historia libris XVI* (Frankfurt: Andreas Wechel, 1576). On the 1534 title page the blurb appears as follows: 'Des. Erasmi roterodami de Saxone censura. In Daniam nauigare malo, quæ nobis dedit Saxonem Grammaticū, qui suæ gentis historiam splendide magnificećq contexuit. Probo uiuidum & ardens ingenium, orationem nusquam remissam aut dormitantem, tum miram uerborum copiam, sententias crebras, & figurarum admirabilem uarietatem, ut satis admirari non queam, unde illa ætate homini Dano tanta uis eloquendi.' In 1576, the passage appears at the end of the prefatory materials, facing the first page of Saxo's text.

[3] 'Harangue d'Amleth à la Reine Geruthe sa mere' and 'Harengue d'Amleth aux Danoys', pp. 159 and 176, respectively, in *Le Cinquiesme Tome des Histoires Tragiques... par François Belle-forest Comingeois* (Paris: Jean Hulpeau, 1572). The highlighting of speeches is a characteristic feature of Belleforest's *histoires*.

[4] Belleforest's attention may well have been drawn to Saxo by Nannini. Nannini's earlier collection, the 1557 *Orationi Militari* served as the model for Belleforest's 1572 *Harengues Militaires*, a debt explicitly admitted in Belleforest's dedication. See Nathalie Hester, 'Scholarly Borrowing: The Case of Remigio Nannini's *Orationi Militari* and François de Belleforest's *Harangues Militaires*', *Modern Philology*, 101 (2003), 235–58.

shows that Erasmus's praise only captures one aspect of Saxo's rhetorical appeal. Some facets of the Latin eloquence of the *Gesta Danorum* may be lost in translation, but its attention to the political import of oratory could not be more apparent in these modern vernacular versions. What Nannini's anthology brings into clear focus is that in Saxo's history of Amlethus, political action is answerable not only to the tradition and topics of prudential reasoning, but also to public arguments of legitimacy.

Shakespeare's *Hamlet* features no public moment equivalent to 'Amlethi oratio'. Although the central political conflict—between Hamlet and his uncle—remains the same, this conflict is never allowed to emerge into public view within the world of the play, because the play stops short of Hamlet's public self-justification.[5] The suppression of public political oratory signals a change of perspective on politics. In the play, the legitimacy of political aims and actions is no longer scrutinized with regard to one's office, to the interests of the commonwealth, or to publicly recognized forms of justice; instead, Shakespeare's *Hamlet* confines itself to an exploration of such actions from the perspective of political prudence and personal loyalties. This change amounts to a new approach to the realm of politics, both in the history of the Hamlet narrative and in the history of English drama.

POLITICAL HAMLET, 1609

Although it muffles the registers of public oratory, Shakespeare's *Hamlet* by no means withdraws from the reach of political conversation that takes place among its audience. In fact, some contemporary references to and borrowings from *Hamlet* show that early modern readers were indeed reading the play with an interest in what it suggested about their political environment. But the mode of political reading, observation, and discussion facilitated by the play has a focus quite distinct from the public arguments about legitimacy, tyranny, and treason rehearsed in Saxo's *faux*-classical oratory.

In a little treatise called *The Sixe-folde Politician*, published in 1609, John Melton seeks to establish the nature of true expertise in statecraft by presenting his reader with character sketches of insubstantial performers of political proficiency—newsmongers, travellers, scholars, and Jesuits (the usual suspects of anything evil in Protestant England)—contrasting their pretended knowledge to the true wisdom of the 'deepe discerning politician', that is, of 'such as haue such insight into the State as by indirections they can finde directions out, though they were hid fathome deepe',[6] 'By indirections find directions out' (2.1.66), a phrase apparently

---

[5] The play's distance from the political oratory of Saxo's narrative and from its readings in Nannini and Belleforest is considerable even in the case of the closet scene. In Shakespeare's version, Hamlet talks about being mad in craft and makes very clear what he thinks of Claudius, but he never proceeds to discuss his plans for revenge, focusing instead on the prudential handling of his mother's relationship to the King: 3.4.190.

[6] *A Sixe-folde Politician. Together with a Sixe-folde Precept of Policy* (London: E.A. for Iohn Busby, 1609), sigs. E5v–E6r. Melton's borrowings from *Hamlet* have gone, to my knowledge, hitherto unnoticed.

original with Shakespeare, is of course among the more memorable lines of Polonius (as we shall see in Chapter 6, at least one other contemporary reader, Edward Pudsey, also found it notable).[7] The old counsellor instructs a somewhat puzzled Reynaldo, whom he is sending after Laertes to Paris, to find out what his son is up to—is he gaming, does he get involved in fights, has anyone seen him '"enter such a house of sale"— / *Videlicet* a brothel'? (2.1.60–1)—by using a 'bait of falsehood' [to take] a carp of truth' (2.1.63). The scene, a training session in the practice of intelligence-gathering, identifies the cunning search for information as the distinctive skill of the class of politicians—a class that now also promises to include Reynaldo:

> And thus do we of wisdom and of reach,
> With windlasses and with assays of bias,
> By indirections find directions out.
> So by my former lecture and advice
> Shall you my son. (2.1.64–8)

Melton, who clearly paid close attention to his *Hamlet*, puts the borrowed phrase to the same use as Polonius, and in doing so, assumes the role of the experienced politician offering instruction to his audience: that is, to his nominal addressee, a young aristocrat eager to enter the political arena, and also to the reading public eager to acquire some form of competence at least in the discussion of the same.[8] That he does so confirms the suggestion, made in the previous chapter, that Polonius's foolishness consists not in his lack of political experience but in its misapplication.

Melton's 'substantiall states-men',[9] although virtuous and godly, are characterized first and foremost by their professional expertise in political analysis and governance, in the application of their experience to emerging new situations. Book learning may provide general rules, and 'the ordinarie and generall propositions maximees, and entercourse of state affaires, is matter of discourse for the trauailer and Student in pollicye' (E5v), but the 'truly wise' person is he 'that can distinguish rightly the times and seasons of vsing his theorie in perticular actions'.[10] And such wisdom, he argues in a way that can be traced back to Aristotle and to Plato's Socrates, cannot be had from books, from conversation, or even from the experience of one's travels, but like other arts and crafts, like that of the carpenter, the seafarer or the apothecary, it needs to be obtained from a master of the profession, to whom the aspiring would-be politician is apprenticed.[11]

---

[7] He copies it as 'Men of wisedome & of reach doe with windelesses with assayes of bias by indirections find directions out'—see Shakespeare Birthplace Trust Record Office ER/82/1/21 f. 2r.

[8] If the quotation is based on reading rather than hearing the play, Melton was probably using the 1604/5 second quarto edition of *Hamlet*: the first quarto has 'by indirections find directions forth': Shakespeare, *The Tragicall Historie of Hamlet Prince of Denmarke* (London: Valentine Simmes for Nicholas Ling and John Trundell, 1603), sig. D2v.

[9] Melton, sig. H6r.   [10] Melton, sigs. E5v, E7r.   [11] Melton, sigs. E8r–F1v.

Presenting himself as such a master, after his critique of the 'vain-glorious, friuolous, deluding mountibankes, and showemakers of policy, and state-learning' who trade in generalities but lack the experience necessary for putting them into practice, Melton in the second half of his book responds to his interlocutor's request for positive guidance on political conduct by offering him 'a sixe-fold precept of policy'.[12] The guidelines he offers closely resemble the set of precepts Polonius wants Laertes to 'character' in his memory in 1.3, as well as similar collections of wise saws which elder statesmen and aristocrats addressed to their sons.[13] However, Melton is not advising his son here, and by printing the exchange of letters in which his advice is solicited and then offered, he also swerves from the model of the grave counsellor whose sphere of activity is in public office. Far from a disinterested gesture, his advice appears as a private service rendered in exchange for the personal favours he has enjoyed. In articulating his sense of obligation to his patron, he once again turns to *Hamlet*, revising Hamlet's avowal of his filial duty in 1.5 into a language of affiliation, of favours extended and acknowledged: 'I haue wiped away from the Table of my remembrance all formes and effigies, that first, middle and last, at all times & aboue all things I might prescribe fresh in my memorie your faithfull favours, so liberally and so freelye expended vppon me, a man of so little worth and respect.'[14]

---

[12] Melton, sig. K4r.

[13] *Basilikon Doron* is the best-known English example of such paternal advice from the period. The precepts attributed to William Cecil, Lord Burghley, and addressed to Robert Cecil, were in wide MS circulation throughout the period (see for example Folger MS V.a.381, ff. 12–20; and Folger MS V.a.402, ff. 21–24) and also printed as *Certaine Precepts or Directions, for the Well Ordering and Carriage of a Mans Life:... Left by a Father to His Son at His Death, Who Was Sometimes of Eminent Note and Place in This Kingdome. And Published from a More Perfect Copy, then Ordinary Those Pocket Manuscripts Goe Warranted by* (London: T. C[reede] and B. A[lsop] for Ri. Meighen, and Thom. Iones, 1617). Another, earlier letter of advice by Burghley to his elder son reflects the latter's tendency to excess: 'A Memorial for Thomas my son, 1561', BL MS Harley 3638, ff. 106r–108v. Further examples from the period include the advice of Charles Cornwallis to a grandson (Folger MS X.d.539); Sir William Wentworth's advice to his son: *Wentworth papers 1597–1628*, ed. J. P. Cooper (Camden 4th series, vol. 12, London: Royal Historical Society, 1973), 9–24; Virgil B. Heltzel, 'Richard Earl of Carbery's Advice to His Son', *The Huntington Library Bulletin*, 11 (1937), 59–105; Henry Percy Ninth Earl of Northumberland, *The Wizard Earl's Advices to His Son*, ed. Gordon R. Batho and Stephen Clucas (The Roxburghe Club, 2002). The advice by Burghley to Robert Cecil, as well as similar texts by Walter Raleigh and Francis Osborn are reprinted in Louis B. Wright (ed.), *Advice to a Son* (Ithaca: Published for the Folger Shakespeare Library by Cornell University Press, 1962). For discussions of the genre, see the introduction to the 2002 edition of Northumberland's advice and Lee Ustick, 'Advice to a Son: A Type of Seventeenth-Century Conduct Book', *Studies in Philology*, 29 (1932), 409–41; G. K. Hunter, 'Isocrates' Precepts and Polonius' Character', *Shakespeare Quarterly*, 8 (1957), 501–6; Theodore S. Beardsley, Jr, 'Isocrates, Shakespeare, and Calderón: Advice to a Young Man', *Hispanic Review*, 42 (1974), 185–98; Mary Thomas Crane, *Framing Authority: Sayings, Self, and Society in Sixteenth-Century England* (Princeton: Princeton University Press, 1993) 116–36. The instructions of Charles V to Philip II, primarily on matters of government and international politics, were in wide circulation throughout Europe; copies of English translations in MS include Huntington MS EL 1612, ff. 95–140; a version was later printed as *The Advice of Charles the Fifth, Emperor of Germany, and King of Spain, to His Son Philip the Second upon His Resignation of the Crown of Spain to His Said Son* (London: for H. Mortlock, 1670); but a shorter set of instructions, much closer in form and content to the genre modelled upon Isocrates's *Ad Demonicum* is also in circulation, see Roger B. Merriman, 'Charles V's Last Paper of Advice to His Son', *American Historical Review*, 28 (1923), 489–91.

[14] Sig. K7v; cp. '...from the table of my memory / I'll wipe away all trivial fond records, / all saws of books, all forms, all pressures past / That youth and observation copied there, / and thy commandment all alone shall live / Within the book and volume of my brain...' (1.5.98–103).

In Melton's book, Shakespeare's play serves *both* as a source of expert knowledge about the conduct of politics and as a template for the conduct of the knowledge transactions, for intellectual work performed in the hope of service and patronage in which such expertise is deployed. Although Melton insists on the high moral seriousness of the trade, his description of politics as a practical art exemplifies what John Pocock described as 'a shift of emphasis, perceptible and important in the Jacobean mind, away from counsel and toward statecraft',[15] and more broadly, a shift from a participatory political rhetoric to an instrumental mode of discussion concentrating on the agents' and the state's interests—that is, to what contemporaries called the reason of state.[16] Melton's borrowings are particularly instructive here, because they link this change of emphasis to the needs, interests, and personal loyalties of the person engaged in thinking about statecraft. His use of *Hamlet*, and indeed his book as a whole, is primarily concerned with the personal success of individuals in the business of politics, be they high-level players, their clients, or (as the readers of the book) people hoping to achieve some degree of competence in the discussion of such topics. What he offers is not a framework for the evaluation of political decisions from the perspective of morality, justice, or the interest of the commonwealth or the crown. Rather, he understands political knowledge primarily as an intellectual asset, and his book makes clear that the pragmatic value of this asset is realized in private exchange, as the currency of personal relationships in the context of the system of patronage. The print circulation of such advice books as Melton's, like Melton's own reliance on the commercial stage for his phrasing, indicates the broad public interest in this intellectual currency (in overhearing in print, as it were, the private advice Melton is offering) and more generally in the political world—a world understood as an arena of employment and personal advancement, rather than as a space where questions of legitimacy, constitutional conflicts, the common good, or the rights of the ruler and the subject would be contested.[17] Taking the long-term view, the public interest in these service-oriented political handbooks is prompted by the rise of the bureaucratic apparatus of the modern state: that is, by the interconnected emergence of the modern state and of its servants, of professional state bureaucracies and of the ideal of the good public servant.[18]

What follows traces the rise to prominence of the self-interested yet loyal political employee in the drama of Hamlet's moment, by repeating the movement encapsulated in the shift from Nannini's to Melton's reading of the play. The account is schematically chronological, with the emphasis on the schematic. My aim is not to reconstruct an actual history, but to show how the implications of the

---

[15] Pocock, *The Machiavellian Moment* 353; Viroli, *From Politics to Reason of State*.

[16] Tuck, *Philosophy and Government* and cp. Peltonen, *Classical Humanism and Republicanism in English Political Thought, 1570–1640*.

[17] The advertised purpose of Barnabe Barnes's *Foure Bookes of Offices: Enabling Priuat Persons for the Speciall Seruice of all Good Princes and Policies* (London: George Bishop, T. Adams and C. Burbie, 1606) is a case in point.

[18] Cp. 'Grundzüge der Beamtenethik', in Stolleis, *Staat und Staatsräson in der Frühen Neuzeit* 197–231.

much longer story of the emergence of the political profession become clearly visible in Hamlet's moment. What I seek to describe are the social and political consequences of the establishment of politics as a distinct field of expert knowledge and a profession, as reflected in the dramatic representation of political agents. The chapter argues that in Hamlet's moment, and in Shakespeare's *Hamlet*, even as the attention turns to professional political activity and a specifically political style of argument, the figure of the career politician—of the political employee or professional state servant—rises from its earlier marginality and demonized abjection to centrality on the political stage. This rise becomes clear if we compare Shakespeare's play both to earlier versions of the Hamlet story and also to some earlier political or court-centred plays often considered as representing analogous situations. Shakespeare's transformation of the cast of characters—of their perspective on the world, their social situation, their style of interaction, and their ambition—results in a shift in the understanding of political action from public contestation to private and interested intellectual activity: a shift exemplified in the demise of the Polonius clan and the concurrent rise of Horatio.

POLEMICAL HAMLET: BELLEFOREST

François de Belleforest's *histoire tragique* of Amleth, first published in 1570, is a modernized version of Saxo's story. As there is nothing in *Hamlet* that would have required first-hand access to Saxo's work instead of the version in Belleforest, the *histoire tragique* is generally considered as the source of Shakespeare's *fin de siècle* tragedy, and it is often discussed with regard to what the play owes to it in terms of plotting and characterization.[19] But the political implications of Shakespeare's use of this *histoire tragique* are rarely discussed, although Belleforest's text is self-consciously couched in a field of political polemics, and it would clearly have been imagined, by its author as well as by its contemporary readers, in England as well as in France, as an intervention in such controversies.

Belleforest himself was not perceived as a politically neutral figure in late sixteenth-century England. Although remembered today by scholars of English literature only for his continuation of Pierre Boaistuau's *Histoires Tragiques*, to late sixteenth-century readers he was at least as important as the author–compiler–translator of various compendia of the history and geography of France and the world, which were widely used and cited as important authorities on continental politics throughout the period.[20] In such scholarly work as well as in more ephemeral

---

[19] Arthur P. Stabler, 'The Sources of *Hamlet*: Some Corrections of the Record', *Research Studies: A Quarterly Publication at Washington State University*, 32 (1964), 207–16; Jenkins (ed.), *Hamlet* 82–96.
[20] See for example John Eliot, *The Suruay or Topographical Description of France* (London: John Wolfe, 1592), sigs. B1v–B2; and Raphael Holinshed, *The First and Second Volumes of Chronicles…* (London: John Harrison and others, 1587), sig. B2. Belleforest was also the main source of Edward Tillney's massive project of geography and heraldry; see W. R. Streitberger, 'The Tyllney Manuscript at the Folger Library', *Papers of the Bibliographical Society of America*, 69 (1975), 449–64 at 455.

pieces, Belleforest was writing as an apologist of the St Bartholomew's Night's Massacre of 23 August 1572, describing it as the just execution of Huguenot conspirators and rebels and a great victory of God's cause.[21] The final pages of the 1573 *Chroniques et Annales de France*, an early sixteenth-century chronicle that he brought up to date under this new title, offer a narrative of the providential discovery and punishment of the Protestant plot in August 1572, and a graphic account of the fate of Gaspard de Coligny, 'the chief of all the traitors in this realm... who was sowing the seeds of the discord that afflicts all of Europe.'[22] Belleforest was keenly aware of the international ramifications of the confessional struggle and put the closely related and historically parallel developments in Britain to analogical use in his chronicle, explicitly contrasting the 'just punishment' exerted over Coligny and his accomplices to the betrayal and extradition to England of the 'good Catholic' Earl of Northumberland by the Scots, and to the unjust accusations of conspiracy brought against the Duke of Norfolk, which served as a pretext for the beheading of this 'good and innocent lord'.[23]

The political implications of Belleforest's partisan narrative were identified in the preface to the English edition of an account of the massacre by the great Huguenot political theorist and polemicist François Hotman: 'How many histories written in Latine, Italian & French, by Iouius, Paradine, Belleforest and other, are printed in Italie, Fraunce and Flaunders, and published & freely had and read in your land', Hotman asks, 'although they contain matter expresly to the sclander of your state and princes?'[24] Hotman's reference is to the vindication of the Massacre Belleforest formulated in the *Chroniques et Annales* and also in pamphlet form,[25] but in the upcoming years, the fierce disagreement between the two authors also extended to the theoretical questions prompted by the conflict. Brandishing his title of royal historiographer, in his 1579 *chef d'oeuvre*, the *Grandes Annales et Histoire Generale de France* Belleforest attacked the Huguenot *monarchomaque* Hotman's influential and highly controversial *Franco-gallia* (1573),

---

[21] Julie Maxwell, 'Counter-Reformation Versions of Saxo: A New Source for *Hamlet*?', *Renaissance Quarterly*, 57 (2004), 518–60 at 544–54. Maxwell uses Belleforest's confessional allegiances to argue for an analogical, topical application of the Hamlet story.

[22] Belleforest, *Les Chroniques et Annales de France... par Nicole Gilles... Reueuës Corrigées & Augmentées... par Francoys de Belleforest* (Paris: Nicolas du Chemin, 1573) f. 529v. Cp. François Hotman, *Francogallia*, ed. Ralph E. Giesey, trans. J. H. M. Salmon (Cambridge: Cambridge University Press, 1972) 59.

[23] Belleforest, *Les Chroniques et Annales*, ff. 529v–530r.

[24] François Hotman, *A True and Plaine Report of the Furious Outrages of Fraunce & the Horrible and Shameful Slaughter of Chastillion the Admirall, and Diuers Other Noble and Excellent Men, and of the Wicked and Straunge Murder of Godlie Persons, Committed in Many Cities of Fraunce, without any Respect of Sorte, Kinde, Age, or Degree. By Ernest Varamund of Freseland. At Striveling in Scotlande* [i.e. London: Printed by Henry Bynneman], 1573 (STC 13847), A2r. In 1573 Bynneman also published the Latin original both under a false Edinburgh imprint (STC 13845) and under his own (STC 13846); a French translation also appeared in England (STC 13847.5). On the original context of the pamphlet, see Donald R. Kelley, *François Hotman: A Revolutionary's Ordeal* (Princeton: Princeton University Press, 1973) 218–38; on the significant afterlife of Hotman's account in England, see Paul H. Kocher, 'François Hotman and Marlowe's *the Massacre at Paris*', *PMLA*, 56 (1941), 349–68.

[25] Belleforest, *Discovrs svr l'Hevr des Presages Advenuz de Nostre Temps Signifiantz la Felicité du Regne de Nostre Roy Charles Neufiesme* (Paris: Le Mangnier, 1572), the new edition of an earlier text, repurposed to serve the post-massacre moment.

contesting Hotman's claim that the ancient constitution of the Franks allowed for the active participation of the people in government, especially in the creation, and, if necessary, deposition of the king. The *Grandes Annales* challenges Hotman on the Calvinist jurist's home turf. In an introductory chapter about the origins of the French, Belleforest offers the most detailed discussion and critique of the historical evidence for the supposed elections of French kings to be found in the works of all sixteenth-century proponents of successive, hereditary kingship. Even though some of the coronation ceremonies may have had the appearance of election, Belleforest contends that 'this was to better approve & confirm the succession, and to pay homage to him who succeeded their late prince.'[26] This argument amounts to a refutation of the supposed historical precedents for the 'laws of election'—precedents which, as Belleforest puts it, some (i.e. people like Hotman) were working hard to discover in order 'to insolently arm the people against their King, and to give more authority to the nobility than they have'.[27] The book's dedication to Henri III makes this polemical intervention the political rationale of the two massive volumes of the work.

As a result of his engagement in political polemics and his detailed exposition of historical evidence, Belleforest became one of the most important points of reference in English debates about theories of succession and resistance at the end of the sixteenth century.[28] Because of the strong sympathies for Mary Queen of Scots voiced again and again in his historical narratives, he was also suspected to have anonymously intervened in the 1568–72 pamphlet war about her title. In 1572, an anonymous collection of three polemical tracts was published under the title *L'Innocence de la Tresillvstre Tres-chaste, et Debonnaire Princesse, Madame Marie Royne d'Escosse*.[29] The volume was aimed against the official English position, promoted in recent publications by George Buchanan and Thomas Wilson, who sought to represent the deposition of Mary Queen of Scots as a legitimate action, an instance of the subjects exercising their right to resist.[30] *L'Innocence* defended

---

[26] Belleforest, *Les Grandes Annales, et Histoire Generale de France, de la Venue des Francs en Gaule, iusques au Regne du Roy Tres-Chrestien Henry III. . . . par François de Belle-Forest Comingeois, & Annaliste de sa Majesté Tres-Chrestienne*, 2 vols. (Paris: Gabriel Buon, 1579) vol. 1, sigs. A1r–B4r, the quote at B3r. Cp. Richard A. Jackson, 'Elective Kingship and Consensus Populi in Sixteenth-Century France', *The Journal of Modern History*, 44 (1972), 155–71 at 166–7; Georges Weill, *Les Théories sur le Pouvoir Royal en France pendant les Guerres de Religion* (Paris: Hachette et cie, 1891) 184–9.

[27] Belleforest, *Les Grandes Annales*, vol. 1, sigs. ã2r–v.

[28] He features prominently in Robert Parsons, *A Conference about the Next Succession* (N.p.: 1594). Of Parsons's 101 authorities, Belleforest is the fourth most often cited, preceded only by the Old Testament, Polydore Vergil and John Stow: see Peter Holmes, *Resistance and Compromise: The Political Thought of the Elizabethan Catholics* (Cambridge: Cambridge University Press, 1982) 151.

[29] The full descriptive title reads: *L'Innocence de la Tresillvstre Tres-chaste, et Debonnaire Princesse, Madame Marie Royne d'Escosse; ou Sont Amplement Refutées les Calomnies Faulces, & Impositions Iniques, Publiées par Vne Liure Secrettement Diulgé en France, l'An 1572. Tovchant tant la Mort du Seigneur d'Arley Son Espouse, que Autres Crimes, dont Elle est Faulcement Accusée. Plus, un autre Discours auquel Sont Descouuertes Plusieurs Trahisons tant Manifestes, que iusques Icy, Cachées, Perpetrées par les Mesmes Calomniateurs* (N.p: n.p, 1572).

[30] James Emerson Phillips, *Images of a Queen: Mary Stuart in Sixteenth-Century Literature* (Berkeley: University of California Press, 1964); John D. Staines, *The Tragic Histories of Mary Queen of Scots, 1560–1690: Rhetoric, Passions, and Political Literature* (Farnham and Burlington, VT: Ashgate, 2009). The major account of the English language political pamphlets around Mary Queen of Scots is the

Mary and represented the English establishment as a nest of traitors, dominated by evil counsellors plotting to subvert Elizabeth's reign. One of the main targets of the attack, William Cecil, Lord Burghley, made a considerable effort to discover who was behind it, but had little success until at last in 1574 Thomas Wilson found out that the collection 'was polyshed, and turned into frenshe by Belforest',[31] and sponsored 'by the meanes of the Byshoppe of Glasgo'. That in 1572 Bellforest did in fact dedicate one of his translations—a compilation of exemplary political correspondence—to James Beaton, archbishop of Glasgow and Mary's ambassador, does not exactly question the results of Wilson's investigations.[32]

Belleforest's notoriety as a French royalist and a staunch opponent of theories of election and resistance suggests something of the expectations his readers were bringing to the *Histoires Tragiques*. Not that the fictional work was particularly reticent about its political motives. Lorna Hutson has argued that such short fiction, regardless of its claims to historical verity or lack thereof, offered itself for prudential application, providing models for interpreting hypothetical states of contingency in the interests of a fortunate outcome.[33] But the majority of Belleforest's *histoires* in *Le Cinquiesme Tome des Histoires Tragiques*—that is, the fifth volume of the series begun by Boaistuau and continued after two volumes by Belleforest—are at least as closely related to Belleforest's work as a historian and cosmographer as to the *novelle* in the earlier volumes in the series. These are narratives lifted from historical writing and therefore stories with a plausible claim to record political experience. They are also heavily editorialized to highlight their political implications, directly reflecting not only on matters of prudence, but also on current debates and on matters of political principle—on questions of succession, of tyranny and of treason, or on the need to punish rebels. Of the twelve narratives in this collection, the history of the treason against Kanut, King of Denmark (another story taken from Saxo's chronicle),[34] and the *histoire tragique* of

---

first three chapters of Peter Lake, *Bad Queen Bess? Libels, Secret Histories and the Politics of Publicity in the Reign of Queen Elizabeth I* (Oxford: Oxford University Press, 2016). I thank Peter Lake for sharing with me earlier drafts of his book.

[31] Thomas Wilson to Burghley from Bruxelles, 12 December 1574: TNA SP 70/132, ff. 133–4, at f. 133v; cp. *CSP Foreign 1572–1574*, p. 579, no. 1612.

[32] Bellforest, *Epistres des Princes, Lesquelles, ov Sont Addressees Avx Princes, Ov Traittent les Affaires des Princes, ou Parlent des Princes. Recueillies d'Italien par Hieronyme Ruscelli, & Mises en François par F. de Belle-forest, Commingeois* (Paris: Iean Ruelle, 1572), the dedication at sigs. †iir–†ivr. A few months later Wilson provides Burghley with a completely different account of how the book was probably compiled, suggesting another translator, 'one Mownse, born in Calais, servant to the Duke of Norfolk'. See Wilson to Burghley, *CSP Foreign 1575–1577*, pp. 10–11, no. 21, 1 February 1575, and Phillips, *Images of a Queen* 267n238. In his great catalogue of French authors, La Croix du Maine attributed the anonymous book to Belleforest, listing it among his original works: *Premier Volume de la Bibliothèque du Sieur de La Croix Du Maine, Qui Est un Catalogue Général de Toutes Sortes d'Autheurs Qui Ont Escrit en François depuis Cinq Cents Ans* … (Paris: Abel L'Angelier, 1584) 90.

[33] Lorna Hutson, 'Fortunate Travelers: Reading for the Plot in Sixteenth-Century England', *Representations*, 41 (1993), 83–103.

[34] The political implications of the eleventh *histoire* in the 1572 collection, devoted to Kanut, are discussed in François de Belleforest, *Le Cinquiesme Tome des Histoires Tragiques*, ed. Hervé-Thomas Campangne (Textes Litteraires Français; Geneve: Droz, 2013) xlv–l.

Amleth are the most strongly inflected by Belleforest's partisan engagement in contemporary political polemics.

The 'Argument' prefacing the *histoire* of Amleth is a long list of historical examples illustrating the point that 'the desire of rule causeth men to become traytors and murtherers'—so much so indeed, that 'without respect of consanguinitie, friendship, or favour whatsoever, they forget themselves so much as that they spared not to defile their hands with the blood of those men, who by all law and right they ought chiefly to defend and cherish.'[35] Examples of the murderous desire to obtain or hold on to power—ranging from Romulus murdering his brother to the sultan Soliman having his son Mustapha strangled with a bow string—conclude with an invitation for the reader to consider

> what tragedies have bin plaid to the like effect in the memorie of our ancestors [in Scotland and England], and with what charitie and love the neerest kindreds and friends among them have bin intertained. If you had not the hystories extant before you, if the memorie were not in a manner fresh, [if a King had not untimely died, and if the most tyrannical men, and who had no right to the lands and estates of their sovereigns, if children had not been conspiring to murder their fathers, and wives their husbands, if all this were not] known almost to every man, I would make a long discourse thereof.[36]

Although some of this passage is rather confused and confusing, with a verb apparently missing at the most important point, the reference to recent tragedies in England and Scotland might easily have been construed as a reminder of the 1567 murder of Henry Stewart, Lord Darnley, who was proclaimed King of Scots the day he married Mary, Queen of Scots.[37] That the translator or publisher thought it wiser to omit all the material enclosed in brackets in the quotation above from the 1608 English edition also indicates that the passage was seen as a reference to the family history of King James VI and I, son of Darnley and Mary.

---

[35] *Le Cinqviesme Tome des Histoires Tragiqves ... par François de Belle-forest Comingeois* (Paris: Iean Hulpeau, 1572), f. 146. Wherever possible, the translation comes from the 1608 *Hystorie of Hamblet* (London: Richard Bradocke, for Thomas Pauier); I cite the edition in Sir Israel Gollancz, *The Sources of Hamlet, with an Essay on the Legend* (London: H. Milford, Oxford University Press, 1926).

[36] Gollancz, *The Sources of Hamlet* 172–3. The passages in square brackets are omitted from the 1608 English version; the translation of those passages is mine. '...pour considerer quelles tragedies ont esté iouées pour ce mesme cas de la memoire de nos peres [en Escosse & Angleterre,] & auec quelle charité se sont carressez les plus proches parens ensemble: [si vous n'auiez les histoires en main, si la memoire n'en estoit comme toute fresche, si vn Roy n'estoit mort hors de saison, & si les plus tyrans, & qui n'ont aucun droit es terres & seigneuries de leurs peres, les femmes celles de leurs espoux, si tout cela] n'estoit presque cogneu à chacun, i'en ferois vn long discours: mais les choses estant si claires, la verité tant descouuerte, la peuple presque abreuué de telles trahisons, ie passeray oultre pour suiure mon proiet...' Belleforest, *Le Cinqviesme Tome des Histoires Tragiqves*, f. 148.

[37] On the death of Darnley, see John Guy, *Queen of Scots: The True Life of Mary Stuart* (Boston and New York: Houghton Mifflin, 2005) 208, 226–32, 253. The modern editor of *Le Cinqviesme Tome* correctly suggests that the events remembered by our fathers must be succession struggles marking the reigns of James III and James IV of Scotland at the turn of the sixteenth century. The second half of the passage, however, with its emphasis on the events being fresh in memory, would inevitably have reminded readers of more recent occurrences between Scotland and England. See Belleforest, *Le Cinqviesme Tome des Histoires Tragiqves*, ed. Hervé-Thomas Campangne, 320.

Belleforest was closely familiar with the events of 1567; in fact, he appears to have been the first to discuss them in print in France. The last pages of his 1568 *L'Histoire des Neuf Roys Charles* contains a detailed account of 'the death of the King of Scotland' and the accusations that Mary was involved in the conspiracy against Darnley. Belleforest compares the Scottish Lords' attempt to control the Queen and benefit from her unmarried state to the way the English are keeping their own Queen in check, and he also relates various hypotheses about the culprits of the assassination. Although he does not commit himself to any of them, he is clear throughout that Mary is innocent of his husband's murder, which is therefore a straightforward case of treason.[38]

Rather than offering further commentary on the Darnley murder, in the *histoire tragique* of 1570 Belleforest uses the story of Amleth to reflect more generally upon treason, tyranny, and the vengeance of God upon those who engage in them. In doing so he carefully positions himself as an opponent to arguments about the subjects' right to resist their tyrannical rulers—arguments the narrative could be construed as endorsing. For Belleforest, tyranny is a word with a broad spectrum of meaning: as the reference to the 'most tyrannical men' in the Argument suggests, it may refer to illegitimate rule, violent behaviour, or an abuse of power, all of which are for the sovereign to avenge. In Belleforest's *histoire*, Fengon (the equivalent of Shakespeare's Claudius) is repeatedly called both tyrant and traitor, and it is his treason—that is, his usurpation of the throne—that his nephew, Amleth, the *de jure* king, 'the true and undoubted heire of the valiant and vertuous king Horvendile'[39] (Belleforest's Hamlet Sr) punishes by killing him. As Amleth explains to his mother, 'if I lay handes upon Fengon, it will neither be fellonie nor treason, hee being neither my king nor my lord, but I shall justly punish him as my subject, that hath disloyally behaved himselfe against his lord and soveraigne prince.'[40]

The term 'tyranny' is as central to this *histoire tragique* of Amleth (and to other *histoires* in the same collection) as it was to the legally and constitutionally oriented controversies about government and succession. In the classic distinction elaborated by Bartolus, Fengon's rule can be described as a tyranny of usurpation (*ex defectu tituli*). Medieval and sixteenth-century theorists of resistance and tyrannicide often allowed the subjects of such tyrants to resist and overthrow the usurper—it was the subjects' opposition to tyrants of exercise (*ex parte exercitii*), i.e. to legitimate monarchs whose rule was despotic and unjust, that required a recourse to a higher principle than royal sovereignty, posing a serious challenge to political thought.[41] But in Belleforest's *histoire*, Amleth's killing of Fengon is carefully

---

[38] François de Belleforest, *L'Histoire des Nevfs Roys Charles de France* (Paris: Jean Le Blanc pour Pierre L'Huillier, 1568) 672–4, and cp. Alexander S. Wilkinson, *Mary, Queen of Scots and French Public Opinion, 1542–1600* (Basingstoke: Palgrave Macmillan, 2004) 86, claiming that no such account was published in French until 1570.

[39] Gollancz, *The Sources of Hamlet* 215.   [40] Gollancz, *The Sources of Hamlet* 225–7.

[41] Ephraim Emerton, *Humanism and Tyranny, Studies in the Italian Trecento* (Cambridge, MA: Harvard University Press, 1925) 126–56; Cecil N. Sidney Woolf, *Bartolus of Sassoferrato, His Position in the History of Medieval Political Thought* (Cambridge: Cambridge University Press, 1913) 163–73;

presented as an example of the former—or perhaps of neither. Through Belleforest's editorial asides and Amleth's orations, the *histoire* redescribes what may appear a successful rebellion against a ruler as the legitimate sovereign's punishment of such a rebellion, making a point about tyranny and about who may or may not legitimately take arms against such troubles and by opposing end them. Belleforest's 1570 text thus anticipates the upsurge of the French polemics about these issues in the wake of the Massacre, and indeed much of the print controversy about the Darnley murder and the deposition of Mary Queen of Scots.[42] Those later developments, and Belleforest's involvement in them, would have made the *histoire*'s polemical edge, its engagement with public arguments about legitimate political action, seem even sharper in retrospect.

A clear sense of Belleforest's polemical point in the *histoire tragique* is particularly significant given his initial reference to the changes in the form of Roman sovereignty and the analogy he sets up between Amleth and Brutus later in the narrative. Selective readings of these analogies have been used to imply Belleforest's republican leanings, and occasionally even the republican leanings of Shakespeare's play.[43] While references to the classical republican tradition are present in both, neither of these texts can in any meaningful sense be understood as republican. Belleforest's arguments about legitimate forms of sovereignty are always historically and locally specific: his disagreement with Hotman is based not on philosophical or Biblical principle, but on the interpretation of French law and custom. When in the Argument of the history of Amleth he invokes Roman examples, he does so to point out the general human tendency to desire and to abuse power, regardless of the form of sovereignty in effect. As he says, sedition and treachery characterized the Roman monarchy, and the corruption 'never ceased nor discontinued in the said principall cittie of the empire, as long as it was governed by the greatest and wisest personages chosen and elected by the people'; nor did it stop 'after the people were deprived of that libertie of election, and that empire became subject to the pleasure and fantasie of one man'.[44] Belleforest sees the constitutional form of sovereignty as irrelevant to the treacherous, seditious, treasonous tendency of humanity. His concern is with the remedies against these ubiquitous tendencies, and the liberty of election (where liberty does not entail automatic endorsement) makes no difference to how rightful government is. In this particular history, he

J. H. Burns and Mark Goldie (eds.), *The Cambridge History of Political Thought, 1450–1700* (Cambridge: Cambridge University Press, 1991) 210, 213–14.

[42] Of the seminal *monarchomach* texts, Hotman's *Franco-gallia* appeared in 1573, the anonymous *Vindiciae Contra Tyrannos* and Buchanan's *De Iure Regni* in 1579. Belleforest's ardently loyalist, anti-Calvinist pamphlets of the 1560s, which anticipated much of the language of the polemical editorializing in the *histoire tragique*, responded to the anti-royalist turn in Huguenot political rhetoric in the decade before the Massacre. On the pre-1572 polemics and Belleforest's role in them as a proponent of sacral hereditary monarchy, see Denis Crouzet, *Les Guerriers de Dieu: la Violence au Temps des Troubles de Religion (Vers 1525–Vers 1610)*, 2 vols. (Seyssel: Champ Vallon, 1990) 2:30–62.

[43] Hadfield, *Shakespeare and Republicanism* 187–91; and cp. the carefully argued reading of the play's republicanism in Kirk Melnikoff, 'Nicholas Ling's Republican *Hamlet* (1603)', in Marta Straznicky (ed.), *Shakespeare's Stationers: Studies in Cultural Bibliography* (Philadelphia: University of Pennsylvania Press, 2013), 95–111.

[44] Gollancz, *The Sources of Hamlet* 169–71.

aims to show how Prince Amleth managed to defeat a case of manifest treason, acting in accordance with the model set up by the greatest ancient example, for 'never any man was reputed by any of his actions more wise and prudent than Brutus, dissembling a great alteration in his minde'. Belleforest readily acknowledges the larger implications of the analogy, reminding the reader that Brutus's actions were intended 'to open a large way to procure the banishment and utter ruine of wicked Tarquinius, and to infranchise the people from the yoake of a great and miserable servitude'.[45] But lest Brutus's actions should be mistaken for models applicable in a Christian setting, Belleforest cites *Romans* 8:21 in support of his formulation of the most important rule to be born in mind here: 'But when I speake of revenging any injury received upon a great personage or superior, it must be understood by such an one as is not our soveraigne, againste whom wee maie by no meanes resiste, nor once practise anie treason nor conspiracie against his life.'[46] Infranchisement from the yoke of servitude means the re-establishment of the rule of the lawful monarch. Furthermore, Brutus and Amleth are held up as exemplary figures not of resistance but of prudent dissimulation through which they escape the onslaught of tyrannical rule. The appeal of this story of Amleth is precisely that by emphasizing Fengon's usurpation and Amleth's right to the crown it adjusts the Brutus story to a monarchical setting where regicide is not an available option. Belleforest's *histoire* of Amleth is a revision of the republican master-narrative into an exemplary account of the monarch's revenge upon traitors.

HAMLET'S SPEECHES AND HORATIO'S SILENCES

Shakespeare's *Hamlet* is an adaptation of Belleforest's *histoire tragique* for the commercial stage. The earliest editions of *Hamlet* call the play a 'tragicall historie'—the first time this phrase was applied in print to an English dramatic work[47]—in a gesture that highlights the play's debt to Belleforest and presents it as a translation between genres and languages. It is all the more surprising, therefore, to find how carefully Shakespeare's play avoids using the public language of political polemics and sidesteps concerns about the definition of, and possibilities of permissible action against, tyranny, which are so characteristic of his source. As recent scholarship has insisted, allusions to a republican tradition of the contestation of monarchical power do appear in *Hamlet*,[48] but it is precisely the displacement and derailment of this stance that defines the shape of the play's political world. Rather than formulating some version of 'republicanism', be that civic or constitutional, endorsing theories of resistance and tyrannicide, or, following Belleforest, making a case against them, Shakespeare's play seems to go out of its way to distance itself from either side of the debate. Unlike Saxo's, Belleforest's, or Nannini's Amleth,

---

[45] Gollancz, *The Sources of Hamlet* 195.   [46] Gollancz, *The Sources of Hamlet* 197.
[47] *Doctor Faustus* was published in 1604 (and after) as *The Tragicall History of D. Faustus*. No other pre-restoration play title uses the term (Marlowe's *Tamburlaine* appeared in 1590 'Deuided into two tragicall discourses').
[48] Hadfield, *Shakespeare and Republicanism* 184–204.

148 Hamlet *and the Profession of Politics*

Hamlet is not a public orator who takes up a stance, but the most famous monologist of Western literature. The public vocabulary of political contestation and polemic that defines the earlier versions of his story is absent even from his private meditations until the final scene.

Although it might be tempting to read *Hamlet* as a play about a tyrant's reign and the legitimate heir's struggle to restore order (and to make up his mind about the arguments for and against taking up arms against the tyrant),[49] apart from the comparison of the immobilized Pyrrhus to a 'painted tyrant' (2.2.476), the only reference to tyranny in Shakespeare's play occurs in the 1603 first quarto edition (Q1), in a speech that became, in the rather different form printed a year later, the best-known monologue in Western drama:

> To be, or not to be, I there's the point,
> To Die, to sleepe, is that all? I all:
> No, to sleepe, to dreame, I mary there it goes,
> For in that dreame of death, when wee awake,
> And borne before an euerlasting Iudge,
> From whence no passenger euer retur'nd,
> The vndiscouered country, at whose sight
> The happy smile, and the accursed damn'd.
> But for this, the ioyfull hope of this,
> Whol'd beare the scornes and flattery of the world,
> Scorned by the right rich, the rich curssed of the poore?
> The widow being oppressed, the orphan wrong'd,
> The taste of hunger, or a tirants raigne,
> And thousand more calamities besides,
> To grunt and sweate vnder this weary life,
> When that he may his full *Quietus* make,
> With a bare bodkin, who would this indure,
> But for a hope of something after death?
> Which pusles the braine, and doth confound the sence,
> Which makes vs rather beare those euilles we haue,
> Than flie to others that we know not of.
> I that, O this conscience makes cowardes of vs all,
> Lady in thy orizons, be all my sinnes remembred.[50]

The nature of the Q1 text and its relationship to the two variants of the more familiar version, as printed in the second quarto and the first folio, has been debated ever since it has been discovered.[51] Scholars have seen it either as an earlier

---

[49] As did Roland Mushat Frye, *The Renaissance Hamlet: Issues and Responses in 1600* (Princeton: Princeton University Press, 1984) 38–75.
[50] Shakespeare, *The tragicall historie of Hamlet* (1603), sigs. D4v–E1r.
[51] Lesser, *Hamlet after Q1*, in its last chapter (157–206) offers a helpful systematization of the approaches to the origins of the Q1 text, and is especially insightful on the dialectic between Q1 as earlier version versus the 'retrograde bibliography' originating with Collier that suggests that Q1 is a derivative of the more familiar texts.

version of the Q2/F play, or as a poor reconstruction derived from it.[52] But whether it is an early draft or a later derivation, what matters for my purposes is that reading Q1 against Q2/F reveals how radically the latter diverges from the more traditional perspective registered by the former. This argument is not about strict chronology: if Q1 is an earlier version, it will of course reflect an earlier intellectual moment, but I want to suggest that even if Q1 is derivative of, and therefore later than, Q2/F, it still provides evidence of earlier conventions, assumptions, and styles of representation, and thus registers the intellectual innovation of the more familiar version. For my purposes, the chronology and exact relationship of the three texts is thus irrelevant. I am working with the now standard assumption that Q1 is derivative of the better-known version because the argument that it is a register of earlier conventions and habits is less intuitively obvious than it would be if we assumed that Q1 was simply an early draft or version.

As even champions of Q1 as the record of an earlier version of Shakespeare's play often admit, the phrases and entire clauses familiar from the second quarto (Q2) and folio (F) versions, couched as they are in the occasionally garbled syntax of this monologue, indicate that it is the product of slapdash reconstruction rather than of carefully considered revision or original composition. Recent work has shifted the terms of our understanding of the transmission and reproduction of play scripts, forcing us to see even a text like Q1 as a product of active writing and reading, whether silent or vocalized, rather than the textual record of some dematerialized mental or perhaps aural process of memorial reconstruction.[53] While no theory has been able to fully and adequately account for the complex relationship between the three texts of the play, it still seems clear that Q1 is a text which appears to intellectually simplify what it is clearly at pains to reproduce. Although it would therefore be of rather limited use in understanding the mindset of the original author of the dramatic version, reading it closely may tell us something about how Shakespeare's text would have been understood, or indeed misunderstood, by some of its contemporaries. If the Q1 text is derived from Q2 or F, its divergences from its source are indicative of the conflicts between these early reader–revisers' expectations and the text they encountered,

---

[52] Terri Bourus, *Young Shakespeare's Young Hamlet: Print, Piracy, and Performance* (Basingstoke: Palgrave Macmillan, 2014), sets out to dismantle the theories of derivation on which the now standard account is based, and to argue that Q1 is the version of *Hamlet* written by William Shakespeare in 1589, which he then revised around the turn of the century. Bourus's critique is often trenchant, but I cannot agree with her positive arguments which are based on the assumptions that authorial revision proceeds from crude, clumsy early formulations to the poetic complexity of a masterpiece, and that the play and the character of Hamlet are autobiographical projections of Shakespeare.

[53] For recent accounts of the material form of transmission, see Scott McMillin and Sally-Beth MacLean, *The Queen's Men and Their Plays* (Cambridge: Cambridge University Press, 1998) 113–15; Simon Palfrey and Tiffany Stern, *Shakespeare in Parts* (Oxford: Oxford University Press, 2007); Tiffany Stern, 'Sermons, Plays and Note-Takers: *Hamlet* Q1 as a "Noted" Text', *Shakespeare Survey*, 66 (2013), 1–23. With the turn to shorthand as the possible medium of reporting, we are returning to Collier's original assumption about how Q1 came about; see Lesser, *Hamlet after Q1* 36–9. For two incisive recent studies of the relationships among the texts of *Hamlet* see Paul Menzer, *The Hamlets: Cues, Qs, and Remembered Texts* (Newark: University of Delaware Press, 2008); Marino, *Owning William Shakespeare* 75–106.

as well as of the habits of mind—these impressions of the past—on which they relied in resolving them.[54]

In spite of its confusions and blunders, the Q1 revision of the monologue follows a consistent logic. Where the Prince of Q2 offers a systematic, if systematically perplexed parsing of our options in the face of the unknown, the Prince of Q1 has no doubts as to what we will awake to from our dream of death. The 'undiscovered country' is here presided over by an 'everlasting judge', 'at whose sight / The happy smile, and the accursed damn'd', and it is in 'the ioyfull hope of' his judgement that Hamlet rehearses an unsurprising, but fairly coherent argument for worldly endurance. Far from being a 'sorry thing' or a 'hopeless garble',[55] the monologue is, if anything, consistently and joyously hopeful of an afterlife in which everything is going to be set right. Although its last lines allow the conflict between Christian acquiescence and the dictates of honour to emerge, the speech as a whole is motivated by a clear vision of how the injustices suffered in this world will be rectified.

The confidence of divine justice affords the Hamlet of Q1 a perspective on the forms and causes of human suffering that include poverty, hunger, the loss of husbands and parents: an unproblematically orthodox Christian view that is both transhistorical and socially inclusive.[56] The 'whips and scorns of time' in the Q2 and F monologue, on the other hand, suggest a different perspective, attributed to a historically and sociologically specific subject:

> For who would bear the whips and scorns of time,
> Th'oppressor's wrong, the proud man's contumely,
> The pangs of dispriz'd love, the law's delay,
> The insolence of office, and the spurns
> That patient merit of th'unworthy takes,
> When he himself might his quietus make
> With a bare bodkin? Who would fardels bear,
> To grunt and sweat under a weary life,
> But that the dread of something after death,
> The undiscover'd country, from whose bourn
> No traveller returns, puzzles the will,
> And makes us rather bear those ills we have
> Than fly to others that we know not of? (3.1.70–82)

---

[54] According to David Scott Kastan, the Q1 monologue shows 'unmistakable signs of logical and syntactic jumble that seem more a function of the troubled transmission of the text than of the troubled mindset of the hero', Kastan, *Shakespeare and the Book* 27. Although I take Q1 to be the product of the reconstruction of a more sophisticated text similar to the monologue as printed in Q2 or F, I am not making any assumptions here about the Q1 text as a whole, most of which is in fact perfectly coherent, and which also has unique features which cannot be blamed on the vagaries of transmission.

[55] G. R. Hibbard quoted by Alan C. Dessen, 'Weighing the options in *Hamlet* Q1', in Thomas Clayton, *The Hamlet First Published (Q1, 1603): Origins, Form, Intertextualities* (Newark: University of Delaware Press, 1992) 65–78, at 65; Robert Hapgood, review of *Hamlet: The First Quarto, 1603*, ed. Albert B. Weiner, *Educational Theatre Journal*, 19:2 (May 1967), 209–10, at 210.

[56] Lesser, *Hamlet after Q1* 195–206 makes a very similar argument about the perspective of Q1, focusing on the word 'conscience' in the monologue and elsewhere in the versions of the play.

The afterlife here is contemplated with 'dread' rather than 'hope', and with an agnosticism that often puzzles readers who point out that Hamlet has already received 'the most vivid confirmation of the nature of the afterlife'[57] in his encounter with the Ghost. In the absence of the promise of an ultimate settling of accounts, the Prince of Q2 rationalizes passive endurance through the casuistic evaluation of imperfectly known variables in the calculus of affliction. This sceptical, indeed cynical line of argument emerges from a series of complaints whose subject is also recognizably different from that of the Q1 monologue.

Especially when taken as a coherent list, the grievances in the familiar Q2/F version are specific to the social world of early modern gentlemen aspiring to promotion or at least survival in service. They are the complaints of a person who explains the cause of his distemper with the phrase 'I lack advancement' (3.2.331): the words of the underdog in a patronage economy, of the malcontent courtier whose services are unrewarded and whose suits unsuccessful, who bristles with a frustrated sense of justice and entitlement—and who seems to have no access to an overarching vision that would organize his experience into a meaningful and perhaps ultimately just whole from a perspective that would transcend the world he inhabits. The Q2/F monologue's view of the polity is limited to the hierarchies and dependencies of patronage, excluding both the dispossessed and the sovereign: the 'oppressor' whose 'wrong' Hamlet mentions here refers in contemporary usage not to a despotic supreme power, but to lords, people 'of the greatest rank of subjects in the land' domineering over their tenants—a practice James VI in *Basilikon Doron* advised his son to repress.[58]

This is not to suggest that the monologue is defined by James's concerns—quite the contrary. Whereas James sought to justify his vision of a 'free' (by which he means absolute) monarchy by stressing its benefits for the entire nation, the monologue concentrates on the world of the court, on the injustices rampant there—on the 'spurnes that patient merit of the unworthy takes'—without reference to such broader concerns as good government or the well-being of the people. The Folio text even qualifies the one gesture in the Q2 speech that seems to be pointing, if only metaphorically, beyond this courtly environment, revising 'who would fardels bear' to 'who would these fardels bear', as if to make sure the audience won't sneer at what might be misunderstood as Hamlet's disingenuous concern about actual physical labour.

Even 'dispriz'd love' ('despiz'd' in Q2), often read as a reference to the Prince's rejection by Ophelia, is in this context more immediately part of the vocabulary of loyalty and advancement than of a web of references to romantic entanglement: 'love' is a term for the devoted service of a patron.[59] In this speech famously oblivious of its own dramatic context, the phrase resonates more with Rosencrantz's anxious 'My Lord, you once did love me' (3.2.326) than with Hamlet's vicious

---

[57] Stephen Greenblatt, *Hamlet in Purgatory* (Princeton: Princeton University Press, 2001) 252.
[58] James VI and I, *Political Writings* 24.
[59] The discourse of patronage here represents 'the economic relations of patron and petitioner in terms that must be indistinguishable from other kinds of purer, more ideal relationships of love': John Barrell, *Poetry, Language, and Politics* (Manchester: Manchester University Press, 1988) 30.

'I did love you once...you should not have believed me' (3.1.115–19) game that he plays with Ophelia. This is the language Hamlet uses as he implores Rosencrantz and Guildenstern to confess that they were sent for by 'the obligation of our ever-preserved love'—a love and loyalty they so obviously despise by obliging Claudius (2.2.285–6). Similarly, when Hamlet promises Horatio, Marcellus, and Barnardo that he 'will requite [their] loves' (1.2.251), he expects them to manifest that love by loyally guarding a secret the sentinels have immediately recognized as boding 'some strange eruption to our state' (1.1.72)—and which it would be their office to make public. This is a language in which intimacy, loyalty, and power are inextricably intertwined, where power relations and political dependencies are articulated in private, personal terms, rather than in the public, institutional vocabulary of office.

When Hamlet encounters Horatio in the next scene, he praises his friend in the same 'anti-court' discourse used to express the tensions of a precarious environment of climbing, of kissing up and kicking down.[60] In this speech, the recognition of the perils of life at court—the only setting where an active, political life is conceivable—leads to its familiar consequence in the espousal of a Stoic perspective. In this context, flattery is the shorthand for the discursive efforts driven by a desire for advancement, and being 'passions slave' (3.2.72) the condition of someone unable to extricate himself from the constant existential pressures, the rewards, anxieties, frustrations, and desperations of this irrational and uncontrollable social world. If in his soliloquy Hamlet was still searching for a rationale for suffering the 'slings and arrows of outrageous fortune', he now takes stoic equanimity as a virtue beyond doubt and goes on to suggest that their friendship is a function, on the one hand, of Horatio's willingness to live up to such expectations, and on the other, of his own honest, disinterested recognition of Horatio's perfection, an admiration whose honesty is guaranteed by Horatio's social inferiority:

> Nay, do not think I flatter,
> For what advancement may I hope from thee
> That no revenue hast but thy good spirits
> To feed and clothe thee? Why should the poor be flatter'd?
> No, let the candied tongue lick absurd pomp,
> And crook the pregnant hinges of the knee
> Where thrift may follow fawning. Dost thou hear?
> Since my dear soul was mistress of her choice,
> And could of men distinguish her election,
> Sh'ath seal'd thee for herself, for thou hast been
> As one in suffring all, that suffers nothing,
> A man that Fortune's buffets and rewards

---

[60] Claus Uhlig, *Hofkritik im England des Mittelalters und der Renaissance: Studien zu einem Gemeinplatz der europäischen Moralistik* (Berlin and New York: Walter de Gruyter, 1973). For a reading that understands this discourse as 'oppositional', see Albert H. Tricomi, *Anticourt Drama in England, 1603–1642* (Charlottesville: University Press of Virginia, 1989); for a more sophisticated understanding of anti-court rhetoric see Annabel Patterson, '*Quod Oportet*, Versus *Quod Convenit*: John Donne, Kingsman?', *Reading between the Lines* (Madison: University of Wisconsin Press, 1993), 160–209.

> Hast ta'en with equal thanks; and blest are those
> Whose blood and judgment are so well commeddled,
> That they are not a pipe for Fortune's finger
> To sound what stop she please. Give me that man
> That is not passion's slave, and I will wear him
> In my heart's core, I in my heart of heart
> As I do thee.

—and then, as if this man was editor of himself: 'Something too much of this' (3.2.56–74). Seemingly picking up on Hamlet's self-chastising comment on his own garrulity in Q2/F, Q1 extricates the speech from its recognizable sociopolitical environment in the early modern system of patronage. Shorn of the neo-stoicism that served as the ideology of self-adjustment to the exigencies of this world, the speech becomes a flat argument about the expectable gains of flattery:[61]

> Nay why should I flatter thee?
> Why should the poore be flattered?
> What gaine should I receiue by flattering thee,
> That nothing hath but thy good minde?
> Let flattery sit on those time-pleasing tongs,
> To glose with them that loues to heare their praise,
> And not with such as thou *Horatio*.[62]

The Q1 version of the 'To be or not to be' monologue can be seen as a similar redaction, a revision indicative of the radical novelty of Q2's inside view of the murky corridors of power: a novel view of politics which has no interest either in the common good or in the transcendental justification of actions by way of the common good. As it attempts to reconstruct Hamlet's puzzled and puzzling ruminations, Q1 gets rid of the perspectivally constrained conceptual framework of the Q2 speech and falls back on a popular political rhetoric which was ubiquitous, indeed dominant, in the representation of politics on the public stage, but which was carefully relegated to the margins of the Q2/F texts of the play, and which doesn't even appear in their version of this particular speech.

Late sixteenth-century drama habitually viewed social evils as the effects of bad government, of the breakdown of the structures of counsel and consent. Its staging of political conflict was underpinned by the terms of the public contestation of the legitimacy of rule, which unfolded between the monarch and the counsellors who represented the interests of the realm. In this mode, the common good or the transcendental justification of actions provided the moral control over political considerations. References to tyranny were frequently deployed as part of this vocabulary of public conflict, and its emergence in Q1 is a sign of a reflexive recourse to a perspective the Q2 and F versions are clearly at pains to avoid, but one which a

---

[61] The classic argument about the role of neo-stoicism in the early modern state as an ideology of self-adaptation to political pressures is by Gerhard Oestreich, *Neostoicism and the Early Modern State*, ed. Brigitta Oestreich and H. G. Koenigsberger, trans. David Mclintock (Cambridge: Cambridge University Press, 1982).

[62] Shakespeare, *The Tragicall Historie of Hamlet* (1603), sig. F2v.

capable actor or playmaker would just as clearly be able to rely on in an improvised riff on human suffering. Accordingly, the courtly subject implied in the better-known version of the monologue is here replaced by subjects of an almost biblical generality: by the widow, the orphan, people who are starving, and who are (indeed because they are) subjects of tyrants. (It is an awkward sign of Q1's efforts to be universal that it mentions both poverty and the inconvenience of being resented by the poor.) The reference to a 'tirants raigne' should be seen as part of the formulaic vocabulary to which Q1 resorts in reducing the speech to the familiar vision of the political drama of the period, rather than as a sign of the redactor's (or Shakespeare's) dissatisfaction with the reign.[63] The distance between this vision and the perspective of Q2 shows how far Shakespeare's *Hamlet* (the play of Q2 and F) has wandered from the beaten path of late sixteenth-century political drama.

When drama written for the public stage deploys references to tyranny, they have an obvious exhortatory or accusatory valence, and tend to signal the imminence of open conflict. In *Julius Caesar*, accusations of Caesar's tyranny are voiced in a public space, in political debate, in arguments against Caesar and as a rallying cry. The play makes it difficult for its audience to simply identify with those who are attempting to describe Caesar's reign as tyrannical, inviting them, rather, to consider such descriptions as political acts that serve to legitimate the resort to extralegal measures.[64] Even in *Richard III*, the Shakespeare play which, along with *Macbeth*, is most obviously about a tyrant, public accusations of tyranny are not matter-of-fact accounts of the state of the realm, but the foundations of a partisan intervention. Open talk of tyranny surfaces at moments when a political agent appears on the scene ready to challenge the succession or depose the reigning monarch. Thus, in 3.7, Buckingham reports to Richard how he has talked to the citizens about Edward's 'tyranny for trifles', and then, in 5.2, Richmond addresses his 'fellows in arms...bruised underneath the yoke of tyranny', never referring to the king by his name, only as 'this wretched, bloody, and usurping boar', 'this foul swine'.[65] The charges against Richard are most fully voiced before the battle, in a piece of public rhetoric adapted from Holinshed, one which would have fit in Belleforest's or Nannini's collection of such harangues and is even labelled, rather

---

[63] The latter was suggested by e.g. Lilian Winstanley, *Hamlet and the Scottish Succession: Being an Examination of the Relations of the Play of Hamlet to the Scottish Succession and the Essex Conspiracy* (Cambridge: Cambridge University Press, 1921); Schmitt, *Hamlet Oder Hekuba* 26.

[64] Robert S. Miola, '*Julius Caesar* and the Tyrannicide Debate', *Renaissance Quarterly*, 38 (1985), 271–89. The accusatory nature of tyranny is analogous with that of treason, about which Harrington famously suggested that 'it doth never prosper, what's the reason? For if it prosper, none dare call it treason.' People may self-identify not only as republicans and conservatives, but also as communist dictators or absolute rulers, but no one would willingly call oneself a tyrant (or a traitor). Atheism, puritanism, and popery had somewhat similar characteristics in the early modern period, although these terms were indeed adopted as labels people were willing to identify with; cp. the overview of the methodological debates and historiography in Michael Hunter, 'The Problem of "Atheism" in Early Modern England', *Transactions of the Royal Historical Society, Fifth Series*, 35 (1985), 135–57; Peter Lake, 'Anti-Puritanism: The Structure of a Prejudice', in Kenneth Fincham and Peter Lake (eds.), *Religious Politics in Post-Reformation England: Essays in Honour of Nicholas Tyacke* (Woodbridge: Boydell Press, 2006), 80–97.

[65] John Jowett (ed.), *The Tragedy of King Richard III* (The Oxford Shakespeare, Oxford: Oxford University Press, 2000) 3.7.7, 5.2.1–2, 7, 10.

unusually for a playbook, as 'His oration to his souldiers', where Richmond reminds his men that 'God and our good cause fight upon our side', and that they are engaging in a battle against 'A bloody tyrant, and a homicide'.[66] Richmond's oration forges a link between God and country, uniting them in an apocalyptic fight against a common enemy, with references to the soldiers' wives and children (the potential widows and orphans of Hamlet's Q1 musings) leading inexorably to Richmond's battle cry that emphatically hinges on the claim of public legitimacy: 'In the name of God and all these rights, / Advance your standards, draw your willing swords.'[67] In *Richard III*, as in Belleforest's *histoire*, where Amleth gets to justify his deed before the Danes who look pale and tremble at the sight of the murdered Fengon, public talk of tyranny serves as a speech act that seeks to establish the legitimacy of the new reign. Such legitimating acts take place in a rhetorical space of public controversy: *Richard III* carefully juxtaposes Richmond's oration with a no less compelling (and similarly labelled) set piece by King Richard, which uses patriotism to fuel its rhetoric, whereas Amleth needs to defend himself against potential accusations of brutal murder and rebellion.

Although Shakespeare's *Hamlet* is as much about the transfer of political power, succession, and the legitimacy of rule, as are *Julius Caesar*, *Richard III*, or Belleforest's *histoire*, the play's central protagonist never has a chance to engage in a confrontation that would require or even allow for such public declarations of opposition and for the use of the language in which such declarations can be phrased. Hamlet dies before he could rehearse 'th'occurrents more and less / Which have solicited' his one public speech act, in which he gives his dying voice to Fortinbras (5.2.360–3), and his death makes it impossible for the play to rehearse the public, ideological discourses about the accountability of princes, tyrannicide, and political intervention in the course of the succession in general (5.2.360–3). Until his last, public moment, Hamlet lives and acts in the world of dependencies characterized by his monologue in Act 3, Scene 1, a world of private loyalties with no room for the public oratory that would allow the language and the concerns of political polemic to enter the play. If Hamlet has a public persona, that persona is fully subsumed in the existing political order; the frustrations he voices concern advancement, affiliation, and loyalty, not an open crisis of legitimacy. Claudius may have 'Pop't in between th'election and [Hamlet's] hopes' (5.2.65), but, as he insists at the beginning of the play, the 'better wisdoms' of the Council 'have freely gone / With this affair along', incontrovertibly establishing his title (1.2.15–16). As no less a legal authority than William Blackstone argued, Hamlet calls Claudius a drunkard, a murderer, a villain, but never a usurper—because in the elective monarchy of

---

[66] Jowett (ed.), *The Tragedy of King Richard III* 5.4.211, 219, 225, and the editorial comments in Appendix D, 384–5.

[67] Jowett (ed.), *The Tragedy of King Richard III* 5.4.242–3. This language appears earlier in the play, intoned by Queen Margaret, especially in 4.4: but while her prophetic voice prepares the ground for Richmond's return, from her position in the ghostly margin of the play she counterpoints, rather than participates in, the world of politics and political discourse. For a nuanced argument about the place of female voice in general, and Margaret's in particular, in Shakespeare's play, see Jean E. Howard and Phyllis Rackin, *Engendering a Nation: A Feminist Account of Shakespeare's English Histories* (London and New York: Routledge, 1997) 105–10.

Denmark, he appears to be an incontestably legitimate king.[68] It is true that the constitution of Denmark is not foregrounded by the play—the election is referred to only in passing, and its mechanisms are not discussed. But its effects are clear and incontrovertible: instead of Hamlet, the deceased king's son, it is his brother, Claudius who now sits on the throne, and yet the only character ever explicitly referred to as a 'usurper' in the play is the Ghost, who is seen as usurping the form of Hamlet Sr (1.1.49). There is no objection that could publicly be made against the legitimacy of Claudius's reign, because only the Ghost, Claudius, and by the end of the play, Hamlet, actually know the most important fact about it.[69] Throughout, the kingdom of Denmark exists in dramatic irony, ruled by a usurper without anyone realizing it.

As a result, Hamlet's desire for the crown remains the subject of oblique remarks, the murder of his father remains his private grievance, and Marcellus's suggestion that there might be 'something rotten in the state' a mere hint in a private conversation, none of which is ever turned into the pretext for the formation of an oppositional political community, or for political action publicly questioning the legitimacy of Claudius's reign. After learning how his father was murdered, Hamlet makes his companions swear on his sword: a powerful symbolic act that is often used in the period to represent the formation of a political community aiming to redress public wrongs. Shakespeare's *Lucrece*, as well as two near-contemporary plays, the *Revenger's Tragedy* and *Antonio's Revenge*, feature episodes where a group of men swear an oath upon a sword to turn against a tyrant. Shakespeare's *Hamlet* reiterates the topos while evacuating it of its political content. As Michael Neill has pointed out, the play stages 'an oddly disjunctive version of the original rite', since Hamlet's companions only swear to keep their knowledge secret, not to act upon it, and the scene also makes it clear that they have no idea what the Ghost might actually have revealed to the Prince. As Neill's careful reading shows, this revision of the convention emphasizes 'the prince's isolation even as it ostensibly denies it'.[70] And although the sworn companions leave the stage suspending—at Hamlet's insistence: 'Nay, let's go together' (1.5.198)—the formalities required by the hierarchical relationship between the Prince and his entourage, they are never to meet again in the play: the oath, rather than establishing a political community, a community of agents willing to take up a common, public cause, disperses it at its incipience. What I am arguing is that this revision of the familiar topos and the turn away from the rhetoric of public action is of a piece with the play's turn to the

---

[68] Blackstone's note was first published in Edmond Malone (ed.), *Supplement to the Edition of Shakspeare's Plays Published in 1778 by Samuel Johnson and George Steevens*, 2 vols. (London: C. Bathurst, W. Strahan, and others, 1780), 1:350–1.

[69] On the constitution of Hamlet's Denmark, see Honigmann, 'The Politics of *Hamlet* and "the World of the Play"'. Eric S. Mallin argues that the play mystifies the procedure whereby Claudius came to power: *Inscribing the Time: Shakespeare and the End of Elizabethan England* (Berkeley, Los Angeles, London: University of California Press, 1995) 112.

[70] Michael Neill, '"He That Thou Knowest Thine": Friendship and Service in *Hamlet*', in Richard Dutton and Jean E. Howard (eds.), *A Companion to Shakespeare's Works, Volume 1: The Tragedies* (Malden, MA: Blackwell, 2003), 319–38 at 328–9.

conditions and pressures of political service, of Shakespeare's effort at imagining politics as a profession.

INDEPENDENCE AND DEPENDENCE: THE FALL OF THE POLONIUS CLAN

Margreta de Grazia has convincingly argued that the focus of post-1800 readings of *Hamlet* on the inwardness of the Prince is the result of a radical revision of the understanding of the tragedy which its first audiences must have seen as a play revolving around the problem of the succession. This post-Romantic reading, de Grazia suggests, is the reinterpretation of Hamlet's performance of a secret, unspeakable desire, which in the early modern play was understood as Hamlet's frustrated expectation to succeed his father, an expectation made unspeakable by the public legitimacy of Claudius's reign. It is this uncontested legitimacy that makes it impossible for Hamlet to openly articulate his desires: to speak his desire for the crown would amount to questioning Claudius's succession, which would be synonymous with treason.[71] As my reading of the two versions of the 'To be or not to be' monologue indicates, Hamlet's political situation does not need to be considered in merely negative terms, something that only began to distinguish the play from other early modern political plays in Romantic interpretations. Hamlet's disappointment also had a clear contemporary effect: it allowed the play to engage the political world from the perspective of the private individual who inhabits the world of political activity without playing a public role, who works in the realm of politics without being a political agent in the strong, public sense, someone whose experience cannot find expression in the public political language of office, and whose frustrations cannot be addressed by a discussion about issues of common concern, about the legitimacy or illegitimacy of rule. This perspective, the one opened up by Shakespeare's *Hamlet*, is also the perspective of those members of early modern audiences who sought to prosper in political careers: of John Melton and his readers. This is not an argument about Hamlet's 'character'. The Prince is not the only figure in the play whose trajectory points away from the public contestation of power. Rather, in Shakespeare's play the Prince's frustrated political ambition aligns him with a whole cast of characters who are themselves revised versions of earlier, publicly engaged character types of the political stage, now entirely private in their political activities, or captured by the play in the moment of their turning away from public engagement.

Politics on the public stage before *Hamlet* was viewed in the terms provided by the rhetoric of counsel, and by an understanding of government in which the

---

[71] Few critics are willing to engage in the kind of radical historicism so characteristic of de Grazia's work; see Hamlet *without Hamlet* 85–108. Maus's important *Inwardness and Theater in the English Renaissance* ties the construction of interiority to the political pressures upon conscience and religious identity in the late sixteenth century. See also the polemical take on the critical problem of the play's construction of selfhood and inwardness in Lee, *Shakespeare's Hamlet and the Controversies of the Self*.

sovereign is advised and controlled by the lords of the realm.[72] In most pre-1600 histories and revenge tragedies, it is these counsellors and magistrates of the realm who are invested with the authority to manage the transfer of royal power, or to enter into conflict with the king. Their independent action on behalf of the commonwealth is underpinned by the late sixteenth-century understanding of the realm, in Patrick Collinson's term, as a 'monarchical republic', which in extreme cases allows for public action motivated by the civic consciousness of a limited circle of subjects.[73] Collinson's argument is based on the example of the 1584 Bond of Association, the signatories of which, peers as well as thousands of gentlemen and citizens, swore 'to act the utmost Revenge upon them' that 'shall attempt any Act, or counsel or consent to any thing that shall tend to the harm of her Majesty's Royal Person',[74] hypothetically assuming the role of the sovereign magistrate who can call a state of exception. It is the task of these magistrates to take revenge for a crime against the commonwealth or against a king, and it is this office that engages them in public discussion about the grievances caused by tyranny and treason. It is important to emphasize the strong monarchical limits on this 'republicanism', or rather, to recognize it—in order to avoid confusion—as emergency action conceivable within a mixed monarchy.[75]

On the stage, as in the contemporary understanding of the *regnum politicum*, the mixed monarchy, such acts of retribution were authorized by senior magistrates of the realm. Even such seemingly private stage-revengers as Titus or Hieronymo are carefully invested with the authority of public office, Titus by election, Hieronymo by acting as Lord Marshal (the highest civil law magistrate of England), to suggest their reliance on a participatory model of government and thus at least partially legitimate their emergency action. Although both Titus and Hieronymo are launched on trajectories of revenge that lack the public sanction of office, their initial investment with the effect of the elder statesman acting in the interest of the commonwealth implies a strong residual connection between office and political intervention.

Polonius is recognizable as just such an elder statesman, whose office demands that he advise, and if necessary also resist, the monarch. Not that he was ever likely

---

[72] For a short analysis of the basic structure and presuppositions of this rhetoric, see Conal Condren, *The Language of Politics in Seventeenth-Century England* (Basingstoke: Macmillan, 1994) 120. Cp. John Guy, 'The Rhetoric of Counsel in Early Modern England', in Dale Hoak (ed.), *Tudor Political Culture* (Cambridge: Cambridge University Press, 1995), 292–310. On the centrality of the interest in counsel to the pre-1600 English stage, see Dermot Cavanagh, *Language and Politics in the Sixteenth-Century History Play* (New York: Palgrave Macmillan, 2003) esp. 36–79.

[73] Collinson, 'The Monarchical Republic of Queen Elizabeth I', 407–8, and McDiarmid (ed.), *The Monarchical Republic of Early Modern England: Essays in Response to Patrick Collinson*.

[74] *A Complete Collection of State-trials, and Proceedings for High-treason,...the Fourth Edition...* Volume the First (London: T. Wright; for C. Bathurst [etc.]: and sold by G. Kearsly, 1776), col. 143. On the 1584 Bond, see David Cressy, 'Binding the Nation: The Bonds of Association, 1585 and 1696', in Delloyd J. Guth and John W. McKenna (eds.), *Tudor Rule and Revolution* (Cambridge: Cambridge University Press, 1982), 217–34 at 217–26.

[75] Johann P. Sommerville, 'English and Roman Liberty in the Monarchical Republic of Early Stuart England', in John F. McDiarmid (ed.), *The Monarchical Republic of Early Modern England: Essays in Response to Patrick Collinson* 201–16.

to have proved a particularly independent-minded counsellor: but with his death the play eliminates not only the hypothetical possibility of participatory action, but also the last vestige of the dramatic structures built on the rhetoric of official counsel that survive into the play, signalling the distance of Shakespeare's *Hamlet* from the public-oriented vision of the world of politics as articulated by the earlier dramatic tradition. Shakespeare's play puts the burden of revenge on the shoulders of Laertes and Hamlet, young men who lack both the actual office and its residual affect that could authorize their turning against their sovereign. Even in *Antonio's Revenge*, a play that, like *Hamlet*, pits a private revenger against a sovereign, the final act coordinates the carefully plotted revenge with parliamentary action. Antonio's revenge is aligned with the grievances of

> The States of Venice...so swoll'n in hate
> Against the Duke for his accursed deeds
> ...
> That they can scarce retain from bursting forth
> In plain revolt,

and in the decisive moment they 'join hearts unto [the revengers'] hands'.[76] In *Hamlet*, the Prince has no such ties to the political community of the Danish monarchy; he conceives of his revenge as a task imposed on a private person. His popularity, while it constitutes a threat to the stability of the realm, does nothing to authorize his actions or to invest them with public legitimacy. His only engagement in official business is an act of forgery that involves counterfeiting the royal signature as well as the royal seal;[77] and Shakespeare carefully times the arrival of the English ambassadors so as to avoid the eruption of the public scandal. When they show up, there remains no one to be scandalized or embarrassed by their news.

After the death of Polonius, it is not Hamlet, but Laertes, the son of the old counsellor, who attempts to set things right in a way that is familiar from earlier political plays. Laertes is the one major character with no precedent in Belleforest, and his introduction does a lot to reinforce the political tendency of the play's revision of the narrative history. Unlike Hamlet, Laertes is granted his moment of public confrontation with the King, when arriving in Elsinore at the head of a riotous crowd who cry 'Choose we! Laertes shall be king' (4.5.106). The rebellion he leads, prompted by the doubtful death of the King's counsellor, falls within the logic of the public accountability of the monarch to the community of the realm. The court's breach of constitutional norms, leaving Polonius's death uninvestigated, logically leads to the withdrawal of public consent from the reign. Some of the outlines of the scenario are most familiar from an earlier play by Shakespeare: *2 Henry VI*, where the commoners, suspecting that the good Duke Humphrey, one of Shakespeare's most memorable elder statesmen, may in fact have been

---

[76] John Marston, *Antonio's Revenge*, ed. W. Reavley Gair (Manchester: Manchester University Press, 1978) 5.1.17–23, 5.5.7.

[77] Stewart, *Shakespeare's Letters* 272–6, 290–4.

murdered, and that the circumstances of his death are being covered up, are threatening open rebellion unless the death of the old counsellor be investigated.[78]

But instead of questioning, or even actually addressing the King in public, Laertes chooses to confront him behind closed doors (albeit behind doors guarded by his own men), and by allowing him to do so the play also closes the door on the possibility of public contestation of grievances. Mentioning treason and rebellion, Claudius clearly gestures at the risks Laertes is running, and pacifies him by an offer to subject himself to the judgement of a jury selected from Laertes's 'wisest friends', promising that

> If by direct or by collateral hand
> They find us touch'd, we will our kingdom give,
> Our crown, our life, and all that we call ours
> To you in satisfaction. (4.5.203–6)

After this overwhelming show of honesty, Laertes's slightly awed and almost apologetic reiteration of what prompted his noisy entry begins to revise his original demand. When he enters, his cry is, 'Let come what comes, only I'll be reveng'd / Most thoroughly for my father' (4.5.135–6); at the end of the scene, he asserts that 'His means of death, his obscure funeral…Cry to be heard, as 'twere from heaven to earth', but this cry is no longer a call for revenge. Laertes's inversion of the direction of the proverbial cry of the victim's blood for vengeance, which in *Genesis* 4:10 sounds from earth to heaven, anticipates his revision of his original commitment to revenge into a call for inquiry in the final clause: 'That I must call't in question' (4.5.214). But even after listening (offstage) to the King's account of the murder, Laertes is still not sure why Claudius 'proceeded not against these feats, / So crimeful and so capital in nature' (4.7.6–7). It is Claudius's explanation that redirects the consideration of the problem from questions of justice and accountability to pragmatic issues. What stops him from going to 'a public count', Claudius says, is Hamlet's popularity, 'the great love the general gender bear him' which threatens to 'revert' Claudius's actions against himself (4.7.17–24): that is, if the circumstances of the murder would come to light, the 'distracted multitude, / Who like not in their judgment but their eyes' (4.3.4–5) would refuse to accept the facts and turn against their beloved Hamlet's prosecutors.

In the encounter between Claudius and Laertes, then, the claims of justice and public accountability are trumped by the concerns for the preservation of rule and security. His confrontation with the King lands Laertes in the space Hamlet has inhabited from the beginning, a space where insistence on the monarch's accountability to the commonwealth is reasonably and convincingly shown by the King to be counterproductive, and in the absence of any other available perspective, from the point of view of the play, moot.

The analogies between Hamlet and Laertes show the latter perhaps less a dupe, and both of them more the courtiers who have been socialized to take the political

---

[78] Hutson, *The Invention of Suspicion* 12–15, 241–58.

status quo as the unquestionable limit on their operation. So rather than seeing Laertes as a 'foil' to Hamlet, a hero whose history parallels that of the Prince and in doing so offers an alternative to Hamlet's supposed inaction, we should take Hamlet's suggestion, only present in the folio version—'by the image of my cause I see / The portraiture of his' (5.2.77–8)—as referring to a closer resemblance: it is not only their cause, but also the separation of that cause from the support of a political community that makes their position, and their decision to resort to private action, analogous. Returning to the court, his head no doubt full of crazy French ideas about election and about the subject's right to resist a tyrant—ideas proposed by Hotman and refuted by Belleforest that Laertes would have encountered during his stay in Paris, ideas that to Shakespeare's audiences may well have seemed radicalized versions of the native English idea of the mixed monarchy, or indeed of the emergency scenario of the 'monarchical republic'—Laertes has his moment of public action and open opposition. But as soon as he comes in from the cold, he recognizes himself as part of the system his father has taught him how to work. Polonius's spirit would not be the kind of ghost to incite anyone against his king.

HORATIO'S MOMENT

After Polonius's death, his place as the *confidant* of the royal couple is filled by Horatio, the humanist-educated scholar, and by Laertes and Osric, resulting in a court filled with a new generation of courtiers who lack traditional, constitutional authority, are completely dependent on their employers, and show not a trace of individual judgement or consciousness. With the death of Polonius, the Danish court becomes irreversibly monofocal. From a shadowy version of a king-and-council, checks-and-balances structure, it is transformed into an environment defined by the hierarchy of employment and patronage.

Horatio's role is particularly instructive here: a penniless, upwardly mobile scholar, he is granted his place in return for his loyalty and learning. As we have seen in the previous chapter, having hastened to Elsinore at the beginning of the new reign, he uses his intelligence—both personal and diplomatic—to manoeuver himself into Hamlet's presence and then quickly into his favour. Over the course of the play's four acts, he quietly advances to a position where he can advise the Queen on the 'dangerous conjectures' Ophelia's behaviour may give rise to 'in ill-breeding minds' (4.5.15). Just how astute this observation is, we recognize a few minutes later when we learn from the King about 'the people muddied, / Thick and unwholesome in their thoughts and whispers' as they rail against the Polonius family's grievances, with 'pestilent speeches' of Polonius's death stoking Laertes's resentment (4.5.78–94). Horatio's anticipation of the king's analysis of the political situation, of the dangerous murmurings of a public opinion driven by malcontent commentators, shows him a shrewd advisor, and someone with as good an understanding of the political importance of Ophelia as her father was ever capable of. Always aware of his place in the court, a place he holds not by right but by personal favour, Horatio attends to the interests of his betters whom he prudently advises but never presumes to contradict or control.[79]

In 3.2, reciprocating Horatio's 'Here, sweet lord, at your service' with his effusive speech which we have already glanced at earlier in this chapter and which has often been understood as a matter-of-fact account, an instance of motiveless generosity, Hamlet reads his friend's polite attention to his betters' needs as an exemplary instance of stoic equanimity, as a sign of disinterestedness. Their conversation concludes in the agreement that they will watch Claudius's reaction to the Mousetrap closely. As one of the most influential books on the play puts it, Horatio will be 'required to act as an independent witness'.[80] But if you want to make sure that a witness is truly independent, should you really remind him, your inferior, that you wear him in your 'heart of heart'?

We tend to read Hamlet's descriptions as straightforward statements of fact and thus to ignore the dramatic implications of those descriptions as speech acts. We also tend either to overlook Horatio's quiet advancement at court or to read it as greatness thrust upon him.[81] Horatio is of course neither passion's slave nor a pipe for Fortune's finger, but an attentive, self-effacing, loyal servant, fully aware of the benefits attendant upon loyalty. In Hamlet's and Horatio's relationship, the performance of equanimity and selflessness become the key to greatness: Hamlet's dying words publicly reward Horatio's stoic gestures of loyalty by bestowing upon him the task of inviting the conqueror to the throne: an office that does not necessarily bode ill for a courtier at the beginning of a new reign.

Horatio is first and foremost Hamlet's friend, and throughout the play, Hamlet defines himself in his relationships as a loving friend. But in contradistinction to readings of *Hamlet* that describe the friendship between Hamlet and Horatio as an intimate relationship of equals, I argue that their friendship is shot through with a sense of hierarchy and with the demands and benefits of political loyalty. In this, theirs is like all other intimate relationships in the play. In fact, Horatio's cautiously obliging attitude resembles Polonius's conduct in his own interactions with Hamlet—a solicitousness the Prince makes fun of at the end of 3.2, where he gets Polonius to recognize a whimsical array of animals, first a camel, then a weasel, and finally a whale, in the shape of a single cloud. However playful the conversation, it is not easy for a courtier to disagree with his prince, and in this insignificant-looking moment of the play, Hamlet is taking cruel, bratty pleasure in his ability to command attention and agreement.[82]

In an essay that explores the conceptual resonances between the election of the monarch and the election of a friend in *Hamlet*, Julia Lupton argues not only that

---

[79] In his reading of Q1, Kirk Melnikoff briefly compares an assertive Polonius/Corambis to a servile Horatio in terms similar to my account here: Melnikoff, 'Nicholas Ling's Republican *Hamlet*', 109.

[80] Nigel Alexander, *Poison, Play, and Duel: A Study in Hamlet* (Lincoln: University of Nebraska Press, 1971) 77.

[81] See the otherwise excellent brief essay by Lars Engle, 'How Is Horatio Just? How Just Is Horatio?', *Shakespeare Quarterly*, 62 (2011), 256–62.

[82] I owe this realization to Péter Dávidházi, 'Teve, Menyét, Cethal', *Holmi*, 6 (1993), 787–96.

'the Hamlet-Horatio couple draws its energy from the classical discourse of friendship', but also that when Hamlet 'elects' Horatio to be his intimate and equal friend, this election locates 'the prince on a horizontal plane defined by genuine instances of equitable encounter'.[83] But to judge whether the relationship is truly equitable, we must ask whether Horatio could have made that election himself, and whether he could have declined Hamlet's election. Hamlet does indeed deploy a version of the classical discourse of friendship, which, as Laurie Shannon has put it, creates a 'virtually civic parity not modelled anywhere else in contemporary social structures'[84]—but that discourse is deployed in a dramatic setting which shows such parity to be wishful thinking at best, and at the (most likely) worst, a tool in the hands of the more powerful party with which to impose an obligation to cooperate. Talking of friendship is Hamlet's way of making Horatio an offer he can't refuse.

The consequences of the social inequality between the two friends has recently been addressed in a fine analysis of their modes of address by Elizabeth Hanson, who has shown how the relationship between Hamlet and Horatio is inscribed in the tensions between poor scholars and young noblemen attending the universities, and how Hamlet uses the claim that his soul 'was mistress of her choice, / and could of men distinguish her election', to distinguish himself through his admiration for the intellectual and moral distinction of his 'fellow student'.[85] But Hanson's interest is in Hamlet, not in Horatio—she wants to know how Horatio benefits Hamlet, not what it means to be Horatio. In that regard, Christopher Warley's analysis of the position of Horatio might be more helpful. He identifies the two distinct, conflicting, or complementary perspectives on him—that of Marcellus, who sees him as the court insider politico, and that of Hamlet, who imposes on him the role of the just scholar, devoid of ambition and flattery. Like Warley, I am suggesting that this coexistence of two descriptions, this two-sidedness of Horatio's character, should be the key to our understanding of Horatio. But instead of trying to understand the logic of the relationship between Horatio and Hamlet in terms of class difference, and thus modelling it on modern social experience, as does Warley, I argue that we should understand it based on the logic of patronage, employment, and political service. As we have seen in the previous chapter, the play's interest is not in what we call class status and in representations of class difference but in avenues of mobility within the system of patronage (avenues that literally involve mobility, travel, and return)—an observation that should perhaps go without saying, or rather, should be understood once we recognize that *Hamlet* is not a bourgeois novel, after all. Rather than making it 'possible to see class', I think the two descriptions of Horatio articulate an understanding of friendship and distinction as interdependent conditions of employment and service. What they make visible is the logic of the use of loyalty and expertise, not of socioeconomic

---

[83] Lupton, *Thinking with Shakespeare* 80, 84.
[84] Laurie Shannon, *Sovereign Amity: Figures of Friendship in Shakespearean Contexts* (Chicago: University of Chicago Press, 2002) 2.
[85] Hanson, 'Fellow Students: Hamlet, Horatio, and the Early Modern University', 224.

status or its cultural accoutrements and articulations.[86] Loyalty and expertise are, of course, the twin virtues of the civil servant, not of the active citizen.[87]

The early modern rhetoric of disinterested friendship, as Alan Bray argued in his deeply melancholy book, was part of a utopian rhetoric. Which is not to say that this rhetoric was insincere, only that it would be naive to mistake such necessary utopias for complete descriptions of the social relationships they envelop.[88] In the world of the play, Hamlet may be describing friendship in this rhetoric, but his friendships so described appear as thoroughly politicized power relationships that serve as informal alternatives to the public formalities of office. Although Hamlet revises Horatio's 'your poor servant ever' by responding 'Sir, my good friend. I'll change that name with you' (1.2.162–3), this ends up reminding us as much of the interchangeability of the notions of service and friendship as of the distinction between the two. Friendship in the play is a term for the relationship between patron and client, and love the emotion that binds a client to his patron.[89]

Throughout the play, Hamlet wields the demands of his love politically, as a loyalty that is frequently in conflict with the duties of office. As we have seen, he requests that the sentinels express their love for him by not reporting what they saw during their watch, as would be their duty; he reminds Rosencrantz and Guildenstern of their love to force them to break their loyalty to their employer, the king, by confessing their secret employment; and he woos Horatio into conspiring with him against the king. Hamlet deploys a political network of clients bound to him by spoken and unspoken promises of later reward—and of course even without such imputed further benefits, the Prince's friendship is a most precious—i.e. pragmatically valuable—asset already, the gift of social prestige of the rarest kind. Last but not least, the King, who obviously relies on a host of office-holding men in his service, also commands the loyalties of clients bound to him informally, and by befriending Laertes, he replaces his dead counsellor with someone who is willing to 'jointly labour' (5.2.208) with him in the face of the 'great love the general gender bear' (4.7.18) to Hamlet.

Claudius's formulation reminds us of the people of Denmark in the background of the events of the play, of 'the people' who just now appeared as 'muddied, / Thick and unwholesome in their thoughts and whispers / For good Polonius' death' (4.5.81–3) and giving their support to Laertes's cause, and who are now seen as equally eager to be enlisted as Hamlet's followers. The apparent fickleness with which they appear to be giving support to any potential challenger to the crown obviously revises the understanding of the public support to Laertes's rebellion as a monarchical–republican movement growing out of the considered opinions and

---

[86] Christopher Warley, *Reading Class through Shakespeare, Donne, and Milton* (Cambridge: Cambridge University Press, 2014) 47–72, the quotation at 70.
[87] Stolleis, *Staat und Staatsräson in Der Frühen Neuzeit* 212–26.
[88] Alan Bray, *The Friend* (Chicago: University of Chicago Press, 2003).
[89] I am deeply indebted here to the elegant and thoughtful analysis of the connections between love and duty, friendship and service in the play in Neill, '"He That Thou Knowest Thine": Friendship and Service in *Hamlet*'. On how Shakespeare's other works explore the complex conceptual relationship between love and service—of which the present discussion is only touching on one aspect—see also David Schalkwyk, *Shakespeare, Love and Service* (Cambridge: Cambridge University Press, 2008).

perceived grievances of citizens hidden inside Claudius's subjects. More importantly still, the description of Hamlet's popularity as 'love' also reminds us of the wider implications of politics conceived in the private, informal terms of affection. Commonly termed 'popularity' in the period, the love of the 'general gender' is an informal, unofficial pressure on the administration of justice and on governance in general—it is a political force outside the bounds of the formal institutions of the monarchy, a force not contained or organized by the established offices of the realm, a force exerted by a community of private participants, rather than by public personae.[90] The value of that 'great love' also answers Hamlet's rhetorical question: 'why should the poor be flattered?' (or rather, since it is a rhetorical question, dismisses it): the poor are precisely 'the general gender' whose love we call popularity.

It is of course such a coming together of private individuals seeking to discuss and perhaps to influence the course of political events that Habermas understood by the term 'public sphere', but the private individuals coming together in his emergent public sphere were also seeing themselves as clearly distanced from, if not necessarily opposed to, the state. In contradistinction to such a Habermasian vision, the language used by the play makes it clear that at this moment, popularity in *Hamlet* is not only unofficial, but also closely affiliated and aligned with the workings of the systems of patronage: in fact, Hamlet's popularity, the politically effective love of the 'general gender' is an extension of the informal patronage relationships he fosters and wields.

The intimate and affective language of love and friendship serves as an alternative to the adversarial public talk of legitimacy and office. The difference between these two modalities, as Shakespeare's *Hamlet* makes clear, has further implications. Being the loyal client of someone great, unlike holding the public office of magistrate or counsellor, involves no obligation to represent the interests of a constituency, be it the commonwealth of the realm or some other political community, and does not entitle one to enter public debate or conflict as an independently responsible agent.[91] The political agency informed by the love between patron and client is personal and private, and is not expected to go 'to a public count' (4.7.17)—but in *Hamlet*, this exemption from accountability no longer serves to undermine its ethos.

---

[90] Peter Lake and Steven C. A. Pincus (eds.), *The Politics of the Public Sphere in Early Modern England* (Manchester and New York: Manchester University Press, 2007); Doty, 'Shakespeare's *Richard II*, "Popularity," and the Early Modern Public Sphere'. The argument about Shakespeare's darkly critical perception of parliamentary representation in Arnold, *The Third Citizen* explores an important aspect of this problematic.

[91] While Julia Lupton once attempted to trace the idea of liberal citizenship to the notion of friendship as it appears in *Hamlet*, I would suggest that of the social *personae* actually available to the characters inhabiting the play, we ought rather to consider how the counsellor, the character effectively eclipsed in the play, might embody analogies, and perhaps anticipations, of such a notion; for her earlier position see Julia Reinhard Lupton, 'Hamlet, Prince: Tragedy, Citizenship, and Political Theology', in Diana Henderson (ed.), *Alternative Shakespeares 3* (London: Routledge, 2007), 181–203. Her formulations have become more cautious in the revised version of the essay in her *Thinking with Shakespeare*, although in that book she is still engaged in rescuing Shakespeare for a genealogy of liberalism, see e.g. 69–95 and 97–9.

Earlier plays viewed such private political agents, the likes of Hamlet, Laertes, and especially Horatio, with a fair amount of suspicion. The conflicts of many early modern political plays revolved around crises that illustrate the consequences of the influence of evil counsellors and flatterers, or of rulers ignoring the advice of good counsellors. The novelty of *Hamlet* is that such a character, a character whose position resembles that of such educated social climbers as the Tresilian of the anonymous *Thomas of Woodstock*, the Ateukin of Robert Greene's *James IV*, the Gaveston of Christopher Marlowe's *Edward II*—that is, of favourites who are contrasted with the born counsellors and lords of the realm, is now represented with an obvious respect and positive affect, without ever suggesting that his access to royalty is in any way made official.[92] That Horatio is the only surviving major character of the play, whose account of the 'accidental judgments, casual slaughters', of 'purposes mistook / Fall'n on th'inventors' heads' (5.2.387, 389–91) is the only one available to posterity, goes a long way to help us see the play's perspective on the realm of politics as the perspective of someone for whom there is only one source of authority: his patron. That until the third act, Polonius and Horatio take turns on the stage, and are for all purposes invisible to each other, never addressing or even mentioning each other, and that with some minor adjustments to exits and entrances in 3.2 an actor could even double in these two roles, is an emblematic indication of the complementary modes of political operation they embody.[93] That in such a hypothetical production this actor would take curtain calls as Horatio indicates the new direction Shakespeare's *Hamlet* has taken.

---

[92] On the question of favouritism and access, see Mario DiGangi, *The Homoerotics of Early Modern Drama* (Cambridge: Cambridge University Press, 1997) 104–25; Blair Worden, 'Favourites on the English Stage', in J. H. Elliott and L. W. B. Brockliss (eds.), *The World of the Favourite* (New Haven and London: Yale University Press, 1999), 159–83; Curtis Perry, *Literature and Favoritism in Early Modern England* (Cambridge: Cambridge University Press, 2006) 55–130. It is his lack of a formal office at the Elsinore court that distinguishes Horatio from other benign climbers, as from the eponymous hero of the 1600 *Thomas Lord Cromwell*, for example.

[93] T. J. King suggests that Polonius doubles as the Clown, and allows the Horatio actor no second role. Such casting is practicable, although obviously motivated by the entrenched reading of Polonius as 'At times, indeed, almost ridiculous— / Almost, at times, the Fool.' At 619 lines, the Polonius–Horatio actor's role would still only be slightly longer than Claudius's 544, and less than half of Hamlet's 1338: a perfectly feasible part, which would reduce the number of principal actors necessary from nine to eight; cp. T. J. King, *Casting Shakespeare's Plays: London Actors and Their Roles, 1590–1642* (Cambridge: Cambridge University Press, 1992) table 60. The Arden 3 editors also see Horatio as 'very unlikely to be doubling any other parts': Ann Thompson and Neil Taylor, '"Your Sum of Parts": Doubling in *Hamlet*', in Lukas Erne and Margaret Jane Kidnie (eds.), *Textual Performances: The Modern Reproduction of Shakespeare's Drama* (Cambridge: Cambridge University Press, 2004), 111–26 at 124. King as well as Thompson and Taylor consider whether two characters appear in the same scene—but there is no reason to assume that early modern stage practice paid more attention to formal scene divisions than to the characters' exits and entrances. Polonius and Horatio never address each other, and when they appear in the same scene, in 3.2, their lines are always separated by marked entrances, exits, or stage business that would allow the actor to exit, change and re-enter in a different role. But my interest here is less in the practicalities of performance, and more in the realization that these two characters' appearances are in what linguists would call 'complementary distribution', appearing as each other's context-dependent equivalents, versions of the political advisor under different regimes of political culture.

PART II

POLITICAL KNOWLEDGE AND THE PUBLIC STAGE IN HAMLET'S MOMENT

4

'Vile and Vulgar Admirations'
Chapman and the Public of Political News

NEWS

In *The Great Assises Holden in Parnassus*, a 1645 satire on the news trade, a series of English newsbooks are arraigned for their profit-driven business of lie-mongering before a tribunal of European men of letters, led by Francis Bacon, and including such luminaries as Philip Sidney, Pico della Mirandola, Erasmus, Jean Bodin, Selden, Grotius, and others.[1] What makes the poem more than a mere rehearsal of the familiar commonplaces about the notorious unreliability of printed news is the composition of the jury: the authors (or personifications) of the news publications are tried before twelve poets, and the poem's main point is that such a jury is indeed a jury of their peers, newswriting being another kind of literary activity, and poetry just another form of lying for profit. As the 'malefactours' try to raise objections to the composition of the jury, 'Histrionicke Poets'—the single largest group of jurors: in fact, if we include Drayton and Davenant, their majority—receive particularly vicious commentary from the dock:

> These mercinary pen-men of the Stage,
> That foster the grand vises of this age,
> Should in this Common-wealth no office beare,
> But rather stand with us Delinquents here:
> Shakespear's a Mimicke, Massinger a Sot,
> Heywood for Aganippe takes a plot:[2]
> Beaumont and Fletcher make one poët, they
> Single, dare not adventure on a Play.
> These things are all but th'errour of the Muses,
> Abortive witts, foul fountains of abuses. (E3r)

These playwrights, celebrities of past decades, should not merely be disqualified from the jury—their offences are such that they belong with *Mercurius Britannicus*, *Mercurius Aulicus*, *The Post*, and the rest of 1640s periodicals. Newsbooks and playbooks, news and plays, are of a kind.

---

[1] (London: Richard Cotes for Edward Husbands). The poem is traditionally attributed to George Wither. For an illuminating reading of the poem in its 1640s context, see Joad Raymond, 'The Great Assises Holden in Parnassus', *Studies in Newspaper and Periodical History*, 2 (1994), 3–17.

[2] i.e. uses other writers' plots as the source of his inspiration.

In comparing plays to news, the satire of *The Great Assises* collapses two distinct historical moments dominated by two mass media: the periodical publications of the 1640s and the theatre of the first couple of decades of the seventeenth century, when Heywood, Shakespeare, Beaumont, and Fletcher were active. Of course, in 1645 there wasn't even a public stage that could offend. What is striking about the conjunction is how clearly it highlights a turning point in the history of news media: the public stage was closed less than a year after the first English newsbook got published.[3]

But the dominance of the stage as a public medium started to wane before the closing of the theatres. By the time they were closed in 1642, they had long lost both their political edge and their centrality to the field of discussion—to print.[4] Printed news had been in wide circulation decades before the first newsbooks appeared, and the printing of the first English language *corantos*—periodical publications of foreign news—even prompted Ben Jonson to write a dramatic satire 'wherein the age may see her own folly or hunger and thirst after published pamphlets of news'.[5] The theme of *News from the New World*, his 1620 masque, received full-length treatment in 1626, in the play *The Staple of News*. The 'folly, or hunger and thirst' at that point was indeed such that the dramatic satire of the emergent news industry was mistaken for the real deal: the preposterous intelligence conveyed by the news-fabricating business to its on-stage customers in Act 3 of the play was lapped up by the theatre audience for real news. Or so Jonson claimed in his note 'To the Readers' inserted between Acts 2 and 3 of the Folio text, in a complaint which is not so much a sign of genuine concern as an extra twist on his complacent satire of undiscriminating consumers of news, and perhaps also a wishful assertion of the power of the stage to hold its own against the press as the truly and properly public, popular medium.[6] But it is nonetheless true that—as D. F. McKenzie pointed out forty years ago—the satire of *The Staple of News* identifies a radical change in the economy of information in the seventeenth century: it marks the rise of the periodical news publication, and the 'end of theatre as the only secular mass medium, the end of the play-house as the principal forum of public debate, the end of the actors' popular function as the abstracts and brief

---

[3] On the importance of 1641, see Joad Raymond, *The Invention of the Newspaper: English Newsbooks, 1641–1649* (Oxford: Clarendon Press, 1996); Zaret, *Origins of Democratic Culture*; Peacey, *Print and Public Politics in the English Revolution*.

[4] David Scott Kastan, 'Performances and Playbooks: The Closing of the Theatres and the Politics of Drama', in Kevin Sharpe and Steven Zwicker (eds.), *Reading, Society and Politics in Early Modern England* (Cambridge: Cambridge University Press, 2003), 167–84.

[5] *The Staple of News*, 'To the Readers', in Jonson (2012) 6:78.

[6] Stuart Sherman, 'Eyes and Ears, News and Plays: The Argument of Ben Jonson's *Staple*', in Brendan Dooley and Sabrina A. Baron (eds.), *The Politics of Information in Early Modern Europe* (London and New York: Routledge, 2001), 23–40 at 34–6; Marcus Nevitt, 'Ben Jonson and the Serial Publication of News', *Media History*, 11 (2005), 53–68; Alan B. Farmer, 'Play-Reading, News-Reading, and Ben Jonson's *The Staple of News*', in Marta Straznicky (ed.), *The Book of the Play: Playwrights, Stationers and Readers in Early Modern England* (Amherst & Boston: University of Massachusetts Press, 2006), 127–58.

chronicles of the time. The dramatic poet, as rhetor in the truest sense, had lost his vocation to a journalist.'[7]

The plays discussed in this book were written before this transformation. When thinking about their place in the circulation of information, we will of course first remember that their successes and failures, the scandals they created, and even their performances, as public events, were obviously news. So when Polonius excitedly but belatedly reveals to Hamlet, 'My lord, I have news to tell you. [...] The actors are come hither, my lord', Hamlet's seemingly sceptical 'Buzz, buzz!' serves to keep the old man going, letting this 'father of good news' (2.2.42) make a fool of himself by embellishing a report whose only fault is that it is already known (2.2.385–400). But around the turn of the century, the theatre was itself an important news medium. Trying to secure the best possible treatment for the players, Hamlet reminds Polonius not of their artistry, but of their power to shape public opinion by broadcasting current information: '...let them be well used, for they are the abstract and brief chronicles of the time. After your death you were better to have a bad epitaph than their ill report while you live' (2.2.519–22).

In Hamlet's moment, the English stage was likely a more important purveyor of news than the extant corpus of published plays implies. Plays disseminated both information that centuries later would have belonged in the gossip column, and also political news—mostly, it seems, news from abroad. To a much-travelled eye-witness, the London stage around 1599 seemed uniquely invested in the circulation of international news. Although he saw Italian, Spanish, and French troupes perform across Western Europe, and commented on them extensively in his journals, the Swiss medical graduate Thomas Platter singled out the English as the people who 'learn from the comedies [i.e. plays] what is happening in other countries'.[8] Of course in plays like *The Jew of Malta* or *The Merchant of Venice*, fictional plots are set in richly imagined and increasingly specific foreign locations (where the repeated question 'What news on the Rialto?' makes the foreign sound reassuringly familiar to news-talking Londoners). Political events of the recent and still acutely relevant past were also dramatized in such plays as Peele's *Battle of Alcazar*, the anonymous *A Larum for London, or the Siedge of Antwerpe*, or Marlowe's *Massacre at Paris*, and the interest in international politics gave rise to historical plays that viewed current conflicts in the distant mirror of medieval history.[9] But

---

[7] Donald F. McKenzie, '"The Staple of News" and the Late Plays', in William Blissett, Julian Patrick, and R. W. Van Fossen (eds.), *A Celebration of Ben Jonson* (Toronto: University of Toronto Press, 1973), 83–128 at 126. McKenzie, like most critics and historians, equates (to my mind problematically) the conduct of public debate with being the 'abstracts and brief chronicles of the time', public polemics with the circulation of information. In quoting *Hamlet* here, McKenzie is using the Folio 'abstracts' where the plural clearly nominalizes what in the Quarto reads as an adjective. Intellectually, I prefer the Folio reading—I am not sure what an 'abstract chronicle' might be like—but my text is Jenkins, whose edition is based on Q2.

[8] Thomas Platter d. J., *Beschreibung der Reisen durch Frankreich, Spanien, England und die Niederlande, 1595–1600*, ed. Rut Keiser (Basler Chroniken, 9; Basel & Stuttgart: Schwabe & Co. Verlag, 1968) 795.

[9] Andrew M. Kirk, *The Mirror of Confusion: The Representation of French History in English Renaissance Drama* (New York: Garland, 1996); Alan Stewart, 'The Forms of News from France in Shakespeare's *3 Henry VI*', in Allison K. Deutermann and András Kiséry (eds.), *Formal Matters:*

occasional references to lost plays about current events (a few of which I will discuss in this chapter) indicate that the most timely plays of the period never got published, and that (as I would argue: unsurprisingly) most instances of this important element of London's mediascape in Hamlet's moment probably disappeared without a trace.

In what follows, I will try to imagine what it meant for people outside of the realm of politics to experience political information before the periodical print publication of news and what it meant for drama to represent such news. The logic of the circulation of news in this pre-newspaper moment was fundamentally different from the news culture defined by the dominance of the printed periodical press: the ideal type developed several decades later is simply not applicable to the context of the political drama of Hamlet's moment, while the logic of this earlier setting played an often underestimated role in creating the demand for the industrial production of political information in the first place.[10]

Our own political culture, which (at least in its public rhetoric) valorizes openness and transparency, might make it hard for us to imaginatively enter a regime of thought of which the value and virtue of secrecy is constitutive. The texts and contexts of the political drama of the first decade of the seventeenth century are instructive in this regard. As if to acknowledge their dependence on the characteristically restricted circulation of political information, the plays most intensely interested in the business of politics are also the ones that cast the products of the manuscript culture of diplomacy and government in decisive roles. Shakespeare's *Hamlet*, with Claudius's commission carried by Rosencrantz and Guildenstern, and the new commission devised by Hamlet to replace it, is followed by other plays representing frenzied political and diplomatic activity conducted through writing, delivering, intercepting, purloining, forging, or copying letters and documents that decide the fates of people and countries. While they both dramatized such activity and depended on its textual products for their 'sources', on occasion these plays themselves also contributed some grist to the mill of diplomatic correspondence through their perceived offences to the foreign notables they represented.

Reading the Materials of English Renaissance Literature (Manchester: Manchester University Press, 2013), 149–69.

[10] Pre-newspaper is a key term here. My understanding of the circulation of news in the specific *milieux* of the late sixteenth century and the turn of the seventeenth, and of the connections and continuities among the various news media, is much indebted to the work of Fritz Levy, see especially his 'How Information Spread among the Gentry, 1550–1640', 'The Decorum of News', 'Staging the News'. On the intersections between political plays and the first periodical news organs: the *corantos*, and on the 1620s and Thirty Years War as the context in which the stage took an active role in the polemical presentation of news, see especially (in addition to work already cited): Limon, *Dangerous Matter: English Drama and Politics in 1623/24*; Werner, 'The Hector of Germanie'; Sherman, 'Eyes and Ears, News and Plays'; Nevitt, 'Ben Jonson and the Serial Publication of News'; Farmer, 'Play-Reading, News-Reading, and Ben Jonson's *The Staple of News*'. In this chapter, my emphasis is on the continuities and discontinuities of the social world and culture of political news of Hamlet's moment with the public sphere and the culture of news later in the seventeenth century. This may have the effect of apparently collapsing later, historically distinct periods into one, so I ought to make clear that I do not argue that the public sphere and political culture of the period after the appearance of the earliest serial and periodical news publications were without radical ruptures and transitions.

In this chapter I focus on transfers of information among various textual media and among various settings of secrecy, privacy, and publicity. Locating the plays in the network of these information transfers in Hamlet's moment, when the public, critical, polemical aspects of news culture were not yet its dominant features, changes our understanding of the function of the stage in this economy of political knowledge. Whereas Shakespeare's *Hamlet* was primarily interested in the production, reproduction, and use of secretive political correspondence—that is, in the powers of political writing in its primary, courtly, professional context—and postponed the public revelation of the textual intrigue to which Rosencrantz and Guildenstern fall collateral victims until the end of the play, other plays in the period also explored the tensions and problems involved in the dissemination and discussion of letters and documents beyond their originally intended sphere of circulation.

News is by its very nature ephemeral, and the plays about current affairs that got published and therefore survived are most likely exceptions. They are texts marked by their effort to negotiate and transcend their ephemerality as performance scripts and as news, to become 'news that STAYS news',[11] and in doing so, to reflect on how plays function as a news medium and how they relate to other news media. Through their concern with the dialectic of secrecy and curiosity, of the withholding of information and the display of access that defined the public circulation of political knowledge in the period, they are theorizing their own condition. The avid interest in foreign politics and foreign news throughout the late sixteenth and early seventeenth centuries has been particularly resistant to explanation through the category of the public sphere as a scene of public-minded debate about issues of common concern. The argument that the preponderance of foreign affairs in publicly circulating news could be understood as a result of the censorship of information about the country's own government only partly addresses this problem: it does not explain why audiences would have been excited by the materials they were allowed to see, so much so that—as Fritz Levy suggests—'news replaced (or at least supplemented) clothes as a new social marker'.[12] A focus on the polarization of public opinion as the force that drove the demand for political news has tended to obscure the extent to which the display of political knowledge functioned as evidence of one's participation in the exchange of political information, and thus as a sign of one's access to the centres of power: as a form of social and then cultural capital, produced and reproduced through circulation. Attending to the stage as a medium in which information about foreign countries was revealed to London audiences, and to what the plays suggest about the social logic of the circulation of

---

[11] The capitalization is Pound's own. On poetry and news in modernity, see Jahan Ramazani, *Poetry and Its Others: News, Prayer, Song, and the Dialogue of Genres* (Chicago: University of Chicago Press, 2014) 63–125. The poetry–news opposition seems like an unfortunate thinning out of a discussion, resulting from the erasure of the notion of 'the classic' that used to articulate the field of poetry itself, as a spectrum from what is meant to be ephemeral to what lasts.

[12] Levy, 'The Decorum of News', 17. In addition to essays by Fritz Levy, Paul Yachnin's work has asserted the importance of news as a social accessory; see especially Dawson and Yachnin, *The Culture of Playgoing in Shakespeare's England* 182–207.

such information, we can adjust our perception of the significance of the dominance of news from abroad in the post-reformation, pre-newspaper public sphere.[13]

ON STAGES AND BOOKSTALLS

The public theatres' efforts to capitalize upon the rising demand for news from abroad ran parallel with the first major outpouring of news from the London printing presses. By the late 1580s, non-periodical, occasional pamphlets discussing foreign affairs, printed whenever some commercially viable document was brought to a publisher's attention, had begun to appear as a recognizable commodity, only somewhat less ephemeral than an afternoon theatre performance under slightly overcast late spring skies.[14] If the closeness of the parallel is a little hard for us to recognize, it is because news was soon assimilated to the print medium, which came to be seen as its native form of circulation, and by the nineteenth century, the name for the machinery of reproduction, 'the press', became the term for the periodical publications in and for which news was produced—whereas the stage ceased to be a medium for the dissemination of information about current affairs, and became instead, in so far as it still had a political function, a venue for commentary on what was already known from other sources—viz. from the press.[15] To us, the political stage appears as a critical arena, and plays seem to comment on, endorse, project, or undermine ideologies and political positions: they are partisan interventions in a well-established field articulated by ideological fault lines. But in 1600, their most obviously immediate political function was publishing what happened. In spite of the rapidly widening oral and written circulation of news in the period, to a significant segment of their audiences, the news performed on the public stages could easily be still news.[16] Just as importantly:

---

[13] As late as in the early eighteenth century, foreign affairs still dominated the news that were recorded by provincial Englishmen, cp. D. R. Woolf, 'News, History, and the Construction of the Present in Early Modern England', in Brendan Dooley and Sabrina Baron (eds.), *The Politics of Information in Early Modern Europe* (London and New York: Routledge, 2001), 80–118 at 93–4. My suggestions here run parallel with, and to some degree complement, Joad Raymond's argument about a cosmopolitan and international readership of news, a public that was following European developments with critical attention: 'International News and the Seventeenth-Century English Newspaper', in Jeroen Salman, Joad Raymond, and Roeland Harms (eds.), *Not Dead Things: The Dissemination of Popular Print in England and Wales, Italy, and the Low Countries, 1500–1820* (Leiden and Boston: Brill, 2013), 229–51.

[14] Although the first English news pamphlet was printed in 1513, the last decade of the sixteenth century saw a sudden growth in the volume of such publications. D. C. Collins, *A Handlist of News Pamphlets, 1590–1610* (London: South-West Essex Technical College, 1943); Richard Streckfuss, 'News before Newpapers', *Journalism and Mass Communication Quarterly*, 75 (1998), 84–97; Paul J. Voss, *Elizabethan News Pamphlets: Shakespeare, Spenser, Marlowe & the Birth of Journalism* (Pittsburgh: Duquesne University Press, 2001); Joad Raymond, *Pamphlets and Pamphleteering in Early Modern Britain* (Cambridge: Cambridge University Press, 2003) 101–8.

[15] Sherman, 'Eyes and Ears, News and Plays', 24.

[16] The theatre is in this respect once again parallel with other commercial popular media, especially with ballads and printed news pamphlets, although not entirely in agreement with Angela McShane's formulation. She has argued that ballads were 'not the "mass journalism" of the people—they were the

both printed news pamphlets and the news on the stage were understood to be dependent on a logically and empirically prior, primary mode of circulation, on the exchange of news in an exclusive, personal setting, and it was this setting that was understood to be the native form of circulation of news, whereas the stage or the press appeared as commercial media that divulged information first processed in this personal, political sphere.

Contemporaries clearly understood the stage and print as closely comparable media for the dissemination of current political intelligence. Writing in 1600, Ben Jonson associated popularity with the situation when people are 'not content to be generally noted in court, but will press forth on common stages and brokers' stalls to the public view of the world'.[17] As the Earl of Essex experienced that year, such divulging of information from court circles to a wider public via the stage and booksellers' stalls could not only be used as self-advertisement but also as an attack directed against others. Writing to the Queen to ask for her protection, the disgraced earl described the dire condition of his affairs, explaining that he was

> subject to their malicious informations that first envied me your favour and now hate me out of custom.... The prating tavern haunter speaks of me when he list: the frantick libeller writes of me when he list: already they print me, and make me speak to the world; and shortlye they will play me in what formes they list upon the stage. The least of these is a thousand tymes woorse than death ...[18]

Essex's despair was caused by the orchestrated breakdown of the decorum normally controlling and restricting the circulation of information about England's great and about the internal workings of the regime, information that the period understood to be appropriately private in nature, as secrets of state or *arcana imperii*. Peter Lake has shown in a series of studies that the pre-civil war, and especially the pre-Thirty Years War political public sphere in England is best understood as the setting into which political information and polemical interventions were released according to the needs of the factions of the political elite, generating public controversy and thus public pressure to advance the cause or interest of one party or another. Essex did not see the public circulation of stories about him as an accident, and certainly not as the autonomous doing of a critical public, but as a

---

street and alehouse theatre, the poetry and the counsellors of the people—and not just those without the discretion to know any better. ... Ballads depended upon and participated in an already informed and widespread debate about state affairs.' While I would not want to argue with this conclusion, I do think that plays as well as ballads did in fact *also* serve as a vehicle for the dissemination of news at least for some of their audience, and that people were not only learning about events from plays and ballads, but also acquiring the strategies of responding to what they heard, both from the plays or the ballads, and from their better-informed peers commenting on them. Angela McShane Jones, '*The Gazet in Metre; or the Rhiming Newsmonger*. The English Broadside Ballad as Intelligencer: A New Narrative', in J. W. Koopmans (ed.), *News and Politics in Early Modern Europe (1500–1800)* (Leuven: Peeters, 2005), 131–51 at 146; for an argument similar to that of McShane Jones, about early news pamphlets building on prior familiarity with the events, see Margaret Meserve, 'News from Negroponte: Politics, Popular Opinion and Information Exchange in the First Decade of the Italian Press', *Renaissance Quarterly*, 59 (2006), 440–80.

[17] *Cynthia's Revels*, 4.3.94–6, Jonson (2012) 1:509.
[18] Essex to the Queen, 12 May 1600, TNA SP 12/274/138, f. 232r.

scandalous attack by his political enemies, precisely the kind of pitch-making Lake identifies as the communicative act that defines late sixteenth-century public politics. In Essex's view—a view so obviously well-informed by the Earl's own active pursuit of popularity that we ought to consider it authoritative—the public to which this information is released is not an autonomous public sphere distinct from the state, sitting in critical judgement of its operations, but rather a public called into being by those targeting it with political information or with a contentious policy pitch, one which is understood to be reacting to, and indeed playing out, the internal conflicts of the regime. And last, the commercial mechanisms of the release and circulation of such politically sensitive, and therefore originally private, restricted information, far from setting the terms of the discussion or driving the debate by their own commercial logic of publication and polemics, are merely the relatively passive if increasingly efficient tools in the hands of the primary agents of such release.[19] In all these important respects, the publicity of political information in the late sixteenth century was radically different from the public sphere of politics that began to emerge around 1620 and especially after 1641, and therefore also from the ideal type of the public sphere that Jürgen Habermas so influentially (if by now also very controversially) established. Political news and political information in this regime are by definition scarce: even when a piece of political information was not scandalous in nature, the very fact that it entered into public circulation (whether in print or on the stage) calls for explanation in terms of the intentions of those releasing them.[20]

Two pamphlets and a lost play about a battle might serve as an example of the release of political news through the various media outlets in London under this regime of popularity. The battle of Turnhout, in January 1596/7, was one of the most successful interventions of the English forces in the war in the Low Countries.[21] The forces of Maurice of Nassau, supported by English troops led by Sir Robert Sidney and Sir Francis Vere, defeated the soldiers of Archduke Albert on 14 January, taking

---

[19] This model of pre-civil war public sphere as the stage on which the internal tensions of the regime were being played out was developed by Peter Lake in Lake and Pincus (eds.), *The Politics of the Public Sphere in Early Modern England*, especially the Introduction, also published as Lake and Pincus, 'Rethinking the Public Sphere in Early Modern England', his contribution to that collection: 'The Politics of "Popularity" and the Public Sphere: The "Monarchical Republic" of Elizabeth I Defends Itself', 59–94. Lake's fuller treatment of the subject is *Bad Queen Bess? Libels, Secret Histories and the Politics of Publicity in the Reign of Queen Elizabeth I*. For a slightly later moment, see Bellany, *The Politics of Court Scandal in Early Modern England*. On the problem of popularity—understood in this moment as an inherently suspect appeal to a general public—see also Doty, 'Shakespeare's *Richard II*, "Popularity," and the Early Modern Public Sphere'; Jeffrey S. Doty, '*Measure for Measure* and the Problem of Popularity', *English Literary Renaissance*, 42 (2012), 32–57; Gajda, *The Earl of Essex and Late Elizabethan Political Culture* 200–9.

[20] For a recent overview, from a broad European perspective, of the circulation and commercialization of confidential news in the sixteenth century, see Andrew Pettegree, *The Invention of News: How the World Came to Know About Itself* (New Haven: Yale University Press, 2014) 96–116.

[21] Millicent V. Hay, *The Life of Robert Sidney, Earl of Leicester (1563–1626)* (Washington, DC: Folger Shakespeare Library, 1984) 102–5; Clements R. Markham, '*The Fighting Veres.*' *Lives of Sir Francis Vere, General of the Queen's Forces in the Low Countries, Governor of the Brill and of Portsmouth, and of Sir Horace Vere, General of the English Forces in the Low Countries, Governor of the Brill, Master-General of Ordnance, and Baron Vere of Tilbury* (Boston and New York: Houghton, Mifflin & Co., 1888) 254–62.

the castle of Turnhout in Brabant the next day. All major centres of the English political establishment were promptly notified of the events.[22] With so many reports surviving among state papers, we can only guess at the sheer volume of correspondence participants and observers of the battle sent home. One report was acquired by the London bookseller Paul Linley, who entered it in the Stationers' Register on 29 January 1596/7, with his business partner John Flasket soon published it, and even decided to follow it with 'A discourse more at large' of the same battle 'Translated out of French'.[23] The first pamphlet is the printed version of a letter in English from 'a Gentleman of account, that was present at the seruice, to a friend of his in England', as the title page puts it, and from someone who is clearly aware of his addressee's loyalty to Robert Sidney, the governor of Flushing: he is sending the letter hoping 'it will be pleasing vnto you, both for the generalitie in respecte of the cause, as also for the reputation my Lorde Gouernour of Flushing hath gotten by it, to whome the greatest part of the honor of that daies victory is by all men attributed'.[24]

Although the printed newsletter does not indicate this, from the Stationers' Register entry we know that the letter was originally addressed to a Mr White.[25] A Mr White who would have been a particularly appropriate addressee of a report framed to highlight Sidney's role was Rowland Whyte, who was, in the words of the first editor of his letters, 'employed by Sir Robert Sydney, to sollicit his Affairs at the Court, and to relate to him what passed there'.[26] Whyte's correspondence testifies to his solicitous attention to Sidney's reputation. He advised Sir Robert on the particulars of how to further his court career from a distance, he reported

---

[22] Essex, a patron of both Sidney and Vere, was the addressee of detailed accounts dated 17 January from Francis Vere and George Gilpin, 19 January from Prince Maurice, 20 January from John Chamberlain, and 21 January from Robert Sidney. HMC Hatfield 7, pp. 24–6, 26, 28, 29, and 31–2, respectively (all dates O.S.). Vere, Gilpin, and Sidney also wrote to Cecil on the same dates, and John Wheeler wrote to William Waad, clerk of the Privy Council, on 21 January. TNA SP 84/54, ff. 15–18, 19, 28–30, and 26–7, respectively.

[23] *A True Discourse of the Ouerthrovve Giuen to the Common Enemy at Turnhaut, the 14. of Ianuary Last 1597. by Count Moris of Nassaw and the States, Assisted with the Englishe Forces. Sent from a Gentleman of Account, that Was Present at the Seruice, to a Friend of His in England* (London: Printed by Peter Short, and are to be sold in Paules Churchyard, at the signe of the blacke Beare, 1597); *A Discourse More at Large of the Late Ouerthrovve Giuen to the King of Spaines Armie at Turnehaut, in Ianuarie last, by Count Morris of Nassawe, Assisted with the English Forces whereunto is Adioined Certaine Inchauntments and Praiers in Latine, Found about Diuerse of the Spaniards, Which Were Slaine in the Same Conflict: Translated out of French According to the Copy Printed in the Low Countries* (London: to be sold in Paules Churchyarde, at the signe of the black Beare, 1597). Some of the material in this section has been used in András Kiséry, 'An Author and a Bookshop: Publishing Marlowe's Remains at the Black Bear', *Philological Quarterly*, 91 (2012), 361–92.

[24] *A True Discourse of the Ouerthrovve*, sig. A2.

[25] Linley's entry is for 'newes in a letter to master WHITE of the overthrowe of the Enemyes in Brabant in this Ianuarye 1596': Edward Arber, *A Transcript of the Registers of the Company of Stationers of London: 1554–1640, A.D.*, 5 vols. (London and Birmingham: Priv. print., 1875) 3:79.

[26] Arthur Collins (ed.), *Letters and Memorials of State, in the Reigns of Queen Mary, Queen Elizabeth, King James . . .* (London: T. Osborne, 1746) 2:4 footnote. For Whyte and his relationship with Sidney, see Michael G. Brennan, '"Your Lordship's to Do You All Humble Service": Rowland Whyte's Correspondence with Robert Sidney, Viscount Lisle and First Earl of Leicester', *Sidney Journal*, 21/2 (2003), 1–37; Michael G. Brennan, Noel J. Kinnamon, and Margaret P. Hannay (eds.), *The Letters (1595–1608) of Rowland Whyte* (Memoirs of the American Philosophical Society, 268; Philadelphia: American Philosophical Society, 2013) 1–27. On Collins's editorial work, see Brennan, Kinnamon, and Hannay (eds.), *The Letters (1595–1608) of Rowland Whyte* 35–6.

to him court news that had an impact on his prospects, along with the gossip circulating about him and about the governorship of Flushing, and recorded his own regular intercessions at court on Sir Robert's behalf. No letter from Whyte to Sidney survives from the period between 2 October 1596 and 14 February 1596/7, so the record of his efforts to publicize Sidney's success are lost, but based on his active attention to his master's interests (around the time, he was trying to help him to the Lord Wardenship of the Cinque Ports), we can assume that Whyte was instrumental in getting into print the reports of his master's success at Turnhout.

Two years after Flasket and Linley's pamphlets, Sidney's performance at Turnhout was still central to his military reputation, a reputation that did not go uncontested. In spite of Whyte's efforts to advertise Sidney's valour, Francis Vere, who was the commander of all the English troops in the Netherlands except in Flushing, and whose reputation constantly seemed to overshadow Sidney's, managed to take most of the credit for the victory. Vere's self-aggrandizement and the resulting bitterness between him and Sidney were publicly known.[27] Given Vere's success at promoting himself, Sidney's friends were eager to please him with reports of occasions when his honour was mentioned or remembered in private or in public.[28] On 26 October 1599, Whyte mentions that

> Two days ago, the overthrow of Turnhout was acted upon a stage and all your names used that were at it, especially Sir Francis Vere's, and he that played that part got a beard resembling his, and a watchet satin doublet with a hose trimmed with silver lace and was full of quips. I saw it not, but I heard it was so. Sir Francis goes to his government.[29]

The comment at the end of the paragraph clarifies the significance of the performance: it took place at a time when Francis Vere was spending several weeks in London—at a time when, after Essex's return from Ireland, the names of Vere as well as of Sidney were floated as potential candidates for Lord Deputy of Ireland.[30] Whyte was closely following how Vere's future was being decided at court, reporting his every move to Sidney. Under these circumstances, a play representing the exploits of Vere and Sidney would obviously have appeared as having immediate propagandistic function, whether performed with the approval, and perhaps encouragement of Sir Francis Vere, or rather, of some of his clients or henchmen.[31]

---

[27] See the *ODNB* article by D. J. B. Trim, and Brennan, Kinnamon, and Hannay (eds.), *The Letters (1595–1608) of Rowland Whyte* 330.

[28] In June, while he was in London, his deputy governor William Browne reported to Sidney that 'Monsieur de Aschicourt, whose regiment was defeated at Turnholt, where your honor was a chief actour, should now be slayne before Bommel.' HMC *Report on the Manuscripts of Lord De L'Isle & Dudley* (London: H.M. Stationery Office, 1934) 2:366 (to Robert Sidney from Flushing, 6 June 1599).

[29] Brennan, Kinnamon, and Hannay (eds.), *The Letters (1595–1608) of Rowland Whyte* 362–3.

[30] Mountjoy was chosen but was trying to excuse himself—Sidney was rumoured to be an alternate.

[31] Which is presumably why Whyte was eager to learn more about it, going to see it the next day: on Saturday 27 October he writes to Sir Robert again, and in the postscript reports that 'This afternoon

Such transfers from private correspondence into commercial news, from manuscript into print and onto the stage, disseminating information so that the dissemination itself became an event significant enough to become news sent from London, exemplify the carefully managed and controlled processes of how things were made public, as well as the chain of agencies that made publication possible. Over the course of the seventeenth century, commercial publication transformed the protocols of secrecy and privilege that governed the circulation of political knowledge.[32] Around 1600, this process of democratization had barely even started yet: the stage could be—could appear to be—so influential a medium for the occasional publication of political information precisely because of the socially and geographically limited reach of parallel public media. What is striking about the news of the battle of Turnhout is how unique it is, how difficult it is to reconstruct such transfers.

A PUBLIC OF POLITICS AND A SCENE OF EXCHANGE

The wide variety of domestic and foreign political information circulating orally and in correspondence was rarely disseminated publicly. The exchange of news outside official channels was predominantly a form of sociability, and the manuscript newsletter a form which re-personalized anonymous information through its rhetoric as well as through its mode of transmission. Even professional intelligencers serving multiple clients understood their communication to be personal and in some sense exclusive.[33] The rhetoric of the newsletter, which depended on the notion of sharing personally acquired information with a personally known addressee, persisted even in print: early news pamphlets were commonly presented as printed versions of letters to a recipient known to the correspondent—that is, as personal communication that was made public after the fact, although they were commonly anonymized by removing the name of the addressee as well as of the writer. That this trait carried over from manuscript to print reflects more than the

---

I saw the overthrow of Turnhout played, and saw Sir Robert Sidney and Sir Francis Vere upon the stage, killing, slaying, and overthrowing the Spaniard. There is most honorable mention made of your service in seconding Sir Francis Vere being engaged.' Brennan, Kinnamon, and Hannay (eds.), *The Letters (1595–1608) of Rowland Whyte* 365.

[32] Zaret, *Origins of Democratic Culture*; Peacey, *Print and Public Politics in the English Revolution*.

[33] As Sheila Lambert argues, John Pory asked John Scudamore to burn his newsletters in order to prevent them from being recopied or otherwise recirculated, and from thus being made anonymously—and in commercial terms damagingly—available: Sheila Lambert, 'Coranto Printing in England: The First Newsbooks', *Journal of Newspaper and Periodical History*, 8/1 (1992), 3–17 at 5, but cp. Sabrina A. Baron, 'The Guises of Dissemination in Early Seventeenth-Century England: News in Manuscript and Print', in Brendan Dooley and Sabrina A. Baron (eds.), *The Politics of Information in Early Modern Europe* (London: Routledge, 2001), 41–56 at 49–50. On the degrees of difference between personal correspondence and anonymous uniformity, see Richard Cust, 'News and Politics in Early Seventeenth-Century England', *Past & Present*, 112 (1986), 60–90 at 62; Ian Atherton, 'The Itch Grown a Disease: Manuscript Transmission of News in the Seventeenth Century', in Joad Raymond (ed.), *News, Newspapers and Society in Early Modern Britain* (London: Frank Cass, 1999), 39–65 at 41; David Randall, 'Epistolary Rhetoric, the Newspaper, and the Public Sphere', *Past & Present*, 198 (2008), 3–32.

inertia of cultural forms: while printed news clearly democratized the access to information and political discussion, the desire it catered to was a desire for the prestige that manuscript circulation promised. And the stage as a medium of political information had a similar affective function—while the political elite was putting it in the service of a politics of popularity, the theatre-going public was not watching plays in order to become pawns of the regime's factional politics, or in order to subject themselves to the intentions of the centres of power, but in order to feel included in the political realm, to imaginatively assume an insider's position.

One can think about the experience of the circulation of news in this personal mode by thinking about what this experience was not. It was certainly not the experience of a group of private individuals unknown to each other but in reading and thinking about the news each of them recognizing him or herself as one among many simultaneous recipients, and by virtue of that, imagining themselves as members of a large anonymous community.[34] It was not the experience of belonging to a horizontal organization of people understanding their relation to each other as a news-reading public by virtue of being addressed by the discourse. Such would be the effect and experience of reading newspapers, and indeed of being engaged with the pamphlet culture after the explosion of print after 1640. Recipients of the news in the personal mode were imagining themselves as members of a different community. Consuming news before 1640, and especially before the 1620s, was not just a quantitatively but also qualitatively different experience.

In late sixteenth- and early seventeenth-century London, the precincts of St Paul's Cathedral were the centre of the exchange of news. They were 'the most densely semiotized space' of the city,[35] and the character-writer John Earle described them in 1628 as 'the great exchange of all discourse'.[36] Earle called the nave of the Cathedral itself, Paul's Walk, 'the eares Brothell', mentioning it in the same breath as the 'Playes, Tauerne, and a Baudy-House'. Unlike those institutions, however, this space of discursive promiscuity is an all-male environment: 'The Visitants are all men without exceptions, but the principall Inhabitants and possessors, are stale Knights, and Captaines out of Seruice, men of long Rapiers, and Breeches, which after all turne Merchants here, and trafficke for Newes.'[37] And the trade is intense: as John

---

[34] This is of course the vision of a national newspaper-reading public in Benedict Anderson, *Imagined Communities: Reflections on the Origin and Spread of Nationalism* (Rev. edn.; London: Verso, 1991) 22–36, 61–5.

[35] See Gail Kern Paster, 'The Children's Middleton', in W. Speed Hill (ed.), *New Ways of Looking at Old Texts II: Papers of the Renaissance English Text Society, 1992–1996* (Tempe, AZ: MRTS, 1998), 101–7 at 103. Paster's important paper argues for seeing theatre-going at Paul's as 'one in a complex of *locally* specific practices dependent for their social and material potency on the Cathedral's agreed-upon centrality in early modern London' (107).

[36] *Micro-cosmographie, or, A Peece of the World Discovered in Essayes and Characters* (London: Printed by William Stansby for Edward Blount, 1628), sig. I11v. Earle's anonymously published *Micro-cosmographie* was to become, along with the earlier collection of characters posthumously attributed to Thomas Overbury, one of the most successful instances of the genre.

[37] Earle sigs. I11r–I12v. When in *Westward Ho* women enter this male world, it is an index of their transgression, and thus confirms, rather than questions, the claim that the space was exclusively male. See Jean E. Howard, 'Women, Foreigners, and the Regulation of Urban Space in *Westward Ho*', in

Chamberlain wrote to Dudley Carleton in 1603, 'Powles is so furnisht that yt affords whatsoever is stirring in Fraunce, and I can gather there at first hand to serve my turne sufficiently'—so much so that he does not even need Carleton to keep him up to date on French politics by writing to him from Paris.[38] Both Chamberlain and Rowland Whyte regularly go there—their letters to Carleton and to Sidney are rich archives of the domestic and international news that circulated around Paul's.

The two parallel commercial institutions for the public dissemination of news, the printing presses and the stage, were also feeding off, and contributing to, the circulation of political intelligence in Paul's Walk. This is also the environment where Whyte's letter about Turnhout entered print circulation. John Flasket, the co-publisher of the two news pamphlets about Turnhout, was a bookbinder who owned a shop in the churchyard, across from the North Door of the Cathedral. He was among those who sought to profit from their direct access to Paul's, the epicentre of the circulation of news, both as a source of manuscripts they could print, and as a market where news publications could be expected to find an audience. Of the thirty-two titles published at the Black Bear during Flasket's career between 1594 and 1607, eight fall immediately into the category of 'news pamphlets', and the Turnhout letters may be representative of how Flasket acquired the materials he published—whether manuscript letters or pamphlets printed abroad, they were pieces of paper someone must have brought to Paul's to share.[39]

But for a vivid picture of the experience of circulation, and for an understanding of the motives of those who were not trying to use the venue to influence public opinion, or to make money off it like Flasket, we must turn to other sources. Reminiscing about his youth under the reign of James I, Francis Osborn writes about the habit of

> men of all professions not meerely Mechanick, to meet in Pauls church... during which time some discoursed of Businesse, others of Newes.... I being very young, and wanting a more advantagious imployment, did, during my aboad in London, which was three fourth parts of the yeare, associate my selfe at those hours with the choicest company I could pick out, amongst such as I found most inquisitive after affairs of State; who being then my self in a daily attendance upon a hope (though a rotten one) of a future preferment, I appeared the more considerable, being as ready to satisfy, according to my weak abilities, their Curiosity, as they were mine.[40]

Osborn stresses the relative social exclusivity of the exchange of news, and he also clarifies the motives for participation in the exchange, making explicit the link

---

Lena Cowen Orlin (ed.), *Material London, ca. 1600* (Philadelphia: University of Pennsylvania Press, 2000), 150–68 at 157–8.

[38] McClure (ed.), *The Letters of John Chamberlain* 1:183–4.

[39] These numbers include titles published by Flasket as well as by his partner Linley, and include second and third editions but exclude reissues of earlier publications with an updated title page.

[40] Francis Osborn, *Historical Memoires on the Reigns of Queen Elizabeth, and King James* (London: J. Grismond, to be sold by T. Robinson Bookseller in Oxon., 1658) sigs. K1r–v. On Osborn's *Memoirs* and their influence on our perception of the reign of Elizabeth and James, see John Watkins, *Representing Elizabeth in Stuart England: Literature, History, Sovereignty* (Cambridge: Cambridge University Press, 2002) 110–16.

between the circulation of news and social ambition that is the commonplace target of contemporary satirical commentary, of Dekker's *Gull's Hornbook* as well as in Jonson's *Volpone*, to mention the most familiar texts. Access to political news, to news from the court and from abroad, meant access to the information circulating at the court and its satellites, among members of the political elite—it signalled access to that elite. The community of which consumers of political news around 1600 were imagining themselves to be members—some of them with more, some with less justification—was the court. Hearing and sharing news, being inquisitive about affairs of state, is a sign of being part of the political realm or is driven by a desire to belong there: in Osborn's case, it is imagined as an effort to acquire the competence necessary for entering political service and perhaps a career. Osborn understands curiosity as a transgressive desire for knowledge—an appetite fuelled by social ambition.[41]

Members of the localized public at Paul's were not the only consumers of news, of course—but in a crucial sense, they were its primary public, the addressees of the turn of the century news trade who defined its culture and its public perception.[42] At a time when this public is not yet describing itself as a competent judge of affairs of state, nor does it yet see itself as representative of a larger, national public, its members are driven to participate in the competitive sociability of talking news by a desire to distinguish themselves. By participating in the exchange of news, one is positioned on this threshold of politics.

But while Osborn and others may have been hoping for entry to court, the real traffic through this gateway was passing in the opposite direction, in the form of political information entering public circulation. As Osborn explains, 'these newsmongers, as they called them, did not only take the boldnesse to weigh the publick but most intrinsick actions of the State, which some courtier or other did betray to this society.'[43] Osborn's sentence perfectly encapsulates my main point here. What became news were either actions done in a ceremonial or otherwise public form, and were intended to be 'public' to begin with—in the form of proclamations, for example—or they were 'intrinsic' and had to be 'betrayed', released from their proper sphere to the public of Paul's Walk in order to be discussed. The more interesting the information, the more valuable in this setting, the more likely it circulates in breach of the established rules of public communication, inviting private persons to reflect upon affairs of state and upon what was synonymous with that, the affairs of the great, that is, engaging in scandalous activity.

In general terms, then, political information available outside of government circles was, first and foremost, information circulated by people in political office

---

[41] The scholarship on the early modern cultures of curiosity have emphasized this connection—although political curiosity, the interest in news and in political affairs, has generally been marginal to the arguments of such studies as Benedict, *Curiosity: A Cultural History of Early Modern Inquiry*; Marjorie Swann, *Curiosities and Texts: The Culture of Collecting in Early Modern England* (Philadelphia: University of Pennsylvania Press, 2001).

[42] See Cogswell, *The Blessed Revolution* 20ff on their importance in shaping (or standing in for) public opinion in the 1620s.

[43] Osborn, *Historical Memoires* sig. K1v.

or employment to their patrons, friends, familiars: it was official knowledge, in the sense of being knowledge gathered by someone as part of discharging their office—or in certain cases unofficial knowledge proper to a theoretically closed circle of insiders—that was brought into private circulation outside of its primary, originary context. Intelligencers were both spies and news reporters—there being no news industry, the categories of intelligence gathering and reportage have not formally, institutionally separated yet. In such a setting, any act of publicity is understood as an occasional offshoot of a personal exchange of intelligence, a deliberate release of information, a discovery or leak from the realm of politics, knowledge that would and should normally have been kept secret suddenly escaping—or plucked—from where it belonged. This sense of published information being the function of a deliberate disclosure also applied to the circulation of political news even if they were not deployed to make the kinds of policy pitches to a national or international public that Peter Lake has discussed in his work about the 'post-reformation public sphere'. Under a regime of information where publicly held political knowledge is the result of betrayal, access to political knowledge is a sign of social access. Having knowledge means someone in the know let you know.

News from abroad, which was being published both in print and on stage far more widely than domestic political news, was not exempt from this logic—and this may very well have been part of its appeal, which sometimes seems a bit difficult to account for otherwise. The proliferation of news from abroad fits notoriously badly with narratives about the emergence of the public sphere as the result of the concerned interest of private individuals in affairs of state, in how their country was governed.[44] Although it would be hard to deny the part played by the domestic ramifications of international politics, the sometimes quite striking analogies between domestic and foreign situations, or the deep sympathies for the cause of fellow protestants in creating an appetite for foreign news, an understanding of the interest in news from abroad in such *political* terms should, I believe, be complemented by an emphasis on their *social* function. Before newspapers, news about affairs of state was experienced as secrets of state, the secrets of princes and their ministers. The fiction enveloping the publication of such news was the fiction of inside knowledge being leaked to outsiders—and this fiction projected an aura of social prestige and cultural capital upon the information thus acquired. But while printed news pamphlets were imitating the personal style of the newsletter, and thus allowing readers to continue experiencing the news, if they so wanted, as (a knock-off of) privileged communication, the theatre forced them to face themselves and each other as members of an anonymous public, and to face the performance as an act of commercial publication—and also forced plays to take the effect of such betrayals into account.

---

[44] Farmer, 'Play-Reading, News-Reading, and Ben Jonson's *The Staple of News*'; Raymond, 'International News and the Seventeenth-Century English Newspaper'.

BETRAYALS

Chapman's *The Conspiracy and Tragedy of Byron* tells the story of one of the most talked-about political scandals of the turn of the century, the treasonous conspiracy, trial, and execution of Charles de Gontault, Duc de Biron, *maréchal de France*, in 1602. Feeling constrained by the peace-oriented diplomacy of Henri IV, France's greatest commander conspired with Savoy and Spain to overthrow his king. When his treason was exposed by one of his *confidants*, Biron put up a spectacular performance denying the charges to the very end. The king also made the most of the opportunity, and by delaying the execution, he strove to convince all parties that although he had to follow the dictates of state interest, sending Biron to the block meant to him an enormous personal loss.

The conspiracy and fall of Biron revealed not only the fragility of the ongoing diplomatic efforts (including the efforts made by the English government) to establish peace in Western Europe[45] but also the changing nature of monarchical power and of its methods of operation in an emerging public sphere. Ralph Winwood, the English agent in Paris, promptly noted that the 'proceeding is termed *un coup d'état* [in the sense of a successful political manoeuvre] and as it is presumed, will strongly establish the Soveraign authority, which did begin to *branler* and totter up and down, and...hereby the Majestie of the King shall be freed from a generall contempt, into the which it was likely headlong to fall.'[46]

The exposure of Biron's conspiracy was an act of publicity, a PR-manoeuvre immediately recognized as such, whose echoes reverberated throughout Europe, but outside France they perhaps resonated most immediately with the English public, for several reasons. A little more than a year earlier Biron had visited England as ambassador to Queen Elizabeth, leaving an enormous impression on the court and on the London public. Just as importantly, the similarity of the fate of Biron to the fall of the Earl of Essex, and to a lesser extent, to the demise of the Earl of Gowrie (whose conspiracy and death was a major event in Scotland in 1600) struck contemporary observers as rather conspicuous—Chamberlain immediately noted the analogy among the conspiracies and deaths of Gowrie, Essex, and Biron,[47] and the similarities were also alluded to in French and continental pamphlets.[48]

---

[45] News from Rome, 1602, 24 July/3 Aug., CP 184/63, reporting discussions of the possibility of Henri going to war against the foreign powers apparently involved in the conspiracy. See also Robert Cecil's draft 'Minute for Scotland concerning the Lady Arabella', ca. 1602/3, discussing the French king's 'disposition to keep upright all terms of amity between those two crowns (notwithstanding all his discoveries of Spanish practices with Biron, Janville and the Count d'Auvergne)', CP 82/104_2–4.

[46] Winwood to Cecil, 4 June 1602, in Edmund Sawyer (ed.), *Memorials and Affairs of State in the Reigns of Q. Elizabeth and K. James I., Collected (Chiefly) from the Original Papers of the Right Honourable Sir Ralph Winwood, Kt.*, 3 vols. (London: W. B. for T. Ward, 1724) 1:415.

[47] John Chamberlain to Dudley Carleton, 4 November 1602, in McClure (ed.), *The Letters of John Chamberlain* 1:168.

[48] See e.g. the 'lettre mistique', an account of the conspiracy by Jean Boucher, in several editions, e.g. *Lettre Mistique. Responce, Replique. Mars Joue son Rolle en la Premiere; en la Seconde la Bande & le Choeur de l'Estat, la Troisieme Figure l'Amour de Polytheme Galathee, & des Sept Pasteurs* (Leiden: 1603),

Reports about Biron's fate were the most important foreign news that summer. After Biron was arrested on 12 June 1602, his trial was the main topic of the reports from Paris, but newsletters sent to Elizabeth's Secretary of State by agents in Italy and Scotland also included information about the case.[49] Information from such newsletters quickly entered circulation in England, sometimes revealing their reliance on hearsay and guesswork: less than two weeks after the arrest, by 17 June (O.S.), John Chamberlain already heard rumours that Biron had been beheaded, and three more weeks later, that he had been pardoned.[50] After Biron's execution on 31 July, the initial guesswork and hearsay gave way to longer narratives, with new details and fuller histories of the events arriving well into the autumn of that year,[51] and with manuscript separates and printed pamphlet publications of various letters and documents related to the trial enclosed in the correspondence.[52]

While his fate was hotly discussed throughout France, and even became a subject of popular ballads,[53] accounts of Biron's arrest, trial, and death were also printed and reprinted throughout Europe in broadsheets and pamphlets,[54] and

the reference to Essex on sig. A2r. In 1603, a new edition of an old-fashioned Latin collection of tragic histories, i.e. stories of the fall of great men, concluded with accounts of the deaths of Gowrie, Essex, and Biron, even featuring the addition of the latter on the title page: [John Dickenson]: *Speculum Tragicum. Regum, Principum, & Magnatum Superioris Sæculi Celebriorum Ruinas Exitusque Calamitosos Breviter Complectens... Tertio Editum & Adauctum. Accessit Etiam Bironij Exitus, & Alia.* (Lugduni Batavorum: Elzevir, 1603), sigs. I5r–K2v. Within a few years, the parallels between Essex and Biron were reason enough to issue accounts of their lives together in French, and to translate them into German together. The *Histoire de la Vie et Mort dv Comte d'Essex avec vn Dicovrs Grave et Eloqvent de la Royne d'Angleterre, au Duc de Biron sur ce Subiect. La Conspiration, Prison, Iugement, Testament, & Mort du Duc de Biron: Trahison Mort & Procez de Nicolas Loste, Prison du Comte d' Auuergne & de Madame Marquise de Vernueil.* n.p., n.d. [1607] is bibliographically an issue of a life of Biron, prefaced with materials about Essex. This composite volume was translated into German as *Denckwürdige, Warhaffte und Eigentliche Historische Beschreibung, welche Sich bey Lebzeiten Elisabetha Königin in England, so Wohl auch unter jetzt Regierendem König in Franckreich Begeben und Zugetragen* (Speyer: Johann Taschner, 1608), reprinted in 1609 and 1611 in Speyer and Frankfurt.

[49] The documents preserved in the State Papers (France) for June and July 1602, in TNA SP 78/46, ff. 127–284, are dominated by news about Biron in the form of newsletters and separates, many of them in multiple copies. Among the Cecil Papers there survives a similarly rich array of materials, indicative of the international scope of the news circulation; see e.g. News from Venice, 1602, 30 July/9 Aug., CP 184/72r–73v, reporting rumours that Biron may have been pardoned by Henri, and will be going to Hungary. Italian newsletters in CP 184 and 199 from the summer of 1602 were all reporting news circulating about the fate of Biron.

[50] John Chamberlain to Dudley Carleton, 17 June 1602 and 8 July 1602, McClure (ed.), *The Letters of John Chamberlain* 1:150, 156.

[51] Dudley Carleton to John Chamberlain, 30 Sept./10 Oct. 1602, TNA SP 78/47 ff. 103–4.

[52] *Lamento, et Esclamatione fatta dal Duca di Birone avanti la Sua Morte.* Di G. C. C. [i.e. Giulio Cesare Croce] (Bologna: Gli heredi di Gio. Rossi, 1603). See the documents and letters in the contemporary compilation of state papers by Sir Peter Manwood, BL MS Add 38139, 3v–10r, 18r–19r.

[53] Gilles Bertheau, 'Chansons Populaires et Incidences Politiques: le Cas de *The Conspiracy and Tragedy of Byron* (1608) de George Chapman', *Études Anglaises*, 52 (1999), 259–74 at 260–5.

[54] *Embleme contre les Ambitievx* (Paris: Jacques Granthome [1602], copy in Koninklijke Bibliotheek, Den Haag, KW Pflt 1180); *Spectatori: Carl de Gontaut Her von Biron, Gemacht ward zu eim Hertzog schon...* (Franz Hogenberg, 1602, copy in ULB Düsseldorf, shelfmark: his/7943, no. 344—see Figure 4.1); *Gründtlicher Bericht dero durch den Marschalck von Biron gegen Königlicher Mayestat in Franckreich vorgenommener Conspiration, dessen gefenglicher Einziehung und Erfolgter Execution Urtheil'* (1602, copy in Forschungs- und Landesbibliothek, Gotha, shelfmark Biogr gr 2° 00593/02 (584) verso);

some of these no doubt also contributed to the sheer volume of information about the case of Biron that reached the English public through various channels. (See Figure 4.1 for a German illustrated broadsheet.) On 5 August 1602 (O.S.), a mere two weeks after the execution, a collection of such papers, printed in at least two editions in French and in an Italian translation, was already entered in the Stationers' Register, to be soon translated into English, supplemented by copies of letters with narrative accounts, and printed as *A True and Perfect Discourse of the Practises and Treasons of Marshall Biron together with the Particulars of his Arraignment and Execution. Faithfully Translated out of the French*.[55] The stage was not lagging much behind the printing press: while Shakespeare's earlier use of the name Biron in the fictitious Navarrese court of *Love's Labour's Lost* indicates its usefulness in creating an effect of foreignness, now the story of the life and downfall of the *maréchal* became the subject of an entire play. On 25 September 1602, the theatrical entrepreneur Philip Henslowe's diary lists the expense of buying 'a black sewt of satten for the playe of burone' (Biron's black outfit was so striking that it became a fashion in London after his embassy), and on 2 or 3 October 1602, carpenters were already being paid for making 'a scafowld & bare for the play of Berowne', indicating that the plot is indeed revolving around Biron's downfall, and also how far the preparations had advanced for the new play.[56] We will probably never learn who wrote the script of this 1602 performance, or whether 'The unfortunate general: French history' written by Richard Hathaway, Wentworth Smyth, John Day & 'the other poet'[57] in January 1602/3 might not be another play on the same topic, and were it not for Henslowe's entries, we would have no knowledge of these plays whatsoever.

Chapman's two-part tragedy, published in 1608, might appear to be situated at several removes from this scene of excited contemporary discussion, since it builds on narrative histories of France printed a few years later.[58] It follows closely, and

Exécution du duc de Biron (title from catalog, n. p., n. d., in BNF Richelieu—Estampes et photographie, Hennin 1244); *Gründtliche Relation und Bericht welcher massen die wider den... Herrn Heinrichen deß Namens den vierdten Königen in Franckreich un[d] Navarra mit Hispanien Savoien und etlichen der Cron Franckreich Fürsten und Adel gemachte Conspiration und MordtPractic an Tag kommen und derenwegen derselben Häupter der Mareschal de Biron und Conte d'Auvergne gefänglichen eingezogen worden* (1602; copy in HAB Wolfenbüttel, shelfmark Xb 2056).

[55] (London: P.S., 1602). *Recueil Memorable: de ce Qui s'Est Passé pour le Faict du Sieur Duc de Biron, Mareschal de France* (Langres: J. Des Preyz, 1602; multiple reprints; copies at BNF and, a slightly abbreviated version from a different press, n.l., n.n., at Brigham Young University); *Recueil Memorable de tout ce Qui s'Est Passé pour le Faict du Sieur Duc de Biron, Mareschal de France: Contenant l'Arrest Donné de la Cour de Parlement de Paris, contre ledit Sieur Duc de Biron* (A Aix, 1602; a copy at the library of the Université de Liège, shelfmark: XXII.87.8(X)(Variétés 3) [16°]); the collection seems to have been translated as *Raccolta Memorabile di Tutto Quello, ch'è Passato per il Fatto del Sig. Duca di Biron... Con la Sentenza definitiva de i Presidenti... Di Francese tradotta in Italiano per G. Bindoni* (Bologna, 1603, copy in BL, 10604.aa.12.(2.)). The English translation includes several additional letters.

[56] R. A. Foakes, *Henslowe's Diary* (2nd edn.; Cambridge: Cambridge University Press, 2002) 216, 217. Berown is the spelling of the name in Shakespeare; 'bare' is most probably 'bar'—the scene which calls for these props is the execution.

[57] 7, 10, 16, 19, and 24 January 1602/3: Foakes, *Henslowe's Diary* 221–3.

[58] Such narratives include the one printed in *Traicte dv Mariage de Henry IIII. Roy de France et de Navarre, avec la Serenissime Princesse de Florence. Des Ambassades de Part & d'Autre de Son Heureuse*

Fig. 4.1. Intaglio broadsheet about the arrest and execution of the Duke of Biron. Franz Hogenberg: *Spectatori: Carl de Gontaut Her von Biron...*, 1602.
Universitäts- und Landesbibliothek Düsseldorf, urn:nbn:de:hbz:061:1-92649.

occasionally verbatim, parts of Edward Grimeston's 1607 compilation of French contemporary history,[59] itself based on Pierre Matthieu's and Pierre-Victor Palma-Cayet's accounts, extended narratives rather than accounts of a single momentous event, allowing Chapman a sustained analytic retrospective glance at the fate of Biron, something that was unavailable in 1602.[60] This does not mean, however, that Chapman lost interest in the scandalously newsworthy. While the details of

Arriuee en France, à Marseille, & Ses Entrees en Auignon & Lyon. Plus la Conspiration Prison, Iugement & mort du Duc de Biron, auec vn Sommaire de sa vie, & pareillement le procez de Ian l'Hoste (A Honneflevr, de l'Imprimerie de Iean Petit [1606]); this was also issued with *Histoire de la Vie et Mort dv Comte d'Essex* in 1607, which in turn formed the basis for the 1608 *Denckwürdige, Warhaffte und Eigentliche Historische Beschreibung*. The story of Biron published in *Traicte dv Mariage* was also reprinted separately, as *La Conspiration, Prison, Ivgement Et Mort Dv Dvc De Biron* (Iouxte la copie imprimee à Honnefleur par Iean Petit. M.DC.VII).

[59] This means that even if Chapman was involved in the production of the 1602 play, his *Conspiracy and Tragedy of Biron* cannot be taken as a revision of that earlier play, at most as a complete rewriting of it.

[60] The notes in Parrott (ed.), *The Plays and Poems of George Chapman: The Tragedies*, and George Chapman, *The Conspiracy and Tragedy of Byron*, ed. John Margeson (Manchester: Manchester University Press, 1988) trace the indebtedness passage-by-passage.

Biron's treason and fall follow the interpretation that the French government publicized in an effort to stem competing accounts that appeared throughout the summer in the form of libels that accused a courtly conspiracy of fabricating the evidence against the general,[61] Chapman's play also divulges material that was not published before, offering its audience a peek behind the public facades of power. Chapman's unflattering on-stage representation of living members of the court of Henri IV, and especially the scene in which the Queen slaps the face of the King's mistress, Henriette d'Entragues, Madame de Verneuil, caused the French Ambassador, Antoine Lefèvre de La Boderie, to complain to the Secretary of State, Sir Robert Cecil. As La Boderie reported home on 8 April 1608, Cecil promptly took action against the company, and he had three of the actors imprisoned, although the author managed to escape. The scandal put an end to the representation of contemporary politics on the stage, and to the short but tumultuous and often scandalous existence of the boy companies that transformed the London theatre scene between 1599 and 1608.[62]

We only know about this incident from a letter La Boderie wrote home: the slap on the face was court gossip that was never before published, should have been kept from public circulation, and in the wake of the scandal was left out of the published text of the play. But while the offence itself disappeared, the scandal of circulation, of documents and information being diverted from their intended course, is a concern that is integral to the plot of the play as we have it. The dramatic intrigue of the Biron plays is identical with the intrigue of international diplomacy: the plot of the two-part play consists in forging and disrupting secret alliances, in conducting and intercepting secret correspondence, in the sharing and withholding of knowledge and textual evidence about conspiracies. Biron delivers his elaborate oratory of heroic resentment and self-justification against this background of intrigue—a background he is so obviously part of that when he decides to visit an astrologer *incognito*, he arrives 'disguised like a Carrier of letters' (*Conspiracy* 3.3.19 SD). The circulation of information is the true focus of this play—what ultimately destroys Biron is not anything he does or even actually plans to do, but his inability to keep his involvement in treasonous diplomatic

---

[61] *A True and Perfect Discourse of the Practises and Treasons of Marshall Biron*, (1602) sigs. C1v–C2v.

[62] In La Boderie's understanding, actors were ordered to 'no longer perform any modern histories nor speak of contemporary affairs on pain of death', and Blackfriars' boys seem to have been forced out of business shortly after, and perhaps by, this scandal. Cp. Munro, *Children of the Queen's Revels* 21. But cp. Richard Dutton, *Mastering the Revels: The Regulation and Censorship of English Renaissance Drama* (London: Macmillan, 1991) 188, pointing out that although they lose their lease of the Blackfriars playhouse in 1608, the company in fact survives and performs at court next winter. For a transcript of the original letter, a translation, and an account based on further evidence, see J. J. Jusserand, 'Ambassador La Boderie and the "Compositeur" of the Byron Plays', *Modern Language Review*, 6 (1911), 203–5; Chapman, *The Conspiracy and Tragedy of Byron* 10–13, 276–7. The command forbidding the representation of 'anie modern Christian kings in those Stage-plays' that (according to Secretary Conway) King James remembered in 1624, during the *Game at Chess* scandal, may have been the order the French ambassador referred to—which would mean that the Biron plays effectively put an end to the possibility of performing plays about current political affairs. See TNA SP 14/171, f. 53, Chambers, *The Elizabethan Stage* 1:327; Dutton, *Mastering the Revels* 182–7. Note, however, how hypothetical all this is.

negotiations secret. Knowledge is power, and it is lost or acquired through betrayal, through the passing on of information in the form of documents.

In a moment whose consequences are emblematic of the play's logic, Biron entrusts his ominously named confidant La Fin with the destruction of his papers, 'considering worthily that in your hands / I put my fortunes, honour, and my life' (*Tragedy* 1.2.99). The next scene, however, begins with King Henri IV poring, with obvious consternation, over the same documents, the records of Biron's ferocious private diplomacy with Savoy, Spain, and Archduke Albert, handed to him by La Fin. Seeking to minimize the fallout from the imminent political scandal, Henri makes a selection of them, choosing twenty-seven that only incriminate Biron and no other member of the French court and discarding the rest of the presumably quite considerable pile. He then entrusts his Chancellor with the safekeeping of this evidence against the man who used to be his most trusted general, and the Chancellor promises to sew the entire correspondence in his doublet in order to keep them from sight 'Till need or opportunity requires' (*Tragedy* 1.3.76–80).

Biron's betrayal of Henri is exposed by La Fin's betrayal of Biron's correspondence, and the existence of these twenty-seven betrayed letters defines the movement of the rest of the play. In performance, as an ominous bulge in the Chancellor's doublet, they might serve as a constant reminder both of the king's control over the situation and of the gap between Biron's actions and his heroic rhetoric. Unaware of having been betrayed, Biron persists in his assertions about his 'true service' (*Tragedy* 4.1.56), about 'Maintaining still the truth of loyalty' (*Tragedy* 3.2.81), in spite of repeated invitations to confess and beg for pardon. During his trial he more ambiguously claims that 'for two months' space I did speak and write / More than I ought, but have done ever well' (*Tragedy* 5.2.111–12) but he refuses to confess until he is at last confronted by La Fin and by his testimony against him, at which point he starts to blame his former client for bewitching him and thus leading him astray, and (accurately) accuses the king and his court for using 'tyrannous and impious policy' (*Tragedy* 5.2.188) to bring him down.

La Fin himself, whom Henri earlier called an 'ill-aboding vermin' (*Conspiracy* 3.2.215) is a dubious and demonic presence, who trades Biron's trust for returning to the king's qualified favour after having been banished. His association with sorcery and his betrayal of Biron are, in this play as in the opinion of the time, of a piece, aspects of the same force destructive of human life and integrity. A 1602 English pamphlet mentioned a contemporary French libel that claimed that Biron was to be executed 'through the sole testimonie & witnes of the most wicked traitor in the kingdome, a murtherer, a parricide, a sorcerer'.[63] When Chapman's Henri remarks that he ought to be called 'La Fiend, and not La Fin' (*Conspiracy* 3.2.226), the punning verdict recalls the series of contemporary epigrams that play with the name that remained 'a by-word for treachery'.[64]

---

[63] *A True and Perfect Discourse of the Practises and Treasons of Marshall Biron*, sig. C2v; cp. the description of La Fin as 'un mechant homme magicien qui communiquoit avec les diables et quill'avoit seduit par charmes lui lui mordant plusierurs fois l'oreille gauche', in BL MS Kings 109, f. 56r.

[64] A. R. Braunmuller, *Natural Fictions: George Chapman's Major Tragedies* (Newark: University of Delaware Press, 1992) 91. One such epigram, preserved in TNA SP 78/46 f. 223, begins: 'Finement

In other plays by Chapman, the same qualities are seen as even more explicitly fiendish. Like Biron, the rest of Chapman's tragic heroes—Bussy d'Ambois, Claremont d'Ambois, and Chabot—meet their end through their inability to control or stop the circulation of crucial documents. In Chapman's first and best-known tragedy, the 1603 *Bussy d'Ambois*, the fate of the eponymous hero starts to unravel when Monsieur, the king's scheming malcontent younger brother, prepares to reveal Bussy's love affair with Tamyra to her husband, the Count of Montsurry, by writing up his accusations in 'a secret paper' (4.2.21).[65] Tamyra is aware of the danger—as the 1641 Quarto has her elaborate: 'Our love is knowne, / Your Monsieur hath a paper where is writ / Some secret tokens that decipher it' (4.2.9–9b)—so she and Bussy turn to Friar Comolet, her confessor, asking for his help in preventing their betrayal. The Friar summons Behemoth, 'great Prince of darkness' (4.2.66), to whom, according to his Latin conjuration, 'the letter-boxes of Great Ones are accessible' (4.2.36: 'cui pervia sunt Magnatum scrinia'). Behemoth, the 'Emperor / Of that inscrutable darkness, where are hid / All deepest truths, and secrets never seen' relegates the task of seizing the incriminating document to a devil who specializes in charters and paperwork: Cartophylax. He instructs this expert from hell, 'thou that properly / Hast in thy power all papers so inscrib'd, / Glide through all bars to it and fetch that paper' (4.2.63–5). Promptly returning from his mission, Cartophylax reports that he failed to intercept the document, as Monsieur 'hath prevented me, and got a spirit, / Rais'd by another, great in our command, / To take the guard of it before I came' (4.2.73–5). This somewhat baffling scene imagines Monsieur's court policy as a quite literally diabolic control over paperwork, which outpaces the desperate efforts of Bussy, Tamyra, and the Friar. It is Monsieur who, having shared the paper with the jealous husband, prompts him to resort to further paper-based scheming, and devise a way to entrap Bussy by forcing Tamyra to invite him to meet her. Readers of the play are aware of the synecdochic significance of the warning he receives but does not understand: 'Her hand shall be thy death' (5.2.56). Although Tamyra writes the letter in her own blood, thus seeking to alert Bussy to the deceit, he misunderstands it as 'a sacred witness of her love' (5.2.90). The letter killeth.[66]

Cartophylax, the infernal 'protector of documents'[67] presides over Chapman's plays about court politics. Whatever combination of diplomacy, vendetta, and love intrigue they focus on, their plots all hinge on the technologies of the production,

d'vn Francois la Fin la fin hastá; / mais a la fin la Fin finira sa Veillesse / si finement ne faict; car desia [*sic*] le fin a / Finy de deffinir ceste fine finesse.'

[65] I cite the play by act, scene, and line numbers from George Chapman, *Bussy d'Ambois*, ed. Nicholas Brooke (The Revels Plays; London: Methuen, 1964).

[66] It even does so in the 1611–12 *Chabot, Admiral of France*. Although the play's honest and upright hero is pardoned when the evidence used against him is revealed to be corrupt by the signs inserted in the document by those forced to sign it against their will, this revelation of the fundamental corruption of justice and the king's implicatedness in it by still offering to *pardon* a crime not committed makes Chabot reject the pardon and die loyal to his king but even more to justice.

[67] Or 'guardian of papers', as Boas translates the post-classical Greek compound word: George Chapman, *Bussy d'Ambois and The Revenge of Bussy d'Ambois*, ed. Frederick S. Boas (Boston and London: D. C. Heath & Co., 1905) 158.

judgement and true experience, and especially if they are then also aired in print. What should be observed should not necessarily be written down, and should certainly not be made public.[71] There was plenty of material in circulation to explain Wicquefort's indignation. Printed collections of (usually) Venetian relations were published on the Continent since 1589, in collections circulating under the title of *Tesoro Politico*, and more systematic compendia, like Giovanni Botero's international bestseller, the *Relazioni Universali*, or Pierre d'Avity's *Estats, Empires, et Principautez du Monde*, were often advertising their origins in *relazioni*.[72] Around the turn of the century, surveys of individual states began to appear in print in England as well, providing readers with the information necessary for making sense of recent political developments, about cities and princes, about alliances and conflicts.[73]

This transition of political intelligence into print posed new challenges: the blunt assessment that was a strength of a document offered to one's betters suddenly became a breach of decorum, and the reaction could be fierce. Robert Dallington, who served as a tutor accompanying the 5th Earl of Rutland on a continental tour in 1595–7, and then also his younger brother (the future 6th Earl) in 1598–1600, wrote two *relazioni*, one about France and one about Tuscany. When his account of Tuscany appeared in 1605, Edward Blount somewhat unusually prefaced the book by a letter to its author, asking for his forgiveness for publishing it without his permission. That Blount was later to publish Dallington's great *Aphorismes Civill and Militarie* (a collection of politic maxims illustrated with passages from Guicciardini), and that they were still good friends in the 1620s, suggests that this was as much a preventive ruse and a marketing ploy as a genuine admission of a transgression.[74] Such a prefatory manoeuvre was clearly necessary: Dallington's *Suruey* suggested that under the Grand Duke, the government of Tuscany '(to speake in one word, and not to vse a harder terme) is meerely

---

[71] *L'Ambassadeur et Ses Fonctions. Par Monsieur de Wicquefort*, 2 vols. (The Hague: Jean & Daniel Steucker, 1680) 2:408.

[72] Simone Testa, 'From the "Bibliographical Nightmare" to a Critical Bibliography. *Tesori Politici* in the British Library, and Elsewhere in Britain', *eBLJ* (2008), 1–33.

[73] Giles Fletcher's *The Russe Commonwealth* (1591) is among the earliest such works; there are a number of *relazioni* included in Hakluyt; Botero's *Relazioni Universali* were first published in English in 1601 and then in seven further editions through 1630 (STC 3398–404), first as *The Travelers Breviat* (London: Iohn Iaggard, 1603), and from 1608 on, as *Relations*; d'Avity's book was translated into English by Grimeston as *The estates, empires, & principallities of the world Represented by ye description of countries, maners of inhabitants, riches of prouinces, forces, gouernment, religion; and the princes that haue gouerned in euery estate. With the beginning of all militarie and religious order*. (London: Adam Islip for Mathewe Lownes and Iohn Bill, 1615); Robert Dallington, *The Vievv of Fraunce* (London: Symon Stafford, 1604), and his *A Suruey of the Great Dukes State of Tuscany* (London: Edward Blount, 1605); Sir Thomas Ouerbury his *Obseruations in His Trauailes vpon the State of the XVII. Prouinces* ([London]: [Bernard Alsop for John Parker], 1626), which also contains a report of the state of France); Jean François Le Petit, *The Low-Country Common Wealth Contayninge an Exact Description of the Eight Vnited Prouinces. Now made free. Translated out of French by Ed. Grimeston* ([London]: G. Eld, 1609).

[74] Blount to Trumbull, 15 June 1621, BL MS Add 72361 ff. 68–9, and cp. Gary Taylor, 'The Cultural Politics of Maybe', in Richard Dutton, Alison Findlay, and Richard Wilson (eds.), *Theatre and Religion: Lancastrian Shakespeare* (Manchester and New York: Manchester University Press, 2003), 242–58. (Taylor's citations are based on an earlier arrangement of this unbound MS.)

authentication, reproduction, alteration, transmission, interception, and recirculation of letters and documents, and on the secrets they transmit and reveal. The tantalizing complexity and treacherousness of the uses of letters and documents in these tragedies is not only a philosophical and theological reflection on the nature of writing in general, but also, and perhaps more pointedly, an exploration of the perilous dynamics of the use of information and intelligence in the life of the political elite.[68] In them, state power—the power that destroys aristocratic independence and identity in seventeenth-century tragedies of nobility, in the tragedies of Corneille and Racine, but also in Shakespeare's *Antony and Cleopatra* and *Coriolanus*—manifests itself in the uncontrollable operation of the medium of modern politics, of political writing and political intelligence.[69] Chapman's plays identify the circulation of political information as the material reality of the abstract ubiquity of modern state power, the power that threatens heroic individuality even as it promises advancement to anyone willing to participate in its operations. For Chapman, policy is in fact synonymous with the manipulation of information, and the betrayal of intelligence a diabolic act. But while the plays represent specific, targeted betrayals taking place within the court, these betrayals figure the intelligence transfers the plays themselves perform. Like the demonic agents they feature, Chapman's tragedies are a medium for the betrayal of political intelligence. The motives for such betrayals can, of course, be several, even at once—but as the scandalous slap on the face of the royal mistress indicates, we could do much worse than use a scandalous revelation on *Gawker* rather than the Snowden files passed on to *The Guardian* as our contemporary analogy for understanding what Chapman is doing here.[70]

SCANDALOUS RELATIONS

As the scandal of Chapman's Biron plays indicated, what Osborn calls the betrayal of the 'most intrinsick actions of the State' often had complicated consequences, and in this respect, publication on the stage and in print were once again analogous. The publication of the ambassadorial reports whose production was discussed in Chapter 2 is an example of this. In his great late seventeenth-century treatise about diplomacy, Abraham van Wicquefort expresses his indignation over ambassadors' 'impertinent and gross, injudicious and ostentatious' descriptions of the courts where they are posted. Observations about 'the genius, the inclinations, the virtues and vices of princes' in *relazioni* become problematic when made without

---

[68] James Kearney's *The Incarnate Text: Imagining the Book in Reformation England* (Philadelphia: University of Pennsylvania Press, 2009) attends to the religious associations of the medium, and to the understanding of 'the graphic dimension of language' as 'an aspect of the fallen world' (23).
[69] For a powerful and suggestive overview of early modern tragedy's engagement with the fate of the aristocracy, understanding such plays as the genre that articulates the experience of the loss of tragic possibility with the rise of political modernity in the seventeenth century, see David Quint, 'The Tragedy of Nobility on the Seventeenth-Century Stage', *Modern Language Quarterly*, 67 (2006), 7–29.
[70] But 'today's gossip is tomorrow's news': my analogy seems dated already.

Despoticall', and ended with an elaborate witticism about the name of the ducal family, concluding with the punch line 'Qui sub Medicis viuit, misere viuit.'[75]

When the *relazione* appeared early in 1605, the Florentine ambassador Ottaviano Lotti immediately alerted the Grand Duke, bestowing upon Dallington's treatise the dubious honour of a prompt translation into Italian, making it one of a very select group of texts written in English to receive such treatment.[76] Lotti also complained to Cecil, and by May 1605, Dallington was under arrest and questioned by a commission of privy councillors. In his defence he insisted that

> he had noe intent, or meaning in anie sort, to publish the same. But a very deare ffreind of his haveing (by chaunce) gotten the sight thereof, did borrow it, and (unwitting to him) tooke a copie thereof; who being sithence deceased, that copie falling into the handes of some indiscreet person, had put it in printe wthout his consent or privity.

Dallington proved innocent of the crime of publication, but the book itself was burnt in Paul's Churchyard, in the presence of the ambassador. This book-burning, however, remained mostly symbolic, as they only found three copies to destroy—it is little surprise, therefore, that Florentine diplomats continued to harbour suspicions about the honesty of the proceedings of the English government in this matter.[77]

In May–June 1605, just as the diplomatic scandal around Dallington's *Suruey* was erupting, Don Giovanni de'Medici, nephew of the Grand Duke of Tuscany, was visiting London, and was received by the King, the Queen, as well as by Prince Henry, which obviously made the English government more sensitive to the topic, and the London *politicos* more excited about Dallington's book.[78] Arguably, the most important effect of the book-burning was that it advertised Dallington's tract as genuine, and genuinely important, and thus guaranteed that Edward Blount

---

[75] Sigs. F4r, L1v.

[76] Preserved in the Archivio di Stato di Firenze, Miscellanea Medicea, Filza 90, as 'Falsissima Relatione dello Stato del Gran Duca di Toscana… Composto l'anno 1596 da uno Inglese chiamato Ruberto Dalington servitore del Conte di Rutland et dato alla stampa nella città di Londra in Inghliterra l'anno di nostro Signore 1605. Dove malamente si può far Giuditio di quello che sia maggiore, la temerità, Arroganza, malignità o, Ignoranza di questo mendacissimo scrittore'. Cited by Anna Maria Crinò, *Fatti e Figure del Seicento Anglo-Toscano: Documenti Inediti sui Rapporti Letterari, Diplomatici, Culturali fra Toscana e Inghilterra* (Biblioteca dell' Archivum Romanicum, I: 48; Firenze: Olschki, 1957) 43–4.

[77] The Florentine archival documents are published in Crinò, *Fatti e Figure del Seicento Anglo-Toscano* 41–8, the quotation at 43. The Venetian ambassador mentioned the case in his letters of 18 May and 1 June, *CSP Venetian* 10 (1603–7), nos. 368 and 374. The case is discussed in F. J. Levy, 'Hayward, Daniel, and the Beginnings of Politic History in England', *Huntington Library Quarterly*, 50 (1987), 1–34 at 15, 31.

[78] See e.g. *CSP Venetian* 10 (1603–7), no. 373, and the letters of Don Giovanni de'Medici in the Medici archives, filza 5157/336 (8 April 1605), 375 and 376 (15 June 1605), 377 (23 June 1605), as calendared by the Medici Archives project. On Don Giovanni, see Brendan Dooley, 'Sources and Methods in Information History: The Case of Medici Florence, the Armada, and the Siege of Ostende', in J. W. Koopmans (ed.), *News and Politics in Early Modern Europe* (Leuven: Peeters, 2005), 29–46; Brendan Dooley, 'Making It Present', in Dooley (ed.), *The Dissemination of News and the Emergence of Contemporaneity in Early Modern Europe* (Farnham and Burlington, VT: Ashgate, 2010), 95–114.

would make a quick profit on the remaining copies. But *relazioni* needed no topical reason to enter commercial circulation in London, whether in print or indeed in manuscript copies. The bookseller Robert Martin published a series of sale catalogues of foreign books from 1633; at first, he only mentioned that he also had manuscripts for sale, but in 1635 and 1639, he also included lists of his manuscripts, including dozens of Italian *relazioni*.[79] As we shall see, some of the information Chapman disseminated through his political plays can also be traced to such manuscripts passing through the bookshops in Paul's Churchyard, providing another example of the connection between the stage and the circulation of political manuscripts.

How Chapman knew what he made public in his plays is almost impossible to tell, but in the case of the plot of his two Bussy plays, *Bussy d'Ambois* (1603) and *The Revenge of Bussy d'Ambois* (1610), we can get a glimpse of the knowledge economy he was tapping into, and thus recognize that the plays' concern with the publication of political intelligence was, depending on how we are disposed, a serious reflection on the condition of his plays or an ostentatious gesture advertising that condition. The story of the adulterous affair of Louis de Clermont, Sieur de Bussy d'Amboise with Madame Monsoreau (Chapman's Tamyra, Duchess of 'Montsurry') and his death at the hands of her husband had a rich literary afterlife, from the history of de Thou, the memoirs of Marguerite de Valois and of Pierre l'Estoile, to the nineteenth century historical novels of Alexandre Dumas *père*. Chapman's *Bussy d'Ambois* is a remarkably accurate dramatization of the story which was not publicly available in any form either in English or in French at the time he was working on the play. It was Chapman's play that betrayed to the public of Paul's Boys—and it is perhaps relevant that their theatre was located on the cathedral precinct, right across Paul's Walk from Paul's Churchyard—the story of Bussy's betrayal.[80] So how did he know?

Bussy d'Amboise was a figure reasonably well-known to England's political elite. Described in Grimeston's compilation of the history of France as a 'bloudie, wicked, and a furious man'.[81] Bussy lead the troops of Monsieur, François, duc d'Alençon and (from 1576) d'Anjou, in the 1578 French expedition to Flanders.

---

[79] *Catalogus librorum quos (in ornamentum reipublicae literariae) non sine magnis sumptibus & labore, ex Italia selegit Robertus Martine, Bibliopola Londinensis: apud quem in coemiterio Divi Pauli prostant venales* (London: Augustin Mathewes, 1633); *Catalogus librorum tam impressorum quam manuscriptorum, quos ex Roma, Venetiis, aliisque Italiae locis, selegit Robertus Martine Bibliopola Londinensis. Apud quem vaeneunt in coemiterio Divi Pauli* (London: John Haviland, 1635); *Catalogus librorum, ex praecipius Italiae Emporiis selectorum. Per Robertum Martinum. Apud quem venales habentur. Londini: In Old Bayly, non procul ab aquaeductu sub Venetiis* (London: Thomas Harper, 1639). Martin's 1640 catalogue lists fewer MSS, and in 1650, there are none. On Martin, see Graham Pollard and Albert Ehrman, *The Distribution of Books by Catalogue from the Invention of Printing to A.D. 1800: Based on Material in the Broxbourne Library* (Cambridge: The Roxburghe Club, 1965) 90–1.

[80] For accounts of the historical events and Chapman's potential sources, see Chapman, *Bussy d'Ambois and The Revenge of Bussy d'Ambois* xii–xviii; Jean Jacquot, *George Chapman, 1559–1634: Sa Vie, Sa Poésie, Son Théâtre, Sa Pensée* (Paris: Les Belles Lettres, 1951) 123–6; George Chapman, *Bussy d'Amboise*, ed. Jean Jacquot (Paris: Aubier, 1960) xxii–xxvii.

[81] *A General Inuentorie of the History of France from the Beginning of that Monarchie, vnto the Treatie of Veruins, in the year 1598. Written by Ihon de Serres. And Continued vnto these Times, out off the Best Authors which Haue Written of that Subiect. Translated out of French into English, by Edward Grimeston*

He was in charge of the negotiations with Walsingham about the French intervention in the Low Countries, about the possibility of Monsieur becoming the sovereign of Flanders, and about his proposed marriage to Queen Elizabeth, the 'Anjou match' that was the cause of so much controversy in England.[82] If we remember Chapman's Bussy as a character with rather large speeches, and perhaps take pleasure in them, we seem to be in agreement with the Queen, who responded to Walsingham's 'longe declaration of your conference with Bussy d'Amboise' saying she found 'nothing to be misliked in your diligent report of Bussies large speaches in his masters behalf'.[83] Intelligence reports sent to Walsingham over the next few years often mentioned Bussy.[84] Although these references only cohere into something like a fragmentary narrative in archival hindsight, they indicate that the subject of Chapman's play—Bussy's tempestuous connections with the key figures in the late sixteenth-century French political landscape, his transfer of allegiance from Henri III to Monsieur, his affair, and his demise—would have received some attention in England.

Other than writing home with news, English diplomats also produced *relazioni* as well as other compendia of background information intended to help make sense of the most recent developments. During his political apprenticeship in Paris in 1584, the young Robert Cecil was compiling and updating a set of political documents that provide a survey of the constitution and networks of the French political elite, with essential information about their alliances and loyalties, and short narrative vignettes about the most important affairs they were involved in over the past few decades, stories that serve to clarify the connections and long-standing conflicts among various political players.[85] This group of manuscripts mentions such momentous events as the death of the King of Navarre, Antoine de Bourbon, father of the future Henri IV, who fell victim to a follower of Henri de Guise while he was pissing against a wall in Rouen, but the compiler also considered Bussy important enough to discuss his complicated family connections

---

Gentleman (London: George Eld, 1607), 674 (sig. 4L2v). Grimeston skips the events of 1579, both d'Alençon's visit to England and the murder of Bussy.

[82] Cp. Baron Kervyn de Lettenhove (ed.), *Relations Politiques des Pays-Bas et de l'Angleterre, Sous le Règne de Philippe II*, 10 vols. (Bruxelles: F. Hayez, 1882–1900) 10:673–705; Léo Mouton, *Bussy d'Amboise et Madame Montsoreau* (Paris: Hachette et cie, 1912) 187–212; Mack P. Holt, *The Duke of Anjou and the Politique Struggle During the Wars of Religion* (Cambridge: Cambridge University Press, 1986) 100.

[83] Kervyn de Lettenhove (ed.), *Relations Politiques Des Pays-Bas et de l'Angleterre* 10:698–9. (BL MS Cotton, Galba, C. VI, 2nd part, no. 127.)

[84] See also the *CSP Foreign* for the relevant years, indexed under Clermont and Bussy.

[85] Cecil copied and augmented the second part of a document called 'Traité des princes, conseillers et autres ministres de l'estat de France', drawn up at the English embassy in Paris around 1579. The original is now BL MS Cotton Vespasian F v, ff. 1–47, Cecil's version of the second part is TNA SP 78/12 no. 82, ff. 221–37; in the same SP volume there is also a list of the titled nobility and office holders of France, TNA SP 78/12, no. 84, ff. 237r–242v, printed in David Potter (ed.), *Foreign Intelligence and Information in Elizabethan England: Two English Treatises on the State of France, 1580–1584* (Camden Fifth Series, Cambridge: Cambridge University Press, 2004) 169–83; and an account of the clans and alliances of the nobility, TNA SP 78/12, no. 85, ff. 244r–249r, printed in Potter (ed.), *Foreign Intelligence and Information in Elizabethan England* 183–92, both in Cecil's hand, from October 1584.

and also explain that he was having an affair with Monsoreau's wife, and was killed by Monsoreau when he was on his way to her. This is where Chapman's first *Bussy* play ends. While scholarly consensus has treated both the plot of *The Revenge of Bussy d'Ambois* and Clermont, the hero of that play the somewhat tedious figments of Chapman's imagination, Cecil's note also provides the basics for this revenge plot, explaining that Bussy's daughter was given in marriage to Baligny on the condition that he would kill Monsoreau, the murderer of her father—which is precisely the situation represented at the beginning of *The Revenge*, although Chapman's more plausible version makes Baligny marry Bussy's sister rather than his daughter (Bussy d'Amboise wasn't even thirty when he died).[86] While Cecil's 1584 compendium has nothing to say about the revenge itself, on 7 December 1582, Cobham, the English Ambassador to Paris, had already written to Walsingham about it as a fait accompli: 'I heare told that Balligni hath caused Monsr de Monsoreau to be murdered, revenginge thereby the death of Monsr de Boussi.'[87] Chapman's second Bussy play builds on this revenge narrative, and complicates it by making Baligny unwilling to perform his obligation, and by adding another revenger, Bussy's brother Clermont, whose reluctance is philosophical rather than cowardly, and who finally performs the task. The name Clermont d'Ambois is usually described as part of Bussy's full name and title, but it appears as a name in its own right at the end of Cecil's note on the family, while in another document in Cecil's hand, Bussy d'Ambois is the head of a clan that also includes a first cousin (*cousin germain*) called Clermont d'Amboise, and another near relation, a 'conte d'Aubigeon', all sharing the name and coat of arms of the d'Ambois.[88]

Far from being fictions, Chapman's Bussy plays were publishing a story that was of obvious interest not only to those in English government circles who were involved in diplomacy with France (which means just about everyone involved in any sort of diplomacy) but also to members of the wider public of political news. These were plays that wore their origins in diplomatic writing on their sleeve, and this may have been an important part of their appeal. Their plots often seem mere devices to evoke major figures of late sixteenth-century French politics: their names, connections, alliances, and their most important deeds; to produce, that is, a stage version of the kind of material Daniel Rogers, Robert Cecil, and their colleagues were collecting and writing up in their *relazioni*. The bizarre masque of

---

[86] 'D'Amboise. Le jeune fille d'amboyse a donne sa soeur a mons. de Baligny en beauvoisin a condition de tuer mons. de Monsereau qui tua son pere allant voir sa femme dudict Monsereau. Messieurs de Clermont d'amboyse de ceste maison ont porte les armes contre le Roy mais a present ils ne bougent.' f. 247r, Potter (ed.), *Foreign Intelligence and Information in Elizabethan England* 191–2.

[87] TNA SP 78/8 f. 115v (*CSP Foreign* Eliz., vol. 16, May–Dec. 1582, p. 490). Cobham is the diplomat Sir Henry Brooke (1537–92), who succeeded Sir Amias Paulet as resident ambassador in France in October 1579. His brother, William Brooke, was the tenth Baron Cobham, but as the DNB puts it, Henry 'pursued a family eccentricity (or pretension) with unusual determination in using as a surname the family title rather than Brooke'. *ODNB*, *s.v.*

[88] TNA SP 78/12, f. 230v: 'Bussi damboise est cousin germain de Clermont damboyse p[ro]che parent du Conte Daubigon en Languedoc[.] Tous trois de mesme nom et armes dont busy est le Chef,' cp. BL MS Cotton 42r and Potter (ed.), *Foreign Intelligence and Information in Elizabethan England* 104, and cp. 93, 96, 106. Potter's note explains that the 'Daubigon' ('d'Aubigeon' in the BL document) is Louis d'Amboise, comte d'Aubijoux (1536–1614).

ghosts near the end of *The Revenge* is emblematic of this: when Monsoreau (called Montsurry in the play) dies, the stage direction calls for 'Musicke', and then

> the Ghost of Bussy enters, leading the Ghost of the Guise, Monsieur [i.e. the Duc d'Alençon and d'Anjou], Cardinal Guise, and Chatillon [the Admiral Coligny, the Huguenot leader murdered in the St Bartholomew's Night's Massacre], they dance about the dead body [of Montsurry lying on the stage], and Exeunt. (5.5.119 SD)[89]

This ghostly dance—whose participants are then identified and commented upon by a Clermont, who, not knowing they are all dead, is rather baffled to see some of them as ghosts—places the action of *The Revenge* at the centre of late sixteenth-century French politics. It signals that the fates of Bussy and Clermont d'Amboise are determined by the field of forces among the Guise, the Valois, and the Huguenots, and reminds the reader and viewer that the events of the play are defined by, and thus intended to evoke, the larger tensions that may seem marginal to the immediate action. Although Monsieur and the Guise are important characters in the two plays, and the murder of the Guise at the King's command the tragic centre of *The Revenge*, the Cardinal Guise and Coligny don't even appear in them; but the political factions they represent, and the motives and obligations behind the factional conflict are discussed at length by Bussy, Clermont (who praises the Guise for his participation in the Massacre), and their interlocutors. Far from being ancient and therefore politically innocuous history, these late sixteenth-century connections and conflicts were still considered relevant enough to current affairs by George Carew, James's ambassador to Paris, to outline them in the *relazione* about the state of France he prepared for the king in 1609, on his return from his embassy, just around the time Chapman would have been writing *The Revenge*.[90]

Whether Chapman took his plot from papers written up by Robert Cecil or not, we cannot know, but we do know that the information written up in Cecil's intelligence report was also present in other, similar documents produced by others.[91] A collection of papers that includes earlier versions of the documents Cecil was

---

[89] *The Revenge of Bussy d'Ambois* is quoted by act, scene, and line number from Parrott (ed.), *The Plays and Poems of George Chapman: The Tragedies*.

[90] For the date of the play, see Albert H. Tricomi, 'The Dates of the Plays of George Chapman', *English Literary Renaissance*, 12 (1982), 242–66 at 260–1. On Carew's *relazione*, see Chapter 3. Some of the characters and issues of the play were still very much alive at the time: Epernon, the mignon and putative lover of Henry III, for example, was not only at the peak of his power, but was also rumoured to have been involved in the conspiracy that led to the assassination of Henri IV—an event which brought the French court to the centre of contemporary attention, and reignited the debates about regicide, another question addressed by the play. The peace negotiations between the Dutch and Philip III, and then, a couple of years later, the eruption of the Julich-Cleves crisis also helped to make an earlier French court which actively sought to control the Low Countries a topic of interest to London audiences, and Chapman's *Revenge of Bussy* clearly speaks to these interests in the region, both by representing Monsieur's departure for Bruxelles in the *Tragedy*, and by choosing Cambrai as the setting for *The Revenge*.

[91] See for example the similar compendium surviving in Folger MS V.a. 146 and in a partial English translation in Folger MS V.b. 41, published in Potter (ed.), *Foreign Intelligence and Information in Elizabethan England* 123–61 and in David Potter and P. R. Roberts, 'An Englishman's View of the Court of Henri III, 1584–1585: Richard Cook's "Description of the Court of France"', *French History*, 2 (1988), 312–44, respectively.

copying and revising also survives among the Cotton manuscripts; on its first page this volume bears the contemporary note, presumably by Robert Cotton: 'Thes things of France I had of Mr Harrison of Pouls 1594.'[92] This note is a crucial piece of evidence of a world that largely vanished without a trace. Cotton's volume is a set of documents produced for government use around 1579, most likely as apprentice work done by someone at an early stage of his career. But instead of remaining within government circles, fifteen years later, they were on sale at the shop of the stationer John Harrison the elder, at the sign of the Greyhound in Paul's Churchyard.[93]

How these materials got in the hands of booksellers in Paul's Churchyard is best explained by Robert Beale's melancholy note about the dispersal of Walsingham's papers: as he says, 'upon the death of Mr. Secretarie Walsingham all his papers and bookes both publicke and private weare seazed on and carried away, perhapps by those who would be loath to be used so themselves.'[94] And we might add: perhaps by someone who, not particularly interested in the documents themselves, but understanding the value of the papers so closely kept by Mr Secretary Walsingham while he was alive, thought there might be someone interested in buying them.[95]

What is certain is that in late sixteenth-century London, the place to go with a bunch of such papers would have been Paul's Churchyard, the centre of the English book trade and of the public exchange of political information, where such manuscripts would be recognized as valuable intelligence, as knowledge helpful in making sense of more recent political developments. If we also consider that the title page of the first edition of *Bussy d'Ambois: A Tragedie* claims to represent the text *As It Hath Been Often Presented at Paules*, and that the playbook itself was also presented to its readers at Paul's, i.e. in Paul's Churchyard, where William Aspley was conducting business from 1608 on, then the Bussy plays become a genuine Paul's phenomenon.

While this is entirely appropriate, it is not entirely an accident, either. What we know about Chapman suggests that he was more than just a casual, occasional visitor to the churchyard: in fact, he had close and well-documented ties to a bookseller especially invested in news and other foreign materials: John Flasket.[96] In

---

[92] BL MS Cotton Vespasian F v, prelim.

[93] Potter surmises that 'Mr Harrison of Pouls' is the antiquarian William Harrison. William Harrison died in Windsor on 9 November 1593, and he would not have been referred to as 'Harrison of Paul's'. The stationer John Harrison rented the shop at the Greyhound, the second shop east of Flasket's Black Bear, between 1582 and 1594; cp. Potter (ed.), *Foreign Intelligence and Information in Elizabethan England* 3 note; Peter W. M. Blayney, *The Bookshops in Paul's Cross Churchyard* (Occasional Papers of the Bibliographical Society, No. 5; London: The Bibliographical Society, 1990) 28.

[94] 'Instructions for a Principall Secretarie, observed by R[obert] B[eale] for Sir Edwarde Wotton: Anno Domini 1592'. BL MS Add 48149 (Yelverton 161 pt 1), f. 1ff., as printed in Read, *Mr. Secretary Walsingham and the Policy of Queen Elizabeth* 423–43, the quoted passage on 431. On the MS, see Taviner, 'Robert Beale and the Elizabethan Polity', at 32–3, esp. n33, and cp. Stewart, *Close Readers* 184–6.

[95] Walsingham's papers were still marketable half a century later: the letters related to his Paris embassies were printed as *The Compleat Ambassador* (London: Tho: Newcomb, for Gabriel Bedell and Thomas Collins, 1654).

[96] Charles Jasper Sisson, *Lost Plays of Shakespeare's Age* (Cambridge: The University Press, 1936) 12–72; Mary C. Erler (ed.), *Ecclesiastical London* (Records of Early English Drama, London and

1601, Flasket paid him to write what ended up being one of the most scandalous of early seventeenth century plays, *The Old Joiner of Aldgate*, an *à clef* city comedy about a girl's multiple suitors and their negotiations with her greedy father, negotiations revolving around the girl's rather considerable dowry. According to the examination conducted by Attorney General Edward Coke in Star Chamber, Flasket, Chapman, and others conspired to have the comedy performed by Paul's Boys in order to embarrass the father of a rich heiress, a certain Agnes How, also living in the neighbourhood, into marrying his daughter to Flasket. The connections between Chapman and Flasket reach back even further, at least to 1598, when the poet's continuation of Marlowe's *Hero and Leander* was published by Flasket. These connections place Chapman right in the middle of the scene where in the first years of the seventeenth century, political intelligence got transferred from one realm, and one medium, to another.

DENIAL, SELF-KNOWLEDGE, AND CURIOSITY

Although it represents events from several decades ago, *The Revenge of Bussy d'Ambois* is a play with obvious relevance to current affairs and to the conduct of foreign politics: it is news that stayed news. The play's main characters, however, seem to consider such concerns, and the handling of information that was key to the business of politics, as mere distractions. Whereas for Chapman 'a great and politicke man... is neuer as he showes', and is an active participant of this Machiavellian textual economy, the rejection of simulation and dissimulation that makes one 'good and wise' starts with a philosophical mistrust of correspondence, diplomacy, intelligence, news, and gossip.[97] Chapman's tragic heroes seek to extricate themselves from this exchange of secret and often deceptive information, to distance themselves from the world of betrayals, and while their efforts only entangle them in it more deeply and fatefully, they often wax eloquent about their deep stoic suspicions of the world of news and policy, and indeed of any information that circulates beyond its originally intended sphere, any piece of paper that reaches others than the original addressee. In their assertions of the claims of constancy and reason over the fickleness of opinion, of the perception of the multitude, they are of course in perfect agreement with the period's satirical writing as well as with anxious politicians who understood the public circulation of news as the hijacking of information, the access of busybodies to knowledge they are not entitled to. Chapman's heroes read the circulation of political intelligence through the spectacles of the stoic dismissal of opinion—and this perspective leads to their downfall.

Toronto: British Library and University of Toronto Press, 2008) 177–202. On Flasket's connections with Chapman, see also Kiséry, 'An Author and a Bookshop'.

[97] Chapman, 'A Great Man' and 'Virgils Epigram of a Good Man', in *Petrarchs Seven Penientiall Psalms*: Phyllis Brooks Bartlett, *The Poems of George Chapman* (New York and London: Modern Language Association of America and Oxford University Press, 1941) 228, 227.

Clermont d'Ambois, the brother and reluctant revenger of Bussy, the character at the centre of the gallery of political portraits called *The Revenge of Bussy d'Ambois*, is the most impeccably stoic of Chapman's protagonists, and his constant philosophizing clearly contributes to the lack of modern interest in the play.[98] The third act of the play finds this high-mindedly passive protagonist in the country. When his friend Renel shows up to visit, Clermont for a fleeting moment appears to be like an ordinary human being, eager to hear court news, and news that circulate at court about foreign affairs:

> You come something later
> From Court, my lord, then I: and since news there
> Is every day increasing with th'affairs,
> Must I not ask now what the news is there?
> Where the Court lies? what stirre, change, what *avise*[99]
> From England, Italy?

Clermont's use of the term 'avise' makes clear that he is asking specifically for the kind of political news disseminated in the manuscript *avvisi* whose commercial production originated in Venice. Renel concedes that asking for such news, for news about the affairs of state from court and from abroad, is indeed something of a social obligation—it is, as the public of Paul's was keenly aware, a way to claim and acknowledge one's status:

> You must do so,
> If you'll be call'd a gentleman well qualified,
> And wear your time and wits in those discourses.

Should it not have been perfectly clear from the beginning that his question was less than genuine, Clermont responds by rejecting the notion of achieving cultural distinction by being conversant in the news. He says

> The Locrian Princes therefore were brave Rulers;
> For whosoever there came new from country,
> And in the city ask'd 'What news?' was punished ...

This reference to the philosopher–kings of Locri derives from Plutarch's essay 'On Curiosity', first published in English in Philemon Holland's translation of the *Moralia* in 1603. The essay was among the more influential pieces of the collection, and the text that provided the conceptual framework for serious as well as satirical commentary on the social vice of curiosity: on newsmongering, gossiping, prying into other peoples' business. It says something about its importance for the political culture of the age that Queen Elizabeth also produced a translation in 1598.[100]

---

[98] Braunmuller, *Natural Fictions* calls it 'pretty poor stuff' (31).
[99] Here I am reverting from Parrott's modernized 'advice', which obscures the point, to the quarto 'auise'.
[100] The translation—based on Erasmus's Latin version—survives in holograph as well as in a scribal copy, which are published in Janel M. Mueller and Joshua Scodel (eds.), *Elizabeth I: Translations, 1592–1598* (Chicago: University of Chicago Press, 2009) 391–447 and Steven W. May (ed.), *Queen Elizabeth I: Selected Works* (New York: Washington Square Press, 2004) 296–314, respectively.

The objections to curiosity are twofold: on the one hand, there is the political anxiety. For Plutarch, an interest in news is synonymous not only with indecorous nosiness, but also with a challenge to the political order:

> For like as Cookes pray for nothing, but good store of fatlings to kill for the kitchin, and Fishmongers plentie of fishes; even so curious and busie people wish for a world of troubles and a number of affaires, great newes, alterations and changes of state: to the ende that they might evermore be provided of gaine, to chase and hunt after, yea and to kill.[101]

Clermont's endorsement of the policing of the exchange of news draws on this thread of Plutarch's essay. But the objections to curiosity also have another frame of reference, one that is also evoked by Ben Jonson, who lists 'gathering and venting news', along with 'scattering compliments, tendering visits, ... following feasts and plays', and with 'making a little winter-love in a dark corner' as the 'cold business' we 'misspend the better part of life in'.[102] Plutarch's central objection to newsmongers or 'busybodies', also shared by Chapman's hero, is that news distracts from the true purpose of life, from stoic self-examination and pursuit of theoretical wisdom. As Clermont argues,

> our wit's sharpness, which we should employ
> In noblest knowledge, we should never waste
> In vile and vulgar admirations. (3.2.4–14, 20–2)

In the understanding of curiosity as a sign of unseemly ambition, an understanding familiar not only from Francis Osborn's memoirs, but also from a wide range of references from the period, a gentleman is in fact 'well qualllified' if he does *not* engage in ephemeral exchanges about current affairs, but stands fast in his proud autonomy. In the 1614 *Andromeda Liberata*, written for the wedding of Frances Howard and Robert Carr, Chapman once again associates the interest in news (and specifically, in seditious news) with 'the ungodly Vulgars'. And it is perhaps not entirely accidental that in Beaumont and Fletcher's *Philaster*, it is another character named Cleremont who apologizes for his 'ignorance in State-policy', only to be profusely praised by his interlocutor for his nature which 'is more constant than to enquire after State news'.[103] While news is sought after and circulated as a marker of status, an 'ignorance in state policy', a refusal to engage in the circulation of news, if performed as a conscious choice, as a marker of the paradigmatic stoic virtue of constancy, places one above and beyond the scene of competition. It is a sign of power and control, like Anna Wintour's flip phone.[104]

---

[101] *The Philosophie, Commonlie Called, the Morals Written by the Learned Philosopher Plutarch of Chaeronea. Translated out of Greeke into English ... by Philemon Holland* (London: Printed by Arnold Hatfield, 1603) 138–9, sigs. M3v–M4r.

[102] 'Jactura vitæ', in *Discoveries*, Jonson (2012) 7:501. There is reason to wax sentimental over the man Edmund Wilson called 'morose Ben Jonson'.

[103] *Philaster. Or, Loue Lies a Bleeding* (London: Thomas Walkley, 1622), sig. B1v.

[104] http://www.dailymail.co.uk/femail/article-2745052/That-s-definitely-not-en-Vogue-Anna-Wintour-spotted-using-fashion-FLIP-PHONE-U-S-Open.html, accessed 25 June 2015, and for the

What better way to assert the fact that you have arrived than refusing to engage in the practices that might mark you as ambitious, eager to advance yourself? But in the logic of all assertions of self-reliance and self-creation, the claims of autonomy that Clermont's social identity is built on are paradoxical to say the least. His disgust with things 'vile and vulgar' finds apt commentary in Adorno's quip in *Minima Moralia*: '*Odi profanum vulgus et arceo*—said this son of a freed slave.' Clermont was first 'rak'd...out of the dung-hill' (1.1.256–7) and brought to court by Monsieur—but by the first scene of the play, he is already described as Guise's 'dear Minion', who 'hangs upon the ear of Guise, / Like to his jewel' (1.1.152–3). As the courtiers hasten to point out, what he is whispering in the ear of the mighty duke on whom he now depends is

> Some doctrine of stability and freedom,
> Contempt of outward greatness and the guises
> That vulgar great ones make their pride and zeal...(1.1.153–6)

A Stoic stance is vital to Clermont's identity and advancement. Should anyone be missing the point of his speeches, in a marginal gloss to 2.1.156, Chapman even cites the *Discourses* of Epictetus, thus closely associating Clermont with this key text of stoicism, which prominently features the Delphic injunction 'Know thyself' in Book I, as the starting point for the ascetic regimen that is supposed to lead to an ability to ignore everything not dependent on one's will, that is, on the one thing that cannot be taken from anyone.[105]

Clermont rises in court patronage because of his discernment between the philosophical and the vulgar, his compelling contempt of social dependencies and of efforts at advancement through them, so much so that he can even posture as a teacher of such philosophical contempt. This stance, however, is seen by others as his conspicuous refusal to know himself. When Monsieur reminds Clermont of the allegiance he owes to him, he takes him to task by asking

> Dost understand thyself? I pray thee tell me,
> Dost never search thy thoughts what my design
> Might be to entertain thee and thy brother,
> What turn I meant to serve with you? (1.1.228–31)

Monsieur's point is that a proper understanding of oneself is an understanding of one's place in a hierarchical network of obligations: what Clermont should know is whose creature he is, to whom he owes his service and obedience. That is the knowledge that ought to determine his every move, rather than the stoic insistence on mental self-sufficiency: it is no surprise that for Monsieur (as for King James), the stoic version of self-knowledge is a rebellious ideology.[106]

---

argument that this is precisely not a sign of being behind, see https://medium.com/matter/the-coolest-girl-you-know-probably-uses-a-flip-phone-8d1151808904, accessed 25 June 2015.

[105] *Disc.* 1.18.

[106] Andrew Shifflett, *Stoicism, Politics, and Literature in the Age of Milton: War and Peace Reconciled* (Cambridge: Cambridge University Press, 1998) discusses the perceived threat of Stoicism to authority and order, 23–4.

Critics have noted the paradoxical tension at the heart of the play, between the philosophical statements and the actions of Clermont d'Ambois, and even between two distinct strands of his moralizing: while he professes the virtues of self-sufficiency and constancy in a series of set speeches, these critics note, on other occasions he also admits his complete dependence on Guise in the language of platonic friendship.[107] Clermont may be a high-minded Stoic, this interpretation recognizes, but he is also entangled in a political world which forces him to act in ways incompatible with his principles, an exigency which scholars then read as a critique either of the 'corrupt' world Clermont lives in, or of the Stoic principles themselves.[108] I suggest that the opposing poles of this apparent ideological conflict are better viewed as competing strategies, responses to the same challenges of the culture of courtly sociability. Contrasted by the play to Monsieur's politic self-knowledge, the denial of the significance of interpersonal dependencies through an emphasis on self-sufficiency turns out to be an effective way of masking both the political interests embodied in those dependencies and the assiduous work that went into their establishment. Such masking helps naturalize existing social bonds and allows those arrived to take the moral high ground over those striving to move up and take their place, dismissing them as vulgar opportunists.[109] And, as the play makes clear, this rhetoric may itself serve as a marker of distinction, a successful bid to advancement: after all, Clermont finds favour with the Guise precisely as his tutor in stoic doctrine, and even late in the play, the Guise praises him for 'His scorn of all things servile and ignoble, / Though they could gain him never such advancement' (4.4.22–3). As a cultural strategy, Clermont's distance from the noise of the world, his contempt for the anxious desire for upward mobility, is a social trope, analogous to *sprezzatura*, of doing things with apparent ease, of rising without seeming to be climbing. It is the stance of someone who has made it and wants to stop others from climbing up in his footsteps. Such an account of the appeal of Stoic notions to those exposed to the social pressures of the early modern state supplements Gerhard Oestreich's top–down model of indoctrination and his argument about the regulative potential of neostoicism in state-formation with an explanation of why it became popular in the first place. In this reading, Clermont's version of Stoic rhetoric is not so much in conflict with, nor merely shielding

---

[107] Alexander Leggatt, for example, argues that 'the inconsistency between his role as a philosopher and his function as a man of action makes Clermont a more attractive character as well as a more convincing one': 'The Tragedy of Clermont D'Ambois', *The Modern Language Review*, 77 (July 1982), 524–36 at 528; cp. the survey of criticism in Richard S. Ide, 'Exploiting the Tradition: The Elizabethan Revenger as Chapman's "Complete Man"', *Medieval & Renaissance Drama in England*, 1 (1984), 159–72 at 159–60.

[108] See Fredson Thayer Bowers, *Elizabethan Revenge Tragedy, 1587–1642* (Princeton: Princeton University Press, 1940) 145; Susanne F. Kistler, ' "Strange and Far-Removed Shores": A Reconsideration of *The Revenge of Bussy D'ambois*', *SP*, 77 (1980), 128–44, respectively.

[109] The choice, as formulated in Epictetus's *Manual*, seems clear: "Thou must either practise thy reason and vnderstanding, or giue all thy seruice to the world, and the worlds dependances.... that is thou must either bee a professed Philosopher, or a direct member of the vulgar.' See Chapter 36 in *Epictetus his Manuall. And Cebes his Table. Out of the Greeke originall, by Io: Healey* (London: [G. Eld] for E. Blunt and W. Barret, 1610), sigs. D3r–v.

against, but also produced by and actively helping in the competition for prestige and position.[110]

Clermont's philosophy, then, has more affinity with the plotting and scheming court around him than he or his interpreters are ready to admit: its deployment allows us to see it as a social strategy—and crucially, as a social strategy manifesting itself in a stance vis-à-vis the public dissemination and circulation of news, a circulation in which this play also participates. Although we may reach for our commonplace books and copy out the lines about the need to appear 'a gentleman well qualified', and about wasting one's 'wit's sharpness' in 'vile and vulgar admirations', Chapman does not allow us to simply register Clermont's tirade against curiosity as an extractable morsel of wisdom. Clermont's friend Renel immediately undercuts it saying "Tis right; but who, save only you, performs it' (3.2.10–23). He recognizes the intellectual appeal, as well as, perhaps, the social advantages, of Clermont's argument, but his comment is less admiring than baffled: how can anyone actually identify with such a pose?

Whether Clermont is interested in news or not, a messenger soon enters with a letter addressed to him. His admiring sister, Charlotte, having clearly missed the lecture, now turns to Clermont, who has already started reading anyway, and asks the vulgar question: 'What news?' The news in the letter is that Clermont has been betrayed by his brother-in-law, and 'Maillard, your brother's Lieutenant...hath letters and strict charge from the King to apprehend you'; he is further advised by the letter to 'Get on your Scotch horse, and retire to your strength...: Believe this as your best friend had sworn it. Fare well if you will. ANONYMOS.'

The letter that arrives here breaks the convention of the letter as personal communication, assimilating it through its anonymity to the condition of the public circulation of news—with the condition of vile and vulgar admiration, the condition that is also the condition of learning the news from the stage. The anonymous letter's use of the epistolary rhetoric of familiarity only serves to highlight how the absence of a personal signature ostentatiously denies the authentication such rhetoric presupposes. Renel, who reads it out, is no philosopher, seems to have no Greek, and hence not to understand the signature. In response to his 'What's that?' Clermont explains: 'Without a name', and then declares: 'I'll not wrong / My well-known Brother for Anonymos' (3.2.68–88). In spite of this initial dismissal, Clermont does make an effort to check the verity of the anonymous tip-off: when Maillard, Baligny's lieutenant comes to invite him to see 'the musters', he wants to search him for 'the letters and strict charge from the King to apprehend him' which the anonymous letter suggested that he will carry on him (3.2.206). Not only is the

---

[110] Oestreich, *Neostoicism and the Early Modern State* 14. Even such a subtle and sophisticated reading as Mario DiGangi's understands the play in terms of a clear opposition between 'court corruption' and 'an idealized homoerotics of favouritism', but the two might be more closely connected than an opposition between an ideal vs. a corrupt version of the same implies; see DiGangi, *The Homoerotics of Early Modern Drama* 129, 130. It is DiGangi's otherwise very productive conceptual framework, his distinction between 'orderly', non-sodomitical homoerotics and subversive sodomy that leads him to reiterate some of the binaries of earlier interpretations. There is obviously much in my argument that is closely compatible with Whigham, *Ambition and Privilege: The Social Tropes of Elizabethan Courtesy Theory*.

message itself anonymous here: as it accuses Baligny of breaking the laws of hospitality and also his word, it calls for the suspension of the structures of trust on which credibility depends in personal communication, and for their replacement with the textual corroboration that is the method of establishing credibility appropriate to the public exchange of news.[111] Clermont, hostile to this vulgar mode, is unable to make this leap: although what is at issue is precisely the credibility of people's word of honour, instead of pushing for the material evidence, Clermont decides to believe Maillard's deeply ambiguous oath 'By all my faith to you' (3.2.237)—which really begs, rather than resolves, the question of his honest dealing. Maillard does, of course, carry the King's command, and Clermont is soon arrested on its orders.

Unlike Shakespeare, some of whose most memorable letters—the commission Hamlet writes up on board the ship sailing to England, Maria's letter to Malvolio, Edmund's forgery of Edgar's letter—are fabrications,[112] Chapman is interested in scenarios where the truth of writing goes wrong: where letters and documents betray important truths to the wrong people, or where their truth remains unheeded. Being diverted or betrayed, disclosed or withheld is the condition of the public life of information. It is a condition upon which drama as a medium for political information is also predicated, and one which Chapman's plays identify as an unavoidable experience of public life. In *The Revenge*, Stoic self-sufficiency is a compelling, distinctive rhetoric, a theatrical stance which appears to effectively dismiss the public circulation of intelligence as an inevitable condition, and summarily dismiss the dangers and vicissitudes inherent to it, a stance, however, which turns out to be fatal when performed to the point. As they attend to the forces giving rise to a public sphere, to the perilous game of achieving distinction through circulation, Chapman's plays recognize that there is no way out of this game.[113]

---

[111] On the anonymity of the sources leading to the radical restructuring of the rhetoric of news in the newspaper regime, see Randall, 'Epistolary Rhetoric, the Newspaper, and the Public Sphere', 26–7.

[112] How letters in Shakespeare refuse to model an ideal (and dematerialized) immediacy of communication, see Stewart, *Shakespeare's Letters* 8–16 and *passim*.

[113] Here as elsewhere, my understanding of the logic of distinction through adept participation in the game of culture is indebted to Zucker, *The Places of Wit*.

5

'The Most Matter with Best Conceyt'
The Publics of Tacitean Observation and the Margins of Politics in Jonson's *Sejanus*

Ben Jonson was intensely preoccupied with the reception of his plays, and he was particularly concerned by the fate of his 1603 *Sejanus*. He designed the elaborately bookish 1605 quarto to define the play as a classical text, an object of study. In the preface 'To the Readers' he wards off anticipated critical objections to the play's structure and to the profuse annotations; then he temporarily yields the stage of the book to his friends, whose 'voluntary labours...have relieved me in much whereat without them I should necessarily have touched'. The well-orchestrated chorus of commendatory verses turns 'the people's beastly rage', the play's apparent failure in early performance, into yet another sign of its erudition and magnificence.[1]

These prefatory verses imply that the play's political purposes were subject to wilful misrepresentation: those who 'are so quick that they will spy / Where later times are in some speech enweaved'—accusing the play of dangerous political application—are 'so unjust, they will deceive themselves'.[2] The issue of analogical reading, of topical parallels between past and present, crops up in the play itself when the historian Cremutius Cordus is put on trial for writing ancient history with a sharply critical modern application; as his accuser puts it, in 'the annals thou hast published...thou bit'st / The present age, and with a viper's tooth' (3.384–5).[3] The scene recalls the predicament of John Hayward, who was thrown into prison two years earlier for Tacitean history of Henry IV, which had ostensible parallels with the Essex rebellion. It also anticipates the fate of Jonson himself, who later claimed that he was charged with 'popery and treason' before the Privy Council for his own Tacitean history, *Sejanus*.[4]

---

[1] Jonson (2012) 2:213, 2:228. Jonson's intense engagement with the conditions of the reception of his own work and the implications of that reception for his writing, has been a central theme of criticism, discussed, among others, by Stanley Fish, 'Authors-Readers: Jonson's Community of the Same', *Representations*, 7 (1984), 26–58; Richard Burt, *Licensed by Authority: Ben Jonson and the Discourses of Censorship* (Ithaca: Cornell University Press, 1993); Richard Dutton, *Ben Jonson. Authority. Criticism* (London: Macmillan, 1996).

[2] Jonson (2012) 2:227.

[3] References to the text of the play are to Jonson (2012) 2:235–391 by act and line number.

[4] 'Informations to William Drummond of Hawthornden', Jonson (2012) 5:375. The self-reflective analogy would be less uncanny if we thought that Jonson elaborated the trial of Cordus and the burning of his books *after* having been 'called before the Council for his Sejanus', as part of his overall and over-determined revision of the play for publication, using the printed text to respond to—and condemn— the hostile reception both from the theatre audience and the authorities. But the trial of Cordus

Since Jonson's comments and his friends' poems present *Sejanus* as a provocation of the theatre-going public as well as of the government, modern interpretations read it as subversive topical–analogical commentary, a bold denunciation of absolute rule and of censorship, and in any case an intervention in a field of political polemic. Such readings are based on an implicit back-projection of the logic of the mid-century public sphere, and on a particular understanding of the function of the theatre in that public sphere as critical, polemical in nature. Without wanting to deny the obviously edgy topicality of the play in its moment of original reception, it is important to note that a historical narrative's topical, polemical applicability does not necessarily qualify it as *une histoire à clef*. The attraction of Tacitean history was the generalizable nature of its observations, and the pointed insight these observations offered into new, emergent political situations: it was this quality that made Tacitus so popular across Europe around the turn of the century. As I will argue in this chapter, *Sejanus* was a deeply conflicted attempt to profit from this popularity.

In his long satirical epigram 'The New Cry', Jonson thought to add the crying of 'ripe statesmen' to the soundscape of London, now that politic busybodies had become as common as cherries and strawberries, apparently growing 'in every street'. Identifying these would-be politicians by what they read—'They carry in their pockets Tacitus, / And the gazetti, or *Gallo-Belgicus*'[5]—Jonson aligns classical historiography with printed news, suggesting not only the wide (and, to him, obviously troubling) popular interest in Tacitus, but also the functional continuity of the two kinds of texts that appear to be so clearly distinguished by genre and cultural aura. Editions of Tacitus were like the corantos in that they could be worn as markers of political competence. Although the matter of classical histories was not, of course, news, Livy, Plutarch, and Tacitus served as models for prudent political analysis, storehouses of political experience. Their antiquity invested them with an authority that was difficult to challenge, and also protected them from being charged with scandalous application or with the kind of irreligiosity of which Machiavelli was often accused. Thus in spite of the growing number of modern vernacular histories, classical historiography played a particularly important role in political education.[6] By the early seventeenth century, Tacitus came to be considered as a quintessential political author, a classic on the *arcana imperii*, and a widely recognized

---

was among the most widely discussed parts of the *Annales*, which makes it unlikely that Jonson left it out to begin with; see Alexandra Gajda, 'Tacitus and Political Thought in Early Modern Europe, *c*.1530–*c*.1640', in A. J. Woodman (ed.), *The Cambridge Companion to Tacitus* (Cambridge: Cambridge University Press, 2009), 253–68 at 258.

As far as the date of Jonson being called before the Council is concerned: Peter Lake has recently shown that the evidence makes 1605 and the Gunpowder Plot a more likely context for it than 1603 and the anticipation of the arrival of the new monarch—and in late 1605, the objections would have been made to the recently published quarto rather than to the performance. See Lake, 'Ben Jonson and the Politics of "Conversion": *Catiline* and the Relocation of Roman (Catholic) Virtue', *Ben Jonson Journal*, 19 (2012), 163–89 at 163–8.

[5] Jonson (2012) 5:158–9, Epigram XCII.

[6] There are countless accounts of Shakespeare's Roman plays; for a broader perspective on the early modern Roman play, see Clifford Ronan, *'Antike Roman': Power Symbology and the Roman Play in Early Modern England, 1585–1635* (Athens and London: University of Georgia Press, 1995).

model for political observation and political commentary. The role of seventeenth-century political drama in the dissemination of Tacitean political analysis would be difficult to overestimate—and political drama would be hard to understand without considering the importance of Tacitus.[7] This is even true of Shakespeare, who turned to Plutarch rather than Tacitus for the subject matter of some his own most politically engaging plays: the Tacitean valences of *Hamlet*, for example, are brought into focus by the fact that the King is called Claudius.[8]

The significance of Jonson's *Sejanus* for early modern political culture has everything to do with its conscious appeal to the authority of Tacitus, and to the commonplacing, fragment-oriented mode of reading associated with it—a mode of reading in the same tradition as Gabriel Harvey's. An octavo notebook now at the Folger Shakespeare Library contains over ten pages of brief extracts taken, as the heading says, 'Ex Sejano. Ben Jonson'.[9] Figure 5.1 is an image of a page of notes paired with the printed passages they record, and may be taken as representative of the dozens of short, pointed observations copied from the play by the notebook's owner, the Buckinghamshire gentleman Sir William Drake (1606–69).

Drake's notebooks are the record of a life spent in political reading and reflection—it is fair to say that he was obsessed with politic literature; his reading was dominated by the works of Machiavelli, Guicciardini, Bodin, Livy, Tacitus, and other politic authors, the major textual sources of political prudence from which one could extract aphoristic points, apt, transhistorically applicable observations about the nature of power.[10] His pragmatic, political focus assimilated even the Bible to such repositories of insight about the uses of dissimulation and the 'force of occasion'.[11] It is not surprising that a reader like Drake would be drawn to a text like *Sejanus*, taking notes from it on at least two different occasions in two different commonplace books. In Jonson's tragedy, characters offer running on-stage commentary on the historical events unfolding in the court of Tiberius, articulating observations on court policy in the aphoristic style of Tacitus, which contemporaries described in terms closely similar to that of Machiavelli. Most of the aphorisms marked by gnomic points in the margins of the 1605 playbook are precisely these observations, and Drake follows the typographical guidance, copying them into his notebook almost without exception.

Some of the play's aphoristic observations can be traced to Jonson's own readings in political literature, allowing us to trace their circuit from commonplace

---

[7] Alan T. Bradford, 'Stuart Absolutism and the "Utility" of Tacitus', *Huntington Library Quarterly*, 46 (1983), 127–55, is an excellent study of the forms in which Taciteanism enjoyed popular circulation in seventeenth-century England.

[8] Fitzmaurice, 'The Corruption of *Hamlet*'.

[9] Folger MS V.a. 263, f. 15r. This notebook was identified as by William Drake, and dated both between and after 1645, in Kevin Sharpe, *Reading Revolutions: The Politics of Reading in Early Modern England* (New Haven: Yale University Press, 2000) 73–4.

[10] On Drake's notebooks see Stuart Clark, 'Wisdom Literature of the Seventeenth Century: A Guide to the Contents of the "Bacon-Tottel" Commonplace Books'. Part I. and II. *Transactions of the Cambridge Bibliographical Society*, 6 (1976), 291–305; 7 (1977), 46–73. For Drake's favourite readings, see Sharpe, *Reading Revolutions* 76–89, 174–80; Sharpe notes that 'extracts from *The Prince*, the *Discourses* and Guicciardini are found in almost every volume', 176n160.

[11] On Drake's reading of the Bible, see Sharpe, *Reading Revolutions* 225–35.

Tacitean Observation and the Margins of Politics in Jonson's Sejanus 209

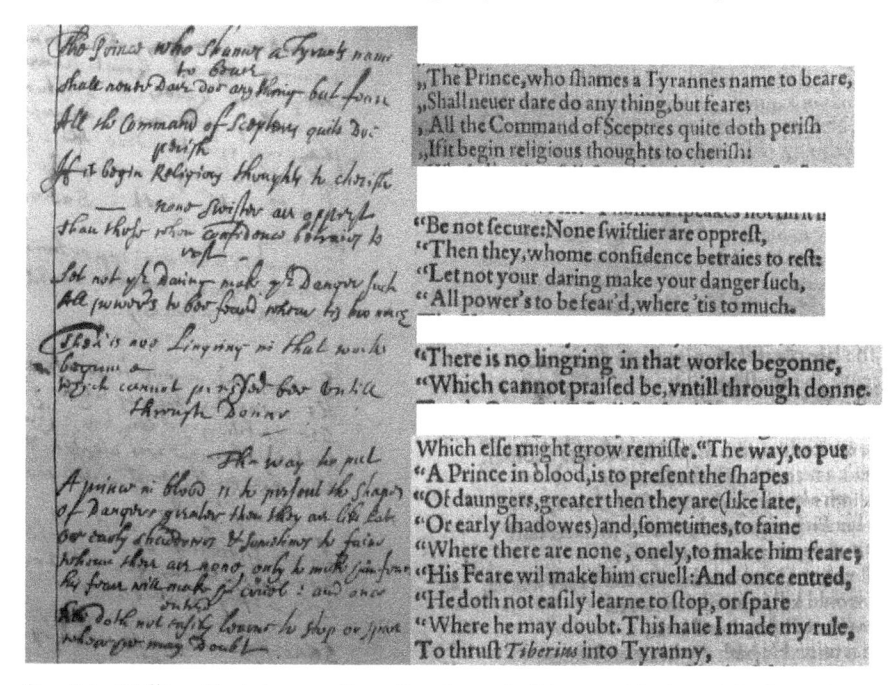

Fig. 5.1. William Drake's notes from Ben Jonson's *Sejanus*, with the original passages as printed in 1605.

William Drake's notebook, Folger Shakespeare Library MS V.a. 263, f. 16v, and *Seianus his fall. VVritten by Ben: Ionson* (London: printed by G. Elld, for Thomas Thorpe, 1605) sigs. D3r, D3v, E1r, E2v.

Photograph by András Kiséry from the collection of the Folger Shakespeare Library, and by Aaron Pratt from the collection of the Beinecke Rare Book and Manuscript Library, Yale University.

book to playtext to commonplace book. Take the first sententious observation that is marked with gnomic pointing, a passage Drake copies into his notebook as

> Tyrants Artes,
> Are to giue flatterers Grace Accusers power
> That those may seeme to kill whom they Deavure (f. 15r)[12]

This rhymed couplet identifying a principle of Tiberius's tyrannical rule is the highly compressed statement of a point that also appears in Jonson's own, carefully organized commonplace book, *Discoveries*, where Jonson also indicates its source:

> A prince should exercise his cruelty not by himself, but by his ministers; so he may save himself and his dignity with his people, by sacrificing those when he list, saith the great doctor of state, Machiavel.

If this more leisurely formulation sounds rather different from the couplet, their shared origin is implied both by their close conceptual similarity and by the fact

[12] Cp. *Sejanus* 1.70–2.

that in *Discoveries*, Jonson's notes from *The Prince* directly follow a discussion of tyranny that cites an incident from the reign of Tiberius.[13] Jonson's approach to forging his 'living line' was to 'strike the second heat / Upon the muses' anvil; turn the same'[14]—as he explained to Drummond, he composed by first writing a draft in prose and then turning that into verse,[15] and the two versions of this maxim might be an example of such paraphrase, a note turned into the couplet of *Sejanus*, and then also copied into the long-term project of *Discoveries* that was published posthumously in 1641. And while in writing *Sejanus* Jonson drew on both the *Discorsi* and *The Prince*, versifying passages from both,[16] for the idea he distils into this particular maxim he did not even need to refer to a Latin or Italian edition of the Florentine secretary's work, since he would also have found it in the English translation *Anti-Machiavel* (hot off the press when he was writing the play), in the list of maxims to which Innocent Gentillet reduced Machiavelli's work, and which served many English readers as a compendium of Machiavellian maxims.[17]

Of all printed English commercial plays, the 1605 quarto of Jonson's *Sejanus* is most heavily and consistently marked by gnomic pointing: this is a text that was designed to be taken up into the cycle of political reading, note-taking, and writing. *Sejanus* is also the only play William Drake ever seems to have excerpted in his dozens of political notebooks, which reminds us how unique Jonson's Roman tragedy is among early modern plays in the sheer intensity of its engagement with politics in the aphoristic mode—or rather, how unique it is among early modern Tacitean or 'politic' histories in being a play written for the public stage.[18] The play's distinctive involvement in the early modern culture of political reading, in the dissemination of political knowledge, and in the circulation of political maxims in particular, is a function of Jonson's efforts to align *Sejanus* with the trend of politic historiography—efforts that result in a work which is uniquely revealing about the logic and the stakes of political reading and of the uses of politic historiography around the turn of the century.

The play performs the functions of politic historiography through the manipulation of some of the genre-specific features of plays written for the public stage around 1600. It combines tragedy's commitment to historical truth with the

---

[13] The quoted passage is *Discoveries* ll. 829–31, Jonson (2012) 7:539; the reference to Tiberius is at ll. 802ff, Jonson (2012) 7:538. On Jonson and Machiavelli, Daniel C. Boughner, *The Devil's Disciple: Ben Jonson's Debt to Machiavelli* (New York: Philosophical Library, 1968); Richard Dutton, 'The Sources, Text, and Readers of *Sejanus*: Jonson's "Integrity in the Story"', *Studies in Philology*, 75 (1978), 181–98.
[14] 'To the Memory of My Belovèd...' ll. 59–61, Jonson (2012) 5:641.
[15] Jonson (2012) 5:378.   [16] Boughner, *The Devil's Disciple* 89–112.
[17] Gentillet 2H1 r–v, based on Chapters 7 and 19 of the *Prince*, where Machiavelli suggests that 'Princes ought to cause others to take upon them the matters of blame and imputation; and upon themselves to take only those of grace and favour.' *Nicholas Machiavel's Prince* (1640) sig. H4v. On Gentillet, see also Chapter 1 of this volume.
[18] Other than the selections from *Sejanus*, he copied a single passage from Suckling's *Aglaura*, directly following the Sejanus material in University College London MS Ogden 7/29, on f. 143. Although headed 'Sir John Suckling', whether it is in fact copied directly from the play or through some form of mediation, is unclear. The passage, the only one marked with gnomic pointing in the first edition of Suckling's play, is a reflection on the nature of political ambition.

deployment of the device of a cast of on-stage political observers, whose chorus-like commentary contrasts them to the self-reflective intriguer Sejanus. The translation of the features of narrative historiography into dramatic form not only produces the plethora of extractable maxims, it also gives rise to the period's most sustained fictionalized analysis of the nature and uses of political observation in the Tacitean mode, and of the implications and effects of political observation becoming available to private persons outside the realm of politics *sensu strico*. In fact, Jonson's investment in writing his own play's reception and use is itself a symptom of how in *Sejanus*, the public medium of commercial drama intersects with the readerly, use-oriented genre of political historiography. This intersection between drama and historiography results in a new understanding of the utility of political knowledge, no longer restricted to those in the position to actually act upon their understanding of the operations of power. Here, Jonson's awareness of drama not only as a classical form but as a public medium marks a new departure, setting *Sejanus* and its readers apart from the world of ambitious learning inhabited by Gabriel Harvey. For Jonson, the lay uses of political knowledge were calling for the controlling and classifying operations of judgement and decorum—but his insistence on the necessity of such operations, his dread of public dissemination spinning out of control, are signs of the political potential of such knowledge.

POLITIC NOTES, POLITIC READERS

Politics was of course always an integral concern of humanist reading, and remained part of the humanist project in its vernacularized literary versions as well. The printed commonplace books produced by the Bodenham circle in London around the turn of the seventeenth century are capacious collections that incorporate materials from classical and vernacular texts on a wide range of subjects of common concern, from the amorous to the political. They are vernacular versions of a humanist construct and, as Heather James has shown, they project a deliberating civic public through their political concerns and through their very capaciousness—a public of readers who resemble the citizens 'concealed within subjects' that according to Patrick Collinson's influential suggestion were produced by the late sixteenth-century scenarios of political emergency, or less dramatically but perhaps in a more habitus-forming way, the deliberating members of the communities of urban and trade corporations and other self-governing entities.[19]

But political note-taking did not remain concealed within a broadly civic enterprise. The proliferation of specialized political notebooks or notebook-sections, analogous to the legal, medical, or theological commonplace books that were

---

[19] Heather James, 'The First English Printed Commonplace Books and the Rise of the Common Reader', in Allison K. Deutermann and András Kiséry (eds.), *Formal Matters: Reading the Materials of English Renaissance Literature* (Manchester: Manchester University Press, 2013), 15–33; Collinson, *De Republica Anglorum or, History with the Politics Put Back* 24; Phil Whitington, *The Politics of Commonwealth: Citizens and Freemen in Early Modern England* (Cambridge: Cambridge University Press, 2005).

important tools of these professions, implies the extent to which politics was—as we saw in the first half of this book—emerging as a separate focus and field of expertise.[20] Such specialized notebooks recorded the fruits of a specialized reading programme to which the study of history was central. Bacon articulated an assumption shared across Europe when he suggested that 'Histories...will best instructe you in matters morrall, politike, and military, by which and in which you must ripen and settle your iudgment.'[21] Over the course of the sixteenth century, history had come to be considered as a form of surrogate experience that informed political counsel. Politic histories, like the works of Machiavelli, Francesco Guicciardini's history of Italy, and Philippe de Commynes' history of France under Louis XI were particularly valuable as *magistra vitae politicae* for their focus on the causes of political events in the motives and considerations of their agents, and on the reasons why specific actions failed or succeeded.[22] Instructing his brother Robert on his studies, Philip Sidney warned him to pay attention to the historian as '*Discourser* which name I giue to who soeuer speaks *non simpliciter de facto, sed de qualitatibus et circumstantijs facti*; and that is it which makes me and many others rather note much with owr penn then with our Minde.'[23] Politic historians were such 'discoursers', sprinkling their narrative with instructive observations on the unfolding events—observations that could easily be lifted again from their context as generalized or generalizable insights about how power operates.

The late sixteenth century discovered Tacitus as the greatest of 'discoursers'. The Earl of Essex praised the special utility of Tacitus among all historians deploying the exact terms in which—as we saw in Chapter 1—he advised the Earl of Rutland on his political education. In the epistle 'To the Reader' that prefaces Savile's great translation, he suggested that Tacitus 'hath written the most matter with best conceyt in fewest wordes of any Historiographer ancient and moderne'[24]—making the Queen's desperate 'more matter with less art' identifiable as a call for the properly politic approach expected of Polonius. In the dedication of his seminal edition of the first-century historian, Justus Lipsius explained that unlike Livy, 'this writer

---

[20] On specialized notebooks, Ian Maclean, *Interpretation and Meaning in the Renaissance: The Case of Law* (Cambridge: Cambridge University Press, 1992); Ann Blair, *The Theater of Nature: Jean Bodin and Renaissance Science* (Princeton: Princeton University Press, 1997); Thomas Fulton, *Historical Milton: Manuscript, Print, and Political Culture in Revolutionary England* (Amherst: University of Massachusetts Press, 2010) 38–81.

[21] Advice to Rutland, Letter 1: Stewart (ed.), *The Oxford Francis Bacon I: Early Writings, 1584–1596* 645–6.

[22] On the political uses of history, see Levy, 'Hayward, Daniel, and the Beginnings of Politic History in England'; Grafton, *What Was History?* 189–254; Popper, *Walter Ralegh's History of the World* 36–76, 239–52.

[23] 18 October 1580, in Kuin (ed.), *The Correspondence of Sir Philip Sidney* 1007.

[24] *The Ende of Nero and Beginning of Galba. Fower bookes of the histories Of Cornelivs Tacitvs. The life of Agricola*, translated by Henry Savile (Oxford: Ioseph Barnes [and R. Robinson, London] for Richard Wright, 1591) sig. ¶3r. The author of the epistle, 'A. B.', has traditionally been identified as Essex, based on Jonson's remarks to William Drummond, 'Informations', Jonson (2012) 5:376. This preface was not Essex's only Tacitean work: around 1603, a set of notes taken from the historian's text was circulating as his. On 12 January 1603, Henry Brooke, Baron Cobham, was writing to someone asking for 'a paper boke of my lo of Essex notations of Cornelius Tacitus' (BL MS Cotton Vespasian F XIII, f. 290r), quoted by Paulina Kewes, 'Henry Savile's Tacitus and the Politics of Roman History in Late Elizabethan England', *Huntington Library Quarterly*, 74 (2011), 515–51 at 526n539.

considers princely courts, the princes' inner life, plans, commands and deeds' and emphasized the utility of the historian by arguing that 'the similarity with our own time being in many respects evident to the reader, he is instructed that the same outcomes result from the same causes.'[25] Robert Johnson, in his 1601 essay 'Of Hystories' similarly admires Tacitus for 'explanation in discouering not only the sequels of things but also the causes & reasons' and for 'enterlacing the *serios* of the tale, with some iudiciall, but strangelie briefe sentences'.[26] Tacitus thus became a central text of the politically oriented version of the humanist commonplace tradition, and it seems primarily for formal, rather than ideological reasons: his aphoristic commentary made him a prime source for the collecting and circulation of political aphorisms, his terse comments on historical events filling the pages of the commonplace books politicians were advised to keep.[27]

Vernacular historians were subject to the same treatment, and while these have received less critical attention, they were just as influential in the period as the classics, and part of the same discursive continuum. A French edition of Guicciardini, for example, came equipped with marginal observations on political and military matters by François de La Noue, and three separate indices, including two *gnomologie*s, i.e. alphabetical lists of all the aphorisms in Guicciardini's text as well as in La Noue's commentary.[28] Although much less known today than Guicciardini or Machiavelli, in the late sixteenth and early seventeenth centuries the *Memoires* of the reign of Louis XI by Philippe de Commynes was at least as important a source of politic maxims as the two Italian authors. His comments on the conduct of politics were so cherished that Pierre Mathieu's history of the reign of the same king, published in 1610, concluded with a generous selection of maxims taken from Commynes's history, presented as commentary on the narrative. The English translation, published in 1614, also includes these 'maximes, ivdgements, and politike observations of Philip de Commines', as well as a reduced version of the rich analytical index of the French original, designed to help the reader to pick out aphoristic observations from the history itself.[29]

---

[25] *C. Cornelii Taciti Opera qvae Exstant: I. Lipsivs Quartum Recensuit* (Antwerp: Plantin, 1588, 1st: 1574), sig. *4r.
[26] *Essaies, or Rather Imperfect Offers, by Rob. Iohnson Gent.* (London: Iohn Windet, for Iohn Barnes, 1601) sig. D4v.
[27] About the uses of Tacitus, see Arnaldo Momigliano, 'The First Political Commentary on Tacitus', *The Journal of Roman Studies*, 37 (1947), 91–101; Peter Burke, 'Tacitism', in T. A. Dorey (ed.), *Tacitus* (London: Routledge and Kegan Paul, 1969), 149–71; Ungerer, *A Spaniard in Elizabethan England* 2:371–7; Kenneth C. Schellhase, *Tacitus in Renaissance Political Thought* (Chicago: University of Chicago Press, 1976); Tuck, *Philosophy and Government, 1572–1651* 65–119; Soll, *Publishing the Prince* 22–40; Gajda, 'Tacitus and Political Thought'.
[28] *Histoire des Gverres d'Italie, Composée par M. François Gvuichardin...Novvelle Edition...à laquelle Ont Esté Adioustees Les Observations Politiques, Militaires & Morales du Sievr de La Nove.... Deux Amples Indices, Contenans par Ordre Alphabetique les Maximes de Guichardin, & Celles du Sieur de La Noue* ([Genève]: Heritiers d'Eustache Vignon, 1593).
[29] *Histoire de Lovys XI... et des Choses Mémorables Advenües en l'Europe durant Vingt & Deux Années de Son Regne. Enrichie de Plusieurs Observations qui Tiennent Lieu de Commentaires* (Paris: P. Mettayer, 1610); the *Maximes, Ivgemens et Observations Politiques de Philippes de Commines* on 573ff. *The History of Levvis the Eleuenth VVith the Most Memorable Accidents which Happened in Europe during the Two and Twenty Yeares of his Raigne. Enricht with Many Obseruations which Serue as Commentaries.... Written in

With the printed circulation of editions, vernacular translations, indices, and aphoristic commentaries, the discourse of political prudence was becoming rapidly popularized, creating a considerable conceptual difficulty for those thinking about the uses of history and of political knowledge. As Montaigne suggested, the works of Tacitus, which contained 'more precepts, then narrations', was 'a seminary of morall, and a magazine of pollitique discourses, for the provision and ornament of those, that possesse some place in the managing of the world'.[30] Lipsius similarly insisted that the Roman historian belonged 'in the hands of those who are holding the rudder and helm of the state'.[31] Written by people with first-hand experience of political events, politic histories were pitched as instruction in affairs of state, understood as the instruction of those entering such careers.

Such an understanding of their function and importance, however, came under serious pressure from the very act of their publication. Thomas Danett, the English translator of the *Memoires* of Commynes 'alleadged many reasons why...bookes of this nature, treating of Princes secrets were vnfit to be published to the vulgare sort'—as he apologetically explained in the preface printed in the first edition of 1596.[32] Danett's remark points to the unintended implications of the publication of political reading material as well as of the dissemination of suggestions about how to process it and about the aims of such processing.[33] When in his 1607 *Hero-Paideia*, a book elaborating the kind of advice offered by Sidney to his younger brother and extending it to a print audience, James Cleland advises young gentlemen to mark up their books by making 'some short annotation vpon the margent', and then to 'write the words of your author into a BOOKE OF COMMONPLACES', he also explains the usefulness of keeping such an organized collection of notes in terms of the action the reader might hope to take: 'herafter when yee shal haue vse of these Maximes, ether in state matters, Policie, or in anie particular affaire, they are in readines.'[34] Absent any notion of a legitimate alternative to the use of political knowledge in political action or in the advising of political agents, the dissemination of the texts and technologies of politic reading appeared to be opening up the opportunity for engaging in political counsel, and perhaps even the prospect of a life in politics, to anyone interested.

Late sixteenth-century political authors articulated their theorizations of the reason of state as a response to an excited conversation about the arts of power. Botero, for example, presents his *Della Ragion di Stato* as a corrective to a flourishing public

French by P. Mathieu...And Translated into English by Edvv: Grimeston... (London: George Eld, 1614), the maxims at sigs. 4C3r–4E6v.

[30] 'Of conferring': Michel Eyquem de Montaigne, *The Essays of Montaigne Done into English by John Florio, 1603*, 3 vols. (London: David Nutt, 1892–3) 3:181–2. On the vexed issue of who Tacitus might be for, see Bradford, 'Stuart Absolutism and the "Utility" of Tacitus'.

[31] *Iusti Lipsi Ad Annales Corn. Taciti Liber Commentarius, Sive Notae* (Antwerp: Plantin, 1581) sig. *3v.

[32] *The Historie of Philip de Commines Knight, Lord of Argenton* (London: Ar. Hatfield, for I. Norton, 1596), sig. A2r. Thomas Danett dedicated a manuscript translation to Leicester and Cecil in 1565. The copy presented to Leicester is now BL MS Add 21579; see Millstone, 'Seeing Like a Statesman in Early Stuart England', n105.

[33] Grafton, *What Was History?* 218–24.   [34] *Hero-paideia* sig. V4v.

Tacitean Observation and the Margins of Politics in Jonson's Sejanus 215

discourse about statecraft formulated and circulated in the form of cynical maxims. As he explains in the preface, during his visits to the various courts of Europe he was

> greatly astonished to find Reason of State a constant subject of discussion and to hear the opinions of Niccolò Machiavelli and Cornelius Tacitus frequently quoted: the former for his precepts relating to the rule and government of peoples, the latter for his lively description of the arts employed by the Emperor Tiberius in acquiring and retaining the imperial title in Rome.[35]

By the turn of the century, such discussion of the precepts of rule and of the arts employed in acquiring and retaining power has spread far beyond court circles, giving rise to complaints that reason of state is now 'on every mouth', that 'not only court advisors and doctors of the schools, but even barbers and the humblest artisans' are avidly discussing 'what was done by reason of state and what was not'.[36] As a Tacitean history, his *Sejanus* is an agent of this dissemination and popularization of political knowledge—but in writing it, Jonson develops a more complex, and more genuinely troubling view of this dissemination than admitted by the 'The New Cry'.

THE POLITIC TRAGEDY OF *SEIANVS HIS FALL*

The 1605 *Sejanus* is a striking object, unparalleled among turn of the century playbooks. It is a learned text with extensive marginal notes, one that occasionally even attempts a verisimilar evocation of Roman inscriptions.[37] This conspicuous re-mediation of the play, its transformation from playscript into a very bookish printed book, has given rise to multiple scholarly narratives. The citations are both an ostentatious indication of Jonson's learning and a defence against censorship, evidence that similarities with any current event or living person are the result of historical coincidence.[38] The presentation is part of Jonson's effort to

---

[35] Botero, *The Reason of State* xiii–xiv.

[36] The quotations are from Antoine de Laval, 1612, and Lodovico Zuccolo, 1621, as quoted by Marcel Gauchet, 'L'État au Miroir de la Raison d'État: la France et la Chrétienté', in Yves Charles Zarka (ed.), *Raison et Déraison d'État: Théoriciens et Théories de la Raison d'État aux XVIe et XVIIe Siècles* (Paris: Presses Universitaires de France, 1994), 193–244 at 195.

[37] As the textual essay of the Cambridge edition, which consolidates research on the production of the 1605 book, points out, 'The history of the early printing of *Sejanus* cannot be divorced from its interpretation'; Tom Cain, '*Sejanus*: Textual Essay', *The Cambridge Edition of the Works of Ben Jonson Online* (2012). Cp. also John Jowett, ' "Fall before This Booke": The 1605 Quarto of Sejanus', *TEXT*, 4 (1988), 279–95; Ben Jonson, *Sejanus: His Fall*, ed. Philip K. Ayres (Manchester: Manchester University Press, 1990) 1–9; John Jowett, 'Jonson's Authorization of Type in *Sejanus* and Other Early Quartos', *Studies in Bibliography*, 44 (1991), 254–65; Stephen Orgel, 'What Is a Text?', in David Scott Kastan and Peter Stallybrass (eds.), *Staging the Renaissance* (New York: Routledge, 1991), 83–7; Thomas O. Calhoun and Thomas L. Gravell, 'Paper and Printing in Ben Jonson's "Sejanus" (1605)', *The Papers of the Bibliographical Society of America*, 87 (1993), 13–64.

[38] See e.g. Annabel Patterson, *Censorship and Interpretation: The Conditions of Writing and Reading in Early Modern England* (Madison: University of Wisconsin Press, 1984) 57–66; Blair Worden, 'Ben Jonson among the Historians', in Kevin Sharpe and Peter Lake (eds.), *Culture and Politics in Early Stuart England* (Stanford: Stanford University Press, 1993), 67–89 at 78–80.

distance his plays from the stage, an attempt at 'validating them as literature, as dramatic poems',[39] and an assertion of Jonson's possessive authorship.[40] As Joseph Loewenstein has suggested, the 1605 *Sejanus* provides a particularly powerful illustration of the Foucauldian argument about censorship bringing about authorship.[41] This particular connection between the politics and the material form of *Sejanus* has become so prevalent that it pre-empts attempts to consider other links between these two most-discussed aspects of the play, links that are not predicated upon an agonistic relationship between the author and the state, or upon a somewhat proleptic understanding of the 'literary'.

The playbook is fronted by a strikingly sparse title page. The information conveyed here is kept to a minimum—we see none of the usual playbook title-page references to other characters or plot lines, no mention of playing company or venue, not even an indication of genre. Indeed, there is nothing here that would even hint at the possibility that *Seianus His Fall* might be a dramatic text.[42] The typography of the play is now habitually read as a manifestation of Jonson's literary ambition. The Cambridge editor summarizes a long-standing consensus when he states that 'in giving copious marginalia to *Sejanus*, Jonson was claiming the status of classical Latin drama for his vernacular play'.[43] But the nature of the marginal notes suggests otherwise. In editions of classical texts, in Thomas Watson's *Antigone* and in Richard Bernard's bilingual Terence—or indeed in E.K.'s commentaries to Spenser's *The Shepheardes Calender* that are modelled on editions of classics—the notes are glosses, discursive explications of linguistic, cultural, historical issues, interpretive supplements to texts whose classical status both authorizes and demands such care and attention. In contrast, Jonson's marginal notes to *Sejanus* are citations intended to authorize the text itself. They point to the sources of the information he dramatizes, authenticating his account of the events. The notes to *Sejanus* (and also to his entertainments published in 1604) are not literary commentary, not even textual apparatus, but supporting reference matter. Rather than the (deserving) object of scholarly elucidation and editorial care, then, the text of Jonson's 1605 *Sejanus* is itself revealed as the product of scholarly labour—a historical work.

Attention to the notes as the register of Jonson's researches can help clarify the specific nature of Jonson's antiquarian achievement. Although the most important source of *Seianus His Fall* is Tacitus, and although in conversation with Drummond

---

[39] Jonas A. Barish, *The Antitheatrical Prejudice* (Berkeley: University of California Press, 1981) 139. Cain concludes his discussion of Q: 'Both the notes and the typography of such passages as 5.514–31 give Q an unmistakable *mos antiqui*, and with it Jonson claims a place for *Sejanus* not in the new and transient tradition of English theatre, on which indeed this text firmly turns its back, but in the pantheon of classical, literary drama.' Cain, '*Sejanus*: Textual Essay', 7.

[40] Loewenstein, *Ben Jonson and Possessive Authorship* 146–60.

[41] Loewenstein, *Ben Jonson and Possessive Authorship* 151. Swinburne understood literariness in another sense when he thought the tragedy should have had in it 'some heat of more than merely literary life'. Algernon Charles Swinburne, *A Study of Ben Jonson* (London: Chatto & Windus, 1889) 31.

[42] The 1607 *Volpone*, the 1611 *Catiline*, and the 1612 *Alchemist* will have similarly textualized, bookish title pages without reference to performance, playing company or dramatic genre. They turn the gesture into a Jonsonian trademark. When it was first made in 1605, the gesture was not yet an authorial signature, but more an announcement of Jonson's filiations with other genres and works.

[43] Cain, '*Sejanus*: Textual Essay'.

he was juxtaposing his play with Grenewey's translation, Jonson's play is not a dramatization of the Roman historian—it cannot be, because the quintessential Tacitean story of the rise and fall of Tiberius's overreaching favourite lacks its more important half, the downfall, that was the subject of the lost fifth book of the *Annales*. As the 1598 English translation of the *Annales* by Richard Grenewey notes: 'There wanteth very much of the story in this place, which hath perished through time.' In the words of the classic twentieth-century monograph on Tacitus, this 'gap robs posterity of a drama unsurpassed in plot and catastrophe'.[44] Jonson's *Sejanus* is a work of restoration, a demonstration of his mastery of the art of historiography through the restoration of a major turning point in the Tacitean narrative, the downfall of a major political figure and his regime.[45]

Among other sources—Dio Cassius, Suetonius, Lipsius's edition of Tacitus (and silently also Grenewey's translation)—Jonson also consulted the seminal text of English Tacitism, Henry Savile's 1591 *The Ende of Nero and Beginning of Galba. Fower Bookes of the Histories Of Cornelivs Tacitvs. The Life of Agricola*, which was included in every edition of Grenewey's translation of the *Annales* to form a complete English Tacitus. Savile's translation is as careful and learned as it is lucid, and is equipped with a historical commentary which Jonson evidently relied on. For example, when Silius describes the experience of being under the constant surveillance of Tiberius's regime saying 'We shall not shortly dare to tell our dreams, / Or think, but 'twill be treason' (1.69–70), he echoes a treason case listed in Savile's commentary on the notion of 'Crime of Maiesty and treason' (a list which also includes a reference to Silius's own downfall), a case in which 'one was arraigned, and condemned of maiesty for dreaming a dreame, another for being dreamed of'.[46]

Jonson was a friend and admirer of Savile. In his epigram to the Oxford scholar, who was tutor to Robert Sidney in the 1580s, and after the fall of Essex, also to Essex's son, Jonson singled out for special praise not his translation and presentation of the Tacitean text itself, but the shorter original work that prefaced it: *The Ende of Nero and Beginning of Galba*, a historical narrative written by Savile to bridge the chronological gap between the two Tacitean works, the *Annales* and the *Histories*, by providing the story of the downfall of Nero. The translation itself would be enough to make Jonson imagine that 'the soul of Tacitus / In thee, most weighty Savile, lived unto us', but it is this work that really thrills him:

> ...when I read that special piece, restored,
> Where Nero falls and Galba is adored,
> To thine own proper I ascribe them more,
> And gratulate the breach I grieved before.[47]

---

[44] *The Annales of Cornelivs Tacitvs. The Description of Germanie* (M.XCVIII), p. 118. Ronald Syme, *Tacitus*, 2 vols. (Oxford: Clarendon Press, 1958) 255.
[45] On Jonson's interests in historiography and on his connections to Camden, Selden, and others, see Worden, 'Ben Jonson among the Historians'.
[46] *The Ende of Nero*, sig. 2B6v.
[47] Jonson (2012) 5:161–3, *Epigrams* XCV: 'To Savile', ll. 3–4, 7–10. For a reading of Savile's work of restoration, see David Womersley, 'Sir Henry Savile's Translation of Tacitus and the Political Interpretation of Elizabethan Texts', *Review of English Studies*, 42 (1991), 313–42.

The gap was so successfully bridged that by the late seventeenth century, Savile's narrative was translated into Latin and included in Latin editions of Tacitus.[48] This canonization by incorporation in the Tacitean corpus recognized Savile's ingenuity in weaving together information gleaned from a plurality of narrative sources reflecting a plurality of stories, and producing a causally structured narrative with a beginning, middle, and end, rather than an annalistic, episodic presentation of domestic and foreign affairs. In a considerable narrative feat, he shaped spatially and temporally expansive events into a tightly plotted account of the overthrow of Nero by Galba. Thus, *The End of Nero* answers not only Savile's own Tacitean reminder that the task of history consists 'not in reporting bare euents, but in discouering the causes of those euents, without which the reader can pick but small profit',[49] but also Jonson's Aristotelian requirement that tragedy should be 'the imitation of one entire and perfect action'.[50] And 'that special piece, restored, / Where Nero falls' provides Jonson with a model for his own enterprise of historiographical restoration, *Sejanus: His Fall*.

To claim that for Jonson tragic drama is a form of historiography is not to deny that it is also a kind of poetry. In fact, it is the controversial neoclassical notion that tragedy ought to represent historical events that here allows Jonson to assume an office to which he is otherwise not entitled. For politic history to serve as an authoritative account of past events, and therefore also be a useful guide to the present, it had to be written by men of experience, either of the events they handled, or at least of the kind of world they were describing. This assumption, first articulated by Polybius, was echoed by such writers as Bacon, the author of a politic history of Henry VII, when he argued that the true understanding and judgement of the reign of a prince is the terrain of 'great officers...and those who have handled the helm of government, and been acquainted with the difficulties and mysteries of state business'.[51] Unlike Tacitus, Commynes, Guicciardini, Machiavelli, or Bacon himself, Jonson was no statesman who could rely on an experience-based insight into the causes of actions and the motives of political agents (even when writing about periods and situations he did not experience at first hand). Jonson's politic history of Sejanus draws its authority from a different source: not from its author's political expertise, but from his identity as a tragedian. As the art of the representation of human action, of all sixteenth- and seventeenth-century genres, tragedy most directly explored the intricate causes of momentous

---

[48] Savile's *Ende of Nero and Beginning of Galba* and his commentaries on the *Histories* (also part of the 1591 edition, these latter were then mostly dropped from later reprints), were published in Latin as *H. Savilivs in Taciti Histor. Agricolae Vitam et Commentarius de Militia Romana* (Amsterdam: Elzevir, 1649); the book starts with 'Mors Neronis, & Initium Principatus Galbae' at pp. 1–50, sigs. A1r–C1v. By 1672, this was incorporated in the Elzevir *Tacitus*; see Burke, 'Tacitism', 153–4.

[49] Annotation 18 to Book 1 in Savile, *Ende of Nero*, sig. 2A3r.

[50] *Discoveries* l. 1903, Jonson (2012) 7:591, a direct borrowing from Heinsius.

[51] 'In felicem memoriam Elizabethae Angliae reginae', James Spedding, Douglas Denon Heath, and Robert Leslie Ellis (eds.), *The Works of Francis Bacon*, 14 vols. (London: Longman and Co., 1857–74) 6:291. 'Ad principes viros pertinet haec cognitio, atque ad eos qui imperiorum gubernacula tractarunt, et rerum civilium ardua et arcana norunt.' I am quoting Spedding's English translation, 'On the fortunate memory of Elizabeth queen of England', 6:305. The *locus classicus* is Polybius 12.25.

events, the motives behind the actions—the chief concerns of politic historiography. Early modern English tragedy was particularly fascinated by the dramatic potential of complex personae with ostensive intentions hiding their true, hidden designs. In creating the figure of Sejanus, Jonson relied on the device of the monologizing, duplicitous character most memorably epitomized by Richard III, Barabbas, or Hamlet,[52] characters who function as the 'discoursers' of historiography, commenting on the motives of others and revealing their own.

While the evolving conventions of (especially tragic) theatre were well suited for the reconstruction of historical characters as multilayered, theatrical beings, Jonson also had at his disposal a critical tradition that closely aligned the aims of tragedy and history. Beyond the numerous rhetorical treatises that viewed poetry in general as a form of historiography or vice versa,[53] a significant strand of Renaissance thought, articulated in discussions of Aristotle, was concerned specifically with the relationship between history and tragedy. For Aristotle, history was merely a relation of a contingent sequence of facts, whereas the tragic plot was characterized by the unity of events couched in probability and necessity, making tragic poetry more philosophical than history. Although a similar valorization of poetry (based on a different argument) is familiar from Philip Sidney's treatise, several Renaissance commentaries challenge the distinction between tragic representation and historical writing. Robortello claims that at their best, both tragedy and history are characterized by the unity of action, and points to Sallust's monograph of Catiline's conspiracy as an example of historical writing attaining to tragic coherence.[54] It is more than simple coincidence that Jonson chose precisely this work for dramatic treatment in the only other tragedy he published, but his choice of the rise and fall of Sejanus for his first surviving tragedy was also prescribed, as it were, by this argument. Tacitus begins Book 4 of the *Annales* with an account of Sejanus's background and character, consciously and clearly alluding to Sallust's treatment of Catiline, and thus promising a study of Sejanus's personal dominance in the form of a well-defined, self-contained monographic treatment, separable from the annalistic texture of the rest of the work.[55] Jonson takes the

---

[52] For the rise of the convention of a hidden interiority as the site of the true motives of action, see Maus, *Inwardness and Theater*.

[53] Cp. Quintilian 10.1.31: 'history has a certain affinity to poetry and may be regarded as a kind of prose poem'; for the assimilation of poetry to history, see Bernard Weinberg, *A History of Literary Criticism in the Italian Renaissance*, 2 vols. (Chicago: University of Chicago Press, 1961) 1:13–16, 87–8, 147–8, 193–4, 196.

[54] Eric MacPhail, 'The Plot of History from Antiquity to the Renaissance', *Journal of the History of Ideas*, 62 (2001), 1–16 at 13.

[55] *Annales* 4.1–2; see the notes on the passage in Cornelius Tacitus, *Annals. Book IV*, eds. Ronald H. Martin and A. J. Woodman (Cambridge Greek and Latin Classics; Cambridge: Cambridge University Press, 1989). Imperial biography structures the *Annales*, a history that begins with the death of Augustus. The death of Germanicus marks the division between Books 2 and 3, the death of Julia Augusta at the beginning of Book 5 signals the onset of the real horrors of Sejanus's rule. Book 6 picks up the narrative with the aftermath of the death of Sejanus. Books 7–10 are lost. Book 11 concludes with the death of Messalina, Book 12 with the death of Claudius, Book 14 with the murder of Agrippina. The need to relate the origins of Sejanus so prominently reflects not only on his importance, but also on the obscurity of those origins, marking him as a true favourite, a low-born climber: members of the imperial family obviously required no introduction.

hint for his play from this narrative signposting. He tracks the interconnected fates of Sejanus and the supporting cast, further selecting and organizing the Tacitean material, and for the last third of the play, piecing together information found in Cassius Dio, Juvenal, and Suetonius, 'restoring' the 'breach' in the *Annales*, and completing it in the form of the self-enclosed and coherent plot of a tragedy of court intrigue.

Discussions about the analogies between historiography and tragedy not only directed Jonson's choice of subject matter, they also provided the rationale for choosing tragedy as the form for the enterprise of historical restoration based on fragmentary evidence. In 'To the readers', by invoking the notion of the 'truth of argument' among the 'offices of the tragic writer' that he discharged in writing *Sejanus*, Jonson aligns himself with Castelvetro's (as well as Scaliger's and others') suggestion that tragic decorum could not be achieved by probable, verisimilar plots, only by plots actually taken from history.[56] Importantly, however, for Castelvetro, verisimilitude and truth become inseparable and interdependent in tragedies based on historical plots, because the representation of historical truth always requires the labours of verisimilar construction and reconstruction. The superiority of historical plots consists precisely in the challenge posed by truthfulness to the writer's artistry and creative skills. Castelvetro illustrates his point through the anecdote of Michelangelo looking at a marble statue of a river god whose beard was broken off. The traces of the beard on the torso were puzzling: 'judged by the part that still remained on the chin, the beard if entire would, if properly proportioned, reach to the navel, though the point of the beard still remained high up on the breast without reaching any further.' Michelangelo solved the problem by using clay to form a properly proportioned beard, reaching to the navel—and then knotting it 'so that the point of the beard formed by him touched high up on the breast in the very same place as the point of the broken beard'.[57] If poetic genius is attested by problem-solving, the genius of the tragic poet becomes the genius of the artist as restorer–conservator–forger epitomized by Michelangelo. It is a mixture of invention and mimicry that fills the gaps, comes up with the words, attitudes, and forms of action to fit the bare (and often broken) bones provided in the historical record, and thus to turn the fragment into a well-shaped, coherent whole that emulates what has been lost—and potentially competes with it, should it be found. This is the work Jonson undertook in *Sejanus*, although one might argue that supplying the fall of Sejanus missing from the Tacitean record was a more substantial and consequential act of restoration than the recreation of a beard, however impressively knotted the facial hair of Michelangelo's ancient river god may have been.

---

[56] On the close parallels between this aspect of Jonson's preface to *Sejanus* and Castelvetro's, see David Farley-Hills, 'Jonson and the Neo-Classical Rules in *Sejanus* and *Volpone*', *Review of English Studies*, 46/182 (1995), 153–73 at 153–7.

[57] Allan H. Gilbert, *Literary Criticism, Plato to Dryden* (New York, Cincinnati etc.: American Book Company, 1940) 321–2, translating pp. 213–14 of the 1576 edition, the commentary on Chapter XI of the *Poetics*.

By choosing to write the tragedy of Sejanus as a restoration of a breach in the *Annals*, Jonson also committed himself to writing a text recognizably Tacitean, characterized by a running aphoristic commentary on the labyrinthine world of court politics—offered by the play's characters. In spite of using different sources, Jonson's treatment follows his model throughout, using the maxims of his chorus of commentators to demonstrate that 'the soul of Tacitus' lived not only in Savile but in him as well.[58] Savile's work may even have influenced the typography of *Sejanus* (see Figures 5.2 and 5.3). Experimenting with a new style to replace the mould established for printed drama, Jonson's title page recalls the ground-breaking, starkly epigraphic style of *The fall of Nero*, imitated by Richard Grenewey's 1598 translation of the *Annales* and the *Germania*, with which it continued to be re-published throughout the seventeenth century, as a feature that distinguished Tacitean publications from other classical or modern histories.[59]

What evidence we have about the early readership of the play suggests that Jonson's efforts paid off, although perhaps not immediately. Reading *Sejanus* in the 1630s and 1640s, William Drake evidently treated it as a work of politic history. Francis Osborn, whose memoirs of the reigns of Elizabeth and James defined the view of the English court for centuries, first 'hissed Sejanus off the stage', but 'after sat it out, not only patiently but with content and admiration'. Osborn mentions his change of mind about *Sejanus* in the preface to his 'secret history' of the scandals around the divorce of Frances Howard, a piece of political pornography in dramatic form that clearly indicates that Jonson's revelations of court politics, most importantly perhaps the scene of make-up and poison in Act 2, may have become a source of inspiration for more contemporary histories.[60] Thomas Fuller's *The Holy State*, a collection of schematic characters and historical portraits of political and professional figures, enlists *Sejanus* as one of the sources of a series of maxims about princes' favourites alongside the histories of Camden and Guicciardini, using a maxim spoken in the play by Tiberius to assert the prerogative of *arcana imperii*.[61]

Sejanus is also listed in the catalogue of the Sidneys' library at Penshurst, as the only playbook published during the lifetime of Robert Sidney (1563–1626) included there.[62] If he ever leafed through the book, Sir Robert, whom his brother

---

[58] For an analogous project, following in the wake of Savile's, see William Fulbecke, *An Abridgement, or Rather, a Bridge of Roman Histories, to Passe the Neerest Way from Titus Livius to Cornelius Tacitus* (London: Richard More, 1608), which supplies what has been lost with the loss of two thirds of Livy. The similarity between Jonson's and Savile's projects of restoration has been noted by Bradford, 'Stuart Absolutism and the "Utility" of Tacitus', 134–5.

[59] The sparse title pages of editions of Tacitus that combine Savile's and Grenewey's translations (1598, 1604, 1612, 1622) can be contrasted with the appearance of Thomas North's *The Lives of the Noble Grecians and Romaines* by Plutarch (1579, 1595, 1603), or Philemon Holland's 1600 Livy, ornamented with the xylographic flourish of the definite article and a woodcut device.

[60] Francis Osborn, *The True Tragicomedy Formerly Acted at Court: A Play*, ed. Lois Potter (New York: Garland, 1983) 4.

[61] (Cambridge: Roger Daniel for John Williams, 1642) IV. 1. maxim 6, sig. 2H4r, quoting (without attribution) *Sejanus* 1.537–40.

[62] The only other potential candidate in the catalogue would be the copy of *Catiline*, but there is no indication of the date of publication, and after the 1611 first edition, *Catiline* was republished in 1635, so the c.1665 catalogue may also refer to this later edition. I would like to thank Germaine Warkentin for information regarding these catalogue entries.

Fig. 5.2. The title page of the 1604–5 third edition of Henry Savile's *The end of Nero and beginning of Galba. Fovre bookes of the Histories of Cornelius Tacitus...* The Third Edition. Published with: *The Annales of Cornelivs Tacitvs. The Description of Germanie* (London: Printed by Arnold Hatfield for Iohn Norton, 1604–5).

LODGE 1604 T118, Rare Book & Manuscript Library, Columbia University in the City of New York.

SEIANVS

HIS FALL.

Writen

by

BEN: IONSON.

Mart. Non hic *Centauros*, non *Gorgonas, Harpyasq́;*
Inuenies : Hominem pagina nostra sapit.

AT LONDON
Printed by *G. Ellde*, for *Thomas*
Thorpe. 1605.

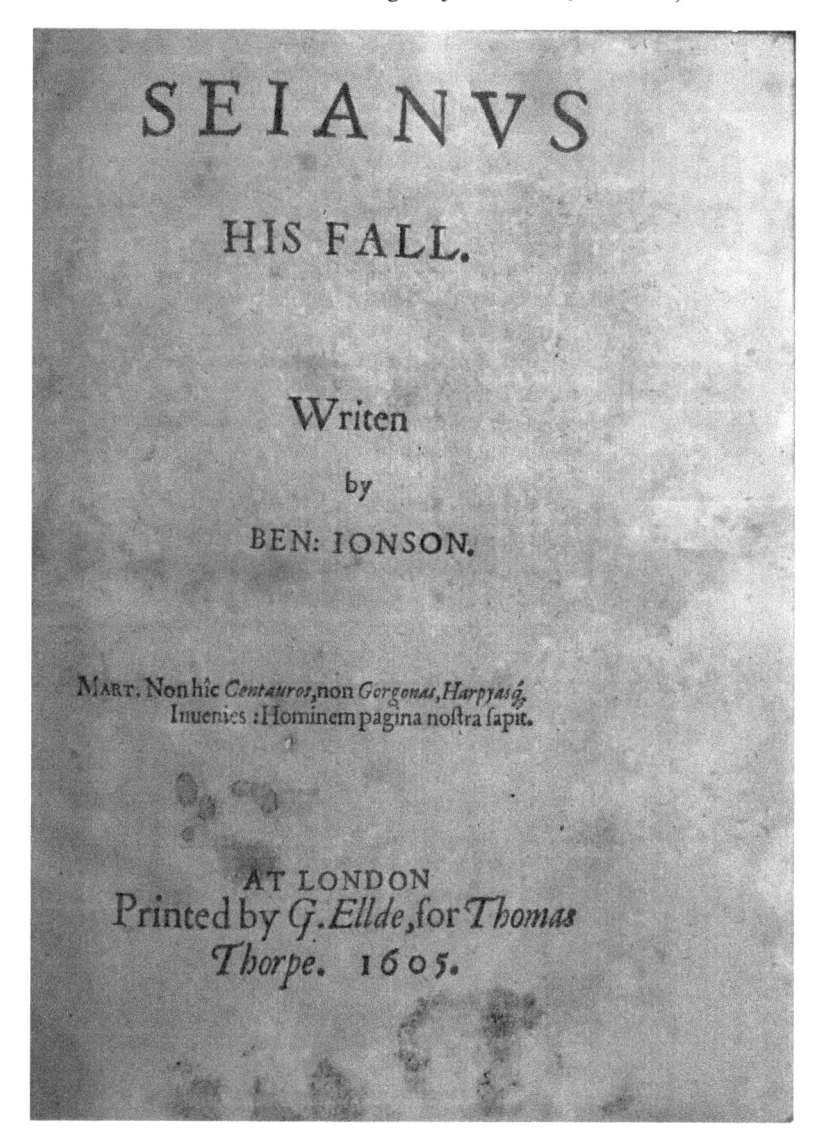

Fig. 5.3. The title page of the 1605 quarto of *Seianus his fall. VVritten by Ben: Ionson* (At London: printed by G. Elld, for Thomas Thorpe, 1605).
Beinecke Rare Book and Manuscript Library, Yale University.

Philip advised in a famous letter of 1580 about his studies, not least about the study of history, would not have been disappointed. The play's aphorisms resonate closely with the extensive marginalia Robert entered in his copy of Tacitus as a personal political commentary on the text in the form of maxims rendered in English, and also with the contents of the two political commonplace books he composed around 1600 and 1613.⁶³ Jonson's presence at Penshurst in 1611, commemorated by his famous poem, probably explains the presence of the copy of *Sejanus* in the collection, and even implies that the (now also lost) *Catiline* listed in the 1665 catalogue was a copy of the 1611 first edition of the play. What better gift could Jonson have brought as tutor to the recently knighted young William Sidney, whom he was hired to prepare for taking over his father's governorship at Flushing, than his own political histories? When Jonson came to Penshurst in 1611, he came as a poet–historian, an artful observer of statecraft, ready to study history for action with William—a scholar–facilitator like Harvey was to the young Thomas Smith, or like Savile himself was to Robert Sidney. But a reading of *Sejanus* also reveals a different understanding of the use of politic historiography, an understanding based on Jonson's awareness of the play as a public, theatrical medium, and of an audience whose members were unlikely (and also not expected) to put their political insight into action.

TO TELL THE TRUTH

Although self-consciously analogous to Savile's enterprise, Jonson's *Sejanus* is separated from *The Ende of Nero* by a dozen years of political change, most importantly, by the experience of the limitations on political agency under Elizabeth's increasingly absolutistic 'second reign'.⁶⁴ In 1591, Savile was focusing on virtuous Romans taking up arms against the most notorious tyrant in history, even in disagreement with the *Homilie Against Disobedience and Wylfull Rebellion* which insisted on the validity of the Pauline injunction to unconditionally submit to the monarch—an injunction which, as the *Homily* reminds its readers, originated under precisely

---

⁶³ Philip Sidney's letter of 18 October 1580 is printed in Kuin (ed.), *The Correspondence of Sir Philip Sidney* 1005–10. Robert Sidney owned the 1585 edition of Lipsius's edition of the works of Tacitus, now BL C.142.e.13; see Joel Davis, 'Robert Sidney's Marginal Comments on Tacitus and the English Campaigns in the Low Countries', *Sidney Journal*, 24 (2006), 1–19; on the commonplace books, see Robert Shephard, 'The Political Commonplace Books of Sir Robert Sidney', *Sidney Journal*, 21 (2003), 1–30. Lipsius, whose edition Jonson also used, was a personal acquaintance of the Sidney brothers. He remarked on the impressive intelligence of Philip (to whom he also dedicated one of his works), and also knew Robert—in 1602, Sir William Browne wrote to Robert referring to 'your Lordships old friend Lypsius'—see Alan Stewart, *Philip Sidney: A Double Life* (London: Chatto & Windus, 2000) 296–8, and HMC Lisle, 2:662.

The Penshurst volume does not seem to be extant, so we cannot know whether anyone in the household in fact read it, and if so, how. There wasn't much time to do so, anyway—William died of smallpox in the winter of 1611/12, and Jonson found new employment as the tutor of Walter Raleigh's son, whom he accompanied on his continental travels in 1612–13. On Jonson and the Sidneys, see J. C. A. Rathmell, 'Jonson, Lord Lisle, and Penshurst', *English Literary Renaissance*, 1 (1971), 250–60; Michael G. Brennan and Noel J. Kinnamon, 'Robert Sidney, "Mr Johnson", and the Education of William Sidney at Penshurst', *Notes and Queries*, 248 (2003), 430–7; Ian Donaldson, *Ben Jonson: A Life* (Oxford: Oxford University Press, 2011) 285–7.

⁶⁴ John Guy, 'Introduction: The Second Reign of Elizabeth I?', in John Guy (ed.), *The Reign of Elizabeth I: Court and Culture in the Last Decade* (Cambridge: Cambridge University Press, 1995), 1–19.

such Roman tyrants as Nero.[65] Informed by the polemical context of the wars of religion and by the debates about the succession, by England's war with Spain as well as by the period's preoccupation with the spectre of civil war, Savile's text imagines political conflict in active, military terms.[66]

By 1603, both the intellectual context and the political situation have changed. Instead of a Savilian effort at weaving together multiple threads of narrative set in distant theatres of action, in *Sejanus His Fall* Jonson sets his scene exclusively in Rome, excising from his account even the little that Tacitus has to say about the world outside the Senate and the Imperial court.[67] Restricted to Rome, the world of the play also restricts the spectrum of conceivable forms of political action. In *The Ende of Nero*, Savile recounts the attempt of Vindex 'to redeeme his cuntrey from tyranny and bondage'. In Jonson's play, the option of armed resistance to the tyrant is only suggested by an *agent provocateur*, and immediately rejected by his virtuous victim, showing that such active valour is now outside the realm of moral possibility (4.161ff). Military action of any sort is only referenced in Silius's Senate trial, where the noble veteran is accused of conspiring with the enemy, an accusation so preposterous that it is quickly dropped in favour of charging him with treasonous notions he is claimed to have uttered in private (3.154–339). In Jonson's play, it is not deeds, but 'words / How innocent soever', that 'are made crimes' (1.67–8), and no virtuous deed remains conceivable other than freely choosing to die, thus denying victory to the tyrant.

In Savile, although the sequence of events set off by Vindex's revolt lead to the overthrow of Nero, Vindex himself commits suicide to avoid certain defeat. Silius's voluntary end, the only on-stage death in Jonson's play, is not a last-ditch private defence against fortune, but a public gesture performed during the Senate trial, committed in defiance of an impending censure for something allegedly said. In the play, political agency takes the form of allegation, simulation, and dissimulation, and Silius's suicide itself becomes a communicative act. As Silius proclaims at the end of his sententious denunciation of Tiberius: 'the coward and the valiant man must fall; / Only the cause, and manner how discerns them'. His public deed thus publicly marks his distinction, while it also intends to teach how 'to mock Tiberius's tyranny', and expose the true nature of a regime that is managed through espionage and show trials (3.334–9).

Silius is a member of a chorus of morally upright but powerless bystanders, members of the senatorial class who were followers of the late Germanicus, repositories of republican virtue, several of whom end up as the regime's victims, but whose insight into the nature of the regime we are clearly invited to cherish. Indeed, while their options are limited to observation and commentary, they are absolutely crucial to Jonson's play, which on the one hand represents the rise and

---

[65] Womersley, 'Sir Henry Savile's Translation of Tacitus', 318–22.
[66] See the revisions to Womersley's account in R. Malcolm Smuts, 'Court-Centred Politics and the Uses of Roman Historians, c.1590–1630', in Kevin Sharpe and Peter Lake (eds.), *Culture and Politics in Early Stuart England* (Stanford: Stanford University Press, 1993), 21–44; Kewes, 'Henry Savile's Tacitus and the Politics of Roman History'.
[67] See Tacitus's comments on his limited scope in *Annals* 4.32–3.

sudden fall of Sejanus, his intimacy with the emperor Tiberius and the emperor's unexpected destruction of the over-ambitious favourite, and on the other, follows the destruction of the virtuous members of the senatorial class as they interpret the political action for us. In Silius's voluntary end, that destruction itself becomes an expression of an astute assessment of the situation, his death his most vocal contribution to the chorus, the extreme form of the agonistic discourse of truth-telling practised by the Germanicans.

The politics of the play is usually approached from the perspective of the strategies of persecution, censorship, suppression, and containment that it models. These strategies make truth-telling, the only conceivable form of political engagement in the play, hopeless and counterproductive. Not only is Silius tried for some comments he made in private: the public gesture of his suicide, rather than stopping the show, is also immediately integrated into the performance of Tiberius, who claims 'this sad accident / . . . hath stallèd and abused our mercy, / Intended to preserve thee, noble Roman' (3.344–6). The emperor thus both divests Silius's act of its communicative content, reducing it to a sign of private despair, and turns it into evidence of the exemplary justice of his reign. The courage of frank, open speech is no more productive: at the end of the trial scene in which Silius has committed suicide, the historian Cordus has been censured, and his books ordered to be burnt, Sejanus advises Tiberius that he should allow Arruntius's bitter criticism and use it to direct the attention away from the oppression of other opponents: 'His frank tongue / Being lent the reins, will take away all thought / Of malice in your course against the rest' (3.498–500).

In Foucault's analysis of the concept and its history, *parrhesia* is a mode of veridiction distinct from other forms of sharing knowledge and telling the truth, in so far as it involves putting a relationship at risk by telling one's partner the truth about themselves. This is a notion fundamentally political in nature: it implies speaking frankly about public matters in a public forum; in its positively valorized form, it is the act of speaking truth to power, of boldly and fearlessly counselling the prince.[68] It is a political act that hinges on the mobilization of personal virtue: the *parrhesiast* may attempt to reveal important if often inconvenient truths to a ruler made blind to the nature of his own rule by personal bias or by evil counsellors—if the ruler still possesses the remnants of virtue which the virtuously bold truth-telling can mobilize. Absent an audience that might be stirred to virtuous action, *parrhesiastic* practice becomes a publicity stunt, the act of publicizing forbidden knowledge.[69]

---

[68] Michel Foucault, *The Courage of Truth: The Government of Self and Others, II* (Lectures at the Collège de France 1983–1984; Basingstoke: Palgrave Macmillan, 2011) 1–71. I want to thank Heather James for teaching me about fearless speech, and for calling my attention to the earlier lectures Foucault gave at Berkeley, published under that title: Michel Foucault, *Fearless Speech* (Los Angeles: Semiotext(e): Distributed by MIT Press, 2001). For the history and plurality of the notion in the Renaissance, see David Colclough, *Freedom of Speech in Early Stuart England* (Cambridge and New York: Cambridge University Press, 2005).

[69] My reading of the situation through the concept of *parrhesia* is in agreement with Peter Lake, who argues that the play shows good counsel to be ineffectual if the monarch being counselled doesn't even have the vestiges of virtue that would allow him to recognize the value of what he is being told:

The aim of such a gesture calls for clarification. The Germanican chorus is fully aware that their game of truth-telling is both pointless and mortally dangerous. As Sabinus notes early on,

> 'It is not safe t'enforce a sovereign's ear:
> 'Princes hear well, if they at all will hear. (1.426–34)

—yet much of the play is nevertheless taken up by characters observing and telling the truth to each other about Rome and the power that controls it. The question that troubles Jonson's *Sejanus* is this question of audience, and how the absence of an active, participatory political public affects the fate and uses of truth-telling in the world—be it the truth-telling of Cordus, of Silius and the Germanicans, or of Jonson himself, be those truths regarding Sejanus or Tiberius or Elizabeth or Essex or James. What is the point of recognizing the nature and abuses of power if we can't hope to find an agent who could act upon this knowledge?

THE KNOWLEDGE OF POWER

The group of the Germanicans is defined by their piercing clarity of vision, their ability to see the unctuous rhetoric for what it is and discern the agenda hidden beneath—their skill at recognizing, in other words, 'Tiberius's art' (4.453) and distilling this art into sharp maxims, often presented as couplets. Their insights, shared in private and—as Penny Geng's analysis of the play's stage directions has shown[70]—occasionally voiced in public as well, give rise to an interpretive community, a group in the margins of political activity whose members are excluded from power but who use such understanding as the distinguishing trait of an exclusive group. Before we can explore the dramatic and cultural significance of this on-stage 'counter-public', however, we should look at the knowledge by whose circulation it is constituted.

In Act 4, Sabinus is set up by Latiaris to speak his mind freely and thus expose himself to two spies. When Latiaris suggests that the 'bright flame / Of liberty might be revived again', and 'It must be active valour must redeem / Our loss, or none' (4.143–4, 157–8, lines which make him the one character in the play who proposes, although deceitfully, the scenario of armed resistance), Sabinus sententiously pronounces that the subjects' duty is to obey:

> 'No ill should force the subject undertake
> 'Against the sovereign, more than hell should make
> 'The gods do wrong. A good man should and must
> 'Sit rather down with loss, than rise unjust—

Peter Lake, 'From *Leicester His Commonwealth* to *Sejanus His Fall*: Ben Jonson and the Politics of Roman (Catholic) Virtue', in Ethan H. Shagan (ed.), *Catholics and the 'Protestant Nation': Religious Politics and Identity in Early Modern England* (Manchester: Manchester University Press, 2005), 128–61 at 146–7.

[70] Penelope Geng, '"He Only Talks": Arruntius and the Formation of Interpretive Communities in Ben Jonson's *Sejanus*', *The Ben Jonson Journal*, 18 (2011), 126–40.

This is one of those rare moments in the play when someone appears to be articulating a universalized moral maxim (rather than an interest-based maxim of the Machiavellian, reason of state modality) to actually guide political action. The cautiously formulated commonplace warning against rebellion then gives way to an afterthought that appears to subvert this sententious submissiveness, but still stops short of proposing anything other than a description of the situation:

> Though, when the Romans first did yield themselves
> To one man's power, they did not mean their lives,
> Their fortunes, and their liberties should be
> His absolute spoil, as purchased by the sword. (4.163–70)[71]

Not only does he not articulate a maxim for action, his remark is nothing but a diagnosis of a state of affairs where the lesson Sejanus earlier volunteered to Tiberius has already been put into effect:

> 'The prince, who shames a tyrant's name to bear,
> 'Shall never dare do anything but fear.
> 'All the command of sceptres quite doth perish
> 'If it begin religious thoughts to cherish:
> 'Whole empires fall, swayed by those nice respects.
> 'It is the licence of dark deeds protects
> 'Ev'n states most hated, when no laws resist
> 'The sword, but that it acteth what it list. (2.178–85)

In discovering the secrets of tyranny, the sententious observations of the Germanican chorus about the motives and considerations of Sejanus and Tiberius identify the strategies that are consciously used and explicitly articulated in the behind-the-scenes scheming and discussion of the emperor and his favourite. The Germanicans' game of truth-telling is a condemning rehearsal of the very suggestions that Sejanus makes in an exhortative modality as his 'Machiavellian' counsel, directly mirroring Sejanus's own understanding and descriptions of the mysteries of state.

The scene of Sabinus's entrapment involves further ironies of truth-telling, as the *agent provocateur* offers some bold observations about Sejanus and Tiberius:

> He that is all, does all, gives Caesar leave
> To hide his ulcerous and anointed face,
> With his bald crown, at Rhodes, while he here stalks
> Upon the heads of Romans and their princes,
> Familiarly to empire.

While we are fully aware of Latiaris's ulterior motive in making these remarks, the margin of Jonson's text shows them to be lifted straight from Tacitus. In other

---

[71] Cp. Geoffrey Hill's reading of the scene in ' "The world's proportion": Jonson's dramatic poetry in *Sejanus* and *Catiline*', in Geoffrey Hill, *Collected Critical Writings*, ed. Kenneth Haynes (Oxford: Oxford University Press, 2008) 50–1.

words, Latiaris is right. Sabinus knows, and responds first with the approval and respect due to the insight of the supreme analyst of princes' courts:

> Now you touch
> A point, indeed, wherein he shows his art
> As well as his power.

—and then reciprocates the valuable comments with his own observations about Sejanus's 'later practice, where he stands / Declared a master in his mystery' (4.173–9, 183–4). The ensuing analysis of Sejanus's tactics verges on admiration due to a masterful performance, and shows Sabinus a discerning if careless commentator on the exemplary use of the arts of power, incriminating himself by rising to his interlocutor's Tacitean challenge.

In his *Ricordi*, a collection of aphorisms and observations on politics, the sixteenth-century Florentine statesman and historian Francesco Guicciardini noted that 'Tacitus teaches those who live under tyrants how to live and act prudently; just as he teaches tyrants ways to secure their tyranny.'[72] As a self-conscious exercise in Tacitean historiography, Jonson's *Sejanus* dramatizes the two-sided or indeed double-edged utility of its own sententious understanding of Tiberius's Rome through the interchangeable observations of the insiders and outsiders of the reign, of the oppressors and the oppressed, an interchangeability that elevates the insights themselves to the status of impartial, non-ideological, non-perspectival knowledge. In the absence of the narrator–historian, Sejanus and the Germanicans take turns in playing the part of—as Sidney puts it—the historian as 'discourser': Sabinus and Sejanus are both experts on the uses and abuses of the arts of power in Rome, and they both formulate aphorisms that identify what Sabinus in the first typographically highlighted sentence of the play calls 'Tyrants' arts' (1.70), that is, the trade secrets of political rule—precisely the kinds of reflections and insights politic readers were instructed to mark in their copies of the *Annales*, and then copy into their notebooks. The typography encourages such reading: the gnomic pointing in the margins of the 1605 quarto of *Sejanus*—which I have throughout added to my quotations from the modern edition of the play—identifies the notable and extractable nuggets of such multivalent practical wisdom, spreading them evenly across the moral spectrum of speakers, from Sejanus and Macro to Arruntius and Lepidus.

As we saw in the first chapter of this book, for late sixteenth-century readers, the tyrant's art is not only an expression of the tyrant's moral character, of his uncontrolled appetites, as it was in the Platonic tradition that dominated the sixteenth-century discourse about tyrants, but increasingly also a pragmatic, instrumental mastery.[73] The self-sufficient aphorisms of Tacitean statecraft reveal

---

[72] *Ricordi* C 18, in Francesco Guicciardini, *Maxims and Reflections (Ricordi)*, trans. Mario Domandi (Philadelphia: University of Pennsylvania Press, 1972) 45.
[73] This tradition has been influentially discussed in Bushnell, *Tragedies of Tyrants*. Writing about *Sejanus*, Bushnell recognizes that the play 'dismantles the Humanist model of the tyrant driven to mad acts of cruelty by his desire' (136), but she does not propose a perspective from which this dismantling happens. For the distinction between a political humanism and the maxim-based political thinking

'what men do, and not what they ought to do', as Bacon put it, explaining the insight for which we are 'much beholden to Machiavel and others'.[74] It is their independence of the specific situation as well as of any larger framework underpinned by ethical considerations that allows the aphorisms of Tacitean statecraft to circulate freely among contexts of application as well as among people deploying them. They are imagined by the play as a fragmentary body of knowledge, consisting of mobile, portable, adaptable, and freely exchangeable parts to be harvested for use under new circumstances.[75]

This notion of true knowledge about the political world in Jonson's *Sejanus* makes it impossible for anyone to conceive of effecting political change by bravely counselling or admonishing the tyrant or his favourite—because all anyone can tell them is what they already know. In this world, *parrhesia* consists in the unauthorized study and dissemination of *arcana imperii*. It is the bravery of knowing, not of doing, and it is a bravery that ultimately erases all political distinctions: whatever your purposes in disclosing the 'tyrants arts', if you are doing it right, you will die for it.

The most crucial insight into the operation of Tiberius's regime concerns how jealously it guards the access to knowledge about the innermost operations of power: this is a regime where 'ignorance is scarcely innocence, / And knowledge made a capital offence' (4.136–7). The emperor's lines about the secrets of the state are crucial here: as he says when he declines to give his reasons for praising Sejanus,

> 'Princes have still their grounds reared within themselves,
> 'Above the poor low flats of common men,
> 'And who will search the reasons of their acts
> 'Must stand on equal bases. (1.537–40)

In Tiberius's Rome, the most visible, most insistently dramatized political acts are acts of interpretation, efforts that seek to understand the regime's true nature, to uncover the technologies with which it maintains its power over its subjects, and to reveal the sources of its success and stability.

As a result of their access to this body of knowledge, Sabinus and Sejanus will both end up sentenced by the Senate, and their bodies on the 'Gemonies', that is, on the Gemonian stairs on the Aventine where cadavers of the condemned

---

cut off from its ethical moorings in England, see, e.g. F. J. Levy, 'Francis Bacon and the Style of Politics', *English Literary Renaissance*, 16 (1986), 101–22; for the continuities of these modes, e.g. Peltonen, *Classical Humanism and Republicanism in English Political Thought, 1570–1640* 135–6.

[74] Vickers (ed.), *Francis Bacon: The Major Works* 254.

[75] This reading points us away from the influential distinction, made by Giuseppe Toffanin early in the twentieth century, between absolutist-Machiavellian 'black' and republican 'red' Tacitisms: Burke, 'Tacitism', 162–7. For a more recent survey of Tacitist writing along similar lines, Tuck, *Philosophy and Government* 65–119. It is also at variance with a particular understanding of the uses of Tacitus in early modern England, one that takes the Tacitism of the Essex circle, and of the earl himself, to suggest that the Roman historian became identified with republican politics and was seen as a 'model of subversion', as in Patterson, *Censorship and Interpretation* 64. Such an understanding of the significance of Tacitus has been challenged by various critics including Sharpe, *Reading Revolutions* 318; Hadfield, *Shakespeare and Republicanism* 44–5.

were dragged before they were at last thrown into the Tiber. As Lepidus reports, Sabinus was

> drawn from the Gemonies,
> And, what increased the direness of the fact,
> His faithful dog, upbraiding all us Romans,
> Never forsook the corpse, but, seeing it thrown
> Into the stream, leaped in, and drowned with it. (4.283–7)

Choosing one's death here re-emerges as the one appropriate act of keeping faith and community, although as an act that the Romans, holding on to the decorum of their citizenship in spite of its vacuity under Tiberius, need to be reminded of by the example of Sabinus's dog. The abjection on the Gemonian steps as a vision of physical and civic annihilation remains on our minds; Arruntius is soon rehearsing an absurd list of potentially incriminating utterances that might land one there:

> May I think,
> And not be racked? What danger is't to dream?
> Talk in one's sleep? Or cough? Who knows the law?
> May I shake my head, without a comment? Say
> It rains, or it holds up, and not be thrown
> Upon the Gemonies? (4.304–9)

So when two hundred and fifty lines later, Terentius warns Sejanus that some of the servants in his escort taking a shortcut 'slipped down the Gemonies, and'—in what is Jonson's addition to the narrative in Cassius Dio—'brake their necks' (5.57–61), we take the omen more seriously than Sejanus, who will of course meet a fate worse than Sabinus, and even his children's 'bodies thrown / Into the Gemonies' (5.838–9). Contrary to what Guicciardini suggests about the practical utility of Tacitus, in Jonson's Rome, such knowledge of the operations of power as articulated by the Roman historian does not guarantee success or even survival: the study of 'tyrants' arts' lands the most astute observers on the Gemonian steps, and their political differences are erased in their final abjection.

THE DISTINCTION OF TRAGICAL SATIRE

Other than their quiet or ineffectually vocal indignation, what the chorus of bystanders can claim as their mark of positive distinction remains their clear understanding of the situation: their truth—both the truth they tell, and the truth about them—is knowledge. Silius, Arruntius, Sabinus, Cordus, and Lepidus recognize the theatre of Tiberius's state for what it is, they see the gap between the mind and the words in the emperor's performance, and stand as tongue-in-cheek connoisseurs and sarcastic commentators of the theatrics of imperial simulation and dissimulation.[76]

---

[76] Jonathan Goldberg, *James I and the Politics of Literature* (Baltimore: Johns Hopkins University Press, 1983) 176–85.

Their reaction to Tiberius's protestations of humility at the beginning of the play is characteristic:

CORDUS: Rarely dissembled!
ARRUNTIUS: Princelike, to the life.
SABINUS: 'When power, that may command, so much descends,
'Their bondage, whom it stoops to, it intends. (1.395–7)

Their insight, distilled into pointed maxims, is cast as dangerous knowledge: what the play's characters are voicing on the public stage and divulging on the printed page, ready for extraction by the play's readers, are observations that will cost them their lives. Jonson effectively suggested to Drummond that they almost cost him his: the assertion that he was 'called before the Council for his Sejanus' lends a certain real-life validation to the play's claim about its own political significance; it seems to put *Sejanus* on a par with Hayward's *Henrie IIII*, as a Tacitean piece with dangerous application.[77] If the play was indeed deserving the attention of the Council, then it really could be considered as *theatrum hodiernae vitae*, 'the theatre of today's life', as Lipsius claimed about Tacitean historiography,[78] the fact of the persecution bestowing upon Jonson the dangerous distinction of being the modern equivalent of Tacitus, who, as he told Drummond, 'wrote the secrets of the council and senate'.[79]

The clearest formulation of the rationale of the characters' engaging in the ineffectual but dangerous game of critical observation appears in what has become the most often discussed or mentioned moment of the play, Cordus's trial for his historical work, referred to as 'th'annals' (3.373). At the heart of the scene is the historian's eloquent defence against accusations of sowing sedition by 'comparing men and times' (3.390–1), a subtly ambivalent protestation of innocence which fails to deny the analogical application of his history of the republican times to the present, and proceeds instead by drawing comparisons between Cordus's own situation and satirical attacks by past writers that were graciously ignored by more gracious Caesars. After rehearsing a series of historical parallels, the speech concludes in Cordus's assertion that his writing about the past rather than the present shows him far removed 'from the time's scandal' (447)—an assertion clearly at odds with the implications of his own practice in the speech. Cordus's oration is a direct translation out of Tacitus, making the moment of *Sejanus* that is most obviously pertinent to Jonson's present situation at the same time the most ostentatiously

---

[77] The assertion reads: 'Northampton was his mortal enemy for brawling, on a St. George's Day, one of his attenders: he was called before the Council for his Sejanus, and accused both of popery and treason by him' (Jonson (2012) 5:375). Whether the accusations were made because of *Sejanus*, or on a different occasion, is not clear, and this is our only information about the case. Ayres admits that the sentence is 'ambiguous', explains that it is 'usually taken to mean that ... Northampton detected "treason" in *Sejanus*' and then proceeds to argue that in Northampton's reading the play 'lent support to a popish treason': Philip J. Ayres, 'Jonson, Northampton, and the "Treason" in *Sejanus*', *Modern Philology*, 80 (1983), 356–63 at 356, 363.
[78] *Iusti Lipsi Ad Annales Corn. Taciti liber commentarius*, sig. *3v.
[79] Jonson (2012) 5:367.

historical—it is a passage that denies the relevance of analogical application through performing such an application.[80]

Cordus is censured, and his books are ordered to be burnt. The Germanican chorus responds to this sentence by channelling Tacitus's own aphoristic remarks, noting that 'the punishment / Of wit doth make th'authority increase' and that those banishing books 'purchase to themselves rebuke and shame, / And to the writers an eternal name' (3.475–6, 479–80).[81] While these comments have often been read as voicing Jonson's heroic belief in the value of free speech and bold condemnation of censorship,[82] in a less idealistic and more pragmatic reading, they identify punishment and 'the cruelty / Of interdiction' as guarantees of cultural authority and an eternal name—distinctions to which Jonson obviously and explicitly aspired, and which his run-in with the authorities allowed him to claim.

Dangerous knowledge also serves as a mark of distinction elsewhere in the play. When, in the last moments of Sejanus's rule, Arruntius reflects on the reasons why 'upstart greatness' might hate him and his like, he claims

> Their breasts
> Are guilty that we know their obscure springs
> And base beginnings. Thence the anger grows. (5.472–4)

Although the play provides no evidence that Sejanus would be particularly anxious about his background, in this last-ditch assertion of the Germanicans' significance, knowledge about people's lineage, since it can be used to arbitrate the legitimacy of their claims upon social status, becomes a mark of social distinction itself.

While courageous truth-telling can be expected to have no impact on the tyrant's or his favourite's reign, then, critical commentary is a practice which is highly effective in bestowing both moral and social distinction upon those engaging in it. As our own response to the play indicates, the Germanicans' insight distinguishes these passive *parrhesiasts* from the unthinking servants of the corrupt tyrannical regime, and also from the ignorant, fickle, easily manipulated multitude. In the last, damning words about the people of Rome, spoken by the messenger who is offering news of the last reverberations of the fall of Sejanus for the Germanicans' commentary, they are 'so stupid, or so flexible, / As they believe him innocent' (5.893–4).

The distinctive importance of a critical stance and knowing distance might even seem to override the modal difference between Sejanus's and the Germanicans' descriptions as cynical insider vs. moral outsider accounts. Early in the play, Sabinus complains how all senators and magistrates in the state

---

[80] 3.407–60, translated from *Annales* 4.34–5; and cp. Jonson (2012) 5:388, where he tells Drummond that 'In his *Sejanus* he hath translated a whole oration of Tacitus.'

[81] Cp. Tacitus, *nam contra punitis ingeniis gliscit auctoritas, neque aliud externi reges aut qui eadem saevitia usi sunt nisi dedecus sibi atque illis gloriam peperere* (*Annales* 4.35): 'The influence [auctoritas] of punished talents swells, nor have foreign kings, or those who have resorted to the same savagery, accomplished anything except disrepute for themselves and for their victims glory [gloriam].' Tacitus, *The Annals*, trans. A. J. Woodman (Indianapolis: Hackett, 2004).

[82] Patterson, *Censorship and Interpretation* 60–1.

> that else not use their voices,
> Start up in public Senate, and there strive
> Who shall propound most abject things, and base,
> So much, as of Tiberius hath been heard,
> Leaving the court, to cry, 'O race of men,
> Prepared for servitude!'—which showed that he,
> Who least the public liberty could like,
> As loathly brooked their flat servility. (1.48–55)

At the very end of the play, Sejanus similarly notes:

> The Senate sat an idle looker-on
> And witness of my power, when I have blushed
> More to command, than it to suffer. (5.257–9)[83]

Sabinus, Tiberius, and Sejanus all see the political class as lacking virtue and independence of mind. They see this fact as the enabling condition of the tyrannical regime, and all three of them are appalled by the blushless, 'flat servility' of the Senate and of the people they represent, even though Tiberius and Sejanus both describe it as something they exploit and benefit from. What is used as a mark of distinction elevating one above the common abjection of Senate and people is not one's actions, but the clarity with which one judges the abjection of others and recognizes its uses for the exercise of power.

The position and role of the Germanicans as urbane, virtuous, discriminating commentators aligns them closely with the on-stage satirists of Jonson's comedies, who provide a stream of reflection on social manners, habits, and follies, modelling the performance and articulation of social judgement and distinction. The choric function of Arruntius, Sabinus, and Lepidus as discerning political observers makes them particularly reminiscent of the commentators designated as *Grex* in *Every Man Out*, a group of characters who not only pass judgement on others, but also make the standards and norms of such judgement the topic of their conversation. Even the temperamental differences among the Germanicans in *Sejanus* can be seen as similar to the spectrum of voices embodied in the characters and described by the names of the Grex in *Every Man Out*, viz. Asper (harsh), Cordatus (wise), and Mitis (gentle). The political commentary that measures appearances against the hidden intentions behind them is thus formally and structurally analogous with social satire for which Jonsonian comedy serves as a medium—the difference between politic tragedy and satiric comedy is one not of form, but of content and social register. Jonson's awareness of the connection is even signalled in *Sejanus* by his address 'To the Readers', which he concludes by assuming Persius's voice, thus adding the persona of the satirist to that of the tragic poet and the historian.[84]

A comment in another major work of 1603 clarifies the analogy Jonson thus proposes between the discussion of state secrets and satire. In *The Advancement of*

---

[83] See Geoffrey Hill's remarks about the 'anatomy of self-abuse', *Collected Critical Writings* 47ff.
[84] He translates an excerpt from the first Satire, asserting that although he loves praise, 'that I should plant my felicity in your general saying "Good", or "well", etc., were a weakness which the better sort of you might well contemn, if not absolutely hate me for.'

Learning, Bacon complains about the deficiency of learning in the area of 'the frauds, cautels [i.e. tricks], impostures and vices of every profession'. These have been discussed in writing, but, as he puts it, 'rather in a satire and cynically, than seriously and wisely'. And for serious attempts at the discussion of corruptions 'with integrity and truth', he argues, 'we are much beholden to Machiavel and others, that write what men do and not what they ought to do'.[85] Machiavellian politic analysis was promising a view behind the veil of ceremonial appearances, behind the public display of virtue put on by political agents.[86] As Bacon's formulation reveals, 'cynical satire' and Machiavellian analysis could be understood as two modalities of revealing the hidden nature of the social and political world, of exposing how appearances are manipulated in the interest of personal ambition. In *De Augmentis Scientiarum*, the expanded Latin version of his tract, Bacon makes the connection even more explicit. That book includes a list of *desiderata*, something of a Borgesian library catalogue of the titles of books yet to be written in each area of knowledge.[87] There, in the section that corresponds to the section quoted, he puts down the title *Satyra seria, sive de interioribus rerum*, a treatise about the inside of things, a serious exposition of what people do. It may be due to the influence of this list of *desiderata* that in 1638, a Latin translation of Bacon's *Essays*—that is, of his book of civil, politic wisdom—was published as *Sermones Fideles, sive Interiora Rerum*.[88] Bacon's understanding of satire is at apparent variance with our own, to which—if we are to believe the OED—'ridicule' seems central, making the very notion of *satyra seria* sound like a contradiction in terms. But if we recognize that ridicule is achieved by a mode of writing that exposes hidden qualities, we are better prepared to understand Bacon's idea of satire as a project of unmasking, which may take comic as well as serious form. The choric political commentary in Jonson's *Sejanus* is best understood as precisely such *satyra seria*, a discourse which treats *de interioribus rerum politicum*.

Jonson's and Bacon's suggestive linking of the two seemingly disparate modes of writing of 'cynical satire' and analysis of state secrets as analogous forms of knowledge about society also invites us to consider the analogy between their social use. The game of political truth-telling in *Sejanus* is a version of the game of wit in the 'comical satires', where the on-stage commentary of critic–observers designates them as a masters of a particular field of cultural competence. While the Germanicans' choric political observation may be republican in its content and perspective, its social and theatrical function is exactly the same as that of their counterparts in

---

[85] Vickers (ed.), *Francis Bacon: The Major Works* 253–4.
[86] Millstone, 'Seeing Like a Statesman in Early Stuart England', 89–90.
[87] On *desiderata*, see Vera Keller, 'The "New World of Sciences": The Temporality of the Research Agenda and the Unending Ambitions of Science', *Isis*, 103 (2012), 727–34.
[88] *Francisci Baconi, Baronis de Verulamio, Vice-Comitis Sancti Albani, operum moralium et civilium tomus Qui continet… Sermones fideles, sive interiora rerum* (Londini: Excusum typis Edwardi Griffini, prostant ad Insignia Regia in Coemeterio D. Pauli, apud Richardum Whitakerum, 1638). Cp. also the collection of essays on the Baconian model, published in 1640, called *Satyrae seriae, or, The Secrets of things written in morall and politicke observations* (London: Printed by J. Okes, for Abel Roper, and are to be sold at his shop at the blacke spread Eagle over against St. Dunstans Church in Fleetstreet, 1640).

Every Man Out: their recognition of the techniques and tactics of imperial power elevates them above naive or ignorant onlookers, while their on-stage discussion invites, indeed forces the reader and the theatre audience to participate in the performance of discernment, emulating the characters' judgement.[89] But while on Jonson's stage, the social use of political competence is analogous to other cultural skills, the dramatic genre of its rehearsal keeps it apart, marking it off as a distinct field. Political insight is tested on the tragic stage: the Germanicans are put in mortal danger by their performance of political observation, and it is precisely this danger that establishes their performance as authentic.

To enjoy the benefits of the distinction of being versed in the 'tyrants' arts', one needs to deploy another, complementary art. In Act 4, having heard Lepidus's account of Sabinus's body, drawn from the Gemonies, being followed by his faithful dog, Arruntius asks the grave and wise observer: 'What are thy arts—good patriot, teach them me— / That have preserved thy hairs to this white dye'? (4.290–1). As Lepidus explains: 'Arts, Arruntius? / None but plain and passive fortitude / To suffer, and be silent' (4.293–5). As an early seventeenth-century English gentleman reflected on his own experience at the English court, 'too late I find...Tacitus his opinion confirmed, that safety dwelleth not in doing well or ill, but in doing nothing.'[90]

In a complex twist on the tenets of the debate about the merits of the active and contemplative lives, which the fate of Chapman's Clermont brought into focus for us in the previous chapter, Jonson here revises the simple opposition.[91] The art of the observer of the tyrant's art consists in steadily maintaining silence and inaction while still keeping an eye on the world of politics—in being a good critical spectator of the stage of power. Although Lepidus claims his secret is to 'live at home, / with mine own thoughts, and innocence about me', we first encounter him advising Tiberius on how to 'show humanity' in disposing of Silius's estate (3.362), and by the time he pronounces the importance of living at home, we have been watching him on stage for most of Act 4 as well as for the second half of Act 5, away from home, observing and discussing a world obviously devoid of innocence. The point seems to be not in actual retreat, but in reflection without the intention to intervene, in taking notes without intending to use them in action. The neostoic position Lepidus articulates, which various modern readers have seen as the Jonsonian ideal of 'the composure of the gathered self',[92] is therefore neither to be taken entirely at

---

[89] My understanding of the cultural work of comical satire, and of the role of stage as modelling and generating cultural competence is indebted to O'Callaghan, *The English Wits* 35–59, and to Zucker, *The Places of Wit*.

[90] P. R. Seddon (ed.), *Letters of John Holles 1587–1637*, 3 vols. (Thoroton Society Record Series, Nottingham, 1975–86) 1:85. On Holles, see Linda Levy Peck, *Court Patronage and Corruption in Early Stuart England* (Boston: Unwin Hyman, 1990) 20–8.

[91] For a useful overview of the history of the debate and its late sixteenth-century applications see Cathy Curtis, 'The Active and Contemplative Lives in Shakespeare's Plays', in David Armitage, Conal Condren, and Andrew Fitzmaurice (eds.), *Shakespeare and Early Modern Political Thought* (Cambridge: Cambridge University Press, 2011), 44–63.

[92] Thomas M. Greene, 'Ben Jonson and the Centered Self', *SEL: Studies in English Literature, 1500–1900*, 10 (1970), 325–48 at 333; Paul Yachnin, *Stage-Wrights: Shakespeare, Jonson, Middleton, and the Making of Theatrical Value* (Philadelphia: University of Pennsylvania Press, 1997) 113.

face value, nor to be seen as contrary to engaging in a discussion about the reason of state: rather, it appears as the stance which enables the safe conduct of such a discussion. And conversely, the Tacitean analysis performed by the play's choric figures becomes a game of social and cultural distinction by virtue of being practised amidst protestations of withdrawal from political action. They are interdependent aspects of the work of producing social and cultural distinction through political observation and commentary. The politically masterful Sejanus reveals himself a social climber, a blatant beast, by seeking to put his knowledge to active political use, by, as it were, climbing from the pit onto the stage.

William Drake's admiration for the play must have been informed by his affinity for Jonson's understanding of the complementary nature of distinction and political action. In *Reading Revolutions*, Kevin Sharpe proposed two different arguments about the political reading evidenced by Drake's notebooks. On the one hand, Drake's sustained attention to Machiavelli and other key politic authors suggested to Sharpe that early modern readers were in fact 'reading for action in the public realm; they all read politically'. The syntax here unproblematically equates 'reading for action' with 'reading politically'—as does the assertion that readers like Drake 'were able to construct meanings for themselves, and constitute themselves as political agents'.[93] But whereas the status and anticipated career of someone like Robert Sidney makes it clear that his political commonplace books were compiled with the expectation of their usefulness in decision-making, the tendency to project the same motive behind the political note-taking of most early modern readers seems warranted more by hope than evidence. Sharpe's own hero, Sir William Drake, was taking his politic notes on the Continent, where he spent most of the 1640s and 1650s, cross-referencing Guicciardini with Tacitus at a safe distance from the theatre of political action. There can, of course, be no shred of doubt that Drake was a politic reader—but it would appear that his long life of note-taking was a function of precisely not making action the point of his reading. More compelling is therefore the subtler version of Sharpe's interpretation of what filling dozens of notebooks with politic notes really amounts to. Here, 'Drake's reading teaches us that politics was not just an activity but a type of consciousness' and Drake himself appears as a subject 'with capacity to understand the psychology of power and to formulate his own political thought'.[94] Like Lepidus, Drake survived the political turmoil of his age by staying out of it even as he was eagerly reflecting on it and polishing his techniques of observation, not least by reading and re-reading *Sejanus*.

POPULAR DISSEMINATION

When it is combined with a repudiation both of agency and of participation in public commentary, political observation becomes a mark of distinction—a form

---

[93] Sharpe, *Reading Revolutions* 306, 307.
[94] Sharpe, *Reading Revolutions* 334, 340. Noah Millstone's work is the exploration of politics as a type of consciousness in this sense.

of cultural capital. As we have seen in this book's Introduction, satirical treatments of would-be politicians and barbershop politicos also predicated the political competence of outsiders on the disavowal of their desire for political involvement. In *Sejanus*, Jonson extends his exploration of the significance of access to knowledge about political power to the people of Rome, and through a familiar trope of identification, to the play's real and imagined audiences. In the final section of the play, precisely where the dramatization of the existing Tacitean narrative gives way to a Jonsonian restoration from parallel accounts and fragments, this ideal of powerless knowledge is reasserted by being contrasted to a nightmarish scenario where public access combines with public agency.

Absent from the stage and, with the oblique exception of scattered references to some characters' popularity, absent even from the discussion taking place on the stage, the many-headed monster of the fickle crowd swings into horrid action when it learns about Sejanus's deeds and his trial, and in an ecstatic scene of lynching, outdoes even the servile Senate in enacting the tyrant's unspoken desires. The furious crowd becomes the uncontrollable agent of Tiberius, with whom it is aligned also through its absence from the stage—two figures whose aims and intentions are discussed but prove inscrutable and also unalterable through rational negotiation, and who are both resistant to the game of *parrhesia*: truth does not move them.[95]

Like *Julius Caesar*, or *Coriolanus*, *Sejanus* stages the joint threats of tyranny and democracy to the monarchical–republican ideal of the mixed constitution. Unlike those plays, however, it figures those threats as they emerge in the modern system of political communication: not simply as problems of theatrical deception and manipulation, but as problems of mediated dissemination and of the incalculable public reach of the disseminated information. In *Julius Caesar*, the people's rage is clearly imagined as incited, or rather ignited, by Antony's masterfully theatrical intervention, by his controlled mobilization of linguistic invention and his dramatization and effective personation of Caesar's wounded body. At the end of his performance, he can expect that his playhouse audience, like Brutus and Cassius, 'Belike...had some notice of the people, / How I had moved them' (3.2.259–60). In Shakespeare, the multitude may be fickle, but even in *Coriolanus*, they are reassuringly controlled by performance—Coriolanus's problem is that he refuses to perform. In *Sejanus*, Tiberius withdraws from Rome, and with it, from political analysis. The surprise condemnation of Sejanus by the Senate is brought about by the dramatic oratorio of the reading of his letter, and even the earlier instances of political performance take place before the limited and perfectly controlled audience of the Senate. Sejanus's dismemberment by the crowd is taking place off stage, not as the extension of a carefully orchestrated performance, but the seemingly unpredictable eruption of violence. There is no direct, theatrical relationship here between ruler and ruled, the tyrant and the mob. Their harmony is mysterious: the play does not engage in the fantasy of the world outside the Senate being

---

[95] On the problem of *parrhesia* in democracy, see Foucault, *The Courage of Truth: The Government of Self and Others, II* 33–55.

conceivable as the familiar, wondrous world of the theatre, controlled by the art of the 'royal actor'. The public constituted by the people outside the doors of the Senate and the court in *Sejanus* is a monster—as an immaterial, absent, invisible, and unknowable monster, it might rightly be called a phantom. Its motives and reasons are unavailable to the observer. The play's subtle commentators have no insight to offer—they are analysts of the reason of state, and expositors of state secrets, but here, they are faced with an open secret that defies their reason, because it does not operate according to reason. What political knowledge this phantom lays its many hands on, it will put to unforeseeable and inexplicable uses. Jonson's senatorial commentators are therefore more comfortable with the knowable and condemnable entity of Sejanus, the man they love to hate, and whose reasons they can state, than with the ominous crowd.

Both Jonson and contemporary commentators suggested that the play was victim to a twofold malice, coming from the court as well as from the audience. The unfavourable early reception—'the people's beastly rage' as well as being accused, from up high, 'of such crimes' which the author of a commendatory poem dared 'By all his muses swear be none of his'[96]—is put down to selective misreading, to a failure to attend to the coherence of the play, or (less generously) to readers' and audiences' attempts to destroy that coherence by taking its lines out of context. Those who 'would offer to urge his own Writings against him' before the council, Jonson argues, did so 'but by pieces...as if any mans Context, might not seem dangerous, and offensive, if that which was knit, to what went before, were defrauded of his beginning.'[97] As in Jonson's England, under Tiberius's and Sejanus's regime one's 'looks are called to question' and one's 'words, how innocent soever, are made crimes' (1.67–8) by being torn out of context and accused of a dangerous topical application: this is the nightmarish condition of one's words starting to live a life of their own, of one's intentions being irrelevant to how one is understood.

The language of physical fragmentation that pervades the play resonates closely with this experience.[98] From the very beginning, people are presented as grotesque assemblages of body parts which are endowed with autonomy and even agency. Not only words, but mouths, ears, eyes live a life of their own, in a dark, disintegrative parody of the anthropomorphic metaphorics of the body politic. The condition of life under constant surveillance, eavesdropping, and suspicion is one where 'Nothing hath privilege 'gainst the violent ear' (3.311), where faces betray the hearts' intentions, or indeed intentions have treacherous faces and inscrutable hearts—as do those of Sejanus, of whom someone says 'I do not know / The heart of his designes; but, sure, their face / Looks farther than the present' (1.250–2), or of Tiberius: 'the

---

[96] Commendatory verses, 'To the most understanding poet' and 'To his worthy Friend, the Author', Jonson (2012) 2:228 and 224, respectively.
[97] *Discoveries* ll. 965–9, Jonson (2012) 7:545, 'De innocentia'.
[98] Christopher Ricks, 'Sejanus and Dismemberment', *Modern Language Notes*, 76 (1961), 301–8 catalogues the examples of this imagery, through which 'the play anticipates and works towards the final scene', and which he sees as a register of the dismemberment of the Roman body politic. Leonard Barkan, *Nature's Work of Art: The Human Body as Image of the World* (New Haven: Yale University Press, 1975) 90–5 offers a reading of the play along these lines.

space, the space / Between the breast, and lips—Tiberius' heart / Lies a thought farther than another man's' (3.96–8). But the imagery is more pervasive than to be reduced to this particular symbolic significance; it is a tendency which leads to people being described as the sum total of their organs, as when Sejanus rescues Tiberius 'with his knees, hands, face, / O'erhanging Caesar' (4.53–4). The linguistic dismemberment of individuals so powerfully defines the play that it even forces characters to assert their own moral integrity in negative terms, denying their participation in the physical and moral disintegration which they see as pervasive and which they thus vividly invoke: 'We have no shift of faces, no cleft tongues, / No soft, and glutinous bodies, that can sticke, / Like snails, on painted walls; or, on our brests, / Creep up, to fall from that proud height' (1.7–10).

This figurative obsession of the play assumes monstrous dimensions when the Roman mob appears as a magnified and multiplied equivalent of the individual disintegration that is the condition of the imperial court, as 'A thousand heads, / A thousand hands, ten thousand tongues and voices' (5.793–4), and is then literalized to horroristic effect when Sejanus, falling from the emperor's favour, is being physically torn to pieces by this crowd. The people incited against him

> Run quite transported by their cruelty—
> These mounting at his head, these at his face,
> These digging out his eyes, those with his brain,
> Sprinkling themselves, their houses, and their friends.
> Others are met, have ravished thence an arm,
> And deal small pieces of the flesh for favours;
> These with a thigh; this hath cut off his hands;
> And this his feet; these fingers, and these, toes;
> That hath his liver; he his heart: there wants
> Nothing but room for wrath, and place for hatred. (5.799–808)

Although it is now a physical reality, dismemberment is still informed by the nightmare of involuntary action—the butchering crowd is 'transported' by its own cruelty, losing itself to the trance of physical violence. When they at last regain their consciousness, 'some, whose hands yet reek with his warm blood, / And gripe the part which they did tear of him, / Wish him collected, and created anew' (5.867–9). Their remorse seems to continue the fury: tearing Sejanus apart seems already to have been driven by a desire to have a piece of him—they were after all dealing 'small pieces of the flesh for favours'—and wishing him collected with his pieces still in hand suggests just more of the same furious activity, perhaps requiring more trading of pieces for favour. As a practising Catholic, Jonson would probably have remembered that the adoration of relics presupposes some butchery of human cadavers.

This extended spectacle of dismemberment is recounted by Terentius to the appalled Arruntius and Lepidus, no friends of Sejanus but astounded by the people's inhumanity and lack of dignity, which is an enabling condition of Tiberius's tyrannical exercise of power. There is an important anticipation of this monstrous scene of off-stage mob violence. Early in the play, Arruntius effectively threatens to dismember Sejanus, throw around his remains torn to tiny scraps, much in the way it happens at the hands of the multitude. But this hypothetical vivisection would be motivated by a need to discover the truth about Sejanus's hidden intentions, to get at 'the heart of his designs', i.e. his suspected ambition to become emperor:

> If I could guess he had but such a thought,
> My sword should cleave him down from head to heart,
> But I would find it out; and with my hand
> I'd hurl his panting brain about the air,
> In mites as small as atomi, to undo
> The knotted bed—(1.253–8)[99]

As Ian Munro points out, this intention 'is marked by its focus on the pursuit of knowledge; Sejanus must be dissected and dispersed in order to discover what truth lies beneath his dissembling surfaces. The dismemberment of Sejanus by the Roman crowd, in contrast, produces no revelation, only dissemination.'[100] More importantly still, the crowd's actions literalize the darkest figurations of the discerning observer's fantasies—in this sense, as well as literally, they only act upon what they snatch from the centres of power, upon human bodies and upon bodies of knowledge that are thrown for them. In Jonson's *Sejanus*, then, the classical view of tyranny and democracy as analogous and related phenomena is situated in a pessimistic understanding of what we might term the economy of political knowledge, where the production of such knowledge always runs the risk of contributing to the conditions of democratic access and excess.

Jonson's reflections on the circulation and use of political knowledge thus include not only a vision of its instrumentality, of its utility in creating social distinction, but also a clear sense of its openness to radical appropriation. This is also to say that Jonson seems to have understood, and dreaded, the full implications of Plutarch's objections to *polypragmosyne*, and the potential of the dissemination of sententious, Tacitean or Machiavellian politic knowledge to foment rebellion. It is through its reliance on this tradition that *Sejanus* foreshadows the well-known mid-seventeenth-century description of the intellectual origins of the civil wars. Plutarch's account of curiosity as envious aspiration was put to sharp contemporary application by Thomas Hobbes, who claimed that in the early seventeenth century, a volatile combination of ambition and the thirst for knowledge resulted in

> gentlemen envying the privy-council, whom they thought less wise than themselves. For it is a hard matter for men, who do all think highly of their own wits...to be persuaded that they want any ability requisite for the government of a commonwealth, especially having read the glorious histories and the sententious politics of the ancient popular governments of the Greeks and Romans.[101]

---

[99] 'The knotted bed'—i.e. 'the heart of his designs'.
[100] Ian Munro, *The Figure of the Crowd in Early Modern London: The City and Its Double* (New York: Palgrave Macmillan, 2005) 169.
[101] Thomas Hobbes, *Behemoth: Or, the Long Parliament*, ed. Ferdinand Tönnies (Chicago: University of Chicago Press, 1990) 23.

or, as he put it a few years later:

> as to Rebellion in particular against Monarchy; one of the most frequent causes of it, is the Reading of the books of Policy.[102]

In the dedication to the 1616 Folio, Jonson compares his play's reception (presumably at the theatre) to Sejanus's dismemberment, claiming that it 'suffered no less violence from our people here than the subject of it [that is, Sejanus himself] did from the rage of the people of Rome'.[103] But if Jonson was genuinely distressed by his tragedy being torn apart by his audiences, when he published it as a Tacitean history, he was nonetheless asking it to be read 'by pieces', to be fragmented for copying into commonplace books in advance of future, unforeseeable uses, to be broken up for recycling as it breaks up and recycles Machiavelli, Tacitus, or Gentillet—that is, Jonson was precisely asking 'that which was knit, to what went before' to be 'defrauded of his beginning' in the reading of his play. Fragmentation is both the intended and ideal use of Jonson's Tacitean history as a source of portable political insights, and the dreaded condition of misinterpretation and abuse. The technologies of distinguished observation and the 'people's beastly rage' are ultimately inseparable from each other, the latter always potentially implicated in the former. This is a text that dreads its own utility being turned against it.

Many of the sententious passages, Tacitean aphorisms, marked for extraction in *Seianus His Fall*, Jonson's book of policy, are spoken by Sejanus, who is thus waiting to be dismembered again, the dissemination of his insights predicated upon the violence of their being ripped out of context. After Orpheus was torn to pieces by fierce maenads, his scattered limbs continued singing as they were swept along by the river in which they were thrown. In Jonson's play, Sejanus emerges as the alter ego of the Tacitean poet–historian, the veritable Orpheus of politic discourse, whose scattered parts will go on singing their Machiavellian song, gathered up in the pages of the play's readers.

---

[102] Thomas Hobbes, *Leviathan*, ed. Richard Tuck (Rev. edn.; Cambridge: Cambridge University Press, 1996) 225.
[103] Jonson (2012) 2:212. In 'The Argument' printed both in the Quarto and the Folio, Jonson uses the same phrase to describe Sejanus's end, when he says Tiberius 'in one day hath him suspected, accused, condemned, and torn in pieces by *the rage of the people*', Jonson (2012) 2:230, my emphasis.

6

'For Discourse's Sake Merely'
Political Conversation on the Stage and Off

In the theatre of Hamlet's moment, members of the audience became spectators of affairs of state, appraising and discussing the performance of political actors. The central claim of this book has been that the drama engaged with the media and genres of professional political knowledge so closely in response to the growing public interest in these materials, and that this interest was in turn fuelled by the appeal (or fantasy) of a career in the political profession as an avenue to social advancement. Diplomatic reports, politic histories, and collections of political maxims were invested with social prestige because of their utility in advancement in the business of politics—and plays capitalized on this prestige by putting on display the forms of political knowledge such professional writing embodied.

The effect of such publication on the stage—and on the pages of playbooks—was not exclusively, or even primarily, the transmission of propositional content. Like comedies of manners and social satires (and, perhaps, in a sense, like any kind of performance) political plays conveyed to their readers and audiences an awareness of vocabularies and skills—in this case, a familiarity with the language, the categories, and the *habitus* of political life—provided them with examples of their uses, and invited them to judge how successfully they were performed on stage. The audiences of political drama were thus prepared to judge politics and—as Plutarch and Jonson and Hobbes and many others feared—also to meddle in it. Such fears were based on the interdependence of judgement and competence: discussing and judging stage politics *is* talking politics. While it offered its audiences an imaginary involvement in the realm of politics, the theatre also trained them in political conversation among themselves.

Early modern theatre audiences were virtually educated in the affairs of their own state and in the exercise of their political judgement. My argument however is not that these audiences were therefore a proleptic version of the public constitutive of modern representative politics, i.e. spectator–critics who sit in judgement of political acts and actors and make their might felt by uttering their judgement in public.[1]

---

[1] Hannah Arendt shows the centrality of the spectator–critic to Kantian political philosophy as an analytic of judgement; Hannah Arendt, *Lectures on Kant's Political Philosophy*, ed. Ronald Beiner (Chicago: University of Chicago Press, 1982) 44–77. The Habermasian concept of the public sphere is also rooted in this Kantian notion of political spectatorship—exemplified for Arendt by Kant's remarks about the French Revolution in *The Conflict of the Faculties*—which is itself the culmination but also the radical revision of the early modern understanding of the political world as theatre. As Arendt succinctly puts it, 'the public realm is constituted by the critics and the spectators and not by

The theatrical moment I am describing clearly belongs to the genealogy of this development, but in my emphasis I differ from earlier critics in that I am imagining audience members who were judging not only stage politics, but also each other's commentary. In talking politics and judging political actions, whether in a playhouse or elsewhere, they were also subject to each other's political judgement, as well as to each other's judgement of social and verbal abilities and performance. This difference in emphasis results in a different understanding of the dynamics of public political conversation, and ultimately, of the emergence of the public sphere. I suggest that while the subject of performance and judgement was political, the nature and regulative power of judgement was social and aesthetic. In a scene of such discussion, the question is not simply how right you are, but how well you are making your point. As a model for linguistic and social conduct as well as an object of judgement, the political stage presented itself to an audience that encompassed both the learned and the ignorant, both the younger and the wiser sort, and transformed the professional knowledge it divulged into a social competence to be used in a conversational arena in which one seeks social recognition through judging and being judged.

I emphasize the conversational advisedly. Much more than most other types of writing in the period, the dramatic medium was defined by the necessary and conscious imitation of the cadences of spoken language. The only exceptions are dialogues, and conversation manuals in particular, like John Florio's *First Frutes*, John Eliot's *Orthoepia Gallica*, and Claudius Hollyband's *Rules and Dialogues...for the Learner of th'Italian Tong*: parallel-text publications produced for English people learning foreign languages, whose explicit intention was to provide models for conversation in those languages, although the nature of the parallel text manual is that someone could also have used it as a lesson on how to converse in English. Editions of classical plays that included translations can in fact be considered as the earliest foreign language conversation manuals, and as we shall see, vernacular playtexts are also known to have been used as models for spoken language.[2]

Gabriel Harvey's books provide some important clues here. First of all, they show the close connection between language learning and the art of conversation. Not only does Harvey make reference to Eliot's French textbook in his copy of Guazzo's hugely popular late sixteenth-century dialogue *La Civil Conversazione*, showing that *Orthoepia Gallica* was valuable both as a language manual and a guide to conversation across languages—his Italian copy of Guazzo is actually bound with Hollyband's *Rules and Dialogues*: the literary dialogue that presents the

---

the actors or the makers.' See Hannah Arendt, *The Life of the Mind*, 2 vols. (New York: Harcourt Brace Jovanovich, 1981) 2:262. On the theatrical concept of the public sphere in the second half of the seventeenth century, see Sándor Bene, *Theatrum Politicum: nyilvánosság, közvélemény és irodalom a kora újkorban* (Debrecen: Kossuth Egyetemi Kiadó, 1999). For an analysis of a different model of the early modern English stage as a metaphor for what Habermas would call 'representative publicness', see Stephen Orgel, *The Illusion of Power: Political Theater in the English Renaissance* (Berkeley: University of California Press, 1975).

[2] Nicholas Udall's *Floures for Latyne Spekynge selected and gathered oute of Terence, and the same translated in to Englysshe...* (London: Thomas Berthelet, 1533, and several editions throughout the sixteenth century) is a phrase book based on Terence.

ideal of social distinction as being based on conversational, cultural, and social virtues rather than on birth, with a textbook for learners of Italian.[3]

The alignment of textual units with bound objects, of their beginning and end with a front and back cover, is revealed as a modern development by the widespread early modern practice of binding (especially small) books into *Sammelbände* which bring together several titles under the same cover.[4] *Sammelbände* sometimes highlight uses of books and connections among them that are often obscured by the conceptual boundaries of genre and subject categories that organize our understanding of the field of reading. Harvey liked to keep together the books he used in learning modern languages: in one *Sammelband*, he bound together French and Spanish grammars, dictionaries, language manuals, and bilingual parallel-text books.[5] His Italian grammar was originally part of a similar, generically diverse but recognizably use-oriented *Sammelband*. On the title page of this volume, which received its current binding in 1867 and is now at the Huntington, there is a note in Harvey's hand indicating what other texts were bound with it originally: 'Gabrielis Harueij. 1579. mense Aprjli. Axiophili prima ars Linguae Italicae. Grammatica. Comoediae. Tragoediae. Poco, y bueno.'[6] Grammar, comedies, tragedies: the sequence of books that were bound together; and the verso of the last page of the grammar refers to the excellent Aldine edition of the translation of Terence, making it clear that the collection of comedies whose title page was facing this blank page is the volume now at the Houghton Library.[7] The tragedies that concluded the *Sammelband* would almost certainly have been those contained in a copy of Lodovico Dolce's Italian adaptations of five classical tragedies, of which only a two-play fragment survives at the Folger.[8]

---

[3] *La Civil Conversatione del Signor S. G. … Divisa in Quattro Libri* (Vinegia, 1575), BL shelfmark C 60 a 1. References to Eliot (as *Le Parlement des Babillards*, the subtitle used at the beginning of both books of the work, as well as in the running head of the second) at 310, 353. In Harvey's copy, Guazzo is followed by the guide to pronunciation and by the phrase book starting on sig. V2 of *The Pretie and Wittie Historie of Arnalt & Lucenda with Certen Rules and Dialogues Set Foorth for the Learner of th'Italian Tong: And Dedicated vnto the Worshipfull, Sir Hierom Bowes Knight. By Claudius Hollyband scholemaster, teaching in Paules Churcheyarde by the signe of the Lucrece* (London: By Thomas Purfoote, 1575). Harvey disposes of the parallel Italian–English text of *Arnalt & Lucenda*, the longer first part of the Hollyband publication, leaving it out of the *Sammelband*.

[4] Jeffrey Todd Knight, *Bound to Read: Compilations, Collections, and the Making of Renaissance Literature* (Philadelphia: University of Pennsylvania Press, 2013).

[5] This *Sammelband* is now broken up; its parts are (in the order of Harvey's arrangement) Huntington 60231, 53922, 56974, 53880, 56972; see Caroline Brown Bourland, 'Gabriel Harvey and the Modern Languages', *Huntington Library Quarterly*, 4 (1940/1), 85–106 at 85–6.

[6] *An Italian Grammer; vvritten in Latin by Scipio Lentulo a Neapolitane: and turned in Englishe: by H.G.* (London: By Thomas Vautroullier dwelling in the Blackefrieres, 1575), Huntington 62184. See Bourland, 'Gabriel Harvey and the Modern Languages', 91–4. *Poco, y bueno* was Harvey's motto for the studying of languages, frequently written in the margins of texts he was reading for language instruction; along with '*petit a petit*' (in his copy of *A Treatise in Englishe and Frenche…made by Peter du Ploiche*, London: by Ihon Kingston for Gerard Dewes, 1578, Huntington 53922, at sigs. A2v–A3r) it is perhaps best understood as a version of the Erasmian '*festina lente*'. Axiophilus is one of Harvey's fictionalized *personae*.

[7] *Le Comedie di Terentio Volgari; di Nuovo Ricorette, et a Miglior Tradottione Ridotte* (Venice: Aldus, 1546), Houghton *EC.2623 Zz546t.

[8] *Le Tragedie di M. Lodouico Dolce: cioe, Giocasta, Didone, Thieste, Medea, Ifigenia, Hecuba*. Di Nuouo Ricorrette et Ristampate (Venetia: Appresso Domenico Farri, 1566) Folger PQ4621.D3 M4 1566a—the copy now only includes *Medea* and *Thieste*.

The recto of the last page of the *Italian Grammer* is a list of 'interjections': 'Of ioye: *Oh*. Of laughing: *Ah, Ah*.... Of Desier: *Deh*. Of dreade: *Bàco Bàco*: *Oh Oh Dio*.' Below the concluding 'FINIS', Harvey explains the relationship between the textbook and the rest: 'No finer, or pithier Examples, then in ye Excellent Comedies, & Tragedies following: full of sweet, & Wise Discourse. A notable Dictionarie, for the Grammer.'[9] This reconstructed *Sammelband* is emblematic of Harvey's understanding of the usefulness of drama as an exemplary form of conversation—an understanding which can be traced back to Erasmus's suggestions that Terence was an exceptionally valuable model for the language of conversation, and which defined the use of comedy in the period.[10] Harvey's markings in the Dolce volume show that vernacular tragedy could also be used this way: they are limited to underlining words and expressions (presumably for their novelty or difficulty) as well as highlighting some felicitous formulations and sententious insights about various topics, as a form of conversational ammunition. In the margin, he occasionally marks witty repartee as being said 'argutamente' that is, sharply, with perspicuous wit,[11] and adds gnomic pointing to such lines as 'Femina essendo, instabile, e leggiera'—a commonplace contribution to the ongoing *querelle des femmes*, a timeless piece of misogyny half way between Hamlet's 'frailty, thy name is woman' and the Duca di Mantova's 'La donna è mobile' from *Rigoletto*.

It wasn't only Harvey who considered his playbooks as exemplary conversations: the typography of early seventeenth-century English playbooks encouraged such readings. While it is frequently argued that early modern writing generally and characteristically points back at its origins in speech, so much so that written language could readily be construed as speech, Holger Syme has shown that playbooks led the way in treating print as a medium of verbal performance. Not only were both stage performance and print understood as 'publications': in the early years of the seventeenth century, Marston and Jonson were experimenting with the *mise-en-page* of their plays to achieve 'a theatrical effect in print—a surrogate sense of embodiment'. This theatrical embodiment centrally included voice, and at its most adventurous, it created the cacophonous effect of simultaneous events and conversations.[12] And it was in playbooks printed around 1600—and in the work of the same playwrights—that typography also began to be used to represent the delivery of spoken language. Jonson's early comedies—and thus, not incidentally, plays associated with the war of the theatres—were the first to deploy dashes and parentheses to record the sound of speech on the page, to register and modulate

---

[9] *An Italian Grammer* (Huntington 62184) sig. L2r.

[10] See Stephen Orgel, *The Reader in the Book: A Study of Spaces and Traces* (Oxford: Oxford University Press, 2015) 36–40.

[11] In the margin of Folger MS H.a. 2, 147v (i.e. Lodovico Guicciardini, *Detti, et Fatti Piacevoli et Gravi, di Diversi Principi Filosofi, et Cortigiani*, Venice: Christoforo de'Zanetti, 1571, p. 118), Harvey points to another dramatic source of *argutia*: 'Arguta altercatio: quales multa in Senecae tragoedijs.'

[12] Holger Schott Syme, 'Unediting the Margin: Jonson, Marston, and the Theatrical Page', *English Literary Renaissance*, 38 (2008), 142–71 the quotation at 152; Syme, 'The Look of Speech', *Textual Cultures: Text, Contexts, Interpretation*, 2/2 (2007), 34–60, discusses the representation of the spoken word as a material presence in late medieval and early modern images as an apparently paradoxical function of the understanding of writing as silent speech.

our metrical and dramatic sense of spoken language: the pauses, interruptions, hesitations, confusions, the improvisational movements of people thinking on the spot.[13] Although scholarship has often emphasized playwrights' and publishers' efforts to turn plays into literary artefacts, the printed playtext of Hamlet's moment was just as often trying to transcend its condition as 'literature', as writing, and assert itself as a form of oral performance, as conversation taking place on the page—and to challenge its audiences to judge its success.[14]

How plays modelled political conversation, what perspective they offered on its styles and functions, depended on their genre. Chapman's and Jonson's political tragedies present what they ask us to understand as dangerously serious intelligence drawn from within the realm of professional politics. These 'serious satires' attend to the uses and abuses of political knowledge in its originary contexts, casting their audiences in the roles of passive, informed, critical spectators of political activity. The comedies written in the period trace the fate and functions of this knowledge in social interaction *outside* the professional, courtly setting where it originates, in the broader conversational setting into which it is released by the mechanisms of commercial drama and other vehicles of dissemination. They show how people not involved in the business of politics grapple with political ideas and political information, with knowledge associated with the profession of politics, and how they use what they know among themselves, off the political stage, outside the realm where such knowledge is produced and whose operation it is meant to enable. Through representing such scenes of sociability and the functions of political conversation in it, these plays seek to discern and critique the benefits or advantages such knowledge may accrue in social interaction: in other words, they investigate the role of professional knowledge among laypeople as a form of cultural capital.

Satirical comedies perform this cultural work by pinpointing competent and incompetent uses of knowledge and skills in social interaction—which on the stage always means conversation. Laughing at ineptitudes does not merely make a distinction: it confirms the audience's sense of their own distinction, their sense of being distinguished from whomever they are laughing at, thus also reaffirming the cultural mechanisms of distinction that are in effect. As Adam Zucker argues in his important book on early modern comedy, when it invites us to judge how characters perform in social interactions, when it incites us to roll our eyes 'at characters who have no idea that eyes are meant to be rolled at all', comic form not only

---

[13] For an attentive reading of the dramatic and poetic effects of dashes, see Graham Bradshaw, 'Appendix: Dashing Othello's Spirits', *Misrepresentations: Shakespeare and the Materialists* (Ithaca and London: Cornell University Press, 1993), 258–82. Parkes, *Pause and Effect* 55–6 suggests that the dash, the triple en rule, and the triple point as marks of suspension first appear in dramatic texts, and also points out that in the typographical representation of the features of spoken language in novels, Richardson 'drew upon his taste for the drama' (p. 93). In an unpublished essay 'Designs for play-reading: typographic experiment and performance innovation in early modern England'—which is based on her systematic survey and analysis of the typographic conventions of playbooks—Claire Bourne discusses how print, and the use of dashes in particular, registered verbal performance as well as action that exceeded it. I want to thank her for sharing her unpublished work with me.

[14] Deutermann, *Audiences to This Act*, Chapter 2.

represents and comments on social interactions, and the social relations shaped by those interactions: it also practises those relations through the judgements it elicits.[15] When we read comic representations of political competence for the judgements and distinctions it makes, we access the framework in which the empirical theatrical publics were judging the deployment of political competence on stage and off.

The comic judgement of political competence is a judgement about ambition and purpose, about whether people are entitled to do and say what they are doing and saying, whether they are acting and speaking within their competence, whether they are qualified or sufficient to say what they are saying. Such judgement of the decorum of political discussion entails the demarcation of the spheres where political competence is displayed. The definition of a separate, cultural, rather than political use of political competence is the most important function of comedy with regard to political discussion.

Plays, especially the plays written around 1600, in the intensely self-reflective context of the war of the theatres, thus provide us with as close an access to early modern talking as we can hope for, albeit with considerable reflective mediation—in what follows, I will be listening for what they suggest about political conversation. This series of readings traces how politics was talked about among those who couldn't call politics their business, and how the theatre shaped such political conversation. Whether in performance or in print, early modern plays represented people in conversation—to audiences and readers who would judge the conversational success on display and model their own linguistic skills on whatever seemed valuable. The chapter follows an outward trajectory: it starts with Marston's *Malcontent*, a tragicomedy that stages court intrigue to model a style of political observation for outsiders, continues with comedies by Chapman and Jonson that explore the decorum of the unofficial political conversation fashioned after professional models, and concludes with a look at a playreader's notebook, and in it, the aestheticization of political commentary in social use—at its transformation from a professional analytic into a conversational aesthetic.

INSIDER TALK AND THE INTERESTS OF CONVERSATION: *THE MALCONTENT*

John Marston and Ben Jonson were close readers, friends, collaborators, and occasional enemies, and *Sejanus* was particularly important to their complicated literary relationship. Marston was among those who wrote commendatory verses for *Sejanus*, but in 1606, in his preface to *Sophonisba*, he also insisted that in this, his own Roman historical tragedy, he did not attempt 'to relate any thing as an historian, but to enlarge everything as a poet', adding that 'to transcribe authors, quote authorities, and translate Latin prose orations into English blank verse, hath,

---

[15] Zucker, *The Places of Wit* xii, 10.

in this subject, been the least aim of my studies'.[16] Although he was emphatically distancing himself from the historiographical responsibilities Jonson undertook in *Sejanus*, his only tragedy also bears close resemblance to that play, not least as a medium in which a large quantity of political aphorisms are served up to a commonplacing readership.[17] The difference Marston seeks to maintain between the work of the poet and the historian makes no difference to the participation of both *Sophonisba* and *Sejanus* in the pointed politic style. They are both representatives of a Machiavellian aesthetic whose roots are social rather than literary or artistic.

Marston's engagement with *Sejanus* actually began before the publication of the 1605 quarto. His best-known play, *The Malcontent*, was produced and published in 1604, and in a highly unusual gesture that is characteristic of Marston's strategies of self-presentation, it was dedicated to a fellow playwright—Ben Jonson. The play is often described as one of the most distinguished examples of the cluster of 'disguised duke plays' that also includes Shakespeare's *Measure for Measure*, Marston's *The Fawn*, and Middleton's *The Phoenix*, all of them predicated on a ruler keeping an eye on developments unfolding in his supposed absence, testing his subjects and finally restoring himself to power.[18] This sequence of tragicomic, satiric plays started in 1604, following closely in the wake of the tragedy of *Sejanus*, both chronologically and in terms of their formal and thematic affinities, although they added a comic twist to the Jonsonian model of political commentary.[19] Like Jonson's Tacitean satiric tragedy, the disguised duke plays deploy passive on-stage critical observers of the political scene, using the disguised dukes to expose the intrigue and corruption that pervert government in times of peace, much like the Germanican chorus does in Jonson's play. Like *Sejanus*, the disguised duke plays promise 'Of government the properties to unfold', and articulate political and social observations in quotable aphoristic insights, often pointed by marginal commas.[20] But as tragicomedies, plays with no historical, experiential basis, they couldn't be accused of trying to compete with historiography as a source of politically useful knowledge. In unfolding the properties of government, the disguised duke plays are less concerned with the practicalities of power than with the savviness, the competences of those involved in it. What they offer is not a perspective on how sovereignty is constituted, but a sovereign perspective (literalized as the

---

[16] John Marston, *The VVonder of VVomen or The Tragedie of Sophonisba as It Hath Beene Sundry Times Acted at the Blacke Friers* (London: Iohn Windet and are to be sold neere Ludgate, 1606) sig. A2r.

[17] Marta Straznicky, *Privacy, Playreading, and Women's Closet Drama, 1550–1700* (Cambridge: Cambridge University Press, 2004) 53–6.

[18] Thomas A. Pendleton, 'Shakespeare's Disguised Duke Play: Middleton, Marston and the Sources of *Measure for Measure*', in John W. Mahon and Thomas A. Pendleton (eds.), *Fanned and Winnowed Opinions: Shakespearean Essays Presented to Harold Jenkins* (London: Methuen, 1987), 79–97; Ivo Kamps, 'Ruling Fantasies and the Fantasies of Rule: *The Phoenix* and *Measure for Measure*', *Studies in Philology*, 92 (1995), 248–73; Kevin A. Quarmby, *The Disguised Ruler in Shakespeare and His Contemporaries* (Farnham and Burlington, VT: Ashgate, 2012).

[19] This analogy between *Sejanus* and the disguised duke plays has been noted by Gail Kern Paster, *The Idea of the City in the Age of Shakespeare* (Athens: University of Georgia Press, 1985) 114.

[20] *Measure for Measure* 1.1.1. Shakespeare's play may not seem as aphoristic as Marston's plays or Middleton's *The Phoenix*, yet it is one of only two plays by Shakespeare in the 1623 folio that carry gnomic pointing.

perspective of a disguised sovereign) on how people touched by power constitute their personal world. Politics, political knowledge, enters the picture primarily as the stuff of private, social relationships. These turn-of-the-century tragicomedies follow in the wake of *Sejanus* as some of the earliest plays that represent the modern condition of politics, the condition of a split between actors and spectators—but in the device of the disguised duke, they forcibly (and conservatively) reunite the observer with the sovereign actor, the Germanicans with Tiberius, investing the political commentary of the former with the princely authority of the latter.

The Malcontent retains more of the claustrophobia of *Hamlet* and *Sejanus* than other examples of the genre. Its complicated intrigue plot focuses on three figures struggling to acquire or keep the dukedom of Genoa. Of the three, it is Altofront, the play's central character, the exiled duke, who haunts Genoa masquerading as the malcontent Malevole, who might have the strongest claim to the throne, but the play is interested less in the question of legitimacy than in the practicalities of how he reassumes power. And that is decided by a fourth duke: the duke of Florence, who never makes an appearance but whose sovereign command creates and deposes the dukes of Genoa. The will of the duke of Florence is relayed in letters as frighteningly beyond the characters' control as are the papers circulating in Chapman's *Bussy d'Ambois*. The court of Genoa is a world ruled by an inscrutable, decisive force which only reveals itself occasionally—much as Rome is ruled by the letters of a Tiberius withdrawn to Capri in *Sejanus*. As a result of this limitation of public agency, the options of the play's characters for prudent political activity are limited to constant self-positioning and self-adjustment in anticipation of a window of opportunity, and to reflection on the intrigue of furious self-positioning, reflections performed through sententious, aphoristic observations.

Marston's plays seem to have been written to be fragmented and quoted. Of English Renaissance playwrights, his *oeuvre* is most persistently pointed with commonplace markers: every single playbook associated with his name carries some highlighted lines. Of all the lines of *The Malcontent*, six per cent are marked by italicization or commas, and to these, an attentive reader could easily add a comparable number of lines that are extractable as standalone pieces of pointed wisdom or sharp observation.[21] The two most sententious characters of *The Malcontent* are Mendoza, a sinister conspirator who is an endless resource of cynical remarks about court politics and female virtue (nor are the two separable here), and Altofront, the deposed and disguised duke. Mendoza's aphorisms include such unsentimental Machiavellisms as 'Who cannot feign friendship, can never produce the effects of hatred' (1.7.82) and disillusioned advice as '... those whom Princes do once groundly hate, / let them provide to die. / As sure as fate, prevention is the heart of policy' (2.5.70–2). Although the disguised duke's utterances (sometimes confusingly) alternate between two *personae*, i.e. between the duke himself and the assumed malcontent character Malevole, the rhetoric of the 'genuine' Altofront

---

[21] Of the play's 2315 lines, 133 are marked by inverted commas or italics—the line count is based on the shorter text that does not include the extensive additions attributed to Webster. All references to the play are to John Marston, *The Malcontent*, ed. G. K. Hunter (London: Methuen, 1975).

persona itself seems to oscillate between an optimistic providentialism, the notion that virtue is rewarded on earth, and the morally sceptical politic vision that allows him to finally reclaim his title, while the Malevole persona's perspective similarly shifts between the scornful critique of court flattery and aphorisms more directly Machiavellian in origin, that is, between observations like 'honesty and courtship straddle as far asunder as a true Frenchman's legs' (2.5.138–9) and maxims like 'For he that strikes a great man, let him strike home, or else 'ware, he'll prove no man' (4.3.80–1).[22]

Since the play revolves around the disguised duke, the irreducible plurality of his constant reflection on the unfolding of the plot, on its characters, and on his own motives posed a major interpretive problem for most of the play's twentieth-century critics, who sought to find in it an expression of a consistent political vision, tacitly understood to be shared by the central character, the play as a whole (its implied author), and its actual (biographical) author. But Altofront/Malevole resists such efforts: he remains a duke of shreds and patches, his pronouncements the snippets of incompatible discourses. On closer look, they turn out to be gambits chosen according to the expectations of whomever he is talking to. He plays the depraved Machiavel, talks of the moral wisdom of withdrawal from the court, or reflects on the workings of providence, as his interlocutor and his own purposes require. *The Malcontent* displays a massive amount of aphoristic insight, but rather than being positioned as choric commentary on the events, as in Jonson's *Sejanus*, it is presented as a rhetorical toolkit for self-preservation, self-presentation, and self-promotion through a variety of conversational registers.

Malevole plays many parts, but he is first introduced as a satirist, and his railing against the court of Genoa has been seen as exemplary of the ideal of free speech.[23] Dissatisfied with everything, Malevole's 'highest delight is to procure others vexation', and his speech 'is halter-worthy at all hours'. Although such courageous truth-telling and rejection of social decorum is in apparent contradiction with the opportunistic self-fashioning of the malcontent, Malevole's strategic deployment of his satiric persona indicates that in Marston's play, more clearly than in *Sejanus*, *parrhesia* is understood as social strategy, not an existential stance. What is understood as the most radical form of truth-telling is yet another mode of self-promoting political commentary in the malcontent observer's repertory.

The play opens as Pietro and his courtiers gather under Malevole's window, the source of 'the vilest out-of-tune music', and call for him to join them: 'Come down, thou ragged cur, and snarl here. I give thy dogged sullenness free liberty; trot about and bespurtle whom thou pleasest' (1.2.10–12). Through this belaboured series of puns, Pietro emblematically identifies Malevole as the dog allowed to bark at society, as the Cynic (literally, dog-like) sage, an outcast living on the margin of society whose position makes his unbridled tongue unthreatening even

---

[22] Cp. 'any injury done to a man must be such that there is no need to fear his revenge'. Machiavelli, *The Prince* 9.
[23] Janet Clare, 'Marston: Censure, Censorship, and Free Speech', in T. F. Wharton (ed.), *The Drama of John Marston: Critical Re-Visions* (Cambridge: Cambridge University Press, 2000), 194–211 at 200–4, 209.

as it is relentlessly critical. Marston's play thus establishes a clear link between Malevole and the archetype of the *parrhesiast*, the Cynic Diogenes. The image of Diogenes that emerges from the classical sources as transmitted by the compilations of the 'ryght famous clerke Maister Erasmus of Roterodame' is well summarized by the prefatory poem in Samuel Rowlands's *Diogenes Lanthorne*, a collection of satirical characters, first published in 1608, and reprinted several times throughout the century:

> ... bould to speake his minde, who euer found,
> Hee spake as free to Alexanders face,
> As if the meanest plowman were in place,
> Twas not mens persons that he did respect,
> Nor any calling: Vice he durst detect.[24]

In his *Arte of Rhetorique*, Thomas Wilson also presents Diogenes as the paradigm of the *parrhesiast*: 'Freenesse of speache, is when wee speake boldely, and without feare, even to the proudest of them, whatsoever we please, or have list to speake. Diogenes herein did excel, and feared no man when he sawe just cause to saie his mynde.'[25] This heroizing view of the cynic's free speech emphasizes the virtue of *parrhesia* over its breach of *decorum*, and assumes that it is motivated by a 'just cause'. The Diogenes of this tradition is the witty, plain-speaking critic of the ills of civilization, who turns his exile from Sinope into a metaphoric exile from human society, offering his ascetic life less an example to be followed than an authentic point of reference, and a perspective from which social standards and practices could be judged. The honesty of fearless speech is the ideal form of political counsel, a political deed of exemplary virtue derived from true understanding.

This exilic incisiveness is also understood to define Malevole's doggedly satiric performance. When Pietro describes Malevole as 'one of the most prodigious affections that ever conversed with nature,... more discontent than Lucifer when he was thrust out of the presence', his comparison identifies the actual motive behind this cynic persona, a persona that is—as even the play's audience will only realize a few scenes later—assumed by the deposed, exiled, powerless ex-duke Altofront. According to Pietro, Malevole considers 'whosoever in this earth can be contented... a slave and damned; therefore does he afflict all in that to which they are most affected' (1.2.19–26). The fantasy of intellectual clarity produced by exilic freedom associates the figure of the Cynic not only with Juvenal, whose exile

---

[24] Samuel Rowlands, *Diogenes Lanthorne* (London: [Edward Allde] for Thomas Pauier, 1608), and reprinted in 1608, 1615, 1628, 1631, 1634, and 1659. For a philosopher whose written work does not survive, Diogenes the Cynic had a remarkable presence in early modern literary culture. The two substantial accounts of his life and teaching, in Diogenes Laertius's *Lives of the Philosophers*, and in the orations of Dion of Prusa (Dio Chrysostom), provided Erasmus with far more apophthegms than he associated with any other character of classical antiquity. In Nicholas Udall's translation of the *Apophthegmata*, the sayings of Diogenes take up ninety leaves; Socrates is second with thirty-nine, Augustus third with thirty-seven, followed by Cicero with thirty leaves: *Apophthegmes That is to Saie, Prompte, Quicke, Wittie and Sentencious Saiynges ... Gathered and Compiled in Latine by the Ryght Famous Clerke Maister Erasmus of Roterodame. And now translated into Englyshe by Nicolas Vdall* (Ricardus Grafton, 1542).

[25] Thomas Wilson, *The Arte of Rhetorique*, ed. Thomas J. Derrick (New York: Garland, 1982) 396.

Marston held up as a potential model for himself in his own satiric poetry, but with an entire tradition of cultural criticism that extends from Hugo of St Victor into the present. Edward Said's frequent invocations of Hugo's *Didascalicon* as a model for intellectual autonomy provide useful modern formulations of the idea. In the last page of *Culture and Imperialism*, for example, Said argues that critical independence and detachment, 'the negative freedom of real knowledge', can be achieved by using exile as a model for understanding: by regarding experiences '*as if* they were about to disappear'. This time-honoured tradition considers exile as a necessary fiction that enables an authentic because disinterested critical consciousness, even if it is also the lived experience of Diogenes and Juvenal, of Auerbach and Said, who are thus tacitly invested with a critical authority to which fictional exiles can never lay claim.[26]

The Malcontent identifies Malevole as an exilic figure, a dog, a free-speaking outsider, but swerves from the heroizing tradition in representing truth-telling as fundamentally instrumental and interest-driven: a performance with an ulterior motive. Malevole's freedom of speech is the source of obvious enjoyment to many in the city, first and foremost to the usurper Pietro, the current Duke, who fully appreciates the 'negative freedom of real knowledge' the exilic persona allows. Pietro is willing to play Alexander to this Diogenes and give the dog 'free liberty' because he expects from him something more than the comic relief afforded by such railing: 'I like him, faith; he gives good intelligence to my spirit, makes me understand those weaknesses which others' flattery palliates' (1.2.28–30). Whether the weaknesses are his own or those rampant in his environment, Pietro realizes that he is better off if he is aware of them.

Malevole thus speaks truth to power—and speaks truth that is seen as useful for power: it is 'good intelligence'. He performs the satiric repertory of the cynic, touching upon 'the public place of much dissimulation, the church' (1.3.4–5), the talk of the town, and the courtly affectation of cosmopolitanism. He 'afflict[s] all in that to which they are most affected' (1.2.25–6), identifying the trait on which a personality hinges, offering satire as a form of knowledge about character. The effect of this performance is not Pietro's reformation, but Malevole's rise to favour. Having thus secured access to Pietro, he switches to another form of truth-telling, and informs him that his wife is cheating on him. He uses his proclaimed unwillingness to flatter anyone to torment the usurper Pietro, who, unable to resist the knowledge offered, finally collapses under its weight and is ready to give up his dukedom—to Altofront, biding the time behind the mask of Malevole, waiting for his chance to return to power.

As the self-interested performance of disinterestedness, the use of cynic *parrhesia* as aimed by Malevole at Pietro might serve as a general model of Malevole's

---

[26] Edward W. Said, *Culture and Imperialism* (New York: Knopf, 1993) 335–6. Erich Auerbach is quoting Hugo in an essay translated by Maire and Edward Said as 'Philology and "Weltliteratur"', *The Centennial Review*, 13 (1969), 1–17, the quotation on 17. Diogenes Laertius actually derives Diogenes's way of life and his teaching from his being an exile (VI. 21). Juvenal's Third Satire is a classic of exilic social criticism, and the biographical information of his exile may well be a reflection of its power.

conversational strategies and of his deployment of pointed observations. This re-purposing of a mode of political intervention, hailed for its exemplary virtuousness, into a tool of self-advancement, is clearly analogous with Malevole's social use of Machiavellism when talking to Mendoza. To this malcontent Machiavel, Malevole brags about being 'banished the court' (2.5.108), following up his self-identification as an exile by a performance of bold disregard for religious pieties—as he says, churches were made 'to scour plough-shares. I ha' seen oxen plough up altars' (2.5.125–6). His *recherché* sarcasm gradually ingratiates him with Mendoza, who considers such cynical remarks as the impeccable credentials of an aspiring assassin.

When Malevole reports his mission accomplished and Pietro dead, Mendoza seeks to get rid of him, but only after a final clash of tyrannical wit that works as a caricature of the fantasy of political employment-seeking through a performance of political competence. Mendoza discloses the Machiavellian rationale of his next plan, the murder of Altofront's wife, using a translation of a Senecan line, pronouncing that 'Black deed only through black deed safely flies'. Malevole ups the ante by dismissing the posture as derivative and unsurprising, citing the original back at him: 'Pooh! *Per scelera semper sceleribus tutum est iter*' (5.4.13–15). The exchange doesn't merely undercut a conventional rhetorical stance by revealing it to be just that, it also calls attention to the kind of persona such cynical tags help to fashion. Seeing that he is beaten at his own game by Malevole, Mendoza projects a social identity upon his opponent—after all, not only are such lines merely conventional, but facility with them is also a conventional marker of the politic intriguer. He exclaims: 'What! Art a scholar? Art a politician? Sure thou art an arrant knave' (5.4.16–17), adding a few lines later for clarification: 'canst thou empoison? canst thou empoison?' (5.4.35). Malevole's impertinent familiarity with the politic style appears to recommend him for further employment by Mendoza. His linguistic performance identifies him as a 'politician', the caricature of the professional man of business as a scheming mercenary devoid of conscience, earning him the appropriate, and appropriately murderous, employment. The scene turns out to be a theatrical farce based on familiar motives: as soon as Malevole offers his services as a poisoner and produces a box of poisonous vapour as his weapon, his employer appears to kill him by holding it to his face—emulating a trope familiar from *Alphonsus*. After Malevole's collapse, Mendoza rehearses a series of self-congratulatory maxims, starting from 'Mischief that prospers, men do virtue call' and concluding in 'The chiefest secret for a man of state / Is to live senseless of a strenghtless hate' (5.4.76–83), and victoriously exits, his politic ingenuity once again asserted by the display of his repertory of Machiavellian tags. It is only after he leaves that we find out that of course the little box was emitting no poison: proving himself truly 'senseless' to Mendoza's 'hate', Malevole jumps up and rejoices in having once again shown himself one step ahead, a better player at Machiavellian one-upmanship.

Here, Machiavellism (reduced to its stereotypical image of scheming immorality) appears as a competitive rhetorical and social performance rather than an intellectual framework for planning political action, or even simply a sign of cunning evil, as with earlier examples of the stage Machiavel. It is part and parcel of the malcontent's strategy of targeted truth-telling, of his delivery of pointed aphoristic observations that unmask social pretences, sexual transgressions, and political stratagems, whose purpose is not to intervene, but to impress. *The Malcontent* lays bare the logic of the cultural value of satiric and politic wit by making it the tool of self-advancement, the instrument that helps the malcontent to a better position at court in which to wait the change of his fortune.

Where such lines come from says a lot about their value. Although Mendoza's 'Machavellism' is among the registers in Malevole's aphoristic repertory, the two characters are joined by more than their competitive cynicism. The social position they occupy in the margins of the court of Genoa marks them as malcontents, melancholy characters with a frustrated desire for upward mobility.[27] Lurking in the dark corners of Genoa's court society, they observe and wait for their moment to arrive. In their aphorisms modelled on, and often also borrowed from, the textual arsenal of people employed in the business of politics, their environment is transformed into an object of interested observation and knowledge. They produce and perform ostentatiously unflinching remarks and piercing insights, deploying them in a stylized social game of wit which sees itself as analogous and sometimes identical to the use of prudential discussion in political decision-making. But unlike the political maxims offered as advice to princes, the malcontents' insights are not instrumental, but rhetorical: in accordance with the conservative structure of these tragicomedies, their hope of achieving greatness lies in someone noticing their performance and thrusting greatness upon them.

Altofront's return to power at the end of the play is not achieved by a successful manipulation of power through Machiavellian tactics, but by the arbitrary command of the duke of Florence. His success is nevertheless predicated upon his rise to a social position where he can receive the favour without opposition, marking his verbal performance of cynical revelation a powerful social tool, a practice that commands attention and respect, and results in social mobility. As political agency is replaced by the social performance of insight, the Tacitean aphorisms and Machiavellian maxims also become part of a larger continuum of the verbal genres of the kind of pointed truth-telling called 'wit'.[28] In this context, the power of such remarks is in their well-appointed pointedness, an aesthetic quality, and in being wielded with an acute sense of purpose.

Although in the world of *The Malcontent*, political aphorisms are seen in circulation in a court setting, their utility is imagined in a way that allows for a much broader social application. The malcontent persona is the product of the variegated commonplaceable discourse circulated by the play to its audience, and it is also a site where the play's politicking reader may hypothetically insert himself. It is a subject position in which the public is inscribed, not least by the typography that invites them to borrow and deploy these extractable observations. When they accept the invitation to take mental or written note of Malevole's and Mendoza's

---

[27] For an overview see Mark Thornton Burnett, 'Staging the Malcontent in Early Modern England', in Arthur F. Kinney (ed.), *A Companion to Renaissance Drama* (Oxford: Blackwell, 2002), 336–52.

[28] See Ian Munro's excellent 'Knightly Complements: *The Malcontent* and the Matter of Wit', *English Literary Renaissance*, 40 (2010), 215–37.

aphoristic lines, members of *The Malcontent*'s public confirm their own role as observers of court politics from its margins. Like Malevole, this public follows and reflects on the events at Marston's Genoa. And like Malevole, perhaps, they aim to articulate their insights in the snappy, aphoristic style of the reason of state, both about the stage world, and, more importantly, also about their own, as they jockey for the attention of their betters and their peers.

TOBACCO AND FOREIGN AFFAIRS: *MONSIEUR D'OLIVE*

In *The Malcontent*, dreams of social climbing are, on the one hand, manifest in the use of political conversation among those seeking to acquire or retain power over the dukedom of Genoa, while on the other, they are kept under control by the fact that the person successfully advancing himself—and advancing from critical spectator to the lead actor on the stage of Genoa—is Malevole/Altofront, who has a legitimate claim to the title. The self-conscious generic doubleness of Marston's tragicomedy, its split *personae*, and its split styles gesture at the divide between serious and comical satire, and at the divide between esoteric and exoteric uses of politic discourse, while (at least seemingly) engaging in both. In satiric comedies, political topics appear in purely hypothetical, and usually parodic form, and fantasies of the direct efficacy of political talk are either revealed to be just that, fantasies, or, less gently, ridiculed for their presumptuousness.

George Chapman's *Monsieur d'Olive*, a comedy written around 1604–5, shortly after Chapman's *Bussy d'Ambois*, just when the quartos of *Hamlet* went on sale in Paul's Churchyard, is a play which appears to promise a glance behind the scenes of court politics and diplomacy, but whose true focus turns out to be on the conversations of private individuals, and on the social conditions and uses of political conversation among those not involved in the business of government. In one important scene, the eponymous hero of the play, a wit who has been leading a life withdrawn from the court, is describing the various positions taken in a 'private conventicle' that debated 'the high point of state'

> Whether in an aristocracy,
> Or in a democratical estate,
> Tobacco might be brought to lawful use. (2.2.144, 145, 166–8)[29]

D'Olive's long-drawn-out and self-consciously ornate account of this discussion concludes in his ecstatic praise of the fume that fills empty brains for its power to draw out sociable discourse:

> Besides the excellent edge it gives a man's wit (as they can best judge that have been present at a feast of tobacco) what variety of discourse it begets, what sparks of wit it yields, it is a world to hear! (2.2.267–72)

---

[29] References to *Monsieur d'Olive* are by act, scene, and line number to Thomas Marc Parrott (ed.), *The Plays and Poems of George Chapman: The Comedies* (London: George Routledge & Sons, 1914).

Proposing the consequences of democratic and aristocratic constitutions for tobacco use as a topic for debate satirically identifies political conversation with the symbolically empty talk about smoke, an opportunity for the performance of wit, for the display of conversational competence, which tobacco and political topics both seem to stimulate. D'Olive's account specifically imagines the convivial exchange as taking place in a 'private conventicle' of

> All sorts of men together:
> A squire and a carpenter, a lawyer and a sawyer,
> A merchant and a broker, a justice and a peasant.
> And so forth, without all difference. (2.2.155–8)

As d'Olive has explained earlier, 'wit's become a free trade for all sorts to live by' (1.1.285–6)—which means that a socially stratified group can converse as equals,

> drink sack, and talk satire, and let our wits run the wild-goose-chase over Court and country. I will have my chamber the rendezvous of all good wits, the shop of good words, the mint of good jests, an ordinary of fine discourse. (1.1.300–4)

A 'high point of state' is thus one of the many subjects traded among an informal group of friends and casual acquaintances, discussed in the setting of private conviviality, a matter of wit that has no part in, or implications for, office, government, or the court. In other words, in the classical terminology that was in effect in the early modern period, Chapman's play ironically imagines politics as a topic for a discussion that is emphatically *private* in nature and import: it is unofficial and of no relevance to the actual conduct of politics. In this setting, a point of state is emphatically like tobacco, another 'matter' that generates sociable exchanges across status divisions, promising inclusion and distinction based on 'the sparks of wit' rather than on title, rank, or office. It is a topic whose significance consists in creating an opportunity to practise the competitive skills of reflection and observation without the risk of a consequence: the promise of the enjoyment of pure judgement unadulterated by practical significance or interest. Such disinterestedness is, of course, ultimately an illusion: even as the inconsequential talk about matters of state suspends status distinction, it is also the means to forge distinction of a different sort in the marketplace of words, jests and fine discourse, an opportunity to excel through adept participation in the game of culture.

Debating the benefits and harms of smoking—of 'drinking' smoke, as it was sometimes called—was something of a sociable pastime around the turn of the century, with outcomes that were soon also aired in print. Thomas Dekker's satire of the world of London fashion written in the form of a manual for success, *The Gull's Hornbook*, advised the would-be gallant to go to the booksellers, suggesting that 'if you cannot reade, exercise your smoake, and inquire who has writ against this divine weede'.[30] Satirical writing like Samuel Rowland's *The Letting of Humors Blood* teems with comments on smoking, and early in 1602, *VVork for*

---

[30] Thomas Dekker, *The Gull's Hornbook*, ed. R. B. McKerrow (London: At the De La More Press, 1905) 41.

Chimny-Sweepers: or A Warning for Tabacconists took the conversation into the field of pamphleteering. A series of responses followed, all of them published in the Churchyard, making tobacco the hot (and bestselling) topic of the moment, and John Flasket, the publisher who had (as we saw in Chapter 4) recently commissioned George Chapman to write poetry for publication and a play for performance, joined the fray by putting out Sir John Beaumont's *The Metamorphosis of Tabacco*.[31] The most famous text written on tobacco in the period, the 1604 *Counterblaste to Tobacco*, King James's first work printed after his accession, is best understood as the new king's response to the quarrel in Paul's Churchyard, and his appropriation of the debate for his own purposes.[32]

The form of such a back and forth, in which the king not only felt it necessary to weigh in, but to do so with a pamphlet that remained, at least officially, anonymous until 1616, can be traced back at least to the Marprelate pamphlets of the sixteenth century. This form creates a low-stakes polemical space ironically modelled on religious controversy, a space in which the polemicist's argument, not his identity or power, was to decide, and a space which anyone could enter by addressing the topic, or even, passively, by considering oneself as addressed by it.[33] The debate about tobacco thus appears to be critical, open, disinterested, and can safely be considered non-instrumental (until and unless someone discovers it having been sponsored by some spectacularly forward-thinking future shareholder of the as yet non-existent Virginia Company). When described like this, the tobacco pamphlets and the conversation they were feeding on and giving rise to may appear to constitute a politically radical development, an anticipation of the modern public sphere, a model for the political debates of the mid-seventeenth century. The discussion about tobacco excitedly rehearsed by the eponymous character in the play provides a convenient although perhaps misleading shortcut to tobacco-lore and to this public discussion that was evolving in print and conversation in Flasket's shop and elsewhere in London, for those members of a play-going audience who never got past the title pages of the tobacco pamphlets.

---

[31] *VVork for Chimny-Sweepers: or A Warning for Tabacconists* (London: T. Este [and Thomas Creede], for Thomas Bushell, & are to be sould at the great north dore of Powles, 1602, and reprinted the same year: STC 12571 and STC 12571.5); [Roger Marbecke], *A Defence of Tabacco: vvith a Friendly Answer to the Late Printed Booke called Worke for Chimny-Sweepers, &c.* (London: Richard Field for Thomas Man, 1602); *A Nevv and Short Defense of Tabacco* (London: V[alentine] S[immes] for Clement Knight, 1602); Sir John Beaumont, *The Metamorphosis of Tabacco* (London: [Felix Kingston] for Iohn Flasket, 1602). The Stationers' Register entries show that the defences all appear in spring 1602. I would like to thank Alan Farmer for calling my attention to this series.

[32] Sandra J. Bell, '"Precious Stinke": James I's *a Counterblaste to Tobacco*', in Daniel Fischlin and Mark Fortier (eds.), *Royal Subjects: Essays on the Writings of James VI and I* (Detroit: Wayne State University Press, 2002), 323–43; Jane Rickard, *Authorship and Authority: The Writings of James VI and I* (Manchester: Manchester University Press, 2007) 120–2.

[33] For treatments of the impact of sixteenth-century polemic, see Bruster, 'The Structural Transformation of Print in Late Elizabethan England'; Jesse Lander, *Inventing Polemic: Religion, Print, and Literary Culture in Early Modern England* (Cambridge: Cambridge University Press, 2006); Andrew Hadfield, '"Not without Mustard": Self-Publicity and Polemic in Early Modern London', in Margaret Healy and Thomas Healy (eds.), *Renaissance Transformations: The Making of English Writing, 1500–1650* (Edinburgh: Edinburgh University Press, 2009).

The elaborate speech in which Monsieur d'Olive portrays this scene of sociable discussion of the state of smoke is not itself delivered in such a private setting. At the instigation of his friends, and as a way to prove his eligibility for ceremonial office, he addresses his account of this momentous debate to the highest public forum possible, to the court of the play's Duke, who rewards the extended rhetorical performance by appointing d'Olive his ambassador to France. Throughout the rest of Chapman's comedy, the subplot that features Monsieur d'Olive is concerned with the preparations for his 'great ambassage'. *Monsieur d'Olive* was written in 1604–5, directly after the completion of Chapman's first surviving French tragedy, *Bussy d'Ambois*, and thus, after his first exploration of the channels of diplomatic or para-diplomatic correspondence. Starting around 1604, when the peace treaty was signed with Spain, diplomatic activity gained a particularly high visibility in London: contemporary accounts like John Chamberlain's letters record the buzz surrounding the departing embassies. This widespread excitement is clearly reflected by Chapman's comedy, which expands Shakespeare's exploration of the connections between foreign missions and domestic success (the subject of Chapter 2 in this book) into the realm of private conversation. The endlessly expanding retinue and elaborate preparations of an embassy that never departs is a satire of the ceremonial missions that marked the restoration of England's diplomatic ties with continental states after the peace with Spain.[34] Tobacco and diplomacy are linked as two timely topics of conversation, topics that share a space and each impact the conduct of the other.

Monsieur d'Olive is of course a comic butt: the embassy is never actually meant to depart, his appointment is a practical joke that rewards an empty rhetorical performance with an empty title.[35] But in a gesture ultimately confirming the fundamental social fantasy that drives political conversation in the period, the reward for his report of a private discussion of such a 'high point of state' turns out to be more than smoke and mirrors. In the last moment, the humiliation of Monsieur d'Olive is averted by a princely promise. This well-meaning conversationalist is not only remunerated for the costs accrued in his earnest engagement in the illusory embassy, but at the end of the play, the Duke asks him not to

> let this sudden change
> Discourage the designments you have laid
> For our State's good; reserve yourself, I pray,
> Till fitter times. (5.2.121–4)

---

[34] The topical reference to the embassies departing in 1605 is crucial for the dating of the play; see Parrott (ed.), *The Plays and Poems of George Chapman: The Comedies* 773–5; A. H. Tricomi, 'The Focus of Satire and the Date of *Monsieur d'Olive*', *SEL: Studies in English Literature, 1500–1900*, 17 (1977), 281–94.

[35] John Huntington's perceptive essay compares the social logic of the play to that of *Twelfth Night*, and Monsieur d'Olive to Shakespeare's Malvolio, arguing that Chapman treats his comic hero with a genuine sense of empathy. As he points out, d'Olive is not a transgressing servant like Malvolio, who needs to twist words and letters to make them fit his ambition, because d'Olive really takes his lord's words at face value, as a loyal servant should; see John Huntington, 'Chapman's Ambitious Comedy', *English Literary Renaissance*, 43 (2013), 128–52.

So while in Chapman's comedy, political competence, an ability to impress by speaking well about random political matters, might be exercised and relished in private conversation among other forms of sociable one-upmanship, the wit, the rhetorical skill honed in such settings also holds the promise of political advancement, of employment: of being convertible to something that actually matters. Political topics appear as having an amphibious nature: while their exchange and enjoyment shows them comfortably at home among other subjects of sociable conversation, their importance to political careers also bestows a different sort of significance upon them.

Mark Netzloff has suggested that the variegated list of the participants in the conventicle exemplifies a proto-Habermasian setting, a commonwealth of sorts, allowing us to align Chapman's comedic account of amphibious politic talk with Habermas's normative model of the bourgeois public sphere. As in the Habermasian model of the bourgeois public sphere, where private people are putting reason to use in their arguments about matters of common concern, Monsieur d'Olive's conventicle gathers together those excluded (or excluding themselves) from public affairs.[36] While the social mixture allows us to describe this gathering of 'all sorts of men' as one that came together without regard for status, calling the gathering a 'conventicle' also makes a gesture at its political potential: in a setting where the most powerful model for public argument was confessional controversy, the term playfully describes the meeting as confessionally defined, and dissident in nature. Milton of course compared unlicensed pamphleteering to such religious gatherings in *Areopagitica*, when he warned that 'To startle thus betimes at a meer unlicenc't pamphlet will after a while be afraid of every conventicle, and a while after will make a conventicle of every Christian meeting.'[37] Counterpublics—in early seventeenth-century terms, the coming together of private individuals around issues that appeared to be seeking to elude or oppose the control of civil and church government—were repeatedly described as conventicles. In the 1630s, meetings at Gresham College—which have even been described as 'unique in providing a true public sphere' in pre-civil war London—were persecuted by an anxious Archbishop Laud as conventicles.[38] Such associations invite us to imagine the play's conventicle perhaps not an embryonic version of the Habermasian ideal, the sphere understood to be that of a general public, but rather, as a political counterpublic.[39]

---

[36] Mark Netzloff, 'Public Diplomacy and the Comedy of State: Chapman's *Monsieur d'Olive*', in Jason Powell and Will Rossiter (eds.), *Authority and Diplomacy from Dante to Shakespeare* (Burlington, VT: Ashgate, 2013), 185–97. I would like to thank Mark Netzloff for sharing with me his essay in manuscript.

[37] Don M. Wolfe (ed.), *Complete Prose Works of John Milton* (New Haven: Yale University Press, 1959) 2:541.

[38] Mordechai Feingold, 'Gresham College and London Practitioners: The Nature of the English Mathematical Community', in Francis Ames-Lewis (ed.), *Sir Thomas Gresham and Gresham College: Studies in the Intellectual History of London in the Sixteenth and Seventeenth Centuries* (Aldershot: Ashgate, 1999), 174–88 at 185.

[39] As Thomas Fuller noted, although the word 'conventicle' meant 'nothing else but a small Convention' it came to 'denote the meeting of such (how many soever) in a clandestine way, contrary to the commands of the present lawfull Authority'. *The Church-history of Britain* (London: for Iohn Williams, 1655), sig. 3N1v. Fuller's account also indicates that such a use of the word was already available in the late sixteenth century.

This counterpublic, however, is not defined by its concern for the common good, and its logic is neither critical nor indeed political in the strong sense. As the play makes it clear, d'Olive's self-imposed exile from court, his enjoyment of the sociable company of wits, is to be understood as a waste of his talents, an ineffectual substitute for the deployment of his wit in its proper arena, the ducal court: the d'Olive plot is in fact a stratagem to trick Monsieur d'Olive back to the sphere he truly belongs, to the arena Habermas terms the sphere of 'the representative publicness' of the court, distinct from, and ultimately supplanted by, the modern (bourgeois) public sphere. For Chapman, the discussion of private individuals is not yet a dignified, even less an authoritative alternative to the court public, and it cannot serve as the basis or location of political action. In Chapman's play, political conversation is not a civic-minded critique of the state, as in Habermas, but a pleasurable activity whose only actual interference with the realm of politics is the playful and symbolic recognition of the monarch. By no means opposed to or even critically distanced from the court, this conversation only assumes even this playfully evanescent political authority when it is invoked before the only public that actually matters: the court.

The function of a conversation about politics and tobacco is the production of cultural capital, not political authority. Whatever constitution might be chosen by d'Olive's 'private conventicle' as the best one for smokers, it makes no difference to the government of any actual state, nor is it intended to. What the conventicle does is create a sociable setting where anything from politics to tobacco can be discussed, and where one's argumentative skills can be demonstrated in a hypothetical argument about such an unlikely combination of topics. For the purposes of such sociable performance of wit, the difference between tobacco and politics is immaterial—as are the very topics themselves. Conversation about politics here is not a political activity, but part of the game of culture in which field-specific competence originating in a professional setting is converted into more fluid cultural capital. The endlessly deferred promise of the conversion of such capital into some form of social advancement hovers over this scene in the form of d'Olive's illusory embassy. Through this link, the play marks the idea that this conversion might take the form of preferment in political employment as a naive illusion, and reminds its audiences that the nature of political competence as a form of cultural capital is precisely that the advancement, if it ever happens, comes in the form of recognition of one's peers. Mistaking one's gains in the game of culture for assets in a professional career is a grave error gently corrected in Chapman's play. Others were not so forgiving.

VOLPONE AND THE FOOL'S PROFESSION

The most famous of all would-be politicians is Sir Politic Would-be, Ben Jonson's extended caricature in *Volpone*, and the subplot revolving around this figure is among the best examples of the use of knowledge claims in the control of social aspiration. The play is, among other things, Jonson's satire of the legal and medical professions as knowledge-based practices open to fraudulent use. Volpone's game of promising and deferring inheritance revolves around the legal instrument of the will, and the elaborate court proceedings of the play's *denouement* are predicated upon the performance of Voltore, the corrupt, self-serving legal attorney that bedazzles the group of *avvocatori*. Medicine makes its contribution in the form of the ointments Volpone uses as a make-up to feign illness rather than to cure one. Volpone also approaches Celia as a mountebank, setting up his stage to sell his cure-all 'blessed *unguento*' (2.2.82) directly under her window. Having witnessed her beauty, he then has Mosca claim to her husband that 'the College of Physicians' have prescribed a therapy for Volpone where 'some young woman must be straight sought out, / Lusty and full of juice, to sleep by him' (2.6.27, 34–5), and the jealous Corvino immediately offers Celia for the job. Medicine also joins the law in Volpone's court sentence, according to which his wealth shall

> all be straight confiscate
> To the hospital of the *Incurabili*;
> And since the most was gotten by imposture,
> By feigning lame, gout, palsy, and such diseases,
> Thou art to lie in prison, cramped with irons,
> Till thou be'st sick and lame indeed. (5.12.119–24)

In this play whose world is defined by the well-established, powerful, frighteningly corrupt learned professions whose only utility appears to be destruction (making the dedication to 'the two famous universities' double-edged, to say the least), Sir Pol appears as a hapless gull aspiring for membership in the emerging non-academically defined profession of the career politician. He appears well-versed in the art of travel, he seeks out fresh intelligence, and reads politic authors, mimicking the trajectories of the young and ambitious English gentlemen of the period that we traced in the first three chapters of this book—but his professional formation is of course hampered by the preposterous nature of the information he gathers and of the texts he reads, transmits, and produces. In a move that he will repeat and elaborate on in the *The Staple of News*, where he takes on the producers of the news business, Jonson here discredits the political newsgathering of the outsider by exposing it as reliant on and contaminated by the commercial and public circulation of information, which he represents as sensationalistic, unreliable gossip. So Sir Pol's most precious political intelligence concerns a whale sent by the Archdukes up the Thames to spy on the English fleet, and he claims to have heard about *relazioni* made by baboons returning from their mission in Europe to their 'subtle nation, near to China' (2.1.44–97).

This focus on professional knowledge also defines the play's perspective on Sir Pol's meddling in politics. His transgression is his unfounded pretence to knowledge and the proclaimed use he wants to put it to. That he is a busybody trading in absurd conspiracy theories makes him an exemplary manifestation of human folly—as his befuddled interlocutor Peregrine immediately realizes, Sir Pol

>   would be a precious thing
> To fit our English stage. He that should write
> But such a fellow should be thought to feign
> Extremely, if not maliciously. (2.1.57–60)

Although Sir Pol claims to be drawing his advice on foreign travel and diplomacy from 'Nick Machiavel and Monsieur Bodin' (4.1.26), his 'politic notes' are about such high points of state as bursting a toothpick during 'a discourse / With a Dutch merchant 'bout *ragion' del stato*', and conclude with the momentous fact that 'at St Mark's I urined' (4.1.139–41, 144). What proves this amateur politician deserving of punishment is his pretence that he can convert his insights into a reward or advancement of some sort. He whips up fantastic theories and projects—also meddling in medicine when he proposes to use onions to draw the plague infection from ships destined for quarantine, for example—and hopes to advance by obtaining a pension from the Great Council in return for proposing such 'goods unto the state of Venice, / Which I do call my "Cautions"' (4.1.71–2). Sir Pol misrepresents his competence, and as a sort of quack-Machiavel, he pretends to an effective, professional competence in affairs of state in spite of the fact that he has no access to the true *arcana imperii*. Recognizing Sir Pol for what he is, Peregrine humiliates him by making his pretences seem real. He advises Sir Pol that he is for once taken very seriously by the Senate, as one plotting 'to sell the state of Venice to the Turk' (5.4.38), and is to be put to the rack for this conspiracy. In his desperate panic, Sir Pol admits his dangerous papers to be nothing but 'notes / Drawn out of playbooks…And some essays' (5.4.41–3), and attempts to hide by climbing into the shell of a giant tortoise.

It might be worth observing that Peregrine decides to give Sir Pol a lesson in the true nature of political conspiracy because he assumes that Sir Pol is not just a cuckold, but a bawd whose true trade is to make unwitting victims like himself 'acquainted with his wife' (4.3.20–1)—which is not in fact the case. But what could be a more deliciously appropriate comic punishment for Sir Pol's pretended knowledge of political conspiracies than being erroneously suspected of a scheme of prostitution and thus winding up a collateral victim of a comic conspiracy he is not even aware of?

By making an aspiring character the butt of the joke, Jonson's satire clearly encourages members of its public to congratulate themselves for knowing the difference between the expert political advisor and the barbershop politico, and to align themselves with the former rather than the latter. But risking that I am stating the obvious, let me also add: the realms of the layperson's knowledge and professional expertise only need to be kept apart by satire because political conversation among laypeople is always predicated upon the tacit assumption that we could perhaps do this, and do this better. This is the assumption that makes one's ability to discuss political topics such an effective form of cultural capital. In the absence of institutional forms of certification—of academic degrees, doctorates, bar exams, formal procedures of licensing and ascertaining mastery—political competence is more open to being challenged or claimed by members of the general public, by private, non-professional individuals, than medical or legal knowledge. Political conversation and chatting about legal matters differ, partly, in that the latter is never meant to establish one's professional credentials—whereas in certain situations, the former in fact might. The lack of a fully formalized and institutionalized system of attestation means, on the one hand, that no matter how familiar one might be with affairs of state, one cannot claim to be a member of the profession until and unless one finds employment in political work. On the other hand, the absence of such a system of admission to the profession can also be used to imply that one's entry into it is imminent, and only a matter of not yet having made the right connections. This theoretical possibility invests competent participation in political conversation with social prestige and significance, and allows it to command attention and admiration in sociable interaction. The curious fact about political competence as a form of cultural capital is that it is inseparable and, in terms of its content, effectively indistinguishable from the professional knowledge associated with political careers.

The satiric strategy of Jonson's *Volpone* does not finally deny the possibility of laypeople acquiring a quasi-professional political expertise—it depends on it. When the play presents Sir Pol as trading in manifestly bogus intelligence, as someone who really has no idea what he is talking about, it relies on the quality and sources of his supposed knowledge to mark Sir Pol's way of talking politics as illegitimate, and Sir Pol a harmless con whose comic downfall is carefully aligned with the much more sinister exposure of Volpone's fraudulence. The wonderful effectiveness of this satire of the would-be politician is thus based on the equation of the incompetent with the illegitimate—an equation that allows, indeed encourages the fantasy that true, well-grounded political knowledge, political knowledge derived from the right sources rather than from playbooks and essays, might after all become the grounds for advising the state of Venice profitably.

The emphatic use of playbooks as markers of illegitimate, fraudulent knowledge is a striking, apparently self-defeating move on Jonson's part. His repeated targeting, in several plays, of the use of playbooks as sources of cultural capital—as manuals of conversation, as substitutes for political or historical learning—is a facet of his efforts to define the place of commercial drama in the culture of his moment, and indicative of the growing importance of plays and playbooks in contemporary culture. Gabriel Harvey's habits of reading were not yet influenced by this cultural transformation. He was contemplating *Hamlet* alongside *Lucrece* as appropriate for the 'wiser sort', partly because his academic education made him approach English playbooks on the model of classical texts, and partly because of the simple fact that his formation took place at an earlier moment, before the public stage would have emerged, around 1600, as an arbiter of contemporary culture.

Jonson was not only a witness to that transformation, but also an active participant in it. His sarcastic on-stage reflections on the uses of playbooks as sources of knowledge as well as of compelling expressions and of compliments are part of his effort to establish his theatre as a theatre of judgement: his plays critically judge social and cultural issues and competences, and also ask to be judged critically and with understanding. The authority of this theatre is derived from its ability to make distinctions, and to claim such distinction-making as its exclusive and specialized function. As we saw in the first chapter of this book, Gabriel Harvey invoked political judgement as a sovereign competence operative in the reading of drama. For him, the reading of sententious passages must begin with the question: is this a political or a philosophical insight?—a question that he understood to be political in nature. Jonson's emphasis is elsewhere: whatever the subject, he wants drama to be a challenge to judgement, not a substitute for it in the form of ready-made judgements. Our language and knowledge is all borrowed, of course—*Timber* is the evidence of Jonson's own habit of borrowing: what he seeks to establish is the distinction between mechanical, unthinking borrowing, and discerning, considered appropriation. Plays are not inert heaps of materials to be judged and used—they are models for judgement, they are to be judged for the judgements they perform.

But who is to tell whether the judgement is indeed competent, whether the choices are indeed the right ones? Satirical comedy judges incompetence without at the same time claiming professional competence. In Jonson's comedies, the right use of medicine, of the law, of political knowledge, or of alchemy only make appearances in concluding acts of poetic justice, if at all. It is the frauds, the gulls, the oafish pretenders to discernment who get the plays' attention, that is, the attention of the gallants, wits, and satirists who, in turn, vie for our attention as self-appointed models of judgement. In this economy, cultural competence is established through judging others' performance, through considering their failures from the apparently disinterested perspective of taste. Adam Zucker has shown how Jonsonian wits, on-stage arbiters of social and cultural competence, bracket the economic underpinnings and social advantages of their discernment, positing it as disinterested attention, governed by taste that is abstracted form the world of practical concerns, which he identifies with the economic.[40] Elaborating on this Bourdieusian analysis, we should add that like Jonson himself, Jonsonian on-stage wits and satirists also strive to keep a distance from interfering with professional values and identities. Peregrine's revenge upon Sir Pol punishes his pretence of political competence, but it is performed by someone who carefully avoids claiming such a competence himself. Sir Pol's humiliation is not a professional examination, but a practical joke that forces him to expose himself.

The authority of the wit and the dramatist regulates the social uses of knowledge—the human, ethical, cultural underpinnings of how knowledge is deployed in society—rather than presuming to regulate knowledge itself. This is the distinction that affords drama, and the social use of wit that is modelled on it, a distinct identity, allowing it to pose as a meta-competence over competences. At the same time, and just as importantly, this distinction guarantees that for the purposes of the sociable and agonistic use of wit, politics and gastronomy, diplomacy and the enjoyment of tobacco are all alike as objects of comment, critique, and judgement, gambits in the game of culture. It is a distinction between professional authority and an authority in matters of conduct, civility: of culture in this narrow sense, reflective of the sense of the sudden emergence of the stage as a central institution

---

[40] See the reading of *Epicoene* in Zucker, *The Places of Wit* 58–72.

of the distribution and exchange of cultural capital. Copying professional knowledge out of playbooks is therefore an obvious mistake—and so is the obvious copying of anything else: success at the game of culture presupposes the ability of making it seem natural, effortless. But making it seem effortless is itself an effort, the work of copying, practice, appropriation, and assimilation.

READING PLAYS FOR DISCOURSE'S SAKE

Sir Pol's farcical admission in *Volpone* that his politic notes were taken from playbooks, or the confident claim of Fitzdottrel (the character in *The Devil Is an Ass* so obsessed with the theatre that he willingly mistakes it for life) that playbooks are 'more authentic' sources of genealogical information than the chronicles,[41] are particularly striking for their identification of playbooks as a medium through which knowledge circulates, as well as for their association of incompetent characters with a naive reliance on playhouse or playbook substitutes for the real deal. This is a mistake, however, that was rarely made: like the story of the Southern yokel jumping on stage to rescue Desdemona from the embraces of the Moor, it is a misunderstanding whose preposterousness is used to ridicule another, more vital transgression—as the confusion of theatrical illusion with reality is used by the anecdote to label Jim Crow racism as boorish, so the confusion of playbooks with political literature identifies the aspirations of uninitiated outsiders as gullibility.[42]

Satire should not be mistaken for realism: it reveals the rules of the game by representing striking transgressions, not routine performance. Along with other forms of contemporary reflection and commentary on the use of plays and playbooks, it provides us with the terms in which the links between dramatic texts and political conversation were understood in the early seventeenth century. The evidence from the traces of reading and note-taking—a kind of evidence we have been returning to over the course of this book—may not only confirm and flesh out, but on occasion also revise and reorient our sense of the significance of such literary representations.

The case of the reader who relied on Shakespeare's *Hamlet* in his attempt to clarify the confusing state of the Russian succession,[43] or of John Melton, who—as we discussed in Chapter 3—drew on the same play as he was articulating the task of the serious statesman, offer glimpses of the uses of playtexts in political discussion and writing.[44] Political tragedies were obviously shaping and transforming

---

[41] Jonson (2012) 4:525, 2.4.12–14.
[42] The anecdote is used by Stanley Cavell, *Disowning Knowledge in Seven Plays of Shakespeare* (Updated edn.; Cambridge: Cambridge University Press, 2003) 98ff. Not all such instances of the temporary confusion of, or simultaneous experience of a scene as reality and representation, are necessarily damning, of course. For two beautiful examples, see Lawrence W. Levine, *Highbrow/Lowbrow: The Emergence of Cultural Hierarchy in America* (Cambridge, MA: Harvard University Press, 1988) 30 and note.
[43] de Grazia, Hamlet *without Hamlet* 48; Scott, *The Model of Poesy* xxi–xxv.
[44] William Drake's serious political note-taking from *Sejanus* was probably encouraged by its appearance as a piece of historiography rather than as a play. Another reader copied a whole series of

their audiences' understanding of the realm of politics. The fact that most of us don't take notes when watching *House of Cards*, and only very occasionally come across copies of spy novels in which the aphoristic remarks about the sinister operations of secret services and about the modern bureaucratic state in general are as carefully underlined as in the copy of *Tinker, Tailor, Soldier, Spy* I picked up two decades ago in a second-hand bookshop, doesn't mean that our understanding of Whitehall and Washington politics, of MI6 and the CIA are not fundamentally shaped by such fictional works. But the lines marked in Le Carré were sardonic remarks you wish you could make at a dinner party, not statements to be used in a job interview or in a history of the secret service. The early modern stage did not merely disseminate political knowledge, or the feel of it: plays also contributed to the transformation and re-functioning of such knowledge, to its adaptation to the needs and circumstances of non-professional observers. Drama contributed to the aestheticization of pieces of prudential insight into instances of verbal ingenuity. By revising complex aphorisms into sharp, pointed statements, and thus assimilating them to the pointed style of satirical comedy and to the witty observations these plays were showcasing as models for urbane conversation, these plays were transforming professional political knowledge into the substance of sophisticated conversation, modelling its uses in social—whether competitive or sociable—interactions. And as plays were offering themselves as conversation manuals, and offering political knowledge as matter and form with which to spice up one's conversation, they were also changing the way people were reading and using historical and political publications, encouraging them to read texts intended as repositories of professional or scholarly knowledge, or as interventions in the field of public political debate, not for their original purpose, but for conversational ammunition, for exemplary or imitable bits of linguistic currency.

Having started this book by pondering an academic's reading of *Hamlet*, I will conclude it with a look at a non-academic theatre-goer–playreader's notes taken from *Hamlet* and other plays contemporary with it, thus concluding the trajectory of political knowledge I have been tracing here from professional education to sociable conversation. The notebook of Edward Pudsey (1572–1613), a rather obscure gentleman from Gloucestershire, consists of about ninety leaves, a densely written collection of lines and phrases copied from a wide range of books.[45]

'Machiavellian' remarks from *1 Henry IV* in his notebook: see Hilton Kelliher, 'Contemporary Manuscript Extracts from Shakespeare's *Henry IV, Part 1*', *English Manuscript Studies 1100–1700*, 1 (1989), 144–81, and Doty, 'Shakespeare's *Richard II*, "Popularity," and the Early Modern Public Sphere', 183–5.

[45] Pudsey's notebook is now at the Bodleian Library: that four of its leaves, with passages from Shakespeare's plays, have been removed from it and are now at the Birthplace Trust, in Stratford-upon-Avon, is emblematic of the kind of attention the notebook has received in scholarship. The manuscript is Bodleian MS Eng. Poet. d.3. The missing leaves are in the archives of the Birthplace, SBTRO ER 82/1/21, among Richard Savage's papers. I will be citing these MSS parenthetically, as Bodleian and Stratford.

It seems that Savage, the secretary and librarian of the Birthplace in the late nineteenth century who published the Shakespeare extracts in the notebook, simply held on to the four leaves when the MS was sold by his 'friend' who originally owned it to James Orchard Halliwell-Phillipps around 1888. The manuscript was acquired by the Bodleian in 1889, and, as the correspondence inserted at the end

Pudsey's reading is secular and predominantly political in nature: a selection of works of political philosophy and 'politic history' supplemented by books of English essayists (including Bacon's *Essays*) and other texts of worldly, politic wisdom. He read Tacitus and Livy, Commynes and Guicciardini, Machiavelli and Gentillet's *Anti-Machiavel*, More's *Utopia* and Castiglione's *Courtier*—the familiar canon of pragmatically and politically oriented vernacular humanism.

Pudsey's claim to fame among scholars resides in the section of his notebook which contains extracts from twenty-six plays performed around the turn of the century. This set of notes amounts to the most extensive set of such dramatic extracts surviving from before the mid-seventeenth century, when collections of quotations from plays began to be created commercially—the title of John Cotgrave's *The English Treasury of Wit and Language Collected out of the Most, and Best of Our English Drammatick Poems; Methodically Digested into Common Places for Generall Use* (1655) may epitomize a whole genre of compilations and miscellanies consisting partly, and on occasion exclusively, of dramatic quotations.[46] Professionally produced collections, like the massive mid-seventeenth-century commonplace project called *Hesperides*,[47] sought to capitalize on an evident demand, and they were building on the common practice of note-taking. Pudsey's book is a fascinating early example of this culture and of the interests of the audiences of the London stage of Hamlet's moment.

Most of the plays he excerpts were published around 1600–2 (perhaps reflecting a visit to the city around that time, followed by occasional purchases of further playbooks until his death), but he can't be accused of being random in his selection. He really liked the plays of William Shakespeare, and he also sought out the satirical plays of the 'poetomachia', the 'war of the theatres', a war waged with the weapons of self-conscious theatrical satire and verbal artifice. Pudsey's book includes notes of every single play printed before 1610 that was associated by modern critics with the *poetomachia*, as well as seven plays by Shakespeare—and almost no other plays, even though there were about thirty more printed in the same three-year period, some in more than one edition.[48] He read Jonson's *Every Man*

---

of the MS volume suggests, the library made every effort to recover the leaves that were still part of the MS when Savage published his extracts. Savage claimed he had passed on all the loose leaves to Halliwell-Phillipps—yet they are still at the collection he was in charge of at the time. See the letters at ff. 90–103 of the MS, and Richard Savage (ed.), *Shakespearean Extracts from 'Edward Pudsey's Booke'* (Stratford-Upon-Avon Notebooks No. 1, Stratford-upon-Avon: John Smith, 1887). For valuable recent discussions, see Jean-Christophe Mayer, 'Les Spectateurs de Shakespeare: à la Découverte des Lettres et Carnets de Ses Contemporains', in Patricia Dorval (ed.), *Shakespeare et Ses Contemporains* (Paris: Société Française Shakespeare, 2003), 143–59; Juliet Gowan, '"One Man in His Time": The Notebook of Edward Pudsey', *Bodleian Library Record*, 22/1 (2009), 94–101; Fred Schurink, 'Manuscript Commonplace Books, Literature, and Reading in Early Modern England', *Huntington Library Quarterly*, 73 (2010), 453–69; Katherine Duncan-Jones, *Shakespeare: Upstart Crow to Sweet Swan, 1592–1623* (London: Arden Shakespeare, 2011) 72–83.

[46] See Adam Smyth, '*Profit and Delight*': *Printed Miscellanies in England, 1640–1682* (Detroit: Wayne State University Press, 2004) for a study of these seventeenth-century publications.

[47] Gunnar Sorelius, 'An Unknown Shakespearian Commonplace Book', *The Library 5th ser.*, 28 (1973), 294–308; Hao Tianhu, '*Hesperides, or the Muses' Garden* and Its Manuscript History', *The Library 7th ser.*, 10 (2009), 372–404.

[48] Dekker's *Honest Whore* and the anonymous *How a Man May Choose a Good Wife from a Bad* (frequently attributed to Heywood) are the only other plays. Notes from *The Atheist's Tragedy* and

In and *Every Man Out*, *Cynthia's Revels*, *The Case Is Altered*, and *Poetaster*, Marston's *Jack Drum*, *Antonio 1–2*, and *What You Will*, Dekker's *Satiromastix*, as well as Shakespeare's *Hamlet*, a play that also reflects on the stage quarrel through its reference to the success of the boys' companies, the 'little eyases', as a reason for players' visit to Elsinore.[49] In addition, Pudsey read further satirical comedies from the same couple of years, like Dekker's *Blurt Master Constable* or Chapman's *Blind Beggar*, as well as two comedies by Lyly (older plays in the boys' companies' repertory that featured centrally in the war of the theatres), and Nashe's *Summer's Last Will*, which appears not among the plays but among other writings by Nashe, the writer who did more than anyone except the Marprelate authors themselves to establish the intensely personal satirical mode of 'embodied writing' of which the *poetomachia* became the stage manifestation.[50]

This satiric back-and-forth among plays featuring on-stage caricatures of rival playwrights and their writing styles has been described as a commercially driven conflict between competing company repertories, as an intensely personal affair of name-calling which served to establish and distinguish individual dramatists' voices, styles, and reputations, but also as a debate about the proper function of satire, 'the most complex and thorough transaction of dramatic criticism in the English Renaissance', a literary debate that allowed a group of playwrights to articulate and test their conflicting aesthetic visions.[51] Whatever the motives and intentions behind the production of these often intensely personal satiric reflections, the *poetomachia* resulted in a set of plays deeply concerned with the decorum of satire and with linguistic decorum in general, helping to confirm the theatre as an arena of judgement and sophistication, an arena in which the exposure of excess and incompetence, the display of wit and discrimination, not only reflected but also produced cultural distinction as an emergent marker of status.

Much to the disappointment of the theatre historian, Pudsey's notes from these plays do not appear to register their implicatedness in what critics usually perceive as the true object of the 'war of the theatres'—in fact, it seems that 'Pudsey intentionally avoided all the fleers about poets and poetry',[52] and even adapted some references to players and poets to make them available for more general

---

Webster's *White Devil* are in a different hand—whether taken by an amanuensis or by the nephew inheriting Pudsey's notebooks and continuing his work is impossible to tell. These are also plays published in 1611 and 1612, respectively, that is, very shortly before Pudsey's death. For the other plays printed in these years, see *DEEP: Database of Early English Playbooks*, ed. Alan B. Farmer and Zachary Lesser. Created 2007. Accessed 30 April 2013. http://deep.sas.upenn.edu.

[49] My list follows the reconstruction of the *poetomachia* in Bednarz, *Shakespeare & the Poets' War*. Pudsey's focus on the *poetomachia* has been noted by Gowan, who, following a different account, says 'Of the seven plays in the quarrel, Pudsey quotes from five.' The two plays omitted from this more narrowly defined corpus would presumably be *Histriomastix* (printed 1610) and perhaps *What You Will*, present in the MS but in a different hand; see Juliet Mary Gowan, 'An Edition of Edward Pudsey's Commonplace Book (*c.*1600–1615) from the Manuscript in the Bodleian Library', M. Phil. thesis (University of London, 1967) 69.

[50] Bruster, 'The Structural Transformation of Print in Late Elizabethan England'.

[51] Bednarz, *Shakespeare & the Poets' War* 4. Cp. Alfred Harbage, *Shakespeare and the Rival Traditions* (New York: Macmillan, 1952); Bevington, *Tudor Drama and Politics* 260–88; Roslyn L. Knutson, *Playing Companies and Commerce in Shakespeare's Time* (Cambridge: Cambridge University Press, 2001) 75–146.

[52] Knutson, *Playing Companies and Commerce in Shakespeare's Time* 144.

application. So the lines spoken by the figure of Envy in the Induction to *Poetaster*, 'Are there no players here? No poet-apes, / That come with basilisks' eyes, whose forked tongues / Are steeped in venom, as their hearts in gall?'[53] become 'The envyous have Basiliske eys & forked tonges steept in venom as their harts in gall' (Bodleian 41v). Although Pudsey may have been interested in the personal, personated, embodied aspect of the satire, what he recorded was the language he could repurpose, not its specific local import. He copies the commonplace: sententious lines and couplets the period considered as valuable assets in conversation and composition, lines to be used to embellish or prop up an argument. From *Romeo and Juliet*, he lifts the couplet '*Loue goes toward loue as schoole boyes from their bookes / But Loue from Loue towards schoole with heauy Lookes*' (Bodleian 86v), from *Hamlet*, he copies long passages from Polonius's advice to Laertes (Stratford 2v), and from Jonson's *Every Man Out*, he takes this misogynistic gem: 'offer no Louerites but let wyves still seek theim / For when they come vnsought, they seldom lyke theim' (Bodleian 39v). Pudsey is reading his plays for bons mots—his note-taking is not driven by a recognizable moral or intellectual purpose, or even by an aim to prepare him for future written composition. His interest seems to be in brevity and style—in pointed, aphoristic utterances that seem to be chosen for their formal or linguistic interest: he copies the good words.[54] Auden noted that Oscar Wilde's way of writing was 'to subordinate every other dramatic element to dialogue for its own sake and create a verbal universe in which the characters are determined by the kinds of things they say, and the plot nothing but a succession of opportunities to say them.'[55] Pudsey would have been Wilde's ideal reader.

Dramatic dialogue shows wit in action, modelling conversational brilliance—which poses special difficulties for note-taking. Pudsey occasionally combines lines of a witty dialogue into a single utterance, as for example in the case of this note taken from *Othello*: 'Dangerous to tell where a soldier lyes. yf I should say he lodge theer I lyed ther', a distillation of the first dozen lines of dialogue between Desdemona and the Clown in 3.4,[56] but he is frequently drawn to characters' readily and extractably striking way with words, to exemplary instances of verbal perspicacity, of sharp and original repartee. Reading *Much Ado*, he copies 'we will spare for no wit I warrant you', Dogberry's response to the exhortation 'do it wisely'. Pudsey's focus is on the words, and he is not in the least troubled by the fact that they are spoken by the play's bumbling constable, whose name has become synonymous with comic ineptitude; it is not his character but his lines that he is

---

[53] Jonson (2012) 2:27, ll. 35–7.
[54] One can therefore only claim in a rather general sense that 'Pudsey read published plays as if they were classical texts, studded with bon mots and improving sentiments.' Although he was deploying the technology of the notebook, Pudsey was not at all exercised by the ideology of identifying linguistic with moral excellence associated with the reading of the classics. Cp. Lena Cowen Orlin, 'The Private Lives of Public Plays', in Richard Fotheringham, Christa Jansohn, and R. S. White (eds.), *Shakespeare's World/World Shakespeare* (Madison: Fairleigh Dickinson University Press, 2008), 140–50 at 142.
[55] W. H. Auden, *Forewords and Afterwords*, ed. Edward Mendelson (New York: Random House, 1973) 322–3.
[56] Stratford 1r, printed in E. A. J. Honigmann (ed.), *Othello* (The Arden Shakespeare, Third Series, Walton-on-Thames: Thomas Nelson & Sons, 1997) 388–9.

drawn to, finding them as remarkable as Benedict's response to Beatrice's 'Will yow not eat your woard. *Res.* with no sause that can be deuised to it' (Stratford 1v). From *Hamlet*, he copies Hamlet's reply to Polonius: 'Ile take my leaue. *Respon.* Yow cannot take from me any thing that I will not more willingly part withall except my life', as well as his response to Ophelia: 'Yow are keen my L. *respon.* yt wil cost yow a groaning to take of my edge' (Stratford 2r, v).

Pudsey's eagerness for misogynous *double entendre* and sexual innuendo, his interest in witty responses (in the obvious paradox of the commonplace genre, this is an interest in models for improvisation, in templates for thinking on one's feet), is combined with an attention to apt, surprising, or novel words and phrases— Jonson's *Every Man In* yields 'Wriggle into acquaintance', 'dearth of Iudgmt' as well as 'inimitable' (Bodleian 41r), and on the verso of the same leaf, among his notes from John Marston's two Antonio plays, we find such formulations as 'a smart speaking ey', 'Keele your mouth it runs ouer', and such words as 'lyfen it' and 'exist'—it may seem surprising, but the sentence from which he takes the latter: '… most things that morally adhere to soules, / Wholly exist in drunke opinion' is the *OED*'s first recorded use of the verb.[57]

From sentences through phrases to individual words, Pudsey's notes record the verbal innovations traded on the early modern stage. The period considered and used the stage as a linguistic marketplace, an exchange of linguistic capital.[58] Satirists often remarked upon this: in his satires published in 1599, Marston lampooned the oafish character whose amorous talk is 'naught but pure Juliat and Romio', because he has 'made a common-place booke out of plaies, / And speakes in print, at least what ere he sayes / Is warranted by Curtaine plaudit[e]s,... / He writes, he railes, he jests, he courts, what not, / And all from out his huge long scraped stock / Of well penn'd playes.'[59] In a satiric vein, Dekker advised the addressee of his *Gull's Hornbook*, to

> hoard up the finest play-scraps you can get, upon which your lean wit may most savorly feed for want of other stuff, when the Arcadian and Euphuired gentlewomen have their tongues sharpened to set upon you. That quality (next to your shuttlecock) is the only furniture to a courtier that's but a new beginner, and is but in his ABC of compliment.[60]

Satirical comments register the practice of accumulating linguistic capital at the theatre, and in doing so, are themselves moves in the game of distinction: by inviting the reader to join the author in sneering at the linguistically less endowed trying to make up for their disadvantage, they establish a cultural high ground of confidence in distinction. Stage characters who proclaim that they woo 'with compliments drawn from the plays I see at the Fortune and Red Bull, where I learn all

---

[57] OED s.v. *exist*, Bodleian 41v.
[58] On newly coined words as a commodity in the 'knowledge marketplace' of the theatre, see Robert N. Watson, 'Coining Words on the Elizabethan and Jacobean Stage', *Philological Quarterly*, 88 (2009), 49–75, and 'Shakespeare's New Words', *Shakespeare Survey*, 65 (2012), 358–77.
[59] John Marston, *The Scourge of Villanie: Three bookes of satyres* (London: I[ames] R[oberts] and are to be sold by Iohn Buzbie, 1598) H4r.
[60] Dekker, *The Gull's Hornbook* 32.

the words I speak and understand not'[61] reassure readers and play-goers of their own superior wit.

The authors and plays involved in 'the war of theatres' were particularly preoccupied with the role of the theatre as 'the *Mint* that daily coyns new *words*',[62] and—reflecting on their function as a cultural institution—with the circulation and distribution of linguistic capital more generally. One of the most memorable moments of the *poetomachia* is the scene in Jonson's *Poetaster* in which Crispinus, the character clearly representing Marston, is purged with the help of a pill, making him vomit dozens of newly coined, indigestible words into a basin—novelties which have since either become familiar, or disappeared without any other trace than this play. Crispinus throws up 'retrograde', 'reciprocal', 'incubus', 'glibbery', 'lubrical', 'defunct', 'magnificate', 'spurious', 'snotteries', 'chilblained', 'clumsy', 'barmy froth', 'puffy', 'inflate', 'turgidous', 'ventosity', and several others, amidst the commentary of the Horace, Gallus, Tibullus, and Caesar who administered the medication.[63]

The first quarto of Shakespeare's *Hamlet* contains a passage about play-goers taking down the punchlines of the jokes spoken by the clown, and ruining his performance by showing off their stolen wit. The traffic in individual words is also thematized: when the First Player comes to Hecuba, and exclaims 'But who—ah, woe!—had seen the mobbled queen', Hamlet seems to be struck by the word and Polonius expresses approval:

>HAMLET: The mobbled queen?
>POLONIUS: That's good: mobbled queen is good.

We will never quite recover how to read this moment (does Hamlet find this a particularly apt phrase, is he baffled by an unfamiliar, inappropriate or dated expression, or is he suddenly reminded of his own queen and mother?)—but picking up or relishing new words in these plays is usually a clear sign of the character's exclusion from the community of wit and of fashionable conversation. Marston may have been indecorously given to coining and picking up new words, but he took as much pleasure in pinpointing their abuse as Jonson. Balurdo, the notorious malaprop of the Antonio plays, is someone who stops mid-sentence to savour his own eloquence in speaking banalities: '...love, the nigher it is to the flame, the more remote—there's a word, "remote"—the more remote it is from the frost' (5.2.133–5). He is a character memorable for his uncomprehending aping of verbal sophistication, and is characterized in the play's Induction as 'one whose foppish nature might seem great only for wise men's recreation...a servile hound

---

[61] Thomas Tomkis, *Albumazar: A Comedy presented before the Kings Maiestie at Cambridge, the ninth of March, 1614* (London: Nicholas Okes for Walter Burre, 1615) 2.1.
[62] Richard Flecknoe, *Miscellania* (1653) 103–4, quoted by Tiffany Stern, *Making Shakespeare: From Stage to Page* (London: Routledge, 2004) 22.
[63] On this scene, and Marston's verbal style in general, see Joseph Loewenstein, 'Marston's Gorge and the Question of Formalism', in Mark David Rasmussen (ed.), *Renaissance Literature and Its Formal Engagements* (New York: Palgrave, 2002), 89–112.

that loves the scent of forerunning fashion, like an empty hollow vault still giving an echo to wit' (*Antonio and Mellida*, Induction 34–8). In the second part of the play, *Antonio's Revenge*, he is so taken by the expressions used by Matzagente to deride him that he starts writing them down ecstatically:

> MAT. I scorn to retort the obtuse jest of a fool.
> *Balurdo draws out his writing tables and writes*
>
> BAL. 'Retort' and 'obtuse'; good words, very good words.
> (1.3.21–2)[64]

'Good words'—neologisms, preferably Latinate, polysyllabic words—are what Balurdo is after, as markers of the status he is aspiring to, although as later scenes reveal, he doesn't necessarily know what they mean or how to use them. In 3.4, he offers Maria the following compliment:

> Lady, with a most retort and obtuse leg,
> I kiss the curled locks of your loose hair.

Throughout the play, he keeps picking up words, 'respective', 'pathetical', and 'unvulgar', being some he considers 'very pretty words' (3.4.25) and deploying them to comic effect. And of course he has no doubts about the power of his dazzling eloquence. Making what he considers a particularly successful compliment, 'More than most honeysuckle-sweet ladies, pine not for my presence. I'll return in pomp,' he congratulates himself: 'Well spoke, Sir Geoffrey Balurdo. As I am a true knight, I feel honourable eloquence begin to grope me already' (*Antonio and Mellida* 5.2.41–4).

It seems appropriate that Edward Pudsey considers 'Eloquence begins to grope him already' worthy of inclusion in his notebook. His third-person rendering is unaware of the contextual irony of the expression's presence among the notes of a person eagerly collecting 'good words, very good words' from any text he can lay his hands on. By the mid-century, printed publications begin to capitalize on the common assumption that from plays one might draw such 'very good words': they may be seen a 'help to discourse' or indeed a 'treasury of wit and language', as the titles of such collections suggest.[65] In these publications, the radical decontextualization of the quotations sometimes leads to similar results—in the 1648 *Wits Labyrinth*, lines from such tragedies as *Titus Andronicus*, *Mariam*, and *A Woman Kill'd with Kindness* are enlisted in a collection of amorous compliments.[66] When

---

[64] Mayer, 'Les Spectateurs de Shakespeare'; Peter Stallybrass et al., 'Hamlet's Tables and the Technologies of Writing in Renaissance England', *Shakespeare Quarterly*, 55 (2004), 379–419 at 410–14.

[65] The circulation of jests is another, closely related aspect of this culture; Ian Munro, 'Shakespeare's Jestbook: Wit, Print, Performance', *English Literary History*, 71 (2004), 89–113; Lucy Munro, *Children of the Queen's Revels* 55–95; Adam Smyth, ' "Divines into Dry Vines": Forms of Jesting in Renaissance England', in Allison K. Deutermann and András Kiséry (eds.), *Formal Matters: Reading the Materials of English Renaissance Literature* (Manchester: Manchester University Press, 2013), 55–76.

[66] This book contains (or probably consists of) extensive (and unmarked) runs of quotations from a variety of plays from the period; some of the lines from Shakespeare are listed in John Munro (ed.), *The Shakspere Allusion-Book*, 2 vols. (London: Oxford University Press, 1932) 1:515.

the theatres were to be closed in the early 1640s, the actors' argument that 'the most exact and natural eloquence of our English language [was] expressed and daily amplified' by the stage was no exaggeration.[67]

Because of their tendency to read the play extracts—and especially the extracts from Shakespeare—in isolation from the rest of the material,[68] scholars have often assumed that the notes are evidence of Pudsey's play-going, and his frequent divergence from the surviving printed text an indication that he was jotting things down from performance.[69] The focus on the theatre as a scene of note-taking, in combination with the desire for something that might pass for early modern critical commentary on the theatre of the period, resulted in readings of Pudsey's notes as evidence of his sympathy or antipathy for various characters, or—rather implausibly—of Pudsey trying to 'remind himself of a memorable piece of stage action'.[70] However, while the length of his extracts does allow for the hypothesis that he used a table-book, i.e. an erasable tablet with a silver or lead stylus to jot down remarkable bits while at the theatre, later transcribing these notes into his book, there are some indications that Pudsey was mostly working from printed playtexts. Most importantly, his manuscript sometimes clearly follows the typography of the playbook, switching to an italic hand where a word or phrase is printed in italics.[71] And while notes from plays are grouped together, such generic organization makes no difference to Pudsey's approach to the texts themselves: whether he is taking notes from plays or other texts, he is working through each sequentially, copying short extracts, sometimes using keywords to identify their topic in the margin. His notes from volumes of classical and modern historiography are just as selective and fragmentary as his play extracts, and they diverge from the printed texts just as often: as we have learnt to expect from commonplacing readers, he is decontextualizing, often rephrasing, and occasionally also compressing his materials for more general usefulness, retaining what he can hope to redeploy in a new context.

In fact, Pudsey's participation in the culture of play-reading and play-use for acquiring linguistic competence casts an interesting light on the rest of his readings, showing the power of the theatre to shape specific areas of discourse. In his

---

[67] Quoted by Stern, *Making Shakespeare* 22.
[68] A transcription of these were published in 1887: Savage (ed.), *Shakespearean Extracts from 'Edward Pudsey's Booke'*.
[69] Andrew Gurr, *Playgoing in Shakespeare's London* (3rd edn.; Cambridge: Cambridge University Press, 2004) 240.
[70] Duncan-Jones, *Shakespeare: Upstart Crow to Sweet Swan* 81. The passages from *Othello* are the most compelling evidence that Pudsey may have been copying from performance: he died in 1613, and the play only got printed in 1622. But even here, the changes, unusually radical even by Pudsey's standards, can be explained by the fact that the material from *Richard III* and *Othello* is crammed into a tiny space left blank earlier. Pudsey is here writing ten lines in a two-inch section remaining at the bottom of the page, where he would normally have fitted six or seven lines, and he is omitting even the usual indication of the title for *Othello* as it would have taken up an extra line (Stratford 1r). In other words, while in this case we must assume that he was working from a source other than print, what the idiosyncrasies of the notes reflect are the exigencies not of jotting things down ineptly from performance, but of the note-taker having run out space.
[71] So in Bodleian 40r, the italics of '*mercuried*', '*pride and ignorance*', and '*iustices*' follow the typography of the 1601 quarto edition of *Cynthia's revels*; this is further evidence to support the argument put forward by Gowan, 'An Edition of Edward Pudsey's Commonplace Book' at 68.

notebook, the commodification of wit in drama seems to provide a model for the reading of political texts, and for the transformation of politic history into another source and another form of verbal, conversational ingenuity. Alongside the notes from plays, a large part of Pudsey's book is taken up by the standard texts in politic historiography and civil wisdom: Guicciardini, Machiavelli, and Gentillet's *Anti-Machiavel*, Livy and Tacitus, the essays of Bacon and of Robert Johnson. In his notes, Pudsey treats plays and classical histories in ways that are closely comparable. Plays have more current, interesting turns of phrase; Tacitus and Machiavelli of course yield larger quantities of sententious observations and points that are strictly speaking political. On occasion, Pudsey copies lexical and factual information from the histories, but his reading of history and political writing is informed by the same, dominantly formal, aesthetic concerns as his play-reading. The lines he copies from Polonius, the crafty politician: 'Men of wisedome & of reach doe with windelesses with assayes of bias by indirections find directions out' (Stratford 2r) are exemplary of the combination of the verbal ingenuity and vaguely 'politic' knowingness that characterizes Pudsey's collection as a whole—qualities that (as we saw in Chapter 3) made these lines memorable and notable to John Melton as well. Although one of his first excerpts from Livy reminds him that 'Wee ought to stand vppon the trewth of things rather then vppon (I / wot not what) gloses & goodly shews of words' (Bodleian 9r), this follows directly upon the goodly show of the isolated phrase 'ffaythles frends & hartles foes'. The maxims he extracts from the most politic of his authors fit in with the rest of the book as a medley of witty and entertaining material, curiosities, and compliments—the repertory of a worldly-wise politic wit.

Because he copies his notes *seriatim* (i.e. rather than organizing extracts from various books under topical headings), Pudsey's tendency to read for language rather than argument, for form or expression rather than the larger purpose of the text is perceptible throughout—but it is most striking when he is reading texts directly implicated in current affairs, as in the case of the small cluster of texts in the notebook revolving around the 1601 Essex rebellion, the most obviously and famously political event of Hamlet's moment, whose reverberations remained audible throughout the period and beyond. It is therefore not surprising to find that Pudsey read William Barlow's funeral sermon of Essex preached at Paul's Cross on 1 March, as well as Bacon's *A Declaration of the Practices and Treasons... of the Late Earle of Essex*, published as part of the government's campaign to disseminate the official account of Essex's rebellion, of his subsequent confession to treason, and of his repentance. What our own expectations about the political culture of the period may not have prepared us for is the form of Pudsey's attention to these texts. In his book, Barlow's and Bacon's commentaries are reduced to just one page of densely written notes, instances of witty phrasing and sententious observations that are obviously shorn of almost all sense of specificity. The commonplace, as Lesser and Stallybrass observe, is the opposite of the topical.[72] But the commonplaces Pudsey derives from these directly and obviously political texts do not constitute a

---

[72] Lesser and Stallybrass, 'The First Literary *Hamlet*', 412.

sustained set of generalizations drawn from the tragic example of the Essex rising, either—notes that would show him reading for the political argument, weighing its merits, or contemplating its larger ramifications. In Pudsey's notes, Barlow's argument for obedience to God's magistrate, his dismissal of theories of resistance, and his account of the earl's treason become the source of such phrases as 'our harried passions', 'some with more virulence though with lesse violence', 'Grudging marres Charitye: *Vertit amorem in amorerem*' (and here he notes, following Barlow, that the Latin is from St Bernard). Even the most directly political sentence lifted from the sermon seems to have been selected for the phrasing:

> Subiects must nether *occidere* or *excidere* kill their liege or fall from him
>
> *Aut deponere a throno, aut exponere periculo.*

Because of Bacon's own tendency to draw sententious conclusions from the evidence presented in narrative form, the snippets Pudsey considers extractable from Bacon's *Declaration* amount to a damning miniature portrait of a malcontent traitor, but even here, what drives the selection is a transparent attention to form: in the account of Essex's campaign in Ireland, it is Bacon's use of alliteration in making the damning point that 'His desires too strong for his dissimulacions' that sends Pudsey copying (*Declaration* B2r, Bodleian 64v), and it is his own single-minded desire for balanced or pointed expressions that makes him pass over almost twenty pages until he finds the next portable formulation: 'An ancient principle of Traytors: *To prepare many & to acquaint few*' (*Declaration* D3r, Bodleian 64v). While he retains the italics of the printed original which highlights the sentence, he is not interested in mentioning that this is a principle set down in discussion between Cuffe and Essex—Pudsey's reading is not oriented at the recent events, but at future use (use, that is, in discussion rather than action); the reason why he is copying this sentence is not because it explains Essex's activities, but because it might be used to comment on similar occurrences in the future.

Pudsey's unwillingness to record topical readings in his notes from playbooks is most clearly exemplified by his treatment of Shakespeare' *Richard II*. While Barlow's sermon is published with Essex's scaffold speech as its appendix, Bacon's narrative is followed by accounts of the court proceedings on which it is based and which it references in the marginal notes. The summary of the evidence given against Sir Gelly Merrick mentions that Merrick 'procured to be played before' the conspirators on the eve of the rising 'the play of deposing King Richard the second...which hee thought soone after his Lord should bring from the Stage to the State' (K2v–K3r).

Pudsey's readings could thus obviously prepare him for an analogical, political reading of the play, but even if he overlooked the reference in Bacon's pamphlet, the tendencies of contemporary reference to Richard II make such a reading appear inevitable. In the late sixteenth century, Bolingbroke's deposition of Richard II and his succession to the throne as Henry IV was a prime historical example of baronial resistance against the monarch: in one possible reading, of the legality of the deposition in which the resistance concluded, and in another, of the devastating long-term consequences of this conclusion. The contemporary relevance of the history was made disturbingly clear by Robert Parsons in 1596: his discussion of the competing claims of the potential heirs of Elizabeth in *A Conference abovt the Next Succession* (a text not incidentally dedicated to Essex) hinges on a lengthy argument that Richard's deposition was justified. Shakespeare's play, first performed around the time Parsons' tract came out, and published in three quarto editions in 1597–8, was clearly troubled by this issue, and the 'Parliament scene', i.e. the scene of Richard's deposition, was probably censored in the early editions, to be printed only in 1608.[73]

The play also engages closely with Bolingbroke's eagerness to win the love of the common people. This focus has long been understood as a reflection on Essex's 'popularity', that is, his efforts to mobilize public support for his militaristic political agenda.[74] The analogy between Bolingbroke and Essex was a crucial part of the contemporary significance of the play, so much so that contemporary political satire borrowed its language both to criticize and to praise Essex's popularity. The book-length account of Henry's succession, John Hayward's *First Parte of the History of Henry IV*, published in 1599, seems itself to have been drawing upon Shakespeare's *Richard II*, not least for its description of how Henry courted the non-elite public.[75] The book's dedication to Essex drew a parallel between the earl and Bolingbroke and the Preface to the reader emphasized the value of the history as a pattern for political action—assertions that the government eagerly pounced on, hoping to use the history in constructing a treason charge against Essex, presenting it as 'a seditious prelude to put into the people's heads boldness and faction'.[76] Attorney General Coke read Hayward's book closely for the analogies between Bolingbroke's and Essex's concerns, and argued that it provided a model for the deposition of the Queen. Essex's rising ultimately provided easier grounds for the prosecution, but the results of these exercises in analogical reading, the Essex–Bolingbroke, Elizabeth–Richard parallels remained central to the government's propaganda campaign in the weeks that followed. Not only did Cecil rehearse them in Star Chamber, and Bacon in the pages of the *Declaration*: the clergy was also instructed to invoke the analogies from the pulpit—as does Dr Barlow in his sermon.[77]

Shakespeare's play itself can hardly be mistaken for a piece propagating the overthrow of a monarch, and if it was indeed the play performed on 7 February, on the eve of the Essex rising, the political significance of such a performance is far from clear.[78] But whether it was Shakespeare's play or not, and whether it was sponsored

---

[73] Cyndia Susan Clegg, '"By the Choise and Inuitation of Al the Realme": *Richard II* and Elizabethan Press Censorship', *Shakespeare Quarterly*, 48 (1997), 432–48.

[74] Doty, 'Shakespeare's *Richard II*, "Popularity," and the Early Modern Public Sphere'.

[75] Paul E. J. Hammer, 'The Smiling Crocodile: The Earl of Essex and Late Elizabethan "Popularity"', in Peter Lake and Steve Pincus (eds.), *The Politics of the Public Sphere in Early Modern England* (Manchester: Manchester University Press, 2007), 95–115 at 103–4; Jonathan Bate, *Soul of the Age: A Biography of the Mind of William Shakespeare* (New York: Random House, 2009) 259–62.

[76] James Spedding (ed.), *The Letters and the Life of Francis Bacon Including All His Occasional Works* (London: Longmans, Green, Reader, and Dyer, 1868) 3:150.

[77] Cyndia Susan Clegg, 'Archival Poetics and the Politics of Literature: Essex and Hayward Revisited', *Studies in the Literary Imagination*, 32 (1999), 115–32 at 125–6. Barlow sig. D5v.

[78] Blair Worden, 'Which Play Was Performed at the Globe Theatre on 7 February 1601?', *London Review of Books*, 25/13 (10 July 2003), 22–4.

in order to encourage a rebellion (as not only Bacon but also most modern critics assume), or as an example of an aristocratic intervention going dangerously far, a premonitory depiction of the kind of action the earl and his followers thought they should avoid at all cost (as Paul Hammer has argued recently[79]), after the winter of 1600/1, any account of Bolingbroke and Richard inescapably resonated with the Essex rising. This remained the case for decades. The famous comment Queen Elizabeth made to the antiquary William Lambarde as they were glancing at a list of records related to Richard's reign: 'I am Richard 2nd, know ye not', may well be a 1650 embellishment or outright fabrication—but this only means that the scene is not another instance of Elizabeth's apparent obsession with this self-comparison, but rather, a register of the persistence of the commonplace analogy which the anecdote seeks to authenticate by attributing it to the Queen.[80]

Because Pudsey was taking notes in the immediate aftermath of the Essex rising, and especially since his notebook testifies to his familiarity with Bacon, Barlow, as well as with Hayward's book, we may very well expect to find him attending to the political aspects of *Richard II*, i.e. to the topics and questions that elicited controversy in the period. But his eight short quotations from Shakespeare's play contain nothing that could be described as political material; in fact, he can even be seen removing the vaguely political valences of the passages he touches. In his notebook, Green's lines registering the insecurity of the king's favourites turn into an observation about being the target of jealousy: 'our nearness to the King in love / Is near the hate of those love not the King' (2.2.126–7) becomes 'My neerenes to yow in loue ys neer to the hatred of & c' (Stratford 1v), notable for its juxtaposition of two senses of being near to suggest that love for one person might be the cause of being hated by another. If Shakespeare's *Hamlet*—as we saw in Chapter 3—distanced itself from the topics of the polemics about succession, resistance, and election, Pudsey's notes from a play that preceded Hamlet's moment and participated in that earlier debate register a lack of interest in the same.

Nor is Pudsey's tendency limited to his reading of the play: his reading of other types of political writing are similarly depoliticized. Bacon famously explained to Queen Elizabeth that Hayward's crime was not treason but felony, because 'the author had committed very apparent theft, for he had taken most of the sentences of Cornelius Tacitus, and translated them into English, and put them into his text.'[81] Modern research confirms the claim, showing that about three quarters of Hayward's own text is made up of quotations, and almost one fifth of the work lifted piecemeal from Tacitus.[82] Even Pudsey's own notes testify to this: he is repeatedly found copying sentences from Hayward that he previously copied from

---

[79] Paul E. J. Hammer, 'Shakespeare's *Richard II*, the Play of 7 February 1601, and the Essex Rising', *Shakespeare Quarterly*, 59 (2008), 1–35.
[80] Clegg, 'Archival Poetics and the Politics of Literature', 118–20; Bate, *Soul of the Age* 263–7.
[81] Or rather, Bacon famously claimed, retrospectively, that he had said so: Spedding (ed.), *The Letters and the Life of Francis Bacon* 3:150.
[82] Edwin B. Benjamin, 'Sir John Hayward and Tacitus', *Review of English Studies*, 8 (1957), 275–6.

Tacitus as well.[83] In taking notes from Hayward, Pudsey doesn't simply reverse Hayward's compositional procedure, tracing the sentences to their sources in Tacitus. While Hayward's borrowing is on the whole driven by the subject, his quotations being used in his commentary on the narrative of the events, Pudsey's selection is made on aesthetic grounds, with an ear for the apt formulation, whatever the subject matter might be. Absent any argumentative context, formulations like 'Rather to desire than hope for victory', 'Priuate respects oft passe vnder publike pretences', or 'Rather extenuating his fact than extolling it', are in Pudsey's notes interspersed with such observations and maxims as 'Earnest is the lesse offensive if it bee deliuered in iest' or 'The overruling of princes oft proceeds to their overthrowing, and cutting them short turns to cutting them off' and further remarkable turns of phrase like 'A rough deniall to a rude demand' (17r). While many of these excerpts can obviously be put to analytic or deliberative use, as templates for prudent argument, in copying them Pudsey seems to be exercising himself in the art of making well-balanced, aptly phrased remarks, readying himself for an arresting performance of verbal ingenuity, rather than for getting at the heart of the political matter. His interest in the reason of state is not in the rigorous, professional political analysis it was understood to provide, but in the conversational success it promised.

In this notebook, the stuff of politic history, Machiavellian and Tacitean thought, while avidly read, is thus assimilated to the conversation-oriented interests of a play-goer. The aphoristic discourse about the reason of state, a popular discourse circulating in printed and manuscript collections of 'Machiavellian' maxims, and finding its way into notebooks as well as into the texts of plays, appears here as part of a repertory of witty conversation, asking us to imagine the distinctly non-political and aesthetic motives behind the interest in political texts and political knowledge. Edward Pudsey's notebook shows a reader fascinated by playbooks as models, indeed manuals for conversational success, and looking for the same materials in a range of other texts, books we would not usually think of as resources for stylish conversation. But we should recall how Sir Politic Would-be tried to excuse himself when he is taken to task for his plan to 'sell the state of Venice to the Turk', and is threatened that warrants have been signed 'to apprehend you and to search your study for papers'. In his despair, he urges that 'I have none but notes / drawn out of playbooks...And some essays', and then adds: 'I but talked so / For discourse's sake merely' (5.4.35–47). Talking politics for 'discourse's sake merely', sociably, is probably a more important form of political discussion than morose Ben Jonson admits and also more common than our morose scholarly selves are inclined to believe. Whereas plays are of limited use as manuals for ambassadors, they do provide 'words, good words' for people eager to talk about ambassadors and their missions. Peregrine notes that Sir Pol must have read 'many proclamations / And studied them for words' (5.4.25–6), and his notes drawn from political documents would not have been much different from what he copied out of playbooks.

---

[83] Gowan, 'An Edition of Edward Pudsey's Commonplace Book', at 159–61.

Political drama not as an expression of oppositional radicalism and seething rebellion, but as the medium that helped turn politics into the subject of a lively, and competitively sociable discussion: this is the contribution of Hamlet's moment to the history of English political culture. Out of the knowledge of politicians, the theatre forged a politic style, an aesthetic which encouraged members of a contemporary public to assume the role of the would-be politician—and of course we never know when such role-play might turn serious.

Bibliography

MANUSCRIPTS AND COPIES OF PRINTED BOOKS WITH MARGINALIA

Bodleian Library MS
Eng. Poet. d.3

British Library MSS
Add. 4466, 32494, 35846, 36444, 39853, 42518, 48062, 48094, 48149, 48152, 72361, 72390, 81083
Cotton Nero B III, Vespasian F v, Vespasian C x
Egerton 921
Harley 36, 38, 252, 290, 588, 3638, 6893
Lansdowne 52, 57, 60, 65, 112
Royal 18 B. I
Sloane 1710
Stowe 150

British Library, Printed Books
C 60 l 11, C 60 a 1

Folger Shakespeare Library MSS
H.a. 2
V.a. 146, 381, 402
V.b. 41
X.d.539
Y.d.623, folder 16

Folger Shakespeare Library, Printed Books
PQ4621.D3 M4 1566a

Houghton Library
*EC H2623 Zz507e
*EC 2623 Zz546t

Huntington Library MSS
EL 1608, 1612, 2805
Huntington 41951

Huntington Library Rare Books
62184, 53922

Princeton University Library
Rare Books (Ex) Oversize PA 6452.A2 1555q

Shakespeare Birthplace Trust Record Office MS
ER 82/1/21

University College London MS
Ogden 7/29

WORKS PRINTED BEFORE 1700

Aristotle (1598), *Aristotles Politiques, or Discourses of Gouernment. Translated out of Greeke into French,... By Loys Le Roy, called Regius*, trans. I. D. (London: Adam Islip).
Ascham, Roger (1570?), *A Report and Discourse Written by Roger Ascham, of the Affaires and State of Germany and the Emperour Charles his Court, Duryng Certaine Yeares While the Sayd Roger was There* (London: Iohn Daye).
Avity, Pierre d' (1615), *The estates, empires, & principallities of the world Represented by ye description of countries, maners of inhabitants, riches of prouinces, forces, gouernment, religion; and the princes that haue gouerned in euery estate. With the begining of all militarie and religious orders* (London: Adam Islip for Mathewe Lownes and Iohn Bill).
Bacon, Francis (1605), *Two Bookes of Francis Bacon of the Proficience and Aduancement of Learning, Diuine and Humane* (London).
Bacon, Francis (1638), *Francisci Baconi, Baronis de Verulamio, Vice-Comitis Sancti Albani, operum moralium et civilium tomus Qui continet... Sermones fideles, sive interiora rerum* (London: Edward Griffin for Richard Whitaker).
Bacon, Francis (1640), *Of the Advancement and Proficience of Learning* (Oxford: Leon. Lichfield, for Rob. Young & Ed. Forrest).
Barnes, Barnabe (1606), *Foure Bookes of Offices: Enabling Priuat Persons for the Speciall Seruice of all Good Princes and Policies* (London: George Bishop, T. Adams and C. Burbie).
Belleforest, François de (1568), *L'Histoire des Nevfs Roys Charles de France* (Paris: Jean Le Blanc pour Pierre L'Huillier).
Belleforest, François de (1572), *Le Cinquiesme Tome des Histoires Tragiques* (Paris: Jean Hulpeau).
Belleforest, François de (1572), *Discovrs svr l'Hevr des Presages Advenuz de Nostre Temps Signifiantz la Felicité du Regne de Nostre Roy Charles Neufiesme* (Paris: pour Robert Le Mangnier).
Belleforest, François de (1572), *Epistres des Princes, Lesqvelles, ov Sont Addressees Avx Princes, Ov Traittent les Affaires des Princes, ou Parlent des Princes. Recueillies d'Italien par Hieronyme Ruscelli, & Mises en François par F. de Belle-forest, Commingeois* (Paris: Iean Ruelle).
Belleforest, François de (1573), *Les Chroniques et Annales de France... par Nicole Gilles... Reueuës Corrigées & Augmentées... par Francoys de Belleforest* (Paris: Nicolas du Chemin).
Belleforest, François de (1579), *Les Grandes Annales, et Histoire Generale de France, de la Venue des Francs en Gaule, iusques au Regne du Roy Tres-Chrestien Henry III. ... par François de Belle-Forest Comingeois, & Annaliste de sa Majesté Tres-Chrestienne*, 2 vols. (Paris: Gabriel Buon).
Bodley, Thomas (1647), *The Life of Sr Thomas Bodley, the Honourable Founder of the Publique Library in the Vniversity of Oxford. VVritten by Himselfe* (Oxford: Henry Hall).
Botero, Giovanni (1603), *The Travelers Breviat* (London: Iohn Iaggard).
Burghley, William Cecil, Lord (1617), *Certaine Precepts or Directions, for the Well Ordering and Carriage of a Mans Life: ... Left by a Father to His Son at His Death, Who Was Sometimes of Eminent Note and Place in This Kingdome. And Published from a More Perfect Copy, then Ordinary Those Pocket Manuscripts Goe Warranted by* (London: T. C[reede] and B. A[lsop] for Ri. Meighen, and Thom. Iones).

Camden, William (1614), *Remaines, concerning Britaine but especially England, and the inhabitants thereof* (2nd edition, 1st edn. 1605; London: John Leggatt for Simon Waterson).

Chapman, George (1654), *The Tragedy of Alphonsus, Emperour of Germany as it hath been very often Acted (with great applause) at the Privat house in Black-Friers by His Maiesties Servants* (London: for Humphrey Moseley).

Charles V (1670), *The Advice of Charles the Fifth, Emperor of Germany, and King of Spain, to His Son Philip the Second upon His Resignation of the Crown of Spain to His Said Son* (London: for H. Mortlock).

Cleland, James (1607), *Hero-paideia, or The Institution of a Young Noble Man* (Oxford: Ioseph Barnes).

Commynes, Philippe de (1596), *The Historie of Philip de Commines Knight, Lord of Argenton* (London: Ar. Hatfield, for I. Norton).

Commynes, Philippe de (1610), *Histoire de Lovys XI... et des Choses Mémorables Advenuës en l'Europe durant Vingt & Deux Années de Son Regne. Enrichie de Plusieurs Observations qui Tiennent Lieu de Commentaires* (Paris: P. Mettayer).

The Compleat Ambassador (London: Tho: Newcomb, for Gabriel Bedell and Thomas Collins, 1654).

Croce, Giulio Cesare (1603), *Lamento, et Esclamatione fatta dal Duca di Birone avanti la Sua Morte* (Bologna: Gli heredi di Gio. Rossi).

Crosse, Henry (1603), *Vertues Common-vvealth: or The High-way to Honour* (London: Printed [by Thomas Creede] for Iohn Newbery).

Dallington, Robert (1604), *The Vievv of Fraunce* (London: Symon Stafford).

Dallington, Robert (1605), *A Suruey of the Great Dukes State of Tuscany* (London: Edward Blount).

Daniel, Samuel (1606), *A Funerall Poem Vppon the Death of the Late Noble Earle of Deuonshyre* (London).

Denckwürdige, Warhaffte und Eigentliche Historische Beschreibung, welche Sich bey Lebzeiten Elisabetha Königin in England, so Wohl auch unter jetzt Regierendem König in Frankreich Begeben und Zugetragen (Speyer: Johann Taschner, 1608).

Dickenson, John (1603), *Speculum Tragicum. Regum, Principum, & Magnatum Superioris Sæculi Celebriorum Ruinas Exitusque Calamitosos Breviter Complectens... Tertio Editum & Adauctum. Accessit Etiam Bironij Exitus, & Alia* (Lugduni Batavorum: Elzevir).

A Discourse More at Large of the Late Ouerthrovve Giuen to the King of Spaines Armie at Turnehaut, in Ianuarie last, by Count Morris of Nassawe, Assisted with the English Forces whereunto is Adioined Certaine Inchauntments and Praiers in Latine, Found about Diuerse of the Spaniards, Which Were Slaine in the Same Conflict: Translated out of French According to the Copy Printed in the Low Countries (London: to be sold in Paules Churchyarde, at the signe of the black Beare, 1597).

Earle, John (1628), *Micro-cosmographie, or, A Peece of the World Discovered in Essayes and Characters* (London: William Stansby for Edward Blount).

Eliot, John (1592), *The Suruay or Topographical Description of France* (London: John Wolfe).

Epictetus his Manuall. And Cebes his Table. trans. Io: Healey (London: [G. Eld] for E. Blunt and W. Barret, 1610).

Erasmus (1542), *Apophthegmes That is to Saie, Prompte, Quicke, Wittie and Sentencious Saiynges*, trans. Nicholas Udall (London: Richard Grafton).

Essex, Robert Devereux Earl of, Sir Philip Sidney, William Davison (1633), *Profitable Instructions Describing What Speciall Obseruations Are to be Taken by Trauellers in All Nations, States and Countries* (London: for Beniamin Fisher).
Fletcher, Giles (1591), *Of the Russe Common Wealth. Or, Maner of Gouernement of the Russe Emperour, (Commonly Called the Emperour of Moskouia) with the Manners, and Fashions of the People of that Countrey* (London: T[homas] D[awson] for Thomas Charde).
Freeman, Thomas (1614), *Rubbe, and a Great Cast* (London: [Nicholas Okes], to be sold [by L. Lisle]).
Fulbecke, William (1608), *An Abridgement, or Rather, a Bridge of Roman Histories, to Passe the Neerest Way from Titus Livius to Cornelius Tacitus* (London: Richard More).
Fuller, Thomas (1642), *The Holy State* (Cambridge: Roger Daniel for John Williams).
Gentili, Alberico (1585), *De Legationibus, Libri Tres* (London: Thomas Vautrollerius).
Gentillet, Innocent (1602), *A Discourse vpon the Meanes of VVel Governing and Maintaining in Good Peace, a Kingdome, or Other Principalitie...Against Nicholas Machiavell the Florentine*, trans. Simon Patericke (London: Adam Islip).
The Great Assises Holden in Parnassus (London: Richard Cotes for Edward Husbands, 1645).
Guicciardini, Francesco (1593), *Histoire des Gverres d'Italie... à laquelle Ont Esté Adioustees Les Observations Politiques, Militaires & Morales du Sievr de La Nove.... Deux Amples Indices, Contenans par Ordre Alphabetique les Maximes de Guichardin, & Celles du Sieur de la Noue* ([Genève]: Heritiers d'Eustache Vignon).
Harvey, Gabriel (1578), *Gratulationum Valdinensium libri quatuor* (London: Henry Binneman).
Harvey, Gabriel (1593), *Pierces Supererogation or A New Prayse of the Old Asse* (London: Iohn VVolfe).
Hentzner, Paul (1612), *Itinerarium Germaniae; Galliae; Angliae; Italiae* (Nürnberg: Abraham Wagenmann).
Histoire de la Vie et Mort dv Comte d'Essex avec vn Dicovrs Grave et Eloqvent de la Royne d'Angleterre, au Duc de Biron sur ce Subiect. La Conspiration, Prison, Iugement, Testament, & Mort du Duc de Biron: Trahison Mort & Procez de Nicolas Loste, Prison du Comte d' Auuergne & de Madame Marquise de Vernueil (N.p., [1607]).
Holinshed, Raphael (1587), *The First and Second Volumes of Chronicles...* (London: John Harrison and others).
Hotman, François (1573), *A True and Plaine Report of the Furious Outrages of Fraunce & the Horrible and Shameful Slaughter of Chastillion the Admirall, and Diuers Other Noble and Excellent Men, and of the Wicked and Straunge Murder of Godlie Persons, Committed in Many Cities of Fraunce, without any Respect of Sorte, Kinde, Age, or Degree. By Ernest Varamund of Freseland* (At Striveling in Scotlande [i.e. London: Henry Bynneman]).
Hotman, Jean (1603), *The Ambassador* (London: V[alentine] S[immes] for Iames Shawe).
Hotman, Jean (1613), *De la Charge et Dignite d l'Ambassadeur: par Ian Hotman Sieur de Villiers. Troiseme edition augmentée, & meilleure* (Dusseldorp: Bernard Busius).
L'Innocence de la Tresillvstre Tres-chaste, et Debonnaire Princesse, Madame Marie Royne d'Escosse; ou Sont Amplement Refutées les Calomnies Faulces, & Impositions Iniques, Publiées par Vne Liure Secrettement Diulgé en France, l'An 1572. Tovchant tant la Mort du Seigneur d'Arley son Espouse, que autres Crimes, dont Elle est Faulcement Accusée. Plus, un autre Discours auquel Sont Descouuertes Plusieurs Trahisons tant Manifestes, que iusques Icy, Cachées, Perpetrées par les Mesmes Calomniateurs (N.p.: n.p., 1572).
Johnson, Robert (1601), *Essaies, or Rather Imperfect Offers* (London: Iohn Windet, for Iohn Barnes).

La Croix du Maine, François Grudé de (1584), *Premier Volume de la Bibliothèque du Sieur de La Croix du Maine, Qui est un Catalogue Général de Toutes Sortes d'Autheurs Qui Ont Escrit en François depuis Cinq Cents Ans...* (Paris: Abel L'Angelier).
La Noué, François de (1587), *The Politicke and Militarie Discourses*, trans. E. A. (London: for T[homas] C[adman] and E[dward] A[ggas] by Thomas Orwin).
Le Petit, Jean François (1609), *The Low-Country Common Wealth Contayninge an Exact Description of the Eight Vnited Prouinces, Now made free*, trans. Edward Grimeston (London: G. Eld).
Lettre Mistique. Responce, Repliqve. Mars Joue son Rolle en la Premiere; en la Seconde la Bande & le Choeur de l'Estat, la Troisieme Figure l'Amour de Polytheme Galathee, & des Sept Pasteurs (Leiden: 1603).
Lipsius, Justus (1581), *Ad Annales Corn. Taciti Liber Commentarius, Sive Notae* (Antwerp: Plantin).
Lipsius, Justus (1594), *Sixe Bookes of Politickes or Ciuil Doctrine*, trans. William Jones (London: Richard Field for William Ponsonby).
M.P. (1661), *A Character of Coffee and Coffee-Houses* (London).
Machiavelli, Niccolò (1584), *I Discorsi* (Palermo: Heredi d'Antoniello degli Antonielli [i.e. London: John Wolfe]).
Machiavelli, Niccolò (1640), *Nicholas Machiavel's Prince. Also, the life of Castruccio Castracani of Lucca. And the meanes Duke Valentine us'd to put to death Vitellozzo Vitelli, Oliverotto of Fermo, Paul, and the Duke of Gravina*, trans. E.D. (London: R. Bishop, for William Hils, sold by Daniel Pakeman).
Marston, John (1598), *The Scourge of Villanie: Three bookes of satyres* (London: I[ames] R[oberts] and are to be sold by Iohn Buzbie).
Marston, John (1601), *Iacke Drums Entertainment: or The Comedie of Pasquill and Katherine* (London: Richard Oliue).
Marston, John (1606), *The VVonder of VVomen or The Tragedie of Sophonisba as It Hath Beene Sundry Times Acted at the Blacke Friers* (London: Iohn Windet).
Martin, Robert (1633), *Catalogus librorum quos (in ornamentum reipublicae literariae) non sine magnis sumptibus & labore, ex Italia selegit Robertus Martine, Bibliopola Londinensis: apud quem in coemiterio Divi Pauli prostant venales* (London: Augustin Mathewes).
Martin, Robert (1635), *Catalogus librorum tam impressorum quam manuscriptorum, quos ex Roma, Venetiis, aliisque Italiae locis, selegit Robertus Martine Bibliopola Londinensis. Apud quem vaeneunt in coemiterio Divi Pauli* (London: John Haviland).
Martin, Robert (1639), *Catalogus librorum, ex praecipius Italiae Emporiis selectorum. Per Robertum Martinum. Apud quem venales habentur. Londini: In Old Bayly, non procul ab aquaeductu sub Venetiis* (London: Thomas Harper).
Mathieu, Pierre (1614), *The History of Levvis the Eleuenth VVith the Most Memorable Accidents which Happened in Europe during the Two and Twenty Yeares of his Raigne. Enricht with Many Obseruations which Serue as Commentaries*, trans. Edward Grimeston (London: George Eld).
Melton John (1609), *A Sixe-folde Politician. Together with a Sixe-folde Precept of Policy* (London: E.A. for Iohn Busby).
Meres, Francis (1598), *Palladis Tamia* (London: P. Short, for Cuthbert Burbie).
Meyer, Abrecht (1589), *Certaine Briefe, and Speciall Instructions for Gentlemen, Merchants, Students, Soldiers, Marriners, & c. Employed in Seruices Abrode*, trans. Philip Jones (London: Iohn Woolfe).
Nannini, Remigio (1561), *Orationi in Materia Civile, e Criminale, Tratte da gli Historici Greci, e Latini, Antichi, e Moderni, Raccolte, e Tradotte per M. Remigio Fiorentino... Nelle*

Quali, oltre alla Cognitione dell'Historie, S'ha Notitia di Gouerni di Stati, e di Republiche, d'Accusare, e Difender Rei, e di Molte altre Cose Utili a Ciasuno, ch'Attende alla Vita Ciuile (Vinegia: Gabriel Giolito de'Ferrari).

Osborn, Francis (1658), *Historical Memoires on the Reigns of Queen Elizabeth, and King James* (London: J. Grismond, to be sold by T. Robinson Bookseller in Oxon.).

Overbury, Thomas (1626), *Sir Thomas Ouerbury his Obseruations in His Trauailes vpon the State of the XVII. Prouinces* ([London]: [Bernard Alsop for John Parker]).

Parsons, Robert (1594), *A Conference about the Next Succession* (N.p.).

Plutarch (1603), *The Philosophie, Commonlie Called, the Morals*, trans. Philemon Holland (London: Arnold Hatfield).

Recueil Memorable: de ce Qui s'Est Passé pour le Faict du Sieur Duc de Biron, Mareschal de France (Langres: J. Des Preyz, 1602).

Rowlands, Samuel (1608), *Diogenes Lanthorne* (London: [Edward Allde] for Thomas Pauier).

Satyrae seriae, or, The Secrets of things written in morall and politicke observations (London: J. Okes, for Abel Roper, 1640).

Savile, Henry (1591), *The Ende of Nero and Beginning of Galba. Fower bookes of the histories Of Cornelivs Tacitvs. The life of Agricola* (Oxforde: Ioseph Barnes [and R. Robinson, London] for Richard Wright).

Saxo Grammaticus (1514), *Danorum Regum Heroumque Historiae* (Paris: Jodocus Badius).

Saxo Grammaticus (1534), *Danorum Historiæ Libri xvi* (Basel: Johannes Bebel).

Saxo Grammaticus (1576), *Danica Historia Libris XVI* (Frankfurt: Andreas Wechel).

Serres, Jean de (1607), *A General Inuentorie of the History of France from the Beginning of that Monarchie, vnto the Treatie of Veruins, in the year 1598. . . . And Continued vnto these Times, out off the Best Authors which Haue Written of that Subiect*, trans. Edward Grimeston (London: George Eld).

Shakespeare, William (1603), *The Tragicall Historie of Hamlet Prince of Denmarke* (London: Valentine Simmes for Nicholas Ling and John Trundell).

Shakespeare, William (1605), *The Tragicall Historie of Hamlet, Prince of Denmarke* (London: James Roberts for Nicholas Ling).

Tacitus, C. Cornelius (1588), *Opera qvae Exstant: I. Lipsivs Quartum Recensuit* (Antwerp: Plantin, 1st: 1574).

Tacitus, C. Cornelius (1598), *The Annales of Cornelivs Tacitvs. The Description of Germanie*, trans. Richard Grenewey (London: Arn. Hatfield, for Bonham and Iohn Norton).

Tomkis, Thomas (1615), *Albumazar: A Comedy presented before the Kings Maiestie at Cambridge, the ninth of March, 1614* (London: Nicholas Okes for Walter Burre).

A True and Perfect Discourse of the Practises and Treasons of Marshall Biron together with the Particulars of his Arraignment and Execution (London: P.S., 1602).

A True Discourse of the Ouerthrovve Giuen to the Common Enemy at Turnhaut, the 14. of Ianuary Last 1597. by Count Moris of Nassaw and the States, Assisted with the Englishe Forces. Sent from a Gentleman of Account, that Was Present at the Seruice, to a Friend of His in England (London: Printed by Peter Short, and are to be sold in Paules Churchyard, at the signe of the blacke Beare, 1597).

Valerius Maximus (1502), *Dictorum et Factorum Memorabilium Libri Novem* (Venice: Aldus).

Wicquefort, Abraham de (1680), *L'Ambassadeur et Ses Fonctions*, 2 vols. (The Hague: Jean & Daniel Steucker).

WORKS PRINTED SINCE 1700

Adorno, Theodor W. (1991), *Notes to Literature*, ed. Rolf Tiedemann, trans. Shierry Weber Nicholsen, 2 vols. (New York: Columbia University Press).
Alexander, Nigel (1971), *Poison, Play, and Duel: A Study in Hamlet* (Lincoln: University of Nebraska Press).
Alford, Stephen (1998), *The Early Elizabethan Polity: William Cecil and the British Succession Crisis, 1558–1569* (New York: Cambridge University Press).
Alford, Stephen (2007), 'The Political Creed of William Cecil', in John F. McDiarmid (ed.), *The Monarchical Republic of Early Modern England: Essays in Response to Patrick Collinson* (Aldershot: Ashgate), 75–90.
Anderson, Benedict (1991), *Imagined Communities: Reflections on the Origin and Spread of Nationalism* (Rev. edn.; London: Verso).
Andreas, Willy (1943), *Staatskunst und Diplomatie der Venezianer im Spiegel Ihrer Gesandtenberichte* (Leipzig: Koehler & Amelang).
Anglo, Sydney (1969), *Machiavelli: A Dissection* (London: Victor Gollancz).
Anglo, Sydney (2005), *Machiavelli: The First Century: Studies in Enthusiasm, Hostility, and Irrelevance* (Oxford: Oxford University Press).
Antonibon, Francesca (1939), *Le Relazioni a Stampa di Ambasciatori Veneti* (Istituto Veneto di Scienze Lettere e Arti. Opera Della Bibliografia Veneziana. Collana di Bibliografie Minori, 1: Tipografia del Seminario di Padova).
Arber, Edward (1875), *A Transcript of the Registers of the Company of Stationers of London: 1554–1640, A.D*, 5 vols. (London and Birmingham: Priv. print.).
Archer, John Michael (1993), Sovereignty and Intelligence: Spying and Court Culture in the English Renaissance (Stanford: Stanford University Press).
Arendt, Hannah (1981), *The Life of the Mind*, 2 vols. (New York: Harcourt Brace Jovanovich).
Arendt, Hannah (1982), *Lectures on Kant's Political Philosophy*, ed. Ronald Beiner (Chicago: University of Chicago Press).
Arendt, Hannah (2005), *The Promise of Politics*, ed. Jerome Kohn (New York: Schocken Books).
Arnold, Oliver (2007), *The Third Citizen: Shakespeare's Theater and the Early Modern House of Commons* (Baltimore: Johns Hopkins University Press).
Ash, Eric H. (2004), *Power, Knowledge, and Expertise in Elizabethan England* (Baltimore: Johns Hopkins University Press).
Atherton, Ian (1999), 'The Itch Grown a Disease: Manuscript Transmission of News in the Seventeenth Century', in Joad Raymond (ed.), *News, Newspapers and Society in Early Modern Britain* (London: Frank Cass), 39–65.
Attridge, Derek (1988), *Peculiar Language: Literature as Difference from the Renaissance to James Joyce* (London: Methuen).
Auden, W. H. (1973), *Forewords and Afterwords*, ed. Edward Mendelson (New York: Random House).
Auerbach, Erich (1969), 'Philology and "Weltliteratur"', *The Centennial Review*, 13, 1–17.
Axton, Marie (1977), *The Queen's Two Bodies: Drama and the Elizabethan Succession* (London: Royal Historical Society).
Ayers, P. K. (1993), 'Reading, Writing, and *Hamlet*', *Shakespeare Quarterly*, 44, 423–39.
Aylmer, G. E. (1961), *The King's Servants: The Civil Service of Charles I, 1625–1642* (New York: Columbia University Press).

Aylmer, G. E. (1980), 'From Office-Holding to Civil Service: The Genesis of Modern Bureaucracy: The Prothero Lecture', *Transactions of the Royal Historical Society, 5th ser.*, 30, 91–108.

Ayres, Philip J. (1983), 'Jonson, Northampton, and the "Treason" in *Sejanus*', *Modern Philology*, 80, 356–63.

Barish, Jonas A. (1981), *The Antitheatrical Prejudice* (Berkeley: University of California Press).

Barkan, Leonard (1975), *Nature's Work of Art: The Human Body as Image of the World* (New Haven: Yale University Press).

Baron, Sabrina A. (2001), 'The Guises of Dissemination in Early Seventeenth-Century England: News in Manuscript and Print', in Brendan Dooley and Sabrina A. Baron (eds.), *The Politics of Information in Early Modern Europe* (London: Routledge), 41–56.

Baron, Samuel H. (1991), 'Fletcher's Mission to Moscow and the Anthony Marsh Affair', *Forschungen zur osteuropäischen Geschichte*, 46, 107–30.

Barrell, John (1988), *Poetry, Language, and Politics* (Manchester: Manchester University Press).

Barrell, John (2004), 'Coffee-House Politicians', *Journal of British Studies*, 43, 206–32.

Barthes, Roland (1986), 'The Reality Effect', *The Rustle of Language* (Oxford: Blackwell), 141–8.

Bartlett, Phyllis Brooks (1941), *The Poems of George Chapman* (New York and London: Modern Language Association of America and Oxford University Press).

Barton, Anne (1984), *Ben Jonson, Dramatist* (Cambridge: Cambridge University Press).

Baschet, Armand (1862), *La Diplomatie Vénitienne: Les Princes de l'Europe au XVIe Siècle: François Ier, Philippe II, Catherine de Médicis, Les Papes, Les Sultans, etc. etc. d'après les Rapports des Ambassadeurs Vénitiens* (Paris: Henri Plon).

Bate, Jonathan (2009), *Soul of the Age: A Biography of the Mind of William Shakespeare* (New York: Random House).

Bawcutt, N. W. (1970), 'Machiavelli and Marlowe's *the Jew of Malta*', *Renaissance Drama*, n.s. 3, 3–49.

Bawcutt, N. W. (2004), 'The "Myth of Gentillet" Reconsidered: An Aspect of Elizabethan Machiavellism', *The Modern Language Review*, 99, 863–74.

Beame, Edmond M. (1982), 'The Use and Abuse of Machiavelli: The Sixteenth-Century French Adaptation', *Journal of the History of Ideas*, 43, 33–54.

Beardsley, Theodore S., Jr (1974), 'Isocrates, Shakespeare, and Calderón: Advice to a Young Man', *Hispanic Review*, 42 (2), 185–98.

Bednarz, James P. (2001), *Shakespeare & the Poets' War* (New York: Columbia University Press).

Bell, Gary M. (1990), *A Handlist of British Diplomatic Representatives, 1509–1688* (London: Royal Historical Society).

Bell, Gary M. (1994), 'Elizabethan Diplomacy: A Subtle Revolution', in Malcolm R. Thorp and Arthur J. Slavin (eds.), *Politics, Religion and Diplomacy in Early Modern Europe* (Sixteenth Century Essays and Studies; Kirksville, MO: Sixteenth Century Journal Publishers), 267–88.

Bell, Gary McClellan (1974), 'The Men and Their Rewards in Elizabethan Diplomatic Service, 1558–1585', PhD thesis (UCLA).

Bell, Sandra J. (2002), '"Precious Stinke": James I's *A Counterblaste to Tobacco*', in Daniel Fischlin and Mark Fortier (eds.), *Royal Subjects: Essays on the Writings of James VI and I* (Detroit: Wayne State University Press), 323–43.

Bellany, Alastair (2002), *The Politics of Court Scandal in Early Modern England: News Culture and the Overbury Affair, 1603–1660* (Cambridge: Cambridge University Press).
Belleforest, François de (2013), *Le Cinquiesme Tome des Histoires Tragiques*, ed. Hervé-Thomas Campangne (Textes Litteraires Français; Geneve: Droz).
Belling, Catherine (1998), 'Reading *The Operation*: Television, Realism, and the Possession of Medical Knowledge', *Literature and Medicine*, 17, 1–23.
Bene, Sándor (1999), *Theatrum Politicum: nyilvánosság, közvélemény és irodalom a kora újkorban* (Debrecen: Kossuth Egyetemi Kiadó).
Benedict, Barbara M. (2001), *Curiosity: A Cultural History of Early Modern Inquiry* (Chicago: University of Chicago Press).
Benjamin, Edwin B. (1957), 'Sir John Hayward and Tacitus', *Review of English Studies*, 8, 275–6.
Benjamin, Walter (1977), *The Origin of German Tragic Drama* (London: NLB).
Berlin, Isaiah (1980), 'The Originality of Machiavelli', *Against the Current: Essays in the History of Ideas* (New York: Viking Press), 25–79.
Berry, Lloyd E. (ed.) (1964), *The English Works of Giles Fletcher, the Elder* (Madison: University of Wisconsin Press).
Bertheau, Gilles (1999), 'Chansons Populaires et Incidences Politiques: le Cas de *The Conspiracy and Tragedy of Byron* (1608) de George Chapman', *Études Anglaises*, 52 (3), 259–74.
Bevington, David M. (1968), *Tudor Drama and Politics: A Critical Approach to Topical Meaning* (Cambridge, MA: Harvard University Press).
Biagioli, Mario (1993), *Galileo, Courtier: The Practice of Science in the Culture of Absolutism* (Chicago: University of Chicago Press).
Binns, J. W. (1974), 'Seneca and Neo-Latin Tragedy in England', in C. D. N. Costa (ed.), *Seneca* (London and Boston: Routledge and Kegan Paul), 205–34.
Biow, Douglas (2002), *Doctors, Ambassadors, Secretaries: Humanism and Professions in Renaissance Italy* (Chicago: University of Chicago Press).
Biow, Douglas (2015), *On the Importance of Being an Individual in Renaissance Italy: Men, Their Professions, and Their Beards* (Haney Foundation Series; Philadelphia: University of Pennsylvania Press).
Birch, Thomas (1749), *An Historical View of the Negotiations between the Courts of England, France, and Brussels, from the Year 1592 to 1617* (London: A. Millar).
Birch, Thomas (1754), *Memoirs of the Reign of Elizabeth, from the Year 1581 till Her Death*, 2 vols. (London: A. Millar).
Blair, Ann (1997), *The Theater of Nature: Jean Bodin and Renaissance Science* (Princeton: Princeton University Press).
Blayney, Peter W. M. (1990), *The Bookshops in Paul's Cross Churchyard* (Occasional Papers of the Bibliographical Society, No. 5; London: The Bibliographical Society).
Blumenberg, Hans (1983), *The Legitimacy of the Modern Age*, trans. Robert M. Wallace (Cambridge, MA: MIT Press).
Bly, Mary (2000), *Queer Virgins and Virgin Queans on the Early Modern Stage* (Oxford: Oxford University Press).
Borges, Jorge Luis (1998), *Collected Fictions*, trans. Andrew Hurley (New York: Penguin Books).
Botero, Giovanni (1956), *The Reason of State*, trans. P. J. Waley and D. P. Waley (New Haven: Yale University Press).
Boughner, Daniel C. (1968), *The Devil's Disciple: Ben Jonson's Debt to Machiavelli* (New York: Philosophical Library).

Bourdieu, Pierre (1984), *Distinction: A Social Critique of the Judgement of Taste*, trans. Richard Nice (London: Routledge and Kegan Paul).

Bourland, Caroline Brown (1940–1), 'Gabriel Harvey and the Modern Languages', *Huntington Library Quarterly*, 4, 85–106.

Bourus, Terri (2014), *Young Shakespeare's Young Hamlet: Print, Piracy, and Performance* (Basingstoke: Palgrave Macmillan).

Boutcher, Warren (2002), 'Humanism and Literature in Late Tudor England: Translation, the Continental Book and the Case of Montaigne's *Essais*', in Jonathan Woolfson (ed.), *Reassessing Tudor Humanism* (Basingstoke: Palgrave Macmillan), 243–68.

Boutcher, Warren (2005), 'Literature', in Jonathan Woolfson (ed.), *Palgrave Advances in Renaissance Historiography* (Basingstoke: Palgrave Macmillan), 210–40.

Boutcher, Warren (2006), 'Unoriginal Authors: How to Do Things with Texts in the Renaissance', in Annabel S. Brett, James Tully, and Holly Hamilton-Bleakley (eds.), *Rethinking the Foundations of Modern Political Thought* (Cambridge: Cambridge University Press), 73–92.

Boutcher, Warren (2012), 'L'Objet Livre à l'Aube de l'Époque Moderne', *Terrain*, 59, 88–103.

Boutcher, Warren (2013), 'Literary Art and Agency? Gell and the Magic of the Early Modern Book', in Liana Chua and Mark Elliott (eds.), *Distributed Objects: Meaning and Mattering after Alfred Gell* (New York and Oxford: Berghahn Books), 155–75.

Bowers, Fredson (1933), '*Alphonsus, Emperor of Germany*, and the *Ur-Hamlet*', *Modern Language Notes*, 48, 101–8.

Bowers, Fredson (1933), 'The Date and Composition of *Alphonsus, Emperor of Germany*', *Harvard Studies and Notes in Philology and Literature*, 15, 165–89.

Bowers, Fredson Thayer (1940), *Elizabethan Revenge Tragedy, 1587–1642* (Princeton: Princeton University Press).

Bradbrook, Muriel C. (1969), *Shakespeare the Craftsman* (London: Chatto & Windus).

Bradford, Alan T. (1983), 'Stuart Absolutism and the "Utility" of Tacitus', *Huntington Library Quarterly*, 46, 127–55.

Bradshaw, Graham (1993), 'Appendix: Dashing Othello's Spirits', *Misrepresentations: Shakespeare and the Materialists* (Ithaca and London: Cornell University Press), 258–82.

Braudel, Fernand (1982), *Structures of Everyday Life: The Limits of the Possible*, trans. Siân Reynolds (Civilization and Capitalism, 15th–18th Century; New York: Harper and Row).

Braunmuller, A. R. (1992), *Natural Fictions: George Chapman's Major Tragedies* (Newark: University of Delaware Press).

Bray, Alan (2003), *The Friend* (Chicago: University of Chicago Press).

Brennan, Michael G. (2003), '"Your Lordship's to Do You All Humble Service": Rowland Whyte's Correspondence with Robert Sidney, Viscount Lisle and First Earl of Leicester', *Sidney Journal*, 21 (2), 1–37.

Brennan, Michael G. and Kinnamon, Noel J. (2003), 'Robert Sidney, "Mr Johnson", and the Education of William Sidney at Penshurst', *Notes and Queries*, 248, 430–7.

Brennan, Michael G., Kinnamon, Noel J., and Hannay, Margaret P. (eds.), (2013), *The Letters (1595–1608) of Rowland Whyte* (Memoirs of the American Philosophical Society, 268; Philadelphia: American Philosophical Society).

Brown, Cedric C. (2004), 'Sons of Beer and Sons of Ben: Drink as a Social Marker in Seventeenth-Century England', in Adam Smyth (ed.), *A Pleasing Sinne: Drink and Conviviality in Seventeenth-Century England* (Cambridge: D. S. Brewer), 3–20.

Brown, Keith (1968), 'Hamlet's Place on the Map', *Shakespeare Studies*, 4, 160–82.

Bruster, Douglas (2003), 'The Structural Transformation of Print in Late Elizabethan England', *Shakespeare and the Question of Culture: Early Modern Literature and the Cultural Turn* (Basingstoke: Palgrave Macmillan), 65–93.

Buck, August (1985), *Machiavelli* (Darmstadt: Wissenschaftliche Buchgesellschaft).

Bullough, Geoffrey (ed.) (1978), *Narrative and Dramatic Sources of Shakespeare* (London: Routledge and Kegan Paul).

Burke, Peter (1969), 'Tacitism', in T. A. Dorey (ed.), *Tacitus* (London: Routledge and Kegan Paul), 149–71.

Burke, Peter (1991), 'Tacitism, Scepticism, and Reason of State', in J. H. Burns and Mark Goldie (eds.), *The Cambridge History of Political Thought, 1450–1700* (Cambridge: Cambridge University Press), 479–98.

Burke, Peter (2000), 'Early Modern Venice as a Center of Information and Communication', in John Jeffries Martin and Dennis Romano (eds.), *Venice Reconsidered: The History and Civilization of an Italian State, 1297–1797* (Baltimore: Johns Hopkins University Press), 389–409.

Burnett, Mark Thornton (2002), 'Staging the Malcontent in Early Modern England', in Arthur F. Kinney (ed.), *A Companion to Renaissance Drama* (Oxford: Blackwell), 336–52.

Burns, J. H. and Goldie, Mark (eds.) (1991), *The Cambridge History of Political Thought, 1450–1700* (Cambridge: Cambridge University Press).

Burrow, Colin (2004), 'Shakespeare and Humanistic Culture', in Charles Martindale and A. B. Taylor (eds.), *Shakespeare and the Classics* (Cambridge: Cambridge University Press).

Burrow, Colin (ed.) (2002), *The Complete Sonnets and Poems* (The Oxford Shakespeare, Oxford: Oxford University Press).

Burt, Richard (1993), *Licensed by Authority: Ben Jonson and the Discourses of Censorship* (Ithaca: Cornell University Press).

Bushnell, Rebecca W. (1990), *Tragedies of Tyrants: Political Thought and Theater in the English Renaissance* (Ithaca: Cornell University Press).

Cahill, Patricia A. (2008), *Unto the Breach: Martial Formations, Historical Trauma, and the Early Modern Stage* (Oxford: Oxford University Press).

Cain, Tom (2012), '*Sejanus*: Textual Essay', The Cambridge Edition of the Works of Ben Jonson online.

Calderwood, James L. (1983), *To Be and Not to Be: Negation and Metadrama in Hamlet* (New York: Columbia University Press).

Calhoun, Thomas O. and Gravell, Thomas L. (1993), 'Paper and Printing in Ben Jonson's "Sejanus" (1605)', *The Papers of the Bibliographical Society of America*, 87, 13–64.

Camden, William (1970), *The History of the Most Renowned and Victorious Princess Elizabeth, Late Queen of England: Selected Chapters*, ed. Wallace T. MacCaffrey (Chicago and London: University of Chicago Press).

Carter, Charles H. (1965), 'The Ambassadors of Early Modern Europe: Patterns of Diplomatic Representation in the Early Seventeenth Century', in Charles H. Carter (ed.), *From the Renaissance to the Counter-Reformation* (New York: Random House), 269–95.

Castellani, Arrigo (2009), *Nuovi Saggi di Linguistica e Filologia Italiana e Romanza (1976–2004)*, ed. Valeria Della Valle et al., 2 vols. (Roma: Salerno Editrice).

Cavanagh, Dermot (2003), *Language and Politics in the Sixteenth-Century History Play* (New York: Palgrave Macmillan).

Cavell, Stanley (2003), *Disowning Knowledge in Seven Plays of Shakespeare* (Cambridge: Cambridge University Press).

Cervantes Saavedra, Miguel de (2001), *The Ingenious Hidalgo Don Quixote de La Mancha*, trans. Roberto González Echevarría (New York: Penguin Books).

Chabod, Federico (1958), 'Machiavelli's Method and Style', *Machiavelli and the Renaissance* (London: Bowes & Bowes), 126–48.

Chambers, E. K. (1945), *The Elizabethan Stage* (Oxford: Clarendon Press).

Chapman, George (1905), *Bussy d'Ambois and The Revenge of Bussy d'Ambois*, ed. Frederick S. Boas (Boston and London: D. C. Heath & Co.).

Chapman, George (1960), *Bussy d'Amboise*, ed. Jean Jacquot (Paris: Aubier).

Chapman, George (1964), *Bussy d'Ambois*, ed. Nicholas Brooke (The Revels Plays; London: Methuen).

Chapman, George (1988), *The Conspiracy and Tragedy of Byron*, ed. John Margeson (Manchester: Manchester University Press).

Cheney, Patrick (2004), *Shakespeare, National Poet-Playwright* (Cambridge: Cambridge University Press).

Chesterfield, Philip Dormer Stanhope, Earl of (1774), *Letters Written by the Late Right Honourable Philip Dormer Stanhope, Earl of Chesterfield, to his Son, Philip Stanhope, Esq.*, 2 vols. (4th edn., London: Printed for J. Dodsley).

Clare, Janet (2000), 'Marston: Censure, Censorship, and Free Speech', in T. F. Wharton (ed.), *The Drama of John Marston: Critical Re-Visions* (Cambridge: Cambridge University Press), 194–211.

Clark, Peter (1983), *The English Alehouse: A Social History, 1200–1830* (London and New York: Longman).

Clark, Stuart (1976–7), 'Wisdom Literature of the Seventeenth Century: A Guide to the Contents of the "Bacon-Tottel" Commonplace Books'. Parts I and II, *Transactions of the Cambridge Bibliographical Society*, 6, 291–305, and 7, 46–73.

Clayton, Thomas (1992), *The Hamlet First Published (Q1, 1603): Origins, Form, Intertextualities* (Newark: University of Delaware Press).

Clegg, Cyndia Susan (1997), '"By the Choise and Inuitation of al the Realme": *Richard II* and Elizabethan Press Censorship', *Shakespeare Quarterly*, 48, 432–48.

Clegg, Cyndia Susan (1999), 'Archival Poetics and the Politics of Literature: Essex and Hayward Revisited', *Studies in the Literary Imagination*, 32, 115–32.

Clover, Carol J. (2000), 'Law and the Order of Popular Culture', in Austin Sarat and Thomas R. Kearns (eds.), *Law in the Domains of Culture* (Ann Arbor: The University of Michigan Press), 97–119.

Cogswell, Thomas (1989), *The Blessed Revolution: English Politics and the Coming of War, 1621–1624* (Cambridge: Cambridge University Press).

Cogswell, Thomas and Lake, Peter (2009), 'Buckingham Does the Globe: Henry VIII and the Politics of Popularity in the 1620s', *Shakespeare Quarterly*, 60, 253–78.

Colclough, David (2005), *Freedom of Speech in Early Stuart England* (Cambridge and New York: Cambridge University Press).

Collins, Arthur (ed.) (1746), *Letters and Memorials of State, in the Reigns of Queen Mary, Queen Elizabeth, King James…* (London: T. Osborne).

Collins, D. C. (1943), *A Handlist of News Pamphlets, 1590–1610* (London: South-West Essex Technical College).

Collinson, Patrick (1986–7), 'The Monarchical Republic of Queen Elizabeth I', *Bulletin of the John Rylands Memorial Library*, 69, 394–424.

Collinson, Patrick (1988), 'Puritans, Men of Business and Elizabethan Parliaments', *Parliamentary History*, 7, 187–211.

Collinson, Patrick (1990), *De Republica Anglorum or, History with the Politics Put Back* (Cambridge: Cambridge University Press).
Collinson, Patrick (1994), 'The Elizabethan Exclusion Crisis and the Elizabethan Polity', *Proceedings of the British Academy*, 84, 51–92.
A Complete Collection of State-trials, and Proceedings for High-treason,... the Fourth Edition...Volume the First (London: T. Wright; for C. Bathurst [etc.]: and sold by G. Kearsly, 1776).
Condren, Conal (1994), *The Language of Politics in Seventeenth-Century England* (Basingstoke: Macmillan).
Condren, Conal (2006), *Argument and Authority in Early Modern England: The Presupposition of Oaths and Offices* (Cambridge: Cambridge University Press).
Condren, Conal (2011), 'Reason of State and Sovereignty in Early Modern England: A Question of Ideology?', *Parergon*, 28 (2), 5–27.
Cook, Megan (2012), 'How Francis Thynne Read His Chaucer', *Journal of the Early Book Society*, 15, 215–43.
Corfield, Penelope J. (1995), *Power and the Professions in Britain, 1700–1850* (London: Routledge).
Cormack, Bradin (2007), *A Power to Do Justice: Jurisdiction, English Literature, and the Rise of Common Law, 1509–1625* (Chicago: University of Chicago Press).
Cowan, Brian (2004), 'Mr. Spectator and the Coffeehouse Public Sphere', *Eighteenth-Century Studies*, 37, 345–66.
Craigwood, Joanna (2013), 'Shakespeare's Kingmaking Ambassadors', in Jason Powell and William T. Rossiter (eds.), *Authority and Diplomacy from Dante to Shakespeare* (Farnham: Ashgate), 199–217.
Crane, Mary Thomas (1993), *Framing Authority: Sayings, Self, and Society in Sixteenth-Century England* (Princeton: Princeton University Press).
Creighton, Gilbert (1967), 'When Did a Man in the Renaissance Grow Old?', *Studies in the Renaissance*, 14, 7–32.
Cressy, David (1982), 'Binding the Nation: The Bonds of Association, 1585 and 1696', in Delloyd J. Guth and John W. McKenna (eds.), *Tudor Rule and Revolution* (Cambridge: Cambridge University Press), 217–34.
Crinò, Anna Maria (1957), *Fatti e Figure del Seicento Anglo-Toscano: Documenti Inediti sui Rapporti Letterari, Diplomatici, Culturali fra Toscana e Inghilterra* (Biblioteca dell' Archivum Romanicum, I: 48; Firenze: Olschki).
Croft, Pauline (2006), 'Rex Pacificus, Robert Cecil, and the 1604 Peace with Spain', in Glenn Burgess, Rowland Wymer, and Jason Lawrence (eds.), *The Accession of James I: Historical and Cultural Consequences* (Basingstoke: Palgrave Macmillan), 140–54.
Crouzet, Denis (1990), *Les Guerriers de Dieu: la Violence au Temps des Troubles de Religion (vers 1525–vers 1610)*, 2 vols. (Seyssel: Champ Vallon).
Curtis, Cathy (2011), 'The Active and Contemplative Lives in Shakespeare's Plays', in David Armitage, Conal Condren, and Andrew Fitzmaurice (eds.), *Shakespeare and Early Modern Political Thought* (Cambridge: Cambridge University Press), 44–63.
Curtis, Mark H. (1959), *Oxford and Cambridge in Transition, 1558–1642: An Essay on the Changing Relations between the English Universities and English Society* (Oxford: Clarendon Press).
Curtis, Mark H. (1962), 'The Alienated Intellectuals of Early Stuart England', *Past & Present*, 23, 25–43.

Cust, Richard (1986), 'News and Politics in Early Seventeenth-Century England', *Past & Present*, 112, 60–90.

Cust, Richard and Hughes, Ann (eds.) (1989), *Conflict in Early Stuart England: Studies in Religion and Politics, 1603–1642* (London and New York: Longman).

Daniel, Drew (2009), '"I Am More an Antique Roman Than a Dane": Suicide, Masculinity and National Identity in *Hamlet*', in Maria Del Sapio Garbero (ed.), *Identity, Otherness and Empire in Shakespeare's Rome* (Farnham: Ashgate), 75–87.

Daniel, Drew (2013), *The Melancholy Assemblage: Affect and Epistemology in the English Renaissance* (New York: Fordham University Press).

Dávidházi, Péter (1993), 'Teve, Menyét, Cethal', *Holmi*, 6, 787–96.

Davin, Solange (2003), 'Healthy Viewing: The Reception of Medical Narratives', *Sociology of Health & Illness*, 25, 662–79.

Davis, Joel (2006), 'Robert Sidney's Marginal Comments on Tacitus and the English Campaigns in the Low Countries', *Sidney Journal*, 24, 1–19.

Davison, Francis (1826), *The Poetical Rhapsody: To Which Are Added Several Other Pieces*, ed. Nicholas Harris Nicolas, 2 vols. (London: William Pickering).

Dawson, Anthony B. and Yachnin, Paul Edward (2001), *The Culture of Playgoing in Shakespeare's England: A Collaborative Debate* (Cambridge: Cambridge University Press).

de Grazia, Margreta (2007), Hamlet *without Hamlet* (Cambridge: Cambridge University Press).

de Vivo, Filippo (2007), *Information and Communication in Venice: Rethinking Early Modern Politics* (Oxford and New York: Oxford University Press).

de Vivo, Filippo (2011), 'How to Read Venetian *Relazioni*', *Renaissance and Reformation*, 34, 25–59.

Dekker, Thomas (1905), *The Gull's Hornbook*, ed. R. B. McKerrow (London: At the De La More Press).

Deutermann, Allison K. (forthcoming), *Audiences to This Act: Listening for Form in Early Modern Theater* (Edinburgh: Edinburgh University Press).

DiGangi, Mario (1997), *The Homoerotics of Early Modern Drama* (Cambridge: Cambridge University Press).

Dollerup, Cay (1975), *Denmark, Hamlet, and Shakespeare: A Study of Englishmen's Knowledge of Denmark Towards the End of the Sixteenth Century with Special Reference to Hamlet*, 2 vols. (Salzburg: Universität Salzburg).

Donaldson, Ian (1982), *The Rapes of Lucretia: A Myth and Its Transformations* (Oxford: Clarendon Press).

Donaldson, Ian (2011), *Ben Jonson: A Life* (Oxford: Oxford University Press).

Donaldson, Peter Samuel (1988), *Machiavelli and Mystery of State* (New York: Cambridge University Press).

Donne, John (1993), *Pseudo-Martyr*, ed. Anthony Raspa (Montreal and Buffalo: McGill-Queen's University Press).

Dooley, Brendan (2005), 'Sources and Methods in Information History: The Case of Medici Florence, the Armada, and the Siege of Ostende', in J. W. Koopmans (ed.), *News and Politics in Early Modern Europe* (Leuven: Peeters), 29–46.

Dooley, Brendan (2010), 'Making It Present', in Brendan Dooley (ed.), *The Dissemination of News and the Emergence of Contemporaneity in Early Modern Europe* (Farnham and Burlington, VT: Ashgate), 95–114.

Doty, Jeffrey S. (2010), 'Shakespeare's *Richard II*, "Popularity," and the Early Modern Public Sphere', *Shakespeare Quarterly*, 61, 183–205.

Doty, Jeffrey S. (2012), '*Measure for Measure* and the Problem of Popularity', *English Literary Renaissance*, 42, 32–57.
Doty, Jeffrey S. (forthcoming), *Shakespeare, Popularity, and the Public Sphere* (Cambridge: Cambridge University Press).
Dover Wilson, John (1935), *What Happens in Hamlet?* (Cambridge: Cambridge University Press).
Dover Wilson, John (ed.) (1934), *Hamlet* (The Works of Shakespeare, Cambridge: University Press).
Duncan-Jones, Katherine (2011), *Shakespeare: Upstart Crow to Sweet Swan, 1592–1623* (London: Arden Shakespeare).
Dutton, Richard (1978), 'The Sources, Text, and Readers of *Sejanus*: Jonson's "Integrity in the Story"', *Studies in Philology*, 75, 181–98.
Dutton, Richard (1991), *Mastering the Revels: The Regulation and Censorship of English Renaissance Drama* (London: Macmillan).
Dutton, Richard (1996), *Ben Jonson. Authority. Criticism* (London: Macmillan).
Dutton, Richard (2008), *Ben Jonson, Volpone and the Gunpowder Plot* (Cambridge: Cambridge University Press).
Dzelzainis, Martin (1999), 'Shakespeare and Political Thought', in David Scott Kastan (ed.), *A Companion to Shakespeare* (Oxford: Blackwell), 100–16.
Eamon, William (1994), *Science and the Secrets of Nature* (Princeton: Princeton University Press).
Edwards, Philip (ed.) (1985), *Hamlet* (Cambridge: Cambridge University Press).
Ehrenberg, Victor (1947), 'Polypragmosyne: A Study in Greek Politics', *The Journal of Hellenic Studies*, 67, 46–67.
Eliot, T. S. (1951), 'Hamlet', *Selected Essays* (London: Faber and Faber), 141–6.
Ellis, Aytoun (1956), *The Penny Universities: A History of the Coffee-Houses* (London: Secker & Warburg).
Ellis, Markman (2001), 'Coffee-Women, *The Spectator*, and the Public Sphere in the Early Eighteenth Century', in Elizabeth Eger et al. (eds.), *Women, Writing and the Public Sphere, 1700–1830* (Cambridge: Cambridge University Press), 27–52.
Emden, Christian and Midgley, David R. (eds.) (2013), *Beyond Habermas: Democracy, Knowledge, and the Public Sphere* (New York: Berghahn Books).
Emerton, Ephraim (1925), *Humanism and Tyranny, Studies in the Italian Trecento* (Cambridge, MA: Harvard University Press).
Empson, William (1953), '*Hamlet* When New', *Sewanee Review*, 61, 15–42, 185–205.
Engle, Lars (2011), 'How Is Horatio Just? How Just Is Horatio?', *Shakespeare Quarterly*, 62, 256–62.
Enterline, Lynn (2000), *The Rhetoric of the Body from Ovid to Shakespeare* (Cambridge and New York: Cambridge University Press).
Enterline, Lynn (2012), *Shakespeare's Schoolroom: Rhetoric, Discipline, Emotion* (Philadelphia: University of Pennsylvania Press).
Erler, Mary C. (ed.) (2008), *Ecclesiastical London* (Records of Early English Drama, London and Toronto: British Library and University of Toronto Press).
Erne, Lukas (2003), *Shakespeare as Literary Dramatist* (Cambridge: Cambridge University Press).
Erne, Lukas (2008), 'Reconsidering Shakespearean Authorship', *Shakespeare Studies*, 36, 26–36.
Erne, Lukas (2013), *Shakespeare and the Book Trade* (Cambridge: Cambridge University Press).
Everett, Barbara (1977), '*Hamlet*: A Time to Die', *Shakespeare Survey*, 30, 117–23.

Falco, Raphael (2007), '*Hamlet*'s Narrative Infrastructure', *The Shakespearean International Yearbook*, 7, 123–39.
Farley-Hills, David (1995), 'Jonson and the Neo-Classical Rules in *Sejanus* and *Volpone*', *Review of English Studies*, 46 (182), 153–73.
Farmer, Alan B. (2006), 'Play-Reading, News-Reading, and Ben Jonson's *The Staple of News*', in Marta Straznicky (ed.), *The Book of the Play: Playwrights, Stationers and Readers in Early Modern England* (Amherst & Boston: University of Massachusetts Press), 127–58.
Fedorowicz, J. K. (1980), *England's Baltic Trade in the Early Seventeenth Century: A Study in Anglo-Polish Commercial Diplomacy* (Cambridge: Cambridge University Press).
Feingold, Mordechai (1984), *The Mathematicians' Apprenticeship: Science, Universities and Society in England, 1560–1640* (Cambridge: Cambridge University Press).
Feingold, Mordechai (1999), 'Gresham College and London Practitioners: The Nature of the English Mathematical Community', in Francis Ames-Lewis (ed.), *Sir Thomas Gresham and Gresham College: Studies in the Intellectual History of London in the Sixteenth and Seventeenth Centuries* (Aldershot: Ashgate), 174–88.
Felperin, Howard (1974), 'O'erdoing Termagant: An Approach to Shakespearean Mimesis', *The Yale Review*, 63, 372–91.
Fish, Stanley (1984), 'Authors-Readers: Jonson's Community of the Same', *Representations*, 7, 26–58.
Fissel, Mark Charles (2001), *English Warfare, 1511–1642* (Warfare and History; London and New York: Routledge).
Fitter, Chris (2005), 'Emergent Shakespeare and the Politics of Protest: *2 Henry VI* in Historical Contexts', *English Literary History*, 72, 129–58.
Fitzmaurice, Andrew (2009), 'The Corruption of *Hamlet*', in David Armitage, Conal Condren, and Andrew Fitzmaurice (eds.), *Shakespeare and Early Modern Political Thought* (Cambridge: Cambridge University Press), 139–56.
Foakes, R. A. (1956), '*Hamlet* and the Court of Elsinore', *Shakespeare Survey*, 9, 35–43.
Foakes, R. A. (2002), *Henslowe's Diary* (2nd edn.; Cambridge: Cambridge University Press).
Foucault, Michel (2001), *Fearless Speech* (Los Angeles: Semiotext(e): Distributed by MIT Press).
Foucault, Michel (2011), *The Courage of Truth: The Government of Self and Others, II* (Lectures at the Collège de France 1983–1984; Basingstoke: Palgrave Macmillan).
Fox, Adam (2013), 'Food, Drink and Social Distinction in Early Modern England', in Steve Hindle, Alexandra Shepard, and John Walter (eds.), *Remaking English Society: Social Relations and Social Change in Early Modern England* (Cambridge: Boydell & Brewer), 165–87.
Freidson, Eliot (2001), *Professionalism: The Third Logic* (Chicago: University of Chicago Press).
Frigo, Daniela (2008), 'Prudence and Experience: Ambassadors and Political Culture in Early Modern Italy', *Journal of Medieval and Early Modern Studies*, 38, 15–34.
Frye, Roland Mushat (1984), *The Renaissance Hamlet: Issues and Responses in 1600* (Princeton: Princeton University Press).
Fulton, Thomas (2006), 'Speculative Shakespeares: The Trials of Biographical Historicism', *Modern Philology*, 103, 385–408.
Fulton, Thomas (2010), *Historical Milton: Manuscript, Print, and Political Culture in Revolutionary England* (Amherst: University of Massachusetts Press).
Fussell, Paul (1983), *Class: A Guide through the American Status System* (New York: Summit Books).

Gajda, Alexandra (2009), 'Tacitus and Political Thought in Early Modern Europe, c. 1530–c. 1640', in A. J. Woodman (ed.), *The Cambridge Companion to Tacitus* (Cambridge: Cambridge University Press), 253–68.

Gajda, Alexandra (2012), *The Earl of Essex and Late Elizabethan Political Culture* (Oxford: Oxford University Press).

Garber, Marjorie (1987), *Shakespeare's Ghost Writers: Literature as Uncanny Causality* (London: Methuen).

Gasquet, Emile (1974), *Le Courant Machiavelien dans la Pensée et la Littérature Anglaises du XVIe Siècle* (Études Anglaises 51; Paris, Montréal, Bruxelles: Didier).

Gauchet, Marcel (1994), 'L'État au Miroir de la Raison d'État: la France et la Chrétienté', in Yves Charles Zarka (ed.), *Raison et Déraison d'État: Théoriciens et Théories de la Raison d'État aux XVIe et XVIIe Siècles* (Paris: Presses Universitaires de France), 193–244.

Gehring, David Scott (2013), *Anglo-German Relations and the Protestant Cause: Elizabethan Foreign Policy and Pan-Protestantism* (London: Pickering & Chatto).

Gehring, David Scott (ed.) (forthcoming), *Diplomatic Intelligence on the Holy Roman Empire and Denmark During the Reigns of Elizabeth I and James VI: Three Treatises* (Camden Series, Cambridge: Cambridge University Press).

Geng, Penelope (2011), '"He Only Talks": Arruntius and the Formation of Interpretive Communities in Ben Jonson's *Sejanus*', *The Ben Jonson Journal*, 18, 126–40.

Gentili, Alberico (1924), *De Legationibus Libri Tres*, trans. Gordon J. Laing, 2 vols. (New York: Oxford University Press).

Gieskes, Edward (2006), *Representing the Professions: Administration, Law, and Theater in Early Modern England* (Newark: University of Delaware Press).

Gilbert, Allan H. (1940), *Literary Criticism, Plato to Dryden* (New York, Cincinnati etc.: American Book Company).

Ginzburg, Carlo (1976), 'High and Low: The Theme of Forbidden Knowledge in the Sixteenth and Seventeenth Centuries', *Past & Present*, 73, 28–41.

Goldberg, Jonathan (1983), *James I and the Politics of Literature* (Baltimore: Johns Hopkins University Press).

Gollancz, Sir Israel (1926), *The Sources of Hamlet, with an Essay on the Legend* (London: H. Milford, Oxford University Press).

Gowan, Juliet (2009), '"One Man in His Time": The Notebook of Edward Pudsey', *Bodleian Library Record*, 22 (1), 94–101.

Gowan, Juliet Mary (1967), 'An Edition of Edward Pudsey's Commonplace Book (c. 1600–1615) from the Manuscript in the Bodleian Library', M. Phil thesis (University of London).

Grafton, Anthony (2007), *What Was History? The Art of History in Early Modern Europe* (Cambridge: Cambridge University Press).

Grafton, Anthony and Jardine, Lisa (1986), *From Humanism to the Humanities: Education and the Liberal Arts in Fifteenth- and Sixteenth-Century Europe* (London: Duckworth).

Graves, M. A. R. (1983), 'The Management of the Elizabethan House of Commons: The Council's "Men-of-Business"', *Parliamentary History*, 2, 11–38.

Graves, M. A. R. (1989), 'The Common Lawyers and the Privy Council's Parliamentary Men-of-Business, 1584–1601', *Parliamentary History*, 8, 189–215.

Greenblatt, Stephen (1988), *Shakespearean Negotiations: The Circulation of Social Energy in Renaissance England* (Berkeley: University of California Press).

Greenblatt, Stephen (2001), *Hamlet in Purgatory* (Princeton: Princeton University Press).

Greene, Thomas M. (1970), 'Ben Jonson and the Centered Self', *SEL: Studies in English Literature, 1500–1900*, 10, 325–48.

Grosart, Alexander B. (ed.) (1884), *The Works of Gabriel Harvey, D.C.L.*, 3 vols. (London and Aylesbury: Printed for private circulation only).
Guicciardini, Francesco (1972), *Maxims and Reflections (Ricordi)*, trans. Mario Domandi (Philadelphia: University of Pennsylvania Press).
Guillory, John (2000), '"To Please the Wiser Sort": Violence and Philosophy in *Hamlet*', in Carla Mazzio and Douglas Trevor (eds.), *Historicism, Psychoanalysis, and Early Modern Culture* (New York: Routledge), 82–109.
Gurr, Andrew (2004), *Playgoing in Shakespeare's London* (3rd edn.; Cambridge: Cambridge University Press).
Guy, John (1995), 'Introduction: The Second Reign of Elizabeth I?', in John Guy (ed.), *The Reign of Elizabeth I: Court and Culture in the Last Decade* (Cambridge: Cambridge University Press), 1–19.
Guy, John (1995), 'The Rhetoric of Counsel in Early Modern England', in Dale Hoak (ed.), *Tudor Political Culture* (Cambridge: Cambridge University Press), 292–310.
Guy, John (ed.) (1995), *The Reign of Elizabeth I: Court and Culture in the Last Decade* (Cambridge: Cambridge University Press).
Guy, John (2005), *Queen of Scots: The True Life of Mary Stuart* (Boston and New York: Houghton Mifflin).
Habermas, Jürgen (1989), *The Structural Transformation of the Public Sphere: An Inquiry into a Category of Bourgeois Society* (Cambridge, MA: MIT Press).
Hadfield, Andrew (2006), 'The *Ur-Hamlet* and the Fable of the Kid', *Notes & Queries*, 53, 46–7.
Hadfield, Andrew (2008), *Shakespeare and Republicanism* (Cambridge: Cambridge University Press).
Hadfield, Andrew (2009), '"Not without Mustard": Self-Publicity and Polemic in Early Modern London', in Margaret Healy and Thomas Healy (eds.), *Renaissance Transformations: The Making of English Writing, 1500–1650* (Edinburgh: Edinburgh University Press).
Halpern, Richard (1991), *The Poetics of Primitive Accumulation: English Renaissance Culture and the Genealogy of Capital* (Ithaca: Cornell University Press).
Halpern, Richard (2004), 'Marlowe's Theater of Night: *Doctor Faustus* and Capital', *English Literary History*, 71, 455–95.
Halpern, Richard (2008), 'Eclipse of Action: *Hamlet* and the Political Economy of Playing', *Shakespeare Quarterly*, 59, 450–82.
Halpern, Richard (2009), 'The King's Two Buckets: Kantorowicz, *Richard II*, and Fiscal *Trauerspiel*', *Representations*, 106, 67–76.
Hammer, Paul E. J. (1994), 'The Earl of Essex, Fulke Greville, and the Employment of Scholars', *Studies in Philology*, 91 (2), 167–80.
Hammer, Paul E. J. (1994), 'The Use of Scholarship: The Secretariat of Robert Devereux, Second Earl of Essex, c. 1585–1601', *The English Historical Review*, 109, 26–51.
Hammer, Paul E. J. (1996), 'Essex and Europe: Evidence from Confidential Instructions by the Earl of Essex, 1595–6', *The English Historical Review*, 111, 357–81.
Hammer, Paul E. J. (1999), *The Polarisation of Elizabethan Politics: The Political Career of Robert Devereux, 2nd Earl of Essex, 1585–1597* (Cambridge: Cambridge University Press).
Hammer, Paul E. J. (2003), *Elizabeth's Wars: War, Government and Society in Tudor England, 1544–1604* (Basingstoke: Palgrave Macmillan).
Hammer, Paul E. J. (2005), 'The Crucible of War: English Foreign Policy, 1589–1603', in Susan Doran and Glenn Richardson (eds.), *Tudor England and Its Neighbours* (Basingstoke: Palgrave), 235–66.

Hammer, Paul E. J. (2007), 'The Smiling Crocodile: The Earl of Essex and Late Elizabethan "Popularity"', in Peter Lake and Steve Pincus (eds.), *The Politics of the Public Sphere in Early Modern England* (Manchester: Manchester University Press), 95–115.

Hammer, Paul E. J. (2008), 'Shakespeare's *Richard II*, the Play of 7 February 1601, and the Essex Rising', *Shakespeare Quarterly*, 59, 1–35.

Hammill, Graham L. and Lupton, Julia Reinhard (eds.) (2012), *Political Theology and Early Modernity* (Chicago: University of Chicago Press).

Hampton, Timothy (2009), *Fictions of Embassy: Literature and Diplomacy in Early Modern Europe* (Ithaca: Cornell University Press).

Hanson, Elizabeth (2011), 'Fellow Students: Hamlet, Horatio, and the Early Modern University', *Shakespeare Quarterly*, 62, 205–29.

Harbage, Alfred (1952), *Shakespeare and the Rival Traditions* (New York: Macmillan).

Harbage, Alfred and Schoenbaum, Samuel (1964), *Annals of English Drama, 975–1700* (Rev. edn.; London: Methuen).

Harkness, Deborah E. (2007), *The Jewel House: Elizabethan London and the Scientific Revolution* (New Haven: Yale University Press).

Hartman, Geoffrey H. (1975), *The Fate of Reading and Other Essays* (Chicago: University of Chicago Press).

Hattenhauer, Hans (1980), *Geschichte des Beamtentums* (Handbuch des Öffentlichen Dienstes; Köln, Berlin, Bonn, München: Carl Heymanns Verlag).

Haverkamp, Anselm (2006), 'The Ghost of History: Hamlet and the Politics of Paternity', *Law and Literature*, 18 (2), 171–98.

Hay, Millicent V. (1984), *The Life of Robert Sidney, Earl of Leicester (1563–1626)* (Washington, DC: Folger Shakespeare Library).

Helms, Mary W. (1988), *Ulysses' Sail: An Ethnographic Odyssey of Power, Knowledge, and Geographical Distance* (Princeton: Princeton University Press).

Heltzel, Virgil B. (1937), 'Richard Earl of Carbery's Advice to His Son', *The Huntington Library Bulletin*, 11, 59–105.

Herendeen, Wyman H. (2007), *William Camden: A Life in Context* (Woodbridge: Boydell Press).

Hester, Nathalie (2003), 'Scholarly Borrowing: The Case of Remigio Nannini's *Orationi Militari* and François de Belleforest's *Harangues Militaires*', *Modern Philology*, 101, 235–58.

Hill, Geoffrey (2008), *Collected Critical Writings*, ed. Kenneth Haynes (Oxford: Oxford University Press).

Hillman, David (2007), *Shakespeare's Entrails: Belief, Scepticism and the Interior of the Body* (Basingstoke: Palgrave Macmillan).

Hirrel, Michael J. (2012), 'When Did Gabriel Harvey Write His Famous Note?', *Huntington Library Quarterly*, 75, 291–9.

Hobbes, Thomas (1990), *Behemoth: Or, the Long Parliament*, ed. Ferdinand Tönnies (Chicago: University of Chicago Press).

Hobbes, Thomas (1996), *Leviathan*, ed. Richard Tuck (Rev. edn.; Cambridge: Cambridge University Press).

Holderness, Graham (2011), '"The Single and Peculiar Life": Hamlet's Heart and the Early Modern Subject', *Shakespeare Survey*, 63, 296–307.

Holmes, Peter (1982), *Resistance and Compromise: The Political Thought of the Elizabethan Catholics* (Cambridge: Cambridge University Press).

Holt, Mack P. (1986), *The Duke of Anjou and the Politique Struggle During the Wars of Religion* (Cambridge: Cambridge University Press).

Honigmann, E. A. J. (1956), 'The Date of *Hamlet*', *Shakespeare Survey*, 9, 24–34.
Honigmann, E. A. J. (1963), 'The Politics of *Hamlet* and "the World of the Play"', *Stratford-upon-Avon Studies*, 5, 129–47.
Honigmann, E. A. J. (ed.) (1997), *Othello* (The Arden Shakespeare, Third Series, Walton-on-Thames: Thomas Nelson & Sons).
Höpfl, H. M. (2002), 'Orthodoxy and Reason of State', *History of Political Thought*, 23, 211–37.
Horkheimer, Max and Adorno, Theodor W. (2002), *Dialectic of Enlightenment: Philosophical Fragments*, ed. Gunzelin Schmid Noerr, trans. Edmund Jephcott (Stanford: Stanford University Press).
Hörnqvist, Mikael (2004), *Machiavelli and Empire* (Cambridge: Cambridge University Press).
Horrocks, John Wesley (1908), 'Machiavelli in Tudor Political Opinion and Discussion', (University of London).
Hotman, François (1972), *Francogallia*, ed. Ralph E. Giesey, trans. J. H. M. Salmon (Cambridge: Cambridge University Press).
Howard, Jean E. (2000), 'Women, Foreigners, and the Regulation of Urban Space in *Westward Ho*', in Lena Cowen Orlin (ed.), *Material London, ca. 1600* (Philadelphia: University of Pennsylvania Press), 150–68.
Howard, Jean E. (2007), *Theater of a City: The Places of London Comedy, 1598–1642* (Philadelphia: University of Pennsylvania Press).
Howard, Jean E. and Rackin, Phyllis (1997), *Engendering a Nation: A Feminist Account of Shakespeare's English Histories* (London and New York: Routledge).
Hughes, Charles (1905), 'Nicholas Faunt's Discourse Touching the Office of Principal Secretary of Estate, &c. 1592', *The English Historical Review*, 20, 499–508.
Huizinga, Johann (1910), 'Rosenkranz und Güldenstern', *Jahrbuch der deutschen Shakespeare-Gesellschaft*, 46, 60–8.
Hunter, G. K. (1951), 'The Marking of Sententiae in Elizabethan Printed Plays, Poems, and Romances', *The Library 5th ser.*, 6, 171–88.
Hunter, G. K. (1957), 'Isocrates' Precepts and Polonius' Character', *Shakespeare Quarterly*, 8, 501–6.
Hunter, Judith (2002), 'English Inns, Taverns, Alehouses and Brandy Shops: The Legislative Framework 1495–1797', in Beat Kümin and B. Ann Tlusty (eds.), *The World of the Tavern: Public Houses in Early Modern Europe* (Aldershot: Ashgate), 65–82.
Hunter, Michael (1985), 'The Problem of "Atheism" in Early Modern England', *Transactions of the Royal Historical Society, Fifth Series*, 35, 135–57.
Huntington, John (2013), 'Chapman's Ambitious Comedy', *English Literary Renaissance*, 43, 128–52.
Hutson, Lorna (1993), 'Fortunate Travelers: Reading for the Plot in Sixteenth-Century England', *Representations*, 41, 83–103.
Hutson, Lorna (2008), *The Invention of Suspicion: Law and Mimesis in Shakespeare and Renaissance Drama* (Oxford: Oxford University Press).
Ide, Richard S. (1984), 'Exploiting the Tradition: The Elizabethan Revenger as Chapman's "Complete Man"', *Medieval & Renaissance Drama in England*, 1, 159–72.
Jackson, Richard A. (1972), 'Elective Kingship and Consensus Populi in Sixteenth-Century France', *The Journal of Modern History*, 44, 155–71.
Jacquot, Jean (1951), *George Chapman, 1559–1634: Sa Vie, sa Poésie, son Théâtre, sa Pensée* (Paris: Les Belles Lettres).

James, Heather (2013), 'The First English Printed Commonplace Books and the Rise of the Common Reader', in Allison K. Deutermann and András Kiséry (eds.), *Formal Matters: Reading the Materials of English Renaissance Literature* (Manchester: Manchester University Press), 15–33.
James VI and I, King (1994), *Political Writings*, ed. Johann P. Sommerville (Cambridge: Cambridge University Press).
Jameson, T. H. (1941), 'The "Machiavellianism" of Gabriel Harvey', *PMLA*, 56, 645–56.
Jardine, Lisa (1986), 'Gabriel Harvey: Exemplary Ramist and Pragmatic Humanist', *Revue des Sciences Philosophiques et Théologiques*, 70, 36–48.
Jardine, Lisa and Grafton, Anthony (1990), '"Studied for Action": How Gabriel Harvey Read His Livy', *Past & Present*, 129, 30–78.
Jardine, Lisa and Sherman, William (1994), 'Pragmatic Readers: Knowledge Transactions and Scholarly Services in Late Elizabethan England', in Anthony Fletcher and Peter Roberts (eds.), *Religion, Culture, and Society in Early Modern Britain: Essays in Honour of Patrick Collinson* (Cambridge: Cambridge University Press), 102–24.
Jed, Stephanie H. (1989), *Chaste Thinking: The Rape of Lucretia and the Birth of Humanism* (Bloomington: Indiana University Press).
Jenkins, Harold (ed.) (1982), *Hamlet* (Arden Shakespeare, London: Methuen).
Jones, Richard Foster (1953), *The Triumph of the English Language: A Survey of Opinions Concerning the Vernacular from the Introduction of Printing to the Restoration* (Stanford: Stanford University Press).
Jonson, Ben (1990), *Sejanus: His Fall*, ed. Philip K. Ayres (Manchester: Manchester University Press).
Jonson, Ben (2012), *The Cambridge Edition of the Works of Ben Jonson*, ed. David M. Bevington, Martin Butler, and Ian Donaldson, 7 vols. (Cambridge and New York: Cambridge University Press).
Jorgensen, Paul A. (1956), *Shakespeare's Military World* (Berkeley: University of California Press).
Jowett, John (1988), '"Fall before This Booke": The 1605 Quarto of *Sejanus*', *TEXT*, 4, 279–95.
Jowett, John (1991), 'Jonson's Authorization of Type in *Sejanus* and Other Early Quartos', *Studies in Bibliography*, 44, 254–65.
Jowett, John (ed.) (2000), *The Tragedy of King Richard III* (The Oxford Shakespeare, Oxford: Oxford University Press).
Jusserand, J. J. (1911), 'Ambassador La Boderie and the "Compositeur" of the Byron Plays', *Modern Language Review*, 6, 203–5.
Kahn, Coppélia (1997), *Roman Shakespeare: Warriors, Wounds, and Women* (New York: Routledge).
Kahn, Victoria (1994), *Machiavellian Rhetoric: From the Counter-Reformation to Milton* (Princeton: Princeton University Press).
Kahn, Victoria (1994), 'Reading Machiavelli: Innocent Gentillet's Discourse on Method', *Political Theory*, 22, 539–60.
Kahn, Victoria (2014), *The Future of Illusion: Political Theology and Early Modern Texts* (Chicago: University of Chicago Press).
Kamps, Ivo (1995), 'Ruling Fantasies and the Fantasies of Rule: *The Phoenix* and *Measure for Measure*', *Studies in Philology*, 92, 248–73.
Kantorowicz, Ernst H. (1955), 'Mysteries of State: An Absolutist Concept and Its Late Mediaeval Origins', *The Harvard Theological Review*, 48, 65–91.

Kastan, David Scott (1986), 'Proud Majesty Made a Subject: Shakespeare and the Spectacle of Rule', *Shakespeare Quarterly*, 37, 459–75.
Kastan, David Scott (1987), '"His Semblable in His Mirror": *Hamlet* and the Imitation of Revenge', *Shakespeare Studies*, 19, 111–24.
Kastan, David Scott (1999), 'Shakespeare in Print', *Shakespeare after Theory* (London: Routledge), 71–92.
Kastan, David Scott (2001), *Shakespeare and the Book* (Cambridge: Cambridge University Press).
Kastan, David Scott (2003), 'Performances and Playbooks: The Closing of the Theatres and the Politics of Drama', in Kevin Sharpe and Steven Zwicker (eds.), *Reading, Society and Politics in Early Modern England* (Cambridge: Cambridge University Press), 167–84.
Kastan, David Scott (2007), 'Humphrey Moseley and the Invention of English Literature', in Sabrina Alcorn Baron, Eric N. Lindquist, and Eleanor F. Shevlin (eds.), *Agent of Change: Print Culture Studies after Elizabeth L. Eisenstein* (Amherst & Boston: University of Massachusetts Press), 105–24.
Kastan, David Scott (2008), '"To Think These Trifles Some-Thing": Shakespearean Playbooks and the Claims of Authorship', *Shakespeare Studies*, 36, 37–48.
Kastan, David Scott (2014), *A Will to Believe: Shakespeare and Religion* (Oxford: Oxford University Press).
Kearney, James (2009), *The Incarnate Text: Imagining the Book in Reformation England* (Philadelphia: University of Pennsylvania Press).
Keller, Vera (2012), 'The "New World of Sciences": The Temporality of the Research Agenda and the Unending Ambitions of Science', *Isis*, 103, 727–34.
Kelley, Donald R. (1973), *François Hotman: A Revolutionary's Ordeal* (Princeton: Princeton University Press).
Kelliher, Hilton (1989), 'Contemporary Manuscript Extracts from Shakespeare's *Henry IV, Part 1*', *English Manuscript Studies 1100–1700*, 1, 144–81.
Kelso, Ruth (1929), *The Doctrine of the English Gentleman in the Sixteenth Century: With a Bibliographical List of Treatises on the Gentleman and Related Subjects Published in Europe to 1625* (University of Illinois Studies in Language and Literature; Urbana: University of Illinois Press).
Kempner, Nadja (1928), *Raleghs Staatstheoretische Schriften: Die Einführung des Machiavellismus in England* (Beiträge zur Englischen Philologie; Leipzig: B. Tauchnitz).
Kenny, Neil (1998), *Curiosity in Early Modern Europe: Word Histories* (Wolfenbütteler Forschungen; Wiesbaden: Harrassowitz).
Kervyn de Lettenhove, Baron (ed.) (1882–1900), *Relations Politiques des Pays-Bas et de l'Angleterre, sous le Règne de Philippe II*, 10 vols. (Bruxelles: F. Hayez).
Kerwin, William (2005), *Beyond the Body: The Boundaries of Medicine and English Renaissance Drama* (Amherst: University of Massachusetts Press).
Kewes, Paulina (2011), 'Henry Savile's Tacitus and the Politics of Roman History in Late Elizabethan England', *Huntington Library Quarterly*, 74, 515–51.
Kiernan, Michael (ed.) (2000), *The Advancement of Learning* (The Oxford Francis Bacon, Oxford: Oxford University Press).
King, T. J. (1992), *Casting Shakespeare's Plays: London Actors and Their Roles, 1590–1642* (Cambridge: Cambridge University Press).
Kirk, Andrew M. (1996), *The Mirror of Confusion: The Representation of French History in English Renaissance Drama* (New York: Garland).
Kirschbaum, Leo (1937), 'The Date of Shakespeare's *Hamlet*', *Studies in Philology*, 34, 168–75.

Kiséry, András (2012), 'An Author and a Bookshop: Publishing Marlowe's Remains at the Black Bear', *Philological Quarterly*, 91, 361–92.

Kistler, Susanne F. (1980), '"Strange and Far-Removed Shores": A Reconsideration of *The Revenge of Bussy d'Ambois*', *SP*, 77, 128–44.

Klein, Lawrence E. (1996), 'Coffeehouse Civility, 1660–1714: An Aspect of Post-Courtly Culture in England', *Huntington Library Quarterly*, 59, 31–51.

Knight, Jeffrey Todd (2013), *Bound to Read: Compilations, Collections, and the Making of Renaissance Literature* (Philadelphia: University of Pennsylvania Press).

Knights, L. C. (1937), *Drama and Society in the Age of Jonson* (London: Chatto & Windus).

Knights, Mark (2005), *Representation and Misrepresentation in Later Stuart Britain: Partisanship and Political Culture* (Oxford: Oxford University Press).

Knutson, Roslyn L. (2001), *Playing Companies and Commerce in Shakespeare's Time* (Cambridge: Cambridge University Press).

Kocher, Paul H. (1941), 'François Hotman and Marlowe's *The Massacre at Paris*', *PMLA*, 56, 349–68.

Kohlndorfer-Fries, Ruth (2009), *Diplomatie und Gelehrtenrepublik: Die Kontakte des Französischen Gesandten Jacques Bongars (1554–1612)* (Tübingen: Niemeyer).

Koselleck, Reinhart (1979), *Vergangene Zukunft: Zur Semantik geschichtlicher Zeiten* (Frankfurt am Main: Suhrkamp).

Kuin, R. J. P. (ed.) (2012), *The Correspondence of Sir Philip Sidney*, 2 vols. (Oxford: Oxford University Press).

Kyle, Chris R. (2012), *Theater of State: Parliament and Political Culture in Early Stuart England* (Stanford: Stanford University Press).

Lake, Peter (2004), 'The King (the Queen) and the Jesuit: James Stuart's *True Law of Free Monarchies* in Context/s', *Transactions of the Royal Historical Society*, 14, 243–60.

Lake, Peter (2005), 'From *Leicester His Commonwealth* to *Sejanus His Fall*: Ben Jonson and the Politics of Roman (Catholic) Virtue', in Ethan H. Shagan (ed.), *Catholics and the 'Protestant Nation': Religious Politics and Identity in Early Modern England* (Manchester: Manchester University Press), 128–61.

Lake, Peter (2006), 'Anti-Puritanism: The Structure of a Prejudice', in Kenneth Fincham and Peter Lake (eds.), *Religious Politics in Post-Reformation England: Essays in Honour of Nicholas Tyacke* (Woodbridge: Boydell Press), 80–97.

Lake, Peter (2007), 'The Politics of "Popularity" and the Public Sphere: The "Monarchical Republic" of Elizabeth I Defends Itself', in Peter Lake and Steve Pincus (eds.), *The Politics of the Public Sphere in Early Modern England* (Manchester: Manchester University Press), 59–94.

Lake, Peter (2012), 'Ben Jonson and the Politics of "Conversion": *Catiline* and the Relocation of Roman (Catholic) Virtue', *Ben Jonson Journal*, 19, 163–89.

Lake, Peter (2016), *Bad Queen Bess? Libels, Secret Histories and the Politics of Publicity in the Reign of Queen Elizabeth I* (Oxford: Oxford University Press).

Lake, Peter and Pincus, Steve (2006), 'Rethinking the Public Sphere in Early Modern England', *Journal of British Studies*, 45, 270–92.

Lake, Peter and Pincus, Steven C. A. (eds.) (2007), *The Politics of the Public Sphere in Early Modern England* (Manchester and New York: Manchester University Press).

Lambert, Sheila (1992), 'Coranto Printing in England: The First Newsbooks', *Journal of Newspaper and Periodical History*, 8, 3–17.

Lander, Jesse (2006), *Inventing Polemic: Religion, Print, and Literary Culture in Early Modern England* (Cambridge: Cambridge University Press).

Larkin, James Francis and Hughes, Paul L. (eds.) (1973), *Royal Proclamations of King James I, 1603–1625* (Stuart Royal Proclamations, Oxford: Clarendon Press).

Lee, John (2000), *Shakespeare's* Hamlet *and the Controversies of the Self* (Oxford: Clarendon Press).

Lee, Maurice (1967), 'The Jacobean Diplomatic Service', *American Historical Review*, 72, 1264–82.

Lee, Maurice (ed.) (1972), *Dudley Carleton to John Chamberlain, 1603–1624: Jacobean Letters* (New Brunswick: Rutgers University Press).

Lee, Patricia-Ann (1970), 'Some English Academies: An Experiment in the Education of Renaissance Gentlemen', *History of Education Quarterly*, 10, 273–86.

Leggatt, Alexander (1982), 'The Tragedy of Clermont d'Ambois', *The Modern Language Review*, 77, 524–36.

Leo, F. A. (1890), 'Rosenkrantz und Guldenstern', *Jahrbuch der deutschen Shakespeare-Gesellschaft*, 25, 281–6.

Leo, F. A. (1891), 'Rosenkrantz und Gyldenstern', *Jahrbuch der deutschen Shakespeare-Gesellschaft*, 26, 325–36.

Lesser, Zachary (2011), 'Playbooks', in Joad Raymond (ed.), *The Oxford History of Popular Print Culture, Vol, 1: Britain and Ireland to 1660* (Oxford: Oxford University Press).

Lesser, Zachary (2015), *Hamlet after Q1: An Uncanny History of the Shakespearean Text* (Philadelphia: University of Pennsylvania Press).

Lesser, Zachary and Stallybrass, Peter (2008), 'The First Literary *Hamlet* and the Commonplacing of Professional Plays', *Shakespeare Quarterly*, 59, 371–420.

Levin, Harry (1959), *The Question of Hamlet* (New York: Oxford University Press).

Levine, Lawrence W. (1988), *Highbrow/Lowbrow: The Emergence of Cultural Hierarchy in America* (Cambridge, MA: Harvard University Press).

Levy, F. J. (1964), 'The Making of Camden's *Britannia*', *Bibliothèque d'Humanisme et Renaissance*, 26, 70–97.

Levy, F. J. (1965), 'Daniel Rogers as Antiquary', *Bibliothèque d'Humanisme et Renaissance*, 27, 444–62.

Levy, F. J. (1982), 'How Information Spread among the Gentry, 1550–1640', *Journal of British Studies*, 21, 11–34.

Levy, F. J. (1986), 'Francis Bacon and the Style of Politics', *English Literary Renaissance*, 16, 101–22.

Levy, F. J. (1987), 'Hayward, Daniel, and the Beginnings of Politic History in England', *Huntington Library Quarterly*, 50, 1–34.

Levy, Fritz (1999), 'The Decorum of News', in Joad Raymond (ed.), *News, Newspapers, and Society in Early Modern Britain* (London and Portland, OR: Frank Cass), 12–38.

Levy, Fritz (2000), 'Staging the News', in Arthur Marotti and Michael Bristol (eds.), *Print, Manuscript and Performance* (Columbus: Ohio State University Press), 252–78.

Limon, Jerzy (1986), *Dangerous Matter: English Drama and Politics in 1623/24* (Cambridge: Cambridge University Press).

Loewenstein, Joseph (2002), *Ben Jonson and Possessive Authorship* (Cambridge: Cambridge University Press).

Loewenstein, Joseph (2002), 'Marston's Gorge and the Question of Formalism', in Mark David Rasmussen (ed.), *Renaissance Literature and Its Formal Engagements* (New York: Palgrave), 89–112.

Long, Pamela O. (2001), *Openness, Secrecy, Authorship: Technical Arts and the Culture of Knowledge from Antiquity to the Renaissance* (Baltimore: Johns Hopkins University Press).

Lupton, Julia Reinhard (2007), 'Hamlet, Prince: Tragedy, Citizenship, and Political Theology', in Diana Henderson (ed.), *Alternative Shakespeares 3* (London: Routledge), 181–203.
Lupton, Julia Reinhard (2011), *Thinking with Shakespeare: Essays on Politics and Life* (Chicago: University of Chicago Press).
MacCaffrey, Wallace T. (1992), *Elizabeth I: War and Politics, 1588–1603* (Princeton: Princeton University Press).
McClure, Norman Egbert (ed.) (1939), *The Letters of John Chamberlain*, 2 vols. (Philadelphia: American Philosophical Society).
McCoy, Richard (1995), 'Lord of Liberty: Francis Davison and the Cult of Elizabeth', in John Guy (ed.), *The Reign of Elizabeth I: Court and Culture in the Last Decade* (Cambridge: Cambridge University Press), 212–28.
McDiarmid, John F. (2007), *The Monarchical Republic of Early Modern England: Essays in Response to Patrick Collinson* (Aldershot: Ashgate).
Machiavelli, Niccolò (1988), *The Prince*, ed. Quentin Skinner, trans. Russell Price (Cambridge: Cambridge University Press).
Mack, Maynard (1952), 'The World of *Hamlet*', *The Yale Review*, 41, 502–23.
McKenzie, Donald F. (1973), '"The Staple of News" and the Late Plays', in William Blissett, Julian Patrick, and R. W. Van Fossen (eds.), *A Celebration of Ben Jonson* (Toronto: University of Toronto Press), 83–128.
McKeon, Michael (2005), *The Secret History of Domesticity: Public, Private and the Division of Knowledge* (Baltimore: Johns Hopkins University Press).
Maclean, Ian (1992), *Interpretation and Meaning in the Renaissance: The Case of Law* (Cambridge: Cambridge University Press).
McMillin, Scott and MacLean, Sally-Beth (1998), *The Queen's Men and Their Plays* (Cambridge: Cambridge University Press).
MacPhail, Eric (2001), 'The Plot of History from Antiquity to the Renaissance', *Journal of the History of Ideas*, 62, 1–16.
McRae, Andrew (2004), *Literature, Satire, and the Early Stuart State* (Cambridge: Cambridge University Press).
McShane Jones, Angela (2005), '*The Gazet in Metre; or the Rhiming Newsmonger*. The English Broadside Ballad as Intelligencer: A New Narrative', in J. W. Koopmans (ed.), *News and Politics in Early Modern Europe (1500–1800)* (Leuven: Peeters), 131–51.
Malcolm, Noel (2007), *Reason of State, Propaganda, and the Thirty Years' War: An Unknown Translation by Thomas Hobbes* (Oxford: Clarendon Press).
Mallin, Eric S. (1995), *Inscribing the Time: Shakespeare and the End of Elizabethan England* (Berkeley, Los Angeles, London: University of California Press).
Malone, Edmond (ed.) (1780), *Supplement to the Edition of Shakspeare's Plays Published in 1778 by Samuel Johnson and George Steevens*, 2 vols. (London: C. Bathurst, W. Strahan, and others, 1780).
Marino, James J. (2011), *Owning William Shakespeare: The King's Men and Their Intellectual Property* (Philadelphia: University of Pennsylvania Press).
Markham, Clements R. (1888), *'The Fighting Veres.' Lives of Sir Francis Vere, General of the Queen's Forces in the Low Countries, Governor of the Brill and of Portsmouth, and of Sir Horace Vere, General of the English Forces in the Low Countries, Governor of the Brill, Master-General of Ordnance, and Baron Vere of Tilbury* (Boston and New York: Houghton, Mifflin & Co.).
Marston, John (1975), *The Malcontent*, ed. G. K. Hunter (London: Methuen).

Marston, John (1978), *Antonio's Revenge*, ed. W. Reavley Gair (Manchester: Manchester University Press).
Mattingly, Garrett (1955), *Renaissance Diplomacy* (London: Jonathan Cape).
Maus, Katharine Eisaman (1995), *Inwardness and Theater in the English Renaissance* (Chicago: University of Chicago Press).
Maxwell, Julie (2004), 'Counter-Reformation Versions of Saxo: A New Source for *Hamlet*?', *Renaissance Quarterly*, 57, 518–60.
May, Steven W. (ed.) (2004), *Queen Elizabeth I: Selected Works* (New York: Washington Square Press).
Mayer, Jean-Christophe (2003), 'Les Spectateurs de Shakespeare: À la Découverte des Lettres et Carnets de ses Contemporains', in Patricia Dorval (ed.), *Shakespeare et ses Contemporains: Actes du Colloque 2002 de la Société Française Shakespeare* (Paris: Société Française Shakespeare), 143–59.
Mayer, Jean-Christophe (ed.) (2003), *Breaking the Silence on the Succession: A Sourcebook of Manuscripts and Rare Elizabethan Texts (c. 1587–1603)* (Montpellier: Université Paul-Valéry Montpellier 3).
Mayer, Jean-Christophe (ed.) (2004), *The Struggle for the Succession in Late Elizabethan England: Politics, Polemics and Cultural Representations* (Montpellier: Université Paul-Valéry Montpellier 3).
Mears, Natalie (2005), *Queenship and Political Discourse in the Elizabethan Realms* (Cambridge: Cambridge University Press).
Meganck, Tine Luk (2003), 'Erudite Eyes: Artists and Antiquarians in the Circle of Abraham Ortelius (1527–1598)', PhD thesis (Princeton University).
Meinecke, Friedrich (1957), *Machiavellism: The Doctrine of Raison d'État and Its Place in Modern History*, trans. Douglas Scott (New Haven: Yale University Press).
Melnikoff, Kirk (2013), 'Nicholas Ling's Republican *Hamlet* (1603)', in Marta Straznicky (ed.), *Shakespeare's Stationers: Studies in Cultural Bibliography* (Philadelphia: University of Pennsylvania Press), 95–111.
Menzer, Paul (2008), *The Hamlets: Cues, Qs, and Remembered Texts* (Newark: University of Delaware Press).
Merriman, Roger B. (1923), 'Charles V.'s Last Paper of Advice to His Son', *American Historical Review*, 28, 489–91.
Meserve, Margaret (2006), 'News from Negroponte: Politics, Popular Opinion and Information Exchange in the First Decade of the Italian Press', *Renaissance Quarterly*, 59, 440–80.
Meyer, Edward Stockton (1897), *Machiavelli and the Elizabethan Drama* (Weimar: E. Felber).
Millstone, Noah (2014), 'Seeing Like a Statesman in Early Stuart England', *Past & Present*, 223, 77–127.
Millstone, Noah (2015), *Manuscript Circulation and the Invention of Politics in Early Stuart England* (Cambridge: Cambridge University Press).
Miola, Robert S. (1985), '*Julius Caesar* and the Tyrannicide Debate', *Renaissance Quarterly*, 38, 271–89.
Momigliano, Arnaldo (1947), 'The First Political Commentary on Tacitus', *The Journal of Roman Studies*, 37, 91–101.
Montaigne, Michel Eyquem de (1892–3), *The Essays of Montaigne Done into English by John Florio, 1603*, 3 vols. (London: David Nutt).
Morris, Christopher (1970), 'Machiavelli's Reputation in Tudor England', *Machiavellismo e Antimachiavellismo nel Cinquecento* (Firenze: Olschki), 87–105.

Moss, Ann (1996), *Printed Commonplace-Books and the Structuring of Renaissance Thought* (Oxford: Clarendon Press).
Motley, Mark Edward (1990), *Becoming a French Aristocrat: The Education of the Court Nobility, 1580–1715* (Princeton: Princeton University Press).
Mousley, Andrew (1991), 'Self, State, and Seventeenth-Century News', *Seventeenth Century*, 6, 149–69.
Mouton, Léo (1912), *Bussy d'Amboise et Madame Montsoreau* (Paris: Hachette et cie).
Moyn, Samuel (2014), 'Imaginary Intellectual History', in Darrin M. McMahon and Samuel Moyn (eds.), *Rethinking Modern European Intellectual History* (Oxford: Oxford University Press), 113–30.
Mueller, Janel M. and Scodel, Joshua (eds.) (2009), *Elizabeth I: Translations, 1592–1598* (Chicago: University of Chicago Press).
Mukherji, Subha (2006), *Law and Representation in Early Modern Drama* (Cambridge: Cambridge University Press).
Munro, Ian (2001), 'Making Publics: Secrecy and Publication in *A Game at Chess*', *Medieval & Renaissance Drama in England*, 14, 207–26.
Munro, Ian (2004), 'Shakespeare's Jestbook: Wit, Print, Performance', *English Literary History*, 71, 89–113.
Munro, Ian (2005), *The Figure of the Crowd in Early Modern London: The City and Its Double* (New York: Palgrave Macmillan).
Munro, Ian (2010), 'Knightly Complements: *The Malcontent* and the Matter of Wit', *English Literary Renaissance*, 40, 215–37.
Munro, John (ed.) (1932), *The Shakspere Allusion-Book*, 2 vols. (London: Oxford University Press).
Munro, Lucy (2005), *Children of the Queen's Revels: A Jacobean Theatre Repertory* (Cambridge: Cambridge University Press).
Murdin, William (ed.) (1759), *A Collection of State Papers Relating to the Reign of Queen Elizabeth, from the Year 1571 to 1596. Transcribed from Original Papers and other Authentic Memorials* (London).
Neale, J. E. (1958), *Essays in Elizabethan History* (London: Jonathan Cape).
Neale, J. E. (1963), *The Elizabethan House of Commons* (Revised edn.; Harmondsworth: Penguin Books).
Neill, Michael (2003), '"He That Thou Knowest Thine": Friendship and Service in *Hamlet*', in Richard Dutton and Jean E. Howard (eds.), *A Companion to Shakespeare's Works, Volume 1: The Tragedies* (Malden, MA: Blackwell), 319–38.
Netzloff, Mark (2013), 'Public Diplomacy and the Comedy of State: Chapman's *Monsieur d'Olive*', in Jason Powell and Will Rossiter (eds.), *Authority and Diplomacy from Dante to Shakespeare* (Burlington, VT: Ashgate), 185–97.
Nevitt, Marcus (2005), 'Ben Jonson and the Serial Publication of News', *Media History*, 11, 53–68.
Nicolas, Nicholas Harris (1823), *Life of William Davison, Secretary of State and Privy Counsellor to Queen Elizabeth* (London: J. Nichols & son).
Nolan, John S. (1994), 'The Militarization of the Elizabethan State', *Journal of Military History*, 58 (3), 391–420.
Norbrook, David (2002), *Poetry and Politics in the English Renaissance* (Rev. edn.; Oxford: Oxford University Press).
Northumberland, Henry Percy Ninth Earl of (2002), *The Wizard Earl's Advices to His Son*, eds. Gordon R. Batho and Stephen Clucas (The Roxburghe Club).

O'Callaghan, Michelle (2007), *The English Wits: Literature and Sociability in Early Modern England* (Cambridge: Cambridge University Press).
Oestreich, Gerhard (1982), *Neostoicism and the Early Modern State*, eds. Brigitta Oestreich and H. G. Koenigsberger, trans. David McLintock (Cambridge: Cambridge University Press).
Ong, Walter J. (1971), 'Latin Language Study as a Renaissance Puberty Rite', *Rhetoric, Romance, and Technology: Studies in the Interaction of Expression and Culture* (Ithaca: Cornell University Press), 113–41.
Orgel, Stephen (1975), *The Illusion of Power: Political Theater in the English Renaissance* (Berkeley: University of California Press).
Orgel, Stephen (1982), 'Making Greatness Familiar', *Genre*, 15, 41–8.
Orgel, Stephen (1991), 'What Is a Text?', in David Scott Kastan and Peter Stallybrass (eds.), *Staging the Renaissance* (New York: Routledge), 83–7.
Orgel, Stephen (2015), *The Reader in the Book: A Study of Spaces and Traces* (Oxford: Oxford University Press).
Orlin, Lena Cowen (2008), 'The Private Lives of Public Plays', in Richard Fotheringham, Christa Jansohn, and R. S. White (eds.), *Shakespeare's World/World Shakespeare* (Madison: Fairleigh Dickinson University Press), 140–50.
Ormsby-Lennon, Theresa Suriano (1977), 'Piccolo, ma con Gran Vaghezza: A New Source for *Hamlet*?', *The Library Chronicle*, 41 (2), 119–48.
Orsini, Napoleone (1946), '"Policy": Or the Language of Elizabethan Machiavellism', *Journal of the Warburg and Courtauld Institutes*, 9, 122–34.
Osborn, Francis (1983), *The True Tragicomedy Formerly Acted at Court: A Play*, ed. Lois Potter (New York: Garland).
Osborn, James M. (1972), *Young Philip Sidney: 1572–1577* (New Haven: Yale University Press).
Ottmann, Henning (2004), 'Was ist neu im Denken Machiavellis?', in Herfried Münkler, Rüdiger Voigt, and Ralf Walkenhaus (eds.), *Demaskierung der Macht: Niccolò Machiavellis Staats- und Politikverständnis* (Baden-Baden: Nomos), 145–56.
Palfrey, Simon and Stern, Tiffany (2007), *Shakespeare in Parts* (Oxford: Oxford University Press).
Palonen, Kari (2006), *The Struggle with Time: A Conceptual History of 'Politics' as an Activity* (Hamburg: Lit).
Parkes, M. B. (1993), *Pause and Effect: An Introduction to the History of Punctuation in the West* (Berkeley: University of California Press).
Parrott, Thomas Marc (ed.) (1910), *The Plays and Poems of George Chapman: The Tragedies* (London: George Routledge & Sons).
Parrott, Thomas Marc (ed.) (1914), *The Plays and Poems of George Chapman: The Comedies* (London: George Routledge & Sons).
Paster, Gail Kern (1985), *The Idea of the City in the Age of Shakespeare* (Athens: University of Georgia Press).
Paster, Gail Kern (1998), 'The Children's Middleton', in W. Speed Hill (ed.), *New Ways of Looking at Old Texts II: Papers of the Renaissance English Text Society, 1992–1996* (Tempe, AZ: MRTS), 101–7.
Patterson, Annabel (1984), *Censorship and Interpretation: The Conditions of Writing and Reading in Early Modern England* (Madison: University of Wisconsin Press).
Patterson, Annabel (1989), *Shakespeare and the Popular Voice* (Oxford: Basil Blackwell).
Patterson, Annabel M. (1993), *Reading between the Lines* (Madison, University of Wisconsin Press).

Peacey, Jason (2013), *Print and Public Politics in the English Revolution* (Cambridge: Cambridge University Press).
Peck, Linda Levy (1990), *Court Patronage and Corruption in Early Stuart England* (Boston: Unwin Hyman).
Peltonen, Markku (1995), *Classical Humanism and Republicanism in English Political Thought, 1570–1640* (Cambridge: Cambridge University Press).
Pendleton, Thomas A. (1987), 'Shakespeare's Disguised Duke Play: Middleton, Marston and the Sources of *Measure for Measure*', in John W. Mahon and Thomas A. Pendleton (eds.), *Fanned and Winnowed Opinions: Shakespearean Essays Presented to Harold Jenkins* (London: Methuen), 79–97.
Perry, Curtis (2006), *Literature and Favoritism in Early Modern England* (Cambridge: Cambridge University Press).
Pettegree, Andrew (2014), *The Invention of News: How the World Came to Know About Itself* (New Haven: Yale University Press).
Phillips, James Emerson (1964), *Images of a Queen: Mary Stuart in Sixteenth-Century Literature* (Berkeley: University of California Press).
Picciotto, Joanna (2010), *Labors of Innocence in Early Modern England* (Cambridge, MA: Harvard University Press).
Pincus, Steve (1995), '"Coffee Politicians Does Create": Coffeehouses and Restoration Political Culture', *The Journal of Modern History*, 67, 807–34.
Pincus, Steve (2007), 'The State and Civil Society in Early Modern England: Capitalism, Causation and Habermas's Bourgeois Public Sphere', in Peter Lake and Steve Pincus (eds.), *The Politics of the Public Sphere in Early Modern England* (Manchester: Manchester University Press), 213–31.
Platt, F. Jeffrey (1988), 'The Elizabethan Diplomatic Service', *Journal of the Rocky Mountain Medieval and Renaissance Association*, 9, 93–116.
Platter d. J., Thomas (1968), *Beschreibung der Reisen durch Frankreich, Spanien, England und die Niederlande, 1595–1600*, ed. Rut Keiser (Basler Chroniken, 9; Basel & Stuttgart: Schwabe & Co. Verlag).
Plutarch (1939), *Moralia*, trans. W. C. Helmbold (Loeb Classical Library; Cambridge, MA: Harvard University Press).
Pocock, J. G. A. (2003), *The Machiavellian Moment: Florentine Political Thought and the Atlantic Republican Tradition* (2nd edn.; Princeton: Princeton University Press).
Pollard, Graham and Ehrman, Albert (1965), *The Distribution of Books by Catalogue from the Invention of Printing to A.D. 1800: Based on Material in the Broxbourne Library* (Cambridge: The Roxburghe Club).
Pollnitz, Aysha (2009), 'Educating Hamlet and Prince Hal', in David Armitage, Conal Condren, and Andrew Fitzmaurice (eds.), *Shakespeare and Early Modern Political Thought* (Cambridge: Cambridge University Press), 119–38.
Pop, Iggy (1995), 'Caesar Lives', *Classics Ireland*, 2, 94–6.
Popper, Nicholas (2005), 'The English Polydaedali: How Gabriel Harvey Read Late Tudor London', *Journal of the History of Ideas*, 66, 351–81.
Popper, Nicholas (2012), *Walter Ralegh's History of the World and the Historical Culture of the Late Renaissance* (Chicago: University of Chicago Press).
Potter, David and Roberts, P. R. (1988), 'An Englishman's View of the Court of Henri III, 1584–1585: Richard Cook's "Description of the Court of France"', *French History*, 2, 312–44.
Potter, David (ed.) (2004), *Foreign Intelligence and Information in Elizabethan England: Two English Treatises on the State of France, 1580–1584* (Camden Fifth Series, Cambridge: Cambridge University Press).

Powell, Jason (2013), 'Astrophil the Orator: Diplomacy and Diplomats in Sidney's *Astrophil and Stella*', in Jason Powell and William T. Rossiter (eds.), *Authority and Diplomacy from Dante to Shakespeare* (Farnham: Ashgate), 171–84.

Praz, Mario (1958), 'The Politic Brain: Machiavelli and the Elizabethans', *The Flaming Heart* (New York: Doubleday), 90–145.

Prest, Wilfrid R. (ed.) (1987), *The Professions in Early Modern England* (London: Croom Helm).

Quarmby, Kevin A. (2012), *The Disguised Ruler in Shakespeare and His Contemporaries* (Farnham and Burlington, VT: Ashgate).

Queller, Donald E. (1972), 'How to Succeed as an Ambassador: A Sixteenth Century Venetian Document', in Joseph R. Strayer and Donald E. Queller (eds.), *Post Scripta: Essays on Medieval Law and the Emergence of the European State in Honor of Gaines Post* (Studia Gratiana; Roma: Libreria Ateneo Salesiano), 653–71.

Queller, Donald E. (1973), 'The Development of Ambassadorial Relazioni', in John Rigby Hale (ed.), *Renaissance Venice* (London: Faber and Faber), 174–96.

Quint, David (2006), 'The Tragedy of Nobility on the Seventeenth-Century Stage', *Modern Language Quarterly*, 67, 7–29.

Raab, Felix (1964), *The English Face of Machiavelli: A Changing Interpretation, 1500–1700* (London: Routledge and Kegan Paul).

Ramazani, Jahan (2014), *Poetry and Its Others: News, Prayer, Song, and the Dialogue of Genres* (Chicago: University of Chicago Press).

Randall, David (2008), 'Epistolary Rhetoric, the Newspaper, and the Public Sphere', *Past & Present*, 198, 3–32.

Ranke, Leopold (1853), *The Ottoman and the Spanish Empires in the Sixteenth and Seventeenth Centuries*, trans. Walter K. Kelly (London: Whittaker and Co.).

Ratcliffe, Stephen (2010), *Reading the Unseen: (Offstage) Hamlet* (Denver: Counterpath Press).

Rathmell, J. C. A. (1971), 'Jonson, Lord Lisle, and Penshurst', *English Literary Renaissance*, 1, 250–60.

Raymond, Joad (1994), 'The Great Assises Holden in Parnassus', *Studies in Newspaper and Periodical History*, 2, 3–17.

Raymond, Joad (1996), *The Invention of the Newspaper: English Newsbooks, 1641–1649* (Oxford: Clarendon Press).

Raymond, Joad (2003), *Pamphlets and Pamphleteering in Early Modern Britain* (Cambridge: Cambridge University Press).

Raymond, Joad (2013), 'International News and the Seventeenth-Century English Newspaper', in Jeroen Salman, Joad Raymond, and Roeland Harms (eds.), *Not Dead Things: The Dissemination of Popular Print in England and Wales, Italy, and the Low Countries, 1500–1820* (Leiden and Boston: Brill), 229–51.

Raymond, Joad (ed.) (1999), *News, Newspapers, and Society in Early Modern Britain* (London and Portland, OR: Frank Cass).

Read, Conyers (1925), *Mr. Secretary Walsingham and the Policy of Queen Elizabeth*, 3 vols. (Cambridge, MA: Harvard University Press).

Reiss, Timothy J. (1997), *Knowledge, Discovery, and Imagination in Early Modern Europe: The Rise of Aesthetic Rationalism* (Cambridge: Cambridge University Press).

Rickard, Jane (2007), *Authorship and Authority: The Writings of James VI and I* (Manchester: Manchester University Press).

Ricks, Christopher (1961), 'Sejanus and Dismemberment', *Modern Language Notes*, 76, 301–8.

Roberts, Sasha (2003), *Reading Shakespeare's Poems in Early Modern England* (New York: Palgrave Macmillan).
Ronan, Clifford (1995), *'Antike Roman': Power Symbology and the Roman Play in Early Modern England, 1585–1635* (Athens and London: University of Georgia Press).
Rose, Mark (1971), '*Hamlet* and the Shape of Revenge', *English Literary Renaissance*, 1, 132–43.
Rospocher, Massimo (2012), *Beyond the Public Sphere: Opinions, Publics, Spaces in Early Modern Europe* (Annali dell'Istituto Storico Italo-Germanico in Trento; Bologna and Berlin: Il Mulino and Duncker & Humblot).
Roth, Cecil (1966), 'Sir Thomas Bodley—Hebraist', *Bodleian Library Record*, 7, 242–51.
Ruffmann, Karl Heinz (1952), *Das Russlandbild im England Shakespeares* (Göttingen: Musterschmidt Wissenschaftlicher Verlag).
Rust, Jennifer (2009), 'Political Theology and Shakespeare Studies', *Literature Compass*, 6 (1), 175–90.
Said, Edward W. (1993), *Culture and Imperialism* (New York: Knopf).
Salingar, Leo (1991), 'Jacobean Playwrights and "Judicious" Spectators', *Renaissance Drama*, 22, 209–34.
Savage, Richard (ed.) (1887), *Shakespearean Extracts from 'Edward Pudsey's Booke'* (Stratford-Upon-Avon Notebooks No. 1, Stratford-upon-Avon: John Smith).
Sawyer, Edmund (ed.) (1724), *Memorials and Affairs of State in the Reigns of Q. Elizabeth and K. James I., Collected (Chiefly) from the Original Papers of the Right Honourable Sir Ralph Winwood, Kt.*, 3 vols. (London: W. B. for T. Ward).
Scaliger, Julius Caesar (1964), *Poetices Libri Septem, Faksimile-Neudruck der Ausgabe von Lyon 1561*, introd. August Buck (Stuttgart-Bad Cannstatt: Friedrich Frommann).
Schalkwyk, David (2008), *Shakespeare, Love and Service* (Cambridge: Cambridge University Press).
Schellhase, Kenneth C. (1976), *Tacitus in Renaissance Political Thought* (Chicago: University of Chicago Press).
Schmitt, Carl (1956), *Hamlet oder Hekuba: Der Einbruch der Zeit in das Spiel* (Düsseldorf-Köln: Eugen Diederichs Verlag).
Schmitt, Carl (1996), *The Concept of the Political*, trans. Tracy B. Strong (Chicago: University of Chicago Press).
Schmitt, Carl (2005), *Political Theology: Four Chapters on the Concept of Sovereignty*, trans. George Schwab (Chicago: University of Chicago Press).
Schmitt, Carl (2009), *Hamlet or Hecuba: The Intrusion of the Time into the Play*, trans. David Pan and Jennifer R. Rust (New York: Telos Press).
Schurink, Fred (2008), '"Like a Hand in the Margine of a Booke": William Blount's Marginalia and the Politics of Sidney's *Arcadia*', *Review of English Studies*, 59 (238), 1–24.
Schurink, Fred (2010), 'Manuscript Commonplace Books, Literature, and Reading in Early Modern England', *Huntington Library Quarterly*, 73, 453–69.
Scott, Edward John Long (ed.) (1884), *Letter-Book of Gabriel Harvey, A.D. 1573–1580* (Camden N.S. 33, London: Camden Society).
Scott, William (2013), *The Model of Poesy*, ed. Gavin Alexander (Cambridge: Cambridge University Press).
Seddon, P. R. (ed.) (1975–86), *Letters of John Holles 1587–1637*, 3 vols. (Thoroton Society Record Series, Nottingham).
Sennett, Richard (1977), *The Fall of Public Man* (Cambridge: Cambridge University Press).
Shagan, Ethan H. (2005), 'Introduction: English Catholic History in Context', in Ethan H. Shagan (ed.), *Catholics and the 'Protestant Nation'* (Manchester and New York: Manchester University Press), 1–21.

Shannon, Laurie (2002), *Sovereign Amity: Figures of Friendship in Shakespearean Contexts* (Chicago: University of Chicago Press).
Shapiro, James (1989), 'Revisiting *Tamburlaine*: *Henry V* as Shakespeare's Belated Armada Play', *Criticism*, 31, 351–66.
Shapiro, James (2005), *1599: A Year in the Life of William Shakespeare* (London: Faber).
Sharpe, Kevin (1979), *Sir Robert Cotton 1586–1631: History and Politics in Early Modern England* (Oxford: Oxford University Press).
Sharpe, Kevin (1992), *The Personal Rule of Charles I* (New Haven: Yale University Press).
Sharpe, Kevin (2000), *Reading Revolutions: The Politics of Reading in Early Modern England* (New Haven: Yale University Press).
Shephard, Robert (2003), 'The Political Commonplace Books of Sir Robert Sidney', *Sidney Journal*, 21, 1–30.
Sherman, Stuart (2001), 'Eyes and Ears, News and Plays: The Argument of Ben Jonson's *Staple*', in Brendan Dooley and Sabrina A. Baron (eds.), *The Politics of Information in Early Modern Europe* (London and New York: Routledge), 23–40.
Sherman, William H. (1996), 'The Place of Reading in the English Renaissance: John Dee Revisited', in James Raven, Helen Small, and Naomi Tadmor (eds.), *The Practice and Representation of Reading in England* (Cambridge: Cambridge University Press), 62–76.
Shifflett, Andrew (1998), *Stoicism, Politics, and Literature in the Age of Milton: War and Peace Reconciled* (Cambridge: Cambridge University Press).
Sidney, Philip (2002), *An Apology for Poetry, or, the Defence of Poesy*, ed. Geoffrey Shepherd and R. W. Maslen (3rd edn.; Manchester: Manchester University Press).
Sisson, Charles Jasper (1936), *Lost Plays of Shakespeare's Age* (Cambridge: The University Press).
Sjögren, Gunnar (1965), '*Hamlet* and the Coronation of Christian IV', *Shakespeare Quarterly*, 16, 155–60.
Sjögren, Gunnar (1968), 'The Danish Background in *Hamlet*', *Shakespeare Studies*, 4, 221–30.
Sjögren, Gunnar (2002), 'The Geography of *Hamlet*', in Gunnar Sorelius (ed.), *Shakespeare and Scandinavia: A Collection of Nordic Studies* (Newark: University of Delaware Press), 64–71.
Slavin, Arthur J. (1994), 'Daniel Rogers in Copenhagen, 1588: Mission and Memory', in Malcolm R. Thorp and Arthur J. Slavin (eds.), *Politics, Religion and Diplomacy in Early Modern Europe: Essays in Honor of De Lamar Jensen* (Sixteenth Century Essays and Studies; Kirksville, MO), 247–66.
Smith, Bruce R. (ed.) (2001), *Twelfth Night, or, What You Will: Texts and Contexts* (The Bedford Shakespeare, Boston: Bedford/St. Martin's Press).
Smith, Emma (2000), 'Ghost Writing: *Hamlet* and the *Ur-Hamlet*', in Andrew Murphy (ed.), *The Renaissance Text: Theory, Editing, Textuality* (Manchester: Manchester University Press), 177–90.
Smith, G. C. Moore (1913), *Gabriel Harvey's Marginalia* (Stratford-upon-Avon: Shakespeare Head Press).
Smith, Logan Pearsall (1907), *The Life and Letters of Sir Henry Wotton*, 2 vols. (Oxford: Clarendon Press).
Smith, Preserved (1921), 'Rosencrantz and Guildenstern', *Modern Language Notes*, 36, 374.
Smuts, R. Malcolm (1993), 'Court-Centred Politics and the Uses of Roman Historians, c.1590–1630', in Kevin Sharpe and Peter Lake (eds.), *Culture and Politics in Early Stuart England* (Stanford: Stanford University Press), 21–44.
Smyth, Adam (2004), *'Profit and Delight': Printed Miscellanies in England, 1640–1682* (Detroit: Wayne State University Press).

Smyth, Adam (2013), '"Divines into Dry Vines": Forms of Jesting in Renaissance England', in Allison K. Deutermann and András Kiséry (eds.), *Formal Matters: Reading the Materials of English Renaissance Literature* (Manchester: Manchester University Press), 55–76.
Soll, Jacob (2005), *Publishing the Prince: History, Reading, & the Birth of Political Criticism* (Ann Arbor: University of Michigan Press).
Sommerville, Johann P. (2007), 'English and Roman Liberty in the Monarchical Republic of Early Stuart England', in John F. McDiarmid (ed.), *The Monarchical Republic of Early Modern England: Essays in Response to Patrick Collinson* (Aldershot: Ashgate), 201–16.
Sorelius, Gunnar (1973), 'An Unknown Shakespearian Commonplace Book', *The Library* 5th ser., 28, 294–308.
Sorlien, Robert Parker (ed.) (1976), *The Diary of John Manningham of the Middle Temple, 1602–1603: Newly Edited in Complete and Unexpurgated Form from the Original Manuscript in the British Museum* (Hanover, NH: Published for the University of Rhode Island by the University Press of New England).
Spedding, James, Heath, Douglas Denon, and Ellis, Robert Leslie (eds.) (1857–74), *The Works of Francis Bacon*, 14 vols. (London: Longman and co. [etc,]).
Spies, Marijke (1999), *Rhetoric, Rhetoricians and Poets: Studies in Renaissance Poetry and Poetics* (Amsterdam: Amsterdam University Press).
Stabler, Arthur P. (1964), 'The Sources of *Hamlet*: Some Corrections of the Record', *Research Studies: A Quarterly Publication at Washington State University*, 32, 207–16.
Stagl, Justin (1995), *A History of Curiosity: The Theory of Travel 1550–1800* (Chur, Switzerland: Harwood Academic Publisher).
Staines, John D. (2009), *The Tragic Histories of Mary Queen of Scots, 1560–1690: Rhetoric, Passions, and Political Literature* (Farnham and Burlington, VT: Ashgate).
Stallybrass, Peter (2001), '"Well Grubbed, Old Mole": Marx, *Hamlet*, and the (Un)Fixing of Representation', in Jean E. Howard and Scott Cutler Shershow (eds.), *Marxist Shakespeares* (London: Routledge), 16–30.
Stallybrass, Peter, et al. (2004), 'Hamlet's Tables and the Technologies of Writing in Renaissance England', *Shakespeare Quarterly*, 55, 379–419.
Steggle, Matthew (1998), *Wars of the Theatres: The Poetics of Personation in the Age of Jonson* (Victoria, B.C.: University of Victoria).
Stern, Tiffany (2004), *Making Shakespeare: From Stage to Page* (London: Routledge).
Stern, Tiffany (2013), 'Sermons, Plays and Note-Takers: *Hamlet* Q1 as a "Noted" Text', *Shakespeare Survey*, 66, 1–23.
Stern, Virginia F. (1979), *Gabriel Harvey, His Life, Marginalia and Library* (Oxford: Clarendon Press).
Stern, Virginia F. (1992), *Sir Stephen Powle of Court and Country: Memorabilia of a Government Agent for Queen Elizabeth I, Chancery Official, and English Country Gentleman* (Selinsgrove, PA: Susquehanna University Press).
Stewart, Alan (1997), *Close Readers: Humanism and Sodomy in Early Modern England* (Princeton: Princeton University Press).
Stewart, Alan (2000), *Philip Sidney: A Double Life* (London: Chatto & Windus).
Stewart, Alan (2005), 'Instigating Treason: The Life and Death of Henry Cuffe, Secretary', in Lorna Hutson and Erica Sheen (eds.), *Literature, Politics and Law in Renaissance England* (Basingstoke: Palgrave), 50–70.
Stewart, Alan (2008), *Shakespeare's Letters* (Oxford: Oxford University Press).
Stewart, Alan (2009), 'The Making of Writing in Renaissance England: Re-Thinking Authorship through Collaboration', in Margaret Healy and Thomas Healy (eds.),

Renaissance Transformations: The Making of English Writing (1500–1650) (Edinburgh: Edinburgh University Press), 81–96.

Stewart, Alan (2013), 'The Forms of News from France in Shakespeare's *3 Henry Vi*', in Allison K. Deutermann and András Kiséry (eds.), *Formal Matters: Reading the Materials of English Renaissance Literature* (Manchester: Manchester University Press), 149–69.

Stewart, Alan (ed.) (2012), *The Oxford Francis Bacon I: Early Writings, 1584–1596* (Oxford: Clarendon Press).

Stimson, Dorothy (1948), *Scientists and Amateurs: A History of the Royal Society* (New York: H. Schuman).

Stolleis, Michael (1990), *Staat und Staatsräson in der Frühen Neuzeit: Studien zur Geschichte des Öffentlichen Rechts* (Frankfurt am Main: Suhrkamp).

Stoye, John (1989), *English Travellers Abroad, 1604–1667: Their Influence in English Society and Politics* (Rev. edn.; New Haven: Yale University Press).

Strauss, Leo (2000), *On Tyranny: Including the Strauss-Kojève Correspondence*, eds Victor Gourevitch and Michael S. Roth (Rev. and expanded edn.; Chicago: University of Chicago Press).

Straznicky, Marta (2004), *Privacy, Playreading, and Women's Closet Drama, 1550–1700* (Cambridge: Cambridge University Press).

Streckfuss, Richard (1998), 'News before Newpapers', *Journalism and Mass Communication Quarterly*, 75, 84–97.

Streitberger, W. R. (1975), 'The Tyllney Manuscript at the Folger Library', *Papers of the Bibliographical Society of America*, 69, 449–64.

Swann, Marjorie (2001), *Curiosities and Texts: The Culture of Collecting in Early Modern England* (Philadelphia: University of Pennsylvania Press).

Swinburne, Algernon Charles (1889), *A Study of Ben Jonson* (London: Chatto & Windus).

Syme, Holger Schott (2007), 'The Look of Speech', *Textual Cultures: Text, Contexts, Interpretation*, 2 (2), 34–60.

Syme, Holger Schott (2008), 'Unediting the Margin: Jonson, Marston, and the Theatrical Page', *English Literary Renaissance*, 38, 142–71.

Syme, Ronald (1958), *Tacitus*, 2 vols. (Oxford: Clarendon Press).

Tacitus (1989), *Annals. Book IV*, eds. Ronald H. Martin and A. J. Woodman (Cambridge Greek and Latin Classics; Cambridge: Cambridge University Press).

Tacitus (2004), *The Annals*, trans. A. J. Woodman (Indianapolis: Hackett).

Taunton, Nina (2001), *1590s Drama and Militarism: Portrayals of War in Marlowe, Chapman and Shakespeare's Henry V* (Aldershot: Ashgate).

Taviner, Mark (2000), 'Robert Beale and the Elizabethan Polity', PhD thesis (University of St Andrews).

Taylor, Gary (2003), 'The Cultural Politics of Maybe', in Richard Dutton, Alison Findlay, and Richard Wilson (eds.), *Theatre and Religion: Lancastrian Shakespeare* (Manchester and New York: Manchester University Press), 242–58.

Testa, Simone (2008), 'From the "Bibliographical Nightmare" to a Critical Bibliography: *Tesori Politici* in the British Library, and Elsewhere in Britain', *eBLJ*, 2008, 1–33, http://www.bl.uk/eblj/2008articles/article1.html, accessed 4 September 2010.

Thomas, Keith (1976), *Age and Authority in Early Modern England* (Proceedings of the British Academy: The Raleigh Lecture on History; London: Oxford University Press).

Thomas, Keith (2009), *The Ends of Life: Roads to Fulfilment in Early Modern England* (Oxford: Oxford University Press).

Thompson, Ann and Taylor, Neil (2004), ' "Your Sum of Parts": Doubling in *Hamlet*', in Lukas Erne and Margaret Jane Kidnie (eds.), *Textual Performances: The Modern*

Reproduction of Shakespeare's Drama (Cambridge: Cambridge University Press), 111–26.

Thompson, I. A. A. (2005), 'Sir Charles Cornwallis y su "Discurso Sobre el Estado de España" (1608)', in Porfirio Sanz Camañes (ed.), *La Monarquía Hispánica en Tiempos del Quijote* (Madrid: Universidad de Castilla-la Mancha: Sílex), 65–101.

Thompson, Michael (1979), *Rubbish Theory: The Creation and Destruction of Value* (Oxford: Oxford University Press).

Tianhu, Hao (2009), '*Hesperides, or the Muses' Garden* and Its Manuscript History', *The Library 7th ser.*, 10, 372–404.

Toscani, Ignazio (1980), 'Etatistisches Denken und erkenntnistheoretische Überlegungen in den Venezianischen Relationen', in Mohammed Rassem and Justin Stagl (eds.), *Statistik und Staatsbeschreibung in der Neuzeit* (Paderborn: Schöningh), 111–29.

Tricomi, A. H. (1977), 'The Focus of Satire and the Date of *Monsieur d'Olive*', *SEL: Studies in English Literature, 1500–1900*, 17, 281–94.

Tricomi, Albert H. (1982), 'The Dates of the Plays of George Chapman', *English Literary Renaissance*, 12, 242–66.

Tricomi, Albert H. (1989), *Anticourt Drama in England, 1603–1642* (Charlottesville: University Press of Virginia).

Trilling, Lionel (2008), *The Liberal Imagination: Essays on Literature and Society* (New York: New York Review Books).

Trim, David J. B. (1998), 'Sir Thomas Bodley and the International Protestant Cause', *Bodleian Library Record*, 16, 314–40.

Trudell, Scott A. (2012), 'The Mediation of Poesie: Ophelia's Orphic Song', *Shakespeare Quarterly*, 63, 46–76.

Tucci, Ugo (1990), 'Ranke and the Venetian Document Market', in Georg G. Iggers and James M. Powell (eds.), *Leopold Von Ranke and the Shaping of the Historical Discipline* (Syracuse: Syracuse University Press), 99–107.

Tuck, Richard (1993), *Philosophy and Government, 1572–1651* (Cambridge: Cambridge University Press).

Turner, Henry S. (2006), *The English Renaissance Stage: Geometry, Poetics, and the Practical Spatial Arts 1580–1630* (Oxford: Oxford University Press).

Uhlig, Claus (1973), *Hofkritik im England des Mittelalters und der Renaissance: Studien zu einem Gemeinplatz der europäischen Moralistik* (Berlin and New York: Walter de Gruyter).

Ungerer, Gustav (1974, 1976), *A Spaniard in Elizabethan England*, 2 vols. (London: Tamesis).

Ustick, Lee (1932), 'Advice to a Son: A Type of Seventeenth-Century Conduct Book', *Studies in Philology*, 29, 409–41.

van Dorsten, J. A. (1962), *Poets, Patrons, and Professors: Sir Philip Sidney, Daniel Rogers, and the Leiden Humanists* (Leiden: Published for the Sir Thomas Browne Institute at the University Press).

Varnedoe, Kirk (1990), *A Fine Disregard: What Makes Modern Art Modern* (New York: Abrams).

Vaughan, Jacqueline D. (2006), 'Secretaries, Statesmen and Spies: The Clerks of the Tudor Privy Council, c. 1540–c. 1603', PhD thesis (University of St Andrews).

Vickers, Brian (ed.) (2002), *Francis Bacon: The Major Works*, ed. Brian Vickers (2nd, rev. edn., Oxford: Oxford University Press).

Villez, Barbara (2005), *Séries Télé, Visions de la Justice* (Paris: Presses Universitaires de France).

Viroli, Maurizio (1992), *From Politics to Reason of State: The Acquisition and Transformation of the Language of Politics, 1250–1600* (Cambridge: Cambridge University Press).
Viroli, Maurizio (1992), 'The Revolution in the Concept of Politics', *Political Theory*, 20, 473–95.
Voss, Paul J. (2001), *Elizabethan News Pamphlets: Shakespeare, Spenser, Marlowe & the Birth of Journalism* (Pittsburgh: Duquesne University Press).
Warley, Christopher (2014), *Reading Class through Shakespeare, Donne, and Milton* (Cambridge: Cambridge University Press).
Warner, Michael (2002), *Publics and Counterpublics* (New York: Zone Books).
Watkins, John (2002), *Representing Elizabeth in Stuart England: Literature, History, Sovereignty* (Cambridge: Cambridge University Press).
Watson, Robert N. (2009), 'Coining Words on the Elizabethan and Jacobean Stage', *Philological Quarterly*, 88, 49–75.
Watson, Robert N. (2012), 'Shakespeare's New Words', *Shakespeare Survey*, 65, 358–77.
Weber, Max (2004), *The Vocation Lectures*, ed. David S. Owen and Tracy B. Strong, trans. Rodney Livingstone (Indianapolis: Hackett).
Weill, Georges (1891), *Les Théories sur le Pouvoir Royal en France pendant les Guerres de Religion* (Paris: Hachette et cie).
Weinberg, Bernard (1961), *A History of Literary Criticism in the Italian Renaissance*, 2 vols. (Chicago: University of Chicago Press).
Werner, Hans (1996), '*The Hector of Germanie, or the Palsgrave, Prime Elector* and Anglo-German Relations of Early Stuart England', in R. Malcolm Smuts (ed.), *The Stuart Court and Europe: Essays in Politics and Culture* (Cambridge: Cambridge University Press).
Whigham, Frank (1984), *Ambition and Privilege: The Social Tropes of Elizabethan Courtesy Theory* (Berkeley: University of California Press).
Whigham, Frank and Rebhorn, Wayne A. (eds.) (2007), *The Art of English Poesy by George Puttenham: A Critical Edition* (Ithaca: Cornell University Press).
Whitington, Phil (2005), *The Politics of Commonwealth: Citizens and Freemen in Early Modern England* (Cambridge: Cambridge University Press).
Wiggins, Martin (2012–), *British Drama, 1533–1642: A Catalogue* (Oxford: Oxford University Press).
Wilkinson, Alexander S. (2004), *Mary, Queen of Scots and French Public Opinion, 1542–1600* (Basingstoke: Palgrave Macmillan).
Willan, Thomas Stuart (1956), *The Early History of the Russia Company, 1553–1603* (Manchester: Manchester University Press).
Williams, Bernard (2002), *Truth and Truthfulness: An Essay in Genealogy* (Princeton: Princeton University Press).
Williamson, Elizabeth Rachel (2012), 'Before "Diplomacy": Travel, Embassy and the Production of Political Information in the Later Sixteenth Century', PhD thesis (Queen Mary, University of London).
Wilson, Bronwen and Yachnin, Paul Edward (2010), *Making Publics in Early Modern Europe: People, Things, Forms of Knowledge* (New York: Routledge).
Wilson, Harold S. (1948), 'Gabriel Harvey's Method of Annotating His Books', *Harvard Library Bulletin*, 2 (3), 344–61.
Wilson, Harold S. (ed.) (1945), *Gabriel Harvey's Ciceronianus*, trans. Clarence A. Forbes (University of Nebraska Studies, Studies in the Humanities, Lincoln: The University of Nebraska).

Wilson, Thomas (1982), *The Arte of Rhetorique*, ed. Thomas J. Derrick (New York: Garland).
Winstanley, Lilian (1921), *Hamlet and the Scottish Succession: Being an Examination of the Relations of the Play of Hamlet to the Scottish Succession and the Essex Conspiracy* (Cambridge: Cambridge University Press).
Winston, Jessica (2006), 'Seneca in Early Elizabethan England', *Renaissance Quarterly*, 59, 29–58.
Wolfe, Don M. (ed.) (1959), *Complete Prose Works of John Milton* (vol. 2; New Haven: Yale University Press).
Wolfe, Jessica (2004), *Humanism, Machinery, and Renaissance Literature* (Cambridge: Cambridge University Press).
Womersley, David (1991), 'Sir Henry Savile's Translation of Tacitus and the Political Interpretation of Elizabethan Texts', *Review of English Studies*, 42, 313–42.
Woodbridge, Linda (2010), 'Resistance Theory Meets Drama: Tudor Seneca', *Renaissance Drama*, 38, 115–40.
Woodfield, Denis B. (1973), *Surreptitious Printing in England 1550–1640* (New York: Bibliographical Society of America).
Woolf, Cecil N. Sidney (1913), *Bartolus of Sassoferrato, His Position in the History of Medieval Political Thought* (Cambridge: Cambridge University Press).
Woolf, D. R. (2001), 'News, History, and the Construction of the Present in Early Modern England', in Brendan Dooley and Sabrina Baron (eds.), *The Politics of Information in Early Modern Europe* (London and New York: Routledge), 80–118.
Wootton, David (2005), review of *Republicanism: A Shared European Heritage*, eds. Martin Van Gelderen and Quentin Skinner, *The English Historical Review*, 120 (485), 135–9.
Worden, Blair (1993), 'Ben Jonson among the Historians', in Kevin Sharpe and Peter Lake (eds.), *Culture and Politics in Early Stuart England* (Stanford: Stanford University Press), 67–89.
Worden, Blair (1999), 'Favourites on the English Stage', in J. H. Elliott and L. W. B. Brockliss (eds.), *The World of the Favourite* (New Haven and London: Yale University Press), 159–83.
Worden, Blair (2003), 'Which Play Was Performed at the Globe Theatre on 7 February 1601?', *London Review of Books*, 25 (13), 22–4.
Woudhuysen, H. R. (2013), 'Gabriel Harvey', in Andrew Hadfield (ed.), *The Oxford Handbook of English Prose 1500–1640* (Oxford: Oxford University Press), 611–30.
Wright, Louis B. (ed.) (1962), *Advice to a Son* (Ithaca: Published for the Folger Shakespeare Library by Cornell University Press).
Wrightson, Keith (1994), '"Sorts" of People in Tudor and Stuart England', in Jonathan Barry and Christopher Brooks (eds.), *The Middling Sort of People* (New York: St. Martin's Press), 28–51.
Wrightson, Keith (2000), *Earthly Necessities: Economic Lives in Early Modern Britain* (The New Economic History of Britain; New Haven: Yale University Press).
Yachnin, Paul (1997), *Stage-Wrights: Shakespeare, Jonson, Middleton, and the Making of Theatrical Value* (Philadelphia: University of Pennsylvania Press).
Yachnin, Paul (2005), '"The Perfection of Ten": Populuxe Art and Artisanal Value in *Troilus and Cressida*', *Shakespeare Quarterly*, 56, 306–27.
Yamada, Akihiro (1998), *The First Folio of Shakespeare: A Transcript of Contemporary Marginalia in a Copy of the Kodama Memorial Library of Meisei University* (Tokyo: Yushodo Press).

Zaret, David (1992), 'Religion, Science and Printing in the Public Spheres in Seventeenth-Century England', in Craig Calhoun (ed.), *Habermas and the Public Sphere* (Cambridge, MA: MIT Press), 212–35.

Zaret, David (2000), *Origins of Democratic Culture: Printing, Petitions, and the Public Sphere in Early-Modern England* (Princeton: Princeton University Press).

Zarka, Yves Charles (ed.) (1994), *Raison et Déraison d'État: Théoriciens et Théories de la Raison d'État aux XVIe et XVIIe Siècles* (Paris: Presses Universitaires de France).

Zucker, Adam (2011), *The Places of Wit in Early Modern English Comedy* (Cambridge: Cambridge University Press).

Index

alehouses 12–16, 18 *see also* coffee houses; taverns
Alençon, François, Duc d' (aka Monsieur) 190, 194, 195, 197, 202, 203
Alphonsus, Emperor of Germanie 7–8, 254
ambassadors 6n8, 91, 92, 96, 99, 101, 103–9, 111–17, 184, 191, 193, 196, 197, 279
  in *Hamlet* 89, 91–3, 124, 125, 159
  in *Monsieur d'Olive* 259
Anglo, Sydney 70
aphorisms, aphoristic style 5, 7, 30, 32, 61, 63, 70–1, 192, 208, 210, 213–14, 221, 223, 229–30, 233, 242, 249, 250–1, 255–6, 267, 270, 279
Archer, John Michael 18n37
Arendt, Hannah 15n32, 22, 243n1
Aristotle, *Poetics* 219, 220n57
Aristotle, *Politics* 5, 53, 55, 56, 57, 65, 68
Armada 24, 100
Arnold, Oliver 3n5, 72n119, 165n90
Aston, Walter 108
authorship, notions of 37n1, 40n8

Bacon, Anthony 118, 122, 123, 124
Bacon, Francis 18, 46, 47, 49, 120, 169, 218, 230, 235, 275, 276
  Advancement of Learning 18, 48, 234–5
  Declaration of the practices… of the late Earl of Essex 275, 276, 277, 278
  Essays 5, 48, 235, 268, 275
Barlow, William 275–6
Barnes, Barnabe 60
  Four Bookes of Offices 5, 139n17
Barthes, Roland 97
Bartolus de Saxoferrato 65n91, 145
Beale, Robert 98, 105, 108, 109, 110, 113, 116, 198
Beaton, James 143
Beaumont and Fletcher, *Philaster* 201
Belleforest, François de 83, 140–7, 154, 161
  and Amleth 31, 83, 90, 91, 92, 95, 134, 135, 140–7, 155, 159
Benjamin, Walter 63n82
Bernard, Richard 216
Biron, Charles de Gontault, Duc de 184–6 *see also* Chapman, George, *The Conspiracy and Tragedy of Byron*
Blackstone, William 155
Blount, Charles *see* Mountjoy, Charles Blount, 8th Baron
Boaistuau, Pierre 140
Boccalini, Traiano 17
Bodin, Jean 5, 55, 56, 169, 208, 263

Bodley, Thomas 10–11, 100, 110, 117, 127n123
Bond of Association 57, 158
Bongars, Jacques 110
Botero, Giovanni 81, 82, 192, 214–15
Bourdieu, Pierre 16–17, 20, 265
Bourus, Terri 149n52
Boutcher, Warren 23n49, 41n11
Bowers, Fredson 7n11, 8
Bradbrook, Muriel C. 95
Braudel, Fernand 119n99
Buchanan, George 142, 146n42
Burghley, William Cecil, Lord 24, 27n62, 53, 57, 99, 102, 113, 115, 117, 118, 121, 138n13, 143
Bussy d'Amboise, Louis de Clermont, Sieur de 194–6 *see also* Chapman, George, *The Revenge of Bussy d'Amboys*; *The Tragedy of Bussy d'Amboys*
busybodies *see* curiosity

Camden, William 42, 110, 223
Carew, George 107–8, 109, 110, 111, 112, 116, 197
Carew, Richard 42
Carleton, Dudley 117, 123, 181
Cary, Elizabeth, *Mariam* 273
Castelvetro, Lodovico 220
Cecil, Robert 12n22, 23, 24, 188, 193, 195–6, 197, 277
Cecil, William *see* Burghley, William Cecil, Lord
Chamberlain, John 123, 181, 184, 185, 259
Chapman, George 4, 7n11, 29, 31–2, 187–8, 194, 197, 198–9, 247, 258
  The Conspiracy and Tragedy of Byron 32, 186–9, 191
  Monsieur d'Olive 256–61
  The Revenge of Bussy d'Amboys 190, 194, 195–6, 199–205, 236
  The Tragedy of Bussy d'Amboys 26, 29, 32, 190, 194, 195, 198, 250, 259
  Tragedy of Chabot 190
Chesterfield, Philip Dormer Stanhope, Earl of 107
Chettle, Henry, *The Tragedy of Hoffman* 96
Christian IV, King of Denmark 99, 105, 127n123
Cleland, James 60, 214
Cobham, Sir Henry Brooke 196, 212
coffee houses 12–13, 14, 18
Coke, Edward 199, 277
Coligny, Gaspard de 141, 197
Collinson, Patrick 57, 158, 211

commonplace 49n35, 59, 213, 228, 246, 255, 270, 271, 275
commonplace book 9, 204, 208–10, 211, 213, 214, 224, 237, 242, 268
commonplace markers, gnomic points 40, 45, 63–4, 74, 79, 88, 208, 209, 229, 246, 249n20, 250
Commynes, Philippe de 32, 212, 213, 218, 268
competence 2, 9–11, 15–17, 25, 27–9, 31, 33, 46–7, 50, 54, 67, 112, 113, 114, 115, 117, 137, 139, 189, 207, 235–6, 238, 243, 244, 248, 249, 254, 257, 260, 261, 263–4, 265, 274 *see also* conversation; distinction, marks of; expert knowledge
conventicles 256–7, 260, 261
conversation 7, 9, 10, 11, 12, 14, 15, 17, 20, 26, 27, 29, 31–3, 54, 136, 137, 162, 214, 234, 243–8, 251, 254, 256–61, 263–4, 266, 267, 272, 275, 279
  drama as model for 244–8
conversation manuals 26, 244, 246, 264, 267, 270
Cook, Megan 42n14
Cornwallis, Charles 108
counterpublics 260–1
Cowell, John 50
Craigwood, Joanna 92n10, 93n11
Cromwell, Thomas 51n39, 53, 57, 116n92
Cuffe, Henry 53, 65, 276
curiosity, *polypragmosyne* 4n6, 13, 17, 18, 50, 50nn37, 39, 173, 181, 182, 182n41, 199–201, 204, 207, 241

Dacres, Edward 69
Dallington, Robert 192–3
Daniel, Samuel 44, 45
Darnley, Henry Stewart, Lord 144–5, 146
Dávidházi, Péter 162n82
Davison, Francis 118, 120, 122–4
Davison, William 113, 116, 120, 121, 122
de Grazia, Margreta 80, 157
Dekker, Thomas
  Blurt Master Constable 269
  Gull's Hornbook 182, 271
  Satiromastix 269
Denmark 83, 89–91, 96–106, 109, 124, 126, 156
Denny, Edward 46
Devereux, Robert *see* Essex, Robert Devereux, second Earl of
DiGangi, Mario 204n110
Digby, John 117
Digges, Thomas 43
Diogenes the Cynic 252
diplomacy 11, 24–5, 30, 53, 70, 91–2, 96, 98, 105–6, 107, 109–12, 113–15, 116, 117, 118, 126, 132–3, 172, 188–9, 196, 259, 263

disciplinarity 43, 54, 67
distinction, marks of social or cultural
  distinction 9, 11–17, 19, 28–9, 41, 42, 46–7, 163, 200, 203, 225, 231–2, 233, 234, 236, 237, 241, 244–5, 247–8, 257, 265, 269, 271
distinction and education 48–51
distinction of politics, the political 55–6, 61, 64–71, 77, 80, 264–5 *see also* Machiavelli, Niccolò, dilemmatic/dichotomizing mode of argument; political knowledge, political expertise
doubling 166
Drake, William 32, 208–10, 221, 237, 266n44
drama, dramatic form 46, 61, 63–6, 264–6
  see also conversation; tragedy
drama as historiography 32, 211, 217–23, 229, 232, 249
Drummond, Willam, of Hawthornden 210, 216, 232
Dzelzainis, Martin 74

Edwards, Thomas 42
Elizabeth, Queen of England 23, 98, 99, 100, 111, 184, 195, 200, 224, 277, 278
Elsinore 89, 90, 99, 100, 130–3
Erasmus 64, 134, 136, 189, 200n100, 246, 252
Erne, Lukas 40n8
Essex rebellion 275–8
Essex, Robert Devereux, second Earl of 5, 23, 24, 37n1, 38, 44, 45, 46, 49, 50, 53, 56, 87, 118–20, 121, 122–3, 175, 176, 178, 184, 212, 217, 227
expert knowledge, expertise 1–2, 5–6, 7–9, 25, 30, 43, 44, 46, 48, 49, 126, 212 *see also* political knowledge; professions, professionalization

Farmer, Alan 258n31, 268n48
Faunt, Nicholas 117–18
Flaskett, John 178, 181, 198–9, 258
  see also Linley, Paul
Fletcher, Giles 109, 110, 111, 116
Florio, John 244
Foord, John 57, 69
Foucault, Michel 226
France 24, 52, 82, 97n21, 107–8, 120, 125, 128, 131, 140, 171, 184–6, 192, 194, 196–8, 259
Frederick II, King of Denmark 98, 99, 100, 127n123
Freeman, Thomas 40
Freud, Sigmund 130

Gehring, David 99n30, 100n32
Geng, Penny 227
Gentili, Alberico 112–13, 120

Index

Gentillet, Innocent, *Antimachiavel* (*A Discourse upon the Meanes of Wel Governing and Maintaining...A Kingdome...*) 8, 59, 62–3, 65, 67, 80, 81, 82, 210, 242, 268, 275
Gilbert, Humphrey 51
gnomic pointing *see* commonplace markers
Gowrie, John Ruthven, 3rd Earl of 184
Grafton, Anthony 38, 54
grammar schools 47–8, 49, 52
Greene, Robert, *James IV* 166
Grenewey, Richard 217, 221
Greville, Fulke 46, 121
Grimeston, Edward 187, 194
Grotius, Hugo 169
Guicciardini, Francesco 5, 32, 192, 208, 213, 214, 218, 223, 229, 231, 237, 268, 275
Guillory, John 41

Habermas, Jürgen 12, 15, 18, 20, 22–3, 165, 176, 243n1, 260, 261
Halpern, Richard 22n46, 93n11
Hampton, Timothy 93
Hanson, Elizabeth 163
Harrison, John 198
Harvey, Gabriel 30, 37–40, 41, 42–6, 48, 49, 52–8, 60–1, 62, 64–8, 69, 71, 77, 82, 85, 87–8, 110, 208, 211, 224, 244, 245, 246, 264, 265
Hawkyns, Henry 118–20, 122, 123, 124
Hayward, John 11, 206, 232, 277, 278, 279
Henri IV 184, 188, 189, 195
Henslowe, Philip 95, 186
Hentzner, Paul 105
historicism 3, 20–3, 157
history, historiography 44, 207, 232, 274; *see also* drama as historiography; politic history
history play (chronicle play, tragedy of state) 4, 24, 131, 158, 266
Hobbes, Thomas 17, 241, 243
Holinshed, Raphael, *Chronicle* 154
Hooks, Adam 41n8, 53n48, 65n90
Hotman, François 101n34, 141, 142, 146, 161
Hotman, Jean 101
humanism, humanists 30, 38, 43, 44, 47–8, 49, 51, 52n43, 54, 56, 111, 113, 120, 134, 211–12, 213, 268
Huntington, John 259n35
Hutson, Lorna 143

James I and VI 4, 4n6, 23, 24, 50, 144, 151, 181, 188n62, 202, 258
James, Heather 211, 226n68
Jardine, Lisa 6, 38, 54
Johnson, Robert 213, 275
Jonson, Ben 63, 175, 201, 206, 217, 218, 223–4, 243, 246, 248–9
  Every Man In 131, 269, 271
  Every Man Out 64, 131, 234, 236, 269, 270
  The New Cry 207, 215
  News from the New World 170
  Poetaster 270, 272
  Sejanus 4, 32, 206–11, 215–42, 249, 250, 251 *see also* drama as historiography
  Staple of News 170, 262
  Timber or Discoveries 210, 265
  Volpone 33, 182, 261–6, 279
judgement 46 *see also* distinction; satire; spectatorship and judgement
Juvenal 220, 252, 253

Kahn, Victoria 21n43
Kalmar Union 126
Kantorowicz, Ernst 4n6
Kastan, David Scott 40n8, 130, 130n132
King, T. J. 166n93
Knights, L. C. 51
knowledge transactions 6, 10, 112n74, 115, 118, 128, 139 *see also* reading practices
Kyd, Thomas, *Spanish Tragedy* 158

La Boderie, Antoine Lefèvre de 188
La Fin 189
La Noué, François de 59–60, 213
Lake, Peter 175–6, 183, 206n4, 226n69
Languet, Hubert 98
Larum for London, or the Siedge of Antwerpe 171
Le Carré, John 2, 267
  Tinker, Tailor, anonymous reader of 267
Le Roy, Louis 53, 55, 56, 65, 68
Leicester, Robert Dudley, Earl of 11, 53, 54, 101, 112
Lesieur, Stephen 105
Lesser, Zachary 41, 63n86, 148n51, 275
L'Estrange, Roger 3n4
Levy, Fritz 172n10, 173
Linley, Paul 177, 178 *see also* Flaskett, John
Lipsius, Justus, *Politicorum Libri Sex* 5, 71n114, 74, 76, 82, 115, 212, 214, 217, 224n63, 232
literature, literariness 19–20, 40–2, 43, 46, 54, 61, 63n86, 70, 216–17, 247, 249
  see also drama, dramatic form; tragedy
Livy 5, 44, 54, 68, 134, 207, 208, 212, 221n59, 268, 275
Lodge, Thomas 95
Lupić, Ivan 64n88
Lupton, Julia 21n43, 162, 165n91

Machiavelli, Niccolò 12, 18n37, 30, 54–8, 59–61, 62, 63, 65, 67, 70, 76, 134, 208–10, 215, 237, 275 *see also* politic thought
  dilemmatic/dichotomizing mode of argument 68–70
  Discourses 54, 55, 116
  The Prince 5, 55, 56, 68, 69, 74, 80–1, 84
McKenzie, D. F. 170–1
McShane, Angela 174n16

Manningham, John 9–11
Marlowe, Christopher 199
  Doctor Faustus 8, 147n47
  Edward II 4, 31, 166
  The Jew of Malta 171
  Massacre at Paris 171
Marprelate 258, 269
Marston, John 246, 248, 271, 272
  Antonio's Revenge 156, 159, 250, 271
  The Fawn 249
  Jack Drum's Entertainment 11–12, 15, 16, 17, 20, 28, 269
  Malcontent 4, 32, 248, 249–56
  Sophonisba 248–9
Marx, Karl 16n34, 22, 38n2, 130
matter and words 49, 54, 56
Maurice of Nassau 176
maxims, sententious political observations 7–8, 19, 32, 61–8, 71, 74, 76, 80, 81, 84, 85, 115, 137, 192, 210, 211, 214, 215, 221, 227, 228, 229, 232, 241, 242, 243, 251, 254, 255, 275, 279
  see also aphorisms
Melanchthon 97
Melton, John, *The Sixe-fold Politician* 5, 136–9, 157, 266, 275
Meres, Francis 42, 44, 59
Merrick, Gelly 123, 276
Meyer, Albrecht 105
Michelangelo Buonarroti 220–1
Middleton, Thomas
  A Mad World 71n115
  The Phoenix 249
Millstone, Noah 5n7, 26
Milton, John 260
modernity 19, 20, 21, 49n34, 67, 70n111, 114n81, 139, 191, 191n68, 243, 250
Monsieur *see* Alençon, François, Duc d' (aka Monsieur)
More, Thomas, *Utopia* 69, 268
Mountjoy, Charles Blount, 8th Baron 44, 45, 178n30
Munro, Ian 241

names as political information 103–6, 196
Nannini, Remigio 134–6, 139, 147, 154
Nashe, Thomas 42, 95, 269
Neill, Michael 156
Netzloff, Mark 260
news 3n4, 5, 7, 8, 10, 11–12, 13, 17, 31–2, 102, 119, 121, 169–74, 175, 176, 179–83, 193, 199–201, 204–5, 207, 262
Norfolk, Thomas Howard, Third Duke of 141
Northumberland, Thomas Percy, Seventh Earl of 141

Oestreich, Gerhard 153n61, 203
Osborn, Francis 181, 182, 191, 201, 221

parrhesia 226, 238, 251–2, 253
Parry, Thomas 123
Parsons, Robert, *Conference about the Succession* 11, 142n28
Paul's boys 194, 199
Paul's Cathedral precinct (Paul's Walk, Churchyard, Cross) 32, 180, 181, 182, 193, 194, 198, 256, 258, 275
Peele, Thomas *Battle of Alcazar* 171
Perez, Antonio 118
philosophy 22, 41, 43, 127, 204
Picciotto, Joanna 18n39
Pico della Mirandola 169
playreaders, notes from plays 223, 263, 264–5, 266n44 *see also* Drake, William; Harvey, Gabriel; Pudsey, Edward; Shakespeare, *Hamlet*, readers of
Plutarch 5, 45, 50n39, 200–1, 207, 208, 221n59, 241, 243
politic history 5, 7, 32, 211, 212, 214, 218, 221, 224, 243, 268, 275, 279
  see also Commynes, Philippe de; Gucciardini, Francesco; Tacitus
politic thought, machiavellianism, reason of state 8, 12, 13, 18, 19, 30, 59–61, 62, 63, 68, 71, 76, 77, 80–7, 115, 139, 199, 207, 210, 215, 228, 235, 237, 239, 242, 249, 250–1, 254, 255–6, 279
Politic Would-be, Sir 33, 261–6, 279
  and *passim*
political knowledge, political expertise 7, 29, 30, 46, 50, 52, 54–5, 67, 93, 95, 97–8, 107, 110–12, 113, 114, 123, 126–8, 136–9, 243–4, 247, 263–4, 267
  see also distinction of politics
politics, the political *see* distinction of politics
politics as a profession 1–3, 6, 10, 15, 27, 29, 61, 112–17, 123, 137–40, 254
polypragmosyne see curiosity
Pop, Iggy 45n23
popularity (as a political concept) 159, 160, 164–5, 175, 176, 277
Powle, Stephen 116
professions, professionalization 6n8, 25, 47, 114–16, 261–5, 267 *see also* expert knowledge
public sphere 12–14, 17–19, 18n39, 50n37, 165, 173, 175, 176, 183, 184, 205, 243n1, 244, 258, 260, 261
  late 17th c., as ideal type 19n39, 172, 176, 207, 260
Pudsey, Edward 267–79

Ranke, Leopold, and *relazioni* 107n51
Rantzau, Heinrich 102, 105
Raymond, Joad 174n13
reading practices 38, 41, 43, 45–7, 52–4, 56, 59–61, 65, 69–70, 180, 206, 208, 210–11, 211–15, 229, 237, 241–2,

245, 266–7 *see also* knowledge transactions; playreaders, notes from plays
reason of state *see* politic thought
relations (ambassadorial reports), *relazioni* 5, 7, 30, 106–12, 117, 118, 119, 121, 122, 123, 124, 126, 191–4, 195, 196, 197, 262
res et verba see matter and words
Revenger's Tragedy 156
Rogers, Daniel 30, 97–105, 106, 109, 110, 111, 113, 114, 116, 120, 121, 126, 196
Rogers, John 97–8
Rutland, Edward Manners, 3rd Earl of 116n91, 121n105
Rutland, Roger Manners, 5th Earl of 46, 49, 53, 121nn.108–9, 192, 212

Said, Edward 253
Sallustius 45, 134, 219
satire 14, 170, 182, 199, 200, 207, 232, 235, 257–8, 266, 268, 269, 271
 as knowledge 253, 263 *see also satyra seria*
 satiric tragedy, tragicomedy 249
  see also satyra seria
 satirical comedy 29, 234, 247, 256, 265, 267
 as social strategy 235–6, 251–5
satyra seria, serious satire 234–6, 247, 256
Savile, Henry, translation of Tacitus and *Ende of Nero* 212, 217–18, 221, 224–5
Saxo Grammaticus, *Gesta Danorum* 90, 91, 134–5, 136, 140, 143, 147
Schmitt, Carl 21, 22, 68n100
Scott, William 44n17, 59, 266
secrets, secrecy 7–8, 18, 19, 50n39, 56, 74, 77, 87, 132, 152, 156, 188, 190, 199
 see also curiosity; expert knowledge
secrets of state, *arcana imperii*, mysteries of state 3–4, 8, 13, 17, 32, 50, 60, 106, 127, 175, 183, 207, 214, 218, 221, 223, 228–30, 232, 234, 239, 263
 see also political knowledge; *satyra seria*
Selden, John 169
Seneca 65, 72, 254
Sennett, Richard 12n23
sententiae 30, 32, 38, 40, 44, 45, 60, 62, 63–5, 72, 73, 74, 85, 134, 227, 228, 246, 265, 270, 276 *see also* maxims
 in playbooks 30, 40–1, 61, 63–5, 71, 79, 84, 88, 209, 225, 250
Shakespeare, William 42, 44, 47, 60, 61, 95, 149n52, 205, 208, 274
 2 Henry VI 31, 159
 Hamlet 77–88, 89–96, 103, 124–33, 136–40, 147–66, 171, 172, 173, 205, 208, 219, 250, 269, 270, 272, 278
  and its differences from 16th-c. tradition 4–5, 79, 94, 153, 156, 159, 166

interiority and inwardness 31, 96, 125, 132–3, 157, 219
 readers of 37–42, 44, 45, 46–7, 60–1, 71, 87–8, 136–9, 266, 267, 270, 271, 275
 versions and textual revision 92–5, 148–54
Henry V 4
Henry VIII 3
Julius Caesar 154, 155, 238
Love's Labour's Lost 186
Lucrece 30, 37, 38–40, 41, 42, 44, 45, 46, 60, 71, 72–7, 78, 79, 82, 88, 156, 264
Measure for Measure 132n140, 249
Merchant of Venice 171
Othello 131n140, 270, 274n70
Richard II 276, 277–8
Richard III 4, 154–5, 219, 274n70
Romeo and Juliet 27n62, 131n140, 270, 271
Titus Andronicus 78, 131n140, 158, 273
Twelfth Night 9–10, 11, 15, 17, 20, 205, 259n35
Venus and Adonis 37, 38–40, 44, 88
Shannon, Laurie 163
Sharpe, Kevin 237
Sherman, William 6
Sidney, Philip 42, 46, 54, 98, 113, 116n91, 121, 169, 212, 229
Sidney, Robert 46, 176, 177–8, 181, 217, 221, 224, 237
Smith, Thomas 44–5, 69
Smith, Thomas Jr 54, 224
Smyth, Edward 120
Southampton, Henry Wriothesley, Earl of 40, 53, 65
Sowerby, Tracey 114n83
spectatorship and judgment 27–8, 243–4, 243n1, 247, 250, 264–6, 269 *see also* theatre as metaphor; theatre, cultural work of
Spenser, Edmund 38, 42, 44, 216
Stallybrass, Peter 41, 63n86, 275
Stanivuković, Zoran 95n18
Stapleton, Thomas 11
Stewart, Alan 91, 92, 121n109
stoicism 152, 153, 162, 199–200, 201, 202, 203, 205, 236

Tacitus 5, 32, 45, 134, 207–8, 212, 213, 214, 215, 217–18, 219–23, 229, 230n75, 232–3, 275, 278–9
taverns 14, 18, 175, 180
Terence 216, 244, 245, 246
theatre, as metaphor 231–2, 236, 239, 244
 see also spectatorship and judgement
theatre, cultural work of 7–9, 17, 26, 27, 28–9, 170–1, 173, 174–5, 179, 180, 183, 207, 219, 236, 243, 248, 271–2
 see also spectatorship and judgement

Thomas, Keith 25
Thomas of Woodstock 4, 31
tobacco pamphlets 257–8
tragedy 61, 63–7, 71, 77, 191, 210, 218–21, 234
travel, instructions on 120–1
Trilling, Lionel 20
Turnhout 176–9, 181

Ur-Hamlet see Shakespeare, *Hamlet*, versions and textual revision

Varnedoe, Kirk 20–1
Vere, Francis 176, 178
Verneuil, Henriette d'Entragues, Madame de 188
Vettori, Francesco 56

Walsingham, Francis 11, 101, 102, 112, 115, 120, 121, 195, 196, 198

war of the theatres 28–9, 33, 131, 246, 248, 268–70, 272
Warkentin, Germaine 223n62
Warley, Christopher 163–4
Warner, William 44
Watson, Thomas 216
Weber, Max 6n8
Wechel, André 110
Whyte, Rowland 177–8, 181
Wicquefort, Abraham van 191–2
Williamson, Lizzy 113n79, 118
Wilson, Thomas 142, 143, 252
Wintour, Anna 201
Wittenberg 82, 84, 90, 97, 125, 127
Wolfe, John 69
Wotton, Henry 3, 116
Wriothesley, Henry *see* Southampton, Henry Wriothesley, Earl of

Yachnin, Paul 8n15